THE PLANETARY GENTRIFICATION READER

Gentrification is a global process that the United Nations now sees as a human rights issue. This new *Planetary Gentrification Reader* follows on from the editors' 2010 volume, *The Gentrification Reader*, and provides a more longitudinal (backward and forward in time) and broader (turning away from Anglo-/Euro-American hegemony) sense of developments in gentrification studies over time and space, drawing on key readings that reflect the development of cutting-edge debates.

Revisiting new debates over the histories of gentrification, thinking through comparative urbanism on gentrification, considering new waves and types of gentrification, and giving much more focus to resistance to gentrification, this is a stellar collection of writings on this critical issue.

Like in their 2010 *Reader*, the editors, who are internationally renowned experts in the field, include insightful commentary and suggested further reading. The book is essential reading for students and researchers in urban studies, urban planning, human geography, sociology, and housing studies and for those seeking to fight this socially unjust process.

Loretta Lees is Director of the Initiative on Cities at Boston University, Boston, USA.

Tom Slater is Professor of Urban Studies at Columbia University, New York City, USA.

Elvin Wyly is Professor of Geography at the University of British Columbia, xʷməθkʷəy̓əm (Musqueam) Territory, Vancouver, Canada.

The Planetary Gentrification Reader

Edited by
Loretta Lees
Tom Slater
and
Elvin Wyly

Routledge
Taylor & Francis Group

NEW YORK AND LONDON

Cover image: The cover image 'Xian Village Guangzhou (2015)' is a photograph by John van Aitken and Jane Brake, Institute of Urban Dreaming (https://iudblog.org). It is part of IUD's ongoing witnessing (through photography, writing and other artistic methods) of the dispossession and displacement produced by contemporary strategies of capital accumulation centred on housing. The photograph was taken when they visited Xian urban village, Guangzhou, China. It captures the dispossessions, 'witnessing everyday life amongst the rubble', caused by planetary gentrification.

First published 2023
by Routledge
605 Third Avenue, New York, NY 10158

and by Routledge
4 Park Square, Milton Park, Abingdon, Oxon, OX14 4RN

Routledge is an imprint of the Taylor & Francis Group, an informa business

© 2023 selection and editorial matter, Loretta Lees, Tom Slater, and Elvin Wyly; individual chapters, the contributors

The right of Loretta Lees, Tom Slater, and Elvin Wyly to be identified as the authors of the editorial material, and of the authors for their individual chapters, has been asserted in accordance with sections 77 and 78 of the Copyright, Designs and Patents Act 1988.

All rights reserved. No part of this book may be reprinted or reproduced or utilised in any form or by any electronic, mechanical, or other means, now known or hereafter invented, including photocopying and recording, or in any information storage or retrieval system, without permission in writing from the publishers.

Every effort has been made to contact copyright-holders. Please advise the publisher of any errors or omissions, and these will be corrected in subsequent editions.

Trademark notice: Product or corporate names may be trademarks or registered trademarks, and are used only for identification and explanation without intent to infringe.

ISBN: 978-1-032-37656-1 (hbk)
ISBN: 978-1-032-37654-7 (pbk)
ISBN: 978-1-003-34123-9 (ebk)

DOI: 10.4324/9781003341239

Typeset in Amasis
by Apex CoVantage, LLC

Contents

Introduction ix

PART ONE THINKING ABOUT GENTRIFICATION TODAY 1

Introduction to Part One 3

1. What time is gentrification? 5
   Suleiman Osman

2. Gentrification 9
   Elvin Wyly

3. Beyond Anglo-American gentrification theory 18
   Hyun Bang Shin and Ernesto López-Morales

4. Revisiting 'the changing state of gentrification' 32
   Manuel B. Aalbers

PART TWO PLANETARY GENTRIFICATION 43

Introduction to Part Two 45

5. Planetary rent gaps 47
   Tom Slater

6. The discursive detachment of race from gentrification in Cartagena de Indias, Colombia 66
   Melissa M. Valle

7. The fire this time: Grenfell, racial capitalism and the urbanisation of empire 82
   Ida Danewid

8. In debt to the rent gap: Gentrification generalized and the frontier of the future 101
   Hamish Kallin

PART THREE GENTRIFICATION AND COMPARATIVE URBANISM — 113

Introduction to Part Three — 115

9   The geography of gentrification: Thinking through comparative urbanism — 117
   Loretta Lees

10   Hybrid gentrification in South Africa: Theorising across southern and northern cities — 132
   Charlotte Lemanski

11   Comparative approaches to gentrification: Lessons from the rural — 147
   Martin Phillips and Darren P. Smith

12   Is comparative gentrification possible? Sceptical voices from Hong Kong — 174
   David Ley and Sin Yih Teo

PART FOUR GENTRIFICATIONS BEYOND ANGLO-AMERICA — 181

Introduction to Part Four — 183

13   Prolonging the global age of gentrification: Johannesburg's regeneration policies — 187
   Tanja Winkler

14   *Desakota* and beyond: Neoliberal production of suburban space in Manila's fringe — 205
   Arnisson Andre C. Ortega

15   Socio-spatial legibility, discipline, and gentrification through favela upgrading in Rio de Janeiro — 226
   Thaisa Comelli, Isabelle Anguelovski, and Eric Chu

16   Housing transformation, rent gap and gentrification in Ghana's traditional houses: Insight from compound houses in Bantama, Kumasi — 248
   Lewis Abedi Asante and Richmond Juvenile Ehwi

PART FIVE PLANETARY GENTRIFICATION AND DIGITAL TRANSFORMATIONS — 271

Introduction to Part Five — 273

17   Holiday rentals: The new gentrification battlefront — 275
   Agustín Cocola-Gant

18   The impacts of Airbnb in Athens, Lisbon and Milan: A rent gap theory perspective — 285
   Alberto Amore, Cecilia de Bernardi and Pavlos Arvanitis

19 Platform-mediated short-term rentals and gentrification in Madrid 300
    Alvaro Ardura Urquiaga, Iñigo Lorente-Riverola and Javier Ruiz Sanchez

20 Postsocialism and the Tech Boom 2.0: Techno-utopics
    of racial/spatial dispossession 317
    Erin McElroy

PART SIX RESISTING PLANETARY GENTRIFICATION **331**

Introduction to Part Six 333

21 Resisting gentrification 336
    Sandra Annunziata and Clara Rivas-Alonso

22 Resisting the politics of displacement in the San Francisco
    Bay Area: Anti-gentrification activism in the Tech Boom 2.0 356
    Florian Opillard

23 A city for all? Public policy and resistance to gentrification
    in the southern neighborhoods of Buenos Aires 374
    María Carla Rodríguez and María Mercedes Di Virgilio

24 When art meets monsters: Mapping art activism and
    anti-gentrification movements in Seoul 390
    Seon Young Lee and Yoonai Han

Index 401

Figure 1 State-led gentrification in Douar Wasti, Casablanca, Morocco.
Photograph: Stefano Portelli

INTRODUCTION

GENTRIFICATION AS A PLANETARY FIELD

It is now over a decade since we first published *The Gentrification Reader* in 2010. This *Reader* is a separate collection but one that follows on from the first. Over the past ten years, gentrification studies have taken off globally. Gentrification studies is becoming less dominated by an Anglo- or Euro-American focus. Scholars around the world are researching this problematic process. Indeed, a recent bibliometric analysis of gentrification that scanned articles published in journals since 1979 shows gentrification to be a 'planetary field' (Uribe-Toril, Ruiz-Real and De Pablo Valenciano, 2018; see Figure 2).

Not surprisingly, this planetary field is dominated by the English-speaking world – in order of influence, the top three being the US, the UK, and Canada. Yet this reflects what has been written since 1979. Moving forward, this is less likely to be the case. In the 2000s, non-English publications on gentrification have been growing. Uribe-Toril, Ruiz-Real and De Pablo Valenciano (2018) found that 'English is the dominant language and only Spanish, German, Portuguese and French have a relevant (<1%) position' but that Chinese is rising fast. Liu, Zhu, Li, Sun, and Huang (2019) analyzed the literature on gentrification in China between 1996 and 2017, again based on bibliometrics, finding it has become 'a topical word in scholarly discussion' (see Figure 3). They argue that a Chinese linguistic scholar introduced the concept of gentrification into China for the first time in 1993, and they discuss subsequent mentions and research on the process: from Zhou and Xu's (1996) 'Shenshi-fication' (*shenshi* means 'gentry' in Chinese), which, as they say, made little sense given there is not a gentry, as such, in Chinese society; to Meng (2000) and Sun's (2000) 'Zhongchanjieceng-fication' (*zhongchanjieceng* means 'middle class' in Chinese), which is also problematic given that there is no uniform definition of 'middle class' in China. Interestingly, there is no uniform definition outside of China either. Liu, Zhu, Li, Sun, and Huang (2019) argue that China's gentrification research took off significantly in 2008, probably impacted by the global financial crisis and accelerating urban transformation in China. They say,

> There are significant signs showing the future trends of gentrification will move to the construction of a theoretical system of gentrification with Chinese characteristics, gentrification consequences evaluation and urban policies, new types of gentrification, gentrification driven by cultural consumption and authenticity protection of gentrification-stricken historical and cultural heritages, application of new technology to gentrification research, and relationship between shantytown renovation and gentrification in China.

But what does building 'a theoretical system of gentrification with Chinese characteristics' mean? How might it be done? These are the kinds of questions that this *Planetary Reader* considers.

Language, and in that the linguistics of gentrification, is important. There has been much debate over whether the English term 'gentrification' translates into other contexts (for example, Ley and Teo, 2014, with respect to Hong Kong), but as Shin and Lopez-Morales (2018: 16) say, 'does it really matter whether or not gentrification as a term exists in a particular locality?' They,

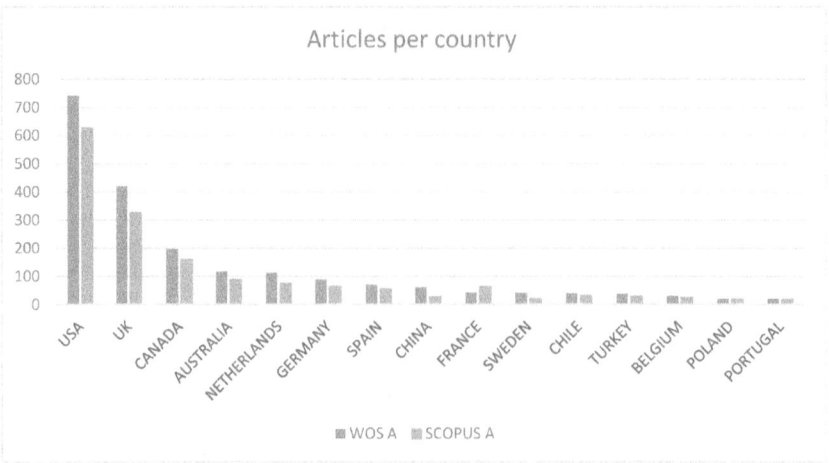

Figure 2 Gentrification articles published since 1979 by country.
Source: Uribe-Toril, Ruiz-Real and De Pablo Valenciano (2018)

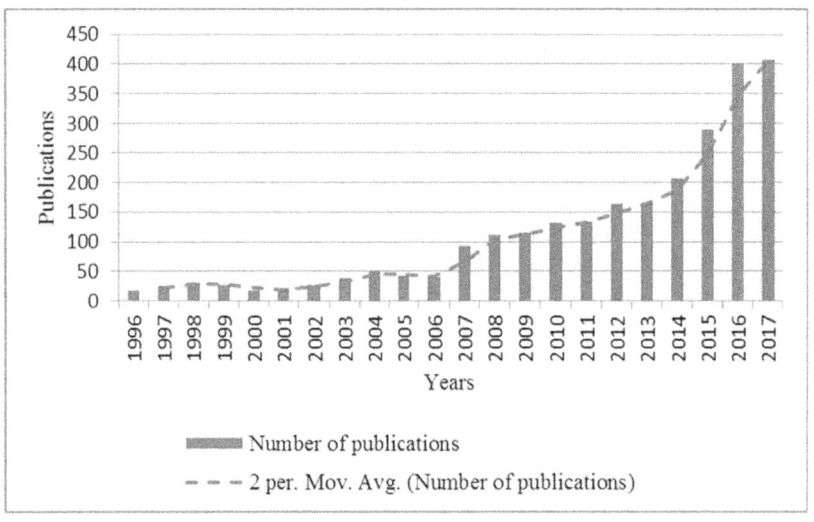

Figure 3 The increase in Chinese publications on gentrification.
Source: Liu, Zhu, Li, Sun, and Huang (2019)

like we also did in our 2010 *Reader*, follow Clark (2005) in calling for a more generic definition of gentrification that is attuned to 'actually existing gentrification' or preferably gentrification*s*.

In this new *planetary* collection, our readers get a more longitudinal (backward and forward in time) and broader (turning away from Anglo-/Euro-American hegemony) sense of developments in gentrification studies over time and space, drawing on key readings that we think reflect the development of cutting edge debates since the 2010 *Reader* was published. This *Reader* is shorter, and our aim is to produce short, updated additional volumes every decade or so going forward.

So what has changed in gentrification studies over the past decade that warrants us producing a new volume? First, as we have already indicated, scholars have properly woken up to the hegemony of Anglo-/Euro-American studies and voices and sought to be properly inclusive of *other* places, geographies, and voices. In our 2010 *Reader* (Chapter 35), we published Neil Smith's discussion of gentrification as a global urban strategy, but since then, there has been recognition that gentrification has not '*gone* global', as Neil Smith stated, but actually it has long been global (Lees, Shin, and Lopez-Morales, 2016). Second, investigation of different mutations of gentrification has continued to grow – in our 2010 *Reader*, we pointed to new debates over, for example, new build gentrification, and in Chapter 32 of that *Reader*, we published Martin Phillip's call for proper recognition of 'other geographies of gentrification', a call to include rural gentrification properly in gentrification studies. Since then, the mutations of gentrification have been numerous – from Airbnbification to greentrification (note that Uribe-Toril, Ruiz-Real, and De Pablo Valenciano, 2018, found that since 1987, the number of papers in environmental studies that focused on gentrification increased at an annual rate of 60.4%) to, most recently, Zoomification. Third, there has been much more of a commitment to working with communities to fight gentrification rather than scholars just theorizing or pontificating on it. Scholar-activist work on gentrification has become more and more important. There has been renewed focus on thinking through resistance theoretically, conceptually, and on the ground.

Reflecting all this, the cover illustration for this *Reader* is a photograph by John van Aitken and Jane Brake, Institute of Urban Dreaming (IUD), who have been investigating gentrification and displacement globally and comparatively using photography, site writing, and other artistic methods. The photograph was taken in Xian Village, Guangzhou, China, in 2015, when IUD visited, and it serves as a witness to and gathering of evidence on gentrification, displacement, and resistance to it; it shows everyday life among the rubble – the destruction caused by gentrification (read Box 1; see also Gransow, 2012; Li and Wu, 2013). This image signifies the planetary nature of this *Reader* in comparison to our 2010 *Reader*, where the cover image, a collage by a New York City artist, was most definitely situated in the US context.

BOX 1 IUD VISIT TO XIAN VILLAGE, GUANGZHOU, CHINA, IN 2015

In April 2015, we took a guided tour of the Xian urban village in Guangzhou, Guangdong Province, China. Our guide was a local journalist with family ties to the village.[1] He discouraged us from spending too long in one place or talking to inhabitants due to local tensions and the risks of being stopped and asked to leave – or worse – by security guards or police.

The photograph shows the stressed landscape, riven by conflict, which we encountered in 2015. There is a striking contrast between the new high-rise structures of Tianhe Central Business District (CBD) in the background and the degraded, apparently abandoned low-rise properties of Xiancun in the foreground.[2] These contrasts are often what attracts photographers to Chinese urban landscapes, but we wanted to understand more about the processes that produce these landscapes and if the photographs themselves can tell us something new or at least produce a cogent account of what is happening.

Chéngzhōngcūn, the Chinese word for urban village, translates literally as 'village encircled by the city'.[3] This specifically Chinese form of urban village was produced in an unprecedented phase of rapid urbanization as villages were absorbed into cities, resulting in displacement and land expropriation of millions of villagers from the countryside and villages in the city.[4] A dual system in China separates urban and rural areas, with residents governed under separate

---

1 Name withheld for security reasons.
2 Cun means village in Chinese. We use this in the absence of village or urban village directly afterwards to avoid any possible confusion with Xi'an the city as the apostrophe is sometimes missed off.
3 Other terms applied to the urban village include: village-in-the-city, informal settlement or migrant enclave.
4 Chen, 2020 (quoting Sargeson) estimates 88 million peasants lost their land between 1990 and 2008. He quotes the (projected) figure for 2020 of 140 million landless peasants.

registration systems, or *hukou*. Many inequalities are embedded in this system, which disadvantages those with rural registration, who are denied access to education, healthcare, and other public services provided in cities. Urban villages are stigmatized as 'slums' in the media and state narratives, which serves to legitimize their clearance.[5] Urban land in China is managed by government officials, whereas rural land, including urban villages, is managed collectively by the villagers, represented by a village committee under the leadership of the village chief.

The first records of Xian Village date back 800 years, and for much of the intervening time, the main crop was cabbage, with later diversification into pig farming. Between the mid-1980s and the mid-1990s, Xian's agricultural land was progressively requisitioned by the city of Guangzhou for residential and commercial projects. Deprived of their agricultural livelihood and ill-equipped to participate in the urban labor market, the villagers' survival strategy was to use compensation money paid by the city to fund the construction of rental properties on their housing plots, to which they retained occupation rights under the collective land tenure system. Thus, the urban village economy came to be based upon the often-lucrative extraction of value from rental properties. The villagers had set out on a course that would make their future dependent on their ability to operate collectively in an international property market, with some of the highest stakes on the planet and endemic corruption. The resulting low-rise properties seen in our photograph were built to poor standards and high levels of density. Mass urbanization of the rural population, arriving in Guangzhou in their millions, looking for low-paying jobs, whose housing needs were not addressed by the state, were able to find cheap accommodation in recently urbanized villages like Xian. At its peak, the village was home to an estimated 40,000 migrant workers, whose labor was vital to the realization of China's economic aspirations.[6]

Despite its location in an area with some of the highest land values in China, villagers received only meager sums in exchange for their land rights and were aware of the settlements offered to other villages when their land was expropriated.[7] Migrants and other village tenants, some of whom were well established in the village, were not entitled to compensation or assistance with relocation. Many Xian villagers were convinced that their village chief and his entourage, in league with a corrupt Guangzhou official, had defrauded them out of the compensation due for the loss of their land.[8] In 2009, the mayor of Guangzhou announced the demolition of Xian urban village and others in the vicinity of the site of the 2010 Asian Games.[9] The announcement caused the departure of tenants, eager to relocate before the demolition started. Villagers recognized the inevitability of the 'development' of the village, which would require the demolition of their homes and rental properties, loss of associated income, and relocation for them. Fearing they would never be fairly compensated for the loss of all that remained of their collective land and distrustful about proposed arrangements for their relocation, the villagers created a petition addressed to the city leaders, filed complaints, and organized protests. Their demands included an investigation into village finances dating back to 1984, as well as the removal of the existing village leadership.[10] This beginning of the villagers' campaign of resistance marked the onset of a period of harassment, arrests, imprisonment, and violence for many of those who stood up for their rights. They were portrayed as antisocial troublemakers, while banners and flyers prepared by the Village Committee reminded

---

5 See Li & Wu page 925.

6 Bettina Gransow p 21- Numbers of migrants are always impossible to verify as some are not registered.

7 Particularly Liede urban village, close by in Guangzhou.

8 See Bandurski, 2015: 28 for figure of 600 million and a detailed account of this narrative and Chinese language sources.

9 Bandurski p 32.

10 Bandurski pp 27 to 37.

11 See photographs of banners in Gransow p 22.

INTRODUCTION

villagers of their obligation to the collective.[11] Nevertheless, the villagers' campaign was successful in preventing the demolition of the village from taking place in time for the 2010 Asian Games.

In 2010, villagers attempted to defend Xiancun Market from demolition but were faced with many hundreds of police and *chengguan*, the local government law enforcement agency, resulting in injuries for some villagers. In 2011, a wall was constructed around the village, which was generally considered the precursor to demolition. The wall functioned as a form of border with checkpoints, where anyone entering or leaving had to show their registration documents to the security guards posted there.[12]

In 2012, when Xi Jinping took over leadership of the Chinese Communist Party, he announced his determination to tackle corruption, which was acknowledged as a serious concern within the party. This created a new context whereby an investigation into the affairs of Xiancun was possible, and in 2013, after four years of campaigning, the village chief was suspended from his role, although it is likely he already had absconded.[13] Later that year, Cao Jianliao, deputy mayor of Guangzhou, was removed from office, dismissed from the Communist Party, and eventually sentenced to life imprisonment for corruption related to Xian Village. In the absence of the village chief, other village officials, mostly his family members, were tried and found guilty of 'serious violations of economic discipline'.[14]

The figure in the foreground of the photograph sits on a camping stool at the base of a mound of rubble.[15] He appears to be contemplating something in the dark waters of the ancient village pond, where the shells of the village rental properties are reflected.[16] Perhaps he is also trying to make a phone call. Other photographs of this spot show residents using cell phones: it is one of the few places in the village where it is possible to get a signal.

At the man's feet, there are a couple of red carrier bags, which make a visual connection to the red flags flying on the roofs of some of the village properties. When we visited in 2015, although the process appeared to have stalled temporarily, parts of the village had been demolished, leaving it resembling a war zone. Many of the low-rise rental blocks that had not been demolished had been gutted internally, making them uninhabitable and explaining the cavernous appearance you can see in the photograph. People had to negotiate tall, sometimes precarious mounds of rubble to get out of their homes and to hang out washing. Washing lines provided some evidence of the extent to which the area was inhabited. We saw construction workers entering the village during their lunch break and were told it was likely that some of them were Xiancun tenants. We filmed shops or at least goods for sale and other commercial activities, such as electronics recycling, street sewing, and barbering, as well as the vegetable market, which had relocated since it was demolished. We also noted the presence of guards as we entered the village. They noted our presence, but we were not stopped, although subsequently we were aware of being followed. Despite the conviction of corrupt village and city officials in the previous year, in 2015 many of the villagers were still campaigning for justice: their demands for a thorough investigation into village finances had not been met, and the scale of what was owed to them had not been addressed by corruption court proceedings. Misinformation, pressure, and financial incentives to sign the agreements to surrender their residential plots to developers had increased divisions among the Xian villagers. Many but clearly not all of the tenants had left, and some urban villagers were already displaced,

12 Bandurski p 96. Although there was barely any wall left in 2015, security guards were positioned at the entrance to the village, but did not ask to see our papers. Bandurski describes the villagers pulling down the wall with their bare hands.

13 Bandurski says the Village Chief had obtained Australian nationality soon after his removal. p 244.

14 See Bandurski p 236.

15 He is probably a monk but we cannot confirm this.

16 The pond is an ancient resource and is a key feature of traditional village design and cultural life. In 2012 villagers petitioned outside the provincial Communist Party Leadership to prevent the pond from being filled. See Bandurski p 97.

although a proportion remained determined to hold out. This meant round-the-clock occupation of their own homes because they were fearful that once empty, even for a short time, they would be demolished.[17] These villagers flew plain red flags, indicating to wrecking crews the location of the homes that were still inhabited, sending a signal to other villagers, who might be considering signing away their land rights, and calling upon the Communist Party to do the right thing.

What has happened to Xian Village now?

In 2019, more of the village had been demolished, and several new high-rise housing blocks are visible on the edge of the old boundary of the Xiancun residential area.[18] These are likely to be so-called social housing blocks, on land that, in order to comply with land tenure legislation, had to be set aside for this purpose when the village was expropriated. It is not clear whether any Xian villagers were relocated into this new housing. We have not yet been able to find a reliable source that really brings the situation in Xiancun up to date.

Figure 4 The contrast between Xian Village and the surrounding skyscrapers in Guangzhou, China 2019.

Source: www.alamy.com/a-sharp-contrast-between-xian-village-and-skyscrapers-around-in-guangzhou-city-south-chinas-guangdong-province-19-november-2019-as-the-last-vill-image336142882.html

17 www.youtube.com/watch?v=TZh3hY5oX2c this video, uploaded on 24th September 2012, shows a high reach excavator in the process of demolishing a building, whilst a woman looks out from an adjacent property. This process of occupation to prevent demolition of one's home is not uncommon in China, so much so that the remaining homes, which stand out amidst the surrounding demolished area are called nail houses.

18 See Figure 4 dated November 2019.

DEFINING GENTRIFICATION GLOBALLY

The term 'gentrification' has long been controversial. In Lees, Slater, and Wyly (2008, 2010) we began both books by referring to the British sociologist Ruth Glass's coinage of the term in 1964, but even back then, we were sensitive to the fact that this now classic conception of gentrification was influenced by the context it came out of – London, England, a specific place at a specific time in its transition to a post-industrial economy, society, and culture. We were clear that gentrification was not necessarily confined to the inner city either. In the 'global turn' in gentrification studies, which recognizes gentrification processes, past and present, around the world, Glass's definition has faced a new wave of intense scrutiny. In moving away from the hegemony of Anglo- or Euro-American research and theorizing on gentrification it seems odd to hinge understanding of gentrification on a time/space specific coinage from nearly 60 years ago now, as Greek sociologist Maloutas (2012) would have us do. Shin and Lopez-Morales (2018: 14) characterize such an understanding as

> an extreme perspective on gentrification that treats it as a historical-cultural process associated primarily with inner city London in the 1960s. Viewed this way, the process of gentrification is effectively fossilized, and disavowed of any applicability outside of a particular time and place/space: it is thus rendered lower than a 'mid-range concept'.

We agree. Shin and Lopez-Morales (2018) also reject other skeptical arguments that gentrification only plays out in formal property markets (for example, Ghertner, 2015), refuting the reality of slum gentrifications around the world. They argue that

> such a viewpoint reflects confusion in the midst of its attempt to intertwine reductionist theorization of urban change with the rich Marxist interpretations of gentrification, and displays a tendency (1) to regard cities in the Global South as qualitatively different and isolated from more general processes of capitalist accumulation; (2) to treat slums and informal settlements as distinct urban spaces where logics of capital accumulation cannot penetrate; (3) to disregard how deeply market and non-market processes are entangled in the same way, how formal and informal processes are fused together in the global economy; (4) to understate how much the operation of speculation and landlordism can be prevalent in informal settlements.

Their critique is spot-on, and we reproduce their essay in Part Two of this *Reader*.

Such skeptical and/or adversarial stands are, perhaps, to some degree, part of a wider kick back against the dominance of gentrification studies in urban studies and maybe the neoliberal positioning and repositioning in academia, where academics increasingly seek out their own contradictory niche to push forward in a saturated field.

In an interview with Neil Brenner,[1] LA-based urbanist Ananya Roy said of terms like 'suburb' and 'gentrification': 'those are very useful concepts – I don't want to let go of those concepts' but at the same time she recognizes that other parts of the world can generate other concepts equally rich – this is a stance we agree with and one to be found in Lees, Shin, and Lopez-Morales's (2016) *Planetary Gentrification* book.

This is a *Planetary* Gentrification Reader and not a *Global* Gentrification Reader, and here we can draw on Jean-Luc Nancy's contrast between the French terms *globalization* and *mondialization*. In opposition to *globality* – 'totality grasped as a whole . . . enclosure in the undifferentiated sphere of a unitotality' – he offers *world-forming* as a 'process in expansion', particularly focused on the world's horizon, a space of relationality and possible meanings held in common and able to become an object of thought specifically *because* globalization is the 'fact' that is destroying the world (Nancy, 2007: 1–2, 35–36).

GENTRIFICATION – ITS HISTORIES AND TRAJECTORIES *TAKE TWO*

There is increasing debate on the histories of the gentrification process (really process*es*). In our 2008 *Gentrification* book, we recognized that there were examples of gentrification before the term was coined—for example, New Orleans and Charleston in the US experienced gentrification in the late 1930s; but the emergence of gentrification proper, we argued, began in postwar advanced capitalist cities. That assertion is more difficult to make now in the context of the planetary gentrification thesis and debates at this time. In a recent book by Dennis Gale (2021), *The Misunderstood History of Gentrification*, he asserts the origins of gentrification in the US to date back to 1915. He argues that gentrification must be understood as an urban phenomenon with historical roots in the very early 20th century and claims he offers a more expansive historical framework. But is this really the historical origins of gentrification in the US? If we say that Haussmannization in the 1850s was an example of state-led gentrification in Paris, might there not be other earlier examples in the US? In the UK context, what about the case of middle-class manufacturers in the 1800s and 1900s purchasing landed estates, displacing the poor, and mixing with the gentry and aristocracy, something British historian Rick Trainor (1989) calls 'gentrification'? In Chapter 5, footnote 3, Trainor (1989) says that the gentrification of industrialists should be distinguished from the geographical usage in which gentrification refers to the social upgrading of residential areas – but should it? The history of gentrification is nebulous and still emerging!

In our 2010 *Reader* we published (in Chapter 8) Hackworth and Smith's stage modelling of gentrification – a very US-focused, indeed New York City–focused, model, yet one that many have generalized to other countries and cities. Hackworth and Smith's model stopped at a third wave in the mid-late 1990s, but in our 2008 *Gentrification* book, we had already identified a fourth wave into the 2000s. Much more recently, Manuel Aalbers (2019) has identified a fifth wave of gentrification in the period 2010 to 2020, one primarily linked to housing financialization (see Part One of this *Reader*, where we reproduce his paper). In the US context, Hyra, Fullilove, Moulden, and Silva (2020) have specified the type of housing financialization taking place during this fifth wave – rental real estate speculation which they connect to fallout from the 2007–2009 Great Recession. Critically they argue that middle class incomers (gentrifiers) are less important in the production of gentrification, and rather that financial speculation is more significant. This fits well with Lees, Shin, and López-Morales (2016: 79–80), who said, 'financial capitalism recovers [and] . . . takes over from [the] crisis', resulting in hyper-gentrification, 'an accelerated taking over of land which is bigger, faster, and much more destructive than the traditional narratives of gentrification'. Yet interestingly, Hyra, Fullilove, Moulden, and Silva (2021) still assume the first wave of gentrification to be the classic, post-war, late 1950s version. Where does that put earlier gentrifications? Osman (2016), like Gale (2021), for example, talks about gentrification in the US in the 1910s to the 1940s. There is much debate and discussion yet to be had on the histories of gentrification globally.

Our 2010 *Reader* was unapologetically urban, as urbanists our main focus was (and, actually for the three of us, still is) on urban gentrification, but in this text, we also highlight and recognize the breakdown of the urban and that rural gentrification is also an important issue. Indeed, the planetary gentrification thesis follows the planetary urbanization thesis in arguing that the distinctions between urban and rural have broken down, for we have all become urban now. As Lees, Shin, and Lopez-Morales (2016) discuss, even Ruth Glass (1964) had begun to point to the inconsistency between urban and rural differences, what Henri Lefebvre (2003) has called 'the final frontier' – the complete urbanization of society, or Brenner and Schmid's (2015) 'the totalization of capital'. One question this does raise, not answered here but rather put out here for discussion and debate, is that if the urban and rural have now broken down, should we just use the term 'gentrification' and not 'rural gentrification' for contemporary processes of gentrification in rural areas? Should we no longer distinguish between urban and rural gentrification as related but different processes? What do we gain or lose from this? Can we say the same for suburban gentrification? What do we lose if we lose the inner city from gentrification? And critically, is this too much (yet again) for the term 'gentrification' to deal with?

The inclusion of a section on digital transformations in Part Five was not even on the table when we collated our 2010 *Reader* and certainly not when Ruth Glass coined the term 'gentrification' in 1964, but it is one of the leading edges of gentrification now. The past decade has seen an explosion in the digital mediation of everyday urban life, so it is not surprising that it has impacted and also created gentrification. A recent book, *The Gentrification of the Internet* (Lingel, 2021), discusses the commercialization of online platforms and the suppression of community. It argues that the internet is gentrified because of shifts in power and control and the prioritization of corporate profits over public good. The internet, like gentrification, raises questions about community and privilege: Who is being actively invited into a space, and who is being displaced? Who benefits from new businesses, new social norms, and new rules, and who loses? Who gets a seat at the table, and who gets left behind? The key features of urban gentrification that Lingel points to in her last chapter – commercialization, isolation, and displacement – all have online counterparts. Lingel states that in both urban and online gentrification, we see power struggles around accessing resources, expressing identity, and the ability of communities to grow and thrive. Apart from showing how the term 'gentrification' has begun to be used outside of classic gentrification studies (see also Schulman, 2012, on the 'gentrification of the mind'), the connection to digital transformation is important. New work is emerging in gentrification studies using big data, machine learning, and artificial intelligence (AI) to try and predict gentrification (see, for example, Reades, De Souza, and Hubbard, 2019); nowcasting, which uses data available virtually in real time, is developing fast (see for example, Glaeser, Kim, and Luca, 2018); and new digital platforms like Airbnb are causing gentrification (see Rozena and Lees, 2021). Short-term accommodation using digital platforms in previously gentrified central urban areas is also playing a significant role in new waves of 'transnational gentrification' in a number of global cities (Urquiaga, Lorente-Riverola and Ruiz Sanchez, 2020). The Zoomification we mentioned earlier could both cause gentrification but also kill it off:

> Nobody *has* to live in New York. There are plenty of places with lower taxes, easier lives, cheaper housing, better weather, and, possibly less racism and corruption, and there will always be ex – New Yorkers who gravitate there. The Zoomification of white-collar work has allowed more people to slip out of its orbit without giving up their professional ambitions. That means New York has to work harder to keep its magnetic force field charged, not just with cheerleading, but by boosting the rewards of living here. The mechanics and politics of gentrification set up repetitive conflicts between newcomers and oldstayers, but the reality is that the city needs both.
>
> (Davidson, 2021)

The trajectories of gentrification are dynamic; they grow and change, triggering new debate and reevaluation.

THE STRUCTURE

The structure of this *Reader* is designed to emphasize contemporary debates in gentrification studies, ones that we feel have emerged as the most important since we published our 2010 *Reader*. The *Reader* contains 24 readings (chapters) on gentrification; each of the six parts include four readings. Each part has an introductory overview that situates the key arguments and contributions within the wider gentrification studies literature. We have also, like we did in our 2010 *Reader*, asked some of the authors included in this *Reader* to reflect back on, and comment on, their work – this *Reader* is, after all, made up of *their* work, as much as our efforts, and hearing what they think now is a valuable exercise.

Part One, 'Thinking about gentrification today', highlights the importance of time, the temporal, and gentrification. It gets us (you) to consider how gentrification today is different to gentrification in the past and to consider whether there were processes of gentrification historically, and indeed are processes currently, not named as such.

Part Two, 'Planetary gentrification', introduces a new thesis that has emerged over the past five to ten years that highlights the complex and often intertwined geographies of gentrification globally. The term 'planetary' is used instead of 'global' to indicate a more open thesis on gentrification, one that reads across diverse geographies and historical periods and, in turn, challenges established ideas.

Part Three, 'Gentrification and comparative urbanism', is a sensible follow-up of Part Two in that it considers how we might *do* planetary research on gentrification. It is not simply a case of looking at similarities and differences; it is a transnational examination that uses one site to pose questions of another, looking at how cities past, present, and future are implicated in each other, posing questions of each other.

Part Four, 'Gentrifications beyond Anglo-America', provides our readers with a selection of journal articles, looking at gentrification in cities outside of the Global North and English-speaking world. A large number of Global South and Global East cities have undergone substantial socio-spatial changes due to intensive state-led and/or private-led investment resulting in the upward and unequal social re-stratification (gentrification) of neighborhoods and communities.

Part Five, 'Gentrification and digital transformations', is a must-have for a new *Reader* on gentrification, as in many ways it is the new gentrification frontier. We just have to think of the Zoomification, mentioned earlier, that was being mooted as a result of COVID-19 – the gentrification of villages, towns, and rural areas, outside of the city, as middle-class professionals were able to work from home. New configurations of gentrification present challenges to gentrification studies, theories, and concepts as they evolve.

Part Six, 'Resisting planetary gentrification', extends Part 7 of the 2010 *Reader* by considering more recent work on resistance and also in contexts beyond Anglo- or Euro-America. The chapters cover how we might conceptualize resistance to gentrification to different kinds of resistance to different kinds of gentrification.

HOW TO USE THIS *READER*

This is a shorter reader, and unlike our 2010 *Reader*, which was partnered with our 2008 *Gentrification* book, it is not partnered with any other book per se. But it would be helpful to our readers if they also read the related text: Lees, Shin, and Lopez-Morales's (2016) *Planetary Gentrification*. Given that this *Reader* is a new volume that extends our 2010 *Reader*, we suggest that people start with the 2010 *Reader* and its partner text and then move on to this *Reader* and its related text; in this way, you will see the progression of ideas on gentrification over time.

This *Reader* provides access to original source academic material related to contemporary debates on gentrification. Instructors/lecturers could organize a full or half unit or module around the six parts in the *Reader*. The further reading sections at the end of each part provide carefully compiled reading lists that can be recommended to students.

But the *Reader* can also be used in more broadly ranging courses, units, or modules, in geography, sociology, urban studies, urban/city planning, anthropology, and so on, where gentrification is featured but not the sole focus.

OUR AUDIENCE

Like with our 2010 *Reader*, our target audience is wide, both academic and indeed non-academic – for example, activists fighting gentrification. Activists fighting gentrification might like to organize discussion around Parts 5 and 6 on the new frontiers of gentrification and resistance to it.

Gentrification studies to date has been dominated by the theorizing of geographers, sociologists, and urban planning scholars, but this is changing as more and more researchers outside of these disciplines are turning their attention to the process. Our audience is deliberately cross-disciplinary, including new disciplinary voices. Related to this the *Reader* itself is deliberately transdisciplinary – it seeks to dissolve boundaries between conventional disciplines, organizing thought on gentrification around the construction of meaning in the context of gentrification as a real-world problem that needs solutions.

Our audience is planetary, yet we are very conscious that this *Reader* has been published in English and includes no non-English gentrification readings. This is an important issue, it continues the Anglo-American hegemony of English language in gentrification studies that concerns us, yet the nature of Anglo-American publishing (and the reality of English as a de facto international lingua franca) meant that we were unable to do otherwise. What we would like to see, if at all possible, is a *Reader* that showcases key writings by scholars in languages other than English.

NOTE

1. https://soundcloud.com/urbantheorylab/utl-podcast-ananya-roy?utm_source=www.urbantheorylab.net&utm_campaign=wtshare&utm_medium=widget&utm_content=https%253A%252F%252Fsoundcloud.com%252Furbantheorylab%252Futl-podcast-ananya-roy

REFERENCES

Aalbers, M. (2019) From Third to Fifth Wave Gentrification, *Tijdschrift voor Economische en Sociale Geografie*, 110:1:1–11.

Bandurski, D. (2015) *Dragons in Diamond Village and Other Tales from the Back Alleys of Urbanising China*. North Sydney, NSW, Australia: Penguin Books.

Brenner, N., and Schmid, C. (2015) Towards a New Epistemology of the Urban? *City*, 15:2–3:151–182.

Chen, A. (2020) The Impact of Land Requisition on Peasant Life in China, *Modern China*, 46:1:79–110.

Clark, E. (2005) The Order and Simplicity of Gentrification: A Political Challenge, in Atkinson, R. and Bridge, G. (eds) *Gentrification in a Global Context: The New Urban Colonialism*, London: Routledge, pp. 256–264.

Davidson, J. (2021) Even before Covid Superstar Cities Were Shrinking, *Curbed*, 27 January, www.curbed.com/2021/01/global-cities-losing-population-nyc-paris-london-tokyo.html.

Gale, D. (2021) *The Misunderstood History of Gentrification: People, Planning, Preservation, and Urban Renewal, 1915–2020*. Philadelphia: Temple University Press.

Ghertner, A. (2015) Why Gentrification Theory Fails in Most of the World, *City*, 19:4:546–556.

Glaeser, E., Kim, H., and Luca, M. (2018) Nowcasting Gentrification: Using Yelp Data to Quantify Neighborhood Change, *AEA Papers and Proceedings*, 108:77–82.

Glass, R. (1964) Introduction: Aspects of Change, in Centre for Urban Studies (ed) *London: Aspects of Change*, London: MacGibbon & Kee, pp. xiii–xlii.

Gransow, B. (2012) Contested Urbanization in China: Exploring Informal Spaces of Migrants-in-the-City, *Harvard Asian Quarterly*, 14:1/2:12–24.

Hyra, D., Fullilove, M., Moulden, D., and Silva, K. (2020) *Contextualizing Gentrification Chaos: The Rise of the Fifth Wave*, www.american.edu/spa/metro-policy/upload/contextualizing-gentrification-chaos.pdf.

Lees, L., Shin, H., and Lopez-Morales, E. (2016) *Planetary Gentrification*, Cambridge: Polity Press.

Lees, L., Slater, T., and Wyly, E. (2008) *Gentrification*, New York: Routledge (republished as e-book in 2013).

Lees, L., Slater, T., and Wyly, E. (2010) *The Gentrification Reader*, London: Routledge.

Lefebvre, H. (2003) *The Urban Revolution*. Translated by Robert Bononno. Minneapolis: University of Minnesota Press.

Ley, D., and Teo, S. Y. (2014) Gentrification in Hong Kong? Epistemology vs. Ontology, *International Journal of Urban and Regional Research*, 38:4:1286–1303.

Li, Z., and Wu, F. (2013) Residential Satisfaction in China's Informal Settlements: A Case Study of Beijing, Shanghai, and Guangzhou, *Urban Geography*, 34:7:923–949.

Lingel, J. (2021) *The Gentrification of the Internet: How to Reclaim Our Digital Freedom*, Berkeley, CA: University of California Press.

Liu, F., Zhu, X., Li, J., Sun, J., and Huang, Q. (2019) Progress of Gentrification Research in China: A Bibliometric Review, *Sustainability*, www.mdpi.com/2071-1050/11/2/367

Maloutas, T. (2012) Contextual Diversity in Gentrification Research, *Critical Sociology*, 38:1:33–48.

Meng, Y. (2000) Gentrification in the Process of Urban Renewal, *Urban Planning Forum*, 1:14–32.

Nancy, J.-L. (2007) *The Creation of the World or Globalization*. Translated by François Raffoul and David Pettigrew. Albany, NY: State University of New York Press.

Osman, S. (2016) What Time is Gentrification? *City & Community*, 15:3:215–219.

Reades, J., De Souza, J., and Hubbard, P. (2019) Understanding Urban Gentrification Through Machine Learning, *Urban Studies*, 56:5:922–942.

Rozena, S., and Lees, L. (2021) The Everyday Lived Experiences of Airbnbification in London, *Social & Cultural Geography*, DOI: 10.1080/14649365.2021.1939124

Schulman, S. (2012) *The Gentrification of the Mind: Witness to a Lost Imagination*, Berkeley, CA: University of California Press.

Shin, H. B., and Lopez-Morales, E. (2018) Beyond Anglo-American Gentrification Theory, in Lees, L. with Phillips, M. (eds) *Handbook of Gentrification Studies*. Cheltenham, UK: Edward Elgar, pp. 13–25.

Sun, S. (2000) Urban Planning Implementation Approach, *Urban Planning Forum*, 1:77–78.

Trainor, R. (1989) The Gentrification of Victorian and Edwardian Industrialists, in Beier, A. L., Cannadine, D., and Rosenheim, J. M. (eds) *The First Industrial Society: Essays in English History in Honour of Lawrence Stone*, Cambridge: Cambridge University Press.

Uribe-Toril, J., Ruiz-Real, J.-L., and de Pablo Valenciano, J. (2018) Gentrification as an Emerging Source of Environmental Research, *Sustainability*, 10:12, www.mdpi.com/2071-1050/10/12/4847

Urquiaga, A., Lorente-Riverola, I., and Ruiz Sanchez, J. (2020) Platform-mediated Short-term Rentals and Gentrification in Madrid, *Urban Studies*, 57:15:3095–3115.

Zhou, C., and Xu, X. (1996) A Summary of Research Progress on Residential Mobility in Western Cities, *Human Geography*, 11:23–27.

PART ONE

Thinking about gentrification today

Gentrification in Seongdong, Seoul, South Korea
(photograph: Hyun Bang Shin)

INTRODUCTION TO PART ONE

> I would like to put in a request to historians to periodize gentrification.
>
> (Schulman, 2012: 18)

> Angkor (in Cambodia) offers one kind of origin story for the process that today we call gentrification.
>
> (Newitz, 2021)

What is gentrification in relation to time and space? What is time-space or space-time? These are questions increasingly being asked by gentrification researchers as they reflect on, critique, and seek to advance over 60 years of scholarship on gentrification. For a long time, despite an explosion in the literature on gentrification, few scholars thought about the phenomenon's origin(s), but this is changing. For those who would stick to Ruth Glass's 1964 definition of gentrification the time and space is 1960s London, a post–Second World War European city (even if back then, it did not really see itself as European as it clung on to the vestiges of a decaying empire). But of course, the history of gentrification did not start in the 1960s, when Glass coined the term; as our 2008 *Gentrification* text discusses, the brownstoning movement in the US predated this and led to gentrification, as did Haussmannization in Paris, as we mentioned earlier.

In recent years, there has been renewed interest and focus on older gentrifications – even if they were not termed that – and newer gentrifications – the constant mutations of this process. This has raised some critical questions – fresh debate on whether we are expanding the definition of gentrification too far, and that it will likely collapse under the weight of this burden. Of course, Bondi (1999) made the same charge over a decade ago, but importantly, it did not collapse under the weight of its supposed burden but quite the opposite – a rich, complex literature on new forms of gentrification developed, from new-build gentrification to green gentrification to digital gentrification, which are a part in this *Reader*. The spaces of gentrification studies are now global, but the process of gentrification has probably been global for some time. Gentrification is a spatial process – it moves across space (and through time). It is also about spatial location and capitalizing on that. In our 2008 and 2010 books, we discussed work on uneven development as related to gentrification, much of this work focused on the scale of neighborhoods, less so whole cities, but with the 'global turn' in gentrification studies, the scale is now planetary. How might we(re)theorize the spatial in gentrification at this scale? The challenge is to refract the theory of uneven development through the planetary. As Smith (2002: 385) said over a decade ago, 'the temporal and spatial limits of gentrification have yet to be explored'; this remains the case today.

The four readings we have chosen for Part One think about the time-space and space-time of gentrification. Osman (2016, Chapter 1 of this book) is clear that gentrification is much older than Ruth Glass and rightly argues that space has been well theorized in gentrification studies, but time has not received the same attention. Wyly (2017, Chapter 2 of this book) takes us away from the long-standing view that gentrification is localized, neighborhood based, and confined to the bounds of cities. He argues that the assumption that gentrification theory began with a neighborhood-scale process in London that was expanded on is flawed. Shin and Lopez-Morales (2018, Chapter 3 of this book) discuss what it means to research gentrification in non-Anglo-American spaces; they rescue gentrification from its confinement to the place specificities of 1960s London. Aalbers (2019, Chapter 4 of this volume) extends forward our discussion of different waves or stages of gentrification in our 2010 *Reader*, identifying a fifth wave of gentrification (which is even more intense and generalized), and is aware of others who question the usefulness of Anglo-/Euro-American state models for periodizing gentrification in say China.

REFERENCES AND FURTHER READING

Aalbers, M. (2019) Revisiting 'The changing state of gentrification' – Introduction to the Forum: From third to fifth-wave gentrification, *Tijdschrift voor Economische en Sociale Geografie*, 110:1: 1–11.

Baeten, G., Listerborn, C., Persdotter, M., and Pull, E. (eds) (2020) *Housing Displacement: Conceptual and Methodological Issues*, Routledge: London.

Bondi, L. (1999) Between the woof and the weft: A response to Loretta Lees, *Environment and Planning D: Society and Space*, 17:3: 253–255.

Brown-Saracino, J. (2017) Explicating divided approaches to gentrification and growing income inequality, *Annual Review of Sociology*, 43: 515–539.

Gale, D. (2021) *The Misunderstood History of Gentrification: People, Planning, Preservation, and Urban Renewal, 1915–2020*. Philadelphia: Temple University Press.

Hammami, F., Jewesbury, D., and Valli, C. (eds) (2021) *Heritage, Gentrification and Resistance in the Neoliberal City*. New York and Oxford: Berghahn Books.

Holgersen, S. (2020) Intervention – the 'middle class' does not exist: A critique of gentrification research, *Antipode* (https://antipodeonline.org/2020/09/09/the-middle-class-does-not-exist/)

Hyra, D., Fullilove, M., Moulden, D., and Silva, K. (2020) Contextualizing gentrification chaos: The rise of the fifth wave (www.american.edu/spa/metro-policy/upload/contextualizing-gentrification-chaos.pdf)

Newitz, A. (2021) Unearthing an origin story of gentrification, *The Atlantic*, May 11 (www.theatlantic.com/ideas/archive/2021/05/angkor-cambodia-gentrification/618848/)

Osman, S. (2016) What Time is Gentrification? *City & Community*, 15:3:215–219.

Schlichtman, J. J., and Patch, J. (2017) *Gentrifier*, Toronto: University of Toronto Press.

Schulman, S. (2012) *The Gentrification of the Mind: Witness to a Lost Imagination*, Berkeley, CA: University of California Press.

Shin, H.B., and López-Morales, E. (2018) Beyond Anglo-American Gentrification Theory, in Lees, L. with Phillips, M. (eds) *Handbook of Gentrification Studies*, Cheltenham, UK: Edward Elgar, pp. 13–25.

Smith, D. (2002) Extending the temporal and spatial limits of gentrification: A research agenda for population geographers, *International Journal of Population Geography*, 8:6: 385–394.

Wyly, E. (2017) Gentrification, in Short, J.R. (ed) *A Research Agenda for Cities*, Cheltenham, UK: Edward Elgar, pp. 113–124.

1
What time is gentrification?

Suleiman Osman

In January 1922, 40 years before sociologist Ruth Glass coined the term, a group of Greenwich Village artists organized one of New York City's earliest protests against gentrification. In an appeal to the District Attorney's office, the League of American Artists complained that rising rents in the bohemian district were pricing out painters and sculptors. The group blamed both landlords and wealthy newcomers. "Real estate agents are booming the studio idea and stressing the idea of the so called 'free-life' of artists to such an extent that bona-fide artists are being denied renewals of leases and are unable to obtain suitable studio quarters," said League secretary Julian Bowes. Pseudo bohemians paid exorbitant rents "in order to win the reputation of being artistic, though they know no art," complained illustrator Howard Chandler Christie. "Prices have gone up so that the poor artist who is struggling to make a start is being driven out of Manhattan," warned Bowes. "Many artists have been driven over to Brooklyn." The League admitted that the connection between urban bohemianism and real estate speculation was not new. "There has always been more or less invasion of the artistic quarters of this city by hypocrites and fakers, but the situation has become acute because of the greed of the landlords in deliberately seeking to supplant genuine artists with wealthy and questionable tenants." Bowes implored the city to raid buildings. The District Attorney pointed out it was perfectly legal for anybody to live in a studio whether an "art- artist" or an art "pretender" (*New York Times*, September 1922).

New York City was not alone. As rents rose in New Orleans' French Quarter, Boston's Beacon Hill, and Charleston's Tradd Street, the *New York Times* predicted that sociologists would one day take interest in the mysterious process that as of yet had no name. "As in Greenwich Village," mused the newspaper in 1922, "the most ardent of the poseurs [in the French Quarter], the youths with the longest and girls with the shortest hair, hail from Peoria and Oshkosh. Someday a patient sociologist will chart the invisible watershed which turns some of these acolytes of art toward New York Bay and some toward the Gulf" (*New York Times*, July 1922).

Gentrification is much older than Ruth Glass. Yet it is a phenomenon still without a history. One can find examples of adaptive reuse of ruins in cities from ancient Greece to Renaissance Italy (Jacks 2008). In the early 20th century, architects and artists rehabilitated townhouses, horse stables, adobe homes, barns, and tenements in New York City, Charleston, New Orleans, Washington DC, and many other cities, often displacing the poor (Osman 2016). Yet despite calls by scholars for more attention to process and change over time (Lees 2000), detailed historical research about the phenomenon is still scant. Scholarship about the "space" of gentrification is theoretically sophisticated with rich debates about displacement, landscape, region and scale. The "time" (Borer 2010) of gentrification is in comparison underexamined.

Gentrification history is still in its infancy. Urban historians have been slow to tackle the subject. But several recent books by young historians are a harbinger of a growing interest (Shkuda 2016; Goldstein 2017). Social scientists have made more progress. Smith (1996) gave the first stab at a "short history" in his seminal *New Urban Frontier*. Lees et al. (2007) distinguish between the small-scale, sweat equity "classical gentrification" first described by Ruth Glass in the 1960s and the more mature and multivaried phenomenon spearheaded today by developers, speculators, and the state. Hackworth and Smith (2001) offer the first periodization of gentrification that, although too strictly bound to neo- Marxist theory (Lees et al. 2007), provides a good foundation to build upon. Others have since modified and added to their three "waves" (Lees 2003; Osman 2016). More detailed research into the legal, political, social, and cultural evolution of gentrification will flesh out these initial frameworks or help develop alternatives.

Aside from the trite observation that gentrification has been around for a long time, what might historical analysis add to what is already an abundant scholarship on gentrification? First, a "long history" complicates theoretical frameworks that point to gentrification as evidence of a "new" city. Second, historical analysis, memory studies, and the sociology of time can help scholars better analyze the politics of space-time that are unique to gentrifying districts. Finally, by examining process and change over time, a historical approach might help break through the "theoretical logjam" and "protracted definitional debates" that hamper the field.

THE NON-NEWNESS OF GENTRIFICATION

In contrast to suburbanization, which scholars consider a long-standing feature of growing cities, gentrification is often mistakenly treated as a break from the past. Many point to the phenomenon thus as evidence to support competing theories about the emergence of a "new" city (Beauregard and Haila 1997) that is neoliberal, postmodern, "inverted" (Ehrenalt 2012), or globalized. Gentrification though is a far older urban process. (In fact, the better research question may be why gentrification slowed during the mid-twentieth century in North America and Europe rather than why it emerged in the late twentieth.) This is not to debunk what are highly sophisticated and useful theoretical frameworks. But as Beauregard and Haila (1997) point out, cities are always incomplete with past and current influences and a mix of old and new processes. A "long history" will help scholars more accurately pinpoint continuities and breaks.

THE SPACE – TIME OF GENTRIFICATION

More historical research will help scholars further analyze the politics of space – time (Clark 2005; Borer 2010) that are particular to gentrifying districts. Gentrification is a phenomenon uniquely invested in history. Gentrifiers are often drawn to "historic" areas and are motivated by a "preservation ethos" that is at times revanchist and at other times genuinely supportive of the poor (Brown-Saracino 2009). Long-time residents similarly draw from the past to fight gentrification in some cases and to market a sense of ethnic authenticity to eager consumers in others (Zukin 2009). Today all residents are influenced by the memory of earlier waves of gentrification. It would be fascinating to trace the evolution of this vernacular "historiography" of gentrification. What are the archives and other sources that residents use? How much of this history is real and imagined? "New arrivals," "old timers," "newcomers," and "original residents" are temporal constructs that in every case study need to be rigorously historicized. In the 1970s, for example, many of the African-American and Latino renters facing displacement pressure from townhouse rehabbers in areas like Boston's South End or Brooklyn's Boerum Hill were relative newcomers. Harlem today has a much longer African-American history with a diverse constellation of African-American old-timers, middle-class newcomers, as well as Caribbean and African immigrants (Jackson 2003). Historical research and memory studies will help scholars more accurately unpack the ways residents mobilize time with varying degrees of power and success (Borer 2010). When do newcomers begin to position themselves as old timers? What groups of old timers do gentrifiers valorize over others? How can history be used to emplace and displace?

TOWARD A HISTORY OF GENTRIFICATION

After a golden age from the 1980s to the early 2000s, gentrification theory has hit a rut. Once groundbreaking debates about why the phenomenon happens on the local level, as well as its benefits and drawbacks, have largely been resolved or reached a "stalemate" (Zukin 1987). Attempts to look at gentrification on a global scale or at a wider array of urban processes are promising but spark criticism that the term has become too protean (Lees et al. 2016). "Protracted definitional debates" (Davidson 2011), rehashed questions, and "continued squabbles" (Slater 2004) have led to an "ontological crisis" and "impasse" (Davidson 2011; Lees 2000). The general public is more preoccupied with the issue than ever. But is there anything new to say? More historical and temporal analysis could perhaps offer one new avenue of research and help break through this "theoretical logjam" (Lees 2000).

Some of the knottiest debates about gentrification may have historical answers rather than purely theoretical ones. Is gentrification beneficial or detrimental for cities? A historical approach would reject a singular answer and instead draw on nuanced empirical studies (Freeman 2006; Newman and Wyly 2006) and qualitative research to examine the changing impact of gentrification on the poor in different locations over time. When has gentrification caused more or less displacement and why? How has the role of the state changed over time and why? The answers likely do not fit into a neat declension narrative. But this does not mean a historical approach is necessarily devoid of critical perspectives, critiques of capitalism, or concerns about social justice (Clark 2005; Slater 2006). A rash of evictions in the late 1970s and early 1980s led to local mobilization against gentrification and condo conversions in cities around the United States for example. Who made up these early anti-gentrification groups? What were their political strategies and tactics? Fifty-four U.S. cities in the late 1970s and 1980s passed ordinances regulating speculation and condominium conversions (Hartman et al. 1982). Did political activism successfully reduce rates of direct displacement (Ley and Dobson 2008)? Did the radicals of the late 1970s later support the social mix policies of the 1990s that displaced public housing residents (Goldstein 2017)?

A historical perspective can also provide a fuller understanding of the shifting cultural landscape of gentrification. Where scholars once debated about whether gentrification is emancipatory or revanchist, most agree now that the ideology and outlook of both new arrivals and long-time residents is quite diverse and nuanced (Brown-Saracino 2009; Freeman 2006; Jackson 2003). A historical analysis could add a temporal dimension to the mix. Different eras, such as the Lower East Side in the 1980s (Smith 1996), were likely more revanchist or emancipatory than others. The meaning of terms such as authenticity, diversity, the frontier, and even gentrification itself have changed over time. The evolving racial and class geography of gentrification could be better historicized. How did the racial, class, gender, and sexual politics of gentrification differ in Greenwich Village of the 1920s, Brownstone Brooklyn of the 1960s, the Lower East Side of the 1980s, and Harlem of the 2000s? One will likely find significant continuities and important differences.

Finally, a historical approach may offer an answer to the intractable debate about how to define gentrification. Should the term be limited to the rehabilitation and adaptive reuse of older buildings or expanded to include all types of development? I would argue that although the difference has blurred today, there does exist a salient historical distinction that should be retained. A purely class-based definition of gentrification fruitfully expands the scope of analysis in the present. But it becomes reductive when traced through the past. Greenwich Village rehabber Jane Jacobs and urban renewal czar Robert Moses may have been both participating in the embourgeoisment of the center city. But their histories intersect with the history of gender, architecture, historic preservation, race, urban politics, and environmentalism in unique ways. Townhouse rehabbers in the 1960s and 1970s, for example, had political and cultural links to antiwar activism, anarchist squatting, anti-expressway protests, urban homesteading, recycling, historic preservation, the "neighborhood movement" and "back to the land" environmentalism. Was their urban project really indistinguishable from Baron Von Haussmann in Paris? More work by historical sociologists can help develop a periodization for gentrification that expands its scope for the present without abandoning its distinct genealogy.

CONCLUSION

The goal of this short essay is not to provide a comprehensive overview of the wide-ranging scholarship on gentrification. I have likely overlooked work that has already addressed these themes. Nor is it to set up an outdated distinction between history and theory. Rather it is to suggest new research questions and to encourage scholars to examine the "time" of gentrification with the same impressive depth that they have its "space." City dwellers around the world are struggling to make sense of gentrification. Time is of the essence.

REFERENCES

Beauregard, Robert A., and Anne Haila. 1997. "The Unavoidable Incompleteness of the City." *American Behavioral Science* 41(3):327–341.

Borer, Michael Ian. 2010. "From Collective Memory to Collective Imagination: Time, Place, and Urban Redevelopment." *Symbolic Interaction* 33(1):96–114.

Brown-Saracino, Japonica. 2009. *A Neighborhood That Never Changes: Gentrification, Social Preservation and the Search for Authenticity*. Chicago and London: University of Chicago Press.

Butler, Tim. 2007. "For Gentrification?" *Environment and Planning A* 39(1):162–181.

Clark, Eric. 2005. "The Order and Simplicity of Gentrification." Pp. 256–264 in *Gentrification in a Global Context: The New Urban Colonialism*, edited by Rowland Atkinson and Gary Bridge. London and New York: Routledge.

Davidson, Mark. 2011. "Gentrification in Crisis: Towards Consensus or Disagreement?" *Urban Studies* 48(10):1987–1996.

Ehrenalt, Alan. 2012. *The Great Inversion and the Future of the American City*. New York: Vintage Books.

Freeman, Lance. 2006. *There Goes the 'Hood: Views of Gentrification from the Ground Up*. Philadelphia, PA: Temple University Press.

Goldstein, Brian D. 2017. *The Roots of Urban Renaissance: Gentrification and the Struggle Over Harlem*. Cambridge, MA: Harvard University Press.

"Greenwich Village on Royal Street." *New York Times*. July 23, 1922.

Hackworth, Jason, and Neil Smith. 2001. "The Changing State of Gentrification." *Tijdschrift voor economische en sociale geografie* 92:464–477.

Hartman, Chester, Dennis Keating, and Richard LeGates. 1982. *Displacement: How to Fight It*. Berkeley, CA: National Housing Law Project.

Jacks, Philip. 2008. "Restauratio and Reuse: The Afterlife of Roman Ruins." *Places* 20(1):10–20.

Jackson, John L. 2003. *Harlemworld: Doing Race and Class in Contemporary Black America*. Chicago, IL: University of Chicago Press.

Lees, Loretta. 2000. "A Reappraisal of Gentrification: Towards a 'Geography of Gentrification'." *Progress in Human Geography* 24(3):389–408.

———. 2003. "Super-gentrification: The Case of Brooklyn Heights, New York City." *Urban Studies* 40(12): 2487–2509.

Lees, Loretta, Hyun-Bang Shin, and Ernesto López-Morales. 2016. *Planetary Gentrification*. Cambridge: Polity Press.

Lees, Loretta, Tom Slater, and Elvin Wyly. 2007. *Gentrification*. London: Routledge.

Ley, David, and Cory Dobson. 2008. "Are There Limits to Gentrification? The Contexts of Impeded Gentrification in Vancouver." *Urban Studies* 45(12):2471–2498.

Newman, Kathe, and Elvin K. Wyly. 2006. "The Right to Stay Put, Revisited: Gentrification and Resistance to Displacement in New York City." *Urban Studies* 43(1):23–57.

Osman, Suleiman. 2016. "Gentrification in the United States." *Oxford Research Encyclopedia of American History*. http://doi.org/10.1093/acrefore/9780199329175.013.135.

"Raid Fake Studios, is Plea of Artists." *New York Times*. September 17, 1922.

Shkuda, Aaron. 2016. *The Lofts of SoHo: Gentrification, Art, and Industry in New York, 1950–1980*. Chicago, IL: University of Chicago Press.

Slater, Tom. 2004. "North American Gentrification? Revanchist and Emancipatory Perspectives Explored." *Environment and Planning A* 36:1191–1213.

———. 2006. "The Eviction of Critical Perspectives from Gentrification Research." *International Journal of Urban and Regional Research* 30(4):737–757.

Smith, Neil. 1996. *The New Urban Frontier: Gentrification and the Revanchist City*. New York: Routledge.

Zukin, Sharon. 1987. "Gentrification: Culture and Capital in the Urban Core." *Annual Review of Sociology* 13: 129–147.

———. 2009. *The Death and Life of Authentic Places*. New York: Oxford University Press.

2
Gentrification

Elvin Wyly

VANCOUVER, SILICON VALLEY, OXFORD, AND NANJING

If average home sales prices are compared to average local incomes, the City of Vancouver, in British Columbia on the West Coast of North America, is often tied with Sydney, Australia, as the world's second most expensive real estate market after Hong Kong. The latest record-setting Vancouver real estate transaction involved a mansion sold by Don Mattrick, CEO of the social media company Zynga, for C$51.8 million; the private sale in the city's elite West Point Grey neighborhood might well have been "the biggest residential transaction ever conducted in Canada" (Young, 2015), perhaps unsurprisingly in light of the fact that CNBC had ranked Mattrick as the second highest paid CEO in the San Francisco Bay Area. But if it was a farming simulation social networking game (Farmville) that put Zynga on the path to success with a suite of games that eventually reached more than 260 million monthly active users, the company's headquarters were quintessentially urban. "The last time I was in San Francisco," reports the journalist Samantha Allen (2014),

> I saw an entire family living in a tent underneath the highway overpass across the street from Zynga's offices. This image of abject poverty set against the headquarters of the social gaming giant . . . is a painfully apt reminder of the social and economic forces that are currently turning San Francisco into a shadow of its former self: Silicon Valley capitalism, gentrification, and the widening income inequality that results from their mutual interaction.

Wall Street capitalism cheered with a 10.4 percent jump in Zynga shares (and another 5.9 percent boost in after-hours action) on the news of recruiting Mattrick, who had been running Microsoft's Xbox division (Rusli and Ovide, 2013).

Mattrick, a native Vancouverite "who lives like a Saudi prince and jets to work" (LaPorte, 2013) and boasts of being friends with Wayne Gretzky and Steven Spielberg (Young, 2015), moved quickly to reposition Zynga towards games played on smart-phones and tablets. The company's shares "soared the most since its initial public offering" (Edwards, 2014) when Mattrick fired 314 people on the same day he sealed a US$527 million deal to buy NaturalMotion, an Oxford University spinoff developed by a neuroscientist pursuing a PhD in Complex Systems and Zoology before he "decided to go in a totally different direction" (Cutler, 2014). Biological expertise yielded advanced 3D animation and a cutting-edge "middleware" enterprise that rendered the stunningly realistic action in the *Grand Theft Auto* series and the *Lord of the Rings* trilogy. Oxford got a 10 percent cut of the NaturalMotion acquisition – part of a wave of innovation that generated more than US$200 million in venture capital raised by Oxford-based startups in 2015.

The Zynga – NaturalMotion – Oxford narrative was then featured prominently in coverage of the advice offered by Professor Andrew Hamilton, outgoing vice-chancellor of Oxford, on how to achieve the full potential of a twenty-first-century university. Part of Oxford's success, we are told, comes from being "one of the most international universities in the world," and part comes from being "at the centre of a 'knowledge spine,' embracing scientific and entrepreneurial establishments" from a vast regional urban network (Rafferty, 2015). Similar "corridors of knowledge" are also fundamental to the success of other "world-class universities, including Cambridge, Stanford, and Harvard-MIT," we learn from a journalist's report of Hamilton's remarks, published as a commentary in the *South China Morning Post*. The commentary is presented as a defense of academic freedom and the "clash of ideas" that "add to the richness of human knowledge" as opposed to Xi Jinping's apparent vision of "universities as teaching machines that preach the party line, didactic Confucianism at work" (Rafferty, 2015).

Within the Chinese People's Political Consultative Conference, though, the Nanjing City representative is a former farmer – a real one, not a Farmville simulation – who worked his way up to create a "skyscraper-building conglomerate" while, according to his corporate website, "pursuing the goal of achieving economic, social, and environmental efficiency and giving back to communities" (quoted in Young, 2015). This is Chen Mailin, who bought that C$52 million Vancouver home from Don Mattrick. "I love Vancouver. It's a very beautiful city," the media-shy Chen told CBC News (2015) in a rare interview: "They have the best education for kids."

In this story, what urban process is at work? Is this about knowledge corridors, creative cities, and Silicon Valley disruptive innovation? Twenty-first century universities? Transnationalism? The rise of China? To be sure, all of these are involved. But in this chapter I suggest that vignettes like these help us gain a fresh perspective on gentrification. There's an enormous academic literature on gentrification, and the keyword is a widely recognized battle cry among policy elites, developers, investors, journalists, and activists. Yet no matter how eloquent and sophisticated it has become over the years, all of this research and debate has reinforced a view of gentrification as a localized, neighborhood-scale process that takes place within the bounds of cities as discrete spatial containers. This way of thinking invariably descends into endless empirical tedium. The family living in a tent next to Zynga's headquarters is a sign of inequality, critics say, but nobody was directly displaced as the new social media giants moved into the patchwork of old industrial buildings, parking lots, and elevated freeways of San Francisco's South of Market (SoMa) district – so how can this be gentrification? Likewise, the Don Mattrick – Chen Mailin transaction may be an interesting case of globalizing real estate markets, but critics will note that Mattrick is hardly a poor renter facing eviction like those constantly on the edge of homelessness in Vancouver's infamous Downtown Eastside, and the elite enclave of West Point Grey is not the downgraded inner-city poor or working-class community that everyone envisions when the word "gentrification" is used.

I suggest that we need to rethink our understandings of gentrification. At the precise moment when gentrification is becoming thoroughly pervasive, transnational, and spatially contingent – manifest in multiple kinds of localized yet often fast-moving spatial contexts – our tradition-bound definitions are blinding us to the true urban significance of contemporary planetary urbanization. "Gentrification" is and should be central to our research agenda on cities, but not in the ways we've been led to believe. We need to stop obsessing over the empirics of precise, neighborhood-level details of *where* urban class succession takes place; instead we must place greater emphasis on *how* class relations evolve. We must see the entire networked constellation of individuals, institutions, and competitive processes as a clear manifestation of contemporary gentrification. Moreover, I argue that while many of the details of today's postcolonial planetary urbanization are new, there is absolutely nothing novel about a cosmopolitan, networked understanding of gentrification: this is an excavation of a forgotten history. Put simply, most discussions of gentrification over the past half century (including my own scribblings on the subject) have been misguided. From the very beginning, we have misunderstood the process that the word "gentrification" tried to capture.

To explain what I mean, I'll reconsider the theoretical and political history of the word and the concept before returning to today's more cosmopolitan forms of planetary gentrification.

WHAT IS GENTRIFICATION?

Everyone who studies gentrification eventually gets around to mentioning that the word was coined by Ruth Glass in the early 1960s, to describe changes underway in parts of post-World War II London. Here's the full paragraph where Glass (1964, pp. xviii–xix) describes what's happening:

> One by one, many of the working-class quarters of London have been invaded by the middle classes – upper and lower. Shabby, modest mews and cottages – two rooms up and two rooms down – have been taken over, when their leases have expired, and have become elegant, expensive residences. Larger Victorian houses, downgraded in an earlier

or recent period – which were used as lodging houses or were otherwise in multiple occupation – have been upgraded once again. Nowadays, many of these houses are being subdivided into costly flats or "houselets" (in terms of the new real estate snob jargon). The current social status and value of such dwellings are frequently in inverse relation to previous levels in their neighbourhoods. Once this process of "gentrification" starts in a district, it goes on rapidly until all or most of the original working-class occupiers are displaced, and the whole social character of the district is changed. There is very little left of the poorer enclaves of Hampstead and Chelsea: in those boroughs, the upper-middle-class takeover was consolidated some time ago. The invasion has since spread to Islington, Paddington, North Kensington – even to the 'shady' parts of Notting Hill – to Battersea, and to several other districts, north and south of the river. The East End has so far been exempt, although before long some of its districts, too, are likely to be affected. And this is an inevitable development, in view of the demographic, economic and political pressures to which London, and especially central London, has been subjected.

An enormous scholarly literature, rich with empirical detail and theoretical debate, has developed in the half century since Glass wrote these words (for samples, see Lees et al., 2010, 2015). If we had to summarize a "consensus" definition, it might look like this: gentrification is a transformation of 1) inner-city neighborhoods, where 2) poor and working-class residents are replaced or displaced by middle- or upper-class residents, through 3) the combined effects of wider societal changes that alter the socio-cultural meanings of urban living, and the land-market economics that can make reinvestment into "downgraded" inner-city districts extremely profitable.

Consensus, however, has always been tenuous and contested. Many who study (or fight) the process define the process broadly to include the upscaling of suburbs, rural areas, commercial/retail spaces, the construction of luxury condos on old waterfront, industrial, and railway lands, and even what Lees calls the "super-gentrification" displacement of the rich by the super-rich. Others question the "meaningless terminological entrepreneurship" (Palen and London, 1984, p. 6) of expanding definitions that conflate "many diverse if interrelated" events and causal processes into a singular and thus fatally "chaotic" concept (Beauregard, 1986, p. 40). At the extreme, the "far broader meaning of gentrification" developed by the "new scholarship" (Sassen, 1991, p. 255) is attacked as "definitional overload." Liz Bondi (1999, p. 255) is the most explicit:

> Ruth Glass's (1964) coining of the term "gentrification" opened up new questions about urban change. But the more researchers have attempted to pin it down the more burdens the concept has had to carry. Maybe the loss of momentum around gentrification reflects its inability to open up new insights, and maybe it is time to allow it to disintegrate under the weight of these burdens.

Recently, more serious criticisms have emerged. Thomas Maloutas (2011, p. 34) argues that gentrification is "highly dependent on contextual causality," and that any attempt to apply a concept that is so deeply enmeshed in the "Anglo-American metropolis" to the different circumstances of cities elsewhere in the world is nothing short of intellectual colonialism. Others warn against a "diffusionist" tendency to see gentrification spreading from the Global North to the Global South (Lees, 2012), and remind us that the language and processes of urban change take very different forms in the developmental states of East Asia (Ley and Teo, 2013; Ong, 2011). Asher Ghertner (2015, p. 552) argues that the concept of gentrification "renders unthinkable and invisible" the legal and regulatory causes of the most violent forms of displacement in societies with legacies of public land ownership, informality, and common property – China, post-socialist Europe, many parts of Southeast Asia and sub-Saharan Africa – and thus gentrification theory "fails in much of the world." In a recent commentary, Matthias Bernt (2016, p. 1) summarizes where the literature now stands:

> While conceptual quarrels over the question whether gentrification as a concept is overstretched are not brand new ... the intensity with which gentrification is challenged as a concept has changed considerably in the last couple of years. Echoing the call of postcolonial thinkers to "provincialize" Western theories, today more and more scholars tend to see gentrification as an urban phenomenon rooted in rather specific

experiences made in a handful of Western metropolises in the last century.

Gentrification has always inspired heated debate, but today's controversies are globally divisive binaries. Either gentrification is a globalizing process, or this assertion is itself a Northern/Western neocolonial imposition. Either the process is what Atkinson and Bridge (2005) label "the new urban colonialism," or the label is itself the product of enduring neocolonial structures in knowledge production. The intensity of this debate makes it clear that the top priority for a research agenda on gentrification involves sustained, comparative, multi-lingual, cross-cultural ethnographic fieldwork to reconcile the standpoint-epistemological divides of positionality and power between theories and experiences of urbanism across the North/South divide. Sadly, I am pathetically unqualified to offer guidance on how to do this (but I am inspired by the valuable but divergent perspectives we get by juxtaposing Smith, 2011, Slater, 2015, and Schafran, 2014, with Roy, forthcoming, Ley and Teo, 2013, Harris, 2008, Ghertner, 2015, Ren, 2015, and Lees et al., 2015). What I offer here is more modest, albeit for certain post-Reaganite American Christians a bit more offensive (Witham, 2002) with insufficient time or space for nuance (Healy, 2016). I offer a reminder that we will never understand today's global gentrification debates if we misunderstand the "contextual causality" of the Global North setting in which gentrification was first diagnosed. Today's debates are flawed insofar as they assume that 1) gentrification theory began with concerns about a neighborhood-scale process that was 2) focused on the particular circumstances of London, and that 3) subsequent researchers "expanded" this original definition.

These assumptions collapse when we stop treating Ruth Glass's (1964) definition as scripture. Everyone cites the eloquent words about shabby mews and cottages being taken over and upgraded, and everyone delights in exploring the contemptuous connotations of the etymology of the English "gentry." But if we actually read the essay – a lengthy introduction to an edited collection of research papers analyzing the results of the Third Survey of London Life and Labour – a very different set of meanings appears. Yes, it's about London. But it's a situated, transitional London at a dramatic historical post-war, post-colonializing moment. The entire purpose of the Centre for Urban Studies that Glass directed was to be deeply critical and cosmopolitan – scrutinizing the cultural and planning histories of urbanism in Britain in the context of what was happening in Asia, Africa, and Latin America (see Glass, 1963). Glass's use of the word "gentrification" appears a few pages into an extraordinary, wide-ranging analysis. She examines regional industrial restructuring, commuting and transportation networks, the consolidation and upscaling of retail and consumption spaces, and the kaleidoscope of occupational, educational, aesthetic, and class subcultures. She analyzes the legacy of imperial rule abroad that now brings the descendants of slaves and indentured servants from the far reaches of the Commonwealth. She analyzes how the segregation, racism, and economic oppression of the empire's racialized citizens expose the flaws of British society – and its reluctance to adapt to "the postcolonial world of today." Glass, who died in 1990, would be a passionate advocate of today's postcolonial calls to provincialize the Global North, the West, and the "developed" world; this was exactly what she was trying to do in the early 1960s (see also Glass, 1962). Every sentence shines with brilliant analytical rigor and unforgiving, mischievous sabotage of an arrogant, frayed imperial hegemony poised between a history of inherited class privilege and the mindless modernism of technological worship, commodified mass communication, and intensified consumption.

Reading Glass's entire essay makes it clear that gentrification is far more than a neighborhood-scale process. While the term is introduced amidst a description of a specific set of sites in central London, the word and the concept are utterly meaningless without an appreciation of the wider context – the newfound post-war affluence of London, the public debates over its creeping "Americanization," and its precarious position as the primate city of a planetary Commonwealth on the edge of decolonization. Over the years, the best work on gentrification has always considered the interdependencies between local and extra-local processes – this is a common theme uniting the otherwise contrasting approaches of David Ley's socio-cultural postindustrial society analysis and Neil Smith's work on circuits of capital, for instance (cf. Lees et al., 2015, pp. 449–450). Yet we must go further, to look past all the details of neighborhoods, housing conditions, occupational groupings, consumption preferences, and even the legal and institutional specifics of displacement, rent, tenure, and property. All of these things matter. But they are all manifestations of a much deeper essence in the ontology – the nature of being – in an urban world: *competition*. Glass repeatedly emphasizes the "competition for space" that has become "more and more intense." She describes many different subcultures of migrants – from other parts of Britain and from all over the world – who have one thing in common: the intense competition for a place to live that renders them targets for ever-worsening exploitation. She describes how spiraling central land values force firms to allocate scarce commercial space to ever-higher tiers of the managerial and executive workforce – amidst a regional suburbanization that stretches journeys-to-work so far that highly paid workers take tiny *pied-à-terre* second homes near their financial-district workplaces (fueling a further spiral of locational competition).

Again and again Glass documents the intensification of competition in urban life, and she makes it clear that upscale "invasions" are by no means *natural*, but they are *inevitable* given certain theories and decisions. The problem lies in the dangerous perversions of how urban thought and planning understood "human nature." Glass sees rising competition as inevitable given the interaction between two factors. First, the Great Depression reinforced deeply entrenched "neo-Malthusian" hopes and fears of population decline, leading to assumptions of a stationary economy and culture that were embedded into Patrick Abercrombie's (1945) *Greater London Plan 1944*. Second, in the early 1950s the first post-war Conservative Government began a series of drastic amendments that transformed the Town and Country Planning Act 1947 into "anti-planning" legislation. Through the 1950s, amendments "denationalised" development rights, relaxed rent controls, required local authorities undertaking public-purpose redevelopment to pay full market price for land assessed at full development potential, and thus "liberated" market speculation. "In such circumstances," Glass (1964, p. xx) observed,

> any district in or near London, however dingy or unfashionable before, is likely to become expensive; and London may quite soon be a city which illustrates the principle of the survival of the fittest – the financially fittest, who can still afford to work and live there. (Not long ago, the then Housing Minister advised those who cannot pay the price to move out.)

For the study of gentrification, Ruth Glass is undisputably what Foucault (1969, p. 387) called a "founder of discursivity." While the gentrification process has a much longer history (and has changed in all sorts of ways in the last 50 years), her essay established certain possibilities conditioning the formation of other texts – setting the parameters in which later generations refine and challenge a discourse and what it seeks to represent and produce. My purpose in undertaking this "return to the origin" (Foucault, 1969) is to excavate the forgotten histories of the time and place in which Glass was writing. That time and place – the first decades after World War II in England – was shaped by the combination of newfound affluence, a collapsing global colonial empire, the new modernist possibilities of Karl Pearson's (Pearson and Moul, 1927) statistical innovations as applied to human populations as envisioned by Francis Galton (1869), and the first Orwellian echos of the "liberating markets" language we now call neoliberalism.

Considering that context makes it clear that the essence of gentrification is the urban evolution of human competition. Glass chose her words carefully, and the evolutionary references are not simply casual metaphors. Elsewhere she wrote of "incessant competition" of land uses, the "takeover" of poor districts by "prosperous colonists," and other aspects of "the process of Social Darwinism in the displacement and succession of population groups." (Glass, 1970, p. 100). Glass was dubious of how "displacement and succession" naturalized inequality in the human-ecological tradition of the Chicago School of Sociology, with its curious theoretical strains of "cognitive Darwinism" (Entrikin, 1980). And even as she narrated the public debates over the "Americanization" of London's post-war society of consumption, communications, and advertising – and how the reorganization of London's "zone in transition" was different from the "urban renewal" bulldozing of US cities – she coyly channeled other American mutations by writing of the "survival of the fittest." Glass and her readers fully understood that this wasn't the wording of the Englishman Charles Darwin; it was the catchphrase of the most influential conservative philosopher of nineteenth-century America, Herbert Spencer. Spencer, who pissed in the gene pool as he built a bizarre precursor of "Intelligent Design" that allowed America's political and religious leaders to avoid the worst implications of the Darwinian revolution for Christian doctrine, became the favored philosophical mouthpiece for America's robber-baron billionaire class. John D. Rockefeller once told children in a Sunday-School class that Spencer's "survival of the fittest" doctrine was a "law of nature and a law of God" justifying the wealth and power he and his peers controlled in the giant corporate trusts of the day.

Today the labels "Social Darwinism" and "survival of the fittest" sound like strange relics from a distant time and place. Perhaps. But that is the time and place where the turnover of shabby mews and cottages to the gentry could only be understood in relation to wider struggles for space throughout the metropolis amidst a dying global colonial order. That colonial empire had been built and defended not just by military force, but also by the cognitive terrorism of Malthusian theological political economy and racist Social Darwinism – and early post-war London was the pivot between the progressive-collective intentions of "managerial" evolutionary thought, from Patrick Geddes to John Maynard Keynes, to a new kind of marketized econometric eugenics promising a world of choice and freedom. It was Keynes, after all, who gave a speech to the British Eugenics Society introducing Sir Alexander Carr-Saunders, the winner of the Society's 1946 Gold Medal. Keynes (1946, p. 40) reminded his fellow eugenicists that Darwin had developed his theories by reading Malthus, but that "Carr-Saunders was led to Malthus through Darwin." Carr-Saunders had achieved fame with a neo-Malthusian treatise on the "quantity and quality" of population, and as Director of the London School of Economics from 1937 to 1957 he paid very close attention to "quality" people. One of them was Friedrich von Hayek, whom he had met during the War at Cambridge, and in later years nearly every aspect of Hayek's theory of human competition and cultural evolution was derived from Carr-Saunders's thesis that "selection operates on acquired habits and tradition" (Angner, 2007, p. 81).

"Acquired habits and traditions" is, of course, the old flawed pre-Darwinian Lamarckianism of Father Malthus's era – but bad science often makes for brilliant politics. In her 1993 autobiography, Margaret Thatcher credits Hayek as the key intellectual figure of the neoliberal revolution that became the new global colonial project – which, like "gentrification," has now evolved to the point where those in the Global North/West who apply the *critique of neoliberalism* to understand urbanization in the Global South are themselves attacked as a new generation of colonizers. Let me be clear. I am inspired by the invigorating plurality of today's postcolonial urban voices "From the South" (Parnell and Oldfield, 2014) – a collective cry of "Our society is unique, our culture is our own" – but the real enemies are not the *critics* of neoliberalism, but those who are working to build, profit from, or encode Thatcher's "There's no such thing as society" sourcecode into the networked, digitized, Android acceleration of competition in today's urban world. Glass (1989) predicted all of this shortly before she died. The Thatcherites dreamed of a "high-tech Britain" with a "miniaturized robotic labour force" as the working classes of all erstwhile industrial societies become "an expendable, even a dying species." While the rich continue to "annex territories of the poor for gentrification," the poor and working classes are sifted and sorted into entrepreneurial "goodies" versus welfare-dependent "baddies," the latter herded into "segregated colonies" and stigmatized as "undesirable, feckless species." A previous century's social divisions of morbidity and mortality reappear with a vengeance, while privatization transforms public education into "programming" of the next generation – forcing a coercive competition among schools for "sponsorships and donations" under the happy banner of "parental choice" and a recrudescence of the systematic "pre-selection of children" for different kinds and "classes" of schools.

THE EVOLUTION OF GENTRIFICATION, AND THE GENTRIFICATION OF EVOLUTION

Let's return to our opening story. A family is living in a tent underneath a highway overpass. Zynga's stock price surges after Don Mattrick fires a few hundred people and buys an Oxford neuroscience-software spinoff. And today's reincarnation of John D. Rockefeller, Chen Mailin, buys the largest house in British Columbia, 9,000 kilometers away from his corporate headquarters in a city that he praises as having the best education for kids. If we look for "gentrification" as conventionally understood in the separate urban locales featured in this story, we'll certainly find enormous contextual contrasts in housing markets, land development practices, histories of colonization and dispossession, ethnoracial and class relations, and roles of the state in Vancouver, San Francisco, Oxford, and Nanjing. Most obviously, the experience in Nanjing is "different from Western countries," because the "evolutionary mechanisms" of the post-reform People's Republic of China (PRC) are driven by a powerful nation-state urban growth machine built for "capital appreciation realized through spatial reproduction"; still, a distinctively non-Western process yields social exclusion, segregation, and marginalization of low-income people – creating a "hindrance to harmonious society" which is "necessary for the state and scholars to seriously consider" (Song and Wu, 2010, pp. 569, 574, 575).

When we look beyond the empiricist spatial details of localized urban change, all of these contrasts – important as they are for people and institutions embedded in particular sites – are irrelevant to the question of whether this constitutes gentrification. Can there be any doubt? Properly understood, as Glass meant it, as the urbanization of intensified competition for the needs of urban life in an unequal world of colonization and capital, every aspect of this story documents the evolutionary essence of gentrification. Rising competition is pervasive. People compete with other people to find and keep a place to live: some wind up living in tents; some wind up living in 25,000-square-foot homes with ten-car garages and commuting by private jet; some live, a few blocks from where I write these words, on a tiny social assistance housing allowance in a dilapidated single room occupancy hotel (SRO) on the verge of collapse, under constant threat of eviction by a slum-landlord family that embodies the very best Canadian multicultural promises of non-European, non-White upward mobility: the family's real estate holdings are assessed at more than C$130 million (Colebourn, 2016), all of it, like all property in this city, built on the stolen, unceded ancestral territories of the Musqueam, Squamish, and Tsleil-Waututh peoples. People compete with other people to succeed, to get a spot on the *Forbes World Billionaires* ranking, or the *Hurun Rich List*. Chen Mailin dropped out of high school and failed in his first venture, a duck farm, but he worked to achieve success in construction and development – his Nanjing Dingye Investment Group is a hybrid of the molecular *neoliberalism* and state-capitalist *neo-dirigisme* that Lefebvre (1970, pp. 78ff.) analyzed in the fields, levels, and dimensions of the production of urban space, and a relational place-making approach now helps us understand the multiple epistemologies of overlapping transnational fields of urban social space (Pierce and Martin, 2015). People compete for jobs, and people must also compete with investors pushing CEOs to cut the "headcount" and with non-human algorithms as Silicon Valley's evolutionary artificial-intelligence "singularity" obsessions (Bostrom, 2014) gradually fulfill Thatcher's dreams of an obedient, miniaturized robotic workforce. And Chen Mailin's praise for Vancouver's "best education for kids" only makes sense when we appreciate how the next generation of people are forced into ever more intense competition in an increasingly competitive transnational educational field (Ley, 2010, pp. 207–213). "Western decay" has become a powerful postcolonial meme to inspire entrepreneurs and tiger-parents, and the PRC's *gaokao* is ruthlessly effective in producing *you xiu ren* ("excellent people"): "Raising the quality of the population was important if China were to catch up to the West and possibly even surpass the United States," an informant tells the anthropologist Susanne Bregnbaek; yet "decay" has its humanistic merits compared to the proliferation of suicides at elite Mainland universities that has become a "public secret" (Bregnbaek, 2011, p. 20). As I read Glass's warnings of Social Darwinist urbanism and Keynes's praise for Carr-Saunders's production of "quality" people like Hayek, I think of the kind, brilliant undergraduate who showed me across campus on my way to deliver a lecture at a university in Shanghai; as we strolled through the crowds chatting about student life, she casually pointed out the tall building on campus where students who couldn't cope with the pressure jumped to their deaths during exam season.

Eugenicist thought and policy is now transnational and cosmopolitan, from the evolutionary justifications for Western neoliberalism peddled by the Hayek-Prize-winning Matt Ridley (2010), to the variegated fusions of Social Darwinism with non-Western cultural histories and nationalist projects in Asia (Chung, 2014). As it was 50 years ago, gentrification is the urbanization of colonialist Social Darwinist competition, and our research agenda must be to expose and challenge the implicit eugenicist logics of urban economics and politics – which today mask a machinery of accelerating competition behind the sunny promises of creativity, diversity, and multicultural meritocracy. We need to continue Smith's (1982, 2011) unfinished project, to integrate Clark and Clark's (2012) insights on participation in our own evolution with Harvey's (2011) comprehensive model of "coevolutionary" capitalism, to advance Boggs and Boggs's (1974) evolutionary humanist project of becoming more kind, compassionate, and egalitarian.

REFERENCES

Abercrombie, Patrick (1945). *Greater London Plan 1944: A Report Prepared on Behalf of the Standing Conference on London Regional Planning.* London: HMSO.

Allen, Samantha (2014). "San Francisco's Gay Culture Is Dying." *The Daily Dot*, 31 October.

Angner, Erik (2007). *Hayek and Natural Law.* New York: Routledge.

Atkinson, Rowland, and Gary Bridge, eds (2005). *The New Urban Colonialism: Gentrification in a Global Context.* London: Routledge.

Beauregard, Robert A. (1986). "The Chaos and Complexity of Gentrification." In Neil Smith and Peter Williams, eds, *Gentrification of the City.* London: Allen & Unwin, 35–55.

Bernt, Matthias (2016). "Very Particular, or Rather Universal? Gentrification through the Lenses of Ghertner and Lopez-Morales." *City*, 7 April, advance online publication.

Boggs, James, and Grace Lee Boggs (1974). *Revolution and Evolution in the Twentieth Century.* New York: Monthly Review Press.

Bondi, Liz (1999). "Between the Woof and the Weft: A Response to Loretta Lees." *Environment and Planning D: Society and Space* 17(3), 253–255.

Bostrom, Nick (2014). *Superintelligence: Paths, Dangers, Strategies.* Oxford: Oxford University Press.

Bregnbaek, Susanne (2011). "A Public Secret: Education for Quality and Suicide among Chinese Elite University Students." *Learning and Teaching* 4(3), 18–36.

CBC News (2015). "Vancouver Mansion Sells for More than $51M." *CBC News*, 10 March.

Chung, Yuehtsen Juliette (2014). "Better Science and Better Race? Social Darwinism and Chinese Eugenics." *Isis* 105(4), 793–802.

Clark, Thomas L., and Eric Clark (2012). "Participation in Evolution and Sustainability." *Transactions of the Institute of British Geographers* NS37, 563–577.

Colebourn, John (2016). "They Thought I Was Going to Back Down and Leave: Tenant Who's Owed $1,675 by His Multimillionaire Landlord Stands Up for His Rights." *The Province*, 10 July, 10–12.

Cutler, Kim-Mai (2014). "Zynga Buys NaturalMotion for $527M, Signaling a New Tack for the Gaming Giant." *Techcrunch*, 30 January.

Edwards, Cliff (2014). "Zynga Buys NaturalMotion to Bolster Mobile, Cut Staff." *Bloomberg*, 31 January.

Entrikin, J. Nicholas (1980). "Robert Park's Human Ecology and Human Geography." *Annals of the Association of American Geographers* 70(1), 43–58.

Foucault, Michel (1969). "What Is an Author?" In Paul Rabinow and Nikolas Rose, eds (2003), *The Essential Foucault.* New York: New Press, 377–391.

Galton, Francis (1869). *Hereditary Genius: An Inquiry Into its Laws and Consequences.* London: Richard Clay and Sons.

Ghertner, D. Asher (2015). "Why Gentrification Theory Fails 'In Much of the World'." *City* 19(4), 552–563.

Glass, Ruth (1962). "Insiders/Outsiders: The Position of Minorities." *New Left Review* I/17, Winter, 34–45.

Glass, Ruth (1963). "Centre for Urban Studies." *Town Planning Review* 34(3), 169–184.

Glass, Ruth (1964). "Introduction." In Centre for Urban Studies, ed, *London: Aspects of Change.* London: McKibben & Gee, xii–xlii.

Glass, Ruth (1970). "Changing Urban Problems in Developed Countries." Discussion paper for WHO Meeting on "Health Effects of Urbanization." Reprinted in Ruth Glass (1989). *Clichés of Urban Doom.* Oxford: Basil Blackwell, 98–105.

Glass, Ruth (1989). "Introduction." In *Clichés of Urban Doom.* Oxford: Basil Blackwell, vii–xxii.

Harris, Andrew (2008). "From London to Mumbai and Back Again: Gentrification and Public Policy in Comparative Perspective." *Urban Studies* 45(12), 2407–2428.

Harvey, David (2011). *The Enigma of Capital and the Crises of Capitalism*. Oxford: Oxford University Press.

Healy, Kieran (2016). "Fuck Nuance." *Sociological Theory*, January, early online publication.

Keynes, John Maynard (1946). "The Galton Lecture, 1946: Presentation of the Society's Gold Medal." *Eugenics Review* 38(1), 39–42.

LaPorte, Nicole (2013). "Meet Former Xbox Boss Don Mattrick, Who Just Left Microsoft to Turn around Zynga." *Fast Company*, 2 July.

Lees, Loretta (2012). "The Geography of Gentrification: Thinking through Comparative Urbanism." *Progress in Human Geography* 36(2), 155–171.

Lees, Loretta, Hyun Bang Shin, and Ernesto Lopez-Morales, eds. (2015). *Global Gentrifications: Uneven Development and Displacement*. Bristol: Policy Press.

Lees, Loretta, Tom Slater, and Elvin Wyly, eds. (2010). *The Gentrification Reader*. New York: Routledge.

Lefebvre, Henri (1970). *The Urban Revolution*. Translated by Robert Bononno, 2003 edition. Minneapolis, MN: University of Minnesota Press.

Ley, David (2010). *Millionaire Migrants: Trans-Pacific Life Lines*. Chichester, UK: Wiley-Blackwell.

Ley, David, and Sin-Yih Teo (2013). "Gentrification in Hong Kong? Epistemology vs. Ontology." *International Journal of Urban and Regional Research* 38(4), 1286–1303.

Maloutas, Thomas (2011). "Contextual Diversity in Gentrification Research." *Critical Sociology* 38(1), 33–48.

Ong, Aihwa (2011). "Introduction: Worlding Cities, or the Art of Being Global." In Ananya Roy and Aihwa Ong, eds., *Worlding Cities: Asian Experiments and the Art of Being Global*. Chichester, UK: Wiley-Blackwell, 1–26.

Palen, John, and Bruce London, eds. (1984). *Gentrification, Displacement, and Neighborhood Revitalization*. Albany, NY: State University of New York Press.

Parnell, Susan, and Sophie Oldfield (2014). "From the South." In Susan Parnell and Sophie Oldfield, eds., *The Routledge Handbook on Cities of the Global South*. New York: Routledge, 1–4.

Pearson, Karl, and Margaret Moul (1927). "The Mathematics of Intelligence: The Sampling Errors in the Theory of a Generalised Factor." *Biometrika* 19(3/4), 246–291.

Pierce, Joseph, and Deborah Martin (2015). "Placing Lefebvre." *Antipode* 47(5), 1279–1299.

Rafferty, Kevin (2015). "What Universities in Hong Kong and the Rest of China Can Learn from Oxford." *South China Morning Post*, 28 December.

Ren, Julie (2015). "Gentrification in China?" In Loretta Lees, Hyun Bang Shin, and Ernesto Lopez-Morales, eds., *Global Gentrifications: Uneven Development and Displacement*. Bristol: Policy Press, 329–347.

Ridley, Matt (2010). *The Rational Optimist: How Prosperity Evolves*. New York: HarperCollins.

Roy, Ananya (forthcoming). "Dis/Possessive Collectivism: Property and Personhood at City's End." *Geoforum*.

Rusli, Evelyn M., and Shira Ovide (2013). "Zynga Founder Mark Pincus Hands CEO Job to Don Mattrick." *Wall Street Journal*, 1 July.

Sassen, Saskia (1991). *The Global City: New York, London, and Tokyo*. Princeton, NJ: Princeton University Press.

Schafran, Alex (2014). "Debating Urban Studies in 23 Steps." *City* 18(3), 321–330.

Slater, Tom (2015). "Planetary Rent Gaps." *Antipode*. http://doi.org/10.1111/anti.12185.

Smith, Neil (1982). "Gentrification and Uneven Development." *Economic Geography* 58(2), 139–155.

Smith, Neil (2011). "The Evolution of Gentrification." In J. Berg, T. Kaminer, M. Schoonerbeek, and J. Zonneveld, eds., *Houses in Transformation: Interventions in European Gentrification*. Rotterdam: NAi Publishers, 15–26.

Song, Weixuan, and Qiyan Wu (2010). "Gentrification and Residential Differentiation in Nanjing, China." *Chinese Geographical Science* 20(6), 568–576.

Witham, Larry (2002). *Where Darwin Meets the Bible: Creationists and Evolutionists in America*. Oxford: Oxford University Press.

Young, Ian (2015). "Former Duck Farmer Revealed as Buyer of US$40 Million Vancouver Mansion." *South China Morning Post*, 19 March.

3
Beyond Anglo-American gentrification theory

Hyun Bang Shin and Ernesto López-Morales

INTRODUCTION

Has gentrification 'gone global'? Has it diffused from its usual suspects (for example, London and New York City) to other non-Anglo-American cities that are more peripheral to global capitalism? What is the meaning of gentrification as a 'global urban strategy' (Smith 2002)? Does it mean gentrification as a neoliberal urban policy colonizing cities outside the core of global capitalism? Or, does it mean that the dominant epistemological horizon has expanded to be more inclusive of non-Anglo-American cities that have seen (historic) endogenous urban processes akin to gentrification? And, what do scholars in the Global North understand about gentrification processes taking place in emergent cities in the Global South, some of which they may not even locate on their world map?

In this chapter, we discuss what it means to study gentrification beyond the Anglo-American domain, emphasizing the possibility of gentrification mutating across time and space, in the same way any other social phenomenon associated with the changing nature of capitalism goes through mutation. We also question here why academia should maintain the Anglo-American cultural region as a necessary comparative framework to talk about gentrification elsewhere. Gentrification is now embedded in urbanization processes that bring together politics, culture, society and ideology. Such urbanization is uneven and place-specific, thus displaying multiple trajectories, hence there is a need to provincialize (c.f. Chakrabarty 2000; cr Lees 2012) gentrification as we know it (namely, the rise of gentrification in plural forms or in other words, *provincial* gentrifications). However, we argue this must be done without losing the most critical aspects of gentrification that need to be investigated, namely the class remaking of urban space involving displacement. For us, gentrification is a reflection of broader political economic processes that result in the unequal and uneven production of urban(izing) space, entailing power struggles between haves and have-nots, be they disputes over the upgrading of small neighbourhoods or larger clashes related to social displacement experienced at the metropolitan or even regional scale.

In this chapter, we focus on four key issues. Firstly, we discuss the epistemology of comparative gentrification studies, explaining what it means to think of gentrification in pluralistic perspectives. In doing so, we remain conscious of how gentrification reflects the more fundamental shift in politics and economics through active circuits of (real estate) capital and policies, which are often dominated by national and transnational economic elites, in spite of widespread dispossession of people across the Global South; thus, we call for *planetary* thinking of gentrification (Lees et al. 2016). Secondly, related to the first point, we discuss the linguistics of gentrification, questioning the extent to which gentrification can be a useful conceptual tool to analyze urban processes in places where gentrification as an expression cannot be easily translated into local expressions. Thirdly, we ascertain the importance of scrutinizing the role of the state and the workings of political elites, for they collectively play a pivotal role in (re-)imagining city-making and deciding how resources are to be allocated in terms of production and consumption. Fourthly, we further elaborate on the state question in gentrification research. The state in the Global South has been of greater significance in gentrification processes because of the vulgar nature of capitalism lacking a historical compromise between dominant and subordinate classes. Finally, we conclude the chapter by thinking about what possibilities there are for seeing social conflicts through the lens of gentrification and how anti-gentrification struggles could be positioned in a broader scheme of societal transformation and defending the right to the city in a manner that is far more socially just than what the current stages of capitalism allow for.

AN EPISTEMOLOGY OF COMPARATIVE GENTRIFICATION STUDIES

Some urban researchers have been struggling to come to terms with the suitability of a gentrification framework as a useful lens to analyze processes of urban restructuring outside of the Global North. Some still see gentrification (somehow unimaginatively) as associated only with specific spatio-temporal contexts, not susceptible to transfer to elsewhere outside the usual suspects. These sceptics have mechanically interpreted London and New York City as the only emblems of gentrification. This is an extreme perspective on gentrification, that treats it as a historic-cultural process associated primarily with inner-city London in the 1960s (for example, Maloutas 2012). Viewed this way, the process of gentrification is effectively fossilized, and disavowed of any applicability outside of a particular time and place/space: it is thus rendered lower than a 'mid-range concept'.

Some sceptics further argue that gentrification is a micro-economic process involving formal property rights and playing out in formal real estate markets only (for example, Ghertner 2015). Such a viewpoint reflects confusion in the midst of its attempt to intertwine reductionist theorization of urban change with the rich Marxist interpretations of gentrification, and displays a tendency (1) to regard cities in the Global South as qualitatively different and isolated from more general processes of capitalist accumulation; (2) to treat slums and informal settlements as distinct urban spaces where logics of capital accumulation cannot penetrate; (3) to disregard how deeply market and non-market processes are entangled in the same way, how formal and informal processes are fused together in the global economy; (4) to understate how much the operation of speculation and landlordism can be prevalent in informal settlements. From this perspective, any effort to apply the gentrification lens to other geographical contexts outside of the United Kingdom (and possibly North America) is seen as the imposition of Anglo-American hegemony. But adhering to such a perspective would also make it difficult to understand that the commodification of decommodified housing stocks has been a major thrust of gentrification in London too, as witnessed by the gentrification of council housing estates (Lees 2014). It also ignores the many other comparable precedents in North America, as well as in Latin America and Asia from the 1970s (for example, Janoschka et al. 2014). The variegated ways in which those occupying informal, non-market housing are dispossessed of their rights in many parts of the world are part and parcel of gentrification processes (see Lees et al. 2015).

Those who deny the application of 'gentrification' to non-Western cities should perhaps revisit the history of how the concept has evolved within the confines of the so-called Global North. By the 1970s, gentrification as a term and concept was appropriated by critics on the other side of the Atlantic, discussed in the context of mainly New York City but also other major cities in the eastern US, and indeed Canada. A number of young North American urban scholars saw gentrification as having resulted from two major forces inherent to capitalism: (1) the socio-cultural transformations in the aftermath of the 'baby boom' era; (2) the emerging importance of the real estate sector that took advantage of widening rent gaps. For more than two decades, gentrification debates battled back and forth over the 'post-industrial, new middle class' thesis and the 'rent gap exploitation' thesis over what had caused the rise of gentrification (see Lees et al. 2008). Importantly, both hypotheses never questioned the stretching of the gentrification concept beyond the domain of inner-city London in the 1960s; they were more concerned about the North American particularities that gave rise to a particular form of mutated gentrification (Ley 1980; Smith 1979; also see Slater 2006, for a full account of this historical debate). In a similar vein, readers should not be surprised by the scale and nature of contemporary gentrification in London, where expensive, new-build, often high-rise redevelopment came to dominate (Davidson and Lees 2010). This mutation has been supported by both New Labour and Tory policies of housing privatization and individual responsibility, and has led to soaring house prices, severe unaffordability issues, and unprecedented rates of displacement, not only of the most deprived segments of society but also of the relatively affluent middle classes.

The fossilization of gentrification also makes it difficult for critics to understand how urban processes coined as gentrification (especially with its focus on real estate capital, the recomposition of class, displacement of original land users and space commodification) have become increasingly pronounced in Asian and Latin American cities. For decades, a large number of non-Anglo-American cities have undergone substantial socio-spatial changes due to intensive state-led and/or private-led investment (often built upon growth coalitions between endogenous political and business elites), which have resulted in upward and unequal social re-stratification of neighbourhoods, *favelas*, *gecekondu* and *lilong* (Lees et al. 2015; López-Morales 2016a, forthcoming; Sánchez and Broudehoux 2013). There is a whole new global context which is seeing the predominance of capital over publicly oriented policy decisions regarding the use of urban space as an asset for the sake of capital accumulation: this is, however, nothing more than the corollary of decades of advancement of a relatively ample and adaptive array of state discourses and policies that range from extreme free-market ideology or neoliberalism (Harvey 2005) to market-oriented state developmentalism in the case of East Asia (Shin et al. 2016). Around the world, gentrification – as an explicit or implicit, or even as a hidden discourse – has become a major justification and goal for urban redevelopment in economies that depend heavily on the circulation of capital for commodification and exploitation of already urban or urbanizing space.

THE LINGUISTICS OF GENTRIFICATION

Attempts to investigate and conceptualize gentrification in non Anglo-American cities face some familiar criticisms; such as, for example, that gentrification is difficult to translate into other languages as the term is too UK-specific. But, does it really matter whether or not gentrification as a term exists in a particular locality? Comparative urban studies on gentrification have produced significant achievements, calling for a more generic definition of gentrification to be adopted (Clark 2005) and asking researchers to pay attention to conjunctural factors that give rise to locally tuned processes of gentrification or actually existing gentrification.

Once we rescue gentrification from its confinement to the place specificities of 1960s London, and build upon the achievements of 20–30 years of comparative gentrification studies, we can broadly define gentrification as 'the commodification of space accompanying land use changes in such a way that it produces indirect/direct/symbolic displacement of existing users and owners by more affluent groups' (Shin et al. 2016: 458; see also the categories proposed by Janoschka et al. 2014). This is in line with Clark's (2005) call not to equate Ruth Glass's particularistic coining of the concept with its origin, calling instead for a more theoretically productive and intellectually inspiring 'generic gentrification' (Clark 2015) that can be applied as both an analytical tool and empowering political goal for the local grassroots to defeat, impede or regulate. The key to this perspective is the realization that generality and particularity are not mutually exclusive and can co-exist in theoretical and political realms. Similar awareness can be considered as one of the major tenets of comparative studies on gentrification; building on the work of the late Doreen Massey, who once argued that 'interdependence [of all places] and uniqueness [of individual places] can be understood as two sides of the same coin, in which two fundamental geographical concepts – uneven development and the identity of place – can be held in tension with each other and can each contribute to the explanation of the other' (1993: 64; cited in Lees et al. 2016: 6). It is perfectly possible to generalize gentrification as a process of land use change that results in the unequal appropriation of rents and causes the displacement of existing land users, while at the same time emphasizing the particular trajectories of how this process is shaped by the workings of the place-specific political, economic and social relations that co-exist in space.

At this point, it is useful to revisit the recent argument made by Ley and Teo (2014), who discuss how in Hong Kong the absence of linguistic expressions of gentrification does not preclude the ontological presence of gentrification as an actually existing urban process. Although the argument might seem a little obvious, we concur with them that it is possible to think of the ontological presence of gentrification in a given society, even though there is no such word as 'gentrification' being circulated in public or academic discourse. A comparative perspective on gentrification can suggest that gentrification as an urban process is often known by more localized forms of expressions such as *blanqueamiento* in Mexico (López-Morales 2016a) and 'urban redevelopment' in Seoul (Shin and Kim 2016). It may also be translated into an expression that is more useful for local populations, while retaining the core principle of gentrification in the translated version. For example, in South Korea, reflecting the growing popularity of gentrification in the media,[1] the National Institute of Korean Language, a government agency that works to translate foreign expressions into standard Korean, has suggested in May 2016 that in Korean, gentrification should be translated as *dungji naemolim*, literally meaning eviction/displacement from one's nest/home.[2] While discussions about gentrification were largely confined to academic discourse, from 2015 it began to receive significant attention in the media and public discourse.

Latin American experiences inform us that theorizing gentrification should be 'sensitive enough to recognize that gentrification also means urban inequalities and segregation accentuated by the state responding to large-scale private interests' (López-Morales 2016a: 571). In Chile, for example, well before the term gentrification started to be used in the analysis of the unequal production of urban space in a highly neoliberalized housing market (López-Morales 2008), ample discussions took place to critically understand the effects of private-led residential redevelopment in the country's major cities (Sabatini et al. 2001). The importance of exploiting the potential to appropriate rents from land development has been historically so pronounced (as part of an institutional design by the state since the early 19th century aimed at increasing property tenure among the lowest strata of society) that there has been frequent conflict between the private exploitation of the commercial value of land and the 'right to stay put' of those living on that land (Wyly et al. 2010), or in simpler terms, between developers and petty landowners who are usually the ones facing unsurmountable barriers (for example, soaring housing prices and lack of financial loans) in finding replacement accommodation within redevelopment areas or nearby after selling their land (López-Morales 2016b). Following Clark (2005: 258), 'any process of change fitting this description is, to my [our] understanding, gentrification.'

THE STATE-DESIGNED NEXUS BETWEEN GENTRIFICATION AND DISPLACEMENT

One of the major characteristics of contemporary capitalism and gentrification is the scaling up of real estate projects. Increasingly it is an entire district or a neighbourhood that becomes subject to the intervention of real estate capital, resulting in wholesale clearance and reconstruction. Real estate capital has grown large in scale, hence the domination of big real estate corporations that have access to state institutions and finance, while smaller firms operate to pick up niche properties in the shadow of scaled-up projects. More importantly, however, the scaling up of real estate projects calls for a dedicated role for local and central states to clear barriers and obstacles, to facilitate the displacement of oppositional voices, creating *tabula rasa* conditions for real estate investment and the production of ideological discourses (Shin 2016; Slater 2014). To help facilitate private sector investment, governments assemble a range of preferential and subsidizing policies. Joined-up efforts by governments, government-affiliated agencies, developers and the media often produce stigmatization of neighbourhoods to be subject to 'revitalization', as if such areas and residents therein have lost their vitality and fallen into eternal disrepute or the so-called 'territorial stigma' (see Shin 2016; Lees 2014; Wacquant et al. 2014). Reinvestment and hence gentrification emerges as an alternative to real or perceived persistent decay and dilapidation, a mythical presumption that forces people to believe that there is no other alternative. In similar vein to Defilippis (2004) and Lees (2014), Slater (2014) calls this a 'false choice urbanism', and says there is an urgent need to 'blast open this tenacious and constrictive dualism of "prosperity" (gentrification) or "blight" (disinvestment)' and reveal the intrinsic relationship between the two in a more fundamental process of uneven capitalist urbanization.

The scaling up of real estate projects leads to the rise of mega-gentrification and mega-displacement, which is enabled by the dispossession of people's rights through the workings of a growth alliance between the (central and/or local) state and (real estate) capital. Obviously, the nature of this alliance will differ across geographies. Very often, in the Global South, governments and developers are fused together through ownership shares or the close ties between developers and ruling families or political figures as in Abu Dhabi and Lebanon. The close nexus between large businesses and political elites in South Korea is another example of this politico-economic fusion (Shin and Kim 2016), and so is the 'state capitalism' that has emerged in mainland China. In Latin America, a more recent example includes the scandal of Adebrecht, the Brazilian construction group that is currently under investigation in several Latin American countries for possible cases of bribery in campaigns and the private accounts of top politicians including national presidents (*The Guardian* 2017).³ Where there is a strong alliance between the state and real estate capital, it becomes increasingly difficult to challenge real estate development and resulting displacement.

As for mega-displacement and gentrification in post-colonial states, ethnic-religious tensions often become the sources of retribution against the marginalized, resulting in mega-displacement to set redevelopment and gentrification in motion. In Mumbai, for instance, the 1995 Maharashtra state elections led to the formulation of the state government's Slum Rehabilitation Scheme (SRS) that was to carry out large-scale slum clearance in order to clear ways for real estate and infrastructure construction in globalizing Mumbai (Doshi 2013). Eligibility for the resettlement of slum dwellers was based on paper-based evidences of residence in Mumbai prior to the cut-off date of the scheme. The SRS was to enable the involvement of real estate developers in redeveloping slums by introducing 'transferable development rights', which allowed developers to produce higher density market rate housing on cleared slums or elsewhere in the suburbs, on condition that developers also provided compensation units for eligible slum dwellers, although off-site resettlement was more popular among those affected. The Vision Mumbai redevelopment programme to transform Mumbai into the 'next Shanghai' resulted in 'Mumbai's "tsunami"' of mass clearance and eviction, demolishing about 45,000–90,000 informal structures and rendering 300,000–350,000 people homeless (see Doshi 2013; Ramesh 2005). Affected were those 'illegal' settlements which emerged after 1995. Xenophobic campaigns by the local political party aggravated the conditions of evictees further, as 'most Vision Mumbai evictees were ethnically North Indian or Muslim' (Doshi 2013: 858).

In promoting mega-gentrification, project financing becomes important, as an individual developer (or even a consortium of developers) will often find it difficult to finance the entire project on its own. In this regard, the origin of capital becomes key to understanding the nature of the state-capital relationship, as well as the state-society relationship. National savings schemes such as the Central Provident Fund in Singapore or the National Housing Fund in South Korea have had a strong role to play in facilitating real estate construction in these countries, while foreign direct investment tends to be highlighted in recent years with regard to the rise of mega urban projects (Shatkin 2008). Surplus from a country or region often gets channelled into other regions in a geographical switching of capital (see Percival and Waley 2012 on Korean investment in Cambodian new town construction, and Kutz and Lenhardt 2016 on inward investment in Morocco). Sovereign wealth funds, as well as savings of middle- or upper-class families in Asia (for example, Singapore and China) have emerged as major investors in cities of the Global North, suggesting that the circulation of real estate capital has become quite complex and involves multiple directions between the Global North and the Global South and within each region.

While financialization plays a key role in the rise of (speculative) real estate projects (see Moreno 2014), how local governments make use of their planning powers to increase the financial viability of real estate projects is pivotal for urban development in the Global South in particular, where endogenous investors and major political elites work together with transnational investors. An exemplary case can be found in Mexico, which involves a public-private corporation called PROCDMX that cooperates with global financial players for the purpose of transforming entire districts in central Mexico City into transport corridors and hubs for luxury real estate investment. In this scheme, the Mexican state has privatized urban lands in core locations as public contributions to the public-private partnership, but at the same time guarantees the private sector's real estate operation by issuing 40-year-long contracts so that the private sector can extract rents from zoned urban space. Researchers and neighbourhood activists together wonder nowadays whether this carefully designed, sanitized new space of exception would be able to host/enlist any type of dissent, social deviation, grassroots cultural expressions or undesired actors (Gaytán 2016).

In many ways, the example of Mexico's PROCDMX chimes with the case of Buenos Aires's Puerto Madero mega-project, initiated in the late 1980s and since then having deeply transformed the city's old and derelict port area, Puerto Madero. It all started in 1989 when the city government transferred public land to the ad hoc, newly created Corporación Antiguo Puerto Madero (hereafter CAPM). The redevelopment of Puerto Madero was carried out under a prevailing neoliberal planning philosophy that widely failed to keep its initial promises of social mixing and public infrastructure provision: the result was a concentration of high-rise luxury condominiums and elite-oriented commercial land use that prevented social mixing. For instance, the highly segregated and enclosed Rodrigo Bueno shanty town located nearby lost access to the newly created 'ecological park' that was supposed to be open for public use according to the law that allowed the Puerto Madero operation (see Cuenya and Corral 2011; Garay et al. 2013). There, experts from Barcelona provided ideas and good-practice strategies for the CAPM operation (see Lees et al. 2016). Critics complain that although Puerto Madero has produced a new landscape pertinent to the world-city status of Buenos Aires, the area is separate from the rest of the city socially and economically, that the masses have been excluded from the project, and that the privatization of public resources such as public lands resulted in private investors' appropriation of enormous returns on their investment with comparatively minuscule collection of tax revenues (Garay et al. 2013).

THE STATE QUESTION

The above discussions about the state-designed nexus between gentrification and dispossession compels us to examine the state question. In Western Europe, there is a legacy of social democratic welfare statism, which has been an outcome of the post-war reconstruction and consensus between labour and capital. In this context, gentrification has a limited role to play if we assume the interventionist role of the state to provide collective consumption including housing welfare. The social democratic orientation of the state, and its legacy in the contemporary neoliberal world, would also create certain barriers to the full exploitation of real estate commodities. The disintegration of the post-war consensus and welfare statism, has therefore, served to accelerate gentrification processes in Anglo-American cities. The demise of Western Keynesian welfare statism has been accompanied by a state rhetoric that argues that gentrification is an inevitable outcome or the only means to revitalize post-industrial urban spaces constrained by a lack of public funding. Lang (1982: 1) goes as far as to claim that 'gentrification comprises one of the few urban success stories that is not dependent on a massive infusion of government moneys.'

The rhetoric of an incompetent state is frequently put forward in the Global South, where corrupt, ineffective or rent-seeking state officials are thought to have failed to provide basic urban services and functions. This is an incompetence that can be very functional for capitalist goals. In the context of a neglectful state that displays impotence in terms of bringing change and maintaining the urban core, private capital initiatives are often regarded as a viable alternative. For instance, Elshahed (2015) is sympathetic to the involvement of real estate capital, especially in a developer's (Al-Ismailia for Real Estate Investments) attempt to reuse and therefore salvage Egypt's modernist heritage building – Cinema Radio – without gentrification impacting on other current users in the vicinity (Elshahed 2015: 137). However, the ability of the private sector, formal or informal, to deliver key urban services needs to be viewed with care, especially with regards to their intervention in land and housing markets.

Contrary to incompetent state rhetoric, East Asian developmental statism is on the other end of the spectrum of understanding in terms of how the state has led the way to provide business-friendly environments as part of nation-building and maintaining state legitimacy (Castells 1992;

Haila 2016; Woo-Cumings 1999). And, it is in this context that the rise of gentrification in East Asia is to be thought of. The lack of a mature civil society in East Asia is often pointed out as a reason for the brutal oppression of protesters against eviction by the state. This had been the case in South Korea, for example, in the early 1980s when there was an all-out attack on tenant protesters against a new redevelopment programme that resulted in large-scale new-build gentrification of dilapidated sub-standard neighbourhoods in Seoul (see Ha 2001; Kim 1999). China's urban redevelopment histories are also full of the violent use of state power to prevent local residents from hindering redevelopment progress (Shao 2013). It is also necessary to remember that in the historical context of urbanization, under the developmental state, the notion of private urbanism may simply be a myth that disguises the underlying and historic intervention of the developmental state in urban development. For example, Shin (2017) examines the case of smart city construction in Songdo, South Korea, and reveals that despite a more recent surge of smart city and private urbanism rhetoric associated with the Songdo City project, the characteristics of developmental state-led urbanization turned out to be persistent. These include the long-term commitment of the (local) state to realize the construction of a brand-new town, the developmental vision repackaged as green growth, and smart city promotion to adjust to the changes of the reigning urbanism. Moreover, profiteering from real estate projects, a key characteristic of speculative Korean urbanization, turned out to be the fundamental motive of both domestic and transnational developers, despite the dominant discourses of smart urban growth (see also Sonn et al. 2017).

On the other hand, a longer trajectory of neoliberalization in Latin America provides a picture that can be contrasted with East Asian states. However, this is not a story of top-down neoliberal imposition but a story of endogenous political and economic interests engaging with global players, on their own terms and conditions. Redeveloping slums (read *slum gentrification*) has involved the workings of the state that often spearhead the changes. The story of Puerto Madero in Buenos Aires, aforementioned, is also one which saw the involvement of the state to eradicate shanty towns and displace local residents. So far, for at least two decades, the southern part of Buenos Aires (La Boca, the Barracas and Parque Patricios neighbourhoods, among others), which previously the state paid no attention to leaving slum dwellers in what became their neighbourhoods (see Rodríguez and Di Virgilio 2016), has increasingly witnessed the expansion of rent-seeking, culturally hip gentrification waves that are transforming the whole central city (Herzer et al. 2015). It is also illuminating to note that such attacks on shanty towns have historic precedents in the city. An unexplored case of state-led gentrification already occurred in 1977 during the eradication of a shanty town in the Bajo Belgrano district: an important reason for this state action was that the main stadium for the 1978 Football World Cup was located next to this *villa miseria*. Subsequently, in the 1990s and 2000s, the land was gradually redeveloped to accommodate luxury condominiums. In this case, mega-event driven displacement and state-led, neoliberal new-build gentrification, seem historically connected. The recent experiences of mega-scale redevelopment in Rio de Janeiro, for example, the ongoing redevelopment of Zona Portuária or Porto Maravilha also demonstrate the rise of state-led gentrification through the sanitization and commodification of urban space, combined with transforming public space into exclusive consumption space for urban elites (Queiroz Ribeiro and dos Santos Junior 2007; Sánchez and Broudehoux 2013).

CONCLUSION

As the real estate economy has become an increasingly dominant arena of capital accumulation, and as city-making has become an increasing part of the political ambition of governing elites, dilapidated and/or undesirable urban spaces have become subject to eradication and further commodification. Gentrification in this regard is a reflection of the state's political, ideological and economic project (Shin forthcoming). This is the story of many countries in the Global South, which are increasingly integrated into the global circuits of capital and people, and as such experiencing the rise of new gentrifications or localized embryonic forms. In this chapter, we have argued that gentrification narrowly understood in a fossilized way (that is, gentrification equated with its classic form in 1960s London) is not a useful barometer through which to evaluate the experiences of other urban processes, either inside or outside of the usual suspects in gentrification studies. What comparative gentrification studies in recent years have taught us is the importance of de-centering the production of knowledge, incorporating emergent contextual discussions from elsewhere (and as it seems, literally from everywhere), and adhering to relational perspectives in order to understand how gentrification interacts with other locally available processes and discourses (see also Bernt 2016; Lees et al. 2016; López-Morales 2016a; Shin et al. 2016; Shin forthcoming). The de-centering of gentrification studies requires researchers to pay more careful attention to the historicity of urbanization and urban contestation. It also requires researchers to accept that gentrification may look completely different in places and societies we researchers do not yet know about or do not understand enough about as of now.

We conclude this chapter with a brief reflection on the construction of political alternatives in the fight against planetary gentrification. While this chapter has largely emphasized the workings of the state and capital in the Global South, it is also premature to simply assume that governments, developers and other state apparatuses are the only agents of mega-gentrification. With the growing affluence and expansion of middle classes in a number of global Southern countries that have seen the generation of wealth by their own industrialization and urban-based accumulation or the transfer of surplus capital from elsewhere (for example, King 2008; Koo 1991; Lett 1998; Tomba 2004), it is equally important to understand how the actions of the state-capital nexus have gained hegemony in their respective territories, and secured consent among a strata of residents, especially the property-owning middle classes who are attracted to securing gains from real estate investment. Such attention to state-society relations is particularly important, as the urban questions in the Global South are hard to detach from broader questions that emerge out of political mobilizations, which occasionally erupt to question state legitimacy. Where the support of the middle classes leans towards is significant in terms of how the state sustains its power vis-à-vis wider social movements. The resulting complexities provide both challenges and opportunities for anti-gentrification struggles in the Global South, which in turn can never be dissociated from those struggles that play out in the Global North.

The experience of Latin American urban struggles can be illuminating in this regard. Historically, Latin America is full of revolutionary moments in its history, starting with the independence wars in the early 19th century, followed by the Mexican and Cuban revolutions in the 20th century. Not only national political movements but also urban-based social uprising and revolutionary insurrection have also been prevalent (see Castells 1985). Latin America is currently seeing complex multi-scalar repertoires of social action, which are unfolding in extremely diverse urban contexts, ranging from Santiago to Buenos Aires to Mexico City, from disputes in micro-neighbourhoods to metropolitan-level conflicts. At a general level, urban social movements in Latin America show certain regularities such as class 'recomposition' on the one hand, exhibiting a growing cross-class consciousness of inequality which has emerged through spatial/local struggles against what Harvey (2010: 181) calls speculative 'landed developer interests' in cities. On the other hand, such urban social movements display a seemingly contradictory, but much more variegated and in many ways 'creative', repertoire of protest performances, where claims are made for space, centrality and housing as social rights, yet somewhat detached from the language and histories of class struggle. These include the successful struggle in Mexico City to fend off the operation of private-public urban renewal agency as a neoliberal government apparatus, which has sought to carry out aggressive urban redevelopment and social cleansing (López-Morales forthcoming), and the creative appropriation of neoliberal urban renewal policies in Buenos Aires to secure housing loans for supporting cooperative-style housing management and producing hundreds of low-cost, good quality social housing units all over the southern part of the city (Rodríguez and Di Virgilio 2016; see also Cociña and López-Morales 2018; López-Morales 2016c). Anti-gentrification agendas increasingly occupy a central position, contributing to the formation of political alternatives and serving as a nexus between everyday struggles over lived space and larger social movement agendas. While we endeavour to locate gentrification in the Global South by not privileging the experience of Anglo-American cities, thinking of anti-gentrification strategies calls for the need to localize anti-gentrification fights while bearing in mind the possibility of the generalizability of such fights for cross-regional alliances. Thus, we envisage planetary use of the concept of gentrification as becoming more than normative.

ACKNOWLEDGEMENTS

Hyun Bang Shin acknowledges the support from the National Research Foundation of Korea Grant funded by the Korean Government (NRF-2017S1A3A2066514). Ernesto López-Morales acknowledges the support from the National Research Fund of Chile (Fondecyt Grant #1151287) and the Centre for Social Conflict and Cohesion Studies (COES, Fondap Grant #15130009).

NOTES

1. According to Lee (2016), there were less than ten reports of 'gentrification' made by the media annually between 2004 and 2011, but the frequency of media reports referring to gentrification exploded, with 45 mentions in 2014, and 813 in 2015.
2. The announcement can be accessed here: http://news.korean.go.kr/index.jsp?control=page&part=view& idx=10332 (last accessed on 13 June 2017).
3. Odebrecht is one of the key operators in the Porto Maravilha mega redevelopment in the (until a few years ago) derelict Zona Portuária (Sánchez and Broudehoux 2013).

REFERENCES

Bernt, M. (2016) 'Very particular, or rather universal? Gentrification though the lenses of Ghertner and López-Morales', *City*, 20(4): 637–644.
Castells, M. (1985) *The City and the Grassroots: A Cross-Cultural Theory of Urban Social Movements*, Berkeley, CA: University of California Press.
Castells, M. (1992) 'Four Asian tigers with a dragon head: A comparative analysis of the state, economy, and society in the Asian Pacific Rim', in Appelbaum, R. and Henderson, J. (eds), *States and Development in the Asian Pacific Rim*, Newbury Park, CA: SAGE, pp. 33–70.
Chakrabarty, D. (2000) *Provincializing Europe: Postcolonial Thought and Historical Difference*, Princeton: Princeton University Press.
Clark, E. (2005) 'The order and simplicity of gentrification: A political challenge', in Atkinson, R. and Bridge, G. (eds), *Gentrification in a Global Context: The New Urban Colonialism*, London: Routledge, pp. 256–264.
Clark, E. (2015) 'Afterword: The adventure of generic gentrification', in Lees, L., Shin, H. and López-Morales, E. (eds), *Global Gentrifications: Uneven Development and Displacement*, Bristol: Policy Press, pp. 453–456.
Cociña, C. and López-Morales, E. (2018) 'Unpacking narratives of social conflict and inclusion: Anti-gentrification neighbourhood organisation in Santiago, Chile', in Rokem, J. and Boano, C. (eds), *Urban Geopolitics – Rethinking Planning in Contested Cities*, London: Routledge, pp. 171–188.
Cuenya, B. and Corral, M. (2011) 'Empresarialismo, economía del suelo y grandes proyectos urbanos: El modelo de Puerto Madero en Buenos Aires', *EURE*, 37(111), 25–45.
Davidson, M. and Lees, L. (2010) 'New-build gentrification: Its histories, trajectories, and critical geographies', *Population, Space and Place*, 16(5), 395–411.
Defilippis, J. (2004) *Unmasking Goliath: Community Control in the Face of Global Capital*, New York: Routledge.
Doshi, S. (2013) 'The politics of the evicted: Redevelopment, subjectivity, and difference in Mumbai's slum frontier', *Antipode*, 45(4), 844–865.
Elshahed, M. (2015) 'The prospects of gentrification in downtown Cairo: Artists, private investment and the neglectful state', in Lees, L., Shin, H.B. and López-Morales, E. (eds), *Global Gentrifications: Uneven Development and Displacement*, Bristol: Policy Press, pp. 121–142.
Garay, A., Wainer, L., Henderson, H. and Rotbart, D. (2013) 'Puerto Madero: Análisis de un Proyecto', *Land Lines*, July. [Online]. Available at: www.lincolninst.edu/pubs/2289_Puerto-Madero-An%C3%A1lisis-de-un-proyecto (last accessed 2 April 2017).
Gaytán, P. (2016) 'Espacio público: Entre el yosmart y la invención urbanita', *Metapolítica*, 20(95), 49–55.

Ghertner, A. (2015) 'Why gentrification theory fails in "much of the world"', *City*, 19(4), 546–556.

The Guardian (2017) 'Brazil's corruption scandal spreads across South America', 11 February. [Online]. Available at: www.theguardian.com/world/2017/feb/11/brazils-corruption-scandal-spreads-across-south-america (last accessed 8 April 2017).

Ha, S.-K. (2001) 'Substandard settlements and joint redevelopment projects in Seoul', *Habitat International*, 25, 385–397.

Haila, A. (2016) *Urban Land Rents: Singapore as a Property State*, Wiley-Blackwell.

Harvey, D. (2005) *A Brief History of Neoliberalism*, New York: Oxford University Press.

Harvey, D. (2010) *The Enigma of Capital and the Crises of Capitalism*, London: Profile Books.

Herzer, H., Di Virgilio, M.M. and Rodríguez, M.C. (2015) 'Gentrification in Buenos Aires: Global trends and local features', in Lees, L., Shin, H.B. and López-Morales, E. (eds), *Global Gentrifications: Uneven Development and Displacement*, Bristol: Policy Press, pp. 199–222.

Janoschka, M., Sequera, J. and Salinas, L. (2014) 'Gentrification in Spain and Latin America – a critical dialogue', *International Journal of Urban and Regional Research*, 38(4), 1234–1265.

Kim, S.-H. (1999) 'The history of evictees' movement in Seoul', *Urbanity and Poverty*, 36, 51–77 [in Korean].

King, V.T. (2008) 'The middle class in Southeast Asia: Diversities, identities, comparisons and the Vietnamese case', *IJAPS*, 4(2), 73–109.

Koo, H. (1991) 'Middle classes, democratization, and class formation: The case of South Korea', *Theory and Society*, 20(4), 485–509.

Kutz, W. and Lenhardt, J. (2016) '"Where to put the spare cash?" Subprime urbanisation and the geographies of the financial crisis in the global South', *Urban Geography*, 37(6), 926–948.

Lang, M.H. (1982) *Gentrification Amid Urban Decline: Strategies for America's Older Cities*, Cambridge, MA: Ballinger Pub. Co.

Lee, S.Y. (2016) 'Neil Smith, gentrification, and South Korea', *Space and Society*, 26(2), 209–234 [in Korean].

Lees, L. (2012) 'The geography of gentrification: Thinking through comparative urbanism', *Progress in Human Geography*, 36(2), 155–171.

Lees, L. (2014) 'The urban injustices of New Labour's "new urban renewal": The case of the Aylesbury Estate in London', *Antipode*, 46(4), 921–947.

Lees, L., Shin, H.B. and López-Morales, E. (eds) (2015) *Global Gentrifications: Uneven Development and Disparity*, Bristol: Policy Press.

Lees, L., Shin, H.B. and López-Morales, E. (2016) *Planetary Gentrification*, Cambridge: Polity Press.

Lett, D.P. (1998) *In Pursuit of Status: The Making of South Korea's 'New' Urban Middle Class*, Cambridge, MA: Harvard University Asia Center.

Ley, D. (1980) 'Liberal ideology and the postindustrial city', *Annals of the Association of American Geographers*, 70(2), 238–258.

Ley, D. and Teo, S.Y. (2014) 'Gentrification in Hong Kong? Epistemology vs. ontology', *International Journal of Urban and Regional Research*, 38(4), 1286–1303.

López-Morales, E. (2008) 'Destrucción creativa y explotación de brecha de renta: discutiendo la renovación urbana del peri-centro sur poniente de Santiago de Chile entre 1990 y 2005', *Scripta Nova*, 12(270). [Online]. Available at: www.ub.edu/geocrit/sn/sn-270/sn-270-100.htm (last accessed on 8 April 2017).

López-Morales, E. (2016a) 'Gentrification in the global South', *City*, 19(4), 564–573.

López-Morales, E. (2016b) 'Assessing exclusionary displacement through rent gap analysis in the urban redevelopment of inner Santiago, Chile', *Housing Studies*, 31(5), 540–559.

López-Morales, E. (2016c) 'Social internalization of risk in the housing market of Santiago, Chile, research on political economy', in Soederberg, S. (ed), *Critiquing Risk Management in Neoliberal Capitalism, Research on Political Economy*, 31, 79–105.

López-Morales, E. (forthcoming) 'Privatization of public and transport space in Mexico City: the birth of a political alternative', in Ahlert, M. and Von Borries, F. (eds), *Mexibility: Estamos en la ciudad, no podemos salir de ella*, Berlin.

Maloutas, T. (2012) 'Contextual diversity in gentrification research', *Critical Sociology*, 38(1), 33–48.

Massey, D. (1993) 'Power-geometry and a progressive sense of place', in Bird, J., Curtis, B., Putnam, T., Robertson, G. and Tickner, L. (eds), *Mapping the Futures: Local Cultures, Global Change*, London: Routledge, pp. 60–70.

Moreno, L. (2014) 'The urban process under financialised capitalism', *City: Analysis of*

Urban Trends, Culture, Theory, Policy, Action, 18(3), 244–268.

Percival, T. and Waley, P. (2012) 'Articulating intra-Asian urbanism: The production of satellite cities in Phnom Penh', *Urban Studies*, 49(13), 2873–2888.

Queiroz Ribeiro, L. and dos Santos Junior, O. (2007) *As metrópoles e a questao social brasileira*, Rio de Janeiro: Revan.

Ramesh, R. (2005) 'Poor squeezed out by Mumbai's dream plan: India's biggest city is razing its shanty towns', *The Guardian*, 1 March. [Online]. Available at: www.theguardian.com/world/2005/mar/01/india.ran deepramesh (last accessed 8 April 2017).

Rodríguez, M. and Di Virgilio, M. (2016) 'A city for all? Public policy and resistance to gentrification in the southern neighborhoods of Buenos Aires', *Urban Geography*, 37(8), 1215–1234.

Sabatini, F., Cáceres, G. and Cerda, J. (2001) 'Segregación residencial en las principales ciudades chilenas: Tendencias de las tres últimas décadas y posibles cursos de acción', *EURE*, 27(82), 21–42.

Sánchez, F. and Broudehoux, A-M. (2013) 'Mega-events and urban regeneration in Rio de Janeiro: Planning in a state of emergency', *International Journal of Urban Sustainable Development*, 5(2), 132–153.

Shao, Q. (2013) *Shanghai Gone: Domicide and Defiance in a Chinese Megacity*, Lanham, MD: Rowman and Littlefield.

Shatkin, G. (2008) 'The city and the bottom line: Urban megaprojects and the privatization of planning in Southeast Asia', *Environment and Planning A*, 40, 383–401.

Shin, H.B. (2016) 'Economic transition and speculative urbanisation in China: Gentrification versus dispossession', *Urban Studies*, 53(3), 471–489.

Shin, H.B. (2017) 'Envisioned by the state: Entrepreneurial urbanism and the making of Songdo City, South Korea', in Datta, A. and Shaban, A. (eds), *Mega-urbanization in the Global South: Fast Cities and New Urban Utopias of the Postcolonial State*, Routledge, pp. 83–100.

Shin, H.B. (forthcoming) 'Studying global gentrifications', in Harrison, J. and Hoyler, M. (eds), *Doing Global Urban Research*, SAGE.

Shin, H.B. and Kim, S.-H. (2016) 'The developmental state, speculative urbanisation and the politics of displacement in gentrifying Seoul', *Urban Studies*, 53(3), 540–559.

Shin, H.B., Lees, L. and López-Morales, E. (2016) 'Introduction: Locating gentrification in the global East', *Urban Studies*, 53(3), 455–470.

Slater, T. (2006) 'The eviction of critical perspectives from gentrification research', *International Journal of Urban and Regional Research*, 30(4), 737–757.

Slater, T. (2014) 'Unravelling false choice urbanism', *City: Analysis of Urban Trends, Culture, Theory, Policy, Action*, 18(4–5), 517–524.

Smith, N. (1979) 'Toward a theory of gentrification: A back to the city movement by capital not people', *Journal of the American Planning Association*, 45, 538–548.

Smith, N. (2002) 'New globalism, new urbanism: Gentrification as global urban strategy', *Antipode*, 34(3), 427–450.

Sonn, J.W., Shin, H. and Park, S.H. (2017) 'A mega urban project and two competing accumulation strategies: Negotiating discourses of the Songdo International Business District development', *International Development Planning Review*, 39(3), 299–317.

Tomba, L. (2004) 'Creating an urban middle class: Social engineering in Beijing', *The China Journal*, 51, 1–26.

Wacquant, L., Slater, T. and Pereira, V.B. (2014) 'Territorial stigmatization in action', *Environment and Planning A*, 46, 1270–1280.

Woo-Cumings, M. (ed) (1999) *The Developmental State*, New York: Cornell University Press.

Wyly, E., Newman, K., Schafran, A. and Lee, E. (2010) 'Displacing New York', *Environment and Planning A*, 42, 2602–2623.

BOX 2 HYUN BANG SHIN REFLECTION

This reflection, although placed in this *Reader* in relation to the chapter I co-authored with Ernesto Lopez-Morales, published in 2018, continues my own critical reflection on what it means to use gentrification as an analytical lens to understand urban processes outside of the Global North. My thoughts build upon and extend the collaborative endeavor that I undertook with the co-authors of *Planetary Gentrification* (Lees, Shin, and López-Morales, 2016), for we pursued a series of *collective* publication projects that brought together a number of researchers from the Global South (from East/Southeast Asia and Latin America in particular), to critically examine gentrification as a process that can be both endogenous (rooted in local capitalistic urbanization) and exogenous (influenced by national/global circuits of investment that increasingly hinge upon speculative real estate accumulation). Our *collaborative* publication projects included not only Shin and López-Morales (2018) or Lees, Shin, and López-Morales (2016), but also a special issue on locating gentrification in the Global East, published in *Urban Studies* (Shin, Lees, and López-Morales, 2016), and another on Latin American gentrifications, published in *Urban Geography* (López-Morales, Shin, and Lees, 2016), as well as a co-edited volume, *Global Gentrifications: Uneven Development and Displacement* (Lees, Shin, and López-Morales, 2015). All of this published work emerged out of two workshops in 2012 – one in London and another in Santiago, Chile – funded by the Urban Studies Foundation. Five to ten years later, it is an appropriate time to reflect on this work and reactions to it from other scholars.

One of the critiques of our collective efforts that emerged came from post-colonial urbanist scholars who argued that cities in the Global South exhibit(ed) distinctively different urban structures and relations from those of the Global North and that the application of the concept gentrification to the Global South could be regarded as academic colonialism. We beg to differ. While we acknowledge the contributions made by post-colonial urbanists for their articulation of the messiness of Southern urbanism, we adopt a critical political economic perspective on the urbanization of post-colonial, Southern cities, to examine the workings of maturing capitalist relations as manifested in urbanizing spaces, identifying gentrification as one of the emergent processes therein, which affects the livelihoods of many urbanites. As noted in Shin and López-Morales (2018), we find it 'perfectly possible to generalise gentrification as a process of land use change that results in the unequal appropriation of rents and causes the displacement of existing land users, while at the same time emphasising the particular trajectories of how this process is shaped by the workings of the place-specific political, economic and social relations that co-exist in space' (p. 16).

Such an understanding *does not* necessarily mean that 'gentrification' is the only useful analytical lens through which to explain urban processes, be they located in the Global South or the Global North. Many studies have centered on the question of whether gentrification exists 'elsewhere', a question that is often inappropriately set up and therefore produces skepticism of gentrification itself. It is imperative that researchers look to locate gentrification in multiple urban processes that are simultaneously at work, both historically and contemporaneously, and also at various geographical scales. Through the aforementioned projects, we tried to reiterate the importance of identifying the evolving trajectories of contemporary capitalism that increasingly commodify land and housing for speculative gain and how this process has become dominant across the globe, creating escalated competition for space and resulting in the severance (i.e., displacement) of people from their communities. We would continue to call for open-minded, planetary thinking on gentrification.

One of the key points that Shin and López-Morales (2018) sought to underline was the issue of *provincializing* gentrification research in Anglo-American cities. Those who question(ed) the applicability of the concept of gentrification to Southern cities tend(ed) to distance themselves from contesting the decades-long evolution of gentrification research in the Global North (in Anglo-American cities in particular). Interestingly, when critics consider the differences between northern Atlantic cities and southern European cities, these differences do not seem to lead to the negation of gentrification in northern Atlantic cities per se. Such an interpretation is contradictory, as it does not acknowledge the differences *within* northern Atlantic cities (e.g., the US versus the UK). The history of gentrification studies is embedded in northern Atlantic cities, but gentrification as a concept has come a long way since Ruth Glass coined the term in 1964. Shin and López-Morales (2018) was a warning against fossilizing gentrification as a concept, a process, and a body of research.

Another key point in the chapter was about the role of the state in facilitating gentrification, acknowledging the differences between the Global North and the Global South/East with respect to the historical formation of the state, its role, and its relations to its societies and markets. For myself, the state question has been particularly pertinent to the Global East, where authoritarian states have shaped the frame of developmental urbanization and class mobility and ensured the creation of a business-friendly environment while striving to achieve a degree of social stability through the use of state violence and co-optation.

While Shin and López-Morales (2018) focused on state-capital relations, upon reflection it would have been helpful to tease out more of the messier conditions of gentrification and how various forms of displacement may occur among diverse social groups entangled in the process of neighborhood change. Let me briefly elaborate further on this point by taking the example of urban redevelopment, especially in the context of East Asia, where such projects have been rampant in recent years. Redevelopment projects involving owner-occupiers are particularly prone to becoming a contested field of gentrification. If owner-occupiers in Seoul, South Korea, join hands with their developer to commercially redevelop their neighborhood, is their neighborhood being gentrified, given the owners are able to stay put? If Singapore's private property owners in high-rise estates agree to *en bloc* sale to a developer that aims to pursue higher-density commercial redevelopment, is their neighborhood being gentrified? Moreover, if local villagers in southern China join hands with their local government and developers and agree to the redevelopment of their village land in return for rehousing units and additional real estate assets that produce economic gains for their village collective, can this be seen as gentrification? The resident or resident group that is chosen as the entry point of analysis for researching and discussing gentrification becomes hugely influential in terms of determining whether a neighborhood is gentrified or not. All too often, cases such as these would lead skeptics to question the use of gentrification as an analytical lens, based on the fact that villagers and owner-occupiers, as well as absentee owners, are not necessarily victims of the neighborhood change, as they have *voluntarily* conceded to sign an agreement to redevelop their neighborhood (and even gain from it financially); at the same time, displacement is also unlikely to happen as they may be able to stay put through securing rehousing units as part of compensation.

However, it might well be that this is too premature a conclusion. For example, the focus on local villagers in China's village redevelopment often excludes migrant tenants, whose number far exceeds those of local villagers and who do not receive access to alternative affordable rental dwellings after their displacement. There is also often a lack of attention to the various tensions and relational oppressions that might produce a coercive environment within which villagers' individual decisions have to be made. Nor is there often attention to intra-family dynamics or gender and kinship relations in terms of how decisions are reached within families and among neighbors. The 'un-homing' experience of each individual, thus giving rise to symbolic or phenomenological displacement, is therefore insufficiently addressed in many existing studies, rendering claims that gentrification is not happening both premature and inconclusive.

In Asia and elsewhere in the world, where (unequal) economic prosperity and efficiency is at the focal point of government policies, there is a need to introduce displacement as a focal point of critical urban studies to capture the frontiers of gentrification at multiple scales (the body, family, community, city, etc.). Too often, we hear stories that emphasize modernity and the material prosperity lifting people out of poverty, treating state-led gentrification as a positive, as societal progress. Attention to displacement would offset this bias in extant scholarship and policy discourse.

Furthermore, while the presence of informal property relations has also led some critics to argue against the applicability of gentrification to cities of the Global South, the complex layers of property rights, alongside the blurring of the boundary between formality and informality, act in both ways: it sometimes facilitates urban redevelopment as informality provides gray rooms for negotiation to overcome the bottleneck of property-rights-related disputes, while, at other times, informality may act as a bulwark against speedy (re)development. All of this suggests that there is no clear-cut case for arguing that gentrification as an analytical lens 'fails' in the Global South.

Those scholars who have criticized the growing work on planetary gentrification ought to be reminded of the purpose of what gentrification as an analytical lens can do for critical urban studies. There are questions to be asked of those using this analytical lens: Is it to confirm the existence of gentrification? *Or* is it to contribute to understandings of the mechanics of social injustice in cities worldwide and the unveiling of socioeconomic and political mechanisms that give rise to such injustice? Gentrification, we would argue, provides an analytical lens through which to dissect the operation of the state, capital, class violence, and those injustices that result from this, but scholars should also be mindful of other urban processes working in tandem with, or alongside, gentrification. Ultimately what the chapter 'Beyond Anglo-American Gentrification Theory' (Shin and López-Morales, 2018) attempts to propose is how extant gentrification studies could benefit from engaging with urban processes outside of the Anglo-American world of gentrification (remember, Lees, 2012, urged urban geographers to talk to development geographers and vice versa) and importantly how cities in the majority world could be sites from which gentrification can be further theorized, thus contributing to ongoing efforts to de-center knowledge production and decolonize urban scholarship.

REFERENCES

Lees, L. (2012) The geography of gentrification: Thinking through comparative urbanism. *Progress in Human Geography* 36(2): 155–171.

Lees, L., Shin, H.B. and López-Morales, E. (eds.) (2015) *Global Gentrifications: Uneven Development and Displacement*. Bristol: Policy Press.

Lees, L., Shin, H.B. and López-Morales, E. (2016) *Planetary Gentrification*. Cambridge: Polity Press.

López-Morales, E., Shin, H.B. and Lees, L. (eds.) (2016) Latin American gentrifications. *Urban Geography* 37(8): 1091–1252.

Shin, H.B., Lees, L. and López-Morales, E. (eds.) (2016) Locating gentrification in the Global East. *Urban Studies* 53(3): 455–625.

Shin, H. B. and Lopez-Morales, E. (2018) 'Beyond Anglo-American gentrification theory', in Lees, L. with Phillips, M. (eds), *Handbook of Gentrification Studies*, Cheltenham, UK: Edward Elgar, pp. 13–25.

4
Revisiting 'the changing state of gentrification'

Manuel B. Aalbers

INTRODUCTION

Our aim in this first *TESG Forum* is to revisit a classic paper published in this journal and take a moment to reflect on the continued importance of this 'classic' to the field. 'The Changing State of Gentrification' (2001) by Jason Hackworth and the late Neil Smith is one of the most influential papers ever published in *TESG*. This paper changed the way we think about gentrification. Hitherto, discussions had been dominated by production-versus consumption-led debates and the process of gentrification itself had been approached as having different stages (starting with marginal gentrifiers (Rose 1984), like artists and students, and ending with full-fledged and later 'super' gentrification; Lees 2003), but Hackworth and Smith discussed how gentrification was qualitatively different in different decades.

The main concept introduced in the article, 'third wave gentrification', sometimes also referred to as state-led or government-sponsored gentrification, was quickly included in discussions of neoliberal urbanism as both paid a great deal of attention to the role of local government in furthering the interests of local elites and developers rather than conceptualising the local authority as primarily interested in welfare. In this wave or phase, gentrification processes, market-led urban public policies and commodification of urban space became 'generalised' as Smith (2002) would later argue. The third wave of gentrification also took gentrification outside the inner city core and into more peripheral urban – and even rural – areas. To me, the concept of third-wave gentrification is more useful than gentrification as a general term; it centres on the role of the (local) state as an instigator, catalyst or sponsor of the socio-spatial restructuring of the city.

The government-sponsored and debt-fuelled gentrification of the late 1990s and early 2000s was at the root of the North-Atlantic financial crisis that started in the US in 2007. Yet, it appears that what we now see in many places, both in those hit hard by the financial crisis and those relatively spared, is the continuation of state-led gentrification. Is this *TESG Forum* we seek to answer the following questions: What has third wave gentrification meant for urban research and what is its meaning today? How can we use 'wave thinking' to understand contemporary urban processes and policies? Are we still in a third wave or have we entered a fourth or fifth wave – and how are the new waves different from the old ones?

In the next section, I will discuss the three waves discussed by Hackworth and Smith (2001) as well as Lees *et al.*'s (2008) proposition for a fourth wave. In the subsequent section I will argue that we have now entered fifth-wave gentrification. As during earlier waves of gentrification, an economic crisis triggered a mutation in the process of gentrification, which led to the emergence of fifth-wave gentrification in which the process is further generalised. Fifth-wave gentrification is the urban materialisation of financialised or finance-led capitalism. The state continues to play a leading role during the fifth wave, but is now supplemented – rather than displaced – by finance.

This *Introduction to the Forum* is followed by three articles and a commentary by Jason Hackworth, the lead author of 'The Changing State of Gentrification'. The editors of *TESG* have invited four authors that previously have used the idea of the third wave in their work on gentrification in, respectively, North America, East Asia and Western Europe. All four have not simply taken the idea of the third wave at face value, but have used

DOI: 10.4324/9781003341239-6

the concept as a starting point to study gentrification rather than as a given, fixed category. We have asked them to discuss the continued usefulness of wave thinking in contemporary gentrification research and debates.

First, Elvin Wyly (this issue) discusses the critiques that have been launched against 'wave thinking' in gentrification. He argues in favour of such wave thinking; to Wyly, gentrification is inseparable from the enduring legacy of evolutionary theory in social science. Shenjing He this issue discusses the meanings and uses of wave thinking to understand gentrification in China. She proposes a different periodisation, differently defined waves, to understand how the interplay between state, market and society produces gentrification in China. Wouter van Gent and Willem Boterman this issue argue that in gentrification debates, class relations should be more visible vis-à-vis the state. Like He, Van Gent and Boterman adapt the periodisation of gentrification to make it fit their case, Amsterdam. They show how Amsterdam was transformed from a radical but largely low-income city into a liberal, middle-class city. Finally, Jason Hackworth this issue responds to the different articles building on or critiquing his taxonomy of gentrification waves. He argues that for Neil Smith and him, gentrification was always about something bigger and should not be separated from broader economic and social processes.

FOUR WAVES OF GENTRIFICATION

In their article Hackworth and Smith introduce a periodisation of gentrification (see Figure 1). Although they provided examples from New York City to illustrate their argument, they stress that their periodisation is based on readings of other cases and has wider applicability: 'Specific dates for these phases will undoubtedly vary from place to place, but not so significant as to diminish the influence of broader scale political events on the local experience of gentrification' (Hackworth & Smith 2001, p. 466). In the first wave the dominant discourse on cities is still one of ame-liorating urban decline, which in NYC was visible in the form of landlord abandonment and arson. As a result, first-wave gentrification was sporadic, highly localised but also significantly funded by the state.

During the recession of the mid 1970s gentrification mutates. In the resulting second wave, federal programmes are scaled back and gentrification takes a more *laissez-faire* form. At the same time, gentrification expands geographically, covering a larger part of the city, but also internationally. Gentrification is no longer simply a process of class-residential change, but extends into cultural and commercial spheres. The presence of arts and culture, either implicitly or explicitly, often functions as a 'soft factor' attracting new flows of capital into these neighbourhoods. The recession that started with the stock market crash of 1987 and the recession of the early 1990s prompted some to speak of the end of gentrification or of 'degentrification', a myth that was already debunked by Smith in 1995. What happens instead is that gentrification mutates again. 'Third-wave', 'post-recession', 'government-sponsored' or 'state-led' gentrification is distinct from first- and second wave gentrification in at least four ways:

First, gentrification is expanding both within the inner-city neighbourhoods that it affected during earlier waves and to more remote neighbourhoods beyond the immediate core. Second, restructuring and globalisation in the real estate industry has set a larger context for larger developers becoming more involved in gentrifying neighbourhoods (Logan 1993; Coakley 1994; Ball 1994). While such developers used to be common in the process only after the neighbourhood had been 'tamed' (Zukin 1982; Ley 1996), they are now increasingly the first to orchestrate investment. Third, effective resistance to gentrification has declined as the working class is continually displaced from the inner city, and as the most militant anti-gentrification groups of the 1980s morph into housing service providers. Fourth, and of most relevance to this paper, the state is now more involved in the process than [in] the second wave.

(Hackworth & Smith 2001, p. 468)

The concept of state-led gentrification made gentrification research more relevant in both academic and political terms. It was no longer about the small-scale and bottom up initiatives of the first wave. Nor was it simply about developers finding a (new?) way to make money on urban land (second wave). Third-wave gentrification

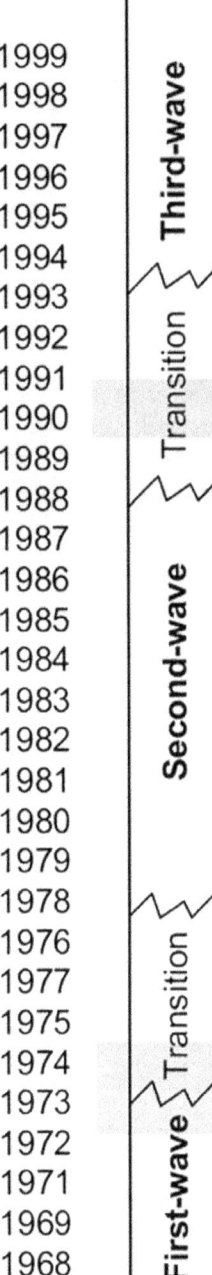

Figure 1 Schematic history of gentrification (recessions in grey).
Source: Hackworth and Smith (2001).

was about how the local authorities and national state use their regulatory and financial powers to enable – and indeed, to boost – profits made by private developers: 'state assistance (or some other form of assistance) is increasingly necessary for the process to swallow "underdeveloped" parcels further from the CBD' (Hackworth & Smith 2001, p. 469). Personally, the heuristic of state-led gentrification has helped me to understand the dynamics of urban change in Amsterdam. In the 'revitalisation' of the infamous Bijlmer housing estate, the local and national state were of Airbnb results in price increases, but also that the potential income from Airbnb may call for bigger mortgage loans for apartments and houses with Airbnb-potential. Airbnb has also pushed the 'touristification' of certain neighbourhoods, not only resulting in house price inflation but increasingly also displacement, as Airbnb is often used throughout the year and thereby relegating long-term tenants to other districts (Gant 2016; Lee 2016; McNeill 2016; Sans & Quaglieri 2016; Lambea Llop 2017; Mermet 2017). Several cities may be trying to regulate Airbnb but so far many Airbnb landlords appear to be bypassing such rules.

In Amsterdam – an Airbnb Top 10 city – an increasing number of locals spends the summer camping at the city edge while renting out their properties through Airbnb, according to a local newspaper (van der Keijl 2017). Furthermore, large corporations are trying to get into the Airbnb market. Residents in central Amsterdam have received flyers of an investor who is willing to pay 25 per cent over current market prices to acquire apartments that can be rented out through Airbnb (van der Meijden 2017). Although this turned out to be a joke, it is a likely future development now that rental housing is increasingly treated as an asset class by international investment funds (Fields 2018; Wijburg *et al.* 2018).

Global mortgage debt

The North-Atlantic financial crisis that started in 2007 has meant a pause in the expansion of mortgage debt, but the pause was short and global mortgage debt has been increasing ever since. Many countries in the Global North as well as in the Global South continue to subsidise mortgaged homeownership, often through fiscal measures. Furthermore, the securitisation of mortgage loans – the technique that allows mortgages portfolios to be resold to investors and pumps more money into the housing market – has been, and continues to be, rolled out to an increasing number of countries. Fiscal subsidies and securitisation do not necessarily result in increasing homeownership rates – in fact, several, mostly Anglophone, countries have seen this rate drop – but mortgage debt has grown exponentially since the crisis as new countries have opened up to more and bigger mortgages loans to an increasing number of households Rolnik 2013; (Fernandez & Aalbers 2016).

Lack of housing affordability

The financialisation of housing (Aalbers 2008), described by Lees *et al.* (2008) as a specificity of the US American fourth wave, increasingly is becoming generalised around the globe in fifth wave gentrification. This results in house price inflation across the board, not only in gentrifying neighbourhoods, but it does imply that increasingly larger social groups are excluded from housing in certain locations as prices are simply out of their reach, resulting in a great deal of indirect displacement. As rents broadly tend to follow the developments in house prices, this also puts pressure on rental properties, again not only in gentrifying neighbourhoods, but more so in those areas as there is more potential to raise rents and rent out properties to higher-income groups than those living there previously.

The role of the (local) state

At first sight, the role of the state in all this may appear somewhat ambiguous. On the one hand, many state institutions have pushed mortgaged homeownership, the securitisation of mortgages (now also at the international state level; see Fernandez & Aalbers 2017) and the spread of REITs. On the other hand, municipalities – that is, the local state – are increasingly trying to regulate Airbnb as well as international capital going into local housing markets. Overall, however, it appears that the state continues to display many of its third and fourth-wave features, that is, state assistance plays an increasingly dominant role in facilitating private investment, not only in inner cities but increasingly also in other parts of the urban region.

The state-support of gentrification is often considered 'natural', as if it is the duty of the state to support private investment. Indeed, in the fifth wave gentrification appears not only generalised but increasingly also naturalised. Local governments may be acting based more on 'potential' than 'need', as van Gent and Boterman this issue show for the City of Amsterdam in their contribution to this Forum. Not only entrepreneurial urbanism but also 'new public management'[2] (that suggests government should be run like corporations) has been fully internalised. It remains to be seen if this is part of a wider trend towards the financialisation of local government (e.g. Weber 2010; Hendrikse 2015; Peck & Whiteside 2016; van Loon et al. 2018). This emerging literature is not just looking into how municipalities are run internally, but also how they sponsor and participate in real estate markets. In some places there appears to be a trend towards the state as not only a sponsor but also a direct agent of gentrification.

The subsumption of alternatives

An alternative way to read consecutive waves of gentrification – bridging cultural and economic readings of gentrification processes – would be to see gentrification as an important 'urban form of capitalism' that, like capitalism itself, increasingly subsumes urban practices that were once developed as alternatives to urban capitalism. The first and second waves of gentrification could be characterised by liberal (in the sense of progressive) values, a 'do it yourself' mentality and a sense of counterculture, but this often developed into what the French so aptly call BoBo: *bourgeois bohemian*. The third wave brought attention to arts and culture, but under urban capitalism this was mutated into 'the creative class' (Florida 2002). Alternative consumption patterns, such as a preference for organic food, popular among many of the new middle classes was also quickly subsumed in new waves of gentrification. Likewise, the promise of the democratisation of the (urban) 'sharing economy' of Airbnb, Uber and other companies is subsumed by a 'cyber-libertarian impulse' (Dahlberg 2010) that is based on a naïve 'technology solutionism' (Morozov 2013) under fifth-wave gentrification.

CODA

Wave thinking in urban research has been criticised for ignoring differences between places (for a discussion, see Wyly this issue). Hackworth and Smith, like others who have advocated a periodisation to gentrification have never claimed their waves explain everything or are globally applicable in the sense that they are the same in different places. What they do claim, is that:

an explanation that invoked *only* local differences would not tell us much either. . . . [B]ut I think we need to be careful about an illicit slippage between levels of abstraction (universal-particular) and geographical scales of experience (global-local). It has become fashionable to assert privilege of 'local knowledge', to use Geertz's (1983) phrase. The irony, of course is that advocating a certain localism . . . can become its own kind of universalist response, threatening a new kind of theoretical stale-mate.
(Smith 1995, p. 124)

Indeed, there are no universally applicable (urban) theories, but there is also no localism that can explain all particularities in a globally connected world. Explanations that suggest all is different and unique are as geographically flat as explanations that suggest that all is universal and the same. Ironically, the latter is often used as a straw-man by the advocates of the former – a straw-man because such claims to universality have long ceased to exist. To understand the particularities of gentrification in different places we need to understand local histories, processes and institutions, but we should be careful to privilege the local and reject the possibility of a 'common trajectory' (Hay 2004; see also Fernandez & Aalbers 2016) a priori. Not all agents of gentrification are locally embedded; policies 'travel'; and Airbnb and REITs are international phenomena. This does not imply their impact is the same everywhere. Policies mutate and agents adapt to local conditions. Yet, policies and agents do not simply embed themselves locally, they also change local practices of gentrification. It would be a loss to urban theory to ignore commonalities, common trajectories and inter-local agents simply because particularities, difference and local agents are considered more worthy explanations of change. As Hackworth this issue writes in his response this Forum: 'The important point is figuring out which are actually local challenges or deviations from larger patterns and which are the residue of similar processes with different local wrapping'.

One of the dominant forces in fifth-wave gentrification is finance; not simply capital, but financial capital, that is, the concentration of capital in the hands of and controlled by financial institutions (cf. Hilferding 1910). It is a period in which urban development is increasingly controlled by financial institutions. Rather than finance replacing the state, finance supplements the state in gentrification. Neither the state nor finance establish a monopoly over urban development, but they have become the dominant powers that give shape to it. Developers remain important, but 'Financial actors can determine *when* cities grow . . . as well as *how* and *where* they grow' (Weber 2015, p. 39, emphasis in original). This does not imply other actors have no agency or that finance capital directs development in the same manner around the world, but it does mean we need to study the dominance of finance capital across cases to understand contemporary gentrification.

NOTES

1. Slater (2015) also sees the predominance of institutional investors with high return expectations as one of the characteristics of what he names 'planetary rent gaps'.
2. On NPM in local government, see Ward (2006) and Weikart (2001).

REFERENCES

Aalbers, M.B. (2008), The Financialization of Home and the Mortgage Market Crisis. *Competition & Change* 12, pp. 148–166.

Aalbers, M.B. (2011), The Revanchist Renewal of Yesterday's City of Tomorrow. *Antipode* 43, pp. 1695–1724.

Aalbers, M.B. (2015), The Great Moderation, the Great Excess and the Global Housing Crisis. *International Journal of Housing Policy* 15, pp. 43–60.

Aalbers, M.B. & M. Deinema (2012), Placing Prostitution: The Spatial-Sexual Order of Amsterdam and its Growth Coalition. *City* 16, pp. 129–145.

Atkinson, R. (2003), Domestication by Cappuccino or a Revenge on Urban Space? Control and Empowerment in the Management of Public Spaces. *Urban Studies* 40, pp. 1829–1843.

Atkinson, R., S. Parker & R. Burrows (2017), Elite Formation, Power and Space in Contemporary London. *Theory, Culture & Society* 34, pp. 179–200.

Ball, M. (1994), The 1980s Property Boom. *Environment & Planning A* 26, pp. 671–695.

Beswick, J., G. Alexandri, M. Byrne, S. Vives-Miro, D. Fields, S. Hodkinson & M. Janoschka (2016), Speculating on London's Housing Future: The Rise of Global Corporate Landlords in 'Post-crisis' Urban Landscapes. *City* 20, pp. 321–341.

Boyer, R. (2000), Is a Finance-led Growth Regime a Viable Alternative to Fordism? A Preliminary Analysis. *Economy and Society* 29, pp. 111–145.

Byrne, M. (2016), 'Asset Price Urbanism' and Financialization after the Crisis: Ireland's National Asset Management Agency. *International Journal of Urban and Regional Research* 40, pp. 31–45.

Calbet I Elias, L. (2017), Financialised Rent Gaps and Public Interest in Berlin's Housing Crisis. In: A. Albet & N. Benach, eds., *Gentrification as a Global Strategy*, pp. 165–176. New York: Routledge.

City of Amsterdam (2011), *Project 1012. Voortgangsrapportage 2011*. Amsterdam: Gemeente Amsterdam.

Coakley, J. (1994), The Integration of Property and Financial Markets. *Environment and Planning A* 26, pp. 99–112.

Dahlberg, L. (2010), Cyber-libertarianism 2.0: A Discourse Theory/Critical Political Economy Examination. *Cultural Politics* 6, pp. 331–356.

Doucet, B. (2014), A Process of Change and a Changing Process: Introduction to the Special Issues on Contemporary Gentrification. *Tijdschrift voor Economische en Sociale Geografie* 105, pp. 125–139.

Fernandez, R. & M.B. Aalbers (2016), Financialization and Housing: Between Globalization and Varieties of Capitalism. *Competition and Change* 20, pp. 71–88.

Fernandez, R. & M.B. Aalbers (2017), Capital Market Union and Residential Capitalism in Europe: Rescaling the Housing-centred Model of Financialization. *Finance and Society* 3, pp. 32–50.

Fernandez, R., A. Hofman & M.B. Aalbers (2016), London and New York as a Safe Deposit Box for the Transnational Wealth Elite. *Environment and Planning A* 48, pp. 2443–2461.

Fields, D. (2018), Constructing a New Asset Cass: Property-led Financial Accumulation after the Crisis. *Economic Geography* 94, pp. 118–140.

Florida, R. (2002), *The Rise of the Creative Class: And How it's Transforming Work, Leisure, Community and Everyday Life*. New York: Basic Books.

Gant, A.C. (2016), Holiday Rentals: The New Gentrification Battlefront. *Sociological Research Online* 21, 10. https://doi.org/10.5153/sro.4071.

Geertz, C. (1983), *Local Knowledge*. New York: Basic Books.

Gotham, K.F. (2006), The Secondary Circuit of Capital Reconsidered: Globalization and the US Real Estate Sector. *American Journal of Sociology* 112, pp. 231–275.

Guironnet, A., K. Attuyer & L. Halbert (2016), Building Cities on Financial Assets: The Financialisation of Property Markets and its Implications for City Governments in the Paris City-region. *Urban Studies* 53, pp. 1442–1464.

Hackworth, J. (this issue), Revisiting the Changing State of Gentrification. *Tijdschrift voor Economische en Sociale Geografie* 110, in press.

Hackworth, J. & N. Smith (2001), The Changing State of Gentrification. *Tijdschrift voor Economische en Sociale Geografie* 92, pp. 464–477.

Harvey, D. (1989), From Manageralism to Entrepreneurialism: The Transformation of Urban Governance in Late Capitalism. *Geografiska Annaler, Series B: Human Geography* 71, pp. 3–17.

Hay, C. (2004), Common Trajectories, Variable Paces, Divergent Outcomes? Models of European Capitalism under Conditions of Complex Economic Interdependence. *Review of International Political Economy* 11, pp. 231–261.

Hay, I. & J. Beaverstock (2016), *Handbook on Wealth and the Super-rich*. Cheltenham: Edward Elgar.

He, S. (this issue), Three Waves of State-led Gentrification in China. *Tijdschrift voor Economische en Sociale Geografie* 110, in press.

Hendrikse, R. (2015), *The Long Arm of Finance: Exploring the Unlikely Financialization of Governments and Public Institutions*. Amsterdam: Offpage.

Hilferding, R. (1910), *Finance Capital: A Study of the Latest Phase of Capitalist Development*. Reprinted, London: Routledge & Kegan Paul (1973).

Ho, H.K. & R. Atkinson (2017), Looking for Big 'Fry': The Motives and Methods of Middle-Class International Property Investors. *Urban Studies* 55, pp. 2040–2056.

ING (2016), *Airbnb Heeft Flink Opwaarts Effect of Amsterdamse Huizenprijzen*. Available at www.ing.nl/nieuws/nieuws_en_pers-berichten/2016/04/airbnb_heeft_flink_op-waarts_effect_op_amsterdamse_huizenprijzen.html. Accessed on 14 July 2017.

Lambea Llop, N. (2017), A Policy Approach to the Impact of Tourist Dwellings in Condominiums and Neighbourhoods in Barcelona. *Urban Research & Practice* 10, pp. 120–129.

Lee, D. (2016), How Airbnb Short-term Rentals Exacerbate Los Angeles's Affordable Housing Crisis: Analysis and Policy Recommendations. *Harvard Law & Policy Review* 10, pp. 229–254.

Lees, L. (2003), Super-gentrification: The Case of Brooklyn Heights, New York City. *Urban Studies* 40, pp. 2487–2509.

Lees, L., T. Slater & E. Wyly (2008), *Gentrification*. New York: Routledge.

Ley, D. (1996), *The New Middle Class and the Remaking of the Central City*. Oxford: Oxford University Press.

Ley, D. (2017), Global China and the Making of Vancouver's Residential Property Market. *International Journal of Housing Policy* 17, pp. 15–34.

Logan, J. (1993), Cycles and Trends in the Globalization of Real Estate. In: P. Knox, ed., *The Restless Urban Landscape*, pp. 33–44. Englewood Cliffs, NJ: Prentice Hall.

McNeill, D. (2016), Governing a City of Unicorns: Technology Capital and the Urban Politics of San Francisco. *Urban Geography* 37, pp. 494–513.

Mermet, A.-C. (2017), Critical Insights from the Exploratory Analysis of the 'Airbnb Syndrome' in Reykjavík. In: M. Gravari-Barbas and S. Guinand, eds., *Tourism and Gentrification in Contemporary Metropolises: International Perspectives*, pp. 52–74. New York: Routledge.

Merrifield, A. (1993), The Canary Wharf Debacle: From 'TINA' – There is No Alternative – to 'THEMBA' – There Must be an Alternative. *Environment and Planning A* 25, pp. 1247–1265.

Mollenkopf, J. (1983), *The Contested City*. Princeton, NJ: Princeton University Press.

Molotch, H. (1976), The City as a Growth Machine: Towards a Political Economy of Place. *American Journal of Sociology* 82, pp. 309–330.

Morozov, E. (2013), *To Save Everything, Click Here: The Folly of Technological Solutionism*. New York: PublicAffairs.

Peck, J. (2012), Austerity Urbanism: American Cities under Extreme Economy. *City* 16, pp. 626–655.

Peck, J. & H. Whiteside (2016), Financializing Detroit. *Economic Geography* 92, pp. 235–268.

Rogers, D. & S.Y. Koh (2017), The Globalisation of Real Estate: The Politics and Practice of

Foreign Real Estate Investment. *International Journal of Housing Policy* 17, pp. 1–14.

Rolnik, R. (2013), Late Neoliberalism: The Financialization of Homeownership and Housing Rights. *International Journal of Urban and Regional Research* 37, pp. 1058–1066.

Rose, D. (1984), Rethinking Gentrification: Beyond the Uneven Development of Marxist Urban Theory. *Environment & Planning D: Society & Space* 2, pp. 118–138.

Rouanet, H. & L. Halbert (2015), Leveraging Finance Capital: Urban Change and Self-empowerment of Real Estate Developers in India. *Urban Studies* 53, pp. 1401–1423.

Sans, A.A. & A. Quaglieri (2016), Unravelling Airbnb: Urban Perspectives from Barcelona. In: A.P. Russo & G. Richards, eds., *Reinventing the Local in Tourism: Producing, Consuming and Negotiating Place*, pp. 209–228. Bristol: Channel View.

Sassen, S. (2014), *Expulsions: Brutality and Complexity in the Global Economy*. Cambridge, MA: Harvard University Press.

Searle, L.G. (2014), Conflict and Commensuration: Contested Market Making in India's Private Real Estate Development Sector. *International Journal of Urban and Regional Research* 38, pp. 60–78.

Smith, N. (1995), Gentrifying Theory. *Scottish Geographical Magazine* 111, pp. 124–126.

Smith, N. (2002), New Globalism, New Urbanism: Gentrification as Global Urban Strategy. *Antipode* 34, pp. 427–450.

Teresa, B.F. (2016), Managing Fictitious Capital: The Legal Geography of Investment and Political Struggle in Rental Housing in New York City. *Environment and Planning A* 48, pp. 465–484.

Van der Keijl, J. (2017), Stadscampings zien Steeds Vaker Airbnb-verhuurders. *Het Parool*, 14 July. Available at www.parool.nl/amsterdam/stadscampings-zien-steeds-vaker-airbnb-verhuurders~a4506254. Accessed on 14 July 2018.

Van Der Meijden, N. (2017), Amsterdams Bedrijf wil Eerste Airbnb-wijk ter Wereld Oprichten. *Het Parool*, 12 June. Available at www.parool.nl/amsterdam/amsterdams-bed-rijf-wil-eerste-airbnb-wijk-ter-wereld-oprichten~a4500483. Accessed on 4 July 2018.

Van Gent, W. & W.R. Boterman (this issue), Gentrification of the Changing State. *Tijdschrift voor Economische en Sociale Geografie* 110: in press. Gentrification of the Changing State. Tijdschrift voor Economische en Sociale Geografie 110, in press.

Van Loon, J. & M.B. Aalbers (2017), How Real Estate Became 'Just Another Asset Class': The Financialization of the Investment Strategies of Dutch Institutional Investors. *European Planning Studies* 25, pp. 221–240.

Van Loon, J., S. Oosterlynck & M.B. Aalbers (2018), Governing Urban Development in the Low Countries: From Managerialism to Entrepreneurialism and Financialization. *European Urban and Regional Studies*, in press.

Waldron, R. (2018), Capitalizing on the State: The Political Economy of Real Estate Investment Trusts and the 'Resolution' of the Crisis. *Geoforum* 90, pp. 206–218.

Ward, K. (2006), 'Policies in Motion', Urban Management and State Restructuring: The Translocal Expansion of Business Improvement Districts. *International Journal of Urban and Regional Research* 30, pp. 54–75.

Webber, R. & R. Burrows (2016), Life in an Alpha Territory: Discontinuity and Conflict in an Elite London 'Village'. *Urban Studies* 53, pp. 1339–1354.

Weber, R. (2010), Selling City Futures: The Financialization of Urban Redevelopment Policy. *Economic Geography* 86, pp. 251–274.

Weber, R. (2015), *From Boom to Bubble: How Finance Built the New Chicago*. Chicago, IL: University of Chicago Press.

Weikart, L.A. (2001), The Giuliani Administration and the New Public Management in New York City. *Urban Affairs Review* 36, pp. 359–381.

Wijburg, G., M.B. Aalbers & S. Heeg (2018), The Financialization of Rental Housing 2.0: Releasing Housing into the Privatized Mainstream of Capital Accumulation. *Antipode* 50, pp. 1098–1119.

Wyly, E.K. (this issue), The Evolving State of Gentrification. *Tijdschrift voor Economische en Sociale Geografie* 110, in press.

Zukin, S. (1982), *Loft Living: Culture and Capital in Urban Change*. Baltimore, MD: Johns Hopkins University Press.

Zukin, S. (1995), *The Cultures of Cities*. Oxford: Blackwell.

PART TWO

Planetary gentrification

State-led Gentrification of Public Housing – Ziwani, Nairobi, Kenya
(photograph: Ashley West)

INTRODUCTION TO PART TWO

> As capitalist urbanisation evolves, so too does gentrification. Theories and experiences that have anchored the reference points of gentrification in the Global North for half a century are now rapidly evolving into more cosmopolitan, dynamic world urban systems of variegated gentrifications. These trends seem to promise a long-overdue postcolonial provincialisation of the entrenched Global North bias of urban theory.
>
> (Wyly, 2015: 2515)

Lees, Shin, and Lopez-Morales's (2016) planetary gentrification thesis unhinges, unsettles, and provincializes Western notions of urban development when looking at it globally. But it does more than that; it also challenges gentrification scholars in the Global North to rethink their own conceptualizations and theorizations. The aim was/is to give gentrification studies new analytical rigor. They make two key claims: first, that the role of the state has been under-conceptualized in gentrification studies and, second, that spatial restructuring provides the breeding grounds for gentrification as capitalism renders certain populations disposable, leading to displacement.

Smart and Smart (2017: 519) criticize 'the urban sprawl of gentrification talk' that they say has become pervasive in contemporary urban studies and has 'displaced and erased alternative idioms and concepts that may be more useful for describing and analyzing local processes'. But the planetary gentrification thesis has not displaced nor erased any such ideas, quite the opposite – it is open to such differences. Lees, Shin, and Lopez-Morales's (2016) planetary gentrification thesis sets out to demonstrate planetary indigeneity (organic gentrifications that are not copies of those in the West) and problematizes translations (West to East, North to South, and vice versa).

The planetary gentrification thesis has emerged from within particular disciplines, and there are calls now for those in other disciplines to take it into account. Valle (2020) has stated that 'in contrast to geographers and other interdisciplinary urbanists, many US-based sociologists have unduly overlooked or minimized two aspects of gentrification that may be more clearly observed in the Global South: the roles of local political-economic forces and the state'. She urges US sociologists to globalize the sociology of gentrification. The 'global turn' in gentrification studies is as yet uneven across disciplines, but it is clear that it is emergent.

The four readings we have chosen for Part Two look at gentrification as a planetary process. Slater (2017) extends our coverage of Neil Smith's rent gap thesis in our 2010 *Reader* by looking at it globally and reminding us of Neil Smith's (2009) essay 'Revanchist planet'. Focusing on the community of Getsemaní in Cartagena de Indias, Colombia, Valle (2018), looks at how Latin American racial ideology has invisibilized racism from gentrification processes; using Racial Attachment Processes (RAP), she reattaches it. Also focusing on racial capitalism, Danewid (2019) discusses the Grenfell Fire in London, connecting it to the colonial dimensions of empire and global city-making that are ongoing. Like in the planetary gentrification thesis, she argues that although gentrification and neoliberal urbanism operate in different ways in different cities, a broader pattern of racialized dispossession and displacement can be discerned. Kallin (2020) also looks again at the rent gap model, arguing that it remains a vital tool for understanding gentrification but only if its sense of time is blown wide open.

REFERENCES AND FURTHER READING

Danewid, I. (2019) The Fire this Time: Grenfell, Racial Capitalism and the Urbanisation of Empire, *European Journal of International Relations*, 26(1):289–313.

Garmany, J. and Richmond, M. (2019) Hygienisation, Gentrification, and Urban Displacement in Brazil, *Antipode*, 52(1):124–144.

Gentile, M. (2018) Gentrifications in the Planetary Elsewhere: Tele-urbanization, Schengtrification, Colour-splashing, and the Mirage of "More-than-adequate" Critical Theory, *Urban Geography*, 39:10:1455–1464.

Gentrification Blog – DRAN (http://mitdisplacement.org/dranblog/tag/Gentrification)

Kallin, H. (2020) In Debt to the Rent Gap: Gentrification Generalized and the Frontier of the Future, *Journal of Urban Affairs*, 43(4):1–12.

Krase, J. and DeSena, J. (eds) (2020) *Gentrification Around the World, Volume 1: Gentrifiers and the Displaced*, Palgrave: London.

Lees, L., Shin, H.B. and Lopez-Morales, E. (eds) (2015) *Global Gentrifications: Uneven Development and Displacement*, Policy Press: Bristol.

Lees, L., Shin, H.B. and Lopez-Morales, E. (2016) *Planetary Gentrification*, Polity Press: Cambridge.

López-Morales, E., Shin, H.B. and Lees, L. [guest editors] (special issue) (2016) Latin American Gentrifications, *Urban Geography*, 37(8).

A New Documentary about Global Gentrification (www.wnyc.org/story/new-documentary-about-global-gentrification/)

Portelli, S. and Lees, L. (2018) Guest Essay and Video: Eviction and Displacement from the Neighbourhood of Douar Wasti in Casablanca, Morocco, *International Journal of Urban and Regional Research* (www.ijurr.org/news/eviction-and-displacement-from-the-neighbourhood-of-douar-wasti-in-casablanca-morocco/)

Shin, H.B. (2019) Planetary Gentrification: What it is and Why it Matters, *Space, Society and Geographical Thought*, 22:127–137. (http://eprints.lse.ac.uk/101124/2/Planetary_gentrification.pdf)

Shin, H.B., Lees, L. and López-Morales, E. [guest editors] (special issue) (2016) Locating Gentrification in the Global East, *Urban Studies*, 53(3).

Slater, T. (2017) Planetary Rent Gaps, *Antipode*, 49(1):114–127.

Smart, A. and Smart, J. (2017) Ain't Talkin' 'Bout Gentrification: The Erasure of Alternative Idioms of Displacement Resulting from Anglo-American Academic Hegemony, *International Journal of Urban and Regional Research*, 41(3):518–525.

Smith, N. (2009) Revanchist Planet, *Urban Reinventors*, 3 (www.urbanreinventors.net/3/smith1/smith1-urbanreinventors.pdf)

Valle, M. (2018) The Discursive Detachment of Race from Gentrification in Cartagena de Indias, Colombia, *Ethnic and Racial Studies*, 41(7):1235–1254.

Valle, M. (2020) Globalizing the Sociology of Gentrification, *City and Community* (https://doi.org/10.1111/cico.12507).

Wyly, E. (2015) Gentrification on the Planetary Urban Frontier: The Evolution of Turner's Noosphere, *Urban Studies*, 52(14):2515–2550.

5
Planetary rent gaps

Tom Slater

Turning and turning in the widening gyre
The falcon cannot hear the falconer;
Things fall apart; the centre cannot hold;
Mere anarchy is loosed upon the world,
The blood-dimmed tide is loosed, and everywhere
The ceremony of innocence is drowned;
The best lack all conviction, while the worst
Are full of passionate intensity.[1]
W.B. Yeats, "The Second Coming" (1919)

SALAD IN A SCOTTISH PUB

A small information board on Rose Street, Edinburgh (midway between Frederick Street and Castle Street), recently installed by Edinburgh City Council, unwittingly offers clues as to why this is an important site in the study of gentrification. Entitled "From low to high fashion", it mentions how a street once renowned as a "seedy backwater, not a place for the respectable to be seen after dark" started to change in the 1960s as "tenement flats gave way to antique shops and boutiques". Two photographs of suddenly fashionable Rose Street, and a telling 1966 quote from *The Edinburgh Tatler* (an equally telling publication), complete the representation (see Figure 1).

Fascinatingly, the information board is located almost directly opposite 119 Rose Street, where in 1972 a young man from Dalkeith (a small working class town south-east of Edinburgh) took a summer job in an insurance office:

> In retrospect I suppose I first saw gentrification in 1972 while working for the summer in an insurance office in Rose Street in Edinburgh. Every morning I took the 79 bus in from Dalkeith and walked half the length of Rose Street to the office. Rose Street is a back street off majestic Princes Street and long had a reputation as nightspot with some long-established traditional pubs and a lot of more dingy howffs – watering holes – and even a couple of brothels, although these were rumoured to have decamped to Danube Street by the early 1970s. It was *the* place in Edinburgh for a pub crawl. My office was above a new bar called *The Galloping Major* which had none of the cheesy décor or saw-dust on the floor of the old-time bars. This one was new. It served quite appetising lunches adorned with salad, still a novelty in most Scottish pubs at the time. And I began to notice after a few days that a number of other bars had been "modernized"; there were a couple of new restaurants, too expensive for me – not that I went to restaurants much in any case. And narrow Rose Street was always clogged with construction traffic as some of the upper floors were renovated. I didn't think much of this at the time, and only several years later in Philadelphia, by which time I had picked up a little urban theory as a geography undergraduate, did I begin to recognise what I was seeing as not only a pattern but a dramatic one. All the urban theory I knew – which wasn't much, to be sure – told me that this "gentrification" wasn't supposed to be happening. Yet here it was – in Philadelphia *and* Edinburgh. What was going on?
>
> (Smith 1996a:xviii).

The Galloping Major is long gone, but I have taken countless undergraduates to 119 Rose Street, which I see as the birthplace of critical gentrification inquiry, and read them sections of *The New Urban Frontier* (see Figure 2: *The Galloping Major* was in the spot now occupied by *Murdo Macleans*, a hair salon).

The "little bit of urban theory" Neil Smith picked up as an undergraduate was dominated by the legacy of the social and spatial theories of the Chicago School of sociology, infused with

Figure 1 Information board on Rose Street, Edinburgh
(*source:* photo by author)

Figure 2 Rose Street pedagogy, February 2013
(*source:* photo by Svenja Timmins; reproduced here with permission)

the methods and assumptions of neoclassical economics. This body of work was inter alia an attempt to account for why certain population categories lived in certain districts of the city, and it laid the foundation for ideas of spatial equilibrium and economic competition that were used to develop neoclassical models of urban land use in the late 1950s and early 1960s. When on a year's exchange program in Philadelphia, and conducting fieldwork for his undergraduate dissertation on the neighbourhood of Society Hill (Smith 1977), Smith became very sceptical of these massively influential models, not just because they showed "half of the ideal city . . . submerged under Lake Michigan" (Smith 1992:110), but because they were linked to a portrayal of the suburbanisation of middle-class and wealthy households as the driving force of urban growth and overall metropolitan housing market dynamics.

The *consumer sovereignty* paradigm undergirding those models was that the "rational choices" of individual consumers of land and housing dictated the morphology of cities. Middle class consumer demand for space apparently "explained" suburbanisation, and this was seen by many scholars to be the future of all urban places. But the empirical reality of Society Hill – gentrification, a process that had also been observed in a few other large Western cities (including London, where the term was coined in 1964) – seemed to call this paradigm into question. Smith could not accept that consumers were suddenly demanding en masse the opposite to what had been predicted, and "choosing" to gentrify central city areas instead.[2] Crucially, in Society Hill he unearthed data showing that many middle class people in Philadelphia had *never left for the suburbs because space was being produced for them*, via state-sponsored private sector development. This created handsome profits for developers and agents of capital, at the expense of working class people who were displaced from central city space. His remarkable undergraduate dissertation was refined and distilled into a punchy paper published in *Antipode* in 1979. In it, Smith argued that the latter day followers of the Chicago School created an "empiricist and ecological quagmire in which substantive theory nearly drowned" (1979a:24). In the next sentence, he went on to note that "[w]ith the help of breathing equipment from various Marxist sources, resuscitation is well under way". The "breathing equipment" resulted in what is surely the most important essay on gentrification ever written (Smith 1979b), where the pivotal theory of the *rent gap* was first articulated.

In this essay I recapitulate the origins, structure, and purpose of the rent gap theory, and assess the frequently discussed but rarely *dissected* empirical studies of the rent gap, in order to trace the key analytical and political shifts Smith effected, as well as posit some possible extensions of the theory vis à vis territorial stigmatisation and displacement. This tracing and extending in place, I then consider the rent gap in the context of the emerging body of work on planetary urbanisation, and argue that the theory helps to expose new geographies of structural violence – planetary rent gaps – where the constitutive power of speculative landed developer interests in processes of capitalist urbanisation can be analysed and challenged. If, as David Harvey (2010:183) has recently argued, rent "has to be brought forward into the forefront of analysis . . . [to] bring together an understanding of the ongoing production of space and geography and the circulation and accumulation of capital", then it is important to consider what we can learn from the rent gap today, rather than relegate it, as so many seem to do, to something that has already been debated or exhausted in the large literature on gentrification.

"MUCH TOO SIMPLE AND DEFINITELY OBVIOUS": THE ANATOMY OF A THEORY

> If the rent gap theory works at all, it works because of its simplicity and its limited claims. It should certainly be subjected to theoretical criticism, but I do think that this will be useful only if the theoretical premises are taken seriously from the start
>
> (Smith 1996b:1202).

It is well known, and widely documented, that David Harvey (Neil Smith's PhD advisor) did not like the rent gap paper when he first read it, and hardly warmed to it later. Smith recalled as follows:

> I thought I was doing the usual journeyman graduate student work of taking on my betters. I was confirmed in this judgement when my advisor let the paper languish for months and months on his desk, water leaking on it from the unfixed ceiling, and especially when he finally delivered the assessment that no-one would ever publish it because my efforts at theory were much too simple and definitely obvious. I had already corrected the journal's proofs
>
> (quoted in Lees et al. 2010:97).

As the paper became increasingly influential, Smith took great joy in teasing his former advisor about his early disapproval. But it is instructive to reflect on precisely *why* Harvey disapproved (which many might find surprising given that, together, Harvey and Smith shaped the present day landscape of human geography and urban studies in such a fundamental way). When he first read it, Harvey was deeply engaged in research for a pivotal chapter of *Limits to Capital* entitled "A Theory of Rent",[3] an elaborate dissection of an issue that "troubled Marx deeply", and Harvey had spent years joining "those few hardy souls who have tried to pick their way through the minefield of his [Marx's] writings on the subject" (1982:330). The chapter Harvey produced for his magnum opus provides a panoramic overview of rent, painstakingly charting a path through issues such as the use value of land, landed property, the various forms of rent under capitalism that Marx identified (and their contradictory roles), class struggle between landlord and capitalist, and land titles as "fictitious capital". It is an exhaustive treatment and a very exhausting read, and given the intellectual labour involved, it is understandable why Harvey let a paper written by one of his postgraduates languish for months and months on his desk. When he did get round to reading it, and found a paper that did not even cite Marx, nor engage specifically with most of the aforementioned issues or any of the Marxian debates on rent, he was unimpressed. This was the basis for the "much too simple" part of his verdict. The "definitely obvious" part refers to the fact that the rent gap was, in Harvey's estimation, little more than a restatement (with different terminology and politics) of what he felt we already knew via the classic Chicago School models of city morphology, specifically the work of Homer Hoyt (1933) on residential "filtering".[4] Harvey's criticisms, at first glance, have some merit. But considered in depth, they miss the point of the rent gap, which, for important analytical and especially political reasons, was *intentionally designed to be both simple and obvious*. Conceptual simplicity is very different from simplistic conceptual thought, and Hoyt's models required a high-dosage injection of radical politics to make the class struggles and injustices behind them transparent. Some elaboration is necessary via further detail on the rent gap and what it teaches students of urbanisation.

In "Toward a Theory of Gentrification", Smith explained that in capitalist property markets, the decisive "consumer preference" (with characteristic mischief he adopted the neoclassical language) is "the preference for profit, or, more accurately, a sound financial investment" (1979b:540). As disinvestment in a particular district intensifies, as had happened in Society Hill, it creates lucrative profit opportunities for developers, investors, homebuyers and local government. If we wanted to understand the much-lauded American "urban renaissance" of the 1970s, the argument and title of the essay went, it was much more important to track the movement of capital rather than the movement of people (the latter movement was the exclusive focus of the "back to the city" rhetoric of the time, and the scholarship on it). Crucial to Smith's argument was the ever-fluctuating phenomenon of *ground rent*: simply the charge that landlords are able to demand (via private property rights) for the right to use land and its appurtenances (the buildings placed on it and the resources embedded within it), usually received as a stream of payments from tenants but also via any asset appreciation captured at resale. Landlords in poorer central city neighbourhoods are often holding investments in buildings that represented what economists and urban planners love to call the "highest and best use" over a century ago; spending money to maintain these assets as low-cost rental units becomes ever more difficult to justify with each passing year, since the investments will be difficult to recover from low-income tenants. It becomes rational and logical for landlords to "milk" the property, extracting rent from the tenants yet spending the absolute minimum to maintain the structure. With the passage of time, the deferred maintenance becomes apparent: people with the money to do so will leave a neighbourhood, and financial institutions "redline" the neighbourhood as too risky to make loans. Physical decline accelerates, and moderate-income residents and businesses moving away are replaced by successively poorer tenants who move in – they simply cannot access housing anywhere else. The lack of maintenance expenditure leads to tough housing conditions for those poorer tenants, amidst myriad other consequences of localised and systematic disinvestment, such as high unemployment, poor schools, inadequate retail services, dismal health outcomes, and so on.

In late 1920s Chicago, Hoyt had identified a "valley in the land-value curve between the Loop and outer residential areas ... [which] indicates the location of these sections where the buildings are mostly 40 years old and where the residents rank lowest in rent-paying ability" (1933:356, 358). For Smith, this "capital depreciation in the inner city" (1979b:543) meant that there is likely to be an increasing divergence between capitalized ground rent (the actual quantity of ground rent that is appropriated by the landowner, given the present land use) and potential ground rent (the maximum that could be appropriated under the land's "highest and best use"). So, Hoyt's land value valley, *radically analysed and reconceptualised*, "can now be understood in large part as the rent gap" (see Figure 3):

> Gentrification occurs when the gap is wide enough that developers can purchase shells cheaply, can pay the builders' costs and profit for rehabilitation, can pay interest on mortgage and construction loans, and can then sell the end product for a sale price that leaves a satisfactory return to the developer. The entire ground rent, or a large portion of it, is now capitalized: the neighbourhood has been "recycled" and begins a new cycle of use
>
> (Smith 1979b:545).

The elegance of the rent gap theory lies not just in what David Ley, one of Smith's more astute interlocutors, has referred to as its "ingenious simplicity" (1996:42), but in its critical edge, its normative thrust. The flight of capital away from certain areas of the city – depreciation and disinvestment – has devastating implications for people living at the bottom of the urban class structure. The "shells" referred to above do not simply "appear" as part of some naturally occurring neighbourhood obsolescence and "decay" –

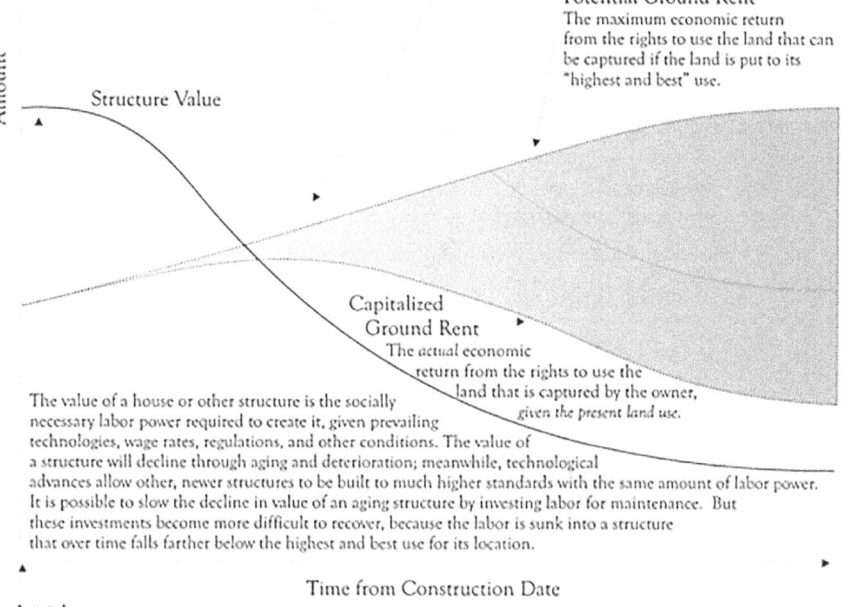

Figure 3 The Rent Gap, redrawn by Elvin Wyly

(*source:* Lees et al. 2008:52; reproduced here with permission)

they are *actively produced* by clearing out existing residents via all manner of tactics and legal instruments, such as landlord harassment, massive rent increases, redlining, arson, the withdrawal of public services, and eminent domain (or "compulsory purchase orders" in the UK). Closing the rent gap requires, crucially, separating people currently obtaining use values from the present land use providing those use values – in order to capitalise the land to the perceived "highest and best" use.[5] The rent gap thus highlights specific social (class) interests, where the quest for profit takes precedence over the quest for shelter.

It is fascinating to note the delightful rascality in where the rent gap paper appeared – the very mainstream *Journal of the American Planning Association*, in a special issue on neighbourhood "revitalization",[6] a term that made Smith wince: "it is often also true that very vital working class communities are culturally *de*vitalized through gentrification as the new middle class scorns the streets in favour of the dining room and bedroom" (1996a:32–33). In an excellent discussion of the rent gap in the book *Gentrification*, Elvin Wyly noted the etymology of the word "gap" – from the Old Norse for "chasm", denoting a breach in a wall or fence, a breach in defences, a break in continuity, or a wide difference in ideas or views. He continued:

> The rent gap is part of an assault to breach the defensive wall of mainstream urban studies, by challenging the assumption that urban landscapes can be explained in large part as the result of consumer preferences, and the notion that neighbourhood change can be understood in terms of who moves in and who moves out. Scholars, therefore, take its implications very seriously
>
> (Lees et al. 2008:55).

It is hardly surprising that the rent gap thesis has been the subject of intense debate for well over 30 years. But those debates, often shot through with intractable ideological confrontations and petty bickering, became rather frustrating for many, leading to many errors of interpretation and cursory, dismissive summaries. However, pinpointing the important scholarship that validates, documents, extends geographically, challenges and complicates the rent gap can aid the overall task of revealing its analytical and political relevance today.

TESTS, REFINEMENTS, AND POSSIBLE EXTENSIONS

> The light work sheds is a beautiful light, which, however, only shines with real beauty if it is illuminated by yet another light
>
> (Wittgenstein 1984:26).

It would be tedious to recite and summarise in any great detail the rent gap debates, and this task has been undertaken elsewhere (Lees et al. 2008:39–86). These debates must not, of course, be considered in isolation from the gentrification debates more broadly, mindful of the booby trap of the stalemate between "production" versus "consumption" explanations, on which I have advanced several observations and critiques (Slater 2006, 2009, 2011). I believe that it is now categorically unhelpful to advance the complaint that the rent gap cannot tell us anything about middle class gentrifiers, when it was never designed to do so. Take this critique by Tim Butler:

> [L]ocal cultures clearly have a continued agency in shaping the gentrification process to an extent far greater than is recognised by those who paint a picture of gentrification as broadly and blandly a process of global urban neocolonialism performed by upper professional groups ... By denying agency to the actors involved, "supply siders" in the gentrification debate (Smith 1979a, 1979b) have long laid themselves open to charges of overdetermination (Hamnett 1991) and continue so to do
>
> (Butler 2007:178).

In point of fact, it is actually those denying power to developers, bankers, and state officials[7] who are "denying agency", for the rent gap points to:

> the various agents involved in supplying "capacities" at given locations, e.g. financiers, developers, property owners ... active in the process insofar as they are the most influential agents in development and redevelopment activities, but also insofar as they actively contribute during the interim to rent gap expansion and the depreciation of building capital
>
> (Clark 1988:246).

Unfortunately, tired critiques refuse to die, for a recent textbook purporting to be a "critical introduction" to urban theory asserts that Smith "later weakened his position" by "acknowledging that gentrification may be explained not only by the actions of advanced capitalists" (Harding and Blokland 2014:148). Yet this was always acknowledged by Smith, as far back as his undergraduate dissertation: "precisely in cases such as Society Hill where housing was appropriated by middle and upper class buyers – the group with the widest choice in the housing market – demand becomes important" (Smith 1977:10). A signal contribution of the rent gap was to show that, first, the individual, personal, rational preferences in the housing market much beloved by neoclassical economists, and second, the "new middle class" dispositions towards a vibrant central city (and associated rejections of bland, patriarchal suburbia) that intrigued liberal-humanist and feminist geographers, are all tightly bound up with larger, collective social relations and investments (core to the rent gap concept is that ground rent is *a product of the labour power invested in land*, and that preferences are not "exogenous" to the structures of land, property, credit and housing). So, highly influential charges of economic "determinism" (Hamnett 1991) seem to be diversions in an epoch of unrelenting capitalist urbanisation, vicious accumulation strategies, and the ever-sophisticated mutation of neoliberalism (Brenner et al. 2010; Harvey 2010) – an economic context that is deeply deterministic. Far more helpful at this juncture is to consider what can be learned from those studies that have grasped the importance of the political thrust of the rent gap from the outset, and understood its theoretical premises in order to conduct detailed empirical studies. Given the intense empirical grafting involved – there are no readily available variables to measure capitalised and potential ground rent, so scholars have to dig into planning archives and land records going back several decades in order to construct their own proxy indicators – few empirical studies exist.

Where Harvey was disappointed by his student's failure to situate the rent gap specifically within the various traditions of urban land rent theory, Eric Clark (1987, 1988, 1994) more than made up for such an omission. Clark's study of 125 years of urban land rent fluctuations in Malmö, Sweden is the definitive work on the history and empirical expression of rent gaps, the creation and closure of which was identified (via combining numerous archival data sources) in several sample blocks in the centre of that city, and then considered in light of the divergent traditions of interpreting land rent between neoclassical economics and Marxist political economy, with the conclusion that "in their empirical form at the level of appearance, the results may be interpreted from either perspective" (1988:86). Clark works firmly in the latter tradition, and his writings on the rent gap are particularly important in terms of how his theoretically informed empirical tests led to some shrewd observations of the gentrification debates, including this powerful reaction to one of the main criticisms of rent gap theory: "The fact that rent gap theory cannot fulfil the dubious wish for a catch-all explanation of various forms of urban redevelopment can, however, hardly be held against it" (1988:81).

Other well known empirical tests were carried out by Ley (1986), who produced a fascinating gentrification index for 22 urban regions in Canada from a multivariate analysis including ratios of inner-city to metropolitan-wide house values and rental costs, but found no evidence for the rent gap thesis (a highly questionable conclusion, given that the ratios did not tell us about potential or capitalised ground rent); by Kary (1988), who mapped a land value valley in Toronto in the 1960s and 1970s, with a striking depth in the Don Vale district that partly explained the class transformation of "Cabbagetown" (one of the earliest neighbourhoods of that city to gentrify); by Badcock (1989) and Engels (1994) in Adelaide and Sydney respectively, who both found evidence of rent gaps whilst pointing to a range of different context-dependent strategies for revaluing a devalorised urban landscape; by Sykora in Prague at the dawn of post-socialist market transition, who charted an emerging land price gradient showing not rent gaps but "functional gaps", "caused by the underutilisation of available land and buildings relative to their current physical quality ... [and] closed in a very short time without making huge investments" (Sykora 1993:288); by Hammel (1999) in Minneapolis, who combined data from deeds of sale and tax assessments on nine groups of land parcels that were assembled and redeveloped for middle class and luxury apartments in the 1960s, and found substantial rent gaps for most of those parcels, mediated by some fascinating local and extralocal scale effects such as neighbourhood reputation (to be discussed later); by Yung and King (1998:540), who drew on several of the studies above to test the rent gap thesis in eight local government areas in Melbourne, and found rent gaps emerging not from the suburbanisation of capital but "the sudden opening of new submarkets for vacant land" in response to a capital-switching crisis that had created new investment opportunities; and by O'Sullivan (2002), who undertook a spatial modelling exercise vis à vis the long-term evolution of the rental and ownership markets in Hoxton, inner-east London, and tentatively identified some links between extremely local events in these markets and broader cycles of disinvestment and reinvestment.

Recent studies proving just as instructive have been undertaken by Darling (2005) in her study of "wilderness gentrification" in New York State's Adirondack Park, where the material production of recreational nature (rather than residential space) by the state management of the local landscape created the conditions within which investment and disinvestment in the rural built environment occurred (the rent gap had a different geographical expression and was closed via New York City-based developers capturing the "bargain-basement property prices" typically found across the Adirondack Park that "made the entire place seem disinvested" [2005:1028]); by Diappi and Bolchi (2008), who deployed agent-based modelling in Milan (specifically, a multi-agent model embedded in a cellular automata framework) and found clear evidence of "the cyclical dynamics of the market induced by investors and developers awaiting better capital returns when the rent gap widens"; and by Porter (2012) in New York City, who deployed a hedonic pricing model based on public use microdata and uncovered two land value valleys between 1990 and 2006 that go some way towards explaining the intensity of gentrification in that city during that time period.

Even though we can only ever obtain proxy data for potential and capitalised ground rent, these empirical studies are all valuable as part of a wider scholarly effort to understand the class transformation of space, wherever and under whatever conditions that transformation might be happening. But reflecting on these studies and on the wider debates about the rent gap, it seems pertinent to highlight something critically important about the theory that is often missed or sidelined. Reflecting on the rent gap paper in 2010, Smith said that the main challenge "was integrating a sense of historical spatiality into an already existing body of theory which, itself, seemed space-blind" (quoted in Lees et al. 2010:97). In this respect it becomes essential to consider that paper in tandem with, and never in isolation from, a later paper that situated the rent gap within a broader articulation of uneven development at the urban scale, entitled "Gentrification and Uneven Development" (Smith 1982). There, three aspects of uneven development were articulated, and gentrification was located within each aspect:

1. *tendencies toward equalisation and differentiation*: capital drives to overcome all spatial barriers to expansion (equalisation), yet a series of differentiating tendencies (divisions of labour, wage rates, class differences, etc.) operate in opposition to that equalisation. At the urban scale, the contradiction between equalisation and differentiation is manifest in the phenomenon of ground rent, which translates into a geographical differentiation (eg in US cities, central city versus suburbs, with higher ground rent in the latter);

2. *valorisation and devalorisation of built environment capital*: the valorisation of capital in cities (its investment in search of surplus value or profit) is necessarily matched by its devalorisation (as the investor receives returns on the investment only by piecemeal when capital is "fixed" in the landscape). However, new development must proceed if accumulation is to occur – so the steady devalorisation of capital creates longer-term possibilities for a new phase of valorisation. The devalorisation of capital invested in the central city leads to a situation where the ground rent capitalised under current land uses is substantially lower than the ground rent that could potentially be capitalized if the land uses were to change. When redevelopment and rehabilitation become profitable prospects, capital begins to flow back into the central city – and then substantial fortunes can be made;

3. *reinvestment and the rhythm of unevenness*: under capitalism there is a strong tendency for societies to undergo periodic but relatively rapid and systematic shifts in the location and quantity of capital invested in cities. These geographical and/or locational "switches" are

closely correlated with the timing of crises in the broader economy (ie when the "growth" much beloved of mainstream economists and politicians does not occur). Crises occur when the capitalist necessity to accumulate leads to a falling rate of profit and an overproduction of commodities (in recent years, these commodities are the various financial products that have emerged vis à vis the buying and selling of debt). The logic of uneven development is that the development of one area creates barriers to further development, thus leading to underdevelopment, and that the underdevelopment of that area creates opportunities for a new phase of development (in spatial terms, Smith called this the "locational seesaw" of capital flows).

An understanding of how neighbourhoods change therefore "requires recognition of the powerful incentives and constraints embedded in the circulation of capital in housing and land markets" (Smith et al. 2001:524). As we have seen, rent gaps are actively produced (especially under current conditions of crisis that have set capitalised ground rent on a downward spiral) through the actions of specific social actors ranging from landlords to bankers to urban property speculators, and the role of the state in regards to these actors is far from laissez-faire but rather one of *active facilitator*, as Smith had found in Society Hill: "The state had both a *political* role in realizing Society Hill, and an *economic* role in helping to produce this new urban space" (1979a:28). In this respect, Ley's statement that the rent gap "overlooks regulatory contexts which may well discipline capital's freedom of expression" (1996:42) becomes very puzzling indeed (Smith's undergraduate dissertation even carried the subtitle, "State Involvement in Society Hill, Philadelphia").

But the rent gap theory is not watertight or without its limitations – no theory is – and therefore can be developed conceptually along multiple fronts. Two immediately stand out. First, the question of *displacement* from space was always implicit in the theory but not explored specifically in Smith's initial formulation and subsequent refinements. To be sure, the very impetus for the production of the theory was the injustice of people losing their homes, and thus Smith provided accompanying nods to Marx's (1990:812) observation that improvements of towns "drive away the poor into even worse and more crowded hiding places", and to Engels' (1872:74) famous passage in *The Housing Question* about poverty being "merely shifted elsewhere" by the bourgeoisie. But Smith's "schematic attempt to explain the historical decline of inner-city neighbourhoods" (1979b:543) via the rent gap invites a closer consideration of "what happens when forces outside the household make living there impossible, hazardous, or unaffordable" (Hartman et al. 1982:3). In addition to his extremely helpful conceptualisation of displacement (identifying four different forms) (Marcuse 1985; see also Slater 2009), Peter Marcuse (2010:187) recently argued that:

If the pain of displacement is not a central component of what we are dealing with in studying gentrification – indeed, is not what brings us to the subject in the first place – we are not just missing one factor in a multi-factorial equation; we are missing the central point that needs to be addressed.

A challenge for students of rent gap theory is to develop and extend it to explain displacement in any or all of the forms identified by Marcuse, to illustrate *specifically* how the opening and closing of rent gaps leads to the agony of people losing their homes (for one such attempt in Seoul, see Shin 2009). How, if at all, might those forms of displacement be incorporated into the simple diagram of the rent gap Smith originally presented in 1979?

A second area where the rent gap theory might be extended is the question of the impact of *territorial stigmatisation*. A tiresome charge against the rent gap theory is that it fails to predict which neighbourhoods will gentrify and which will not (missing completely the fact that it was never designed as a predictive model). But there is an unresolved analytic puzzle requiring attention: why does it appear to be the case that gentrification rarely seems to occur first in the most severely disinvested and parts of a city or a region – where the potential for substantial profit is at its greatest – but proceeds instead in devalorised, working class tracts that are disinvested but by no means the poorest or offering the maximum profit to developers? Hammel (1999:1290) helpfully offered a clue:

Inner city areas have many sites with a potential for development that could return high levels of rent. That development never occurs, however, because the perception of an impoverished neighbourhood prevents large amounts of capital being applied to the land.

Smith was alert to those (frequently racialised) perceptions[8] and explored them thoroughly in a landmark paper on the gentrification of Harlem (Schaffer and Smith 1986). But the challenge remains enticing and urgent – to consider the disparity between potential and capitalised ground rent in the context of how urban dwellers at the bottom of the class structure are discredited and devalued *because of the places with which they are associated*. The negative manner in which certain parts of cities are portrayed (by journalists, politicians and think tanks especially) has become critically important to debates about their future. A mushrooming body of work points to a direct relationship between the defamation of place and the process of gentrification (August 2014; Gray and Mooney 2011; Kallin and Slater 2014; Slater and Anderson 2012; Thörn and Holgersson 2014; Wacquant 2007), where neighbourhood "taint" becomes a target and rationale for "fixing" an area via its reincorporation into the real estate circuit of the city – yet sometimes the "perception" Hammel outlines is so negative and entrenched that it acts as a symbolic barrier or diversion to the circulation of capital. In sum, as territorial stigmatisation intensifies, there are major implications for rent gap theory, but further investigations are needed to understand how the theory might be recalibrated to account for the pressing issue of the symbolic defamation of space. Such defamation serves economic ends, but also vice versa: examples abound under authoritarian urban regimes whereby the economics of inter-urban competition – with gentrification strategies at the core – are serving the brutal and punitive policies directed at working class minorities, and particularly at the places where they live (Ahmed and Sudermann 2012; Kuymulu 2013; Sakizlioglu 2014).

But there is one overarching issue that cannot be ignored when considering the rent gap today. It was formulated in the late 1970s, and we are dealing today with a radically changed context in which cities "now find themselves competing economically with each other across national borders in a way that would have been inconceivable in the 1970s" (Smith 2010:19). These words come from one of the last things Smith wrote about gentrification, an astute essay that reflected upon a "new interscalarity" emerging where cities have "quite different global powers, and a greater global presence", within which gentrification "is now generalised, increasingly planned, somewhat democratised, and of a totally recalibrated scale" (2010:19). The challenge for scholarship and for political action is to think about how, and in what ways, the rent gap thesis might be helpful in an era of planetary urbanisation.

SPECULATIVE PLANET

> We came with visions, but not with sight. We did not see or understand where we were or what was there, but destroyed what was there for the sake of what we desired . . . And this habit of assigning a higher value to what might be than to what is has stayed with us, so that we have continued to sacrifice the health of our land and of our communities to the abstract values of money and industrialism
>
> (Wendell Berry, quoted in Clark 2005:256).

To capture the mutation of gentrification into a "global urban strategy" (Smith 2002), and to provide an illustration of the role of truly global financial systems and the deregulation of the entire global financial apparatus, Smith would often (in person rather than in print) give the example of the 1995 construction of a luxury apartment building in the Lower East Side of New York City which involved an Israeli developer, investment capital from a European-American import bank, a Bangladeshi landlord, and a Long Island architect (and built using non-union labour, which was a first in New York City at the time). But, guided by Lefebvre's dialectical imagination in *La Révolution Urbaine* (particularly the intriguing statement that urbanisation had superseded industrialisation as the major vehicle for capital accumulation [see Lefebvre 2003]), Smith was also acutely aware that global financial transactions were producing extraordinary transformations of, and struggles in, cities such as Shanghai, Mumbai and Mexico City – and on a scale that dwarfed anything ever seen in the theoretical heartlands of gentrification such as New York and London. This immediately raises the theoretical and empirical question of the production of these new urban geographies, and scholarship on this has recently arrived at the *problematique* of "planetary urbanisation" (Brenner 2014a, 2014b; Merrifield 2013). Since the remit of this new body of work is "to replace city- and settlement-centric, population-based models of urbanisation with an exploration of the dynamics of implosion-explosion under capitalism" (Brenner 2014a, 2014b:21), and since evictions, enclosures and dispossessions – what Merrifield (2014) calls "neo-Haussmannisation" – now occur "on the scale of the entire planet" (Brenner 2014a, 2014b:27), it seems prudent to consider rent gaps, and the "rent question" in general (Haila 2015), in this theoretical context and under these social conditions. The realities of neo-Haussmannisation render highly questionable the influential pleas to "unlearn" theories that emerged from global cities in the so-called "Global North". In fact, the postcolonial "new comparative urbanism" has yet to yield any major insights into the global move from use value (somewhere to build and live) to exchange value (something to sell at a profit after the price has risen or something that represents stored capital), and has yet to cast any light upon where surplus value (ie the extraction of social production) gets extracted. This is unfortunate, given pressing and widespread realities of land grabbing and forced eviction. In one of his "dangerous contradictions" of capital, Harvey (2014) addresses the problem of continuous compound growth under long cycles of accumulation. To address this problem, capital has to devalue land to reinvent investment opportunity. The violence and human consequences of these cycles of building and destroying, of creating and tearing apart, surely demand that we jettison sub-disciplinary turf wars over how various parts of the world should be studied and theorised and consider instead the purchase and relevance of theories that have proven more than adequate (analytically and politically) in grasping the function of rent: to underpin investment and reinvestment opportunity, which in turn underpin uneven development under capitalism.

So far there are three *specific* deployments of rent gap theory in parts of the world that have, for too long, been off the radar in gentrification research (see Lees et al. [2015] for a fascinating corrective). Whitehead and More (2007) examined the massive changes visited upon the central mills districts of Mumbai in the context of the 1980s informalisation and decentralisation (to the suburbs) of the textile industry in that city. Aided by an NGO organisation actively supporting the "relocation" of slum dwellers from those districts to the outskirts of Mumbai, mill owners and multinational developers seeking opportunities for commercial real estate realised that the (actively disinvested) land upon which the mills once worked was not at its "highest and best use", and to gain maximum profit from the land they pushed successfully for changes to development regulations (which had stipulated that only one-third of the mill lands could be used for real estate development).[9] The result was an exclusive apartment and shopping mall development in a city where over 70% of residents officially live in "slum" conditions. True to the original formulation of the rent gap thesis, the role of the state was far from *laissez-faire*:

> The state government has changed to become an organisation attracting off-shore and domestic investment to the island city, while service provision becomes secondary. It has been reshaped to enable, facilitate and promote international flows of financial, real estate and productive capital, and the logic of its policies can be read off almost directly through calculations of rent gaps emerging at various spots in the city (Whitehead and More 2007:2434).

The propitious role of the state in creating the disparity between capitalised and potential ground rent has also been illustrated by López-Morales (2010, 2011), in two striking papers on "gentrification by ground rent dispossession" in Santiago, Chile. After the 1990 return to democracy in Chile (following 17 years of military dictatorship), various state policies were designed with a view to attracting professional middle classes into deeply disinvested parts of central Santiago, with varying degrees of success. From the 2000s onwards, however, a second phase of much larger scale state-sponsored entrepreneurial redevelopment has been taking place on formerly industrial sites, and on small owner-occupied plots in traditionally working class peri-central areas known locally as *poblaciones*, all of which exhibit wide rent gaps in the context of a city that has positioned itself as one of the economic powerhouses of Latin America. Drawing upon several years of field and archival research, López-Morales traced and mapped the policy-driven production and accumulation of potential ground rent in Santiago alongside the land devaluation produced by strict national building codes and the under-implementation of previous state upgrading programs. The author identified two forms of capitalised ground rent, the first being what owner-occupiers receive for their plots in a sale under current regulatory conditions, and the second what developers are able to extract from land if they are able to brush aside those conditions (and the upheavals created by that second form led López-Morales to equate it with Harvey's concept of *class monopoly rent*).[10] Just as in the Mumbai case above, the state was critically important in the opening and closing of rent gaps, and also in creating the conditions for national and foreign speculation in urban land markets, for:

> the way developers can acquire and accumulate large portions of inhabited land is by buying, at relatively low prices, from inner city owner-occupiers, and they often hold it vacant while passively waiting (or actively lobbying) to get building regulations loosened
>
> (López-Morales 2010:147).

A third recent deployment of the rent gap thesis has been in a remarkable analysis by Wright (2014) of the gentrification of the *centro historico* of Ciudad Juárez on the Mexico – USA border in the wake of the carnage and devastation caused there by a transcontinental drugs war (2006–2012) instigated by both countries' governments. Wright found rent gap theory to be highly applicable to account for a situation whereby:

> in order to rescue the *centro* and augment its economic value, the city first needed to be economically and socially destroyed. The formerly vibrant downtown, in short, needed to be killed before it could be rescued
>
> (Wright 2014:2).

Particularly striking about this study is the way in which Wright weds feminist and Marxist approaches to accumulation by dispossession to explain a class struggle between, on the one hand, ruling elites intent on a strategy of denigrating the lives and spaces of working class women and their children living in the *centro* in order to expand the rent gap and ultimately "clean up" the area and "re-establish" it as a place for upstanding families (see also Mountz and Curran 2009), and on the other, activists drawing public attention to the exploitation (in *maquiladora* factories and in sex work) of working poor women and especially to *feminicidio* (the killing of women with impunity):

> activists used the language of *feminicidio* to launch a counter-offensive against the political and business elites who minimized the violence by declaring that the victims were not worth remembering. In so doing, they challenged the story that equated women's disappearance from public space, either through their deaths or through municipal social cleansing projects, with value. And, as such, they disabled a key technology for widening the rent gap between the places known for poor women and the places known for their disappearance
>
> (Wright 2014:9).

While gentrification plans were disrupted by activists for some time, this did not last, for those same policy and business elites then targeted young men caught up in the violence of the drugs war:

> Rather than refer to the male youth population that dominates the body count as the resident population of the city's poor working-class families, the mayor referred to them as "venomous vermin" who had descended upon the city . . . Such depictions . . . sought to whitewash the public memory of these young people who were being gunned down on the very streets that had raised them
>
> (Wright 2014:11).

This official "politics of forgetting" is now working to close the rent gap and extract profits from massively devalorized spaces: "the business leaders who are gobbling up the shuttered businesses and overseeing the massive physical reconstruction of the city that has its streets and buildings in rubble declare that everything is officially better as long as we forget about the past" (Wright 2014:12). Powerful legal instruments procured by the state were deeply implicated in this disturbing picture, for "the mayor, and then the state governor, declared in that year that any business that did not sell as part of the development plan would be targeted for eminent domain" (Wright 2014:11).

Reflecting on these three studies in the context of theoretical developments vis à vis planetary urbanisation, and considering the massive dislocation caused by the real estate and construction industry bonanza (buttressed by state power) commonly known as "mega-events" (Porter 2009; Shin and Li 2013), it becomes clear why Neil Smith wrote an essay in 2009 entitled "Revanchist planet":

> [T]he crisis of the state, to which revanchism is in part a response, is integral to a contemporary rescaling of the geography of capital accumulation. The reconnection of the global and the urban, through the tendrils of the state as much as through the dictates of the market, is central to this process. Revanchism is a global reality today in a way it was not ten years ago, and any focus on revanchist urbanism must be squeezed through a recognition of this truth . . . It is vital in this context that our perspective keeps pace with this globalisation of revanchism. The convergence between the revanchist city and a revanchist globalism is still largely unexplored but now represents an urgent political and analytical challenge
>
> (Smith 2009:16–17).

Just as the political challenge becomes clearer via close scrutiny of the sheer variety of remarkable struggles and movements that have erupted across the revanchist planet, the analytical challenge is increasingly transparent: the rent gap, and the structural violence and dispossession visited upon working class people, needs to be considered vis à vis the *speculative landed developer interests* that Harvey has since identified as: "a singular principle power that has yet to be accorded its proper place in our understanding of not only the historical geography of capitalism but also the general evolution of capitalist class power" (2010:180).

Landowners have everything to gain from the global circulation of interest-bearing capital in urban land markets, and from the municipal absorption of surplus capital via all kinds of debt-financed urbanisation projects. Since 2008 it has become clear that vast sums of money in financial services are not made from big bets but from the *circulation* of capital (eg in the immediate aftermath of Ireland's financial collapse, capital markets lent money to the UK government to lend to the Irish government, which then give it back to the capital markets through interest payments and debt retirement – and just "keeping it moving" allows a tiny and disgraced financial elite to get even richer). In his assessment of the "geography of it all", Harvey continues:

> Investments in rents on land, property, mines and raw materials thereby becomes an attractive proposition for all capitalists. Speculation in these values becomes rife. The production of capitalism's geography is propelled onwards by the need to realise speculative gains on these assets
>
> (2010:181).

Whilst the wealth that has arisen out of speculative gains from massive urban development projects is greeted by business leaders, politicians and the media with predictable fanfare and ludicrous promises of "trickle-down", little is heard about those who have been forced to leave to make way for such projects. An illustration of the problem was provided recently in a powerful short film on forced evictions entitled *People Before Profit*,[11] produced by human rights organisation WITNESS, where an activist remarks:

> You have South Korean companies investing in India. You have Indian companies investing in South Africa. If the nature of that transaction and finance and the people causing these evictions are international in nature, then the campaigns ought to be international in nature . . . We have no choice.

Under these conditions, distinctions between the "Global South" and the "Global North" – and squabbles in journals about *who* should say *what* about *where* – appear completely redundant, "requiring an upgrade and a rethink" (Merrifield 2014:x). The "South" is in the "North", and vice versa, but the circulation of capital within secondary circuits of accumulation is everywhere and does not recognise or validate such distinctions. The relevance of the rent gap theory to campaigns and struggles against speculative landed developer interests is that it helps, as Smith (1979a:24) intended, to "redirect our theoretical focus toward the sphere of circulation . . . [where] we can trace the power of finance capital over the urbanisation process, and the patterning of urban space according to patterns of profitable investment". Two illustrations: first, Wright concludes her study of Ciudad Juárez by observing that, in 2012, the Washington DC based Inter-American Development Bank promised a $50 million loan to the city in order to capture profits from a place deliberately scrubbed clean of its working class history; second, in a study of gentrification in Ras Beirut, Lebanon, Ross and Jamil (2011:23) document the currents and contradictions of speculative foreign investment in urban land:

> To the same extent that real estate capital depended upon the deflated prices that urban, national, and regional instability generated, it also needed political stability to protect that which had already been invested. For poorer Beirutis, particularly those who rent, this contradiction meant that the availability of relatively affordable housing depended, in part, on unnerving political tensions and the threat of violence, while the onset of peace and stability brought about much higher housing costs.

The title of Ross and Jamil's essay is as revealing as it is disturbing: "Waiting for war (and other strategies to stop gentrification)".

In sum, as scholarship moves "towards a study of planetary urbanisation", it seems difficult to ignore the emergence of planetary rent gaps in a collective intellectual project that "may prove useful to ongoing struggles – *against* neo-Haussmanisation, planetary enclosure, market fundamentalism, and global ecological plunder" (Brenner 2014a, 2014b:28). The creation of fictitious capital through financial instruments designed to broaden the markets of who can bid and by how much – financialisation – means that expectations of what can be extracted from legally enforced rights to land have drastically increased. Hoyt, Alonso, and von Thunen have been globalised, so have the biases in their theories, and, as a consequence, rent gaps have become *much* wider, woven into causal linkages with processes at much wider spatial scales (Vradis 2013). The scientific challenge is to study planetary rent gaps in relation to how global financiers, developers, states, and local populations work together to produce the conditions for accumulation in a very uneven manner.

DISMANTLING THE NEEDS OF CAPITAL

> If a mark of a good theory is that it compels us to ask illuminating questions of reality, then the rent-gap theory is "a good theory"
> (Yung and King 1998:540).

Smith never wanted the rent gap theory to be about abstract lines and curves on a graph or reduced to squabbles in journals with neoclassical economists or liberal geographers. The rent gap is fundamentally about class struggle, about the structural violence visited upon so many working class people in contexts these days that are usually described as "regenerating" or "revitalizing". Contrary to contemporary journalistic portraits of latte-drinking white "hipsters" versus working class people of colour, the class struggle in gentrification is between those at risk of displacement and the agents of capital (the financiers, the real estate brokers, policy elites, developers) who produce and exploit rent gaps. Housing is class struggle over the rights to social reproduction – the right to make a life. This is a class struggle playing out within the realm of *circulation* largely between, on the one hand, those living in housing precarity, and on the other, finance capital and all its many tentacles.[12] Without the rent gap, we would not understand this class struggle like we do, nor have such a clear set of critical analytic optics through which to interpret and challenge cycles of investment and disinvestment in cities. Smith would be the first to encourage serious critical engagement with his theory, and would welcome and learn from critiques that understood from the outset the roots of the rent gap in Marxist urban theory, whilst offering biting and witty rebuttals to those who did not grasp those roots (eg Smith 1996b to Bourassa 1993). In this essay I have identified some openings, extensions, and political possibilities of the rent gap that are invariably missed in urban studies textbook summaries of the theory, and hopefully this acts as something of a backlash against those participating in the ongoing saga of gentrification debates who are quick to trivialise or abandon the theory, rather than clarify it and consider its relevance today, and those who argue we should "unlearn" certain urban theories simply because of where they were formulated.

The final task is to recognise the importance of the rent gap theory to urban social movements. Take Back the Land is one such movement in the USA, a national network of organisations dedicated to elevating housing to the level of a human right and securing community control over land. Max Rameau (2012:951), one of the movement's leaders, recounts as follows:

> In pursuit of a unified theory of gentrification, among a list of other suggestions, I casually recommended we take a gander at this "rent gap theory". To say it was one of the better readings would woefully understate its importance. Neil Smith's rent gap theory was dazzling. It was academic and complex, while simultaneously refreshingly simple and stripped down to the bare essentials of economic motivations and transactions . . . The rent gap theory served as the core document informing our understanding of gentrification. In addition to helping us understand what gentrification is and why it occurs, the rent gap theory enabled us, through a process of reverse engineering, to divine theories on how to stop gentrification, even if we lacked the power to implement those theories. To this day, Take Back the Land campaigns are substantially designed based on the implications of the rent gap theory.

Identifying rent gaps, and identifying those institutions creating them with a view to capturing profits from them, is clearly vital to the formulation of strategies of resistance and revolt. Therefore it is a critically important challenge for scholars and activists, together, to identify precisely where developers, owners and agents of capital and policy elites are stalking potential ground rent; to expose the ways in which profitable returns are justified among those actors and to the wider public; to raise legitimate and serious concerns about the fate of those not seen to be putting urban land to its "highest and best use"; to point to the darkly troubling downsides of reinvestment in the name of "economic growth" and "job creation"; to examine the possibilities for concerted resistance; and to reinstate the use values (actual or potential) of the land, streets, buildings, homes, parks and centres that constitute an urban community. These concerns were always at the core of Smith's inseparably intellectual and political project. In closing the original rent gap paper, he was prescient when he remarked that gentrification "could be the leading edge . . . of a larger restructuring of urban space", and he identified two opposing scenarios, over which a struggle was to be fought:

> According to one scenario this restructuring would be accomplished according to the needs of capital . . . According to a second scenario, the needs of capital would be systematically dismantled, to be displaced by the social, economic and cultural needs of people as the principle according to which the restructuring of space occurs
>
> (1979b:547).

That second scenario is what the rent gap theory leads us towards, and it is a powerful intellectual legacy to be sustained if "we wish the von Thunen theory of the urban land market to become *not* true" (Harvey 1973:137).

ACKNOWLEDGEMENTS

The title of this essay comes from Elvin Wyly, with profound thanks – yet the interpretations remain my own. Nik Heynen's amazing patience and kindness ensured that this essay saw light of day. I am grateful to three referees for their generous feedback and very constructive engagement. It is a pleasure to express my gratitude to the following comrades who made time to offer their views and insights on a draft of this paper: Eric Clark, Winifred Curran, Eliza Darling, Joe Doherty, Shenjing He, Ernesto López-Morales, Phil O'Keefe, Bob Ross, Bahar Sakizlioglu, Hyun Shin, Catharina Thorn, Antonis Vradis, and Elvin Wyly. My greatest intellectual debt is obvious. It seemed that a light went out in September 2012, but when I take my students to 119 Rose Street to discover and to think, their reactions tell me that Neil's light will always guide attempts to make better theory for a better world.

NOTES

1. This poem appears at the start of Neil Smith's (1977) undergraduate dissertation, the piece of empirical research that provided the foundation for his rent gap theory. He did not comment on the poem, but it is reasonable to assume that "the worst are full of passionate intensity" captures perfectly the agents of capital, stalking potential ground rent, who are intent on gentrifying a neighbourhood without due regard for those currently living there.
2. He once captured the absurdity of this view for me in person when he joked: "Can I please have the phone number of the middle class household that ordered the London Docklands? I want their power!"
3. David Harvey, personal communication, Athens, Greece, 9 May 2014.
4. Hoyt (1933) contended that new houses and new neighbourhoods were almost always built for higher-income households as their previous homes had become "obsolete". He argued that once those previous homes were vacated, they "filtered down" and became more affordable for progressively poorer groups as part of a "vacancy chain". The mainstream urban studies assumption is that, ceteris paribus, this process continues until the last vacancy is an abandoned place that nobody wants. Empirical evidence for this assumption, however, is entirely lacking.
5. The entire concept of "highest and best use" is always unexamined in neoclassical theory, as argued by Blomley (2004) in a very powerful critique.
6. A few years later Smith came up with a shrewd take on exactly what is being "revitalized": "[I]t was suggested that revitalisation was rarely an appropriate term for gentrification, but we can see now that in one sense it is appropriate. Gentrification is part of a larger redevelopment process dedicated to the revitalisation of the profit rate" (Smith 1982:151–152).
7. Throughout his career, Smith remained inspired by the attack on "fat cat sociology" by Martin Nicolaus, particularly this passage: "What if that machinery were reversed? What if the habits, problems, actions and decisions of the wealthy and powerful were daily scrutinized by a thousand systematic researchers, were hourly pried into, analyzed, and cross referenced, tabulated and published in a hundred inexpensive mass-circulation journals and written so that even the 15-year-old high school drop-outs could understand it and predict the actions of their parents' landlord, manipulate and control *him*?" (1969:155).
8. A short blog piece by Smith in 2008 contains many insights along these lines. See: www.enoughroomforspace.org/project_pages/view/198
9. See Date (2006) for some reflections on Smith's visit to Mumbai that year, where he was shown the struggles taking place over the redevelopment of the mills districts.
10. An excellent, provocative overview of (and call for conceptual advances in) class monopoly rent in urban geography can be found in Anderson (2014).
11. See: http://globalurbanist.com/2012/10/02/what-forced-evictions-look-like
12. I am very grateful to Bob Ross and Phil O'Keefe for their helpful reminders and clarifications here.

REFERENCES

Ahmed B and Sudermann Y (2012) *Syria's Contrasting Neighbourhoods: Gentrification and Informal Settlements Juxtaposed*. Boulder: Lynne Rienner Publishers

Anderson M (2014) Class monopoly rent and the contemporary neoliberal city. *Geography Compass* 8(1):13–24

August M (2014) Challenging the rhetoric of stigmatisation: The benefits of concentrated poverty in Toronto's Regent Park. *Environment and Planning A* 46(6):1317–1333

Badcock B (1989) An Australian view of the rent gap hypothesis. *Annals of the Association of American Geographers* 79(1):125–145

Blomley N (2004) *Unsettling the City: Urban Land the Politics of Property*. New York: Routledge

Bourassa S (1993) The rent gap debunked. *Urban Studies* 30(10):1731–1744

Brenner N (ed) (2014a) *Implosions/Explosions: Towards a Study of Planetary Urbanisation*. Berlin: Jovis

Brenner N (2014b) Urban theory without an outside. In N Brenner (ed) *Implosions/Explosions: Towards a Study of Planetary Urbanisation* (pp 14–30). Berlin: Jovis

Brenner N, Peck J and Theodore N (2010) Variegated neoliberalisation: Geographies, modalities, pathways. *Global Networks* 10(2):1–41

Butler T (2007) For gentrification? *Environment and Planning A* 39(1):162–181

Clark E (1987) *The Rent Gap and Urban Change: Case Studies in Malmö, 1860–1985*. Lund: Lund University Press

Clark E (1988) The rent gap and the transformation of the built environment: Case studies in Malmö, 1860–1985. *Geografiska Annaler B* 70:241–254

Clark E (1994) Toward a Copenhagen interpretation of gentrification. *Urban Studies* 31(7):1033–1042

Clark E (2005) The order and simplicity of gentrification: A political challenge. In R Atkinson and G Bridge (eds) *Gentrification in a Global Context* (pp 256–264). New York: Routledge

Darling E (2005) The city in the country: Wilderness gentrification and the rent-gap. *Environment and Planning A* 37(6):1015–1032

Date V (2006) Capital invading spaces of the poor. *CounterCurrents.org*, 18 October. http://www.countercurrents.org/eco-reddy181006.htm (last accessed 18 November 2014)

Diappi L and Bolchi P (2008) Smith's rent gap theory and local real estate dynamics: A multi-agent model. *Computers, Environment and Urban Systems* 32:6–18

Engels B (1994) Capital flows, redlining, and gentrification: The pattern of mortgage lending and social change in Glebe, Sydney, 1960–1984. *International Journal of Urban and Regional Research* 18(4):628–657

Engels F (1872) *The Housing Question*. www.marxists.org/archive/marx/works/1872/housing-question/ (last accessed 18 November 2014)

Gray N and Mooney G (2011) Glasgow's new urban frontier: "Civilising" the population of "Glasgow East". *City* 15:1–24

Haila A (2015) *Urban Land Rent: Singapore as a Property State*. Oxford: Wiley-Blackwell

Hammel D (1999) Re-establishing the rent gap: An alternative view of capitalised land rent. *Urban Studies* 36:1283–1293

Hamnett C (1991) The blind men and the elephant: The explanation of gentrification. *Transactions of the Institute of British Geographers* 17:173–189

Harding A and Blokland T (2014) *Urban Theory: A Critical Introduction to Power, Cities, and Urbanism in the 21st Century*. London: Sage

Hartman C, Keating D and LeGates R with Turner S (1982) *Displacement: How to Fight It*. Berkeley: National Housing Law Project

Harvey D (1973) *Social Justice and the City*. London: Edward Arnold

Harvey D (1982) *Limits to Capital*. Oxford: Blackwell

Harvey D (2010) *The Enigma of Capital and the Crises of Capitalism*. London: Profile

Harvey D (2014) *Seventeen Contradictions and the End of Capitalism*. New York: Verso

Hoyt H (1933) *One Hundred Years of Land Values in Chicago*. Chicago: University of Chicago Press

Kallin H and Slater T (2014) Activating territorial stigma: Gentrifying marginality on Edinburgh's periphery. *Environment and Planning A* 46(6):1351–1368

Kary K (1988) The gentrification of Toronto and the rent gap theory. In T Bunting and P Filion (eds) *The Changing Canadian Inner City* (pp 53–72). Waterloo: Department of Geography, University of Waterloo

Kuymulu M B (2013) Reclaiming the right to the city: Reflections on the urban uprisings in Turkey. *City* 17(3):274–278

Lees L, Shin H B and López-Morales E (eds) (2015) *Global Gentrification: Uneven Development and Displacement*. Bristol: Policy Press

Lees L, Slater T and Wyly E (2008) *Gentrification*. New York: Routledge

Lees L, Slater T and Wyly E (eds) (2010) *The Gentrification Reader*. New York: Routledge

Lefebvre H (2003) [1970] *The Urban Revolution*. Minneapolis: University of Minnesota Press

Ley D (1986) Alternative explanations for inner-city gentrification: A Canadian assessment. *Annals of the Association of American Geographers* 76(4):521–535

Ley D (1996) *The New Middle Class and the Remaking of the Central City*. Oxford: Oxford University Press

López-Morales E (2010) Real estate market, state entrepreneurialism, and urban policy in the gentrification by ground rent dispossession of Santiago de Chile. *Journal of Latin American Geography* 9(1):145–173

López-Morales E (2011) Gentrification by ground rent dispossession: The shadows cast by large scale urban renewal in Santiago de Chile. *International Journal of Urban and Regional Research* 35(2):330–357

Marcuse P (1985) Gentrification, abandonment, and displacement: Connections, causes, and policy responses in New York City. *Journal of Urban and Contemporary Law* 28:195–240

Marcuse P (2010) A note from Peter Marcuse. *City* 14(1):187–188.

Marx K (1990) [1867] *Capital, Vol. I*. London: Penguin

Merrifield A (2013) *The Politics of the Encounter*. Athens: University of Georgia Press

Merrifield A (2014) *The New Urban Question*. London: Pluto

Mountz A and Curran W (2009) Policing in drag: Giuliani goes global with the illusion of control. *Geoforum* 40:1033–1040

Nicolaus M (1969) Remarks at ASA convention. *American Sociologist* 4(2):154–156

O'Sullivan D (2002) Toward micro-scale spatial modelling of gentrification. *Journal of Geographical Systems* 4(3):251–274

Porter L (2009) Planning displacement: The real legacy of major sporting events. *Planning Theory and Practice* 10(3):395–418

Porter M (2012) The rent gap at the metropolitan scale: New York City's land value valleys, 1990–2006. *Urban Geography* 31(3):385–405

Rameau M (2012) Neil Smith: A critical geographer. *Environment and Planning D: Society and Space* 30:951–952

Ross R and Jamil L (2011) Waiting for war (and other strategies to stop gentrification): The case of Ras Beirut. *Human Geography* 4(3):14–32

Sakizlioglu B (2014) Inserting temporality into the analysis of displacement: Living under the threat of displacement. *Tijdschrift voor Economische en Sociale Geografie* 105(2):206–220

Schaffer R and Smith N (1986) The gentrification of Harlem? *Annals of the Association of American Geographers* 76(3):347–365

Shin H B (2009) Property-based redevelopment and gentrification: The case of Seoul, South Korea. *Geoforum* 40(5):906–917

Shin H B and Li B (2013) Whose games? The costs of being "Olympic citizens" in Beijing. *Environment and Urbanization* 25(2):549–566

Slater T (2006) The eviction of critical perspectives from gentrification research. *International Journal of Urban and Regional Research* 30(4):737–757

Slater T (2009) Missing Marcuse: On gentrification and displacement. *City* 13(2):292–312

Slater T (2011) Gentrification of the city. In G Bridge and S Watson (eds) *The New Companion to the City* (pp 571–585). Oxford: Blackwell

Slater T and Anderson N (2012) The reputational ghetto: Territorial stigmatisation in St. Paul's, Bristol. *Transactions of the Institute of British Geographers* 37:530–546

Smith N (1977) *The Return From the Suburbs and the Structuring of Urban Space: State Involvement in Society Hill, Philadelphia*. Unpublished BSc thesis, University of St Andrews. www.geos.ed.ac.uk/homes/tslater/NeilSmithugraddiss.pdf (last accessed 18 November 2014)

Smith N (1979a) Gentrification and capital: Practice and ideology in Society Hill. *Antipode* 11(3):24–35

Smith N (1979b) Toward a theory of gentrification: A back to the city movement by capital, not people. *Journal of the American Planning Association* 45(4):538–548

Smith N (1982) Gentrification and uneven development. *Economic Geography* 58(2):139–155

Smith N (1992) Blind man's bluff, or, Hamnett's philosophical individualism in search of gentrification? *Transactions of the Institute of British Geographers* 17:110–115

Smith N (1996a) *The New Urban Frontier: Gentrification and the Revanchist City*. New York: Routledge

Smith N (1996b) Of rent gaps and radical idealism: A reply to Steven Bourassa. *Urban Studies* 33(7):1199–2103

Smith N (2002) New globalism, new urbanism: Gentrification as global urban strategy. *Antipode* 34(3):427–450

Smith N (2009) Revanchist planet. *Urban Reinventors* 3. www.urbanreinventors.net/3/smith1/smith1-urbanreinventors.pdf (last accessed 18 November 2014)

Smith N (2010) The evolution of gentrification. In J Berg, T Kaminer, M Schoonderbeek and J Zonneveld (eds) *Houses in Transformation: Interventions in European Gentrification* (pp 15–26). Rotterdam: NAi Publishers

Smith N, Caris P and Wyly E (2001) The "Camden Syndrome" and the menace of suburban decline: Residential disinvestment and its discontents in Camden County, New Jersey. *Urban Affairs Review* 36(4):497–531

Sykora L (1993) City in transition: The role of the rent gap in Prague's revitalisation. *Tijdschrift voor Economisce en Sociale Geografie* 84(4):281–293

Thörn C and Holgersson H (2014) *The Urban Frontier Revisited*. Unpublished manuscript, University of Gothenburg

Vradis A (2013) From crisis to gentri-nation. *Political Geography* 40:A1–A2

Wacquant L (2007) Territorial stigmatisation in the age of advanced marginality. *Thesis Eleven* 91(1):66–77

Whitehead J and More N (2007) Revanchism in Mumbai? Political economy of rent gaps and urban restructuring in a global city. *Economic and Political Weekly* 23 June

Wittgenstein L (1984) *Culture and Value* (trans P Winch). Chicago: University of Chicago Press

Wright M W (2014) Gentrification, assassination, and forgetting in Mexico: A feminist Marxist tale. *Gender, Place, and Culture* 21(1):1–16

Yung C-F and King R (1998) Some tests for the rent gap theory. *Environment and Planning A* 30(3):523–542

6
The discursive detachment of race from gentrification in Cartagena de Indias, Colombia

Melissa M. Valle

INTRODUCTION

Claudio said that I was mistaken. His community's impending displacement from Getsemaní in Cartagena, Colombia had *nothing* to do with race and *everything* to do with class. His challenge following my presentation before friends, community residents and scholars did not surprise me. Claudio is hardly alone in believing class to be the primary, if not only, stratifying principal throughout Latin America. Yet my research consistently showed that both race and class hierarchically organized the places in which people like Claudio lived.

Gentrification is the process of spatial, economic and social restructuring that involves the (1) reinvestment of capital, (2) social upgrading of locale by incoming high-income groups, (3) landscape change and (4) direct or indirect displacement of low income groups (Davidson and Lees 2005, 1170). While class is essential to gentrification, race is a critical mediating factor. In racialized spaces, race configures why particular groups are excluded from some neighbourhoods and driven to inhabit others. Race is also key to the economic, political and social capital disparities between those considered native to these spaces and those who later supplant them. How then has race become elided in the aggregation of factors constituting gentrification? To solve this puzzle, I introduce the conceptual framework, *Racial Attachment Processes* (RAP) (Figure 1), which is the addition or removal of race as a constitutive component in the interpersonal, organizational and/or structural processes and relations that stratify social life. RAP examines both discursive and material practices. The former analyses individual or group discourse and their ordering schemas related to the social category of race. The latter traces how individual, organizational or institutional practices manifest beliefs and relations related to the social category of race.

This paper is not a complete explication of the concept of *RAP*, but an empirical example of its utility in social analyses. I employ it as a framework for understanding how individuals reconcile Latin American discourses that suggest race is not a primary stratifying principle, with the material spatial realities of racial hierarchies that counter such discourses. I introduce four of the six features of the RAP concept. The most paramount here, *structural racial detachment* (SRD), is the removal of race as a constitutive component in structural processes and relations that stratify social life. In the case I present, SRD ultimately eliminates racism as an accepted basis of social hierarchies and systems of oppression. SRD is not necessarily a conscious means to rebuke the reification of race – that is, resistance to the ideological or biological-oriented concept of racialization. Instead, SRD can frequently naturalize social divisions, remove racism as a component structure of discrimination and mask the power relations and repercussions of racial categorization.

In this paper, I present the ways actors in various social locations discursively and selectively remove the notion of race from social difference along multiple vectors. I first demonstrate that people accept race as a salient category of difference in day-to-day social interactions, what I term *interpersonal racial attachment* (IRA). I then look at the ways people employ *organizational racial*

Racial Attachment Processes	Micro-level	Meso-level	Macro-level
Attachment	Interpersonal Racial Attachment (IRA)	Organizational Racial Attachment (ORA)	Structural Racial Attachment (SRA)
Detachment	Interpersonal Racial Detachment (IRD)	Organizational Racial Detachment (ORD)	Structural Racial Detachment (SRD)

Figure 1 RAP (discursive and practical).

attachment and *organizational racial detachment* when racially categorizing and assessing neighbourhoods and regions. A racialized geography locating blackness in key regions and time periods results in the attachment of race to specific places and the detachment of race from others. Finally, through examples of SRD, I reveal how Latin American racial ideology ensconces racist practices and prompts people to detach race from the politics of discrimination. In an assay of how people understand varied forms of displacement, I then show how capitalism's "invisible hand" functions as the colour blind force behind gentrification-induced displacement, making the dislocation of residents not about their racialized identities, but market preferences unrelated to race.

This exploration reveals why race is discursively and selectively attached, and the effect that such selectivity can have on perceptions of the constituent factors precipitating displacement. This article builds upon the literature on racialization and contributes to the study of race and ethnicity in Latin America by illuminating the interrelationship between racial ideology, space, identity and inequality.

PROCESSES OF RACIALIZATION

In this article, I frame race as an object that individuals, groups or institutions can attach or detach in a manner that is both non-reifying and non-essentializing. The concept of RAP builds upon scholarship on "racialization," defined as both a socially constructed process that unites physiological differences with social traits, characteristics and issues (Miles 1989) and "the extension of racial meaning to a previously racially unclassified relationship, social practice and group" (Omi and Winant [1986] 2015, 13). For a more exhaustive overview of "racialization," see Barot and Bird (2001); Murji and Solomos (2005) and Shih (2008). RAP bridges a number of theories of racialization by demonstrating how race is a relational process (Fanon 1967; Kim 1999; Lewis and Phoenix 2004), which can be differentiated (Reeves 1983; Brah 1996; Mac an Ghaill 1999; Hesse 1997), and is historically and geographically contingent (Banton 1977; Goldberg [1992] 2010; Omi and Winant [1986] 2015).

I contribute a framework to understand how the addition or removal of race can function at various levels of analysis and the potential rationales for what may appear as contradictory perspectives on race's role in social life. This paper presents an alternative to the binary of racialization and deracialization, demonstrating how these processes can operate simultaneously within the same space. There are three primary advantages to RAP as a core mode of understanding that can be utilized at the micro, meso and macro levels. (1) It is anti-essentialist and removes race from people's beings, instead framing race as something to be detached and attached to individuals, groups or social relations; (2) It reveals the manifold ways actors make meaning of the construct of race and use it in practice and (3) It shows us how race can be very present and absent within the same empirical context.

LATIN AMERICAN RACIAL IDEOLOGIES IN COLOMBIA

Predominant racial ideologies in Latin America result in a stratification system that "promotes racial discrimination while simultaneously denying its existence," (Hanchard 1998, 6). *Blanqueamiento* [whitening] is a belief in the innate racial and biological superiority of those considered white and conditions that esteem and progress in Latin America be achieved through an infusion of European people, descendants and culture (Gros 2000). The *mestizaje* ["race mixture"] ideology seeks to submerge differences and suggests that everyone in Latin America is mixed, in varying degrees, with Pre-Columbian Indigenous, Africans and Europeans (Telles 2014). However, *mestizaje* in Colombia was predicated on the discursive exclusion and invisibilization of blacks (de Friedemann 1984; Restrepo 1998; Wade 1993) and is deeply embedded within Colombian culture (Paschel 2010). Colourism or "pigmentocracy" refers to how skin colour serves as a primary stratifying variable in Latin America and the social disadvantages that are correlated with successively darker skin tones (Telles 2014, 11). Social and racial relations in Colombian society have been greatly influenced by such a colour hierarchy (Urrea Giraldo, Viáfara López, and Vigoya 2014). This study empirically contributes to the research on *blanqueamiento*, *mestizaje* and skin colour-based hierarchies by demonstrating how people reproduce such ideologies and reconcile the contradictions of a visible racial hierarchy with colourblind dogma.

URBAN ETHNOGRAPHY AND RACE SCHOLARSHIP IN LATIN AMERICA

For urban ethnographers in the US, change and development in cities are often analysed utilizing a racial lens (see, e.g. Anderson 1990; Venkatesh 2000; Freeman 2006; Pattillo 2007; Wherry 2011; Woldoff 2011). However, with the notable exceptions of Gregory (2006), Dinzey-Flores (2013) and Perry (2013), urban ethnographic studies in Latin America rarely provide an extensive analysis of race and racism and often focus primarily on violence (e.g. Auyero 2001; Goldstein 2004; Pine 2008). The minimal ethnographic engagement with racial discourses when analyzing economic phenomena is consonant with the minimal role racial discourses play broadly in political and economic discussions in Latin America.

While there is research documenting the pervasive Latin American racial ideology, there is not a great deal of analysis of race's centrality in the (re)production of Latin American urban space, particularly from an ethnographic perspective. Ethnographic works in Latin America that centre race and identity help dissect how people understand racial hierarchies in the Latin American context; however, they typically do not integrate this analysis with one on urban change (see, e.g. Wade 1993; Twine 1997; Sheriff 2001; Escobar 2008). While the ethnographic analysis of Caldeira (2001) explores everyday discourses around spatial transformations in Brazil and illuminates the mechanisms engendering spatial change and inequalities, it ignores race as an essential feature of the change process.

This paper is an ethnographic examination of a community undergoing transformation due to gentrification in the Global South and provides an account of the transformation's relationship to race and racism in Latin America. It demonstrates how the detachment of race from understandings of Colombian socio-spatial, political and economic relations elides the material consequences of racism and the relationship between racial domination and social inequality. By placing race at the forefront of ethnographic work on urban displacements, this paper broadens knowledge about marginalized groups throughout the globe, often racialized, who are vulnerable to the detrimental social, economic and political effects of globalization and neoliberalism.

THE NATIONAL AND NEIGHBOURHOOD CONTEXTS

Colombia has the second largest population of people of African descent in Latin America (Antón et al. 2009). Cartagena served as one of the primary enslaving ports for the influx of enslaved Africans in seventeenth century colonial Spanish America (Meisel Roca 1980). Scholars suggest that the legacy of slavery and enduring racist ideologies and practices exacerbate the contemporary social, political and economic marginalization of Afro-Colombians (Arocha 1998; Dixon 2008). Afro-Colombian settlements are mired by poverty rates that hover around sixty per cent (United Nations Independent Expert on Minority Affairs 2010). There are major inequities in educational attainment and access to high-status occupations between racialized groups.

These are particularly acute in Cartagena (Viáfara López and Urrea Giraldo 2006).

Afro-Colombians constitute approximately twenty-six per cent of the Colombian population and have gained two per cent of the national territory, primarily in the Pacific region (Ng'weno 2007), largely through street demonstrations and other public acts of protest, where Afro-Colombian communities rallied for a "pluriethnic and multicultural nation" (Grueso, Rosero, and Escobar 1998, 197). Law 70 in 1993 legally recognized the cultural rights of all Afro-Colombians and the territorial rights of those in a specific rural region on the Pacific Coast of Colombia (Wade 1993; Paschel 2010). Such territorial rights, however, had little effect on the majority of the urban regions of Colombia's Atlantic Coast, leaving Afro-descendants in these regions minimal legal recourse in their battles over space.

The locus of this study, Getsemaní, is in Cartagena de Indias on Colombia's Atlantic Coast. It sits within the old city walls, yet just outside those of the historic downtown city center, which the national and local government and the private sector redeveloped during the 1960s and 1970s (Rojas 1999). Getsemaní has a population of around 6,000 residents within 631 households. Originally a neighbourhood of lower-class free persons of colour, artisans, seamen and enslaved blacks (Helg 1999), it has long been considered the "popular" barrio of the lower classes and an "arrabal," a somewhat derogatory word that expresses its suburban, peripheral status to the historic center (Guerra 2010). It was the site of political resistance during the revolution against Spain in 1811 and continued to be home to many of the city's poor (Rojas 1999).

In spite of Cartagena's growing reputation for tourism, Getsemaní began to deteriorate significantly, both physically and economically during the 1970s. This followed Cartagena's economic crisis and the city government's decision to transfer the main market from Getsemaní to another neighbourhood (Díaz de Paniagua and Paniagua Bedoya 1993). During the 1980s, the public and private partnerships that urban scholars consider typical of contemporary urban development intensified (Harvey [1973] 2009). Getsemaní's location and classic Spanish architecture has become highly valued in the last two decades, engendering what Smith (2011) calls "the outward diffusion of gentrification from the urban center" (442). Buyers are offering proprietors (about thirty per cent of residents) more than ten times what they would have been offered ten years ago. There is a perceived reduction in crime, which was considered rampant until recently. An increase in access to transportation, retail and economic resources has paired with an increase in taxes, noise, traffic, the cultural segregation of newer and longstanding residents, and the displacement of the latter.

RESEARCH DESIGN

This primarily ethnographic project involved twelve months of sustained fieldwork conducted over the course of three years. I historicized the change process, embedding race, neighbourhoods and social relations within the context of the conditions that produced them. I employed the grounded theory heuristics of fieldnotes, coding along various dimensions and constant comparing, writing, sorting and diagramming memos throughout the project (Tavory and Timmermans 2009).

Getsemaní was my home and I lived adjacent to the heart of the neighbourhood, La Plaza de la Santísima Trinidad, or simply "La Plaza." I spent a great deal of time observing events and chatting with residents and non-residents, including long-term travellers, short-term tourists, business-owners and people from Cartagena who now found it vogue to frequent La Plaza. I also spent a few days a week at both the University of Cartagena and the Technological University of Bolivar.

I conducted sixty-two semi-structured and open-ended interviews with Getsemaní residents, business-owners from within and outside of the community, scholars and government and NGO employees. Most interviews were conducted in two parts. I first used photo-elicitation as a methodological tool to explore the patterns emerging from the repeated use of still photographs. I presented figures that have come to represent people of African descent during festivals (e.g. "Negrita Puloy" and "El Son de Negro"), a neighbourhood graffiti mural of a caricatured scantily clad Afro-descendant woman, and in advertisements. These photographs functioned as prompts for discussions of race, gender, class and community. The responses provided insights into how residents categorize what constitutes blackness and the practices and behaviours associated with it. I also posed questions about neighbourhood history and perceptions in an attempt to understand racialized, gendered and classed understandings of the neighbourhood by those in various positions within it. Approximately one-third of these interviews are reflected within this paper, blending responses from both photo-elicitation and neighbourhood questions.

EMPIRICAL FINDINGS

Interpersonal racial attachment

The racial categories of white, black, Indigenous, Asian or Pacific Islander are not always utilized in everyday conversations in Colombia. However, the physical attributes associated with such categories are regularly employed when describing others. For example, in La Plaza, in Getsemaní, I overheard a woman describe a man as "*el moreno con pelo indio,*" [The dark-skinned or brown guy (presumably of African descent) with Indian hair]. In addition to descriptions, nicknames for those considered black, negro or Afro-descendant – such as "negro bembon" (black with thick lips), "carbón" (carbon), Coca-Cola, Chocorramo (a Colombian chocolate dessert company), "la mona/el mono" (the monkey), "caca" (shit) and "diablo" (devil) – are often based upon phenotypes and stereotypes. Such nicknames reproduce racist thinking by ridiculing, animalizing, hypersexualizing and stereotyping blacks (Restrepo 2007). Through these nicknames, people define and articulate a spectrum of acceptability and make the racial hierarchy visible in daily social life.

Speaking with people about romantic and sexual partnership selection in Colombia regularly brought to the fore the reality of how such preferences reflect both racial and national hierarchies and the deeply embedded *blanqueamiento* [whitening] ideology. One afternoon in La Plaza I interviewed a young man, Yamil, from Getsemaní. He was in his 20s, with a golden-brown complexion and faded cut into his somewhat tightly coiled hair. His facial features and name suggested that he was partially of Arab descent, likely a product of the Syrian, Palestinian and Lebanese migration to the region since the late 1880s. He gave a description of his ideal partner:

. . . ideally 1.65 meters (5′4″) . . . The color isn't important. Well, not too dark. Light or blonde, light or blonde *(pause)* or wheat-colored/tawny [*Clara o rubia. Clara o rubia . . . o trigueña*], but not dark, with curly or straight hair.

In spite of adhering to a plural racial categorization system, the hierarchical nature of the pigmentocracy still means that having darker skin is deemed unacceptable.

Following our discussion, Yamil invited over Matteo, who was selling empanadas in La Plaza. Matteo is in his forties, visibly of Indigenous descent with dark red-brown skin and straight black hair worn to his ears. In a later formal interview with Matteo, he would define his racial/ ethnic classification by saying, "I am Indian, *but a cute* Indian" [*Soy Indio, pero Indio lindo*- emphasis his], a statement that highlights the normalized hierarchy of beauty and the commonplace belief that an Indigenous person is unattractive. In a similar vein, Streicker (1995) found that "the language of physical appearance in Cartagena exalts European/blanco standards of taste while denigrating those of non-European origin" (61). He witnessed the following exchange about mate selection and procreation between young women from Cartagena.

> Lupe teased her cousin about having a negro boyfriend. The cousin bridled, disputing the charge. Lupe sat back in her chair and sighed, "I want to have a really white son [un hijo blanquito], with straight hair and blue eyes." "You'll have a fat, negro one with kinky hair," her cousin laughed.
> (Streicker 1995, 60)

This section provides examples of IRA in Cartagena. It shows that race is a legible category and how the racial hierarchy becomes normalized through everyday parlance. While race as a social construct may be more ambiguous in Latin America than the United States, a triangular racial class order persists, placing whiteness/ Europeanness at the top and blackness and Indianness at the bottom. This racial order closely maps on to the existing class order (Gutiérrez Azopardo 1980; Wade 1993). Next, I will demonstrate how such racial and class orders become crucial to gentrification processes at the organizational level of analysis.

Organizational racial attachment and detachment

To construct a composite of the processes and relations that residents associate with race, I continue with an assessment of how people articulate the connections between racialized groups and physical space. Such associations are partially grounded in the Colombian discourse around regional differentiation, which is both racialized and gendered (Appelbaum 2003), with region serving as, "a powerful language of cultural and racial differentiation" (Wade 1993, 19). Relationships between race and space in Colombia are often articulated via the *mestizaje* ideology, which creates a plural stratification system that allows for a social distancing from the often-stigmatized racial category of black and the selective detachment of race from places such as Colombia's Atlantic Coast. Identity on Colombia's Atlantic Coast is greatly constituted by race and is often relationally and circumstantially defined. As Wade (2000) notes, "Things costeño [Atlantic Coast] can be black or not black – or more or less black – at times or in different contexts, or even in the same time and same place, depending on what one wants to see" (43). This plastic manner of defining place by race was evident in interviews. When questioned about presentations of local culture, a few Getsemaní neighbourhood residents attached racialized blackness to the region, city and neighbourhood, defining the Atlantic Coast as an Afro-descendant place with comments such as, "most of the Coast is of the black race [*la raza negra*]. 95% are brown [*morenos*]." People also described Cartagena as an Afro-descendant city, saying things like, "This is a city of blacks and Indians." Some similarly referred to the community of Getsemaní by saying, "In Getsemaní African descent and culture are represented a lot."

Interviewees also regularly harked back to the notion of *mestizaje* by describing places as "mixed" or detaching defined singular racial categories from Cartagena and the local community. For example, when asked whether a person performing in blackface represented the neighbourhood, one Getsemaní resident said, "No, because there is everything here. It's not only these kinds of people. You find all colours, all races here." Another resident said, "It represents Cartagena. Well, we could say yes, a little, although there is a lot of mixture. But there is also a lot of blackness." Residents often identified the Pacific Coast as being authentically black and therefore relationally defined the Atlantic Coast or those from multiple regions as "mixed". For example, one resident, Jorge said:

> Here on the Caribbean Coast a different phenomenon occurred than on the Pacific. The Pacific black is pure black (emphasis his). You see less of a mixture of black and white. But here in the Caribbean, yes.

Another, when describing his race and ethnicity said, "I'm a mixture. My mother is from Antioquia, a *trigueña* [swarthy, wheat-colored]. My father is black, a *Chocoano* [Person from Chocó on the Pacific Coast]."

Interviews reveal that residents also consider Palenque a quintessentially black place. Located 70 km from Cartagena, El Palenque de San Basilio is one of the known maroon villages established in the Atlantic region by formerly enslaved people of African descent who rebelled between the sixteenth and eighteenth centuries (Moñino and Schwegler 2002). When asked whether photographs of independence festival participants dressed in blackface to depict women from Palenque represented Cartagena, a resident commented, "This represents this area only a little. It represents the black region more. Those people are a color that is really quite dark." Another said, "The people they represent have black skin and so they do this to personify these people."

In interviews, blackness in Cartagena also appeared relegated to the epoch when slavery existed in Colombia (around 1580–1851). When asked whether blackfaced characters represented their local geographies, residents made comments such as "Yes, this represents the old period," "Yes, there were a lot blacks here" and "Yes, because history tells us slaves lived here. Those slaves who built us all the prettiness that we now enjoy." Similar discursive patterns can be seen in Colombian school textbooks, where Soler Castillo (2009) notes that references to blacks are associated with the past, thereby positioning Afro-descendants as irrelevant elements of Colombia's contemporary social, economic and political development. This observation is crucial when evaluating the relationships between neighbourhoods presently inhabited by those of African descent and gentrification-induced displacement.

Unlike places such as El Chocó on the Colombian Pacific Coast, where black space has been concretized through legislation for territorial rights, or El Palenque de San Basilio, whose socio-geographic identity has been attached to its formerly enslaved black founders, Cartagena's racialized identity is often ambiguous and contingent upon the point of comparison. The racialized identity of the neighbourhood of Getsemaní within Cartagena often follows a similar pattern. According to the Bank of the Republic, Cartagena (Pérez Valbuena 2007), the black population in Getsemaní was zero per cent. This suggests that either Getsemaní residents are not self-identifying as black or they do not meet the criteria being used to measure this racialized category. Residents' socio-spatial framings, which selectively detach race at the regional, city and neighbourhood levels based upon relational definitions of blackness, have resulted in the locus of the study being effectively racialized as non-black by many residents. Such a subjective attachment of race to place does not serve to liberate the neighbourhood from the stigma of racialized blackness, which constitutes and is constituted by the racial hierarchy. Instead, it masks the relationship between racial and neighbourhood devaluation and displacement. If people do not recognize their community as externally "raced," then they will not recognize such racialization as contributing to spatial change emanating from external pressures.

SRD: the politics of discrimination

Racism invisibilization frames

By detaching race from discussions about inequality, prejudice and discrimination, people depoliticize race and make the causes and material consequences of structural racism invisible. Interviews and participant observation revealed two primary racial frames, which stem from Latin American racial ideologies: the minimization of racism and the use of cultural racism. Long-term residents, non-residents and neighbourhood newcomers discursively employ these frames to detach race from the politics of discrimination.

Minimization

Racism in Latin American is regularly minimized through a focus on prejudice, which is not systemic. Any disparities that could be considered to reflect racial inequality are regarded as the products of class dynamics (Bonilla-Silva [2003] 2010). People often embrace the language of race, as demonstrated earlier, but say that it is generally of no consequence to outcomes, particularly to those where an economic explanation can be facilely made.

In addition to the denigrating stereotypes of blacks mentioned in the earlier discussion of IRA, further illustrations were visible during carnival and independence festivals on the Colombian Atlantic Coast. In Cartagena, people openly talk about the "blackness" and "Africanness" of those who perform in blackface, but typically consider such displays unproblematic, if not positive. For example, Edgar, a fifty-eight-year-old resident of Getsemaní, said that those in blackface were making exaggerated facial expressions because "they characterize a monkey." When asked what he thought of the expressions and the blackface paint he said, "It's good. It just reminds everybody in Cartagena that most of us come from blacks." Edgar makes an association between blackness and monkeys – an iconographic representation that has historically been employed since Europeans first had contact with Africans (Goff et al. 2008) – but minimizes the racism inherent in this relationship.

A few residents did express some discomfort with the images, but would not link their discomfort to race. For example, another long-term resident, twenty-eight-year-old Julio said, "I don't really find it amusing . . . I think it looks like a human chimpanzee. I don't think it's good to make those faces to represent the celebrations." While Julio recognizes the problem with making the association between those painted in blackface and monkeys, he states that it is not good to represent the *celebrations* as such. About the harm to black people, he is silent, thereby minimizing the maligning of those of African descent.

Cultural racism

Cultural racism as defined by Ryan (1976) and Bonilla-Silva ([2003] 2010) describes the ways culturally based arguments are employed to explain the standing of minorities in society.

Those on Colombia's Caribbean Coast have long been depicted as having a dramatically different and inferior culture when compared to other regions considered "whiter" in Colombia. However, coded language couched in ideals about culture and comportment allows for the discussion of groups without explicitly identifying the racialized categories associated with them. For example, in a number of interviews, people discussed the cultural boundaries between those from places associated with whiteness, such as Colombia's interior (which includes Bogotá and Medellín), and those from places often associated with blackness and mixedness, such as Colombia's Atlantic Coast. This occurred in an interview with Paul, a business-owner in Getsemaní and native of Bogotá. After speaking favourably about the neighbourhood by adhering to a fairly typical script about authenticity, he continued:

> Me, I'm from Bogotá. I now understand the slow pace people have that live here. The weather six months of the year has a humidity of over eighty-five per cent. It's very hard. So it's a lazy society and that reflects on the people. The labor isn't good. It's hard to find good employees . . . The other thing is the lack of culture, of education. So these people are lazy and they don't have any interests. So you see them all day long, sitting on the porches doing shit. Doing nothing.

Paul articulates a common trope about the laziness and lack of culture of those on the Coast and makes a comparison to the interior of Colombia. Paul's comments are reminiscent of those of famed Colombian scientist, Francisco José de Caldas, who discussed how the climate was partially responsible for the "slow-wittedness, barbarism and ignorance" of blacks in Colombia and that the black is, "lazy, he hardly knows life's comforts . . . At times idolater . . . he spends his days in laziness and ignorance" (as quoted in Cunin 2003, 71). However, note that, unlike de Caldas, Paul never mentions race. A legacy of racialized geography that attaches negative stereotypes to the Atlantic Coastal region and its racialized inhabitants makes it unnecessary to make explicit references to race.

Constantine is European and has been living in Cartagena for a few years. He owns homes in Getsemaní, but resides in a nearby high-income neighbourhood. The following interview excerpt highlights the value foreigners place on one another:

> (*Historically, who have the native Getsemanisenses* [residents of Getsemaní] *been?*) Nice people, friendly. I can only say good things. (*Do you find it difficult to rent your homes here?*) No, I would say the opposite. It's quite easy. People are always looking for places or houses to stay. (*Who are your tenants typically?*) Foreigners. (*Do you prefer foreigners?*) Yes, yes. (*Why?*) Foreigners are more respectful of the properties, more polite, see what I mean? (*Do you advertise?*) No. Somebody calls me, "I have a friend from Holland."

Constantine has a clear preference for "foreigners" (i.e. whites from Europe, the US, Australia/New Zealand), but alleges that the inferior culture of local residents is his standard of judgment. Such restrictions on rentals to local people would combine with the displacement of *Getsemanisenses* to further racially and economically segregate Cartagena. Cultural racism justifies the perceived devaluation and disposability of local residents while on the surface detaching race from such practices.

According to developers, gentrifiers, as well as the Cartagena elite, those considered "native" to Getsemaní, do not have the economic, social and cultural capital to make them worthy of staying in the neighbourhood. As a community of poor Afro-descendants, *Getsemanisenses* are undesirable and incapable of contributing to the enhancement of the place because they lack the means, work ethic, aesthetic and moral values to do so. However, the minimization of racism and cultural racism superficially detach race from such political beliefs despite the fact that racism is inherent to them.

SRD: economic processes

Thus far, I have shown how the selective detachment of race from space at various levels, and the detachment of race from the politics of discrimination can foster an interpretive space where residents of Getsemaní understand processes of gentrification as detached from their racial underpinnings. The third context from which people discursively detach race is economics. I found that this detachment is made possible by two primary factors. The first is that the documented high correlation between race and class in Colombia (Wade 1993) allows residents to discuss class without acknowledging race and therefore detach race from economic processes. The need to plainly refer to race is often obviated at times because discussions of class often imply racial differences, as Streicker (1995) found in Cartagena.

People also detach race from economics as a result of how they conceive of the catalysts of displacement. Long-term residents mentioned three sources of residential displacement: (1) displacement by armed conflict, (2) removal by government force due to urban redevelopment projects, and (3) displacement due to market pressures and a concomitant increase in taxes and services. The former two causes have clearly identifiable displacers, which distinguish them from the more inconspicuous cause in the third case, the "invisible hand" of capitalism. I discuss the latter two causes as they distinctly refer to economic processes and are therefore more germane to the discussion of gentrification.

Removal by government force

The neighbourhood of Chambacú was once located near Getsemaní, between the walled city and The Castle of Saint Phillip (San Felipe). In the 1950s, the state and local government believed that the impoverished slum of Chambacú, composed of primarily Afro-Colombian residents (over ninety-five per cent), was its greatest threat to achieving material progress from the tourism industry. The slum was regularly identified as a problem for the city of Cartagena as its inhabitants were consistently characterized as immoral, violent, drug-addicted and promiscuous and it was removed in 1971 (Deávila 2008). The depiction of Getsemaní by Cartagena residents, government officials and the media for decades has closely mimicked that of Chambacú. Nevertheless, as opposed to seeing the similarity between the removal of Chambacú and the imminent displacement of Getsemaní residents, of the only three residents who mentioned the neighbourhood of Chambacú at all, two did so to reinforce its negative reputation and distinguish it from Getsemaní. For example, one long-term resident in her fifties, Mirta, stated:

They had bad customs. They came to live here because Getsemaní was always a neighborhood of working and honest people. But following the transfer (of Chambacú residents) this neighborhood suffered. There were very social changes and suddenly the selling of drugs and the theft began.

By overlooking Chambacú or distinguishing it from Getsemaní in discussions, residents demonstrate that they consider either the composition of the former community or the process by which it was removed as distinct. Next, I will demonstrate how displacement caused by market forces, a process that has far more inconspicuous displacers, can be conceived of differently from the aforementioned removal by government force.

Dislocations through increases in taxes and services

In the 1990s, the recognition of cultural rights and multiculturalism coincided with a major neoliberal restructuring in Colombia. This restructuring, involving trade liberalization, privatization, deregulation and austerity measures, engendered a dramatic increase in poverty and an economic crisis (Hristov 2009). These government decisions contributed to both the blatant removal and relocation of the residents of Chambacú, as well as the tax-driven displacement Getsemaní residents now experience. However, in the former scenario, people witnessed firsthand the individuals and specific groups responsible for the displacements, making it more difficult to dismiss the full menu of factors that contributed to these groups' motives.

Residents of Getsemaní are conscious of being supplanted by those with more financial means. A number of residents shared that taxes and increased prices for utilities were major points of distress. Residents believed that the local government had little regard for the neighbourhood previously and now felt that the government considers the neighbourhood as a place of particular interest. One resident said, "before they looked at the neighbourhood as one without value and now as one with more value. But not for locals, for people from outside." Another shared, "They were not aware that this was an attractive place, but right now they are aware that there is a boom in the city." Unlike the case of

Chambacú, where the local government was the palpable, active perpetrator in the displacement of native residents, in this instance the government is conceived of passively doing little to prevent "market-driven" displacement.

Only one resident expressed an understanding of the relationship between the government's previously held disregard for Getsemaní, its current plan to "revitalize" it, and Getsemaní's perceived racial composition. Interviews demonstrated that residents frame their vulnerable positions as a function of a market-based, capitalist accumulation process. As residents approximate the relationship between their value (or their lack of) and their disappearance from the neighbourhood, race is rarely, if ever, mentioned, as if it were a variable completely detached from their mental economic models. Unlike Bonilla-Silva's ([2003] 2010) finding that an economic liberalism frame is used by both whites and non-whites to attribute racial differences to individualism and choice, which are central tenets of capitalism; in this case, residents regard the economic and spatial differences as having neither racial bases nor consequences. The thinking goes, the place is not "truly" black and even if it were, racism is not a primary stratifying principle. And since capitalism is detached from the racial hierarchy, as opposed to being a mutually constitutive factor in its construction and reproduction, race does not affect how space is shaped in the case of gentrification.

CONCLUSION

The politics of race, development and identity are deeply intertwined in urban space. In this paper, I made manifest this relationship by employing the RAP conceptual framework at the level of discourse to explore how and when people attach race as a constitutive component in interpersonal, organizational and structural processes and relations that stratify social life. By doing so, I demonstrated how people reconcile Latin American discourses that suggest race is not a primary stratifying principle, with the material realities of racial hierarchies that counter such discourses.

I provided examples of race being actively mobilized at the interpersonal level, revealing the role that race and racism play in day-to-day interactions. I contrasted this with the ways that social actors detach and attach race at the organizational levels of neighbourhood, city and region. Colombia's regionalism, racial geography and racial categorization affect whether residents construct their spatial identities as non-black. Latin American racial ideology precipitates the consistent detachment of race from the structural level of the politics of discrimination, thereby invisibilizing racism. Furthermore, residents' economic understandings buttress the notion that capitalism is unrelated to race, thereby eliminating race as instrumental in modern spatial change. The cumulative effect of these processes is that gentrification is viewed by residents as having no relationship to racialization or racism.

RAPs are not unique to the context in which I have presented them. Various facets of these processes are discernible across numerous domains of social life and geographic locations. For example, we see the practical application of RAP in cases where home or business-owners attach race as a crucial factor in determining the criminality of those they encounter. We see law enforcement officers attach race in practice when determining whom to stop and frisk. Yet government officials discursively detach race as a factor when justifying the disproportionate effects of "stop and frisk" policing and instead attribute disparities between racialized groups to differences in rates of criminality. We see institutions such as banks attach race to neighbourhoods to determine their creditworthiness, leading to the practice of redlining. Affirmative action opponents seek to remove race as a factor in determining higher education admission policies. However, similar opponents will attach and essentialize race when attributing differences in acceptance rates to the perceived innate biological intellectual inferiority of marginalized groups lower on the racial hierarchy, as opposed to a history of racial bias, housing segregation and limited educational opportunities.

Race is often not disentangled from other factors of social difference, particularly from gender and class. However, RAP permits us to see where it is useful to attach racial significance to social processes. It also underscores that because race is not being mobilized at one level of analysis does not mean that race is not socially relevant. It may be attached and detached distinctly at different levels of analysis.

DISCLOSURE STATEMENT

No potential conflict of interest was reported by the author.

FUNDING

This work was supported by the U.S. Fulbright Commission, the Fulbright Commission in Colombia, and the Institute of International Education (IIE) [Fulbright U.S. Student Program Study/Research Grant].

REFERENCES

Anderson, Elijah. 1990. *Streetwise: Race, Class, and Change in an Urban Community*. Chicago, IL: University of Chicago Press.

Antón, Jhon, Álvaro Bello, Fabiana Del Popolo, Marcelo Paixrc, and Marta Rangel. 2009. "Afrodescendientes en América Latina y el Caribe: Del Reconocimiento Estadístico a la Realización de Derechos." Santiago de Chile: CEPAL. http://repositorio.cepal.org/bitstream/handle/11362/7227/S0900315_es.pdf?sequence=1.

Appelbaum, Nancy. 2003. *Muddied Waters: Race, Region, and Local History in Colombia*. Durham, NC: Duke University Press.

Arocha, Jaime. 1998. "Inclusion of Afro-Colombians: Unreachable National Goal?" *Latin American Perspectives* 25 (3): 70–89.

Auyero, Javier. 2001. *Poor People's Politics: Peronist Survival Networks and the Legacy of Evita*. Durham, NC: Duke University Press.

Banton, Michael. 1977. *The Idea of Race*. London: Tavistock.

Barot, Rohit, and John Bird. 2001. "Racialization: The Genealogy and Critique of a Concept." *Ethnic and Racial Studies* 24 (4): 601–618.

Bonilla-Silva, Eduardo. (2003) 2010. *Racism Without Racists: Color-Blind Racism and the Persistence of Racial Inequality in Contemporary America*. Lanham, MD: Rowman & Littlefield.

Brah, Avtar. 1996. *Cartographies of Diaspora: Contesting Identities*. London: Routledge.

Caldeira, Teresa P. R. 2001. *City of Walls: Crime, Segregation, and Citizenship in São Paulo*. Oakland: University of California Press.

Cunin, Elisabeth. 2003. *Identidades a Flor de Piel: Lo "Negro" Entre Apariencias y Pertenencias: Categorías Raciales y Mestizaje en Cartagena (Colombia)*. Bogotá: Instituto Colombiano de Antropología e Historia.

Davidson, Mark, and Loretta Lees. 2005. "'New-Build 'Gentrification' and London's Riverside Renaissance." *Environment and Planning A* 37 (7): 1165–1190.

Deávila, Orlando Pertuz. 2008. "Construyendo Sospechas: Imaginarios del Miedo, Segregación Urbana y Exclusión Social en Cartagena 1956–1971." *Cuadernos de Literatura del Caribe e Hispanoamérica* 7: 35–50.

de Friedemann, Nina S. 1984. *Estudios de Negros en La Antropología Colombiana: Presencia e Invisibilidad*. Bogotá: Etno.

Díaz de Paniagua, Rosa A., and Raúl Paniagua Bedoya. 1993. *Getsemaní: Historia, Patrimonio y Bienestar Social en Cartagena*. Cartagena: COREDUCAR.

Dinzey-Flores, Zaire. 2013. *Locked In, Locked Out Gated Communities in a Puerto Rican City*. Philadelphia: University of Pennsylvania Press.

Dixon, Kwame. 2008. "Transnational Black Social Movements in Latin America: Afro-Colombians and the Struggle for Human Rights." In *Latin American Social Movements in the Twenty-First Century: Resistance, Power, and Democracy*, edited by Richard Stahler-Sholk and Glen David Kuecker, 181–196. Lanham, MD: Rowman & Littlefield.

Escobar, Arturo. 2008. *Territories of Difference: Place, Movements, Life, Redes*. Durham, NC: Duke University Press.

Fanon, Frantz. 1967. *The Wretched of the Earth*. Harmondsworth: Penguin.

Freeman, Lance. 2006. *There Goes the 'Hood: Views of Gentrification from the Ground Up*. Philadelphia, PA: Temple University Press.

Goff, Phillip Atiba, Jennifer L. Eberhardt, Melissa J. Williams, and Matthew Christian Jackson. 2008. "Not Yet Human: Implicit Knowledge, Historical Dehumanization, and Contemporary Consequences." *Journal of Personality and Social Psychology* 94 (2): 292–306.

Goldberg, David Theo. (1992) 2010. "The Semantics of Race." *Ethnic and Racial Studies* 15 (4): 543–569.

Goldstein, Daniel. 2004. *The Spectacular City: Violence and Performance in Urban Bolivia*. Durham, NC: Duke University Press.

Gregory, Steven. 2006. *The Devil Behind the Mirror: Globalization and Politics in the Dominican Republic*. Oakland: University of California Press.

Gros, Christian. 2000. *Políticas de la Etnicidad: Identidad, Estado y Modernidad*. Bogotá: Instituto Colombiano de Antropología e Historia.

Grueso, Libia, Carlos Rosero, and Arturo Escobar. 1998. "The Process of Black Community Organizing in the Southern Pacific Coast Region of Colombia." In *Cultures of Politics Politics of Cultures: Re-Visioning Latin American Social Movements*, edited by Sonia E Alvarez and Evelyn Dagnino, 430–447. Boulder, CO: Westview Press.

Guerra, Adriano. 2010. "Getsemaní a 200 Años de Independencia: Exclusion e Inclusion de la Verdadera Cartagena." In *Cuaderno de Bitácora*, 19–32. Cartagena: La Fundación Carolina Colombia y la Universidad Tecnológica de Bolívar.

Gutiérrez Azopardo, Ildefonso. 1980. *Historia del Negro en Colombia: Sumisión o Rebeldía?* Bogotá: Editorial Nueva América.

Hanchard, Michael George. 1998. *Orpheus and Power: The Movimento Negro of Rio de Janeiro and Sao Paulo, Brazil, 1945–1988*. Princeton, NJ: Princeton University Press.

Harvey, David. (1973) 2009. *Social Justice and the City*. Athens: University of Georgia Press.

Helg, Aline. 1999. "The Limits of Equality: Free People of Colour and Slaves During the First Independence of Cartagena, Colombia, 1810–15." *Slavery and Abolition* 20 (2): 1–30.

Hesse, Barnor. 1997. "White Governmentality." In *Imagining Cities: Scripts, Signs, Memory*, edited by S. Westwood and J. Williams, 86–103. London: Routledge.

Hristov, Jasmin. 2009. *Blood and Capital: The Paramilitarization of Colombia*. Athens: Ohio University Press.

Kim, Claire J. 1999. "The Racial Triangulation of Asian Americans." *Politics and Society* 27: 105–138.

Lewis, Gail, and Ann Phoenix. 2004. "Race, Ethnicity and Identity." In *Questioning Identity*, edited by K. Woodward, 115–150. London: Routledge.

Mac an Ghaill, Mairtin. 1999. *Contemporary Racisms & Ethnicities: Social and Cultural Transformations*. Buckingham: Open University Press.

Meisel Roca, Adolfo. 1980. "Esclavitud, mestizaje y haciendas en la provincia de Cartagena: 1533–1851." *Desarrollo y Sociedad* 4: 228–277.

Miles, Robert. 1989. *Racism*. London: Routledge.

Moñino, Yves, and Armin Schwegler. 2002. *Palenque, Cartagena y Afro-Caribe: Historia y Lengua*. Tübingen: Max Niemeyer Verlag.

Murji, Karim, and John Solomos. 2005. *Racialization: Studies in Theory and Practice*. New York: Oxford University Press.

Ng'weno, Bettina. 2007. "Can Ethnicity Replace Race? Afro-Colombians, Indigeneity and the Colombian Multicultural State." *Journal of Latin American and Caribbean Anthropology* 12 (2): 414–440.

Omi, Michael, and Howard Winant. (1986) 2015. *Racial Formation in the United States*. 3rd ed. New York, NY: Routledge.

Paschel, Tianna. 2010. "The Right to Difference: Explaining Colombia's Shift from Color Blindness to the Law of Black Communities." *American Journal of Sociology* 116 (3): 729–769.

Pattillo, Mary E. 2007. *Black on the Block: The Politics of Race and Class in the City*. Chicago, IL: University of Chicago Press.

Pérez Valbuena, Gerson J. 2007. *La pobreza en Cartagena: Un Análisis por Barrios*. Cartagena: Banco de la República. Centro de Estudios Económicos Regionales.

Perry, Keisha-Khan Y. 2013. *Black Women Against the Land Grab: The Fight for Racial Justice in Brazil*. Minneapolis: University of Minnesota Press.

Pine, Adrienne. 2008. *Working Hard, Drinking Hard: On Violence and Survival in Honduras*. Oakland: University of California Press.

Reeves, Frank. 1983. *British Racial Discourse: A Study of British Political Discourse about Race and Race-related Matters*. London: Cambridge University Press.

Restrepo, Eduardo. 1998. "La Construcción de La Etnicidad: Comunidades Negras en Colombia." In *Modernidad, Identidad y Desarrollo: Construcción de Sociedad y Recreación Cultural en Contextos De Modernización*, edited by Maria Lucía Sotomayor, 341–358. Bogotá: Instituto Colombiano de Antropología.

Restrepo, Eduardo. 2007. "Racismo y Discriminación." www.ramn.net/restrepo/documentos/racismo.pdf.

Rojas, Eduardo. 1999. *Old Cities, New Assets: Preserving Latin America's Urban Heritage*. Washington, DC: Inter-American Development Bank, distributed by the Johns Hopkins University Press.

Ryan, William. 1976. *Blaming the Victim*. New York, NY: Vintage Books.

Sheriff, Robin E. 2001. *Dreaming Equality: Color, Race and Racism in Urban Brazil*. New Brunswick, NJ: Rutgers University Press.

Shih, Shu-Mei. 2008. "Comparative Racialization: An Introduction." *PMLA* 123 (5): 1347–1362, Special Topic: Comparative Racialization.

Smith, Neil. 2011. "Uneven Development Redux." *New Political Economy* 16 (2): 261–265.

Soler Castillo, Sandra. 2009. "Racismo y Discurso en Los Textos Escolares." In *Nina S. de Friedemann: Cronista de Disidencias y Resistencias*, edited by Jaime Arocha Rodríguez, 233–266. Bogotá: Universidad Nacional de Colombia.

Streicker, Joel. 1995. "Policing Boundaries: Race, Class, and Gender in Cartagena, Colombia." *American Ethnologist* 22 (1): 54–74.

Tavory, Iddo, and Stefan Timmermans. 2009. "Two Cases of Ethnography: Grounded Theory and the Extended Case Method." *Ethnography* 10 (3): 243–263.

Telles, Edward. 2014. *Pigmentocracies: Ethnicity, Race, and Color in Latin America*. Chapel Hill: University of North Carolina Press.

Twine, France Winddance. 1997. *Racism in a Racial Democracy: The Maintenance of White Supremacy in Brazil*. New Brunswick, NJ: Rutgers University Press.

United Nations Independent Expert on Minority Affairs. 2010, February 12. "Declaración de la Experta Independiente de las Naciones Unidas sobre Cuestiones de las Minorías, Conclusiones Preliminares de su visita oficial a Colombia." Accessed November 19 2015. www.ohchr.org/en/NewsEvents/Pages/DisplayNews. aspx?NewsID=9821&.

Urrea Giraldo, Fernando, Carlos Augusto Viáfara López, and Mara Viveros Vigoya. 2014. "From Whitened Miscegenation to Tri-Ethnic Multiculturalism: Race and Ethnicity in Colombia." In *Pigmentocracies: Ethnicity, Race, and Color in Latin America*, edited by Edward Telles, 81–125. Chapel Hill, NC: University of North Carolina Press.

Venkatesh, Sudhir. 2000. *American Project: The Rise and Fall of a Modern Ghetto*. Cambridge, MA: Harvard University Press.

Viáfara López, Carlos Augusto, and Fernando Urrea Giraldo. 2006. "Race and Gender Effects in the Educational Achievement and Social-Occupational Status for Three Colombian Cities." *Desarrollo y Sociedad* 58: 115–163.

Wade, Peter. 1993. *Blackness and Race Mixture: The Dynamics of Racial Identity in Colombia*. Baltimore, MD: Johns Hopkins University Press.

Wade, Peter. 2000. *Music, Race, and Nation: Musica Tropical in Colombia*. Chicago, IL: University of Chicago Press.

Wherry, Frederick F. 2011. *The Philadelphia Barrio: The Arts, Branding, and Neighborhood Transformation*. Chicago, IL: University of Chicago Press.

Woldoff, Rachael A. 2011. *White Flight/Black Flight: The Dynamics of Racial Change in an American Neighborhood*. Ithaca, NY: Cornell University Press.

BOX 3 MELISSA VALLE REFLECTION

My introduction to understanding the relationships between gentrification and racialization was not the direct result of any academic undertaking but a series of practical ones. The first was my experience as an intern for two community development corporations in Washington, DC, while I was an undergraduate student at Howard University. At Manna Community Development Corporation in 1999, I was first exposed to the fears of Black communities in Northwest DC, who were fighting to protect their places along the famous U Street corridor, and in the LeDroit Park and Shaw-Howard communities. One of the residents' greatest expressed worries was the steady 'encroachment of 14th Street'. This was their way of describing the racial and physical boundaries that separated the Black communities situated east of 14th Street from the white ones to the west.

Five years later, as the public policy director at Abyssinian Development Corporation, another community development corporation, I was again confronted by similar fears held by long-term Harlemites about their impending displacement and dispossession. In both DC and Harlem, residents minced no words, freely analyzing what they felt were the very concrete relationships between their communities' racial categorization as Black and their imminent displacement. This articulation of the explicit relationships between gentrification and neighborhood racial categorization repeatedly echoed in my head as I moved about the world.

It was fortuitous how I ended up in the community that would later become the locus of my dissertation and, subsequently, the article 'The discursive detachment of race from gentrification in Cartagena de Indias, Colombia'. I was conducting a study in Bogotá, examining the Afro-Colombian social movement, and wanted to escape the wet and chilly weather of the mountains of central Colombia. So I ran off to a place that I believed would feel more comfortable and familiar, both in terms of climate and racial population: Cartagena de Indias. While there, I found myself in Getsemaní, a largely Afro-descendant community that sits within the old city walls yet just outside those of the historic downtown city center in Cartagena, Colombia. Due to my professional experiences uncloaking the patterns of gentrification, I immediately recognized the signs of a nascent form of gentrification upon my arrival to Getsemaní. Hip cafes and bars were sparsely sprinkled among dilapidated Spanish-style row homes. European travelers who appeared like the more risk-averse types sashayed through the neighborhood's narrow streets with a relaxed curiosity. Residents also were not yet at the point of worry. Instead, they were reveling in the positive changes and didn't anticipate the more dire consequences that I knew the changes actually portended.

For the next three years, I returned to Getsemaní annually to document what would become a rapidly evolving change process. I expected to tell an all-too-familiar tale of race and gentrification-related displacement, one that involved disinvestment by the state, market devaluation of land, residents who are racialized as Black being stereotyped in familiar ways, and the displacement of long-term residents. And yes, these familiar elements were all present. Yet conducting this work in what appeared to be a gentrifying Afro-Indigenous community in Latin America meant that

I had to meld my own experiences and knowledge with what I was uncovering about how racial identity politics operate in Colombia, as well as how processes of gentrification operate in the Global South.

Upon my first return to Cartagena, I discovered that a great deal had transpired in only a year. Suddenly, Getsemaní was headlining the travel section of the *New York Times*, there were non-profit organizations in the community working with residents to prevent gentrification-related displacement, and the community (or NGOs) had even nicknamed the city's change process 'Getsemanificación', a play on the neighborhood name and the Spanish word for *gentrificación*. This was the same place where, when I mentioned gentrification to residents the previous summer, I received nothing but quizzical looks. Now they were explaining to me what gentrification was and spitting back to me the same examples of places in Puerto Rico that I had mentioned to residents the year before!

As I attempted to grasp the racial landscape of Cartagena (and Colombia more broadly), the community's metamorphosis, and residents' understandings of both things, I had run into a sociological dilemma. I had discovered, or even created, a puzzle for which I initially could not solve. Despite the myths of racial democracy that run rampant throughout Latin America, everyday talk is imbued with racial language, and racist discourse is the norm in countries like Colombia. Space is extremely racialized, with neighborhoods, cities, and regions becoming synonymous with racialized groups and all their concomitant stereotypes. However, I was not hearing Getsemaní residents discuss their displacement in racial terms. In later discussions with vendors, they were not telling me that their removal from the streets of Cartagena was related to their disproportionate identities as Black, poor, and often female. That relationship that felt concrete in the minds of US residents had a much more gossamer feel in the discussions with Cartagener@s. Yet the "why?" evaded me. I resolved this dilemma by constructing the Racial Attachment Processes (RAP) framework discussed in this paper.

In exploring the literature parsing out the relationships between race and displacement, I was surprised to find that there was not a great deal of empirical work on the topic in the United States, especially given the high rates of both racial segregation and gentrification in major US cities. US-based gentrification scholarship, especially quantitative work, frequently minimized the relationships between gentrification-related displacement and neighborhood racial categorization. Therefore, when I was asked to reflect on the contemporary inscription of race on urban space for *International Journal of Urban and Regional Research*'s web series called *Spotlight On*, I elected to focus on the trouble with 'colorblind' or 'race-neutral' urbanism, as described by Christopher Mele (2013). This was in 2017, following the momentum of the Black Lives Matter movement, and I addressed why such relationships would be increasingly difficult to ignore in the years to come, given factors such as the rise of transnational anti-racist movements that explicitly confront racial injustice, unaware of the even more intense racial reckoning and global pandemic that were but a few short years away.

In seeking to uncover how gentrification operated in this community in Cartagena and how race factored into displacement, I was also struck that the literature addressing race and racism as intrinsic features of urban development was virtually non-existent outside of the Global North. Similarly jarring was that there were very few sociological accounts of gentrification in the Global South coming from US scholars. These realizations inspired my article "Globalizing the Sociology of Gentrification," as I continued to understand what made my study of Cartagena unique and what could also be seen as related processes, operating like intricate circuits within the same globalized system. I now have a more profound appreciation for US scholarship that centers the Global South, as well as scholarship coming out of the Global South that tackles the realities of racial inequities and their effects on spatial inequalities, including dispossession.

REFERENCES

Mele, C. (2013). Neoliberalism, race and the redefining of urban redevelopment. *International Journal of Urban and Regional Research*, 37 (2), 598–617.

Valle, M.M. (2017). Revealing the Ruse: Shifting the narrative of colorblind urbanism. "Spotlight on Race, Justice and the City." *International Journal of Urban and Regional Research*. www.ijurr.org/spotlight-on/race-justice-and-the-city/revealing-the-ruse-shifting-the-narrative-of-colorblind-urbanism/

Valle, M.M. (2021). Globalizing the sociology of gentrification. Special Issue: "Global South". *City & Community*, 20 (1), 59–70.

7
The fire this time
Grenfell, racial capitalism and the urbanisation of empire

Ida Danewid

INTRODUCTION: GHOSTS OF GRENFELL

> Grenfell burned for local and global reasons.
> (Ish, former Grenfell resident)

When London awoke on the morning of 14 June 2017, Grenfell Tower had already been burning for several hours. The fire, which began just before 1 a.m. in a fridge-freezer on the fourth floor and quickly spread to engulf the entire building, left at least 72 dead and hundreds more missing. Desperate residents trapped in the burning tower could be heard screaming for help, with some jumping from windows as high as the 15th floor. In those fateful hours, as pictures of the fire went viral and eyewitness accounts began to come in, London was caught in shock: how, in one of the wealthiest boroughs in one of the world's richest cities, could a preventable fire have ripped through a 24-storey building with such devastating results? Indeed, what had made Grenfell possible?

In the days, weeks and months after the fire, 'class' and 'neoliberalism' were the answers most commonly given by the British media (Erlanger, 2017; McRobbie, 2017; Tucker, 2017; Williamson, 2017). Grenfell Tower, it turned out, was owned by the local council, the Royal Borough of Kensington and Chelsea (RBKC), but lacked smoke alarms, sprinkler systems and multiple escape routes. Residents had complained about the building's 'dangerous living conditions and neglect of health and safety legislation' (Grenfell Action Group, 2016) for years but had persistently been ignored by the council. A refurbishment project carried out in 2017 addressed few of these concerns, and instead covered the building in cheap and combustible cladding materials – a cost-effective way to beautify its brutalist appearance for the benefit of wealthier neighbouring residents (Griffin, 2017). The cladding, which failed to meet the manufacturer's own safety standards and is forbidden in the US and many European countries, was later found to be the main reason that the fire spread so quickly: it made the tower burn 'like a fire that you pour petrol on', remembers one resident, and pushed temperatures up to over 1000 degrees (Kirkpatrick et al., 2017). For many commentators, neoliberal ideology and decades of privatisation, cuts, gentrification and deregulation thus formed the context in which the fire had been made possible. The neoliberalisation of the British housing market, it was argued, had created a dangerous climate in which local authorities were incentivised to neglect the needs of their less well-off residents, and chose to put costs and profits before health and safety. The fire, many concluded, was ultimately the terrible result of neoliberal urbanism and 'the class violence embedded in London's rich, gentrifying neighborhoods' (Arabia, 2017).

Two months after the fire, London rapper-activist Lowkey released a song in tribute to the 'ghosts of Grenfell'.[1] The music video, which features local residents and survivors mouthing the lyrics of the song, ends with a name call for the dead and missing. As the names are read out loud and their pictures shown, it is difficult to not notice that the majority of victims were black and brown, Arab and Muslim, and European migrants and refugees from the Global South.[2] On the night of the fire, Grenfell was predominantly occupied by London's racialised poor – by Nigerian cleaners, Somali carers, Moroccan drivers and so on. Yet, in post-Grenfell debates about austerity, urban gentrification and social marginalisation, race was either relatively absent or discussed in isolation from the supposedly more fundamental problem of widening class inequality under neoliberalism.[3]

In this article, I argue that the neglect of race in discussions about Grenfell is indicative of a wider set of racial erasures in the scholarly literature on global cities and neoliberal urbanism. Over the last few years, a growing number of International Relations (IR) theorists have taken an interest in the changing relationship between the urban and the global. The study of global cities has emerged as a focal point for those interested in understanding the accelerating urbanisation of world politics and the challenges that it brings to existing geographies of power. As Keller Easterling (2014: 15) explains, 'some of the most radical changes to the globalizing world are being written, not in the language of law and diplomacy, but rather in the spatial information of infrastructure, architecture and urbanism'. While this literature has been successful in bringing new forms of urban violence, hierarchy and exclusion into view, it has – like most post-Grenfell commentary – largely neglected questions of race and racism. This article argues that this is problematic because although gentrification and neoliberal urbanism operate in different ways in different cities, a broader pattern of racialised dispossession and displacement can be discerned. From London to New York, Mumbai to Cairo, Johannesburg to São Paulo, ethnographic studies tell largely reminiscent stories of racialised evictions, expropriations and police violence (Alves, 2018; Camp, 2012; Cowen and Lewis, 2016; Ghertner, 2014; Johnson, 2014; Samara, 2011; Tilley et al., 2019). Like Grenfell, they highlight how the 'making' of global cities often goes hand in hand with racialised policies and practices designed to 'clean up the streets' through revitalisation programmes and plans to displace actually existing inhabitants, which are cast as deviant, criminal, violent and out of place. Alerting us to the racial structuring of life and death in the global city, they thus underscore the pressing need to engage with the vibrant and diverse scholarship produced in post/decolonial, black and indigenous studies – bodies of thought that remain largely overlooked in urban studies and global cities, in IR and beyond.

This article examines the distinctively racial logics of neoliberal urban governance and, in doing so, makes two contributions. First, it develops a sympathetic critique of IR's theories of the global city, arguing that the violence of neoliberal urbanism cannot be understood without a racial theory of capitalism. Contrary to what the IR literature often seems to suggest, the racialised nature of global cities exceed the existence of discriminatory employers, lenders and landlords; indeed, rather than neutral playing fields where non-white individuals experience occasional forms of discrimination, global cities are themselves a mechanism through which capital produces raced space. In this article, I draw on the literature on racial capitalism to subject the racial logics of the global city to theoretical inquiry and critique (Gilmore, 2007; Goldstein, 2017; Johnson and Lubin, 2017; Kelley, 2015a; Lowe, 2015; Melamed, 2015; Robinson, 2000). Following black Marxists such as Cedric Robinson, Ruth Wilson Gilmore and Robin D.G. Kelley, I argue that capitalism has always been racial capitalism, and that it is through this lens that contemporary urban regeneration programmes must be analysed and understood. In the words of Lisa Lowe (2015: 150), 'capitalism expands not through rendering all labor, resources, and markets across the world identical, but by precisely seizing upon colonial divisions, identifying particular regions for production and others for neglect, certain populations for exploitation and still others for disposal'. Bringing this literature into conversation with global cities scholarship, the article examines the distinctively urban dimensions of racial capitalism, arguing that the rise of global cities is underpinned by a racial and imperial political economy that produces some people and places as 'surplus'. With calls to decolonise urban studies increasingly heard throughout the academy, IR theorists interested in the urban dimensions of world politics cannot afford to overlook this link between race, space and political economy.[4]

Second and relatedly, the article argues that today's neoliberal urbanisation is intimately linked to yesteryear's 'urbanisation of empire'.[5] Global cities should be conceptualised as part of a historical as well as ongoing imperial terrain. While, in IR, there has been a growing interest in questions of race, colonialism and their centrality for the study of world politics (Anievas et al., 2014; Carrozza et al., 2017; Sabaratnam, 2017; Shilliam, 2015; Vitalis, 2015), scholars have predominantly focused their analyses on North – South encounters. As Joseph Turner (2017: 2) explains, this is underwritten by 'a temporal and spatial schema which often treats colonisation as something done by Northern states to the Global South'. This focus is not without its merits, but scholars have sometimes been prone to overlook how 'violence and racism in the Global South is connected to the treatment of populations in the Global North' (Turner, 2017: 2). Responding to this lacunae, in this article, I interrogate the co-constitution of Western 'homelands' and colonial frontiers through a focus on the distinctively imperial political economy of neoliberal urbanism. Examining how global cities and colonial borderlands are bound together through racial capitalism, I show how practices of urban planning, slum administration and law-and-order policing are central to the management of racialised subjects in urban metropoles as well as (post)colonial peripheries. Where the IR literature typically conceives of global cities as a new form of actor or governance structure representing 'a fundamental challenge to some of the core logics of the modern international system' (Curtis, 2011: 1), my analysis thus reveals global cities as part of a historical and ongoing imperial terrain. The failure to account for this link has not only theoretical implications, but also serious political consequences. Indeed, in overestimating the newness of neoliberal urbanism, theorists of the global city inadvertently sanction populist projects that seek to counter the violence of neoliberalism with a nostalgic return to the post-1945 welfare state.

The Grenfell fire forms the background to the theoretical arguments developed in this article. Rather than a formal case study, Grenfell is used here as a heuristic to work from the local to the global and back again. While the fire is often understood as a strictly 'local' tragedy of British class inequality, the article argues that the 'makings' of Grenfell were inherently global-colonial in character (see also El-Enany, 2017). This is not to suggest that the racial logics of Grenfell map onto New York, Nairobi and Singapore in the exact same way; nowhere is exactly like Grenfell because urban processes of racialisation look different in different metropolitan contexts.[6] While the article highlights the racialized forms of expropriation and dispossession that often unfold alongside the 'making' of global cities, my goal is therefore not to reduce urban development to a single set of logics or to deny the existence of variations and particularities in metropolitan life. Indeed, the argument is *not* that Grenfell provides a model for understanding the under-bellies of *all* other cities around the world, but rather that the global city viewed from Grenfell Tower demonstrates the value of studying the local and global logics of race, class and place *together*. As black, post/decolonial and indigenous studies have been at the forefront in developing such analyses, urban studies and global cities scholarship have much to gain from a more sustained engagement with these literatures.

The article proceeds in three parts. The first section introduces the literature on global cities and neoliberal urbanism, as well as its uptake in IR. I argue that although an IR focus on cities has been helpful for challenging the discipline's 'Westphalian common sense', these approaches often rely on an abstract and ahistorical conception of the city that obfuscates the colonial and racial structures that pattern metropolitan life. While a growing critical strand of this literature highlights the dark side of neoliberal urbanism, it is predominantly framed through the lens of class and thus cannot explain why the cost of urban regeneration so often is carried by the racial poor. In order to account for the link between racial differentiation, capital accumulation and urban upscaling, in the second section, I turn to theories of racial capitalism. Racial capitalism highlights the centrality of race-making practices to political economy and therefore helps us re-conceptualise global cities as a mechanism through which capital produces raced space. The final section argues that a focus on the racial ordering of the global city also requires an engagement with colonial and imperial histories. Building on Aimé Césaire's image of the 'boomerang', I probe the colonial logics of three processes that are central to the production of 'surplus' people and places in urban settings: (1) gentrification and urban regeneration programmes; (2) racialised policing; and (3) accumulation by dispossession. When read through the lens of racial capitalism, the global city represents less a new type of international actor or governance structure than an extension and reconfiguration of the domestic space of empire. As North Kensington residents were quick to realise, raced spaces like Grenfell are rendered surplus 'for local and global reasons'.[7]

GLOBAL CITIES, NEOLIBERAL URBANISM AND THE ELISION OF RACE

Since the early 1990s, cities such as London, Tokyo, New York, Dubai, Johannesburg, Mumbai, São Paulo and Shanghai have been conceptualised and understood by political geographers and urban sociologists as representing a new urban form, that is, 'global cities'. Coined and introduced by Saskia Sassen (2013), global cities are nodal points in the global political economy. As Manuel Castells (2001: 225) explains, 'the entire planet is being reorganised around gigantic metropolitan nodes that absorb an increasing proportion of the urban population, itself the majority of the population of the planet'. For Castells and Sassen, global cities are a by-product of the structural transformation of the world economy and the acceleration of economic globalisation. While economic activity has become more dispersed around the world, its 'command and control functions' have increasingly been concentrated in a handful of locations. As local governments compete to maintain or improve their standing within the hierarchy of global cities, the result is a new form of urbanism: a neoliberal mode of urban governance characterised by redevelopment, urban expansion and real-estate speculation.

In recent years, the concept of the global city has been picked up by a number of IR theorists (Acuto, 2013; Curtis, 2016; Kangas, 2017; Ljungkvist, 2015). For most of these thinkers, the rise of the global city entails a challenge to existing geographies of power, yet there exists substantial disagreement as to precisely what this entails. Three main strands of thinking can be discerned. The first is represented by scholars such as Michele Acuto and Kristin Ljungkvist, for whom the emergence of global cities represents a new important actor in world politics. Global cities are *de facto* agents within diplomacy and governance but have been the 'invisible gorillas' in the room of IR for too long. As Acuto (2010: 429) explains, the growing importance of global cities in diplomatic affairs and international relations 'challenge[s] our traditional and IR-dominated theoretical frames of reference, bypassing scalar (globe, state, region) as well as political (supranational, governmental, regional, and local) hierarchies and disrupting the Westphalian system of sovereignty'. The second strand treats global cities as units in a new type of international system. Simon Curtis (2011: 2), for example, argues that global cities are an indication of 'a new development in the long-running tension between capitalism and the territorial state-system within which it developed'. The rise of global cities is, in effect, a sign of how the modern international system is being rapidly transformed. In contrast, the third and last category of IR scholarship conceptualises global cities as a mechanism of power with world-making capacities. Anni Kangas, drawing on the Foucaultian notion of the *dispositif*, argues that global cities function as a governmental technique that normalises and legitimises the idea of hierarchical and competitive city relations. If to be a global city is an 'authoritative image of city success', then urban elites have no choice but to undertake the kind of urban regeneration policies necessary to improve or at least maintain the city's standing within the network of global cities.

While IR scholars variously conceive of global cities as new important political actors, indicators of a new kind of international system or a governmental mechanism, most agree that the rise of the global city is deeply linked to the 'neoliberal project' (Curtis, 2011: 15) and the structural transformation of the world economy. As Delphine Ancien (2011: 2473) explains:

> these cities owe their 'global status' to their very high concentration of the world's financial and related industries, the new pillars of a late capitalism characterised by new conditions of rapidly increasing globalisation, financialisation and deregulation of the world economy.

A central area of concern for many global cities scholars has been the 'dark side' of these processes. As Sassen has demonstrated, global cities cannot function without those who build its urban economy from below: the immigrants, refugees and casual workers who provide their wealthy neighbours with drivers, cleaners and other low-wage services. In the same way that the capitalist world-system splits the globe into core and periphery, global cities similarly shatter the urban landscape into spaces of rich and poor. In drawing attention to the poverty, marginalisations and labour hierarchies that cut through urban life, the literature on global cities thus offers a sobering corrective to liberal approaches that typically portray urban metropoles as nodes of migration and cosmopolitanism where tolerance, multiculturalism and cosmopolitan sensibilities are nurtured (Binnie et al., 2006; Florida, 2005; Sandercock and Lyssiotis, 2003). Indeed, as this literature makes clear, global cities are at once characterised by the emergence of new, shiny corporate citadels and financial centres, glistening high-tech enclaves and quirky high-culture districts, as well as by the gentrification of the city centre, the displacement of the original occupants, the rapid increase in slums and homelessness, and the growing polarisation of wealth.

For many commentators, it is within this (domestic) context of neoliberal urbanism and the 'dark side' of the global city that the Grenfell fire must be analysed and understood. As Brenna Bhandar (2018) explains, Grenfell 'has come to signify the worst aspects of a neo-liberal mode of governance that took hold in Britain from the 1980s onwards'.[8] Four decades of deregulation, privatisation, financialisation, cuts to public services and outsourcing have transformed the UK housing and property market and created acute problems of affordability, overcrowding and homelessness. Consecutive Labour and Conservative governments have sold off and demolished old, worn-down council estates and replaced them with new developments. While regeneration schemes and urban upscaling programmes have been justified as a way to improve housing conditions, the result has been a rapid decline in social housing and the displacement of poor and working-class communities from their own neighbourhoods: at its height in 1979, social housing accounted for 29% of all housing in England; in 2016, it had fallen to 6.8%. While London has become a global capital for financial and real-estate speculation, and the home of 86 billionaires, 338,000 homes rented by people under 35 are now in such poor condition that they put the health and safety of tenants at risk (Booth, 2018). As Nathan Brooker (2017) summarises:

> [i]f the price of food had risen at the same rate as London house prices over the past 40 years, then a chicken would now cost £100. . . . Houses were once places where people lived; today, first and foremost, they are financial assets.

Importantly, this situation is not unique to London, but closely mirrors that in other global cities. From Paris to Mumbai, Johannesburg to New York, São Paulo to Sydney, urban space is quickly becoming more unequal as gentrification and regeneration projects push low-income residents out of the city centre (Atkinson and Bridge, 2004; Lees et al., 2015). The wave of riots that have shaken global cities in recent years – London in 2011, the banlieues of Paris 2005 and Husby in Stockholm in 2013 – are, at least in part, a response to this trend.[9]

Discussions following the Grenfell fire have successfully shone a light on this 'dark side' of the global city. However, while these debates have helped bring problems of urban class inequality into mainstream focus, they have often worked to de-race the violence of neoliberal urbanism. While some commentators have insisted that race is absolutely central for understanding the processes that rendered the Grenfell Tower structurally unsafe, mainstream commentary has often framed the fire as an exclusive question of inadequate fire safety protective measures, combustible cladding, the Fire Brigade's 'stay-put' policy and, more broadly, poverty and marginalisation (MacLeod, 2018; McRobbie, 2017; Madden, 2017; Shildrick, 2018). The public inquiry, set up to 'examine the circumstances leading up to and surrounding the fire' (Grenfell Tower Inquiry, 2017) has largely replicated this focus. While Imran Khan QC, representing the Grenfell survivors, bereaved and relatives, emphasised the need to address 'institutional racism',[10] it has been altogether missing from the inquiry. This is problematic as most indicators confirm that the British urban landscape is highly racialised: in England, the majority of children who live above the fourth floor of tower blocks in England are black or Asian – in a country where 82% of the population is white (Dorling, 2011).

Throughout the UK, children from brown and black families are more likely to live in dilapidated and overcrowded housing than white people, and they are 75% more likely to experience housing deprivation. Out of the 307,000 homeless that live on the streets in London, one in three are non-white (Gulliver, 2016).[11] Important work on other global cities suggests that this racialised urban political economy might not be unique to the UK (even though it does not, of course, look exactly the same in *all* global cities). In the San Francisco Bay area, gentrification has overwhelmingly led to the displacement of poor people of colour and resulted in new concentrations of poverty and a new wave of racial segregation (Urban Displacement Project, 2015). In Southeast Asian cities such as Jakarta, Bandung, Bangkok, Hanoi and Singapore, the disciplining and exclusion of mobile, 'irrational' urban subjects (predominantly migrant and racialised) has been central to the construction of 'clean' and 'orderly' streets (Poon, 2009; Tilley et al., 2019). In Paris, the physical transformation of the urban centre has expelled many poor Arab and African communities to the outskirts of the city (Hazan, 2010). In São Paolo, the bid to overtake Rio de Janeiro has created an urban landscape where 'black bodies are exploited in the job market, segregated in favelas, incarcerated, beaten' and killed by the police (Alves, 2014: 324). Evidence from other global cities, such as Cape Town, Dubai and New York, tells of roughly similar stories of raced forms of exclusion, appropriation and displacement (Alawadi, 2014; Cowen and Lewis, 2016; Davis, 2007; Franck, 2019; Kelley, 2012; Samara, 2011). While, of course, the specificities of urban renewal look different in all these cities, a broader pattern of racialised inclusion and exclusion nonetheless stands out.

In spite of this, scholarship on global cities has relatively neglected the role of race in neoliberal urban governance. Indeed, while this scholarship has been successful in shedding light on new forms of inequality, violence and hierarchy, it has often been resistant to bring race into the debate. As Tom Slater (2009: 576) explains, global cities scholars tend to focus on class-driven fragmentation: 'a rare point of agreement among analysts of gentrification is that *class* should be the central focus'. While there is some recognition that gentrification typically involves the displacement of black and brown communities, and although scholars such as Sassen have examined how global cities depend on a service class of workers typically racialised as non-white,[12] these analyses tend to turn on class-based power relations and issues such as poverty, social marginalisation and stigmatisation. As Laura Pulido (2000: 12) correctly points out, racism is here 'understood as a discrete act that may be spatially expressed' – in residential segregation, employment patterns and so on; however, 'it is not seen as a sociospatial relation' that is 'both constitutive of the city and produced by it'. In essence, race is treated as an individual mentality or as an exception from normality, rather than as a form of structural coercion that is built into capitalist structures and institutions. Ultimately, by reducing racism to a question of discriminatory employers, lenders and landlords, what is forsaken is an analysis of the ways in which the global city might function as a mechanism through which capital produces race as a socio-political category of distinction and discrimination in the first place. In what follows, I argue that the violence of neoliberal urbanism cannot be understood without a racial theory of capitalism. Drawing on Cedric Robinson and Aimé Césaire, I show that global cities are more than merely 'local' or 'regional' landscapes. Neoliberal modes of urban governance often build on practices of urban planning, slum administration and law-and-order policing experimented with in the (post)colonies. Studying these historical and evolving North – South connections should be of key concern to IR scholars as it sheds new light not only on the racial ordering of global cities, but also on the many afterlives of empire.

URBAN (DIS)ORDERS: GLOBAL CITIES AND THE PRODUCTION OF RACED SPACE

When Grenfell Tower was built in 1974, the surrounding area in Ladbroke Grove was known as one of the most degraded places in London. The harsh conditions of the piggeries in the 19th century, the slums of the 1930s and the race riots of 1958 had earned the area a notorious reputation (Whetlor, 1998). Populated by the poorest of the English working class and people of Irish, Jewish and Spanish descent, after 1948 and Empire Windrush, Ladbroke Grove also became home to the Afro-Caribbean immigrants excluded from living elsewhere, alongside a sizeable Moroccan community. While Grenfell quickly became known as the 'Moroccan Tower' – a result of its large number of Moroccan immigrant residents – it was, like the street that runs south of the building, originally named after Field Marshal Lord Grenfell, a senior British Army officer who served in various colonial campaigns in Africa, including the Zulu and Kaffir wars. A strange coincidence it might seem, but, as we shall see, it is deeply revealing of how racial and colonial logics continue to structure global cities like London.

To better understand how race, urban space and capital accumulation interlink, it is helpful to turn to the literature on racial capitalism. In *Black Marxism* from 1983, Cedric Robinson examines the centrality of race, enslavement and colonialism to capitalist formations. Stepping into what Walter Mignolo (2007) has described as Marxism's 'colonial fracture', the book argues that racial violence constitutes a permanent, rather than anterior, condition of capital accumulation.[13] What we typically describe as 'capitalism' has historically always been 'racial capitalism'. As Robinson (2000: 2) explains, since its inception, 'the development, organization and expansion of capitalist society pursued essentially racial directions'. Capitalism emerged – and continues to operate – through racial projects that assign differential value to human life and labour, such as chattel slavery, settler colonial dispossession, racialised indentured servitude and the exploitation of immigrant labour. There was never such a thing as capitalism without slavery, and 'the history of Manchester never happened without the history of Mississippi' (Johnson, 2016). In contrast to conventional Marxist thinking, racism thus forms a constituent logic of capitalism. The concepts of 'race' and 'class' are insufficient to capture this dynamic because the very categorisation assumes that capitalism is not already racialised. As Lisa Lowe (2015: 149–50) explains, 'Racial capitalism captures the sense that actually existing capitalism exploits through culturally and socially constructed differences such as race, gender, region and nationality and is lived through those uneven formations'. Capitalism relies upon the elaboration, reproduction and exploitation of racial difference: on the production of populations that are surplus, expandable and disposable. Capitalism is thus racial not merely because people racialised as non-white are disproportionately impacted and disadvantaged by the 'free' market, although this is true as well (Bassel and Emejulu, 2017). More fundamentally, race-making practices are intrinsic to processes of capital accumulation because racism supplies the precarious and exploitable lives that capitalism needs to extract land and labour. In Jodi Melamed's (2015: 77) formulation:

Capital can only be capital when it is accumulating, and it can only accumulate by producing and moving through relations of severe inequality among human groups – capitalists with the means of production/workers without the means of subsistence, creditors/debtors, conquerors of land made property/the dispossessed and removed. These antinomies of accumulation require loss, disposability, and the unequal differentiation of human value, and racism enshrines the inequalities that capitalism requires.

In other words, there can be no capitalism without racialisations, hence *racial* capitalism. Viewed from the perspective of racial capitalism, the global city is not a race-neutral space. As Sherene Razack (2002; see also Da Silva, 2001) has argued, space is never an empty, natural or innocent category, but always saturated with hierarchies and privileges. To focus on the urban dimensions of racial capitalism is therefore to examine how global cities produce some places and people as disposable and expendable. Consider, for example, how urban regeneration projects often come to be seen as just and necessary through a colonial mentality that conceives of some spaces as 'wastelands', as places of crime, drugs, disease, teenage pregnancy and broken families, prostitution, and pimps – that is, as raced spaces that are 'empty' and lacking in civilised inhabitants, and that therefore need to be 'regenerated, cleansed, and reinfused with [white] middle-class sensibility' (Smith, 2014: 316).[14] In the context of contemporary Britain, it is the high-rise tower block that best captures this image of 'blighted' urban space in need of regeneration and development by urban elites – in Los Angeles, it is the ghetto; in São Paulo, the favela; in Mumbai, the slum; in Paris, the banlieue; in Jakarta, the kampung; and in Cape Town, the township (Alves, 2018; Camp, 2012; Davis, 2007; Samara, 2011; Tilley et al., 2019). As Sarah Keenan (2017) explains, raced spaces such as these come to mean:

> poor, over-crowded, migrant, socially immobile, working class, racialised, ghetto; and its consequences are government and corporate containment and malicious neglect, particularly as these spaces of poverty become blights on a rapidly gentrifying landscape, bringing down property prices and getting in the way of 'regeneration.'

[To belong to such abandoned spaces] means having a materially lower than average standard of living and an identity that will not be listened to or taken seriously by those in power, even when – as the Grenfell Action Group blog shows us – it is a matter of life and death.

Such forms of organised abandonment often unfold alongside organised violence (Gilmore, 2015). Indeed, while neoliberalism is often associated with the withdrawal of the state through privatisation and deregulation, it also – as Stuart Hall and his co-authors (2013) argued in their classic *Policing the Crisis* – entails a roll-out of new forms of interventionism and social control. Aggressive policing in urban areas has been one of the main ways in which global cities foster urban regeneration. As Manissa Maharawal (2017: 349) explains, 'gentrification signifies not just the reinvestment of capital into urban spaces, but also the concomitant security forces which exert violence and spatial control upon poor racialized urban populations'. In New York, the gentrification of Harlem was partly made possible through the introduction of 'broken windows' policing, an escalation of the local war on drugs and the clearing out of 125th street by 400 police dressed in riot gear (Kelley, 2012; see also Cowen and Lewis, 2016; Smith, 2005). This intimate link between gentrification and police violence is not just a New York phenomenon, but can also be seen, as Neil Smith (2002: 442) documents, 'in the antisquatter campaigns in Amsterdam in the 1980s, attacks by Parisian police on homeless (largely immigrant) encampments, and the importation of New York's zero-tolerance techniques by police forces around the world'. In São Paolo, anti-black police terror has become a constant feature of urban regeneration; as Jamie Alves (2018: 1) shows in his ethnography of the Brazilian global city, 'spatial segregation, mass incarceration, and killings by the police are all constitutive dimensions of the reproduction of the urban order'.[15] In Cape Town, Tony Samara (2011) similarly documents how the police and criminal justice system operate to enforce development by 'pacifying' the black urban poor. Throughout the UK and US, 'broken windows' policing disproportionately targets the urban working class, in general, and the racialised urban poor, in particular: in the UK, stop-and-search policies are eight times more likely to target black people (Dodd, 2017); and in New York, 80% of those stopped are black or Hispanic (New York Civil Liberties Union, 2019). In all these cases, urban policing not only operates to enhance the desirability of gentrifying areas by 'cleaning up the streets' and creating 'safe' spaces for capital investment, urban redevelopment projects and middle-class consumer habits. Racialised policing also helps to justify revitalisation programmes and plans to displace actually existing inhabitants as it directly casts them as deviant, criminal and violent. The broken windows metaphor is thus particularly revealing because, as Jordan Camp (2012: 667) explains, 'broken windows are not repaired – they are replaced', in the same way that black, brown, Muslim and poor people are literally removed from gentrifying neighbourhoods. Like the deaths of so many other black and brown people at the hands of the police around the world, the extra-legal killing of Eric Garner in 2014 is symptomatic of this development. Slain on a Staten Island pavement by the New York Police Department (NYPD), Garner had been stopped and harassed for small-scale infractions (such as the sale of 'loosies', i.e., untaxed cigarettes) for several years. While it is his last words – 'I can't breathe' – that have become a rallying cry for protestors, his preceding words are perhaps more telling: 'Every time you see me, you want to mess with me. I'm tired of it' (Capelouto, 2014).

To summarise, how can a focus on racial capitalism help us better understand the Grenfell fire and, more generally, what does it bring to the literature on global cities, in IR and beyond? As we saw in the previous section, the global cities literature has largely overlooked the racial dynamics of neoliberal urban governance. While scholars such as Sassen have taken an interest in urban core – periphery relations, race is often treated as an effect of discriminatory landlords, lenders and employers rather than a constituent logic of capital. In contrast, I have argued that race-making practices are central to the governance and ordering of global cities. While gentrification, of course, looks different in different cities, it is typically underpinned by a set of racialised assumptions about who belongs in certain spaces and who does not. This racial logic ultimately helps explain why Grenfell residents' years of complaints about safety were ignored and why many residents have still to be properly rehoused more than two years after the fire (Mills, 2019).[16]

In the eyes of urban elites, Grenfell was disposable and expendable, 'a racially devalued, surplus place' (Pulido, 2016: 2) standing in the way of gentrification and urban regeneration schemes. To insist that race does not explain what made the fire possible because white people also lived there is thus to miss the point: as Laura Pulido (2016: 8, emphasis in original) has argued, places such as Grenfell come to be considered disposable 'by virtue of being *predominantly* poor and Black'. In what follows, I build on this analysis to argue that the racial ordering of the global city demands an engagement with colonial and imperial histories, because the production of raced urban space builds on technologies and techniques that have long been experimented with in the (post)colonies. Such a focus not only questions the 'newness' of neoliberal urbanism and the accompanying nostalgia for a return to the post-1945 welfare state. As we shall see, it also calls into question IR's standard language of Western 'homelands' and colonial frontiers, and thus challenges dominant narratives of what the global city is and represents.

GLOBAL CITIES, IMPERIAL TERRAINS

As smoke covered the London sky on the morning of 14 June 2017, the first Grenfell victim was identified: Mohammed al-Haj Ali, a 23-year-old Syrian refugee who had come to Britain with his brother in search of a better life. He survived the Syrian revolution, the bombing campaign by ISIS and the dangerous journey across the Mediterranean only to die three years later in a burning tower block in Central London. He was, as it later turned out, far from the only migrant from the global South who lived and died in Grenfell; on the night of the fire, the building was home to a large North African community. While the official death toll stands at 72, locals have continued to claim that it could be more than twice as high as some residents were undocumented migrants. Like Mohammed, they might have come from Syria – or, like so many other of the 1.1 million undocumented migrants in the UK, from Eritrea, Somalia, the Philippines, Sudan and Afghanistan.

Can Grenfell and this 'dark side' of the global city be understood through the same lens as the (post) colonial borderland from which Mohammed and his brother had fled? In his analysis of racial capitalism, Cedric Robinson insisted that such a combined perspective is both possible and necessary. Pointing to the coeval and dialectical relationship between local and global geographies, Robinson noted how the plantations of Mississippi and the factories of Manchester, rather than being separate systems, were differentiated and complementary parts of the *same* global economy. In *Discourse on Colonialism*, Aimé Césaire (2001) developed a similar argument. Offering the haunting metaphor of the 'boomerang', he noted how colonial violence – far from only happening 'out there', in the periphery, beyond the pale – sooner or later will make its way back to the 'veins of Europe', where it sets in like an 'infection' or 'poison'. The colonial project, Césaire reminds us, was never a 'constitutive outside', but a set of political technologies, rationales and institutions that sooner or later will return home like a 'terrific boomerang': one day the bourgeoisie will wake up to find 'the gestapos are busy, the prisons fill up, the torturers standing around the racks invent, refine, discuss' (Césaire, 2001: 36). In what follows, I build on these insights to argue that the global city operates through a racial *as well as* imperial political economy. In particular, by reading imperial metropoles and colonial peripheries as different but fundamentally interlinked spatialisations of racial capitalism, I argue that the global city's gentrifying and ghettoised areas are more than simply 'local' geographies: they constitute domestic spaces of empire that are intimately linked to the production of (post)colonial borderlands. Such a focus on co-constitution and entanglement stands in direct contrast to IR's static categories of borders, inside/outside and sovereignty, which typically treat the 'West' and the 'Rest' as separate containers. Subjecting these categories to theoretical challenge and critique, I examine the colonial dimensions of three areas that are central to neoliberal urbanism: gentrification, urban policing and accumulation by dispossession. Where IR scholars have predominantly focused their analysis of race and colonialism on North – South encounters (through war, development, humanitarianism, etc.), my argument thus reveals the importance of also examining the ways in which 'domestic' landscapes are shaped by empire. As the death of Mohammed al-Haj Ali and other migrants in Grenfell Tower reminds us, the global city's production of raced space is ultimately part of a wider cartography of imperial violence.

Gentrification

Urban regeneration offers a good starting point for unpacking the co-constitution of near and far peripheries under racial capitalism; after all, gentrification is sometimes described as a form of colonisation. Neil Smith, for example, has argued that urban renewal projects are informed by a colonial imaginary that draws on myths of the frontier, *terra nullius*, the 'Wild West' and pioneers. According to Smith (2005: 15), this imaginary 'provides the decorative utensils by which the city is reclaimed from wilderness and remapped for white upper-class settlers with global fantasies of again owning the world – recolonizing it from the neighborhood out'. Other scholars, such as Rowland Atkinson and Gary Bridge (2013: 52), have similarly described gentrification as a 'new urban colonialism':

> Those who come to occupy prestigious central city locations frequently have the characteristics of a colonial elite. They often live in exclusive residential enclaves and are supported by a domestic and local service class. Gentrifiers are employed in . . . 'new class' occupations, and are marked out by their cosmopolitanism. Indeed in many locations, especially in ex-communist European and Asian countries, they often are western ex-patriots employed by transnational corporations to open up the markets of the newly emerging economies.

While these authors correctly identify points of resemblance between gentrification and colonial forms of expansion, they problematically treat colonialism as little more than a metaphor. This overlooks that gentrification, more than just *resembling* previous forms of colonial and mercantile expansion, actually *builds* on distinctively colonial forms of urban housing policy and city planning. Modern forms of urban planning – including ideas of segregation, slum administration and urban renewal – were first experimented with in colonial cities before they were put into use in imperial metropoles. Colonial administrations frequently established separate living quarters for the colonised, who, it was feared, carried infectious disease and epidemic plague (Abu-Lughod, 2014; Jones, 2012; Legg, 2008; Nightingale, 2012). David Theo Goldberg (2013: 48) has shown how the 'sanitation syndrome' often:

caught hold of the colonial imagination as a general social metaphor for the pollution by blacks of urban space. Uncivilized Africans, it was claimed, suffered urbanization as a pathology of disorder and disgeneration of their traditional tribal life. To prevent their pollution contaminating European city dwellers and services, the idea of sanitation and public health was invoked first as the legal path to remove blacks to separate locales at the city limits, and then as the principle for sustaining segregation.

The colonial city thus came to be 'cut in two', as Fanon reminds us. Where the settler's town is 'strongly built' and 'brightly lit', the town that belongs to 'the colonized people, or at least the native town, the Negro village, the medina, the reservation', is 'a hungry town, starved of bread, of meat, of shoes, of coal, of light . . . [it is] a crouching village, a town on its knees, a town wallowing in the mire' (Fanon, 2001: 39).

In the 1950s and 1960s, the principle of racialised urban segregation found its way back to metropolitan centres in the West. As formal imperial rule crumbled and postcolonial subjects migrated to the motherland, the 'administration of racialized urban space in the West began to reflect the divided cityscapes produced by colonial urban planning' (Goldberg, 2013: 49).[17] The post-war period's massive urban renewal and public housing programmes thus came to draw on urban planning rationales developed in the colonies, including techniques of slum clearance and racial segregation. Framed as a question of public health – of disease, criminality, alcoholism, prostitution and other 'dangers' that might 'pollute' the white body politic – these regeneration projects followed their colonial predecessors in displacing the racial poor to the city limits, while simultaneously creating small and highly visibly racial slums, typified by the high-rise tower block.[18] As Goldberg (2013: 53) notes, this left the racial poor 'isolated within centre city space, enclosed within single entrance/exit elevator buildings, and carefully divided from respectably residential urban areas by highway, park, playing field, vacant lot or railway line'. It is ultimately within this imperial context that contemporary processes of urban regeneration and gentrification must be understood: not as processes that simply (and accidentally) mirror prior forms of colonial expansion, but as the continuation of distinctively colonial techniques for organising urban space. The process of realising urban development – in yesteryear's colonial city *as well as* in today's global city – often takes place through the creation of raced space. Consequently, and as Briana L. Urena-Ravelo (2017) has argued, gentrification might not be the 'new colonialism', as is sometimes argued; rather, 'it's just the old one'.

Urban policing

Like gentrification, the urban policing of black, brown, Muslim and other working-class communities builds on distinctively colonial models of pacification, militarisation and control. Colonial cities and peripheries have historically functioned as 'social laboratories' where new security strategies designed to 'pacify' urban geographies could be tested before they were shipped back to the metropole (Barder, 2015; Dixon, 2009; Kaplan, 2005; Khalili, 2010; Sinclair and Williams, 2007). For example: the French Empire regularly used Algeria as a testing ground for forms of population control that were later exported back to the colonial metropolis; the US relied on the Philippines to experiment with new forms of policing tactics; and Britain made use of its domestic colony, Ireland, and later Palestine, Malaya and Kenya. Foreign and homeland security operations have never been distinct and separate, but interlink through empire and racial capitalism. The escalation of aggressive and militarised policing in today's global cities follows this trajectory. Indeed, racialised policing practices such as community surveillance, preemptive stop-and-frisk policies and public order containment draw on techniques and technologies developed in colonial peripheries, and build on a long tradition of imperial exchange. Just as 19th-century colonial powers imported fingerprinting, panoptic prisons and other methods of surveillance and control, today, counterinsurgency technologies and techniques tested in Palestine and on the battlefields of Afghanistan and Iraq are being used in the global city to 'clean up the streets' and protect capital investment in gentrifying areas.[19] As Stephen Graham (2011: xviii) elaborates:

> Israeli drones designed to vertically subjugate and target Palestinians are now routinely deployed by police forces in North America, Europe and East Asia. Private operators of US 'supermax' prisons are heavily involved in running the global archipelago organizing incarceration and torture that has burgeoned since the start of the 'war on terror.' Private military corporations heavily colonise 'reconstruction' contracts in both Iraq and New Orleans. Israeli expertise in population control is regularly sought by those planning security operations for major summits and sporting events. . . . Even the 'shoot to kill' policies developed to confront risks of suicide bombing in Tel Aviv and Haifa have been adopted by police forces in Western cities (a process which directly led to the state killing of Jean Charles De Menezes by London anti-terrorist police on 22nd July 2005).

Like urban regeneration strategies, the link between counterinsurgency and urban policing techniques exceeds IR's standard language of territorial borders, inside/outside and Westphalian sovereignty. These typically depict colonial frontiers and Western 'homelands' as fundamentally separate domains. Yet, from the black American ghetto to the French banlieue and the Brazilian favela, security and military doctrines used to police and pacify 'unruly' urban landscapes are melding with those used in colonial borderlands. What Graham calls the 'new military urbanism' increasingly structures the global city and colonial borderlands, as seen in: the rapid expansion of policing and incarceration, gated communities, fortress suburbs, and detention centres; the proliferation of militarised borders alongside the world's North – South equator; and the growing 'security archipelago' (Amar, 2013) designed to protect the wealthy and powerful from those rendered surplus by the economic dislocations of racial capitalism.

Accumulation by dispossession

Gentrification and racialised urban policing both exemplify what Césaire described as the 'boomerang' effect of colonialism. The global city's role in this exchange has, importantly, been more than a passive and benign recipient. Cities such as London, New York, Frankfurt and Paris occupy a central position in what David Harvey (2003) has described as the 'new imperialism'. Since the

1970s, 'primitive' accumulation has escalated on a global scale, as can be seen in:

> the commodification and privatization of land and the forceful expulsion of peasant populations; the conversion of various forms of property rights (common, collective, state, etc.) into exclusive private property rights; the suppression of rights to the commons; the commodification of labour power and the suppression of alternative (indigenous) forms of production and consumption; [and] colonial, neo-colonial, and imperial processes of appropriation of assets (including natural resources).
>
> (Harvey, 2003: 159)

The prosperous cities of the Global North are crucial to this process of 'accumulation by dispossession'. Not only are they the main sites through which the 'new imperialism' inflicted on the South is financed and orchestrated, but global cities also depend on such neocolonial violence – on the appropriation of land and resources by multinational companies, alongside the exploitation of cheap labour – in order to sustain wealthy urban lifestyles. As Graham (2011: xxix) explains:

> the North's global cities often act as economic or ecological parasites, preying on the South, violently appropriating energy, water, land and mineral resources, relying on exploitative labour conditions in offshore manufacturing, driving damaging processes of climate change, and generating an often highly damaging flow of tourism and waste.

Since the 2003 invasion of Iraq, London and New York have provided the main financial and corporate power through which Western companies have appropriated Iraqi oil reserves. Similarly, global cities also provide the main site through which neocolonial land grabs in sub-Saharan Africa are engineered, at the same time as they benefit from the increased production of food and biofuels for cars that such large-scale land acquisitions are often used for (Graham, 2011: xxiii; see also Gillespie, 2016).

However, these processes are less novel than terms such as the 'new imperialism' might imply. As Paula Chakravartty and Denise Ferreira da Silva (2012: 368–9) have argued, Harvey's account of new forms of dispossession elides 'how neoliberal architectures and discourses of dispossession act on earlier forms of racial and colonial subjugation'. Like gentrification and law-and-order policing, the manner in which dispossession is carried out today cannot be understood outside the 'legacies of colonial expropriation' (Chakravartty and Da Silva, 2012: 369, 374). That is, 'accumulation by dispossession' is less a new stage in the history of capitalism than an intensification of the structural inequalities that have always been necessary for capital accumulation. Similarly, while it might be true that today's global cities function as 'the "brains" of the global war machine' (Graham, 2011: 133), this close relationship between cities and empire is hardly new: cities have arguably always funded, managed and profited from colonialism (Hunt, 2015). As nodes of colonial extraction, they have historically been, and arguably continue to operate as, places where racialized forms of dispossession and expropriation are orchestrated and reproduced – not just in the metropole, but also in the (post)colonies.

CONCLUSION

In this article, I have argued that the Grenfell fire alerts us to the racial structuring of neoliberal urban governance, and the need to draw on black, post/decolonial and indigenous scholarship to make sense of the global city and its place in the world. Where Marxist and liberal scholars point to the salience of neoliberalism in explaining the violence, inequalities and hierarchies that often accompany the 'making' of the global city, I have argued that global cities are part of a historical and ongoing imperial terrain. Although cities such as London, New York, Cape Town, Dubai, Shanghai and Rio de Janeiro have transformed themselves over the last few decades into glitzy centres of financial capital and real-estate speculation, the cost of this transformation has predominantly been carried by racialised 'surplus' people and places. Racialized forms of expropriation, dispossession and policing have made the global city 'cleaner', 'safer' and more amenable to capital investment and middle-class consumer habits. As Cedric Robinson's (2000) *Black Marxism* reminds us, this is not surprising: capitalism has historically operated through racial projects that differentiate between those associated with rights, wages and citizenship and those subject to super-exploitation and dispossession. Capitalism has *de facto* always been racial capitalism. The failure to account for this link between racial differentiation and capital accumulation has ultimately led IR scholars to overestimate the 'newness' of the global city. Notwithstanding the long list of declarations of novelty – of global cities as 'new actors' or indicators of a 'new international system'; of gentrification as a 'new urban colonialism' or 'new military urbanism' – many of the processes that sustain the 'renaissance' of global cities are strikingly un-novel. Strategies of urban regeneration, slum administration and racialised policing draw directly on techniques and technologies experimented with in the (post)colonies. For IR theorists interested in the changing relationship between the urban and the global, this has important implications. Looking through the lens of the global city, I have argued, does not in itself challenge established geographies of power, nor does it yield a radically different image of world politics. Proclaiming the advent of a new global era of cities and urbanising world politics requires accepting, at least to some extent, the previous hegemonic narrative – namely, that of the Westphalian system, with its territorially bounded nation-states in an anarchic realm. Escaping this 'territorial trap' necessitates an engagement with the distinctive ways in which both the global and the urban are structured by the political economy of race and empire. This means looking beyond IR's static categories of territorial borders, inside/outside and Westphalian sovereignty so as to recognise the co-constitution of the global and the local with the colonial. The fire that ripped through Grenfell Tower is, from this perspective, part of a much wider cartography of imperial and racial violence. More than a purely domestic problem of widening class inequality under neoliberalism, the makings of Grenfell were inherently global-colonial in character. Robin Kelley's (2015b) conclusions about Michael Brown – that he was 'collateral damage in a perpetual war whose colonial roots are still alive' – ultimately ring as true here, in North Kensington, as they do in Ferguson, the favelas of São Paulo, the townships of Cape Town, the kampungs of Jakarta and the banlieues of Paris.

ACKNOWLEDGEMENTS

Rahul Rao, Kerem Nisancioglu, Louiza Odysseos, Kirsten Ainley, Sabrina Axster, George Lawson, Keith Feldman, Evelyn Pauls, Will Rooke, Alvina Hoffmann and Kerry Goettlich all read and commented on earlier versions of this article. A special thanks to the editors, two anonymous peer reviewers and Adam Almakroudi.

FUNDING

The author(s) received no financial support for the research, authorship and/or publication of this article.

AUTHOR BIOGRAPHY

Ida Danewid is Lecturer in Gender and Global Political Economy at the University of Sussex, UK. Her work draws on anti-colonial and black radical thought to explore questions of internationalism and the politics of solidarity. She was previously a Visiting Scholar at University of California, Berkeley, and the Editor of *Millennium: Journal of International Studies.*

NOTES

1. The music video of the song is available at: www.youtube.com/watch?v=ztUamrChczQ
2. According to 2011 census data, just over half of the residents in the Grenfell postcode were born outside of England; only seven of the victims were white (Rice-Oxley, 2018; Shilliam, 2018: 170).
3. The deracialised critique of neoliberalism was a leitmotif in many leading British newspapers. Where the racial composition of Grenfell victims was noted, it was typically analysed in separation from the political economy and questions of neoliberal restructuring. For an exception, see Bhandar (2018) and Shilliam (2018). Importantly, the local community in North Kensington has argued from the beginning that race was central to the neoliberal makings of the fire.
4. Important feminist research has suggested that similar questions need to be asked about gender, the sexual and the intimate in urban

settings. For an excellent analysis of the role of heteronormativity and the 'proper' family in the making of Singapore as a 'world-class' city, see Oswin (2014).
5. I borrow this phrase from Davis (2004).
6. In this article, I approach race not as a pre-political, biological characteristic, but as a social construct brought into being by political, economic and colonial forces. Thus conceived, race is not reducible to skin colour (which is one of many possible markers of racism), but instead describes a relation of subordination drawn along the line of the human (Grosfoguel, 2004; Omi and Winant, 2014). For the purposes of this article, this definition is particularly useful as it helps us understand why processes of racialisation might not look exactly the same in London as they do in, say, São Paolo, Dubai, Jakarta and Nairobi.
7. North Kensington local Ish interviewed in the documentary *Failed By The State* (Redfish, 2017).
8. Tracy Shildrick (2018: 787) similarly argues that the Grenfell fire exposed some of the 'worst aspects of contemporary neoliberal capitalism, not just in terms of inequality and social housing, but also in the ways that profits can be put before people's lives and well-being and how cuts to public services such as the police and fire services, made in the name of austerity, can have deadly consequences'. For others, such as David Madden (2017: 2–3), Grenfell exemplifies the 'structural violence of urban life in neoliberal capitalist society'.
9. Some notable work examines these riots as protests against gentrification and rising inequality under neoliberal urbanism (see Angélil and Siress, 2012; Back and Gilroy, 2013; Briggs, 2012; Dikec, 2011). For a discussion of Black Lives Matter as a movement against gentrification, see Maharawal (2017).
10. In his opening statement, Imran Khan QC stated that: 'Our clients firmly believe that it is absolutely vital that the terms of reference are amended so that race, religion and social class are considered, because whilst there will be – and I accept rightly – focus on the construction and refurbishment of the tower which led to the fire, that will not be the full story. That will not explain why it was that these particular people – these particular people – were the ones that died and will not explain what led them to their death' (Siddique, 2018).
11. Similarly, out of the 19% of the urban population that live in poverty in the US, more than 60% are black or Latino (Wilson, 2009: 139).
12. Sassen (1993), in particular, has emphasised that global cities depend on the existence of a service class of workers such as taxi drivers, private nannies, cleaners and so on. Nonetheless, while she recognises that this army of workers is typically racialised as non-white, she refrains from a more thorough analysis of how racial differentiation might be fundamental to processes of capital accumulation and urban regeneration.
13. Anthony Bogues has described this as a black radical heretical practice through which black radicals sought to expose Marxism's incompleteness when it came to the non-white and colonial world. As Bogues (2015: 13) explains, black heretics entailed 'a double operation – an engagement with Western radical theory and then a critique of this theory'.
14. In fact, and as Glen Coulthard (2014: 175) has argued, 'gentrifiers often defend their projects as a form of improvement, where previously "wasted" land and lives are made more socially and economically productive'.
15. As Alves (2018) explains, the most conservative statistics suggest that between 1999 and 2014, 10,152 people were killed by the military police in the state of São Paolo; at least 50% of these deaths occurred in the metropolitan region of São Paolo.
16. Many of the residents that have been rehoused have been moved to new homes far from the area in North Kensington where they previously lived, lending further weight to critiques of social cleansing.
17. Sherene Razack (2002: 129) has similarly documented how the end of the colonial era combined with 1950s' and 1960s' urbanisation policies of segregation to replicate the spatial zones produced by colonisation, whereby 'slum administration replaces colonial administration'.
18. For a comparison between post-war regeneration and contemporary gentrification, see Jones (2008). On the afterlives of colonial architecture, see Kusno (2010).

19. For an analysis of how counterinsurgency methods are routinely deployed to police racialised populations in global cities, see Abourahme (2018), Camp and Heatherton (2016), Graham (2011) and Neocleous and Kastrinou (2016).

REFERENCES

Abourahme N (2018) Of monsters and boomerangs: Colonial returns in the late liberal city. *City* 22(1): 106–115.

Abu-Lughod J (2014) *Rabat: Urban Apartheid in Morocco*. Princeton, NJ: Princeton University Press.

Acuto M (2010) Global cities: Gorillas in our midst. *Alternatives* 35(4): 425–448.

Acuto M (2013) *Global Cities, Governance and Diplomacy: The Urban Link*. London: Routledge.

Alawadi K (2014) Urban redevelopment trauma: The story of a Dubai neighbourhood. *Built Environment* 40(3): 357–375.

Alves JA (2014) From necropolis to blackpolis: Necropolitical governance and black spatial praxis in São Paulo, Brazil. *Antipode* 46(2): 323–339.

Alves JA (2018) *The Anti-Black City: Police Terror and Black Urban Life in Brazil*. Minneapolis, MN: University of Minnesota Press.

Amar P (2013) *The Security Archipelago: Human-Security States, Sexuality Politics, and the End of Neoliberalism*. Durham and London: Duke University Press.

Ancien D (2011) Global city theory and the new urban politics twenty years on. *Urban Studies* 8(12): 2473–2493.

Angélil M and Siress C (2012) The paris 'Banlieue': Peripheries of inequity. *Journal of International Affairs* 65(2): 57–67.

Anievas A, Manchanda N and Shilliam R (2014) *Race and Racism in International Relations: Confronting the Global Colour Line*. London: Routledge.

Arabia T (2017) Disaster at arm's length: An interview with Richard Seymore. *The Jacobin*. Available at: www.jacobinmag.com/2017/06/grenfell-tower-fire-kensington-tories-labour-jeremy-corbyn (accessed 10 February 2019).

Atkinson R and Bridge G (2004) *Gentrification in a Global Context*. London: Routledge.

Atkinson R and Bridge G (2013) Globalisation and the new urban colonialism. In: Brown-Saracino J (ed.) *The Gentrification Debates: A Reader*. London: Routledge.

Back L and Gilroy P (2013) Husby and territorial stigma in Sweden. *OpenDemocracy*. Available at: www.opendemocracy.net/les-back-paul-gilroy-others-see-below/husby-and-territorial-stigma-in-sweden (accessed 8 February 2019).

Barder A (2015) *Empire Within: International Hierarchy and Its Imperial Laboratories of Governance*. London: Routledge.

Bassel L and Emejulu A (2017) *Minority Women and Austerity: Survival and Resistance in France and Britain*. Bristol: The Policy Press.

Bhandar B (2018) Organised state abandonment: The meaning of Grenfell. *Critical Legal Thinking*. Available at: http://criticallegalthinking.com/2018/09/21/organised-state-abandonment-the-–-meaning-of-grenfell/ (accessed 28 September 2018).

Binnie J, Holloway J, Young C et al. (eds) (2006) *Cosmopolitan Urbanism*. London: Routledge.

Bogues A (2015) *Black Heretics, Black Prophets: Radical Political Intellectuals*. London: Routledge.

Booth R (2018) Hundreds of thousands living in squalid rented homes in England. *The Guardian*. Available at: www.theguardian.com/society/2018/jan/28/hundreds-of-thousands-living-in-squalid-rented-homes-in-england (accessed 19 February 2018).

Briggs D (2012) *The English Riots of 2011: A Summer of Discontent*. Hampshire: Waterside Press.

Brooker N (2017) 'Big capital' by Anna Minton – who broke London's property market? *Financial Times*. Available at: www.ft.com/content/82a1af1c-46cc-11e7-8d27-59b4dd6296b8 (accessed 19 February 2018).

Camp JT (2012) Blues geographies and the security turn: Interpreting the housing crisis in Los Angeles. *American Quarterly* 64(3): 543–570.

Camp JT and Heatherton C (2016) *Policing the Planet: Why the Policing Crisis Led to Black Lives Matter*. London and New York, NY: Verso Books.

Capelouto S (2014) Eric Garner: The haunting last words of a dying man. *CNN*. Available at: https://edition.cnn.com/2014/12/04/us/garner-last-words/index.html (accessed 12 February 2019).

Carrozza I, Danewid I and Pauls E (eds) (2017) Racialized realities in world politics. *Millennium: Journal of International Studies* 45(3): 267–510.

Castells M (2001) *The Internet Galaxy: Reflections on the Internet, Business, and Society*. Oxford: Oxford University Press.

Césaire A (2001) *Discourse on Colonialism*. New York, NY: NYU Press.

Chakravartty P and Da Silva DF (2012) Accumulation, dispossession, and debt: The racial logic of global capitalism – An introduction. *American Quarterly* 64(3): 361–385.

Coulthard G (2014) *Red Skin, White Masks: Rejecting the Colonial Politics of Recognition*. Minneapolis, MN: University of Minnesota Press.

Cowen D and Lewis N (2016) Anti-blackness and urban geopolitical economy. *Society and Space*. Available at: http://societyandspace.org/2016/08/02/anti-blackness-and-urban-geopolitical-economy-deborah-cowen-and-nemoy-lewis/ (accessed 1 October 2018).

Curtis S (2011) Global cities and the transformation of the international system. *Review of International Studies* 37(4): 1923–1947.

Curtis S (2016) *Global Cities and Global Order*. Oxford: Oxford University Press.

Da Silva DF (2001) Towards a critique of the socio-logos of justice: The analytics of raciality and the production of universality. *Social Identities* 7(3): 421–454.

Davis M (2004) The urbanization of empire: Megacities and the laws of chaos. *Social Text* 22(4): 9–15.

Davis M (2007) *Planet of Slums*. London and New York, NY: Verso.

Dikec M (2011) *Badlands of the Republic: Space, Politics and Urban Policy*. Oxford: Wiley & Sons.

Dixon P (2009) 'Hearts and minds'? British counter-insurgency from Malaya to Iraq. *Journal of Strategic Studies* 32(3): 353–381.

Dodd V (2017) Stop and search eight times more likely to target black people. *The Guardian*. Available at: www.theguardian.com/law/2017/oct/26/stop-and-search-eight-times-more-likely-to-target-black-people (accessed 19 February 2018).

Dorling D (2011) Unique Britain. *OpenDemocracy*. Available at: www.opendemocracy.net/shinealight/danny-dorling/unique-britain (accessed 19 February 2018).

Easterling K (2014) *Extrastatecraft: The Power of Infrastructure Space*. London and New York, NY: Verso Books.

El-Enany N (2017) The colonial logic of Grenfell. *Verso Blog*. Available at: www.verso-books.com/blogs/3306-the-colonial-logic-of-grenfell (accessed 30 July 2019).

Erlanger S (2017) After Grenfell Tower fire, U.K. asks: Has deregulation gone too far? *The New York Times*. Available at: www.nytimes.com/2017/06/28/world/europe/uk-grenfell-tower-fire-deregulation.html (accessed 19 February 2018).

Fanon F (2001) *The Wretched of the Earth*. London: Penguin.

Florida R (2005) *The Rise of the Creative Class: And How It's Transforming Work, Leisure, Community, and Everyday Life*. London: Harper.

Franck A (2019) The 'street politics' of migrant il/legality: Navigating Malaysia's urban borderscape. *Asia Pacific Viewpoint* 60(1): 14–23.

Ghertner DA (2014) India's urban revolution: Geographies of displacement beyond gentrification. *Environment and Planning A* 46: 1554–1571.

Gillespie T (2016) Accumulation by urban dispossession: Struggles over urban space in Accra, Ghana. *Transactions of the Institute of British Geographers* 41(1): 66–77.

Gilmore RW (2007) *Golden Gulag: Prisons, Surplus, Crisis, and Opposition in Globalizing California*. Berkeley and Los Angeles, CA: University of California Press.

Gilmore RW (2015) Organized abandonment and organized violence: Devolution and the police. *UC Santa Cruz*, 9 November. Available at: https://vimeo.com/146450686 (accessed 18 October 2018).

Goldberg DT (2013) 'Polluting the body politic': Racist discourse and urban location. In: Cross M and Keith M (eds) *Racism, the City and the State*. London: Routledge.

Goldstein A (2017) On the reproduction of race, capitalism, and settler colonialism. In: Davis W (ed.) *Race and Capitalism: Global Territories, Transnational Histories*. Los Angeles: University of California, 20 October 2017, pp. 42–51. Available at: http://criticallegal-thinking.com/2018/09/21/organised-state-abandonment-the-meaning-of-grenfell/

Graham S (2011) *Cities Under Siege: The New Military Urbanism*. London and New York, NY: Verso Books.

Grenfell Action Group (2016) KCTMO – Playing with fire! Available at: https://grenfellaction-group.wordpress.com/2016/11/20/kctmo-playing-with-fire/ (accessed 10 September 2018).

Grenfell Tower Inquiry (2017) About. Available at: www.grenfelltowerinquiry.org.uk/about (accessed 10 September 2018).

Griffin A (2017) Grenfell Tower cladding that may have led to fire was chosen to improve appearance of Kensington block of flats. *The Independent*. Available at: www.independent.co.uk/news/uk/home-news/grenfell-tower-cladding-fire-cause-improve-kensington-block-flats-appearance-blaze-24-storey-west-a7789951.html (accessed 1 March 2018).

Grosfoguel R (2004) Race and ethnicity or racialized ethnicities? Identities within global coloniality. *Ethnicities* 4(3): 315–336.

Gulliver K (2016) *Forty Years of Struggle: A Window on Race and Housing, Disadvantage and Exclusion*. Birmingham: Human City Institute.

Hall S, Critcher C, Jefferson T, et al. (2013) *Policing the Crisis: Mugging, the State and Law and Order*. London: Red Globe Press.

Harvey D (2003) *The New Imperialism*. Oxford: Oxford University Press.

Hazan E (2010) Faces of Paris. *New Left Review* 62: 31–44.

Hunt T (2015) *Ten Cities that Made an Empire*. London: Penguin.

Johnson GT and Lubin A (2017) *Futures of Black Radicalism*. London and New York, NY: Verso Books.

Johnson KS (2014) 'Black' suburbanization: American dream or the new banlieue? *Social Science Research Council Cities Papers*. Available at: http://citiespapers.ssrc.org/black-suburbanization-american-dream-or-the-new-banlieue/ (accessed 10 February 2019).

Johnson W (2016) To remake the world: Slavery, racial capitalism, and justice. *Boston Review*. Available at: https://bostonreview.net/race/walter-johnson-slavery-human-rights-racial-capitalism (accessed 22 June 2017).

Jones BG (2012) Civilising African cities: International housing and urban policy from colonial to neoliberal times. *Journal of Intervention and Statebuilding* 6(1): 23–40. https://doi.org/10.1080/17502977.2012.655560

Jones P (2008) Different but the same? Post-war slum clearance and contemporary regeneration in Birmingham, UK. *City* 12(3): 356–371.

Kangas A (2017) Global cities, international relations and the fabrication of the world. *Global Society* 31(4): 531–550.

Kaplan A (2005) *The Anarchy of Empire in the Making of U.S. Culture*. Cambridge, MA: Harvard University Press.

Keenan S (2017) A border in every street. *The Disorder of Things*. Available at: https://thedisorderofthings.com/2017/06/29/a-border-in-every-street/ (accessed 1 October 2018).

Kelley RDG (2012) Disappearing acts: Harlem in transition. In: Hammett J and Hammett K (eds) *The Suburbanization of New York: Is the World's Greatest City Becoming Just Another Town?* San Francisco, CA: Chronicle Books.

Kelley RDG (2015a) *Hammer and Hoe: Alabama Communists during the Great Depression*. Chapel Hill, NC: The University of North Carolina Press.

Kelley RDG (2015b) Mike Brown's body: Meditations on war, race and democracy. *Princeton University*, 13 April. Available at: www.youtube.com/watch?v=RP8FP8qjKgc (accessed 10 October 2018).

Khalili L (2010) The location of Palestine in global counterinsurgencies. *International Journal of Middle Eastern Studies* 42(3): 413–433.

Kirkpatrick D, Hakim D and Glanz J (2017) Why Grenfell Tower burned: Regulators put cost before safety. *The New York Times*. Available at: www.nytimes.com/2017/06/24/world/europe/grenfell-tower-london-fire.html (accessed 10 October 2018).

Kusno A (2010) *The Appearances of Memory: Mnemonic Practices of Architecture and Urban Form in Indonesia*. Durham: Duke University Press.

Legg S (2008) *Spaces of Colonialism: Delhi's Urban Governmentalities*. London: John Wiley & Sons.

Ljungkvist K (2015) *The Global City 2.0: From Strategic Site to Global Actor*. London: Routledge.

Lees, L, Bang Shin H and Lopez-Morales E (2015) *Global Gentrifications: Uneven Development and Displacement*. Bristol: The Policy Press.

Lowe L (2015) *The Intimacies of Four Continents*. Durham: Duke University Press.

MacLeod G (2018) The Grenfell Tower atrocity. *City* 22(4): 460–489.

Madden DJ (2017) Editorial: A catastrophic event. *City* 21(1): 1–5.

Maharawal MM (2017) Black Lives Matter, gentrification and the security state in the San Francisco Bay area. *Anthropological Theory* 17(3): 338–364.

McRobbie A (2017) Fire in neo-liberal London. *OpenDemocracy*. Available at: www.open-democracy.net/en/transformation/fire-in-neo-liberal-london/ (accessed 10 October 2018).

Melamed J (2015) Racial capitalism. *Critical Ethnic Studies* 1(1): 76–85.

Mignolo WD (2007) Delinking. *Cultural Studies* 21(2/3): 449–514.

Mills J (2019) Grenfell victims still living in temporary accommodation two years later. *Metro*. Available at: https://metro.co.uk/2019/04/09/grenfell-victims-still-living-temporary-accommodation-two-years-later-9141649/ (accessed 29 April 2019).

Neocleous M and Kastrinou M (2016) The EU hotspot: Police war against the migrant. *Radical Philosophy* 200: 3–9.

New York Civil Liberties Union (2019) Stop-and-frisk in the de Blasio era. Available at: www.nyclu.org/sites/default/files/field_documents/20190314_nyclu_stopfrisk_singles.pdf (accessed 29 April 2019).

Nightingale CH (2012) *Segregation: A Global History of Divided Cities*. Chicago, IL: University of Chicago Press.

Omi M and Winant H (2014) *Racial Formation in the United States*. London: Routledge.

Oswin N (2014) Queer time in global city Singapore: Neoliberal futures and the 'freedom to love'. *Sexualities* 17(4): 412–433.

Poon A (2009) Pick and mix for a global city: Race and cosmopolitanism in Singapore. In: Goh DPS, Gabrielpillai M, Holden P et al. (eds) *Race and Multiculturalism in Malaysia and Singapore*. London: Routledge.

Pulido L (2000) Rethinking environmental racism: White privilege and urban development in Southern California. *Annals of the Association of American Geographers* 90(1): 12–40.

Pulido L (2016) Flint, environmental racism, and racial capitalism. *Capitalism Nature Socialism* 27(3): 1–16.

Razack S (2002) When place becomes race. In: Razack S (ed.) *Race, Space, and the Law: Unmapping a White Settler Society*. Toronto: Between The Lines.

Renwick D and Ish (2017) *Failed by the State: The Struggle in the Shadow of Grenfell* (Part 1) (Documentary). Berlin: Redfish.

Rice-Oxley M (2018) Grenfell: The 72 victims, their lives, loves and losses. *The Guardian*. Available at: www.theguardian.com/uk-news/2018/may/14/grenfell-the-71-victims-their-lives-loves-and-losses (accessed 15 May 2018).

Robinson C (2000) *Black Marxism: The Making of the Black Radical Tradition*. Chapel Hill, NC: University of North Carolina Press.

Sabaratnam M (2017) *Decolonising Intervention: International Statebuilding in Mozambique*. London: Rowman & Littlefield International.

Samara TR (2011) *Cape Town After Apartheid: Crime and Governance in the Divided City*. Minneapolis, MN: University of Minnesota Press.

Sandercock L and Lyssiotis P (2003) *Cosmopolis II: Mongrel Cities of the 21st Century*. London: A&C Black.

Sassen S (1993) Rebuilding the global city: Economy, ethnicity, and space. *Social Justice* 20(3/4): 32–50.

Sassen S (2013) *The Global City: New York, London, Tokyo*. Princeton, NJ: Princeton University Press.

Shildrick T (2018) Lessons from Grenfell: Poverty propaganda, stigma and class power. *The Sociological Review* 66(4): 783–798.

Shilliam R (2015) *The Black Pacific: Anti-Colonial Struggles and Oceanic Connections*. London: Bloomsbury Publishing.

Shilliam R (2018) *Race and the Undeserving Poor: From Abolition to Brexit*. Newcastle: Agenda Publishing.

Siddique H (2018) Grenfell Tower: Inquiry fails to consider 'institutional racism', says victim's QC – as it happened. *The Guardian*. Available at: www.theguardian.com/uk-news/live/2018/jun/05/grenfell-inquiry-survivors-opening-statements-begin-live-updates (accessed 10 October 2018).

Sinclair DG and Williams DCA (2007) 'Home and away': The cross-fertilisation between 'colonial' and 'British' policing, 1921–85. *Journal of Imperial and Commonwealth History* 35(2): 221–238.

Slater T (2009) Missing Marcuse: On gentrification and displacement. *City* 13(2/3): 292–311.

Smith N (2002) New globalism, new urbanism: Gentrification as global urban strategy. *Antipode* 34(3): 427–450.

Smith N (2005) *The New Urban Frontier: Gentrification and the Revanchist City*. London: Routledge.

Smith N (2014) Class struggle on Avenue B: The Lower East Side as Wild Wild West. In: Gieseking J, Mangold W, Katz C et al. (eds) *The People, Place, and Space Reader*. London: Routledge

Tilley L, Elias J and Rethel L (eds) (2019) The production and contestation of exemplary centres in Southeast Asia. *Asia Pacific Viewpoint* 60(1): 7–13.

Tucker P (2017) The Grenfell Tower fire was the end result of a disdainful housing policy. *The Guardian*. Available at: www.theguardian.com/commentisfree/2017/jun/20/grenfell-fire-housing-policy-social-housing-tenants (accessed 10 October 2018).

Turner J (2017) Internal colonisation: The intimate circulations of empire, race and liberal government. *European Journal of International Relations* 24(4): 765–790.

Urban Displacement Project (2015) Executive summary. Available at: www.urbandisplacement.org/sites/default/files/images/urban_displacement_project_-_executive_summary.pdf (accessed 8 October 2018).

Urena-Ravelo BL (2017) It's true, gentrification isn't the new colonialism, it's just the old one. *Medium*. Available at: https://medium.com/@AfroResistencia/its-true-gentrification-isn-t-the-new-colonialism-it-s-just-the-old-one-daf7e97a86f0 (accessed 1 October 2018).

Vitalis R (2015) *White World Order, Black Power Politics: The Birth of American International Relations, The United States in the World*. Ithaca, NY: Cornell University Press.

Whetlor S (1998) *Story of Notting Dale: From Potteries and Piggeries to Present Times*. London: Kensington & Chelsea Community History Group.

Williamson C (2017) This is how neoliberalism, led by Thatcher and Blair, is to blame for the Grenfell Tower disaster. *The Independent*. Available at: www.independent.co.uk/voices/grenfell-tower-inquiry-deregulation-thatcher-tony-blair-fire-service-cuts-a7876346.html (accessed 8 October 2018).

Wilson D (2009) Introduction: Racialized poverty in U.S. cities: Toward a refined racial economy perspective. *The Professional Geographer* 61(2): 139–149.

8
In debt to the rent gap
Gentrification generalized and the frontier of the future

Hamish Kallin

> What is expropriated by credit/debt is not only wealth, knowledge, and the "future," but more fundamentally the possible.
>
> (Maurizio Lazzarato, 2015, p. 23)

CHOOSE LIFE, CHOOSE DEBT

In late 2014, a large billboard appeared on the northern side of Niddrie Mains Road in Edinburgh, an artery for traffic that cuts through one of the historically most deprived neighborhoods on the south-west side of the city. Black silhouettes appeared to have waltzed their way out of an iPod commercial, frozen in the embellished poses of an idealized everyday life – cycling, jogging, walking the dog – and contrasted against a neon rainbow in whose center shone a single word: CHOICE. In situ, it stood zealously like a signpost to the good life, framed against grassy fields once home to the city's oldest municipal housing estate and now awaiting redevelopment.

CHOICE was symptomatic of how duplicitous the word *affordable* has become in contemporary housing policy across the UK.[1] Alongside a number of units available at "Mid-Market Rent" (a misleading name, for these rents are pegged at 80% of market rent), prospective residents were offered the option of "buying" a property using a range of shared equity schemes (some backed up by the Scottish government, others by the developer themselves). The third party takes on a portion of the total debt, enabling prospective buyers to reach beyond the maximum price-point enabled by their own mortgage-capacity by as much as 40%. Whilst the lending mechanics are different, the overall function is much like the UK-wide Help to Buy policy, which serves to indirectly subsidize (through state-backed debt) the sales of volume house builders, whilst enabling housing costs to rise. Such schemes are symptomatic of how the older ideal of *making housing more affordable* has given way to what is in effect its opposite: *making residents able to afford housing*, in most instances through debt. The two strategies are at odds with each other, for even though the latter is presented as the historical continuation of the former, it creates multiple new opportunities to extract profit from the cost of living. In this way, housing policies that are dressed in the veil of egalitarianism are essentially parasitic at the same time, creating a stream of rent-based profit extraction through debt. Shortly after the first phase was finished, the developer was able to offer "ownership" in exchange for a deposit of just 5%, promising that "buyers could be moving in for an initial outlay of just £4,080" (Cruden Homes, 2014). In a neighborhood once entirely made up of public housing, the name and marketing for this development played off a series of clichés around consumer sovereignty, undermined by the fact that (of course) the one *choice* missing was for a council home. These debts were offered up as gifts, keys to ontological security forged from financial liquidity. In a city where almost 25,000 people languish on the waiting list for a genuinely affordable home (Shelter, 2016), these gifts were well received.

At first blush, a development like CHOICE does not fit into the notion of gentrification at all. It was a popular scheme, and the homes sold out quickly. There is no doubt that it enabled some people to move into the area who would otherwise have been financially excluded. It brings "homeownership" into reach for people who would be unable to afford a mortgage without additional support. By certain measures, it is therefore a success. To suggest it forms part of a "gentrification" strategy would seem to blur the concept into complete meaninglessness. But, I want to suggest, it also shows us how prescient Smith's (2002) argument around the generalization of gentrification has become, for here even the "affordable" housing relied on rising land values, higher house prices, and the closure of a rent gap. In replacing council tenants with a new cohort of aspiring "homeowners," it completes a drawn-out process of displacement by explicitly marketing an aspirational vision of *becoming* middle class. There are similarities here with Paton's (2018, p. 5) work in Glasgow, on the ways in which working class residents are invited to participate in gentrification, "frequently borne out of the restriction of choice (meanwhile maintaining the seeming illusion of greater choice)." What is clear, however, is that the role of "gentrifier" in this situation is not defined by the fact that these individuals are richer than those they indirectly displaced (even though, broadly speaking, this appears to be true). For it is not their *wealth* that makes this development profitable (and therefore possible), but their *debt*.

Smith's (2002) work on gentrification generalized never mentioned debt, but it should have done. He hinted at this when he noted that the "generalization of gentrification is in part its *democratization*" (Smith, 2006, p. 199, emphasis added), but he neglected to mention that if that "democratization" occurs through increased debt, it is therefore profoundly undemocratic. Across the OECD (2018), the last decade has been overshadowed by unprecedented wage stagnation. Macroeconomic trends demonstrate the exact *opposite* of a democratization of wealth (Piketty, 2014). This same period has seen the supposedly endless proliferation of "middle class" landscapes, lifestyles, and gentrification-like processes in a huge range of contexts where the rent gap is being mercilessly opened and closed again and again. How is this disjunction possible, in social and political terms as well as economically? The answer, of course, is through the availability of credit. The possibility of gentrification becoming truly *generalized* (Smith, 2002) relies on the generalization of indebtedness. The supply of potential "gentrifiers" – those who occupy housing substantially more expensive than their predecessors, whether they want to or not – becomes as limitless as the supply of potential debtors.

To a certain degree, this much is already well documented: the growing pool of literature on financialization has become a staple in accounts of contemporary gentrification (Marcuse & Madden, 2016). It is widely acknowledged that changes to the way that mortgages are packaged, traded and regulated has instituted a kind of turbo-charged (or "super") gentrification across the Global North, pushing the process further and faster, leveraged by the newfound profitability of debt (Lees et al., 2008). The growing field of literature on financialization is adept at explaining this shift in macro-economic terms (Ryan-Collins et al., 2017), whilst the older strain of Marxist geographies on the spatio-temporal fix is adept at explaining *why* there might be a generalized shift of capital into the future and into space (Harvey, 1982). Both approaches are essential, but I believe that they miss something fundamental about the ways in which housing debt becomes politically effective. For debt is never purely an economic relation. It is also always a power relation, manifest in ways at once social, cultural, and psychological (Dienst, 2011; Graeber, 2012; Joseph, 2014; Lazzarato, 2012; Di Muzio & Robbins, 2016).

In this paper, I offer a theoretical reflection on the ways in which debt should change the way we think of gentrification, both as a concept to be explained and a process to be resisted. I advance three interconnected arguments. First, that the availability of credit "liberates" potential land values from social constraints; second, that this institutes the "property mind" as a coercive common sense; third, that this exacerbates class divisions whilst obscuring them. I frame this by returning to the importance of the rent gap model as a way of seeing the connection between debt and gentrification that highlights the wider processes of speculation and accumulation underpinning that relationship, but also the social, cultural, and political power that is *always* necessary to uphold those relations.

The rent gap has had its fair share of criticism lately. It is, we are told, too reductive, and "necessarily leaves aside institutional, social, cultural and political factors" (Bernt, 2016, p. 641). Such accusations are, as I hope to show, absurd (for when has profit ever been made outside of an institutional, social, cultural, and political context?), and a discussion of debt makes this especially clear. Attending to the debt question reasserts the vitality of the rent gap, for it recalls what is at stake in the mutually reinforcing spiral of rising land values and rising debt: not only the future of "gentrification" as a concept, nor "just" the totality of urban space, but every minute of indebted labor for decades and decades to come. This concerns the seeds of the next financial crisis and all the misery it will cause, whilst instituting a trajectory toward perpetual economic growth with truly terrifying ecological implications. All the while, individual dreams of autonomy, security, comfort, and pride are allowed to blossom (for some, for a while). You may call that hyperbole: I hope you are right.

Those caricatures of reductionism that paint the rent gap as a blunt economic vision may contain some unwitting truth however, only relating to the *phenomenon that the rent gap seeks to describe*, and not the model itself. The mechanisms that fuel the ever-rising "potential" value of land and enable (some) people to still live on that land whilst their wages stagnate *are* abstract and *do* subsume everyday life, space and labor under the matrix of capital accumulation. As Joseph (2014) argues, understanding the role of debt and finance in contemporary capitalism requires an engagement with abstractions, and therefore thinking in the abstract. If the value of debt is an abstraction, it is however an abstraction built upon dreams and policy, forged through a coercive common sense, and realized through labor-time. In other words, the rent gap model is not "economistic," in the sense that that is all it is, and yet it *has to be* "economistic" to a certain extent, for the phenomenon it seeks to describe is. Moreover, losing sight of this – bickering over the economistic tendency of the *model* and not the reality it describes – loses sight of the fundamental purpose of the model, which is to inspire us to *change* the reality it describes.

LIBERATING POTENTIAL

The relationship between average house prices (measured in ratio to income) and the amount of mortgage debt outstanding in the UK is umbilical (Ryan-Collins et al., 2017). The two have risen in tandem, reliant on each other. It is worth repeating the figures on rising indebtedness, for they remain striking. In 1994, total household debt levels stood at around £420 billion, of which just over 95% was tied into property. By 2001, that total came to around £730 billion, of which around 85% was tied into property. "From that point," to quote Horsley (2015, p. 31), "rather than describe the figures, it is easier to just add another £100 billion every year until 2007," at which point the collective debt of the British people overshadowed the entire annual output of the British economy for the first time. When the financial crisis hit later that year, the average income-to-debt ratio across the UK was about 160% (Bunn & Rostom, 2014, p. 305), a trend mirrored (and, indeed, magnified) across Europe and much of the Global North (Garciá-Lamarca & Kaika, 2016; Walks, 2013). These figures declined slightly in the years immediately after the last financial crash, but then began to rise once more (Bank of England, 2016). The Office for Budget Responsibility expects household debt-to-income levels across the UK to continue the slow climb back to pre-2007 levels, reaching 153% by 2022, of which almost 80% will be mortgage debt (Harari, 2018).

In the years running up to the last financial crisis, new techniques of financialization had fundamentally (and very profitably) broken the relation between wages and house prices (Rolnik, 2019). As Fitzpatrick and McQuinn (2007, p. 100) point out from Ireland, this was possible because there was a "mutually reinforcing long-run relationship" between debt levels and house prices, or, as Christophers (2019, p. 9) puts it regarding the UK, a "mutually reinforcing cycle." In short, the growth in house prices over recent decades has been underwritten by a growing tide of household debt. Individuals caught in this cycle may take on debt to afford more expensive housing, but this works just as well the other way around, where houses are more expensive because individuals take on more debt. To hold this "swivel" in view is politically important: considered as a technique of power, the debt relation changes our definition of the possible. If it were not for debt, houses would *have to be* cheaper. An alternative vision is found in the final pages of Clifford Simak's (1952) novel *City*, where the entire world is covered in houses that nobody lives in.[2]

The proliferation of gentrification in the cities of the Global North has "evolved within a broader affordability crisis of debt-leveraged financialization" (Wyly et al., 2010, p. 2602). The two processes are closely linked and increasingly reliant on each other. Without the availability of credit, gentrification would have remained a "narrow and quixotic oddity in the housing market" (Smith, 1996, p. 39); without the spiraling frenzy of housing costs, we would never have borrowed so much. Bearing in mind that around 81% of house price increases since 1950 can be explained by rising land prices (Knoll et al., 2017), attending to this relationship shows how fundamentally the rent gap – in a UK context at least – is opened *and* closed by the availability and newfound profitability of debt. In this way, those who own or invest in land can conceive and continuously reconceive of its "highest and best use" unhindered by the stagnating incomes of those who are expected to populate and use that space. As both an exchange-value and an imagined ideal, *potential* is liberated.

Realizing that potential is still fraught with difficulty. The promised "liberation" is therefore always incomplete and always uneven. The trajectory of the housing debt/price cycle looks at first glance to only go "up" – higher prices, more debt, *ad infinitum* – but this does not mean (and cannot possibly mean) that capital has finally found a friction-free plane of accumulation. The challenge is not to imagine a world (or a city) in which debt-fueled gentrification really can occur *everywhere* – becoming, at last, the "rising tide that lifts all boats" (Duany, as cited in Slater, 2006, p. 741), floating on a sea of credit – but rather to excavate the ways in which debt hits up against its own crisis-prone limits, hardening lines of inequality as it does. In the UK, for example, it is clear that mortgage credit is unevenly allocated (Rae, 2015); that it becomes more exclusionary the further house prices rise (Ryan-Collins et al., 2017); that it remains beyond the means of those on low pay and precarious contracts (Dorling, 2014); that the growth of buy-to-let mortgages and the growth of the private rented sector are closely related (Paccoud, 2017); and, in this way, that the growth of debt-financed homeownership fuels its own counter-tendency, "trapping" a generation in rent (Walker & Jeraj, 2016). And as the 2008 financial crisis illustrated with stark clarity, no debt bubble can last forever (Harvey, 2011). In short, debt "liberates" potential land values, but it cannot do so smoothly or equitably.

As Walks (2013) notes, the "urban debtscape" is sharply characterized by uneven development, and could only ever be thus. I will now argue that it also imbues relations between *people* with an unevenness that imbeds the "property mind" as a coercive common sense.

DEBT AS DISCIPLINE

In the years following the financial crisis, there was a notable increase in scholarly attention paid to questions of debt, and mortgage debt in particular. From the disciplinary politics of repossession (Langley, 2009) to the spatial distribution of subprime loans in the U.S. (Aalbers, 2012); from collective resistance in Spain (Garciá-Lamarca & Kaika, 2016) to the mapping of debt liabilities in Canada (Walks, 2013), this work made it clear that questions of housing and spatial justice must attend to the shifting power relations of debt. Understandably, much of this work focused on those loans at the cutting edge of inflating the bubble that burst, namely those of a "subprime" nature, often targeted in a predatory fashion at people least able to pay them back, overlaying (and reinforcing) inequalities of race, class, and gender. In what follows, I am by no means seeking to deflect attention away from those processes (which are vital to study and vital to stop), but the functionality of debt to gentrification – especially in a city like Edinburgh – appears to be in many ways less spectacular. I am not so much concerned by those moments in which the mortgage relation *fails*, but the enduring effect of the belief that it usually, "normally," *works* (though within capitalism, of course, the relation between normally working and occasionally failing is symbiotic).

Here Foucault and Marx walk arm in arm: the debt/gentrification intersection is particularly interesting when viewed through the lens of *governmentality* as well as capital accumulation (for it is always both). By governmentality, I do not mean a sense of the world in which all power relations are devolved down and out to nowhere, but in the vein of those who argue that "it is often the case that when we think we are most free is when we are most governed" (Joyce, 2013, p. 6). Mortgage debt is a particularly striking example of this. As Garciá-Lamarca and Kaika (2016) point out, it is implausible to explain the growth in housing debts purely as a macroeconomic shift, one in which individuals respond automatically to the deregulation of finance capital. But it is equally implausible to presume that this shift represents countless coincidentally aligning decisions to take on more debt. What is needed is a conceptual framework that marries the two, not to triumphantly declare "messiness," but to focus on the extent to which individual aspirations, state policy and the logic of capital(ists) work together to push speculation on housing. In this instance – as Bidet (2016) has argued – the capitalist present is best understood by holding Marx and Foucault in tension together. Debt is structurally fundamental to capitalism and to economic growth. As Di Muzio and Robbins (2016) note, citizens have far more of an obligation to take on debt than they do to pay it back. But, crucially, this comes wrapped in deeply personal discourses – *your* debt, *your* responsibility, *your* guilt. This implicates the individual even whilst their actions are funneled into a trajectory cajoled on all sides by policy, by pressure, by expectation, and by a shrinking range of alternative options. This is a potent form of individualization in action, recalling the late Zygmunt Bauman's beautifully worded diagnosis of the "the vexing, demeaning and infuriating feeling of having been sentenced to *loneliness* in the face of *shared* dangers" (Bauman & Bordoni, 2014, p. 14). Atkinson and Blandy (2017, p. 9) use the phrase "tessellated neoliberalism" to discuss the ways in which the "wider order and values of exchange and economic life expand outwards from the micro-scale of a multitude of owned homes and into the fabric of the macro-economy." I find this an intriguing phrase, and a useful one insofar as it refocuses attention on the *effect* of tenure as a way in which everyday life is connected to the wider functioning of capitalism (though the notion of expanding *outward* needs reversing simultaneously). It links closely with Haila's (2017) discussion around the institutionalization of the "property mind," a phrase she uses to describe the percolation of property ownership and speculation through mainstream culture as a taken-for-granted common sense. Her observations are drawn from Singapore, but they chime well with an older strain of literature from the UK on what Kemeny (1981) called *The Myth of Homeownership*. But if the vast majority of that "ownership" is underpinned by debt, then the institutionalization of the property mind, a normalized and naturalized way of relating to ownership, brings with it the normalization and naturalization of immense debt.

Across the UK, housing debt that goes far beyond personal earnings is routinely and consistently normalized, advertised and encouraged. This normality has been pushed by government policy for several decades, heightened in the early 1980s by the simultaneous assault on public housing via the Right to Buy and the re-regulation of the banking sector to encourage speculation on housing loans (Forrest & Hirayama, 2015; Richard, 2008). In this context, the mortgage remains a uniquely *respectable* form of debt, trading on a series of moralizing discourses around aspiration, health and responsible citizenship, whereby it is considered better to be heavily in debt to a bank than it is to be renting (Flint, 2003; Gurney, 1999; Hunter & Nixon, 1999).

One effect of this tension (between the myth of individualism and the shepherding of individuals) is that people with mortgage debt are politically and economically incorporated into a system where they *want* house prices to keep rising because their personal financial situation gets far worse if they do not. This is never purely a financial pressure, for it is linked closely to questions of psychological wellbeing, mental health, family security and emotional stability, all exacerbated by the degree to which many rely on the rising value of their property in the face of evaporating social security and welfare provision (Kaika, 2017; Lowe et al., 2011). As the vestiges of the welfare state are dismantled, privatized, and siphoned off into last resorts, this reliance will only grow. In a world where *belief* and *faith* play such a fundamental role in keeping prices high and growing higher, this alignment should not be overlooked. The debt-funded private home comes clad in the sheen of opportunity, even whilst it amounts to a contract for the exploitation of decades of labor-time to come. And this contract works, at least in part, because we *want it to*. "What was the expansion of household debt, including consumer debt and subprime mortgages," asks Dienst (2011, p. 175), if not "an attempt by a vast swathe of people to lay claim to their financial heaven on earth?"

Lefebvre's (1976) suggestion that capitalism survives by *producing space* has become a central idea of Marxist geography, and it is important to remember that he never meant this purely in a material sense. The profit rate may be resuscitated through the construction industry, speculation on land and property, the "switch" of capital into real estate, and so on. But capitalism cannot survive on capital alone (it never has done). It requires the production of ideological space, of subservience, hope, investment (in the political sense of having something to lose), internalization of the profit motive as the road to individual dreams, and, of course, the eradication of alternatives that can be glimpsed working. It is for this reason that Lefebvre undertook a critique of everyday life as *part of* a critique of capitalism, and his insistence on doing both was important, and is even more important now.

The availability of credit within the housing sector thus has two particular effects on the process of gentrification. Critical urbanists are very good at identifying the first, where credit functions as a lubricant to the circulation of capital, as well as the stage on which the next round of crisis is rehearsed (Harvey, 2006). What we now call *financialization*, and the debt that underpins it, has enabled the process of gentrification to go further and faster, both socially and spatially. But the coercive impetus written into that debt when it does *not* "fail" is just as important, for the fate of those who are indebted is tied to the trajectory that indebted them. The desire to want property prices to continue to rise – or at last to fear them falling – institutes gentrification as a common sense far beyond policy-makers, mirroring the "dull compulsion" of economic relations that stamps itself so thoroughly on urban policy (Peck, 2014). The so-called law of supply and demand (and the idea of equilibrium it instills) is rendered utterly irrelevant, for the speculative logic invested in housing works to push up prices whilst also pushing up demand (Marazzi, 2011). A new formula is forged, one that disintegrates communities through the promise of individual opportunity: *supply* the credit, and those who scramble onto the "ladder" will *demand* higher prices.

WE ARE ALL MIDDLE CLASS NOW

Gentrification, as Smith (2008; Smith and Williams, 1986) consistently argued, is fundamentally a class phenomenon. Yet there is still a "theoretical ambivalence" (Bridge, 1995, p. 239) in the way that the gentrification literature uses and defines class. The class debate about London which played out in the journal *City* demonstrates this quite neatly. Slater (2009) begins by reasserting the importance of working-class displacement to the process of gentrification. His target is Hamnett's "professionalization" thesis, which emphasizes the changing class structure of the city not only through displacement but also *replacement*, typified by the decline of manual labor and the rise of what are broadly accepted as middle-class occupations. Hamnett (2009) duly responds, bolstering his case with census data that seeks to quantify class changes at the societal level. The debate ricochets back and forth for several years, containing many fascinating points that I will not attempt to summarize here (Davidson & Wyly, 2012, 2013, 2015; Hamnett, 2015; Hamnett & Butler, 2013). Clearly, this was a debate not only about empirical methods of measuring class change, but the politics of how to theorize class: as relation or category? Identity or antagonism? And whilst this discussion was never solely about "gentrification," it was a debate carried out under the shadow of the term, and what it implies vis-à-vis displacement and the class takeover of space.

What particularly interests me here is the invisibility of debt on both sides of this argument. Pages and pages of discussion about changing employment patterns, lifestyle choices and rates of inequality are pitted against each other to discern whether or not the class transformation of urban space in London has been enacted through displacement of the working class *or* their uneven transformation into the new middle class. Most of this is written as if the miraculous trend of "professionalization" either never existed at all or was underwritten by a genuine democratization of wealth. To me, the answer lies somewhere in between, not in the sense of a meek compromise, but through the way that debt ties the two narratives together. How many of those who make up the so-called "new middle classes" are reliant on credit? Certainly not all of them, but as Horsley (2015) clearly demonstrates, probably most of them. This is not a phenomenon unique to London. Across the world (though with significant variation, of course), the lifestyles of the so-called new middle class "is unstable and chained to enormous amounts of debt" (Lees et al., 2016, p. 87).

In 1997, John Prescott (then deputy leader of the Labor Party) famously intoned that "we're all middle class now." This was an aspiration to be powered by the availability of credit, branding for a "third way" that promised unhindered profits and unhindered social mobility at the same time. The roll-out of British neoliberalism functioned as "an economic system geared toward the singular purpose of lending as much money as humanly and mathematically possible" (Horsley, 2015, p. 4), with the "democratization" of consumerism and homeownership as two of its main drivers. This trend was always inherently classed, even whilst it promised to flatten class distinctions. As Pathak (2014, p. 102) notes, "debt and indebtedness in general has now become naturalized" but some forms of debt are still heavily stigmatized. Those whose debts are not backed up by property are treated as deviant, irresponsible citizens, despite the fact that their levels of borrowing are low, both absolutely and proportionately. Those whose debts enable them to "buy" property increasingly augment their incomes, often by as much as a quarter, through *in situ* borrowing off the value of their property, funding lifestyles that cement their class distinction (Ong et al., 2013). If access to housing credit is classed in the first instance, this distinction calcifies over time. As indebted citizens, aspiring homeowners become part of a mechanism that entrenches inequality, for the growth in ownership levels amongst those with access to credit heightens the reliance on private sector renting for those whose incomes are not high or stable enough to guarantee them a mortgage (Ryan-Collins et al., 2017). Moreover, the question of intergenerational inequality – which can be politically framed as inheriting a class position – is closely related to property ownership and the life-changing value that houses can accrue (Christophers, 2018). In the first instance, then, it should be clear that debt augments the division of classes both as an identity and an economic position. I want to argue that it does more than this, however.

Class, of course, is understood in many ways (as the debate around categorization in London demonstrates). Kelly (2012) offers a useful summation: class functions (i) as a *position* in society, where an individual is placed within a hierarchy of wealth, labor, and ownership; (ii) as a *performance*, embodied through consumption and lifestyle; (iii) as a *process*, through which surplus value is extracted from labor; and (iv) as *politics*, through which the first three are consciously molded into a collective claim on the future. The intersection of gentrification and class clearly maps onto these distinctions in multiple ways at the same time, but I am particularly interested in the way that the third category – *class as process* – occurs. Here is where "value" in the urban landscape is produced, where profit is made, that same liquid currency that fuels "fifth-wave gentrification" (Aalbers, 2019) and "Neo-Haussmannization" (Merrifield, 2014), "algorithmically automated" (Wyly, 2019) into the blueprint of progress. For whilst the indebted gentrifier can be incorporated into the "middle class" in the first two meanings (as a *position* and a *performance*), if debt underpins this transformation then in the third sense (as *process*), things are much harder to pin down, and this leaves the fourth sense (as *politics*) wide open. As Di Muzio and Robbins (2016, p. 13) note, on an international scale, debt "essentially divides society into net creditors and net debtors," with the latter underpinning the contemporary monetary system. Through housing debt, all forms of paid labor are incorporated into the urbanization of capital itself (and all forms of unpaid labor that are necessary for paid labor to occur). The seemingly endless supply of gentrifiers that enables the "generalization" of the phenomenon should be seen as the increasingly indebted mass that they are.

I do not say this to deny the very real inequalities of capital (social, cultural, and economic) that cut across society among those in debt, or between those with access to credit and those without. Nor do I want to be misconstrued as someone seeking to emphasize the "suffering" of those who seem, by most accounts, to benefit from gentrification. But "class is a role, not a label that attaches to persons" (Harvey, 2011, p. 232). In the process of gentrification as a capital accumulation strategy, all those who – through their debts – generate untold billions for the owners of the future city take on the role of *labor*, even if they play many other roles during the working day or through their politics, their consumption patterns, their future ownership of property, and so on. In this sense, I do not care if someone likes vegan iced lattes and has a "middle class" job: if their house price is underpinned by a loan from a bank then they are exploited as a producer of surplus value, whether consciously or not, even if they imagine *themselves* as owners of the future city, and even if they *do become* owners of the future city, exploiting others along the way. Such a dynamic is too simple, of course, for there are countless ways in which an individual can be paying their mortgage through the labor of others – whether as boss or landlord – which scatters the impetus to exploit downward. In this way, the creditor/debtor relation reinforces the capital/labor relation at the macro level even whilst it obfuscates it at the social level. As Federici (2014, pp. 235–236) reminds us, "the function of debt as an instrument of labor extraction is masked . . . under the illusion of self-investment." I would only add that this masking is all the more effective when the boundary between *illusionary* investment and "real" investment is harder to pin down. If gentrification is conceived of as a "process of upward mobility that uses urban space to climb over other people" (Wyly, 2019, p. 16), then the stairway "up" (which is framed with so many gilded signposts promising prosperity, security, respectability, pride, and success) is constructed on a conveyor belt of debt. And it is the profitability of that debt, and the enduring nature of the power relationship that it relies on, that entrenches gentrification as a global urban strategy.

Debt atomizes its users, even whilst the ranks of the indebted grow (Federici, 2014). Rethinking the class relation inherent to debt as a process of value extraction may help to conceptualize this as a terrain of struggle, akin to the many anti-debt movements that emerged after the 2008 crisis. Partly what makes the *Plataforma de Afectados por la Hipoteca* so inspiring (above and beyond its concrete victories in claiming housing) is its engagement not "beyond" class boundaries but through a more fluid understanding of who is exploited through their housing debt (García-Lamarca, 2017). Importantly, the power relation at the heart of this debt works both ways. Marx (1990, p. 277) notes that the point at which we do work and the point at which we are paid for it "do not coincide in time." Because most workers are paid *after* a day's work (or an hour's, a week's, a month's, etc.), "everywhere the worker allows credit to the capitalist" (p. 278). This is Marx at his subversive best, flipping a piece of received wisdom so it recasts the moral relation at the heart of wage labor. The debt relation exacerbates this temporal disjunction on a massive scale. The bank lends out money to "help" people find housing, but the opposite is just as true: those who borrow help the bank to create money using the guarantee of their future labor, "secured" by the collective value of the cities they inhabit, and the work that they have not yet done.

CONCLUSION

I started on one particular street, looking at an advert. I ended "nowhere," in the abstract realm of class relations, dreams, and speculation. I have tried to show that the two are impossible to disassociate. Capitalism relies on our desires as well as our fears, mediated through "repetition in daily life" (Lefebvre, 1988, p. 80). Along the way, I framed the relation between debt and gentrification first as a liberation, second as a social relation and third as an extractor of value. Land values can rise faster, decoupled from social constraints; the "property mind" is instituted as a coercive common sense; and the class relation between capital and labor is reconfigured. It is not merely the houses – the places we live – that are financialized, but all the future labor-time of those who will get in debt to live in them.

This opens out the temporality of the rent gap model, bursting these neat lines. The rising line of "potential" (as an ideological, imagined, and continually reinforced idea of what space *could* and therefore *should* be for, as well as a measure of exchange value as-yet unrealized) assumes an overbearing power over whatever is now "capitalized" because it is liberated from social constraints. "Potential" no longer has to bear any rational relation to income, or the affordability of life, but this only serves to amplify its importance as a lens for considering urban land use change. To spatialize this observation, the frontier of gentrification is driven not only by the available land, the buildings on that land, and the potential profit to be made from both, but through the debt-potential of the population which will underscore and extend that profitability through living there, far into the future. Thus the rent-gap is no longer "closed" when gentrification occurs (if it ever was). Instead, its point of closure is dragged forth into the future. The temporality and spatiality of the model is thus altered, subtly but fundamentally. The impetus to gentrify no longer depends on the capitalized ground rent *reaching* its potential level – no longer depends, in other words, on a "moment" of profitability that is easily traceable and finite – for that potential is constantly deferred. And as Marx (1992) argued, stretching the timespan of profit realization may be hugely lucrative, but it is also hugely vulnerable.

The uneven "liberation" of potential land values from social constraints brings with it all the pernicious effects associated with generalized gentrification – a broad affordability crisis, ongoing displacement in many forms, the proliferation of precarious living conditions, the erosion of communities. It also does something far more dangerous. For several decades, critical urbanists have talked about the switching of capital into space, into real estate, and into the future (Harvey, 1982). Scholars have tirelessly documented the extent to which this involves continuous redevelopment, a restless and hyper-speculative urbanism that is constantly chasing promised returns, constantly destroying old landscapes and constructing new ones (Weber, 2002). As I have tried to show, the way debt and gentrification intersect speeds up the proliferation of this process, but it may do more than this: it may "lock in" the pursuit of those potential land values, always beholden to a loan already-borrowed and a future already-imagined, tied to the "persistent popular irrational belief" (Haila, 2017, p. 501) that house prices will keep rising. It is vital not to be fatalistic about this: debt is simultaneously powerful and fragile, and whilst it appears to undermine "old" forms of solidarity, it can engender new ones. The struggle against gentrification – imagined not merely as neighborhood change but as a "politico-economic window" into the wider machinations of capital (Hackworth, 2019) – *must* entail a struggle against debt. Moreover, as Di Muzio and Robbins (2016) note, it is imperative to see the *ecological* implications of generalized indebtedness, for it codifies economic growth as a legal obligation to the past, one which destroys our collective future. Debt not only fuels the rent gap, for it reconstitutes its never-quite-closure as a binding obligation. The urban growth machine shows no signs of stopping in the face of an overwhelming tide of evidence that it must. The "death pledge" of housing debt is socialized to all living creatures, even whilst the promised gains are individualized to (some) working humans: making rent gap theory "not true" (Clark, 2018) has never been more urgent.

ACKNOWLEDGMENTS

I would like to thank Elvin Wyly and Emma Saunders for their feedback on an earlier draft, Eric Clark for his kindness and enthusiasm, and three anonymous reviewers for their sincere engagement with the text.

DISCLOSURE STATEMENT

No potential conflict of interest was reported by the author.

ABOUT THE AUTHOR

Hamish Kallin is a Lecturer in Human Geography at the University of Edinburgh. His work focuses on the myriad ways in which capital remakes the city. He has published on territorial stigmatization, state power, and gentrification.

NOTES

1. As McKee et al. (2017) point out, there is no singular UK housing policy, as the Scottish Government (alongside the legislative chambers in Wales and Northern Ireland) have devolved power in this regard. Nevertheless, at present, the reliance on debt underpinning Scottish housing policy is barely distinguishable from UK policy more broadly, closely linked over multiple generations.
2. Incidentally, Henri Lefebvre (with Ross, 1997, p. 75) suggests that Simak's novel – a cheap paperback sci-fi vision of the far-future – was his "starting point" for discussions with the Situationists around capitalist urbanization after automation.

REFERENCES

Aalbers, M. B. (2012). *Subprime cities: The political economy of mortgage markets*. Wiley-Blackwell.

Aalbers, M. B. (2019). Introduction to the forum: From third to fifth-wave gentrification. *Tijdschrift voor Economische en Sociale Geografie, 110*(1), 1–11. https://doi.org/10.1111/tesg.12332

Atkinson, R., & Blandy, S. (2017). *Domestic fortress: Fear and the home front*. Manchester University Press.

Bank of England. (2016). *Financial stability report – July 2016*. Bank of England. www.bankofengland.co.uk/financial-stability-report/2016/july-2016

Bauman, Z., & Bordoni, C. (2014). *State of crisis*. Polity Press.

Bernt, M. (2016). Very particular, or rather universal? Gentrification through the lenses of

Ghertner and López-Morales. *City: Analysis of Urban Trends, Culture, Theory, Policy, Action*, *20*(4), 634–644. https://doi.org/10.1080/13604813.2016.1143682

Bidet, J. (2016). *Foucault with Marx*. Zed Books.

Bridge, G. (1995). The space for class? On class analysis in the study of gentrification. *Transactions of the Institute of British Geographers, New Series*, *20*(2), 236–247. https://doi.org/10.2307/622434

Bunn, P., & Rostom, M. (2014). *Household debt and spending*. Bank of England. www.bankofengland.co.uk/quarterly-bulletin/2014/q3/household-debt-and-spending

Chatterton, P. (2010). The student city: An ongoing story of neoliberalism, gentrification, and commodification. *Environment and Planning A*, *42*(3), 509–514. https://doi.org/10.1068/a42293

Christophers, B. (2018). Intergenerational inequality? Labour, capital, and housing through the ages. *Antipode*, *50*(1), 101–121. https://doi.org/10.1111/anti.12339

Christophers, B. (2019). A tale of two inequalities: Housing-wealth inequality and tenure inequality. *Environment and Planning A: Economy and Space*. https://doi.org/10.1177%2F0308518X19876946

Clark, E. (2018). Making rent gap theory not true. In A. Albet & N. Benach (Eds.), *Gentrification as a global strategy: Neil Smith and beyond* (pp. 74–84). Routledge.

Cruden Homes. (2014). *A good time to choose choice*. Cruden Homes. www.cruden-ltd.co.uk/homes/news/186/a-good-time-to-choose-choice

Davidson, M., & Wyly, E. (2012). Class-ifying London: Questioning social division and space claims in the post-industrial metropolis. *City*, *16*(4), 395–421. https://doi.org/10.1080/13604813.2012.696888

Davidson, M., & Wyly, E. (2013). Class analysis for whom? *City: Analysis of Urban Trends, Culture, Theory, Policy, Action*, *17*(3), 299–311. https://doi.org/10.1080/13604813.2013.795327

Davidson, M., & Wyly, E. (2015). Same, but different: Within London's "static" class structure and the missing antagonism. *City: Analysis of Urban Trends, Culture, Theory, Policy, Action*, *19*(2–3), 247–257. https://doi.org/10.1080/13604813.2015.1014709

Dienst, R. (2011). *The bonds of debt*. Verso.

Di Muzio, T., & Robbins, R. H. (2016). *Debt as power*. Manchester University Press.

Dorling, D. (2014). *All that is solid: The great housing disaster*. Allen Lane.

Evans. (2018). Housebuilder Barratt reports record profits. *Financial Times*. www.ft.com/content/cabda93c-b0d3-11e8-8d14-6f049d06439c

Federici, S. (2014). From commoning to debt: Financialization, microcredit, and the changing architecture of capital accumulation. *South Atlantic Quarterly*, *113*(2), 231–244. https://doi.org/10.1215/00382876-2643585

Fitzpatrick, T., & McQuinn, K. (2007). House prices and mortgage credit: Empirical evidence for Ireland. *The Manchester School*, *75*(1), 82–103. https://doi.org/10.1111/j.1467-9957.2007.01004.x

Flint, J. (2003). Housing and ethopolitics: Constructing identities of active consumption and responsible community. *Economy and Society*, *32*(4), 611–629. https://doi.org/10.1080/0308514032000107628

Forrest, R., & Hirayama, Y. (2015). The financialisation of the social project: Embedded liberalism and home ownership. *Urban Studies*, *52*(2), 233–244. https://doi.org/10.1177/0042098014528394

García-Lamarca, M. (2017). From Occupying plazas to recuperating housing: Insurgent practices in Spain. *International Journal of Urban and Regional Research*, *41*(1), 37–53. https://doi.org/10.1111/1468-2427.12386

Garciá-Lamarca, M., & Kaika, M. (2016). "Mortgaged lives": The biopolitics of debt and housing financialization. *Transactions of the Institute of British Geographers, New Series*, *41*(3), 313–327. https://doi.org/10.1111/tran.12126

Graeber, D. (2012). *Debt: The first 5,000 years*. Melville House.

Gurney, C. (1999). Pride and prejudice: Discourses of normalisation in private and public accounts of home ownership. *Housing Studies*, *14*(2), 163–183. https://doi.org/10.1080/02673039982902

Hackworth, J. (2019). Gentrification as a politico-economic window: Reflections on the changing state of gentrification. *Tijdschrift voor Economische en Sociale Geografie*, *110*(1), 47–53. https://doi.org/10.1111/tesg.12330

Haila, A. (2017). Institutionalization of "the property mind". *International Journal of Urban and Regional Research*, *41*(3), 500–507. https://doi.org/10.1111/1468-2427.12495

Hamnett, C. (2009). The new Mikado? Tom Slater, gentrification and displacement. *City*, *13*(4), 476–482. https://doi.org/10.1080/13604810903298672

Hamnett, C. (2015). The changing occupational class composition of London. *City: Analysis of Urban Trends, Culture, Theory, Policy, Action, 19*(2–3), 239–246. https://doi.org/10.1080/13604813.2015.1014711

Hamnett, C., & Butler, T. (2013). Re-classifying London: A growing middle class and increasing inequality. *City, 17*(2), 197–208. https://doi.org/10.1080/13604813.2013.765719

Harari, D. (2018). *Household debt: Statistics and impact on economy*. House of Commons Library.

Harvey, D. (1982). *The limits to capital*. Basil Blackwell.

Harvey, D. (2006). *The limits to capital*. Verso.

Harvey, D. (2011). *The enigma of capital and the crises of capitalism*. Profile Books.

Horsley, M. (2015). *The dark side of prosperity: Late capitalism's culture of indebtedness*. Ashgate.

Hunter, C., & Nixon, J. (1999). The discourse of housing debt: The social construction of landlords, lenders, borrowers and tenants. *Housing, Theory and Society, 16*(4), 165–178. https://doi.org/10.1080/14036099950149893

Joseph, M. (2014). *Debt to society: Accounting for life under capitalism*. University of Minnesota Press.

Joyce, P. (2013). *The state of freedom: A social history of the British state since 1800*. Cambridge University Press.

Kaika, M. (2017). Between compassion and racism: How the biopolitics of neoliberal welfare turns citizens into affective "idiots". *European Planning Studies, 25*(8), 1275–1291. https://doi.org/10.1080/09654313.2017.1320521

Kelly, P. F. (2012). Migration, transnationalism, and the spaces of class identity. *Philippine Studies: Historical and Ethnographic Viewpoints, 60*(2), 153–185. https://doi.org/10.1353/phs.2012.0017

Kemeny, J. (1981). *The myth of homeownership: Private versus public choices in housing tenure*. Routledge & Kegan Paul Ltd.

Knoll, K., Schularick, M., & Steger, T. (2017). No price like home: Global house prices, 1870–2012. *American Economic Review, 107*(2), 331–353. https://doi.org/10.1257/aer.20150501

Langley, P. (2009). Debt, discipline, and government: Foreclosure and forbearance in the subprime mortgage crisis. *Environment and Planning A, 41*(6), 1404–1419. https://doi.org/10.1068/a41322

Lazzarato, M. (2012). *The making of indebted man*. Semiotext(e).

Lazzarato, M. (2015). *Governing by debt*. Semiotext(e).

Lees, L., Shin, H.-B., & López-Morales, E. (2016). *Planetary gentrification*. Polity Press.

Lees, L., Slater, T., & Wyly, E. (2008). *Gentrification*. Routledge.

Lefebvre, H. (1976). *The survival of capitalism*. Allison and Busby.

Lefebvre, H. (1988). Towards a leftist cultural politics: Remarks occasioned by the centenary of Marx's death. In C. Nelson & L. Grossberg (Eds.), *Marxism and the interpretation of culture* (pp. 75–88). University of Illinois Press.

Lowe, S. G., Searle, B. A., & Smith, S. J. (2011). From housing wealth to mortgage debt: The emergence of Britain's asset-shaped welfare state. *Social Policy & Society, 11*(1), 105–116. https://doi.org/10.1017/S1474746411000455

Marazzi, C. (2011). *The violence of financial capitalism*. Semiotext(e).

Marcuse, P., & Madden, P. (2016). *In defense of housing*. Verso.

Marx, K. (1990). *Capital: A critique of political economy* (Vol. I). Penguin Books.

Marx, K. (1992). *Capital: A critique of political economy* (Vol. II). Penguin Books.

McKee, K., Muir, J., & Moore, T. (2017). Housing policy in the UK: The importance of spatial nuance. *Housing Studies, 32*(1), 60–72. https://doi.org/10.1080/02673037.2016.1181722

Merrifield, A. (2014). *The new urban question*. Pluto Press.

OECD. (2018). *Rising employment overshadowed by unprecedented wage stagnation*. OECD. www.oecd.org/employment/rising-employment-overshadowed-by-unprecedented-wage-stagnation.htm

Ong, R., Parkinson, S., Searle, B. A., Smith, S. J., & Wood, G. A. (2013). Channels from housing wealth to consumption. *Housing Studies, 28*(7), 1012–1036. https://doi.org/10.1080/02673037.2013.783202

Paccoud, A. (2017). Buy-to-let gentrification: Extending social change through tenure shifts. *Environment and Planning A, 49*(4), 839–856. https://doi.org/10.1177/0308518X16679406

Pathak, P. (2014). Ethopolitics and the financial citizen. *The Sociological Review, 62*(1), 90–116. https://doi.org/10.1111/1467-954X.12119

Paton, K. (2018). *Gentrification: A working-class perspective*. Routledge.

Peck, J. (2014). Entrepreneurial urbanism: Between uncommon sense and dull compulsion. *Geografiska Annaler: Series B, Human Geography*, *96*(4), 396–401. https://doi.org/10.1111/geob.12061

Piketty, T. (2014). *Capital in the twenty-first century*. Belknap Press.

Rae, A. (2015). The illusion of transparency: The geography of mortgage lending in Great Britain. *Journal of European Real Estate Research*, *8*(2), 172–195. https://doi.org/10.1108/JERER-08-2014-0030

Richard, R. (2008). *The ideology of home ownership: Homeowner societies and the role of housing*. Palgrave Macmillan.

Rolnik, R. (2019). *Urban warfare: Housing under the empire of finance*. Verso.

Ross, K. (1997). Lefebvre on the situationists: An interview. *October*, *79*, 69–83.

Ryan-Collins, J., Lloyd, T., & Macfarlane, L. (2017). *Rethinking the economics of land and housing*. Zed Books.

Scottish Government. (2020). *Low-cost initiative for first time buyers (LIFT)*. Scottish Government. www.gov.scot/policies/homeowners/low-cost-initiative-for-first-time-buyers/

Shelter. (2016). *City of Edinburgh*. Shelter Scotland. http://scotland.shelter.org.uk/housing_policy/get_your_housing_facts/city_of_edinburgh

Simak, C. (1952). *City*. Gnome Press.

Slater, T. (2006). The eviction of critical perspectives from gentrification research. *International Journal of Urban and Regional Research*, *30*(4), 737–757. https://doi.org/10.1111/j.1468-2427.2006.00689.x

Slater, T. (2009). Missing Marcuse: On gentrification and displacement. *City: Analysis of Urban Trends, Culture, Theory, Policy, Action*, *13*(2), 292–312. https://doi.org/10.1080/13604810902982250

Smith, N. (1996). *The New Urban Frontier: Gentrification and the Revanchist City*. Routledge.

Smith, N. (2002). New urbanism, new globalism: Gentrification as global urban strategy. *Antipode*, *34*(3), 427–450. https://doi.org/10.1111/1467-8330.00249

Smith, N. (2006). Gentrification generalized: From local anomaly to urban "regeneration" as global urban strategy. In M. S. Fisher & G. Downey (Eds.), *Frontiers of capital: Ethnographic reflections on the new economy* (pp. 191–208). Duke University Press.

Smith, N. (2008). The evolution of gentrification. In J. Berg, T. Kaminer, M. Schonderbeek, & J. Zonnevald (Eds.), *Houses in transformation* (pp. 15–26). NAi Uitgevers.

Smith, N., & Williams, P. (1986). Alternatives to orthodoxy: Invitation to a debate. In N. Smith & P. Williams (Eds.), *Gentrification of the city* (pp. 1–14). Routledge.

Walker, R., & Jeraj, S. (2016). *The rent trap: How we fell into it and how we get out of it*. Pluto Press.

Walks, A. (2013). Mapping the urban debtscape: The geography of household debt in Canadian cities. *Urban Geography*, *34*(2), 153–187. https://doi.org/10.1080/02723638.2013.778647

Weber, R. (2002). Extracting value from the city: Neoliberalism and urban redevelopment. In N. Brenner & N. Theodore (Eds.), *Spaces of neoliberalism: Urban restructuring in North America and Western Europe* (pp. 172–193). Blackwell Publishing.

Wyly, E. (2019). The evolving state of gentrification. *Tijdschrift voor Economische en Sociale Geografie*, *110*(1), 47–53. https://doi.org/10.1111/tesg.12333

Wyly, E., Newman, K., Schafran, A., & Lee, E. (2010). Displacing New York. *Environment and Planning A*, *42*(11), 2302–2623. https://doi.org/10.1068/a42519

PART THREE

Gentrification and comparative urbanism

Rural gentrification in Yamanakako, Minamitsuru District, Yamanashi Prefecture, Japan (photograph: Martin Phillips)

INTRODUCTION TO PART THREE

An understanding of urbanism in all its vagaries historically and geographically is necessary for any understanding of gentrification. A contemporary understanding of gentrification must derive empirical and theoretical inspiration from experiences around the world, past and present. And from this multitude of experiences, comparisons must be made. The question is what kind of comparative strategies are appropriate for a planetary gentrification that is premised on post-colonial critique and learning. The planetary gentrification thesis has sought to decolonize the concepts and practices embedded in gentrification studies, moving toward a properly global gentrification studies. The 'new' comparative urbanism helps with this challenge; it gets us thinking in a 'world of cities', pushing us to build concepts across difference.

Comparative urbanism also reminds us that the urban is not static, its time-space is always emerging and multiple and, as Jenny Robinson's (2021) new book tells us, must be in a constant state of revisability. We must reconsider, change, and modify; gentrification is not a static thing.

In our 2010 *Reader* (Chapter 29), we republished Lees's (2000) paper, which sought a reappraisal of gentrification studies, in particular a deconstruction of the process of gentrification itself and discourses on it, and renewed focus on contextuality and temporality. Twelve years on and Lees (2012) extended these calls; she was reinvigorated by work on 'new' comparative urbanism. When she wrote the 2000 paper, gentrification was 'all but unheard of in the cities of the Global South, and as such gentrification studies were not yet directly confronted with issues around developmentalism and categorization' (Lees, 2012: 156). As we see in this *Reader*, this changed massively in the following decade. Confronted with numerous global gentrifications she began to wonder how we might research them in a less colonial and more cosmopolitan way. Lemanski (2014) continued this new mode of thought in gentrification studies, attempting to theorize across southern and northern cities. Critically, she showed how theories traditionally rooted in northern cities and academies can be challenged and redeveloped by southern perspectives by focusing on downward raiding as gentrification without the name. Phillips and Smith (2018) get us to move beyond the 'metrocentricity' of gentrification studies by looking at how we might do comparative global research on rural gentrification. They identify four 'strategies of comparison' in studies of urban *and* rural gentrification and advocate for a 'genetic approach' that could reinvigorate universalizing comparisons but also be incorporated into individualizing, variation-finding, and relational or encompassing comparisons. In 2014 Ley and Teo published *Gentrification in Hong Kong? Epistemology vs. Ontology*, a thoughtful paper that examines the transferability of the concept of gentrification away from its Anglo-American heartland to the cities of Asia Pacific and specifically Hong Kong. They identified gentrification in Hong Kong but without the name/label. Subsequently, IJURR assembled a special issue to critique this paper; here, Ley and Teo (2018) respond effectively to those critiques. In doing so, they advance a comparative approach for a global gentrification studies that is 'dominated neither by planetary theory nor by regional specificity'.

REFERENCES AND FURTHER READING

Harris, A. (2008) From London to Mumbai and back again: Gentrification and public policy in comparative perspective, *Urban Studies*, 45:12:2407–2428.

Holm, A., Marcínczak, S., and Ogrodowczyk, A. (2015) New-build gentrification in the post-socialist city: Łód´z and Leipzig two decades after socialism, *Geografie*, 120:164–187.

Janoschka, M., Sequera, J., and Salinas, L. (2013) Gentrification in Spain and Latin America – A critical dialogue, *International Journal of Urban and Regional Research*, 38:1234–1265.

Kan, K. (2020) Building SoHo in Shenzhen: The territorial politics of gentrification and state making in China, *Geoforum*, 11:1–10.

Lees, L. (2018) Doing comparative urbanism in gentrification studies: Fashion or progress?, in Lees, L. with Phillips, M. (eds) *Handbook of Gentrification Studies*, Edward Elgar: Cheltenham, UK, pp. 49–62.

Lees, L. (2000) A re-appraisal of gentrification: Towards a 'geography of gentrification', *Progress in Human Geography*, 24:3:389–408.

Lees, L. (2012) The geography of gentrification: Thinking through comparative urbanism, *Progress in Human Geography*, 36:2:155–171.

Lemanski, C. (2014) Hybrid gentrification in South Africa: Theorising across southern and northern cities, *Urban Studies*, 51:14:2943–2960.

Ley, D. and Teo, S. (2014) Gentrification in Hong Kong? Epistemology vs. Ontology, *International Journal of Urban and Regional Research*, 38:4:1286–1303.

Ley, D. and Teo, S. (2018) Is comparative gentrification possible? Sceptical voices from Hong Kong, *International Journal of Urban and Regional Research*, 44:4:166–172.

Lopez-Morales, E., Ruiz-Tagle, J., Santos Junior, O.A., Blanco, J. and Arreortua, L.S. (2021) State-led gentrification in three Latin American cities, *Journal of Urban Affairs* (https://doi.org/10.1080/07352166.2021.1939040)

Nickayin, S.S., Halbac-Cotoara-Zamfir, R., Clemente, M., Chelli, F.M., Salvati, L., Benassi, F. and Morera, A.G. (2020) 'Qualifying peripheries' or 'repolarizing the center': A comparison of gentrification processes in Europe, *Sustainability*, 12:9039 (https://doi.org/10.3390/su12219039)

Phillips, M. and Smith, D.P. (2018) Comparative ruralism and 'opening new windows' on gentrification, *Dialogues in Human Geography*, 8:1:51–58.

Ren, X. (2018) From Chicago to China to India: Studying the city in the C21st, *Annual Review of Sociology*, 44:497–513.

Robinson, J. (2021) *Comparative Urbanism and Global Urban Studies: Theorizing the Urban*, Routledge: London.

9
The geography of gentrification
Thinking through comparative urbanism

Loretta Lees

> One important way of investigating the global spread of gentrification – while remaining sensitive to its different geographically and historically specific manifestations and effects – is to adopt a comparative perspective. Such a perspective already has a rich and productive intellectual tradition within gentrification research, arguably more so than in other strands of urban literature.
>
> (Harris, 2008: 2411)

I INTRODUCTION

Back in 2000 I published a paper in *Progress in Human Geography* that called for a progressive research programme on the 'geography of gentrification'. Part of my argument was that context and temporality had been sidelined in both gentrification research and in urban policies that promoted gentrification. The latter was a critique of one size fits all gentrification models/programmes/policies being launched in the UK, the USA, and elsewhere. I argued that a 'geography of gentrification' must include a consideration of both the spatial and the temporal dimensions of gentrification: international, intranational, and citywide comparisons; and a consideration of the timing of processes. The research programme I was arguing for, and indeed that I had already begun to work through (e.g. Carpenter and Lees, 1995; Lees, 1994), shared/shares many similarities with the renascent research agenda around comparative urbanism – a field of inquiry which seeks the 'systematic study of similarity and difference among cities or urban processes' (Nijman, 2007) both through description and explanation. This 'new' comparative urbanism is a field of inquiry which has perhaps become best known for its attempts to move urban studies towards a postcolonial agenda (see Robinson, 2006); but back in the 1990s when I was working on 'the geography of gentrification' the process was all but unheard of in the cities of the Global South, and as such gentrification studies were not yet directly confronted with issues around developmentalism and categorization.

Over the past decade we have seen the rapid and visceral emergence of state-led gentrification in the Global South – processes of gentrification are now changing the centres of cities in China, India, Pakistan, South America and South Africa (among others). Gentrification began to take off in the Global South (or at least it began to attract the attention of the media and certain academics) at the turn of the 21st century but even then the geographies of a global gentrification presented (e.g. Atkinson and Bridge, 2005; *Urban Studies*, 2003) all but omitted the Global South in any meaningful way. Despite a good discussion in Atkinson and Bridge (2005) about gentrification as a form of neocolonialism – the White Anglo appropriation of the central city – there was no discussion about appropriate theory to analyse this, nor of how it might play out differently in the predominantly non-white cities of the Global South. Porter and Shaw's (2008) excellent collection, which features case studies from Europe, North and South America, Asia, South Africa, the Middle East and Australia, develops a comparative analysis of regeneration/gentrification strategies, their effects, and efforts to resist them, but it still does not pay enough attention to the issues of developmentalism, universalism and categorization in comparative urbanism. As Robinson (2011a: 2) says, 'promising edited collections which take care to juxtapose case studies from different parts of the world still do so without allowing them to engage with each other or with more general or theoretical understandings of cities'. Recent journal special issues on gentrification (my own included) can be criticized likewise (e.g. *Environment and Planning A*, 2007; *Population, Space and Place*, 2010; *Urban Studies*, 2008).

Future comparative work on gentrification needs to attend to the issues around comparative urbanism more critically. This would take us away from an 'imitative urbanism' (from the idea that gentrification in the Global North has travelled to and been copied in the Global South) towards a 'cosmopolitan urbanism' (where gentrification in the Global South has a more expanded imagination). This requires a comparative imagination that can respond to the postcolonial challenge, and it will have implications for how gentrification is conceived (questioning the usefulness and applicability of the term 'gentrification' in the Global South) and how research is to be conducted (this will push us to learn new kinds of urbanism and involve multiple translations throughout the world). Importantly, it entails unlearning (drawing on Spivak, 1993) existing dominant literatures that continue to structure how we think about gentrification, its practices and ideologies. As Harvey (2004: 239) says, 'If our urban world has been imagined and made then it can be reimagined and remade'.

II GENTRIFICATION AND COMPARATIVE URBANISM

When one reads through the renascent literature on comparative urbanism in urban geography (e.g. Ward, 2008) there is no sign of the gentrification literature, of its long tradition of comparative work (between different countries, different cities, and different neighbourhoods within single cities), of its 'geographies of gentrification' (some examples include Butler, 1997; Butler with Robson, 2003; Clark, 1994; Clay, 1979; Lees, 1994; Ley, 1988, 1996; Smith, 1996), even by way of critique. Researchers interested in comparative urbanism will find some of the theoretical and conceptual debates around gentrification illuminating, but more importantly the gentrification literature can learn from the new literature on comparative urbanism, in particular moving towards a postcolonial approach to comparativism.

Despite a lot of new hype around comparative urbanism, the discussions of what it might constitute epistemologically, methodologically, and overall as a research agenda/strategy are disappointingly thin. This is not surprising as there are some complex issues at the heart of such an endeavour. Recent writings are thick with idealism but thin with the practicalities of everyday urban research. Part of the problem is that comparative urbanism means different things to different researchers. Nijman (2007: 1) claims that comparative urbanism is a field of inquiry that aims to develop 'knowledge, understanding, and generalization at a level between what is true of all cities and what is true of one city at a given point in time'. This seems reasonable, but as Robinson (2004) states there are important theoretical and methodological questions to sort out if we are to (re)deploy comparative urbanism in a way that does not fall back into modernist ideas about universalism, scientism and problematic discourses on developmentalism, especially when we are researching the Global South. These theoretical and methodological questions have not yet been sorted out and it might well be that focusing in on a particular urban process, such as gentrification, may help. One reason is that 21st-century gentrification has begun to throw up some complex issues around comparing the process in developed and developing world cities, issues around temporality and difference. Another is that the gentrification literature has also been at the forefront of discussions on how theoretical approaches are changed in different cities and contexts (cf. Robinson, 2002: 549), as can be seen in discussions of the 'emancipatory city thesis' and the 'revanchist city thesis' (see Lees, 2000; Lees et al., 2008; Slater, 2004). Discussions on the 'emancipatory city thesis' and the 'revanchist city thesis' have been clear about the locatedness of these theorizations in particular cities and the problems that come about when they are used out of context. Gentrification researchers have already taken comparison 'not just as a method, but as a mode of thought that informs how urban theory is constituted' (as McFarlane, 2010, asks of urban studies), and we have situated and contested claims around theories of gentrification, and around the way that these theories have 'travelled' (see MacLeod's, 2002, critique of the 'revanchist city' thesis from Glasgow). In fact we have been interested in both how theories of gentrification have travelled and how the process itself has travelled (from the central city to rural or suburban gentrification, from historic architecture to new-build architecture, from metropolitan cities to provincial cities, and from world cities to emerging world cities, etc. – see Phillips, 2004, on the politics of 'gentrification's others'). Like in the comparative urban studies literature more widely (see Ward, 2010) the gentrification literature has acknowledged the challenges of dealing with different geographical scales; for example, gentrification does not always simply cascade down the urban hierarchy from metropolitan to provincial cities – sometimes it happens in both places at the same time (see Lees, 2006), sometimes it is a relational thing (see Dutton, 2003, on the 'uneven socio-cultural relationship' between London and Leeds). As Peck (2002: 332) states, 'a relational and reflexive analysis of scale is necessary – one that is sensitive to geographic, historical, and institutional contingencies, rather than absolutist and categorical approaches in which political-economic functions are rigidly, exclusively and unambiguously fixed at particular scales'.

Like urban studies more generally, the gentrification literature has long positioned comparison to the fore, the term 'gentrification' was coined with respect to the process in London (a particular place, at a particular time) and all literature since has been forced to conceive of gentrification comparatively with the process that the British sociologist Ruth Glass (1964) identified in inner London in the 1950s/1960s. Of course many of the 'past' comparative studies in the gentrification literature have been exactly the type that today's postcolonial comparative urbanists might critique. Nevertheless there is still plenty to learn from them. Take, for example, the problematic of comparing gentrification in London and Paris when until very recently French academics did not use the term 'gentrification', they used 'embourgeoisement' instead (see Preteceille, 2007) and of comparing the process in London and Berlin, where the German 'klasse' means something quite different to the British 'class'. In Spain the terms 'recualificació'n social', 'aburguesamiento', 'aristocratizació'n' and 'elitizació'n residencial' have been used (Garcia, 2001), but in Spanish-speaking countries outside Spain, e.g. Chile, the terms translate differently.[1] What gentrification researchers need to do now is to critically debate the international usefulness of the term 'gentrification' and to consider how comparison might take place with respect to historic gentrifications (there are plenty of new histories to be written) and contemporary processes of gentrification in the Global North *and* the Global South. We should not read gentrification in the Global South as simply the recreation of the periphery (the urban South) in the image of the supposed centre (London or New York).

In addition, we need to pay much more attention to the temporality of processes of gentrification around the world. The stage models of gentrification that emerged in the 1970s are ill suited with respect to contemporary gentrification (see Lees, 2003a, for a critique) and the revised stage models (like Hackworth and Smith, 2001) are very US-centric. As Nijman (2007: 2) states, 'social scientists often formulate "thick theories" defined by complex arguments about sequence and duration ... Yet mainstream social science methods are not well-suited for analysis of these kinds of temporal arguments'. The temporal arguments in gentrification need to be rethought. Nijman also notes that geographers face an even more complex challenge because they have to focus on comparison across spaces/places as well as the temporal. Different stage types of gentrification are emerging in different places at different and indeed the same times, making comparisons complex. For example, in 2011 inner London is experiencing the typical first wave/pioneer sweat equity type of gentrification, alongside third wave, state-led new-build gentrification and stalled gentrification. There are important questions about gentrification types, timing/temporality and scales both for understanding this process more fully, and importantly for having the knowledge and tools we need as critical social scientists to resist it.

Nijman (2007) argues that there are four theoretical questions fundamental to comparative urbanism: (1) questions about the spatial identification of the city itself and of the wider urban, economic and political system it is in; (2) the role of the state or city-state; (3) the relationship between globalization and the urban – the impact of globalization on urban processes, networks and categories; and (4) questioning whether globalization means urban convergence. These are good questions for gentrification research. In addition to these theoretical questions, Dear (2002) demands that we consider comparative urban epistemologies too (he is interested in The Chicago School of Sociology, Marxist urban political economy and postmodern urbanism). Gentrification researchers have long debated urban epistemologies (e.g. Marxism versus humanism, etc.; see Lees et al., 2008, 2010), but they have considered them less in terms of comparative urbanism (although wider discussions of Marxism and humanism touch on this). We need to think again about the comparative value of different theoretical perspectives.

In addition, gentrification research can now be used to reject The LA School's 'paradigmatic city' because their model of a centreless Los Angeles now seems rather naive as gentrification has begun to take off in downtown LA. If anything, the late emergence of gentrification in LA demonstrates the importance of comparative urbanism for gentrification research: why did gentrification come late to LA? Is it because LA is a relatively young city? Is it due to the sustainability (Smart Growth) agenda in a cardominated city? Are contemporary processes of gentrification there the same as or different from other cities in the USA and indeed cities elsewhere in the world? After all, there is no historic 19th-century architecture, LA has a reputation for being inauthentic, and there is little there in the way of authenticity. Indeed, in a city like LA that is dominated by its Latino population perhaps Jenny Robinson's (2006) 'cosmopolitan approach' can be brought to bear on a developed world city. Ironically LA might be a good place to begin to look for 'alternative comparative frames'. After all, as Reiff (1992) states, LA is a 'third world city' in a 'first world city'.

McFarlane (2010) argues that urban studies has inherited an impoverished sense of comparison due to the influence of debates around 'pragmatic urbanism' (e.g. The LA School), but I do not necessarily think we have to step outside of developed world cities completely to develop alternative comparative frames. No matter where our study of gentrification is located, as Ward (2010) makes clear, this involves understanding cities differently from the way they have been theorized comparatively in the past. Ward (2010) advocates a relational comparative approach, arguing that:

> stressing interconnected trajectories – how different cities are implicated in each other's past, present and future – moves us away from searching for similarities and differences between two mutually exclusive contexts and instead towards relational comparisons that use different cities to pose questions of one another.
>
> (Ward, 2010: 480)

Following Clark (2005: 256), I would like to see 'a more inclusive perspective on the geography and history of gentrification', but one informed by the new debates on comparative urbanism. Like Clark (2005; see also Sayer, 2001) I find the social construction of gentrification as 'an object of study' increasingly problematic in the face of the mutation of gentrification (e.g. from an urban to a suburban mindset) and its rapid spread in the Global South. I am concerned that traditional conceptualizations of gentrification from the Global North will dominate and thus distort accounts of gentrification in/from the Global South. Like Clark (2005) I want to see some dispute over the 'conventional truth', the time-space delineations of gentrification. As he argues:

> confident proclamations ring out: Gentrification is now global! The problem with this is not if gentrification can be observed in places around the world, but it is again an issue of time: it is now global ... The extent of occurrence of the phenomenon from a global historical perspective remains however largely uncharted.
>
> (Clark, 2005: 260)

III GENTRIFICATIONS, NEOLIBERALISMS AND ASSEMBLAGES

There has been a lot of research in comparative urbanism around issues of government and governance (e.g. Brenner, 2004) and it is clear now that gentrification researchers need to pay much closer attention to government policies on gentrification as neoliberal models of governance (see Lees and Ley, 2008). Sometimes the state is directly involved in contemporary gentrification, as in the case of state-led gentrification in the UK and the USA (see Lees et al., 2008). At other times it aids rather than directs gentrification (e.g. Moscow; see Badyina and Golubchikov, 2005). In some cases it is even ambivalent about gentrification, as is the case in Switzerland (see Rerat and Lees, 2011). These different forms of governance matter. There is certainly a difference between state-led gentrification that considers what to do with the displaced, even if this means displacing them to the periphery of cities as has happened in Shanghai and other cities in China, and state-led gentrification such as that in Pakistan where no allowance is made for the displaced. Yet 'planned displacements' to the periphery of cities do not necessarily lead to better outcomes for the displacees. Take the case of Istanbul – in 2008, 300 Romani families from Sulukule, a neighbourhood in central Istanbul that had been declared an urban renewal (stateled gentrification) area, were moved to a development called Tas,og˘luk approximately 40 kilometres from the city centre (from which it took an average of three hours to commute back to their neighbourhood, workplaces, relatives and friends). Their neighbourhood was demolished despite massive national and international protest, but after only six months of living in Tas,og˘luk 291 of the families moved back to Sulukule because they could not afford their new rents and there were no jobs on the periphery. The result – the returnees were officially homeless and those who could not fall back on the help of family or friends started to live in tents or in the ruins of their old neighbourhood (see www.tarlabasiistanbul.com for other examples). An examination of the 'practices' of gentrification (whether apparently the same or different to those in the Global North) across a variety of world cities would begin the task of decentring the dominant narratives of gentrification from the Global North (if not from world cities). But this decentring must be sensitive to an exploration of the different neoliberalisms associated with gentrifications around the world. Wyly et al. (2010) point to such differences between the Global North and the Global South:

> the long economic expansion and globalized credit boom across urban systems of the Global North drove gentrification outward from the urban core. The leveraged real-estate frenzy set the stage for an unprecedented crash and a wave of foreclosure driven displacements across many kinds of city neighbourhoods ... At the same time, transnational economic realignments and state-led redevelopment schemes transformed vast sections of the urban built environment of China, India, Brazil and elsewhere in the Global South ... Contemporary urban renewal in the Global South dwarfs the bulldozed landscapes that enraged Anderson (1964) and, even in the US, the phrase is losing its stigma: Robert Moses ... was the subject of a sympathetic, three-museum retrospective in New York in the Spring of 2007. All of these changes suggest that gentrification, displacement, and renewal have been respatialized and intensified in transnational urbanism.
> (Wyly et al., 2010: 2604)

Indeed we need to assess the utility of the term 'neoliberalism' (more often framed in gentrification writings within the North American experience) for the study of gentrification in the Global South. As Arif Hasan[2] of The Asian Coalition for Housing Rights (ACHR) has said:

> Whereas in Pakistan, redevelopment for the sake of keeping up with a globalised economy causes the marginalising of the poor sections ... in Europe they concentrate more on social and environmental issues before planning major city changes.
> (Fernandes, 2006)

Gentrification is embedded in what Peck (2010) calls an emergent regime of 'fast' urban policy formation. Fast policies are designed to travel fast, they are post-ideological (and this is important because it means they can be co-opted by those in any part of the political spectrum), pragmatic, and will propagate themselves spatially. Gentrification is sold to us as something that is creative, it is about urban 'renaissance', the rebirth of the central city. Creative neoliberalism is a feel-good term that is hard to argue against (Peck, 2010). As a 'fast policy' gentrification has become easily recognizable: it is easy to sell, as a creative process it is easily summarized and modelled (there are gentrification blueprints). The process itself has been simplified and essentialized ('gentrification generalized'; see Smith, 2002) and the end results are rather general policies that are often spliced with other rather general (but morally persuasive thus making it hard to argue against such forms of 'positive gentrification') policies such as mixed communities policy (see Bridge et al., 2011). Gentrification policies have been successful because they have coincided with a neoliberal climate, advances in communication technology have meant they have been picked up around the world more quickly and effectively, as have the professionalization and increased mobility of policy elites, and they have also coincided with what Peck calls the 'creativity fix' – for example, 'the creative city' which plays off competitive anxieties like league tables, etc. (on the creative city thesis and gentrification, see Lees et al., 2008: preface; Peck, 2005, 2010). Indeed 'creative gentrification' is seen to be a productive process (Peck, 2010: 216–217). We need to know much more about the mobilities of these policies and ideas, and how different policies and ideas have been spliced together to form policies of 'positive (productive) gentrification'. Here gentrification researchers could work at the forefront of a new literature that merges ideas from the policy mobilities literature with ideas from the comparative urbanism literature – for example, McCann and Ward (2010), who argue that in understanding contemporary urban governance in a global context we need to develop a conceptualization that is equally sensitive to the role of relational and territorial geographies, fixity and flow, global contexts and place-specificities (and vice versa), structural imperatives and embodied practices. Focusing on the specifics of gentrification across a variety of cities worldwide would begin the task of decentring the dominant narratives of gentrification from the Global North. But this in, and of, itself is not enough. We need to explore how urban ideologies of gentrification (for they are not singular) have developed, travelled, translated and diffused. We need a sense of both the fixity and the mobility of processes of gentrification. Harris (2008: 2409) has argued that we need to ask who is responsible for the creation of the gentrification blueprint, but I would take this a step further and ask: can we really identify a singular gentrification blueprint? Are there multiple gentrification blueprints? Are the latter inter-related? Following recent work on the mobility and assemblage of urban policies and policy-making (e.g. Brenner et al., 2010; McCann, 2008, 2011; Ward, 2006) and drawing on the work on 'globalized planning cultures' (e.g. Friedmann, 2005) we can begin this task. Gentrification researchers have long been aware of the circulation of gentrification ideologies and policies – in the UK the Urban Task Force (see Lees, 2003b) travelled around Europe and elsewhere undertaking fact-finding on successful urban renaissance initiatives in other cities (Bilbao and Barcelona dominated). There has been discussion of similar policies of gentrification in different countries (e.g. Porter and Shaw, 2008; *Urban Studies*, 2008) but little detailed research into what McCann (2011) calls 'urban policy mobilities'. And there are important questions we need to ask. How does a gentrification blueprint account for and anticipate the geographical and historical specificity of places? What is the complex geographical contingency to gentrification (as part of neoliberal urbanism)? How do gentrification policies emerge in different countries – is it by repetition (copying), borrowing (aspects that suit) or is it reinvented (for a different context)? Is it indigenous? As Robinson (2011b) states:

> There is much at stake in how we characterise the spatiality of urban policy transfer and learning. It is important to question understandings of policy exchange and innovation which are the inheritance of a deeply divided urban studies shaped by colonial and developmentalist assumptions. Conceptualisations of the power relations of learning (often assumed to be imposed by powerful western or international development agents), deeply embedded assumptions about creativity and mimicry as the preserve of wealthier contexts, and presumptions that the trajectories of learning all need to be questioned. In this regard the very vocabulary we choose to use can perpetuate certain assumptions about power relationships – 'trajectories' of policy learning, for example, imply directionality and thus a sense of a distant origin and mimicry on the part of the receiving context, and can also tend to imply a form of imposition ... we need to explore alternative vocabularies and conceptualisations of the spatialities at work in processes of globalisation.
>
> (Robinson, 2011b: 22)

Robinson makes some good points and researchers are beginning to take heed (see Bunnell and Das, 2010), but the reality with respect to gentrification may often be what Robinson would prefer not to see (in terms of power relations) and in following this thinking such 'traditional' power relations must not and cannot be sidelined or ignored. What we need to aim for is more subtle (less black and white) theorizations of the power relations involved in the circulation of gentrification policies (cf. McCann, 2011). If we are to resist gentrification we need to look closely at the spatial dynamics of policy learning – this is a complex and intriguing process:

> The question which is both intellectually and politically important is, what enables ideas to take hold, connections to be forged, relationships to be formed, municipalities to pursue certain agendas, experiences to be packaged as best practice, and what are the effects of these achievements. This matters politically for two reasons. First humanitarian concern about urban conditions in most of the world means that policy action in the field of urban development needs to be able to be affective. Second concerns about the ambitions of powerful agents in this field make the determination of an appropriate political engagement with apparently hegemonic urban policy important.
>
> (Robinson, 2011b: 28)

IV POLICY, RESISTANCE AND COMPARATIVE URBANISM

In 2005 David Harvey criticized social science's lack of radical spirit, arguing that it had moved too far towards political power and the third way. He claimed that we had lost our revolutionary spirit and had forgotten that critical theory is there to understand the world but also to change it. Harvey was particularly critical of 'being policy relevant', which he asserted was about being in bed with government or political power. Some gentrification researchers, and critical geographers, have followed this ideological line (see the commentaries in the *International Journal of Urban and Regional Research*, 2008). I would argue that taking this position on this issue is problematic in the face of the rapid policy transfer of gentrification worldwide. Gentrification researchers cannot avoid being 'policy relevant' even if we dislike that term, and I do; indeed my recent research has been about the lack of, poor, weak, contradictory, and indeed sometimes false 'evidence' behind so-called 'evidence based policy' (see Bridge et al., 2011; Lees, 2008). There are complex political structures (outlined in the quote from Robinson, 2011b, above) that you can only examine and only come to know about if you actually get inside policy organizations (as Peck, 2006, has done most successfully), undertake policy work, and/or policy critique. Getting inside policy organizations, and importantly they are not just purely governmental we must consider the role of think tanks and NGOs, etc. – helps. This is not sleeping with the enemy, it is learning about the enemy in order to confront, resist, undermine and fight the negative aspects of gentrification, especially displacement and sociocultural homogenization. As Harris (2008) states:

> There has been no mapping, for example, of the significant role for new urban-focused think-tanks in the global spread of policies and practices of gentrification. With close connections to governmental, property and media elites, they have helped to push strategies of gentrification onto and up policy agendas.
>
> (Harris, 2008: 2409)

Resistance is a complex process and more often than not the levels, forms and effects of resistance are modest with respect to gentrification. The end point of resistance to gentrification has rarely been an outright victory (and yes this is disappointing) as the fate of the former Woodwards Department Store in Vancouver, Canada, attests to. This symbol of gentrification in the Downtown Eastside of Vancouver was the focus of anti-gentrification activity at the Inaugural Critical Geography Conference in Vancouver (see Lees, 1999). Its 'rehabilitation' is now nearly complete and it is being promoted as a model of 'social inclusivity'. At the end of the day anti-gentrification activists have had to make significant compromises over the massive private (market condos) component to the newly developed Woodwards (see Bula, 2010). Importantly, resistance to gentrification should be a collaborative project, as it was with respect to Woodwards in Vancouver (international academics, artists, locals and activists all came together to fight gentrification), but this collaboration needs to be extended outwards. I would like to see a form of comparative urbanism in which international (Global North and South) anti-gentrification critiques, movements and groups learn from each other and this can be aided by those of us active in the field and who see our work as politically important (see Slater, forthcoming).

Similarly McFarlane (2010) argues for attention 'not just to different scholarly knowledge on cities from social science around the world, but different activist and public knowledges that are important for the production of a more global, more democratic urban studies characterised by diverse urban epistemes and imaginaries'. This is something that gentrification researchers, especially critical geographers, have tried to do (see Porter and Shaw, 2008), but we have a lot more work to do yet. It is certainly worth learning from activist academics like Michael Edwards. Edwards has been engaged with the regeneration of King's Cross in central London over a 20-year period, through research funded by the King's Cross Partnership, advisory work with local authorities and developers, and through his own and student collaborations with the King's Cross Railway Lands Group (www.kxrlg.org.uk) – an umbrella organization of local groups. Importantly, the latter's local work was 'strengthened and refreshed through international collaborations with similar struggles elsewhere in the world in two networks – BISS and INURA (see Edwards, 2010). This kind of outward-looking attention to wider struggles provides an important and steep learning curve and is the first step on the way to bridging local and global, northern and southern, resistances to gentrification.

Given the visceral nature of gentrification in the Global South it may be that we (in the Global North) can learn more about resistance from cities and neighbourhoods there (Harris, 2008, very briefly discusses anti-gentrification efforts in Lower Parel in Mumbai). Fighting gentrification as if it is some singular form of neoliberalism (see Peck's, 2010, critique of Harvey's singular and unambiguous account of neoliberalization as a class project) is not the way forward, for gentrification is not a singular project! It is polycentric, different in different countries, embedded in the soil and institutions of those countries. Precisely because it is not singular means that it will no doubt survive (cf. Brenner et al., 2010).

Part of resisting gentrification is about resisting dominant paradigms and gentrification is embedded in the paradigm of neoliberalism. This is a difficult paradigm to resist, for as Peck (2010) states neoliberalism cannot live on its own and as such it acts like a parasite grafting itself onto other things, onto different markets, even non-market hybrids. We can no longer view gentrification simply as a 'plague of locusts' (see Smith, 1984) devouring neighbourhoods; we need to see gentrification as mutating, as parasitic, as attaching to and living off other policies (e.g. mixed communities policy, the creative city thesis, modernization policies in cities of the Global South and indeed poorer cities of the Global North). In resisting gentrification, fighting gentrification, we must be sensitive to the complexities of gentrification policy production, circulation and consumption, the complexities of gentrifications (plural). Resistance to gentrification, like resistance to neoliberalism, 'does not always conform to the David-and-Goliath metaphor of plucky, local resistance to a metastasizing global project, alternative politics may take radically different, unanticipated forms, cutting a very different course, and, by the same token, (re)shaping the market offensive' (Peck, 2010: 27).

A turn to comparative urbanism is vital in the fight against gentrification. We need to be attuned to the timings and intricacies of gentrifications (and neoliberalisms) worldwide, as Wyly et al. (2010) discuss: as analysts turn to the large-scale gentrification-induced displacements happening in the Global South, gentrification-induced displacement in the Global North is getting harder to measure and easier to ignore because recent gentrification evolved within the broader affordability crisis of the debt-leveraged financialization of housing. Wyly et al.'s (2010) discussion of displacement shows that researchers must pay greater attention to the politics of measurement (as they argue one of the most effective tactics of neoliberalism involves the statistical disappearance of its costs and victims) and to methodological questions around the definition of gentrifying neighbourhoods and the 'endogeneity of displacees' responses that render them statistically invisible' (p. 2605). Measuring the effects of gentrification worldwide and producing maps to demonstrate this could be used strategically to highlight the right to the city (cf. Harvey, 2008; Marcuse et al., 2009; Wyly et al., 2010).

V A POSTCOLONIAL PERSPECTIVE

If gentrification is the new urban colonialism (Atkinson and Bridge, 2005), what might a postcolonial programme of research on gentrification look like? It is clear that cities like Mumbai, Sao

Paulo, Mexico City and Shanghai are now at the cutting edge of urban change. Active processes of gentrification in the USA and Europe today are nothing compared to the '*mega-gentrification*' and associated '*mega-displacement*' that is happening in these cities. In Shanghai nearly a million people have been 'relocated' from the central city to the outskirts of the city over the past 12 years and 51.02 million square metres of housing has been demolished (He, 2007). The Asian Coalition for Housing Rights has monitored evictions in seven Asian countries (Bangladesh, China, India, Indonesia, Japan, Malaysia and the Philippines) and shown that evictions increased dramatically: between January to June 2004, 334,593 people were evicted in the urban areas of these countries; in January to June 2005, 2,084,388 people were evicted. The major reason for these evictions was/is 'the beautification of the city' (read gentrification). In the majority of cases, people did not receive any compensation for the losses they incurred and where resettlement did take place it was 25–60 kilometres from the city centre (Fernandes, 2006). Gentrification in the Global South is leading to the relocation (either formally or informally) of evicted inner-city populations to peri-urban areas far away from their places of work, educational possibilities, social networks and better health facilities. Of course the loss of home and community (see Davidson, 2009, on displacement and dwelling) will be painful in every individual case but the differences (if they are as they seem) in the sheer volume of these displacements cannot be ignored either. Keeping up with evolving laws on property is also vital if we are to understand the mechanisms of displacement/relocation (see Shih, 2010).

It is time now for gentrification researchers to decolonize the gentrification literature away from Euro-American perspectives and to pay much more attention to gentrification in the Global South. Following McFarlane (2010) this involves a:

> constant process of criticism and self-criticism that reflects on how a particular object of comparison is arrived at, and a commitment to develop new objects, methodologies and typologies of comparison through consideration of different theory cultures and perhaps also through new forms of collaboration.
>
> (McFarlane, 2010: 738)

As Harris (2008: 2423) argues, rather than exporting Euro-centric understandings of gentrification to the Global South we need to learn from the 'new sharp-edged forms' of gentrification emerging in the previously peripheral cities of the Global South – 'in this way some of the more parochial assumptions, practices and language of gentrification research can be "provincialized" and re-examined' (Chakrabarthy, 2000).

We need to be clear that neoliberalism is as much a product of the periphery as the centre (cf. Peck, 2010) and a fresh comparative urbanism of gentrification must be open to the hybridity of neoliberalism everywhere. Gentrification, like neoliberalism, is a product of particular historical, contextual and temporal forces. Contextualizing these neoliberalisms is essential in our fight against gentrification. In Shanghai national and local government is forcing large-scale gentrification on particular central city neighbourhoods, selling it not through mixed communities policies like in the Global North but as modernist progress good for the nation as a whole (e.g. He, 2007, 2010). How are ideas and images around 'modernization' travelling? Speaking on 'Urban development in the 21st century', Arif Hasan, comparing cities such as Beijing, Mumbai and Manila, has said that different cities with varied needs and population sizes have some strong similarities, but that whereas politicians in Mumbai aim to make that city resemble Shanghai, politicians in Karachi are striving to make the city look more like Dubai (see Fernandes, 2006; Hasan, 2007). What are the differences and similarities between these neoliberal urban development paradigms, and their effects? Much of what constitutes state-led gentrification in the Global North today takes the form of large-scale urban renewal, a 21-st century form of slum clearance, and in the Global South 'slums' from Mumbai to Santiago de Chile[3] (see Lopez-Morales, 2010, 2011) are being demolished for the purposes of gentrification; yet currently the vast literature on 'slums' pays little attention to the gentrification literature and vice versa – it is evident that this must change. We need to question what we might mean by 'gentrification' and in so doing assess the usefulness and applicability of the term as a conceptual frame for processes in the Global South. This means reconsidering what processes and cases ought to be discussed under the umbrella of 'gentrification' and which ought to be excluded. The relatively recent debates around new-build gentrification (see the 2010 Special Issue of *Population, Space and Place*) were forced to confront the overly restrictive Anglo definition of gentrification, but this confrontation must now go further, for there are processes in cities of the Global South that share many of the same characteristics of 'gentrification' (see Davidson and Lees, 2005, for a list) but they are not called 'gentrification'. Lemanski (2011), for example, talks about the practice of 'downward-raiding' in low-income housing areas in cities of the Global South – a process where middle-income groups unable to afford to live in more formal parts of the city purchase property in low-income, often informal or state-subsidized, residential areas. Lemanski (2011) argues that theories of gentrification and downward-raiding essentially describe and analyse comparable forms of urban change, 'yet their accompanying literatures and popular use are restricted to wholly separate empirical worlds, suggesting that while gentrification is primarily found in "Western" cities, downward-raiding is exclusively reserved for the Southern city slum'. Of course, extending the term 'gentrification' yet again risks it collapsing under the weight of this burden, but as I have argued before this is a risk worth taking. Also, in extending the term to accommodate similar processes in the Global South we are confronted, yet again, with the politics of the term. Is the term 'gentrification' useful politically with respect to the case of 'downward-raiding' in the South African slum, or not? Whatever the answer may be, it is clear that gentrification researchers need to learn more about processes akin to gentrification happening in cities around the world, especially in the Global South.

A postcolonial perspective might help collapse (or prove?) the myth of the linear development of gentrification as travelling from the Global North to the Global South, replacing it with an ontology of relational multiplicity and an epistemology of multiple forms of knowledge in continual construction. Amin and Graham (1997) warned of the dangers of overemphasizing particular spaces, times and partial representations of the city (see also McFarlane, 2010, on paradigmatic urbanism) – something that those who insist on sticking to Ruth Glass's definition of gentrification ignore at their own cost. We need to look at gentrification from 'outside the box' of the Global North and the western post-industrial city, indeed from outside the box of the rather parochial gentrification literature itself; herein at last we have a real opportunity to escape the confines of the traditional theoretical battlegrounds in gentrification (see Lees et al., 2008, on production and consumption accounts). What new, indigenous or cosmopolitan theorizations can be brought to bear on gentrification in the Global South, and in turn the Global North?

VI CONCLUSION

One of the first gentrification researchers to write about 'comparative urbanism' was Andrew Harris in his work on gentrification in London and Mumbai (see Harris, 2008). Harris's work marked a turn away from work that compared the usual suspects (e.g. London and New York City), comparisons that McFarlane (2010) points out are based on similarity rather than difference. Other work on the Global South (for example, on South Africa, Visser and Kotze, 2008; Winkler, 2009; on China, He, 2007, 2010; Wang and Lau, 2009; Wu and Luo, 2007; on Singapore, Wong, 2006) has tended to view gentrification processes in the Global South through the lens of Anglo-American urban theory. There are a whole host of reasons why researchers in the Global South might do this, from the particularities of their place in the global world of academia, to their particular research training, etc. But I would like to see gentrification researchers learning through different (non Anglo-American) urban theory cultures of the city (cf. Robinson, 2002, 2006, on this politics of learning). McFarlane (2010) is right that urban studies has been slow to analyse how the experience of cities in the South might cause us to rethink urban knowledge and urban theory; gentrification studies can probably be exempt from this criticism to date (due to the supposedly later emergence of gentrification in the Global South) but gentrification researchers must now confront this task. We need to attend to 'ways of knowing' gentrification across the North-South divide – investigating in detail what academics, policy-makers, gentrifiers, and especially the communities being gentrified 'know' about gentrification on the ground. Such a project is not amenable to research at a distance – it would necessitate ethnographic engagement and, as Maringanti and Bunnell (2010) argue, this demands the use of language other than English, all kinds of cultural competencies, conceptual flexibility and a willingness to engage with plural traditions (see also Jazeel and McFarlane, 2010, on the complexities of postcolonial knowledge production).[4] Comparative urbanism requires a proper commitment to global learning, to learning through differences, and to being critically reflexive of the power relations between the Global North and the Global South (Jazeel and McFarlane, 2007).

Rethinking the 'geography of gentrification' through comparative urbanism is more than formulating a postcolonial programme of research, for there remain important comparative studies to be made not just between the Global North and the Global South but also between cities in the Global North (see De Verteuil, 2011, on strong- and weak-centred gentrification in London and Los Angeles, respectively) and between cities in the Global South (see Weinstein and Ren, 2009, on gentrification and housing rights in Shanghai and Mumbai). We should not avoid comparing and learning from the usual suspects altogether, but such comparisons should no longer dominate the gentrification literature. Also, as I argued in 2000, context and temporality remain very important. To give an example, Clark (2005: 263) said: 'visiting Malmo, Neil Smith asked me to show him the battlefields of gentrification. At the time, I was at a loss to explain that there were processes of gentrification in Malmo, but no battlefields'. In 2005 gentrification had more 'benign unwindings' in Sweden, but this is changing as the Swedish welfare state and its public housing are dismantled and privatized (see Johnson et al., 2008). Perhaps those battlegrounds are now coming. The battlegrounds in different places will be different. Given the visceral scale of the (direct) displacements happening in the Global South – what Davis (2004: 23) calls the 'brutal tectonics of neoliberal globalization' – the battlegrounds there may be, and may yet be, more bloody, as authoritarian governments stamp out anti-gentrification protest and resistance. As Clark (2005) states:

> In places characterised by a high degree of social polarization, short on legally practised recognition of the rights of users of place and long on legally practised recognition of the rights of owners of space, the conflict inherent in gentrification becomes inflammatory.
> (Clark, 2005: 262)

Only a truly comparative urbanism of gentrification will tell us how and why gentrification has emerged around the world, why gentrification leads to violent conflict in some places and not in others, how we could and should make urban policy responsible and accountable at the global scale (Massey, 2011), and how we might put the question of what a 'Just City' should be on the day-to-day agenda of urban reform worldwide (see Marcuse et al., 2009).

ACKNOWLEDGEMENTS

This paper was first presented to the Center for Metropolitan Studies, Berlin, July 2010 workshop: 'Between thin ideals and thick practicalities: Discussing regeneration policies and anti-gentrification efforts in London and New York'; special thanks to Alessandro Busa, Tom Angotti, and the participants, for their feedback. It was also presented to the Cities Seminar Series, Department of Geography, King's College London, in November 2010 and the 'Cities are back in town: London in comparative perspective' seminar at Sciences Po, Paris, in December 2010. Thanks to those audiences for their feedback, especially Jenny Robinson. I would also like to thank the three referees who gave very useful suggestions for revisions.

NOTES

1. Thanks to John Turnbull, University of Santiago, for pointing this out.
2. Many thanks to Arif Hasan (Chairman of the Urban Resource Centre in Karachi and founding member of the Asian Coalition for Housing Rights) for taking the time to discuss gentrification in Pakistan with me at the IAPS-CSBE and Housing Network Conference in Istanbul, October 2009.
3. Thanks to Roberto Figueroa for pointing me in the direction of what is happening with respect to gentrification in Santiago de Chile.
4. This will necessitate better cross-cultural institutional linkages between universities and urban researchers. The Cities Group at KCL has begun this difficult task. We now run joint PhD programmes between ourselves and Humboldt University in Berlin, Hong Kong University, and the National University of Singapore, and we are working with colleagues in those places and elsewhere on issues around comparative urbanism.

REFERENCES

Amin A and Graham S (1997) The ordinary city. *Transactions of the Institution of British Geographers* 22(4): 411–429.

Anderson M (1964) *The Federal Bulldozer*. Cambridge, MA: MIT Press.

Atkinson R and Bridge G (eds) (2005) *Gentrification in a Global Context: The New Urban Colonialism*. London: Routledge.

Badyina A and Golubchikov O (2005) Gentrification in central Moscow – a market process or a deliberate policy? Money, power and people in housing regeneration in Ostozhenka. *Geografiska Annaler B* 87: 113–129.

Brenner N (2004) *New State Spaces: Urban Governance and the Rescaling of Statehood*. Oxford: Oxford University Press.

Brenner N, Peck J, and Theodore N (2010) Variegated neoliberalization: Geographies, modalities, pathways. *Global Networks* 10(2): 1–41.

Bridge G, Butler T, and Lees L (eds) (2011) *Mixed Communities: Gentrification by Stealth?* Bristol: Policy Press.

Bula F (2010) From slum to new urban mix. *The Globe and Mail*, 5 January.

Bunnell T and Das D (2010) A geography of serial seduction: Urban policy transfer from Kuala Lumpur to Hyderabad. *Urban Geography* 31(3): 1–7.

Butler T (1997) *Gentrification and the Middle Classes*. Aldershot: Ashgate.

Butler T with Robson G (2003) *London Calling: The Middle Classes and the Remaking of Inner London*. London: Berg.

Carpenter J and Lees L (1995) Gentrification in New York, London and Paris: An international comparison. *International Journal of Urban and Regional Research* 19(2): 286–303. Reprinted in Pacione M (ed.) (2002) *The City: Critical Concepts in the Social Sciences, Vol. 2: Land-use, Structure and Change in the Western City*. London: Routledge, 544–566.

Chakrabarty D (2000) *Provincialising Europe*. London: Routledge.

Clark E (1994) Toward a Copenhagen interpretation of gentrification. *Urban Studies* 31(7): 1033–1042.

Clark E (2005) The order and simplicity of gentrification – a political challenge. In: Atkinson R and Bridge G (eds) *Gentrification in a Global Context: The New Urban Colonialism*. London: Routledge, 256–264.

Clay P (1979) *Neighborhood Renewal: Middle Class Resettlement and Incumbent Upgrading in American Neighbourhoods*. Lexington, MA: DC Heath.

Davidson M (2009) Displacement, space/place and dwelling: Placing gentrification debate. *Ethics, Place and Environment* 12(2): 219–234.

Davidson M and Lees L (2005) New build 'gentrification' and London's riverside renaissance. *Environment and Planning A* 37(7): 1165–1190.

Davis M (2004) Planet of slums. *New Left Review* 26(March/April): 5–34.

Dear M (2002) *From Chicago to LA: Making Sense of Urban Theory*. London: SAGE.

De Verteuil G (2011) Evidence of gentrification-induced displacement among social services in London and Los Angeles. *Urban Studies* 48: 1563–1580.

Dutton P (2003) Leeds calling: The influence of London on the gentrification of regional cities. *Urban Studies* 40(12): 2557–2572.

Edwards M (2010) King's Cross: Renaissance for whom? In: Punter J (ed.) *Urban Design and the British Urban Renaissance*. Abingdon: Routledge, 189–205.

Environment and Planning A (2007) Special Issue 39(1), 'Extending gentrification?' Guest edited by Smith D and Butler T.

Fernandes K (2006) *Some Trends in Evictions in Asia*. Bangkok: Asian Coalition for Housing Rights (ACHR).

Friedmann J (2005) Globalization and the emerging cul-ture of planning. *Progress in Planning* 64: 183–234.

Garcia L (2001) Elitización: Proposal in Spanish for the term gentrificación. *Biblio 3W: Revista Bibliográfica de Geografía y Ciencias Sociales* VI(332), 5 December. Available at: www.ub.es/geocrit/b3w-332.htm.

Glass R (1964) Introduction: Aspects of change. In: Centre for Urban Studies (ed.) *London: Aspects of Change*. London: MacKibbon and Kee, xiii–xlii.

Hackworth J and Smith N (2001) The changing state of gentrification. *Tijdschrift voor Economische en Sociale Geografie* 22: 464–477.

Harris A (2008) From London to Mumbai and back again: Gentrification and public policy in comparative perspective. *Urban Studies* 45(12): 2407–2428.

Harvey D (2004) The right to the city. In: Lees L (ed.) *The Emancipatory City?: Paradoxes and Possibilities*. London: SAGE, 236–239.

Harvey D (2005) The sociological and geographical imaginations. *International Journal of Politics, Culture and Society* 18(3–4): 211–255.

Harvey D (2008) The right to the city. *New Left Review* 53: 23–40.

Hasan A (2007) *Confronting the Urban Development Paradigm*. Available at: www.india-seminar.com/2007/579/579_arif_hasan.htm.

He S (2007) State-sponsored gentrification under market transition: The case of Shanghai. *Urban Affairs Review* 43(2): 171–198.

He S (2010) New-build gentrification in central Shanghai: Demographic changes and socio-economic implications. *Population, Space and Place* 16(5): 345–361.

International Journal of Urban and Regional Research (2008) Issue 32(1).

Jazeel T and McFarlane C (2007) Responsible learning: Cultures of knowledge production and the North South divide. *Antipode* 39(5): 781–789.

Jazeel T and McFarlane C (2010) The limits of responsibility: A postcolonial politics of academic knowledge production. *Transactions of the Institute of British Geographers* 35(1): 109–124.

Johnson K, Clark E, Lundholm E, and Malmberg G (2008) Gentrification and social mixing in Swedish cities 1986–2001. *Paper presented to the ESRC Seminar Series Gentrification and Social Mixing*, 22–23 May, Department of Geography, King's College London.

Lees L (1994) Gentrification in London and New York: An Atlantic gap? *Housing Studies* 9(2): 199–217.

Lees L (1999) Critical geography and the opening up of the academy: Lessons from 'real life' attempts. *Area* 31(4): 377–383.

Lees L (2000) A reappraisal of gentrification: Towards a 'geography of gentrification'. *Progress in Human Geography* 24(3): 389–408. Reprinted in Lees L, Slater T, and Wyly E (eds) (2010) *The Gentrification Reader*. Abingdon: Routledge, 382–396.

Lees L (2003a) Super-gentrification: The case of Brooklyn Heights, New York City. *Urban Studies* 40(12): 2487–2509.

Lees L (2003b) Visions of 'urban renaissance': The Urban Task Force Report and the Urban White Paper. In: Imrie R and Raco M (eds) *Urban Renaissance? New Labour, Community and Urban Policy*. Bristol: Policy Press, 61–82.

Lees L (2006) Gentrifying down the urban hierarchy: 'The cascade effect' in Portland, Maine, USA. In: Bell D and Jayne M (eds) *Small Cities: Urban Experience Beyond the Metropolis*. Abingdon: Routledge, 91–104.

Lees L (2008) Gentrification and social mixing: Towards an urban renaissance? *Urban Studies* 45(12): 2449–2470.

Lees L and Ley D (2008) Introduction: Gentrification and public policy. *Urban Studies* 45(12): 2379–2384.

Lees L, Slater T, and Wyly E (2008) *Gentrification*. New York: Routledge.

Lees L, Slater T, and Wyly E (eds) (2010) *The Gentrification Reader*. London: Routledge.

Lemanski C (2011) Urban theory as empirically embedded: Mutated gentrification and downward raiding in a South African 'slum'. *Paper Presented at the Annual RC21 Conference, 'The Struggle to Belong. Dealing with Diversity in 21st Century Urban Settings'*, Amsterdam, 7–9 July.

Ley D (1988) Social upgrading in six Canadian inner cities, 1981–1986. *The Canadian Geographer* 32(1): 31–45.

Ley D (1996) *The New Middle Class and the Remaking of the Central City*. Oxford: Oxford University Press.

Lopez-Morales EJ (2010) Real estate market, state-entrepreneurialism and urban policy in the 'gentrification by ground rent dispossession' of Santiago de Chile. *Journal of Latin American Geography* 9(1): 145–173.

Lopez-Morales EJ (2011) Gentrification by ground rent dispossession: The shadows cast by large scale urban renewal in Santiago de Chile. *International Journal of Urban and Regional Research* 35(2): 330–357.

Macleod G (2002) From urban entrepreneurialism to a revanchist city? On the spatial injustices of Glasgow's renaissance. *Antipode* 34(3): 602–624.

Marcuse P, Connolly J, Novy J, Ollvo I, Potter C, and Steil J (eds) (2009) *Searching for the Just City: Debates in Urban Theory and Practice*. New York: Routledge.

Maringanti A and Bunnell T (2010) Practicing urban and regional research beyond metrocentricity. *International Journal of Urban and Regional Research* 34(2): 415–420.

Massey D (2011) A counterhegemonic relationality of place. In: McCann E and Ward K (eds) *Mobile Urbanism: Cities and Policymaking in the Global Age*. Minneapolis, MN: University of Minnesota Press, Chapter 1.

McCann EJ (2008) Expertise, truth, and urban policy mobilities: Global circuits of knowledge in the development of Vancouver, Canada's, 'four pillar' drug strategy. *Environment and Planning A* 40(4): 885–904.

McCann EJ (2011) Urban policy mobilities and global circuits of knowledge: Towards a research agenda. *Annals of the Association of American Geographers* 101(1): 107–130.

McCann EJ and Ward K (2010) Relationality/territoriality: Toward a conceptualization of cities in the world. *Geoforum* 41: 175–184.

McFarlane C (2010) The comparative city: Knowledge, learning, urbanism. *International Journal of Urban and Regional Research* 34(4): 725–742.

Nijman J (2007) Introduction – comparative urbanism. *Urban Geography* 28(1): 1–6.

Peck J (2002) Political economies of scale: Fast policy, interscalar relations, and neoliberal workfare. *Economic Geography* 78: 331–360.

Peck J (2005) Struggling with the creative class. *International Journal of Urban and Regional Research* 29(4): 740–770.

Peck J (2006) Liberating the city: From New York to New Orleans. *Urban Geography* 27(8): 681–783.

Peck J (2010) *Constructions of Neoliberal Reason*. New York: Oxford University Press.

Phillips M (2004) Other geographies of gentrification. *Progress in Human Geography* 28(1): 5–30.

Population, Space and Place (2010) Special Issue, 'New forms of gentrification: Issues and debates'. Guest edited by Rerat P, Soderstro"m O, and Piguet E.

Porter L and Shaw K (eds) (2008) *Whose Urban Renaissance? An International Comparison of Urban Regeneration Strategies*. Abingdon: Routledge.

Preteceille E (2007) Is gentrification a useful paradigm to analyse social changes in the Paris metropolis? *Environment and Planning A* 42: 2302–2308.

Reiff D (1992) *Los Angeles: Capital of the Third World*. New York: Touchstone.

Rerat P and Lees L (2011) Spatial capital, gentrification and mobility: Lessons from Swiss core cities. *Transactions of the Institute o f British Geographers* 36(1): 126–142.

Robinson J (2002) Global and world cities: A view from off the map. *International Journal of Urban and Regional Research* 26(3): 513–554.

Robinson J (2004) Cities between modernity and development. *South African Geographical Journal* 86(1): 17–22.

Robinson J (2006) *Ordinary Cities: Between Modernity and Development*. Abingdon: Routledge.

Robinson J (2011a) Cities in a world of cities: The comparative gesture. *International Journal of Urban and Regional Research* 35(1): 1–23.

Robinson J (2011b) The spaces of circulating knowledge: City strategies and global urban governmentality. In: McCann E and Ward K (eds) *Mobile Urbanism: Cities and Policymaking in the Global Age*. Minneapolis, MN: University of Minnesota Press, Chapter 2.

Sayer A (2001) For a critical cultural political economy. *Antipode* 33: 687–670.

Shih M (2010) The evolving law of disputed relocation: Constructing inner city renewal practices in Shanghai, 1990–2005. *International Journal of Urban and Regional Research* 34(2): 350–364.

Slater T (2004) North American gentrification? Revanchist and emancipatory perspectives explored. *Environment and Planning A* 36(7): 1191–1213.

Slater T (forthcoming) *Fighting Gentrification*. Oxford: Blackwell.

Smith N (1984) *Uneven Development: Nature, Capital, and the Production of Space*. Oxford: Blackwell.

Smith N (1996) *The New Urban Frontier: Gentrification and the Revanchist City*. London: Routledge.

Smith N (2002) New globalism, new urbanism: Gentrification as global urban strategy. *Antipode* 34(3): 427–450.

Spivak G (1993) *Outside In the Teaching Machine*. London: Routledge.

Urban Studies (2003) Special Issue 40(12), 'The gentry in the city: Upward neighbourhood trajectories and gentrification'. Guest edited by Atkinson R.

Urban Studies (2008) Special Issue 45(12), 'Gentrification and public policy'. Guest edited by Lees L and Ley D.

Visser G and Kotze N (2008) The state and new-build gentrification in central Cape Town, Africa. *Urban Studies* 45(12): 2565–2593.

Wang J and Lau SSY (2009) Gentrification and Shanghai's new middle class: Another reflection on the cultural consumption thesis. *Cities* 26(2): 57–66.

Ward K (2006) Policies in motion, urban management and state restructuring: The trans-local expansion of business improvement districts. *International Journal of Urban and Regional Research* 30(1): 54–70.

Ward K (2008) Commentary: Towards a comparative (re)turn in urban studies? Some reflections. *Urban Geography* 29(4): 1–6.

Ward K (2010) Towards a relational comparative approach to the study of cities. *Progress in Human Geography* 34: 471–487.

Weinstein L and Ren X (2009) The changing right to the city: Urban renewal and housing rights in globalizing Shanghai and Mumbai. *City and Community* 8(4): 407–432.

Winkler T (2009) Prolonging the global age of gentrification: Johannesburg's regeneration policies. *Planning Theory* 8(4): 362–381.

Wong T (2006) Revitalising Singapore's central city through gentrification: The role of waterfront housing. *Urban Policy and Research* 24(2): 181–199.

Wu G and Luo Y (2007) Comparison of gentrification between Chinese and Western cities. *City Planning Review*. Available at: http://en.cnki.com.cn/Article_ en/CJFDTOTAL-CSGH200708008.htm.

Wyly E, Newman K, Schafran A, and Lee E (2010) Displacing New York. *Environment and Planning A* 42: 2602–2623.

10
Hybrid gentrification in South Africa

Theorising across southern and northern cities

Charlotte Lemanski

INTRODUCTION

The relationship between urban theory and urban experience has recently come under close scrutiny, with a growing critique of the ways in which Global North (or Anglo-American/western) urban experiences dominate urban theory (e.g. Robinson, 2006). Concurrently, the broad brushstroke use of 'development' to explain processes in the Global South that would be considered 'social', 'urban', 'economic', 'political' or 'transport' geography if they were located in London or New York, is similarly critiqued (e.g. Rigg, 2007; Williams et al., 2009). This paper challenges the northern empirical basis of urban theory by examining two theories that, despite conceptualising very similar processes, are rarely considered analogous and are embedded in divergent theoretical and empirical worlds. Gentrification and downward raiding essentially describe and analyse comparable forms of urban (mostly residential) class-based change, yet their accompanying literatures and popular use are separate. While gentrification is acknowledged as a major urban studies theme primarily identified in northern central cities,[1] downward raiding is a minor concept in housing- and development-studies addressing the southern 'slum'.[2]

Over the past four decades, a significant body of gentrification literature has emerged. While the concept's origins are traced to Ruth Glass' 1950s/60s East London commentary, when the middle-classes 'invaded' working class quarters of London, renovating 'modest mews' homes into 'elegant, expensive residences' and displacing working-class tenants (Glass, 1964: 19), the recent revival of interest explores gentrification as a symbol of urban change (e.g. Lees et al., 2008). Although the focus of research has broadened, to address for example new gentrifiers such as students (e.g. Smith and Holt, 2007), non-residential and new-build developments (e.g. Davidson and Lees, 2005), and non-urban locales (e.g. Phillips, 2004), attention primarily addresses northern cities. For example, *The Gentrification Reader*'s (Lees et al., 2010) 40 classic texts include none based on case study material outside North America, Europe or Australia. The recently emerging interest in gentrification in the south (e.g. Lees, 2011)[3] accompanies a longer history of gentrification research in specific southern inner cities (e.g. Harris, 2008; Jones and Varley, 1999; Shin, 2009; Visser and Kotze, 2008) that have typically explored how 'gentrification has travelled from the Global North to the Global South' (Lees, 2011: 155). In contrast, this paper analyses gentrification in a southern 'slum-like' settlement,[4] an area more typically reserved for downward raiding terminology, as an example from which to challenge the northern concentration of urban theory.[5] This critique is developed alongside an exploration of downward raiding – a process whereby the emerging indigenous middle-classes, unable to afford rising land costs in established parts of the city, purchase ('raid') property in low-income, often informal or state-subsidised, areas.

DOI: 10.4324/9781003341239-16

The South African case is used to explore the relevance of both gentrification and downward raiding. Despite addressing similar processes of urban change their use is typically restricted to distinct empirical regions (Global North/South) and specific locales within those regions (central city/slum).[6] In this paper, gentrification and downward raiding are used to analyse the sale of state-subsidised houses by low-income beneficiaries to businesses and wealthy families (as property for employees) in South Africa. The research conceptualises resales as a form of 'hybrid gentrification', whereby processes bearing similarities to both existing downward raiding and gentrification theories and trends combine to reveal a new urban concept and methodology for comparative urbanism. Hybrid gentrification as a concept demonstrates that theories rooted in certain empirical locations are enriched by analyses from elsewhere; and more broadly this example demonstrates a methodology for bridging the North – South theory divide.

The data come from five years of extended research in Westlake village, a state-subsidised housing settlement in Cape Town. Three distinct periods of fieldwork (in 2004, 2006 and 2008) involved qualitative semi-structured interviews with residents, officials and local NGOs. A 2006 housing survey comprising semi-structured interviews with 100 households is also used, supplemented by City of Cape Town deeds office data for the settlement. Deeds data for 1999–2005 were acquired and analysed by the author, and 2006–2009 data accessed via the Affordable Land and Housing Data Centre.[7] The topic of this paper was not an intended fieldwork objective, but results from a growing awareness of changes in the community, alongside increasing frustration with urban theories that reflect the experiences of only certain types of cities and spaces.

The paper commences with a brief overview of gentrification and downward raiding literatures within a comparative urbanism framework. The South African context of housing provision and house resales in the case study settlement are then outlined, providing contextualisation for assessing the relevance of gentrification and downward raiding debates. The paper concludes by exploring hybrid gentrification as a concept and method for theorising across northern and southern cities.

GENTRIFICATION AND DOWNWARD RAIDING IN COMPARATIVE URBANISM

Comparative urbanism

This study embraces the recent urban studies 'turn' towards comparative urbanism (e.g. McFarlane, 2010; Nijman, 2007; Robinson, 2011; Ward, 2008, 2010). Whilst intra- and inter-urban comparative studies are nothing new, comparative urbanism argues the need to embrace interdependent South – North urban theorisation, where all cities are equal sites for the creation of theory. This contrasts with prior tendencies to use the South as an 'exotic' case study for northern-based theorisation. Whilst comparative urbanism is increasingly popular in theory, the epistemological and methodological logistics of implementing such an egalitarian approach hamper practical application (Lees, 2011). The methodological approach in this paper is to analyse processes already occurring in the South as dynamics in their own right, rather than as passive recipients or static containers for trends/theories from elsewhere. Identifying these processes can result in practices and theories traditionally associated with the north being challenged and reinvented. This methodological approach is implicitly comparative, bringing into conversation theoretical developments based on different empirical contexts (Robinson, 2011). In exploring the South African case of state-subsidised house resales, this study challenges the narrow concentration of both gentrification (isolated in northern urban studies) and downward raiding (isolated in southern development/housing studies). Analysis demonstrates comparative urbanism in two linked ways: firstly, by interrogating current theoretical approaches through a southern case; and secondly, by integrating two existing approaches, downward raiding and gentrification, to produce the new concept of 'hybrid gentrification'. In addition, this 'hybrid' method provides a model that can be applied in analysing other context-centric (whether northern or southern) theories.

Defining gentrification

Class change, rather than physical environment, is the defining feature of gentrification (Slater et al., 2004); that is, residents' (and ex-residents') class as well as class-based changes in neighbourhood characteristics (e.g. use of public spaces, cultural amenities, service provision) rather than physical characteristics (e.g. whether structures are pre-existing, the area is residential and/or located in the inner city). Gentrification thus represents a much wider set of processes than middle-class (self)renovation of property in run-down urban areas, embracing multiple actors (e.g. middle-class buyers/renovators, developers, estate agents, landlords, state policies) functioning in multiple locales (e.g. inner city, suburbia, rural, commercial, residential). Within this definition, class and the displacement and exclusion of lower-class groups by higher-class groups are the central markers of gentrification.

Defining downward raiding

Downward raiding is equally defined by displacement and exclusion. As middle-income groups 'raid' lower-income areas (often state-subsidised or informal settlements) and undertake service/infrastructural upgrades, low-income residents are both displaced and excluded. Geoff Payne's literature review of land titling in developing countries argues that while downward raiding of state-subsidised settlements could indicate integration into the formal property market and the upward mobility of low-income vendors, in fact down raiding makes it 'more difficult for low-income households to obtain housing in areas originally intended for them' (Payne, 1996: 21). In particular, there is potential that as higher income purchasers improve and resell property they effectively exclude low-income beneficiaries (for whom the housing was originally designed and often state-subsidised) in the short- and long-term (Lemanski, 2011; Payne, 2001; Thirkell, 1996).

Gentrification and downward raiding: parallel processes?

Before developing the comparison, it is important to recognise that gentrification's larger literature, produced by key scholars and recognised as an urban studies theme, provides great depth to the concept. In contrast, downward raiding is rarely the primary focus of research and certainly not considered an urban theme itself, having received virtually no theoretical critique or development, and thus their analysis is unequal.

At their most basic, both concepts involve higher-income groups moving into lower-income areas. Furthermore, both prioritise in-movers (gentry/raiders), representing a higher class/income than previous residents.

In terms of the process, in both cases higher-income/class households ultimately displace prior (poorer) residents, resulting in settlement-wide upgrading. In terms of differences, the types of housing and transaction processes involved typically contrast, with more informal housing and transactions occurring in downward raiding. Terminology differences in socio-economic profile also exist: while the gentry are depicted in class terms, e.g. well-educated professionals; raiders are described in income-terms, e.g. middle-income workers. This semantic divergence implicitly awards the gentry a higher class and income than raiders, a distinction discussed later. In addition there are empirical differences already noted: while gentrification is traditionally analysed in Global North inner cities that have decayed as a result of low-income occupation (and might previously have had high-income occupation), downward raiding is primarily identified in southern slums, typically on the urban edge in areas explicitly intended for low-income occupation (not previously housing higher-income groups). These empirical differences also relate to differential drivers: while both are essentially driven by spiralling land costs, gentrification is increasingly part of state-led regeneration (e.g. Davidson and Lees, 2005; Shin, 2009), whereas downward raiding is largely led by opportunistic individuals. These differences notwithstanding, gentrification and downward raiding refer to very similar processes of urban change, and the absence of prior comparison is surprising.

SOUTH AFRICAN HOUSING CONTEXT

Gentrification and downward raiding in South Africa

Neither gentrification nor downward raiding terminologies are commonly used to explain urban change in South Africa. This is not because these processes do not exist, but the explicit terms are rarely employed. Instead, debates address city centre urban renewal (e.g. Pirie, 2007), suburban desegregation (e.g. Saff, 1998), and the re-informalisation ('slumification') of state-subsidised housing areas (e.g. Robins, 2002).

Visser and Kotze (2008) investigate the paucity of academic gentrification studies in South Africa, critiquing the handful of studies as 'direct applications of Anglo-American debates' lacking local adaptation (2570). Explicit reference to downward raiding in South Africa's urban literature is equally scant. Several studies express concern about the *potential* for downward raiding, fearing that poor beneficiaries could fall prey to offers of cash, resulting in middle-class ownership of assets designed for the poor (e.g. Bond and Tait, 1997; Dewar, 1997; Marx, 2007; Robins, 2002), but no academic discussion or evidence demonstrates whether such processes *actually* exist.

South Africa's state-subsidised housing: the 'problem' of resales

The post-apartheid government's promotion of housing for the poor is a principal foundation of contemporary South Africa. The National Housing Subsidy Scheme effectively provides newly-built 25–30m^2 houses with electricity and running water (colloquially termed 'RDP houses') to low-income households.[8] Despite impressive construction rates, with 3.25 million government subsidies released from 1994 to 2010 (Urban LandMark, 2011), criticisms of the policy are widespread – for example, the quality and size of units, the peripheral location of settlements, the scheme's inflexibility (e.g. home-ownership as the only option), and the 'slum' quality of life (e.g. mass unemployment). In response, the 2004 'Breaking New Ground' Housing Strategy promised a range of tenure options, larger houses and better located settlements, although implementation is limited.

In addition, concerns regarding state-subsidised houses being sold for low values, with sellers returning to informal settlements, led to a prohibition on RDP house sales for the first eight years of ownership (later reduced to five). However, officials admit that implementing the ban is virtually impossible and that informal RDP house sales thrive (Cape Argus, 2003).

In 2008, South Africa's Housing Minister announced that following a national audit of state-subsidised housing, all beneficiaries who illegally sold or leased their house would face criminal charges, and all non-original beneficiaries living in RDP houses would be evicted (Cape Argus, 2008c).[9] This criminalisation of vendors reveals the government's understanding of agency in RDP resales, problematising beneficiaries as the sole agents in the process, with no recognition of other factors (e.g. beneficiary poverty, pressure from buyers, shortage of affordable housing stock, failings of the housing policy). This negative view of vendors is pervasive amongst housing officials and politicians. For example, the Western Cape's Housing MEC blames RDP resales on poor homeowners' frivolous lifestyles, 'spend[ing] all their money on drinking' (Cape Argus, 2008b), while the City of Cape Town Human Settlement Director argues that 'from a moral point of view it is wrong to sell or lease out your [state-subsidised] house' (Cape Argus, 2005). However, blaming beneficiary vendors not only contradicts government visions of state-subsidised housing as a financial asset for wealth creation by failing to acknowledge vendors as property owners with the authority to sell/let (Lemanski, 2011), but also ignores the perilous financial position of beneficiaries, often forced to sell property in order to cope with unexpected crises or long-standing debts (Barry, 2006; Robins, 2002).

Despite significant media attention on RDP resales, reliable data are scarce and fragmented. Indeed, 'while there is little research on the tradable value of subsidized housing it is widely understood that there has been substantial depreciation in formal sales' (FinMark Trust, 2007). Anecdotal perceptions of RDP resales as: (1) unregistered/illegal; (2) widespread; and (3) under-valued are challenged in the following literature review, indicating that both legal and illegal transactions exist, are less common than anticipated, and that property prices vary significantly.

Firstly, although most RDP transactions are informal (often because of the confusing, lengthy and expensive registration process), these 'unregistered' transactions are witnessed by a neighbour, councillor or police affidavit and thus some transaction record exists (Marx, 2007).

Secondly, in exploring whether resales are widespread, the handful of studies reveal transactions rates ranging from 6 to 30%, which although far lower than scare-mongering media accounts of 50–80% (Cape Argus, 2008b), such a wide range limits its applicability as a baseline. For example, while Boaden and Karam's (2000) research across four Cape Town RDP settlements revealed that 10–30% of RDP houses in each settlement had transacted, more recent research identified much lower RDP transaction rates of 6% (Marx, 2007: 138) and 9% (Vorster and Tolken, 2009: 93).[10] Whilst an initial period of intense property transactions occurs as beneficiaries first arrive, gradually abating as settlements consolidate (Boaden and Karam, 2000), this does not explain the data variability, which arguably stems from limited information on RDP house transactions as well as significant variability between settlements.

Thirdly, while transaction values vary significantly, under-valued sales certainly occur. Whilst RDP houses in well-located areas are highly-valued, most RDP houses transact for a fraction of their 'market value' (ZAR45,000 according to 2007 Cape Town municipal valuation; Cape Argus, 2008a), often below construction costs. Ironically, the prohibition on RDP house sales has had a perverse effect: lowering tradable values (as vendors cannot offer tenure security) and encouraging informal transactions (as sales cannot be legally registered), rather than halting transactions. In 2000 low value transactions were common – up to ZAR10,000 (in some cases considerably less) – representing 33–54% of the house subsidy (Boaden and Karam, 2000). However, average RDP transaction values have risen over time, to ZAR14,000 in 2004 (SDMS, 2004), and ZAR22,000 within the Western Cape province over the 2006–2008 period, though averages of ZAR34,000 in the City of Cape Town for the same period reveal significant location-based variability (Vorster and Tolken, 2009). These averages also conceal under-valued transactions, with approximately 30% of state-subsidised property transactions in 2006–2008 involving amounts below ZAR15,000 (Vorster and Tolken, 2009).[11] Thus while state-subsidised property prices have certainly risen, many sales remain below municipal valuations.

CASE STUDY: RESALES IN A STATE-SUBSIDISED HOUSING SETTLEMENT

Westlake is a state-subsidised housing settlement situated on the fringes of Cape Town's wealthy suburbs and developed in 1999, prior to restrictions on state-subsidised house sales (thus transactions can be legally registered). It is part of a larger development that comprises a business park, office park, gated community, private school and retail centre, and is thus in proximity to employment opportunities. Housing beneficiaries previously resided on the land in informal structures and decaying brick-built buildings, and were awarded certificates of subsidy eligibility in 1997, moving *en masse* to state-subsidised houses in December 1999 (Lemanski, 2008).

Westlake's one-bedroom houses cost ZAR35,000–ZAR40,000 to construct including land, infrastructure and top structure (Constantiaberg Bulletin, 1999), and thus sales below this figure represent financially under-valued transactions. At occupation new homeowners were given leaflets explaining the responsibilities of homeownership, the property value and their ineligibility for future housing subsidies, and virtually all residents interviewed by the author since 2004 have known these facts. Fewer than six months after occupation, local media reported house sales for as little as ZAR10,000–ZAR20,000, blamed on beneficiaries' failure to understand the value of the asset and the one-off nature of the subsidy, as well as their need for cash to finance drug and alcohol vices (e.g. Constantiaberg Bulletin, 2000). However, evidence for sales was largely anecdotal, reported in low-quality newspapers.

Official deeds data for 2000–2006 indicate that of Westlake's 650 houses/plots, 70% (452) were owned by original RDP beneficiaries in November 2006. The remaining 198 residential properties/plots transacted after 1999 occupation, and thus almost one-third of Westlake properties are owned by non-beneficiaries. However, 51 of these properties/plots are empty plots sold by developers to local wine estate owners in 2003–2004 (subsequently building houses for employees) and thus are not resales from RDP beneficiaries (though they may contribute to gentrification and/or downward raiding). The remaining 147 properties represent RDP house resales, of which 24 have transacted more than once, indicating that at least a quarter (25%) of original beneficiaries have sold state-subsidised property.[12] This figure is comparable to suburban turnover rates and disputes media exaggerations.

Furthermore, the number of transactions per year has gradually decreased since 2003 (Figure 1), potentially indicating decreased desire to sell alongside decreased buyer interest.

Westlake's mean house prices have multiplied five times during the nine years of registered property transfers, from an average of ZAR24,458 in 2000 to ZAR123,411 in 2009 (Figure 1). However, average transaction values in other state-subsidised settlements are much lower, for example ZAR48,526 and ZAR48,400 in Delft South and Dunoon respectively in 2009, both large RDP settlements on the fringes of the Cape

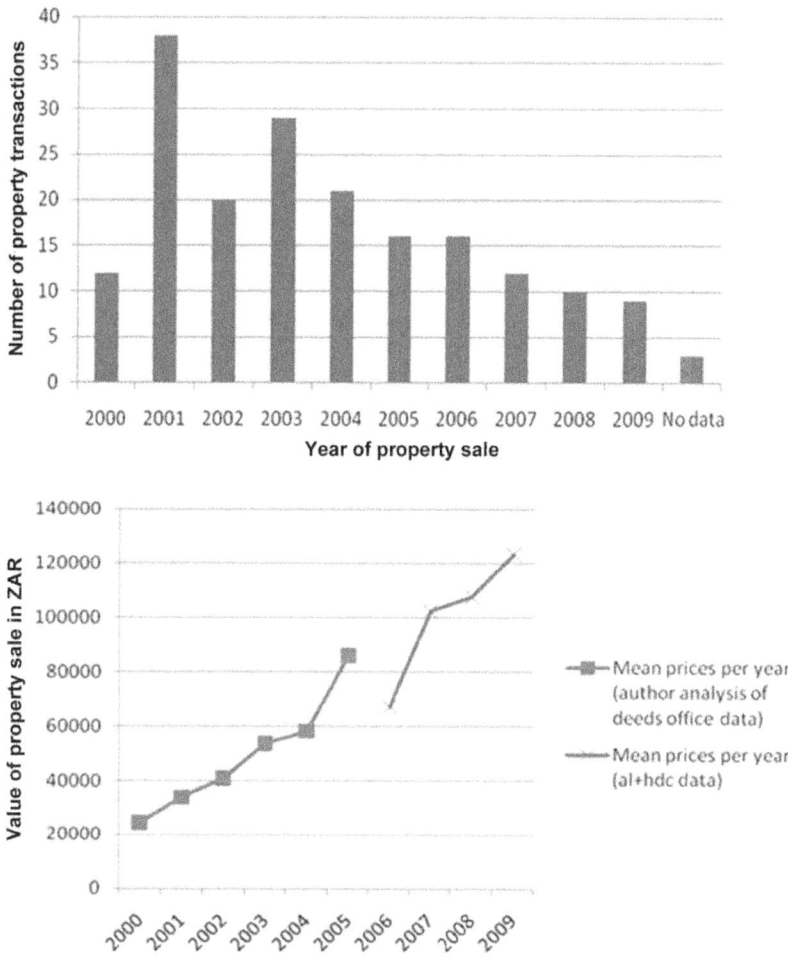

Figure 1 Number and mean prices of property sales, Westlake village, 2000–2009.

Note. These data represent the 147 RDP properties that have transacted (not the newly purchased farm-worker plots). These data are limited because the year in which previous house sales occurred (e.g. the first and second transactions for a property that has changed ownership two or three times respectively) were unavailable so each entry represents a property rather than a transaction per se (however, only 24 properties have changed ownership more than once so this margin of error is minimal).

metropolitan area (www.alhdc.org.za). Westlake's higher property values are explained by its location, close to economic opportunities and on the fringe of wealthy suburbs, and thus attractive to businesses and wealthy families requiring nearby staff. Nevertheless, Westlake's higher prices remain miniscule compared to property prices elsewhere in the city, and do not enable upward mobility for vendors (Lemanski, 2011).

GENTRIFICATION AND DOWNWARD RAIDING IN STATE-SUBSIDISED HOUSING

Three criteria for analysing the extent of gentrification and downward raiding in a new empirical context are identified (these are necessarily broad and not exhaustive). Firstly, both concepts require that property purchasers in a specific area are a higher socio-economic class than vendors. Secondly, the physical and/or economic displacement and exclusion of lower-class residents is an explicit element of gentrification and an implicit consequence of downward raiding. Thirdly, some form of settlement-wide upgrading is essential, with gentrifiers altering the area's class-based nature (e.g. physical and cultural changes), while raiders typically contribute infrastructural upgrades to under-serviced areas.

Class differential

In establishing class differentiation between state-subsidised property vendors and buyers, the former provide the baseline for comparison. Vendors are subsidy beneficiaries and thus household income is below ZAR3500 pcm, with the majority of Westlake household incomes below ZAR1600 pcm (59%), including 15% of households receiving no income (Ngetu, 2003). In contrast, profiling buyers is more complex. Existing literature is silent on state-subsidised house buyers, and deeds office data do not provide socio-economic profiles. However, survey data identified the vast majority of purchasers in Westlake village as wealthy landowners and businesses from nearby areas, purchasing property for employee-occupation.

The 2006 housing survey revealed nearly one-fifth (19%) of houses as owned by non-original residents (slightly below the 25% identified in deeds office data). Most non-original homeowners received property via an employer (84%), with only a handful (16%) purchasing houses independently (with bank loans). Although local elites buy property for employee-occupation (often accompanied by title deeds via salary-sacrifice), their extreme purchasing power (relative to low-income households) arguably dictates Westlake's housing market. Property prices in Westlake vary significantly, but the ZAR123,411 average in 2009 (Figure 1) is almost loose change for large companies with multi-million rand turnovers and families owning homes worth ZAR4–6million (2009 property prices in adjacent Silvertree estate; www.pamgolding.co.za), yet likely to exclude potential low-income buyers. Three employer-types dominate Westlake's property market: local wine estate owners, Westlake business park companies, and wealthy families from nearby suburbs.

In 2003–2004, local wine estate owners purchased empty plots and existing properties in Westlake village. The plots were originally intended to house RDP beneficiaries (and thus were zoned residential and situated within the development), but were excess after all eligible beneficiaries were identified in the late-1990s. In 2000, via settlement-wide leafleting, the remaining plots were offered to Westlake residents (e.g. households ineligible for an RDP house due to arriving in the community after the 1997 housing survey) for ZAR20,000–ZAR25,000 (John Edgar, project manager, 29 April 2004, personal communication).[13] Despite interest from 200 local residents, none bought a plot (Colin Green, developer, 15 April 2004, personal communication). Instead, nearby wine estate owners bought the plots for ZAR20,000 each (Lowell Jooste, farm-owner, 27 October 2006, personal communication) in addition to nine houses from original subsidy beneficiaries for ZAR25,000–ZAR75,000 (average ZAR42,000). Such amounts are beyond the reach of low-income potential buyers (given inability to purchase a plot for less), and thus the arrival of farm-workers caused disgruntlement.

> There was a shortage of homes – there were 50 they didn't build – so people are up in arms that the spare land has gone to the farm people.
>
> (SD, 12 February 2004)

Houses built for farm employees are larger than state-subsidised houses, and the socio-economic profile of new occupants from local farms (i.e. working-class labourers with regular incomes and benefits) is higher than original RDP beneficiaries, who are largely irregularly- and under-employed. Therefore, the physical presence of farmworkers and their larger houses altered the area's class demographics. For example a social worker commented:

> one farmer's wife has started a soup kitchen for the Westlake people. They're not rich people but they contribute to the area, but the poorer people [feel] hostility living with difference.
> (JF, 4 May 2004)

Farmworkers equally identified the difference, with many feeling unsafe in this new 'rowdy' area filled with people and lifestyles so dissimilar to their own.

In 2000 a manufacturing company relocated to the Westlake business park seeking affordable and nearby accommodation for existing factory-level employees. The company leafleted Westlake village requesting sellers, and successfully purchased 35 houses in 2000–2001 (Omnipless representative, 3 May 2004, personal communication). All transactions were legally processed by the deeds office, but as the company made employees the property owners (via a company-sponsored loan paid from employee salaries) they are difficult to identify in deeds data, although interviews indicate that the company paid ZAR35,000–ZAR60,000 per house.

> My son-in-law's mother sold her Westlake house for R50,000 or 60,000 . [The company] bought it for their workers.
> (TC, 7 April 2004)

> [The company] bought the house, they paid R60,000 and I paid R5,000 for the deposit and R2,800 for the transfer fees. I have the deeds and now I pay for the house from my salary.
> (PX, 30 April 2004)

Not only are property purchasers (a commercial business) from a different economic world to sellers (e.g. in terms of available finance), and thus able to influence Westlake's property market, but new occupiers (i.e. factory employees) are of a higher and more stable income than original beneficiaries, able to afford the financial demands of a deposit and monthly house repayments, clearly affecting the area's class profile.

The third type of employer-purchaser, wealthy families seeking accommodation for domestic workers and gardeners, are also difficult to identify in deeds office data, but evidence from interviews indicates this is a common and ongoing trend, also contributing to high prices (by RDP standards) and a market controlled by the non-poor.

> Recently a guy offered me R100,000 – he's a doctor. He was buying for his maid. He came here in a very fancy car.
> (MF, 21 September 2006)

> My wife is a domestic worker. [Her] boss organised this house. He bought it but I have to pay him back. He paid R50,000 for it 2 years ago. I . pay him R700 a month. It will take 4 or 5 years then we're finished.
> (KP, 6 September 2006)

Based on deeds office data and qualitative fieldwork, property ownership in Westlake village is undergoing downward raiding, as companies and individuals far wealthier than the intended low-income market for state-subsidised houses purchase property. However, the lack of purchaser-occupation limits gentrification processes, as the socio-economic profile of occupants is only slightly higher than vendors. The main factor restraining high-income purchaser-occupation is an unwillingness to live in an area that, despite being in proximity to wealthy suburbs, is very poor. Recognising this, in 2005 a developer attempted to buy all 650 houses/plots in Westlake village for ZAR45,000–ZAR50,000 per unit and offered to relocate vendors to a nearby township (*Cape Times*, 2005). Although the community overwhelmingly rejected the proposal, it indicates the extent of interest in well-located state-subsidised settlements as well as the potential for (presumably new-build) gentrification if a developer were willing to buy houses gradually and quietly.

While the class and income difference between poor beneficiary vendors and high-income, often commercial, property purchasers is huge, there is also a small but significant socio-economic distinction between original residents and new occupants. While beneficiary residents are largely un-, under- and informally-employed, new occupiers are formally and regularly employed, resulting in substantial differences in terms of financial security, employment tenure, and housing upgrades. John Harriss (2006: 447–448) makes a similar distinction in urban India, differentiating between the 'informal working class' as the highly vulnerable subaltern lacking employment protection and dependent on casual forms of labour, and the 'labour aristocracy' (in strictly relative terms), in permanent wage work, able to draw on trade union resources and legal protection. Such categories are broadly applicable in the South African case, with vendors and occupiers conceptualised as low- and middle-income respectively (in relative terms).

It is difficult to predict whether this influx of middle-income occupiers (and high-income buyers) is a short- or long-term trend. Although Figure 1 indicates the decreasing frequency of house sales, interviewees indicate continuing demand for state-subsidised houses, particularly from middle-class families seeking accommodation for domestic employees. Indeed, given the shortage of affordable housing in South Africa, this supply – demand mismatch could force prices up, ultimately ensuring that *only* high-income individuals or companies can afford well located state-subsidised property, and perpetuating continued income differentials between original and new occupiers. The ALDHC data differentiate between 'individual' and 'company' purchasers, revealing that although nearly three-quarters (70%) of Westlake village property buyers in 2004–2009 were 'individuals' (many of whom would be middle-class families purchasing property for domestic employees or companies registering occupier-employees as purchaser), companies play a significant role, purchasing nearly one-quarter (23%) of Westlake's state-subsidised properties since 2004.[14]

High demand for state-subsidised houses from companies and wealthy families could be a unique consequence of Westlake's location (proximity to a business park and high-income suburbs). However, similar demand is identified elsewhere, with estate agents interviewed for the Western Cape Occupancy Study commenting on growing interest from business owners in purchasing RDP houses for employees (Vorster and Tolken, 2009). This indicates Westlake as a forerunner for the future rather than a unique outlier, especially given the current policy focus on situating RDP settlements in proximity to economic activity.

Displacement and exclusion

Downward raiding and gentrification processes both result in the physical and economic displacement of lower-income groups as higher-income owners drive up property prices to such an extent that not only are original occupiers displaced (often indirectly; Davidson and Lees, 2005) but low-income potential owners are ultimately excluded. Although these processes of exclusion and displacement are more explicitly acknowledged in gentrification studies (albeit under-researched; see Slater, 2006), they remain a key element of downward raiding, with downward property sales resulting in the exclusion of the poor rather than the upward mobility of vendors or market integration of state-subsidised housing (Payne, 2001).

Westlake vendors face indirect and 'exclusionary displacement' (Slater, 2009: 303) because not only are original state-beneficiaries replaced with higher-income employee-owners, but future low-income residents are also excluded. Although home-owner beneficiaries can ultimately choose not to sell, this 'choice' is constrained by the high costs of homeownership compared to the low incomes required for subsidy eligibility (i.e. beneficiaries are 'cash poor, asset rich'). Following a house sale, subsidy vendors are physically and economically displaced from the area, due to rising property prices as a consequence of high-income purchasers that restrict future low-income households from buying property in the area.[15] Furthermore, the 'once-in-a-lifetime' subsidy means that vendors face permanent exclusion from this element of the welfare state, and potentially from homeownership for life; the consequent exclusion is far more permanent than merely being priced out of the area in the classic

Settlement upgrading

Gentrifying neighbourhoods exhibit visible physical characteristics, for example, renovated/extended houses alongside new services and cultural amenities that reflect changing class demographics. Similarly, raiders bring property upgrades and infrastructural improvements, particularly in settlements with poor service provision.

A significant proportion of Westlake's newly-purchased properties have been physically upgraded (see Figure 2). New owners, financially supported by employers, have extended and improved properties to better suit their middle-income status. All properties purchased by commercial companies and farm-owners were upgraded and extended prior to employee occupation, and newly-built farm-worker houses are slightly bigger than original state-subsidised houses. However, this does not entail settlement-wide upgrading, as no new services or cultural amenities have accompanied the arrival of middle-income residents (basic infrastructure already exists). While specific houses have undergone improvements, the area as a whole remains low-income, hosting mostly run-down houses and few cultural amenities. These physical upgrades, restricted to individual houses rather than the community as a whole, resonate with the early stages of downward raiding and gentrification, but have not (yet) led to service or cultural upgrades in the wider community.

Implications for South Africa

The implications of gentrification and downward raiding in state-subsidised settlements are significant in South Africa in at least two ways. Firstly, the displacement of low-income beneficiaries (sellers) into informal settlements has

Figure 2 Left panel: Original subsidy semi-detached properties, Westlake village; Right panel: upgraded properties, Westlake village.

Note. All photos taken by author, October 2006.gentrification conceptualisation of exclusion. Thus the case study presented confirms the concerns of downward raiding research, that state-subsidised house sales do not result in the upward mobility of vendors (who largely return to informal housing; Lemanski, 2011) or the market integration of state-subsidised housing (as the 'market' is narrowly confined to a handful of wealthy buyers), but rather, the (potentially permanent) exclusion of the poor from housing originally designed and state-subsidised to benefit them.

consequences for the permanence of informal housing (households can only receive one subsidy), an anathema to the South African state vision of formal homeownership and the eradication of informality. Secondly, the concentration of access to property ownership in high-income groups (mostly employers), with the financial strength to dictate and control the state-subsidised housing market, destroys the post-apartheid vision of equality and poverty alleviation via housing. Thus, while the primary focus of this paper is to highlight the limitations of restricting theoretical labels to narrow empirical sites, the case study reveals the importance of this specific process in South Africa.

Furthermore, the transfer of state-subsidised (or recently titled) housing from low- to high-income groups raises important moral/ideological concerns more broadly in the Global South, particularly given the lack of vendor movement up the property ladder (Lemanski, 2011). In other words, the poor are not simply sacrificing their current accommodation but potentially their only chance for decent housing and wealth creation through property, whilst the middle-classes and private sector are benefiting from state investment for the very poor. This moral/ideological perspective is easily overlooked by northern-centric theory's reliance on the capitalist market (albeit sometimes in tandem with the state) as the primary generator of housing investments and processes, thus highlighting the ways in which prioritising context and processes in the South as legitimate in their own right (rather than as examples of northern theories) introduces new challenges for urban theory and practice.

HYBRID GENTRIFICATION

The ways in which property sales in South Africa's state-subsidised market provide distorted echoes, rather than identical duplications, of both gentrification and downward raiding, result in this paper coining the phrase 'hybrid gentrification' (with downward raiding conceptualised as a hybrid form of gentrification). Hybrid gentrification not only explains the non-classic processes demonstrated in the South African case, but also provides a methodology from which to challenge and redevelop context-specific theory (whether based on northern, southern or regional contexts). Three examples of this hybridisation are discussed: the significance of agency, the role of context and process, and the moral/economic status of housing.

Both gentrification and downward raiding debates favour binary agency conceptualisations addressing buyers/sellers and winners/losers. However, the empirical example in this research highlights a third agent: occupiers receiving 'mixed benefits'. While the resale process has clearly displaced and excluded the very poor (as sellers and potential buyers), it has also benefitted 'not-so-poor' occupants who would otherwise be unable to access homeownership – a process and agency that cannot be adequately conceptualised within existing urban theories. Furthermore, the agency of both buyers and occupiers fits neither typical gentry nor raider motivations and profiles. While new occupiers demonstrate classic raider traits (i.e. labourers with regular but small incomes, unable to afford housing elsewhere in the city), their agency is hybridised because they are not a new indigenous middle-class and are not buyers themselves. Instead, the profile and motivations of actual buyers are rather different, being upper- and middle-class households and businesses purchasing property for employee-occupation (and often ownership), and thus fit neither classic raider profiles nor gentrifying motivations. One outcome of these hybrid agency identities is that while property prices have risen due to big business (and wealthy family) buyers, this is not matched by infrastructural/cultural change, an unexpected outcome according to classic theories. Consequently, a 'hybrid gentrification' approach is needed in order to understand and analyse the motivations of various actors.

Hybrid gentrification recognises the importance of context and process in redeveloping theoretical models. For example, two traditional theories of gentrification causality are the 'rent gap' production-side hypothesis, focusing on the gap between current and potential property prices/rents; and consumption-side arguments, focusing on the middle-class agency of buyers seeking a greater quality of life. While both theories have relevance in Westlake (and other well-located state-subsidised settlements), neither is able to adequately explain the specific context.[16] While Westlake's low prices relative to neighbouring suburbs (albeit high relative to other state-subsidised settlements) could potentially soar if the village experienced *significant* alteration (recognised by the developer attempting to buy all properties in 2005), production-side factors are not relevant in this hybridised case because buyers are not seeking to capture the rent gap in value accruing to themselves (most employer-purchasers were passing ownership to employee-occupiers). Similarly, while buyers are seeking a greater quality of life in terms of the proximity of employees (and potentially altruism in improving employees' lives), consumption-side factors are not significant because buyers are not occupiers (and because occupiers have minimal agency in determining their move). However, that is not to suggest that traditional theories are irrelevant, for example rent gap analyses could be used to identify state-subsidised settlements at risk of gentrification and downward raiding, but they would need redefining in relation to a broader range of empirical contexts and processes.

A further theoretical disjuncture exists in approaches to understanding housing markets. While traditional gentrification theory conceptualises housing as an economic opportunity, downward raiding prioritises the welfare role of housing, and both theories rely on the capitalist market to explain change (e.g. motivations for buying/selling). However, hybrid gentrification acknowledges the mixed nature of housing as an economic and welfare asset (for buyers, sellers and occupiers), that functions within both the capitalist and welfare market (i.e. housing produced and subsidised by the welfare market transfers to the capitalist market via transaction processes, but leaves vendors excluded from both welfare and capitalist housing markets). A hybrid method therefore forces analysis to consider a broader range of forces shaping urban space and housing markets, leading to unexpected outcomes (e.g. the permanent exclusion of vendors from homeownership) and challenges northern theory's over-reliance on theorising gentrification in terms of the capitalist market.

The hybrid gentrification concept and method is not exclusively relevant to this specific South Africa case, but serves as a model for expanding gentrification studies beyond their northern concentration, as well as for theorising across northern and southern cities more broadly. By demonstrating the ways in which using diverse and unexpected empirical examples can develop and challenge theoretical labels and accompanying debates, hybrid gentrification provides a template for analysis that bridges the north/south theoretical divide, allowing 'northern' urban theories to be reshaped and refined by 'southern' practices (and vice versa).

CONCLUSION

This paper develops hybrid gentrification as both a concept that highlights the diversity of gentrification/raiding processes across the globe, as well as an analytical method that enables southern trends to challenge northern theories. Until recently there has been a dearth of analysis questioning and challenging the empirical concentration of gentrification debates in the Global North (downward raiding debates are too thin to support self-analysis). At this critical juncture, with gentrification debates starting to recognise the comparative urbanism movement (e.g. Harris, 2008; Lees, 2011) it is crucial that this 'turn' avoids replicating prior tendencies to use the south as an exotic case study for northern-based theory and instead embraces the challenge to redefine gentrification theory using global examples.

This paper explored state-subsidised housing resales in South Africa as an example that demonstrates the need for northern-based urban theory to be redefined by contextual realities in the South. Highlighting the sale of state-subsidised houses to the elite (as accommodation for employees), analysis revealed that processes of upward and downward housing stock filtering involve more complex purchase and occupation patterns than commonly acknowledged. A comparative urbanism perspective illuminates the hybrid nature of gentrification processes in this example, consequently challenging the northern empirical focus of urban theory.

Based on the South African example presented in this paper, there are clear gaps in gentrification theory in terms of the significance of agency, the role of context and process, and the moral status of housing in a welfare/market context. For example, the differentiation between purchasers and occupiers is not adequately addressed in either gentrification or downward raiding literatures, raising questions about whether these processes require the middle-classes to actually occupy or merely purchase property given the consequences for settlement upgrading (or lack thereof). Furthermore, this example also reveals the need for a complex conceptualisation of key players. From a class perspective purchasers are the gentry (i.e. middle-class families and commercial enterprises), while occupiers are raiders (i.e. working class labourers). However, from a dynamic perspective the roles are reversed because while middle-class elites are 'raiding' state-subsidised properties as buyers, new working-class occupiers have the potential to upgrade (or gentrify) the settlement (although settlement-wide upgrading has not occurred in Westlake). Thus, using a southern slum-like case study that is atypical for gentrification reveals challenges and critiques for theoretical debates, highlighting the ways in which theory can be built across different contexts.

At a broader scale, this paper argues that comparative urbanism's call for a more egalitarian urban theory can be implemented by taking context-specific empirical trends and theoretical resources as an analytical starting point (rather than applying theories rooted in the one context to another) from which to challenge existing, and create new, urban theories. This cross-context approach to urban theory prioritises empirical experience and theoretical development as relevant for *all* cities, and entrenches a more dynamic relationship between isolated strands of academic literature. Although this paper uses a southern empirical example to critique northern-based theory, the approach can be reciprocated to critique the relevance of theories rooted in various contexts. Whilst beyond the scope of this paper, the sale of UK council housing to high income/class groups presents a possible case study. The 1980s 'right-to-buy' scheme enabled tenants to purchase council-owned accommodation at a large discount. In the interim thirty years many ex-council properties have since resold on the private market to higher-income buyers, facilitating a transition from working-class to middle-class ownership of former council housing, particularly in well-located areas (Chaney and Sherwood, 2000). Unsurprisingly, downward raiding terminology is rarely employed, though buyers match 'raider' profiles and motivations in terms of their inability to afford property elsewhere. This could be a fruitful line of future enquiry, implementing comparative urbanism by exploring existing processes of urban change as a means to challenge and refine theory.

ACKNOWLEDGEMENTS

The author is grateful for critical comments received from Gustav Visser, Sarah Charlton and Jenny Robinson on earlier drafts of this paper, as well as feedback received on various conference presentations of the paper, and also from the anonymous reviewers.

FUNDING

The research for this paper was spread over several years, incorporating research projects funded by the Economic and Social Research Council, The Leverhulme Trust and the Royal Geographical Society.

NOTES

1. Although gentrification studies now include empirical examples beyond the west (e.g. Lees, 2011) and inner city (e.g. Phillips, 2004), the bulk of research addresses the northern central city.
2. The problematic 'slum' label (Gilbert, 2007) is used here to acknowledge its widespread use as short-hand for the southern city and urban poverty (e.g. Rao, 2006).
3. Also evident from the 2012 seminar series – *Towards an emerging geography of gentrification in the Global South*. Retrieved from www2.lse.ac.uk/geographyAndEnvironment/News%20archive/SeminarSeries.aspx.
4. 'Slum' is rarely used in South Africa (township/informal settlement are preferred), and the state-subsidised housing example in this paper is technically not a slum, but exhibits slum-like characteristics.
5. Harris (2008) equally argues that his Mumbai case provides an example from which gentrification theories and debates can learn.
6. Although gentrification research has expanded beyond the inner city, it remains the primary locale.
7. The ALHDC (www.alhdc.org.za) provides online deeds office data for neighbourhoods with average house prices below ZAR500,000 (ZAR11.1 = GBP1, www.xe.com).
8. Eligible households must: be earning below ZAR3500pcm; be South African citizens; be married or have a dependent; and have not previously owned property or received a subsidy.

9. The occupancy audit was conducted in 2009–2010, covering 262,686 households in seven provinces (Urban Land Mark, 2011, representing approximately 10% of housing units). No charges have been brought against beneficiaries or occupants.
10. The 9% rate from the Western Cape Occupancy Study (which surveyed 2835 RDP houses) is limited by its methodology (surveying only properties where original beneficiaries remained the registered owner).
11. ZAR exchange rate fluctuated between GBP1 = ZAR10–18 from 2000 to 2007 (www.x-rates.com).
12. Unregistered transactions are rare in Westlake village because the local councillor, a lawyer, offered *pro bono* conveyancing to Westlake villagers and because most purchasers (businesses and wealthy families) favour formal procedures. However, as there are likely to be some unregistered transactions, 25% transaction rates are an under-count.
13. Due to the original developer-municipal agreement for Westlake, potential 'spare plot' purchasers could not access a state subsidy.
14. The remaining 6% were purchased by 'government', presumably as part of the 2002 housing amendment requiring vendors to offer provincial government first refusal.
15. A major shortcoming of this research is the absence of interviews with state-subsidised house vendors. Difficulty identifying vendors is linked to the illegality of state-subsidised house sales. Interestingly, gentrification researchers acknowledge similar problems accessing displaced individuals and communities (Slater et al., 2004).
16. While not the first to suggest that consumption and/or production theories of gentrification are irrelevant in many cases, the call for theories rooted in empirical context and process needs adoption.

REFERENCES

Barry M (2006) Formalising informal land rights: The case of Marconi Beam to Joe Slovo Park. *Habitat International* 30: 628–644.

Boaden B and Karam A (2000) *The Informal Housing Market in Three of Cape Town's Low income Settlements*. Cape Town: Cape Metropolitan Council.

Bond P and Tait A (1997) The failure of housing policy in post-apartheid South Africa. *Urban Forum* 8: 19–41.

Cape Argus (2003) Many RDP homes sold to criminals. *Cape Argus*, 16 April, p. 1.

Cape Argus (2005) State puzzles over how to retain RDP homes for social housing. *Cape Argus*, 29 August, p. 12.

Cape Argus (2008a) Turning RDP houses into big business. *Cape Argus*, 6 March, p. 4.

Cape Argus (2008b) Crackdown on RDP homes sales hailed. *Cape Argus*, 21 May, p. 4.

Cape Argus (2008c) Sisulu pledges mass evictions from RDP homes. *Cape Argus*, 1 June, p. 2.

Cape Times (2005) City mum on developer's plans to buy RDP houses. *Cape Times*, 27 July, p. 3.

Chaney P and Sherwood K (2000) The resale of right to buy dwellings: A case study of migration and social change in rural England. *Journal of Rural Studies* 16: 79–94.

Constantiaberg Bulletin (1999) Charming village replaces Westlake shacks. *Constantiaberg Bulletin*, 14 October, p. 1.

Constantiaberg Bulletin (2000) Westlake starter homes being sold for a song. *Constantiaberg Bulletin*, 18 May, p. 3.

Davidson M and Lees L (2005) New build 'gentrification' and London's riverside renaissance. *Environment and Planning A* 37: 1165–1190.

Dewar D (1997) The vexatious question of rental housing. *Urban Forum* 8: 83–91.

FinMark Trust (2007) Access to housing finance: What would it look like when it works? *Access Housing* 6: 1–9.

Gilbert A (2007) The return of the slum: Does language matter? *International Journal of Urban and Regional Research* 31(4): 697–713.

Glass R (1964) Introduction. In: Centre for Urban Studies (eds) *London: Aspects of change*. London: MacGibbon and Kee, pp. xiii–xlii.

Harris A (2008) From London to Mumbai and back again: Gentrification and public policy in comparative perspective. *Urban Studies* 45: 2407–2428.

Harriss J (2006) Middle-class activism and the politics of the informal working class. *Critical Asian Studies* 38: 445–465.

Jones GA and Varley A (1999) The reconquest of the historic centre: Urban conservation and gentrification in Puebla, Mexico. *Environment and Planning A* 31: 1547–1566.

Lees L (2011) The geography of gentrification: Thinking through comparative urbanism. *Progress in Human Geography* 36: 155–171.

Lees L, Slater T and Wyly E (2008) *Gentrification*. New York: Routledge.

Lees L, Slater T and Wyly E (2010) *The gentrification Reader*. New York: Routledge.

Lemanski C (2008) Houses without community: Problems of community (in)capacity in a low-cost housing community in Cape Town, South Africa. *Environment and Urbanization* 20: 393–410.

Lemanski C (2011) Moving up the ladder or stuck at the bottom? Homeownership as a solution to poverty in South Africa. *International Journal of Urban and Regional Research* 35: 57–77.

Marx C (2007) *Do Informal Land Markets Work for Poor People? An Assessment of Three Metropolitan Cities in South Africa*. Pretoria: Urban LandMark.

McFarlane C (2010) The comparative city: Knowledge, learning, urbanism. *International Journal of Urban and Regional Research* 34: 725–742.

Ngetu G (2003) *Community Profile: Westlake Village 2003*. Cape Town: Social Development Directorate.

Nijman J (2007) Introduction: Comparative urbanism. *Urban Geography* 28: 1–7.

Payne G (1996) *Urban Land Tenure and Property Rights in Developing Countries: A Review of the Literature*. Report, Overseas Development Administration.

Payne G (2001) Urban land tenure policy options: Titles or rights? *Habitat International* 25: 415–429.

Phillips M (2004) Differential productions of rural gentrification: Illustrations from north and south Norfolk. *Geoforum* 36: 477–494.

Pirie G (2007) Re-animating a comatose goddess? Re-configuring central Cape Town. *Urban Forum* 18: 125–151.

Rao V (2006) Slum as theory: The South/Asian city and globalization. *International Journal of Urban and Regional Research* 20: 225–232.

Rigg J (2007) *An Everyday Geography of the Global South*. Oxford: Routledge.

Robins S (2002) Planning 'suburban bliss' in Joe Slovo Park, Cape Town. *Africa* 72: 511–548.

Robinson J (2006) *Ordinary Cities: Between Modernity and Development*. Oxford: Routledge.

Robinson J (2011) Cities in a world of cities: The comparative gesture. *International Journal of Urban and Regional Research* 35: 1–23.

Saff G (1998) *Changing Cape Town*. Lanham, MD: University Press of America.

Shin HB (2009) Property-based redevelopment and gentrification: The case of Seoul, South Korea. *Geoforum* 40: 906–917.

Shisaka Development Management Services (SDMS) (2004) *Phase Three: Findings, Conclusions and Implications, Workings of Township Residential Property Markets*. Report, Finmark Trust.

Slater T (2006) The eviction of critical perspectives from gentrification research. *International Journal of Urban and Regional Research* 30: 737–757.

Slater T (2009) Missing Marcuse: On gentrification and displacement. *City* 13: 292–311.

Slater T, Curran W and Lees L (2004) Guest editorial. *Environment and Planning A* 36: 1141–1150.

Smith D and Holt L (2007) Studentification and 'apprentice' gentrifiers within Britain's provincial urban locations: Extending the meaning of gentrification? *Environment and Planning A* 39: 142–161.

Thirkell AJ (1996) Players in urban informal land markets. Who wins? Who loses? A case study of Cebu City. *Environment and Urbanization* 8: 71–90.

Urban LandMark (2011) *Investigation into the delays in issuing title deeds to beneficiaries of housing projects funded by the capital subsidy*. Report, SDMS.

Visser G and Kotze N (2008) The state and new-build gentrification in central Cape Town, South Africa. *Urban Studies* 45: 2565–2593.

Vorster JH and Tolken JE (2009) *Western Cape occupancy Study 2008*. Cape Town: Western Cape Department of Local Government and Housing.

Ward K (2008) Editorial: Towards a comparative (re)turn in urban studies? *Urban Geography* 29: 405–410.

Ward K (2010) Towards a relational comparative approach to the study of cities. *Progress in Human Geography* 34(4): 471–487.

Williams G, Meth P and Willis K (2009) *Geographies of Developing Areas: The Global South in a Changing World*. Oxford: Routledge.

11
Comparative approaches to gentrification
Lessons from the rural

Martin Phillips and Darren P. Smith

INTRODUCTION

There is a growing interest in comparative research, particularly in urban studies where comparative urbanism is a vibrant subject of discussion (McFarlane and Robinson, 2012; Robinson and Roy, 2016; Ward, 2010), albeit one that has not hitherto featured in *Dialogues in Human Geography*. Here we rectify this omission by explicating the application of these debates to one research area where comparative research is prominent, namely the study of gentrification.

As Bernt (2016: 1) observed, the arrival of comparative urbanism into gentrification scholarship raises challenges whose relevance constitutes 'a turning point not only for gentrification research, but also for the way we develop established concepts into a more global body of knowledge'. Bernt highlights how the rise of comparative research has led to an expansion in the geographical focus of gentrification studies, with attention paid to spatial variabilities in the concept, form and extent of gentrification. As Lees (2012: 157–158) comments, this interest preceded the emergence of the notion of comparative urbanism, with gentrification researchers having a long-standing interest in how 'theories of gentrification have travelled and how the process itself has travelled'. She adds that different forms of gentrification emerge 'in different places at different and indeed the same times' and that meanings associated with gentrification in one place may not translate easily, if at all, to other locations. Consequently, she argues, researchers need to 'critically debate the international significance of the term "gentrification"' and 'consider how comparison might take place' (Lees, 2012: 158). As such, gentrification research might be commensurable and reinvigorated by interest in comparative research. Yet, as Bernt (2016: 1) observes, the rise of comparative research has led to calls for abandonment of the gentrification concept, with Ghertner (2015: 522) wondering whether it is now 'time to lay the concept to bed'. Bernt (2016: 1), while drawing back from such arguments, sees value in some of Ghertner's claims and observes that the impact of comparative research on gentrification is 'an increasingly open question'. We address this question via consideration of the potential and value of comparative research on rural gentrification. While identified as a somewhat 'neglected other' to the study of urban gentrification (Phillips, 2004), recent decades have seen increasing reference to rural gentrification, especially in the United Kingdom (e.g. Phillips, 2002; Smith, 2002a; Stockdale, 2010) and North America (e.g. Darling, 2005; Hines, 2012; Nelson and Nelson, 2010), but also in other countries (e.g. Hjort, 2009; Qian et al., 2013; Solana-Solana, 2010). There are, however, many countries where there has been little use of the concept, and even in places where it has been employed, rural gentrification remains a minor motif within rural geography and a peripheral constituent of wider gentrification debates. Theorizing from positions of marginality has been a major point of argument within elaborations of comparative urbanism (e.g. McFarlane, 2010; Roy, 2009, 2016), and we want to stimulate consideration of the extent to which framings other than the urban might contribute to elaborating comparative studies of gentrification. More

DOI: 10.4324/9781003341239-17

specifically, we explore how a comparative study of rural gentrification in France, United Kingdom and United States could be developed to engage with the challenges identified by Bernt (2016).

To develop its arguments, the article begins by considering strategies of comparison as outlined within comparative urbanism and explores how these have been performed within urban gentrification studies. Hitherto, discussions of comparative approaches within these studies have been narrow in focus, particularly when set alongside the literature on strategies, practices and politics of comparison associated with comparative urbanism. Drawing on Tilly (1984) and Robinson (2015), we suggest that practices of comparison enacted in gentrification studies are more diverse than are represented in existing literatures. From this starting point, the article argues that the strategies of comparison identifiable within urban gentrification studies are present within rural studies, albeit with differences in extent and focus. The article then focuses on a comparative study of rural gentrification in France, United Kingdom and United States, drawing on the concept of 'sociologies of translation', outlined by Latour (1999), to explore both the 'geographies of the concept' and 'geographies of the phenomenon' of rural gentrification (Clark, 2005). The article concludes by considering relationships between these two geographies of rural gentrification and strategies of comparison.

COMPARATIVE URBANISM AND URBAN GENTRIFICATION

Comparative urbanism highlights the prevalence and complexity of comparison. Ward (2010: 473), for example, argues that 'comparison is practically omnipresent in much empirical social science research', while McFarlane (2010: 725) asserts that theoretical abstractions inevitably, albeit often implicitly, make comparative assertions, because 'claims and arguments are always set against other kinds of ... possibilities or imaginaries'. Practices such as literature citation, for example, set up comparisons with existing bodies of knowledge. McFarlane claims that comparative practices should be explicitly discussed, with consideration paid to both epistemological methodologies and the politics of comparison. The former involves consideration of the practicalities of comparison, such as language, resources, the delimitation of scope and focus, methods of comparison and the role and construction of comparative typologies.

In relation to this last feature, Lagendijk et al. (2014) argue that comparative studies of gentrification often focus on establishing a metric to actualize interpretations and practices across spatial contexts. Examples include studies by Ley (1986, 1988, 2003) and Wyly and Hammel (1998, 2004), which variously illustrate difficulties in constructing comparative metrics, including 'readily available secondary data' (Wyly and Hammel, 1998: 305) failing to map onto conceptual arguments and/or be available across localities being compared (Ley, 1996).

Metric-based analysis could be characterized as fitting within McFarlane and Robinson's (2012: 767) description of 'quasi-scientific' research focused on the identification of a narrow range of comparative traits, an approach they claim is 'inappropriate' given the 'multi-dimensional, contextual, interconnected, and endogenous nature of urban processes'. In the context of gentrification research, Lees et al. (2015b: 9) similarly argue that structured comparative approaches 'flatten cases' through focusing on 'a limited number of factors or categories'. They make no use of metric-based analysis, but rather propose practices of transnational 'collegiate knowledge production' (Lees et al., 2015b: 13; see also Ló pez-Morales et al., 2016). However, Lagendijk et al. (2014: 362) utilize assemblage theory to propose that, rather than either foster the articulation of generalized metrics or reject them as being 'untrue to reality', comparative studies of gentrification might recognize their presence within the 'worlds of gentrification' and study their 'actualisation and counter-actualisation' within a range of localities. This is a productive position, although it implies that comparative studies would only examine spaces where metrics were present, which might severely limit the scope of such studies.

A range of positions on the value of metrics and typologies to comparative studies are being advanced within gentrification studies, although, as yet, there remains little sustained discussion of their epistemological significance or the practices required for alternative strategies of comparison. There is a significant difference here between discussions of comparative studies of gentrification and the literature on comparative urbanism which contains much greater epistemological reflection,

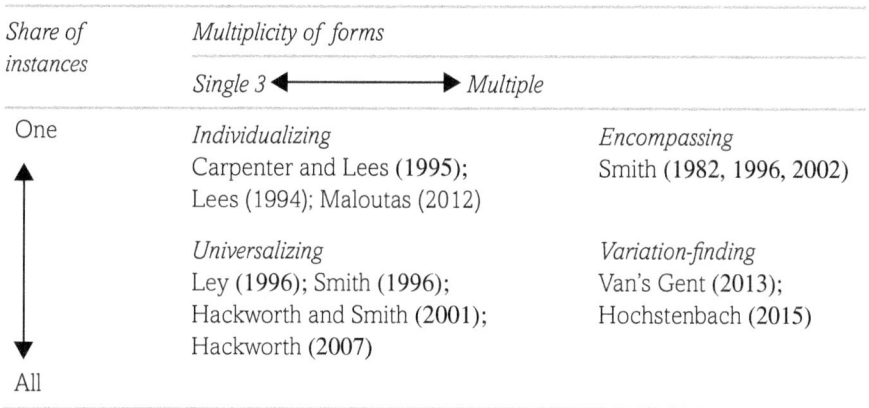

Table 1 Comparative approaches in gentrification research.

with Tilly's (1984) identification of 'individualising', 'universalising', 'encompassing' and 'variation-finding' strategies (Table 1) being widely cited (e.g. Brenner, 2001; Robinson, 2011). We demonstrate that these have applicability to gentrification studies and, hence, can advance the development of comparative studies of gentrification, although as the article develops we layer in other understandings of comparison, derived from comparative urbanism and studies of gentrification.

Individualizing and variation-finding gentrification studies

Ward (2010) suggests that individualizing and variation-finding strategies characterize much of comparative urban studies. The focus in the former is on comparing instances of a phenomenon to identify the particularities of each case. Gentrification examples include the comparisons of Carpenter and Lees (1995: 286) focused on a 'questioning of generalizations about the gentrification process and an emphasis on international differences', Musterd and van Weesep's (1991) examination of whether gentrification in Europe was an instance of a generalized process or involved specifically European dynamics, and Butler and Robson's (2003) study of neighbourhoods in London that emphasized the different compositions of gentrifiers in each locality.

A recent, and epistemologically focused, example is Maloutas' (2012) criticism of the application of the concept of gentrification across contexts. He claims that this, first, leads to a decontextualization of the concept, which becomes increasingly abstract in order to be applicable across cases. An illustration is Clark's (2005: 258) creation, by 'realist abstraction', of 'an elastic yet targeted definition' of gentrification, an argument employed in developing the notion of 'generic gentrification' (Hedin et al., 2012). Maloutas (2012: 38–39) asserts, however, that abstract conceptions of gentrification produce a neglect of 'causal mechanisms and processes', in favour of a superficial focus on 'similarities in outcomes across contexts'.

Second, Maloutas argues that while gentrification scholars have sought to decontextualize the concept, it remains marked by the context of creation. Specifically, he contends that the concept was developed in, and was of considerable significance in understanding changes within, cities such as London and New York. Attempts to make the concept travel to other time-spaces are, he claims, flawed because conditions in these contexts are different. Third, he argues that attempts to make gentrification travel are ideological, acting to project 'neoliberal framings' across contexts.

Maloutas is an exponent of individualizing comparison, viewing concepts as inextricably linked to contexts. Such arguments when advanced within comparative urbanism have been subject to criticism, with Peck (2015: 179) commenting that such work can be particularist rather than comparative, promoting 'hermetically sealed' modes and sites of analysis. With respect to gentrification, Lees et al. (2015b: 7) state that Maloutas creates 'fossilisation not contextualisation', reifying the 'contextual epiphenomena' of gentrification, such as how it 'looked, smelled or tasted in some specific (North American and West European) contexts at very specific times', to create a simplified and static conception of gentrification that cannot be reasonably applied beyond its initial context. They add that while there are lessons to be learnt from comparative urbanism, 'we should not throw the baby out with the bathwater' (Lees et al., 2015b: 9) and seek to 'stand aside' from a 'flat ontology' dedicated to the appreciation of difference in favour of an ontology focused on 'social injustices and power relations'. It is further asserted, 'that a large number of well analysed cases help extract global regularities of the causes of gentrification' (Lees et al., 2015b: 6).

While few gentrification researchers hitherto appear willing to fully embrace Maloutas' individualizing perspective, many studies implicitly employ it by drawing comparisons to pre-existing studies to emphasize the particularities of their study. Instances of variation-finding comparisons, which are identified by Tilly (1984) as strategies that seek to identify causes of variation across cases, include van Gent's (2013) 'contextual institutional approach', which, although focused on Amsterdam, explains variations from other studies of 'third-wave gentrification' via institutional practices (see also Hochstenbach et al., 2015).

Universalizing and encompassing comparisons

While individualizing and variation-finding comparisons can be identified in gentrification studies, universalizing and encompassing perspectives have a stronger presence. Universalizing comparisons focus on establishing that instances share common, and generally independently constituted, properties, with change within them viewed as largely driven by dynamics internal to these cases. The approach generally enacts 'an incipient monism' (Leitner and Shepherd, 2016: 231) in that certain features are seen to be significant to all the identified cases, and universalizing comparisons also often adopt 'developmentalist perspectives', with differences between cases viewed as reflections of differential positions within a common path.

Examples of universalizing perspectives can be identified within gentrification studies. Early decades of gentrification studies, for example, involved 'legislative' debates (Phillips, 2010) concerning the applicability of various monist conceptions of gentrification to a widening number of cases. For authors such as Lambert and Boddy (2002), the spatial extension of locations identified as undergoing gentrification stretched the term to encompass so much difference that, as per Molutas, it lost any specific meaning. For others, commonalities could be discerned within such differences. Reference has already been made to Clark's (2005: 260–261) adoption of realist abstraction, and he sought to use this to identify both generic 'underlying necessary relations and causal forces' associated with gentrification and features which, while crucially significant in understanding the formation and impact of gentrification in particular localities, were contingent in character. Recent years have seen a series of applications of these arguments to comparative studies of gentrification (Betancur, 2014; Lees et al., 2016; Ló´pez-Morales, 2015; Shin et al., 2016). A different, but related, perspective was work, such as Smith (2002b) and Lees et al. (2008), suggesting that the character of gentrification was itself changing, such that early definitions were now inappropriate to identify the presence, processes and varied forms of contemporary gentrification. Strands of continuity, such as class transformation, displacement and capital flows into built environments, were, however, also identified.

In both sets of work, the universalism of identifying continuities and/or abstract commonalities was tempered, to a degree, by recognition that gentrification could take a range of different forms. This was evident in 'stage-theories' of gentrification (Clay, 1979; Gale, 1979; Hackworth, 2007; Hackworth and Smith, 2001). As discussed in Phillips (2005), these interpretations have been criticized for employing developmentalist logics, whereby gentrification is framed as a singular process impacting locations which move, or in some cases fail to move, through a predetermined series of stages, although attention has been drawn to differences in trajectories of change, to instances of non-development and to the multiplicity of gentrification forms present in a location at particular points in time (Ley and Dobson, 2008; Pattaroni et al., 2012; Van Criekingen and Decroly, 2003).

Universalizing comparisons were also enacted in discussions of 'gentrification generalised', which often portrayed gentrification as a singular process 'cascading' both 'laterally' across national borders and 'vertically' down 'the urban hierarchy', until it reached 'even small market towns' (Smith, 2002b: 439) or 'unfurled to include rural settlements' (Atkinson and Bridge, 2005: 16). Such views encouraged the adoption of an implicit, 'imitative urbanism', whereby processes of urban gentrification are seen to have 'travelled to and been copied in the Global South' (Lees, 2012: 156). Such perspectives are viewed as 'western-centric' by comparative urbanists influenced by post-colonialism (e.g. Robinson, 2004; 2011), as well as by gentrification researchers such as Maloutas (2012), Lees (2012) and Lees et al. (2015a, b), who highlight how such interpretations may act as 'deforming lenses' (Maloutas, 2012: 43), projecting occidental concerns and assumptions at the expense of recognizing specificities and differences. However, it can also be argued that these conceptions are overly urban-centric in their focus, viewing gentrification as originating in and diffusing from a selected number of metropolitan sites to other urban and, eventually, rural sites. This imagery neglects the identification of sites of rural gentrification soon after coinage of the term gentrification by Glass (see Phillips, 1993). Just as post-colonialists have highlighted how occidental concerns may be projected over cities of the South, researchers often position the urban as 'a privileged lens through which to interpret, to map and, indeed, to attempt to influence contemporary social, economic, political and environmental trends' (Brenner and Schmid, 2015: 155).

Universalizing comparisons do not have to be coupled with diffusionist perspectives. Brenner et al. (2010: 202), for example, identify the possibility of 'accumulation of contextually specific projects', and Peck (2015: 171) argues for recognition of 'common, cross-contextual patterns and processes', while Robinson (2015) calls for examination of repetition as singular assemblings. In this perspective, repeated appearance is not seen as diffusion of a common process but as a series of singular outcomes of processes, practices and relations in operation within multiple localities.

Such arguments resonate with urban gentrification scholarship. Lees et al. (2015a: 442), for example, argue for recognition of the 'transnational mobility of gentrification' and 'its endogenous emergence' in a range of locations, such that gentrification may be viewed as multiple and multicentric, although there are still said to be 'necessary conditions' (Lees et al., 2015b: 8) that need to be present before gentrification can be said to exist. A similar, and in our view more productive, way of framing such arguments is to suggest that universalizing comparisons be viewed as 'genetic comparisons' (Robinson, 2015), identifying singularly constituted transformations in locations across which there are some recurrent features viewed as constitutive of gentrification, but in each case, these will have been produced within that locality. These recurrent features might be viewed as the abstract 'generic' dimensions of gentrification outlined by Clark (2005), although within a genetic approach these elements would be viewed as contingently created as the other elements of each case, rather than identified as established through some form of necessary relationship. As such, the genesis of the generic dimensions requires explanation in each instance rather than being viewed as foundationally determinant. Furthermore, while each case may involve, or be stimulated by, movement of resources and agents into that locality from beyond, it is likely that there will be at least some spatially and/or temporally specific elements. Such an approach would counter the monism and developmentalism that has been the focus of criticism.

The final form of comparison identified by Tilly is 'encompassing'. Here, the aim is to situate instances of a phenomenon in relationship to each other, in such a way that their form can be seen to be in large part determined by such relationships. Such understandings can be clearly identified within gentrification studies. Examples include Smith's (1982, 1996) conceptualization of gentrification as a facet of uneven development and the globalization of gentrification (Smith, 2002b). In this latter work, Smith argues that gentrification has become global as various forms of capital sought to restructure new localities in their search for continuing profitability, with the vertical and lateral dispersal of gentrification discussed earlier, being seen to stem from an 'influx of new capital' into gentrification projects and disinvestment and reinvestment of existing capitals from one area to another. Similarly, Atkinson and Bridge (2005) suggest that the 'unfurling' of gentrification in an increasing range of spaces, including rural areas, is the result of flows of finance, people, information and ideas from one gentrified area into another (see also Lees, 2006, 2012). More recently, Lees et al. (2016: 13) have identified their examination of 'planetary gentrification' as 'a relational comparative approach' involving investigation of how instances of gentrification are 'increasingly interconnected'. Emphasizing connections rather than similarities between cases of gentrification, these studies can be viewed as advocating encompassing rather than universalizing comparisons, although failing themselves to recognize these differences. Attention also needs to be paid to the status of these connections, with Robinson (2011) promoting use of the term 'incorporating comparisons' to recognize the significance of what she would later describe as the genetic elements of relational connections, that is recognizing their genesis as well as consequences.

Politics of comparison

In addition to fostering discussion of epistemology, comparative urbanism also highlights the politics of comparison. McFarlane (2010: 726), for example, argues that comparison is a political mode of thought because it can be employed 'as a means of situating and contesting existing claims . . . expanding the range of debate, and informing new perspectives'. Comparative urbanism has been particularly associated with postcolonial perspectives (e.g. Robinson, 2004, 2011), it being claimed that comparison fosters the creation of 'readings of theory and the city' (McFarlane, 2010: 735) less marked by the cities and urban theorists of the North. Lees (2012: 155–159) draws heavily upon this argument, claiming that 'gentrification researchers need to adopt a postcolonial approach'. She suggests that work is needed on the mobilities and consequences of ideas of gentrification and on forms and practices of contemporary gentrification, with a key focus being postcolonial informed studies of urbanism in the Global South, although adds that 'there remain important comparative studies to be made not just between the Global North and Global South' (Lees, 2012: 157–158).

The remainder of this article explores the potential and value of comparative studies of rural gentrification, which, as mentioned earlier, have been identified as a neglected other to the study of urban gentrification (Phillips, 2004). Indeed, while postcolonial comparative urbanists have challenged 'metrocentricity', where this is understood as involving a concentration of research on metropolitan centres in the Global North (Bunnell and Maringanti, 2010), the term might also be viewed in urban and rural registers as well. Thomas et al. (2011) have argued that 'a defining element of social science education for a former inhabitant of Rural America is an overwhelming sense that you are ignored by your discipline', a comment that echoes Lobao's (1996: 3) commentary, although she argued that the study of rural space was not only often marginalized as the 'non-metropolitan' but that such a positioning could be a location of 'creative marginality' from which to transform the mainstream.

The following section considers how comparative strategies outlined with respect to urban gentrification relate to studies of rural gentrification. We then explore how these strategies can be deployed in comparative studies of rural gentrification in France, United Kingdom and United States, drawing on Latour's (1999) concept of 'circulatory sociologies of translation' to illuminate the geographies of gentrification and geographies of 'articulating gentrification'.

COMPARATIVE STUDIES OF RURAL GENTRIFICATION

Nelson et al. (2010) argue that rural gentrification studies are marked by localized case studies, with little examination of the distribution or processes of gentrification beyond these locations. This does not mean, however, that comparisons have been absent from rural gentrification studies. Reference has been made to the arguments of McFarlane (2010) that even localized studies make comparative claims, even if individualizing in character. Many rural gentrification studies include cautionary remarks concerning the transfer of ideas of gentrification from urban to rural contexts. Smith and Phillips (2001: 457), for example, coined the term 'rural greentrification', both to stress the 'demand for, and perception of, 'green' residential space from in-migrant' gentrifier households and to suggest that this feature 'stands in contrast to the 'urban' qualities which attract in-migrant counterparts in urban locations'. Smith (2011: 603) later argues that studies reveal 'more and more incommensurabilities between urban and rural gentrification', while Guimond and Simiard (2010) assert that while rural researchers have drawn inspiration from urban gentrification studies, 'important nuances must be taken into consideration when applying urban theories of gentrification to a rural context'. The significance of contextual differences has been highlighted not simply with respect to urbanity and rurality, but within the rural: Darling (2005: 1015) argues that rural areas may be 'sufficiently differentiated to render the idea of an overarching, homogeneous "rural gentrification" suspect', indicating a need for 'a more refined and specific set of labels to indicate a variety of landscape-specific gentrification models'. Consideration might also be paid to the scale of landscape forms and how these connect to particular theorizations of gentrification.

Contextual factors are significant to variation-finding as well as individualizing comparisons. The limited number of rural gentrification studies limits the scope for variation-finding comparisons, although it is possible to identify practices and processes that could cause variations in the gentrification of rural localities. As in urban contexts, governmental regulations and development controls are identified as agencies within the gentrification of rural localities (Gkartzios and Scott, 2012; Hudalah et al., 2016; Shucksmith, 2011) and clearly can be enacted differentially. Likewise, the nature and extent of rural space might condition the presence and/or form of rural gentrification (Darling, 2005; Phillips, 2005; Smith and Phillips, 2001), given differences are evident in the character of areas identified as experiencing rural gentrification: UK studies often focus on localities with extensive commuting, while North American studies tend to be in areas seen to be beyond extensive metropolitan influences (Figures 1 and 2).

Nelson et al.'s (2010) and Nelson and Nelson's (2010) examinations of rural gentrification across the United States provide arguments for the adoption of both universalizing and encompassing comparisons. In connection to the former, Nelson et al. (2010) review existing research on rural gentrification in the United Kingdom, Spain and Australia, in order to identify mappable indicators of gentrification in non-metropolitan areas. This strategy assumes that processes of gentrification have high uniformity across rural contexts, an approach also adopted in Nelson and Nelson (2010). However, this study also enacts an encompassing focus, identifying relational reasons for moving beyond localized case studies. Globalization is viewed as a major driver of rural gentrification because key constituents of urban to rural movements are middle and upper-middle classes who have benefited from globalized capital accumulation and rising land and property values. Nelson and Nelson argue that this positioning in global capital enables these classes to acquire the assets to locate in high-amenity destinations, with gentrification in these remote rural locations being consequential to relationships with, and within, a globalized economy. Nelson et al. (2015) repeat this argument, asserting that rural gentrification in amenity areas of the United States reflects a spatial fix of surplus capital accumulated in high wage urban-based careers in the globalized service sector.

Similar arguments, albeit focused on UK rural restructuring through the settlement of a commuting 'service class', were advanced by Cloke and Thrift (1987), who claimed this movement was driven by changes in the international division of labour. Cloke et al. (1991) also drew attention to how movements of this class could connect into flows of exogenous 'footloose' capital, while Phillips (2002, 2005) stressed flows of capital from agriculture and service provision into the gentrification of properties, as well as flows of labour power, ideas and people. Nelson and Nelson (2010) and Nelson et al. (2015) identify further global connections, with the gentrification of remote amenity locations stimulating movement of low-income Latino populations to, or more often in proximity to, these localities. Parallels with studies of service class migration to accessible UK rural areas can be seen, with Cloke and Thrift (1987: 328) arguing that rural service class growth entails 'growth of members of other classes and class fractions needed to service the service class'.

Rural gentrification studies, like their urban counterparts, enact all four strategies of comparison identified by Tilly (1984: 145), an unsurprising finding given he argues that each strategy of comparison 'have their uses'. Both Ward (2010) and Robinson (2011) have asserted that individualizing comparisons are among the most widespread form of comparison conducted in urban studies, and this appears to be the case also in

Figure 1 Studies of rural gentrification in the United Kingdom.

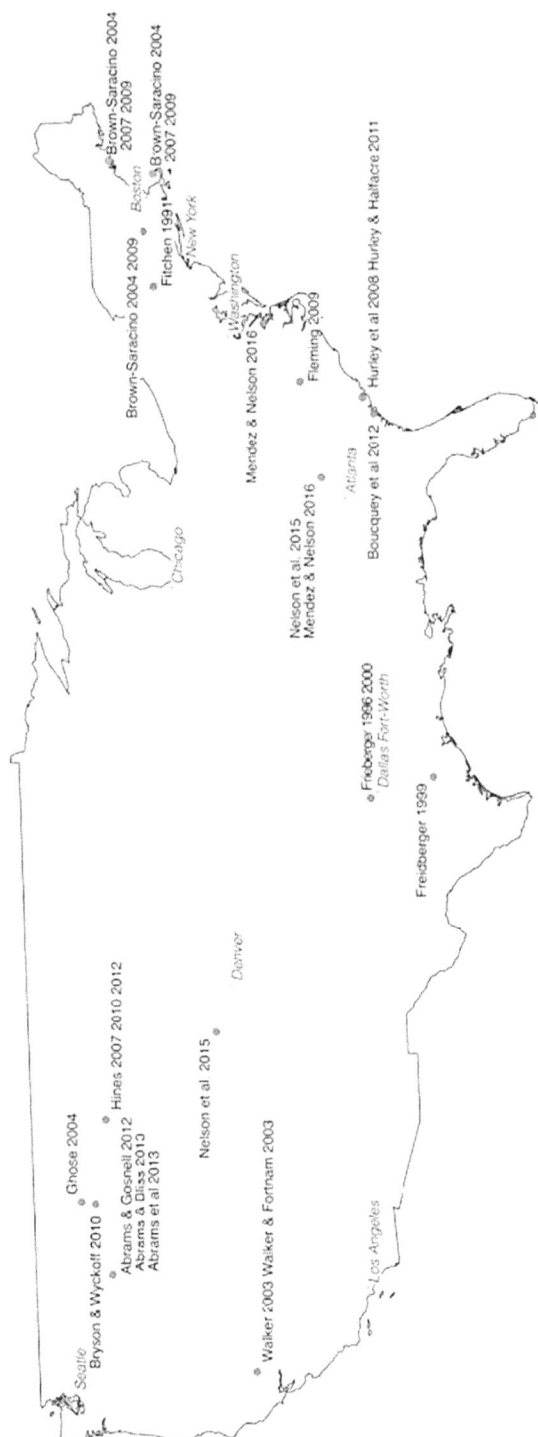

Figure 2 Studies of rural gentrification in the United States.

rural gentrification studies, in part because of the predominance of localized case studies. Adoption of such a strategy provides an implicit critique of universalizing perspectives, although such viewpoints are evident in rural gentrification studies, as are encompassing comparisons. Variation-finding perspectives on rural gentrification are least developed, due in part to the lack of studies from which this approach could draw. All the identified strategies of comparison, and reflections on the value of comparative studies of rural gentrification, could clearly benefit from explicit examples of comparative research. The final section of this article explores how such studies could be developed by considering how a comparative study of rural gentrification could be pursued in France, United Kingdom and United States. In undertaking this, it will draw upon the concept of sociologies of translation as outlined by Latour (1999).

COMPARING RURAL GENTRIFICATION IN FRANCE, UNITED KINGDOM AND UNITED STATES

The United Kingdom and United States have more extensive literatures on rural gentrification, stemming back at least to the late 1970s/early 1980s (Cloke, 1979; Lapping et al., 1983; Parsons, 1980). In France, by contrast, gentrification appears largely absent 'from the vocabulary of French social science' (Fijalkow and Preteceille, 2006: 6), although from the late 1990s, there was some engagement by urban researchers (Authier, 1998; Bidou, 2003; Lacour and Puissant, 2007; Pre´teceille, 2007) and from the 2000s in rural studies (Cognard, 2006; Perrenoud, 2008; Puissant, 2002; Richard et al., 2014).

A comparative study of rural gentrification in France, United Kingdom and United States provides an opportunity to explore reasons for, and consequences of, differential use of this concept, and whether this connects to differences in the presence of the phenomenon or what, following Lagendijk et al. (2014: 358), might be described as 'geographies of the articulation of the concept' and 'geographies of the phenomenon' of rural gentrification. They suggest that assemblage theorizations foster comparative studies exploring 'variations and complexities' associated with use of the term gentrification. Such an approach has parallels with Latour's (1999) concept of

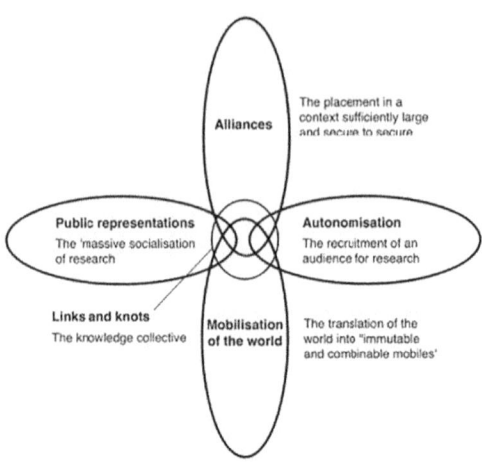

Figure 3 Circulating sociologies of translation.

'circulatory sociologies of translation' employed in Phillips' (2007, 2010) explorations of the use of concepts of gentrification, class and counterurbanization within rural studies. Latour's concept provides an effective way of developing comparisons that recognize the limitations and potentials of travelling theories.

Latour develops his concept of circulatory sociologies of translation as a way of 'enumerating' types of activities and actants that need to be enrolled in constructing concepts and knowledge. He argues that concepts are analogous to a 'heart beating in a rich system of blood vessels' (Latour, 1999: 108), being simultaneously at the centre of a circulating system and dependent on flows from other elements of the system. Drawing on this analogy, Latour argues that concepts be conceived as 'links and knots' at the centre of 'loops' of flow, or 'circulating sociologies of translation', which bring assets to sustain the development of the concept. These circulating sociologies are identified as autonomization, alliance building, public representation and mobilization (Figure 3).

Autonomization

Latour (1999) describes the enrolment of support for a concept or interpretation within worlds of academic activity and discourse as autonomization. Although there are no detailed sociologies of rural studies (although see Murdoch and Pratt, 1993), studies pointing to the significance of autonomization in understanding differential levels of engagement with the concept of rural gentrification in France, United Kingdom and United States can be identified.

Kurtz and Craig (2009) and Woods (2009), for example, identify differential developments in UK and US rural geography. For Kurtz and Craig, the publication industry fostered differential engagements with theory, with UK rural studies being more theoretically inclined due to a focus on journal article and edited book production, while US rural studies were more empirically focused through an emphasis on regional book monographs. Woods (2009), while accepting this differentiation of rural geography, argued that processes of disciplinary institutionalization played an important role, creating in the United States a stronger theoretical orientation among rural sociologists than rural geographers, while UK rural geography became highly engaged in social theoretical debates in part because of institutional marginalization of rural sociology in this country. Thomas et al. (2011) provide a different account of the institutionalization of US rural sociology, stressing its severance from wider sociology. It is evident that geographers have more readily adopted the concept of rural gentrification than sociologists (although see Brown-Saracino, 2009; Hillyard, 2015), while its adoption within UK rural geography may reflect the significance of 'political-economy' perspectives in geography during the 1980s and 1990s. The subsequent turn towards culture that invigorated UK rural studies in the later 1990s also inspired considerations of the role of rural space as a motivator of rural gentrification (e.g. Phillips, 2002, 2014; Phillips et al., 2008; Smith and Phillips, 2001). Important disciplinary differences have been identified within French rural studies (Lowe and Bodiguel, 1990), although in both geography and rural sociology during the 1980s and 1990s, there was an emphasis on empirical studies, with limited engagement with social theory and epistemological reflections (Alphandéry and Billaud, 2009; Papy et al., 2012). This was despite notable French social theorists who have influenced gentrification studies in the Anglophonic world, such as Bourdieu and Lefebvre, undertaking early work in rural sociology (Elden and Morton, 2016; Phillips, 2015).

While differences in levels of theoretical reflection within disciplines at particular moments in time can influence engagement with conceptions of gentrification, other processes are also influential, including enrolment of other concepts. Fijalkow and Préteceille (2006) and Préteceille (2007), for example, argue that gentrification's low uptake in France reflects a preference to use the concept of 'embourgeoisement', conjoined with concerns about the coherence and relevance of the gentrification concept within French contexts (cf. Rousseau, 2009). This preference may, however, have limited applicability within a rural context, where long-standing preoccupations with processes of agricultural change and the status of French peasants and small producers fostered disconnection with notions of embourgeoisement circulating in other social science discourses (Hervieu and Purseigle, 2008; Rogers, 1995).

Another influence on French rural studies was its framing of rural space as a passive subject of urban change. The countryside was viewed as losing its specificity (Berger et al., 2005), either becoming urbanized (sometimes described as rurbanization) or more differentiated, such that there were no clear lines of distinction between the urban and rural (Hervieu and Hervieu-Léger, 1979; Jean and Perigord, 2009; Kayser, 1990). Large areas are ascribed an urbanized identity, without consideration of landscape character or public perceptions (Mathieu, 1990, 1998). These 'peri-urban' areas include accessible localities akin to those that formed the locus of UK studies of rural gentrification (Figure 1). Similarly, in the United States, conceptions of the exurban and the rural as simply non-metropolitan may contribute to rural gentrification being applied primarily in areas with low levels of urban commuting (Figure 2), although as mentioned previously, consideration might also be given to the differences in the scale of areas being characterized as rural: according to the OECD's (2016) 'national area classification', for instance, only 24.1% of the United Kingdom is designated as rural, compared to 77.8% and 40.9% of United States and France, respectively.

Simultaneous with academic movements towards recognition of the peri-urban in France was growing public interest in issues of rural cultural identity (Bonerandi and Deslondes, 2008). Paralleling these changes was movement from quantitative assessments of population numbers/movements to qualitative consideration of how these connect to transformations in popular understandings of the countryside. These include studies of international migrants in French rural places (Benson, 2011; Barou and Prado, 1995; Buller and Hoggart, 1994; Diry, 2008), as well as a few studies explicitly referencing notions of rural gentrification (Cognard, 2006; Perrenoud, 2008; Puissant, 2002). However, across all three countries, discussions have generally been framed in registers other than gentrification, with terms such as amenity migration, counterurbanization, neo-ruralism, peri-urbanization, rural renaissance and social segregation and differentiation being preferred over gentrification.

Alliance building and public representations

Phillips (2010) has discussed relationships between conceptions of rural gentrification and counterurbanization, arguing that in UK and US studies, the latter gained strength over the former not only through widespread circulation within academic channels of autonomization but also through the circulatory sociologies of alliance building and public representation. Counterurbanization, it is claimed, drew strength from alignments with the intellectual contours of governmental statistics production and policymaking, while also making use of 'social abstractions well embedded in, or highly commensurable with, public normative consciousness' (Phillips, 2010: 553). Consequently, counterurbanization circulated relatively easily within public discourses, with Halfacree (2001: 400) highlighting how it 'spun out into popular debate', particularly within the United Kingdom, where narratives of residential migration to the countryside are reproduced across television documentaries and dramas, newspapers and popular fiction. The concept of gentrification, on the other hand, has social connotations of class that may have limited its uptake in public and policy contexts, although at times feeding into both (Phillips, 2002, 2004).

Applying such arguments to comparisons between the United Kingdom, France and United States suggests that circulatory sociologies of alliance building and public consciousness, as well as autonomization, may significantly differ. Reference has, for example, already been made to the significance of concepts such as peri-urbanism within French rural studies, and this concept gained significant academic impetus when included as a category in the *Institut National de la Statistique et des É'tudes É'conomique* official classification of French national spaces in 1996 (Le Jeannic, 1996).

This change both reflected the conceptual success of the peri-urban within academic debates and institutionalized the peri-urban as a category of space deserving not only academic attention but also as a subject for political and public discourse, although with respect to the latter, notions of urban and rural space still predominate. Similar arguments can be made with respect to the *US General Accounting Office* that classifies land using categories (e.g. urban, urbanized, urban cluster, metropolitan, micropolitan, nonmetropolitan and rural) that effectively cast the rural and nonmetropolitan as residual classifications with no consideration given to their material character or public perceptions of these areas. In the United Kingdom, by contrast, governmental spatial classifications have, at least in England and Wales, demonstrated parallels to aspects of popular constructions of rurality since 2004 (cf. Bibby and Shepherd, 2004; Bibby and Brindley, 2016; Phillips et al., 2001). One consequence is that areas close to urban areas have been identified as locations of 'rural' gentrification (Figure 1).

There is evidence pointing to greater popular and policy engagement with the term gentrification in North America than in the United Kingdom or France. Guimond and Simiard (2010), for example, suggest that rural gentrification attracted the attention of television producers, as well as reporters, in Quebec's provincial and regional press. In the United States, rural gentrification research by Nelson figured in an article in the *Wall Street Journal* (Dougherty, 2008), while in relation to alliance building, the *Housing Assistance Council*, in cooperation with *US Department of Housing and Urban Development*, produced a high-profile report on rural gentrification (Housing Assistance Council, 2005). Furthermore, while the term rural might not be applied by academics and policymakers to areas with high commuting to large urban areas, there are numerous cases of literary and filmic representations of such spaces that enact motifs of rurality and gentrification.

Part of the policy interest in rural gentrification within the United States links to what has been described in urban studies as 'positive gentrification' (Cameron, 2003), whereby state agencies perceive there to be benefits from processes of gentrification, such as the influx of capital-rich migrants whose consumption, skills and enterprise might stimulate local development and employment. While subject to considerable criticism within urban studies (Smith, 2002b; Slater, 2006), this conception of rural gentrification has resonances with studies of migration to non-metropolitan areas in the American West (Beyers and Nelson, 2000; Gosnell and Abrams, 2011; Nelson, 1999), to Stockdale's (2006, 2010) work on rural gentrification and the impacts of rural in-migration in Scotland, and to the activities of some French local authorities which have sought to attract particular in-migrants, such as entrepreneurs or other 'project backers' (Richard et al., 2014).

In relation to public representations, Lamont (1992, 2000) and Bennett et al. (2009) suggest there is greater acceptance of notions of hierarchical differentiations in cultural value in France than in the United Kingdom or United States, and conversely, less receptivity to identities constructed around socio-economic distinctions. Such arguments are of clear importance to the study of gentrification given that research has suggested that symbolic distinctions are of crucial significance to its formation (e.g. Butler and Robson, 2003; Rofe, 2003). Furthermore, connections between cultural values and academic interpretations of society have been highlighted by Savage (2010), who presents an historical account of changing concepts of culture within the UK middle classes, connecting these to developments in the conduct of sociology. Among the studies used to develop this argument was Pahl's (1965) research on Hertfordshire villages, which has been viewed as constituting a study of rural gentrification by people such as Paris (2008), despite it making no use of the term. For Savage, Pahl's study represents both a description and enactment of technocratic middle-class culture (Phillips and Smith, forthcoming). Circulatory sociologies of translation are, however, often far from direct: Although the concept of gentrification appears not to have translated readily into French public and academic discourse, the writings of French social theorists such as Bourdieu, Latour, Lefebvre and Waquant have exerted a profound influence on UK and US gentrification studies (e.g. Bridge, 2006; Butler and Robson, 2003; Phillips, 2010, 2015), although not on French rural studies.

Mobilization

The final circulating sociology identified by Latour (1999: 108) relates to practices and processes of inscription and translation through which objects of study become 'progressively loaded into discourse'. This circulation has long been the focus of epistemological and methodological discussion about the ability, or not, of concepts to connect to objects or situations, issues that have been, and continue to be, a focus of debate within gentrification studies. While there have been claims that the ontological debates over the meaning of the concept of gentrification have declined in significance (e.g. Lees et al., 2008; Slater et al., 2004), the rise of comparative research has certainly challenged this, with Ghertner (2015: 552), for example, arguing that the concept 'fails in "much of the world"'. This argument, advanced in relation to studies of the Global South, has relevance even within the studies of the metropolitan North, given that there are both variegated understandings of the concept and numerous criticisms raised about its value. The complex geography to the adoption of the concept has been neglected both by its exponents and critics, as evidenced by use of the term rural gentrification, which not only is far from extensive in France but is also relatively limited even in the United Kingdom and United States.

While processes of autonomization, alliance building and representation may profoundly influence the acceptance and development of the concept of rural gentrification, differential recognition of the concept in France, United Kingdom and United States may also reflect differences in the activities and dynamics of change occurring in the country-side in these countries. As such there is a need to conduct comparative research exploring if conceptions of rural gentrification provide differentially effective mobilizations of the rural 'pluriverse' (Latour, 2004: 40) in each country, or as it might also be expressed, to explore the geographies of the phenomenon, or phenomena, of rural gentrification, as well as its articulations. Clearly, given earlier discussions, there are a host of practical, methodological, epistemological and political issues to be considered in developing such comparative research. In the context of the present article, however, we will restrict ourselves to considering how Tilly's (1984) typology of strategies of comparison, along with Robinson's (2015) differentiation of genetic and generative comparisons, could assist in mobilizations of conceptions of gentrification applicable across rural France, United Kingdom and United States, as well as being of potential wider relevance in studies of gentrification.

Genesis and generation within strategies of comparisons

It has been argued that many studies of rural gentrification implicitly adopt an individualizing comparative perspective, although evidence of national differentials in the focus of studies (Figures 1 and 2) indicates potential for variation-finding comparisons exploring whether differences reflect the influence of contextual processes such as landscapes, planning regulations or property relations. Darling's (2005) work was discussed in relationship to the former, while UK studies have identified the latter two as important influences on the geography of rural gentrification, particularly its focus within smaller rural settlements (Phillips, 2005). Studies in the United States also highlight the significance of rural gentrification in transforming property and land-management practices (Abrams et al., 2013; Gosnell and Travis, 2005).

Such work does not preclude identification of contextually specific understandings and practices and, when combined with analysis of the sociologies of translation operating within such contexts, can produce insights that speak back to prevailing conceptualizations of gentrification. Robinson (2015) argues for the development of comparative approaches that combine 'genetic' and 'generative' tactics of conceptual development. The former, as previously discussed, examine the genesis or emergence of seemingly common/repeated or related outcomes, while the latter explore how examination of 'different singularities or cases' generate insights and problems that provoke new lines of thought that can potentially be bought 'into conversation' with prevailing conceptualizations. These conversations might, as in individualizing comparisons, centre around differences between cases, although Robinson sees scope for generating connections which resonate across and from cases and hence can be of value within other strategies of comparison. Gentrification studies provide illustrations of such conversations. Focusing on the application of stage interpretations, a past conversation will be outlined, before considering a hitherto rather implicit one and one in need of development. In relation to the first, although, as previously argued, stage models are commensurable with universalizing and encompassing comparisons, they have been created generatively. Early-stage models of urban gentrification emerged from comparisons between innercity locations in North America (e.g. Clay, 1979; Gale, 1979). Later-stage models (e.g. Hackworth and Smith, 2001; Hackworth, 2007; Lees et al., 2008) drew on different theoretical understandings of gentrification and from recognizing forms of gentrification that differed from the 'classical' gentrification of the 1960s to 1980s, which came to be viewed as a 'pioneer' phase of gentrification, involving small-scale sporadic transformations of buildings. Pioneer/classical/sporadic gentrification became, and very much still act, as comparators to set against other forms of gentrification.

A second generative conversation that gentrification studies should recognize is that stage interpretations are more multidimensional than often represented. Work of people such as Rose (1984) on 'marginal gentrification', for example, promoted differentiation of gentrification on the basis of assets or capital. Marginal gentrifiers, often associated with the onset of gentrification, were viewed as having limited amounts of economic capital yet relatively high levels of cultural capital. They were seen to be frequently displaced by an 'intensified gentrification', involving larger scale, more professional and capitalized agencies, and gentrifiers with more economic capital and, at least relatively, less cultural capital. In some locations, gentrification was seen to extend in scale to encompass not only large areas of residential properties but also other transformations, with Smith (2002b: 443) coining the phrase 'gentrification generalised' to refer to the formation of 'new landscape complexes' whereby not only housing but also 'shopping, restaurants, cultural facilities, . . . open space, employment opportunities' become gentrified.

This form of gentrification was widely associated with the construction of new-build properties and heightened involvement of state agencies, but has also been connected, within the work of Ley (1996), Butler and Robson (2003) and Bridge (2001, 2003), with a further decline in the significance of cultural capital as a 'channel of entry' (Phillips, 1998) into gentrified spaces. Some areas have also been identified as undergoing 'super-gentrification' (Butler and Lees, 2006) involving people with very high levels of economic capital.

Concepts such as economic and cultural capital facilitate universalizing comparisons through simplifying or 'abbreviating' (Robinson, 2015) the complexity of everyday life by focusing on particular, repeated aspects. Given this, it is unsurprising that studies of the UK countryside have made comparisons between stages and assets identified in urban studies and processes of change observed in rural areas (Phillips, 2005; Smith, 2002a). It appears that many UK rural localities have experienced intensified and generalized gentrification, given their high levels of middle class residence (Phillips, 2007). In the United States, the 'American West' has been a focus of attention within rural gentrification studies (Figure 3), and according to Nelson and Nelson (2010), is an area where it appears most widely present, although also occurring more sporadically across rural areas in the Mid-West, the South and the Eastern seaboard. Even in the American West, however, rural gentrification is shown to be concentrated in a relatively small number of areas, with Hines (2012: 75) likening its geography to an 'archipelago' of change set within 'the midst of a relatively static, conservative, agricultural/industrial "sea"'. In France, the progress of rural gentrification appears even more sporadic, as well as widely perceived via other process descriptors, such as international or neo-rural in-migration, tourism or peri-urban or new-build development. A study of the High Corbie'res has, however, suggested that neo-rural migration reflected an early sporadic phase of gentrification which was followed by inflows of people with both more economic assets and greater levels of cultural capital (Perrenoud and Phillips, forthcoming).

Such research highlights that comparisons can generate connections between studies of rural gentrification and investigations framed through other concepts. They also point to how more multidimensional understanding of gentrification could be constituted by recognizing that economic and cultural capitals take a range of different forms. Ley (1996), for example, argues that gentrification can be associated with 'critical' or 'counter-cultural values'. As outlined in Phillips (2004), such arguments have rural counterparts, not least in the work of Smith and Phillips (2001) which highlighted the presence of what they characterize as 'New Age professionals'. Smith subsequently developed this argument further, highlighting how some areas are experiencing gentrification sparked and reproduced by householders seeking to realize a range of 'alternative' ways of living (Smith, 2007; Smith and Holt, 2005). These arguments chime with aspects of Hines' (2010, 2012) work in a North American context, as well as notions of neo-rural migration employed in France. Drawing on such arguments, it can be argued that some capital/asset-based analyses of gentrification employ what could be described as a three-dimensional differentiation of gentrifiers and gentrification (Figure 4).

Three-dimensions, however, are insufficient, an argument that can be illustrated by considering the concept of 'super-gentrification'. This concept, which has been briefly discussed in a rural context by Stockdale (2010) and potentially has wider relevance, both within rural areas close to global cities such as London, Paris and New York and to remote amenity locations, has generally been used to describe people who are 'super-rich' in economic terms. However, studies suggest that there are a range of cultural dimensions that need fuller investigation. Super-gentrification, for example, has been identified with practices of conspicuous consumption, with Lees (2003: 2487) arguing that it involves 'intense investment and conspicuous consumption by a new generation of super-rich "financifiers"'. As such super-gentrification can be seen to connect to objectified forms of cultural capital (Bennett et al., 2009; Bourdieu, 1986), which, as Phillips (2011) has observed, can be used to frame much of the analysis of culture and class conducted within UK rural studies in the 1980s and 1990s.

Butler and Lees (2006), however, also suggest that, at least in the Barnsbury area of London, super-gentrifiers were predominately drawn from elite segments of the British education system (i.e. public or selective secondary schools and Oxbridge). As such, these gentrifiers had high levels of credentialed or institutional

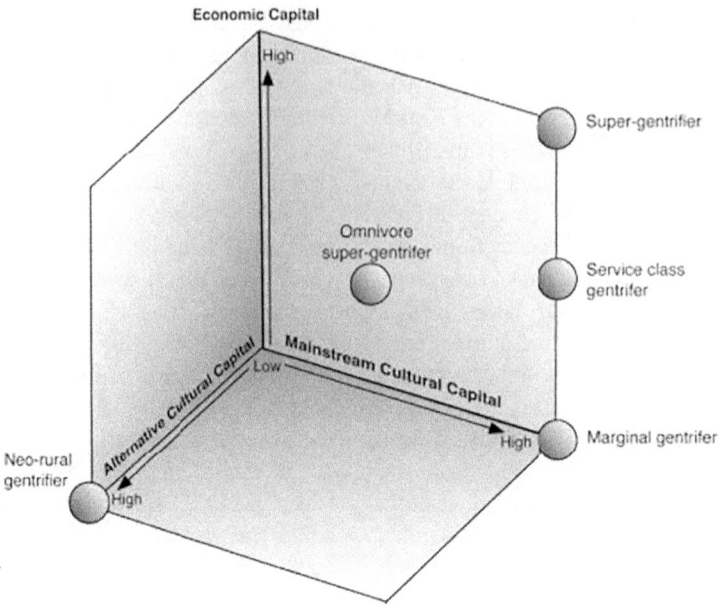

Figure 4 Gentrifiers within a 3-dimensional asset-based theorisation.

capital (Bourdieu, 1986) but also enact a range of embodied forms of cultural and social capital reproduced through this educational system (Bennett et al., 2009; Savage, 2015). Such connections are not universal, with Butler and Lees (2006) drawing contrasts between their study and the work of Rofe (2003) and Atkinson and Bridge (2005) on the habitus of gentrifiers in other global cities, which appear to be more cosmopolitan in origin and cultural orientation. Savage, in a series of works (Bennett et al., 2009; Savage et al., 1992, 2013), has argued for recognition of a range of different forms of cultural evaluation beyond the classical high – low distinction (see also Lamont, 1992, 2000; Warde and Gayo-Cal, 2009). In some contrast, Perrenoud and Phillips (forthcoming) argue that rural areas of southern France are experiencing gentrification by people connected to the production of Parisian 'high culture', and who might be described as 'super-gentrifiers' in a cultural sense, as well as being well endowed with economic assets. Even within the study of super-gentrification, there is a need to move analysis beyond three-dimensions, to recognize a range of different forms of cultural capital, an argument advanced more generally in relation to studies of rural gentrification by Phillips (2015). Also, earlier work (Phillips, 2004) on a 'composite' stage-interpretation of rural gentrification highlighting labour, property and finance capital flows, provides an example as to how multidimensionality can be applied to the concept of economic as well as cultural capital.

Comparison holds the potential for fostering the creation of more multidimensional asset-based studies of gentrification. Petersen's discussions of cultural omnivores provide an interesting example of this, not only suggesting that the concept of people engaging in both high and mass cultural activities could link into gentrification (Petersen and Kern, 1996), but also highlighting its emergence from comparative work inspired by Bourdieu's writings and how it catalysed critiques and revisions of Bourdieu's conceptualizations of cultural capital (Petersen, 2005).

Concepts of capital and flow point to relationality, which is a third generative conversation that gentrification studies should develop. As outlined earlier, relationality is central to encompassing comparisons. However, as Wright (2015) has observed, there is considerable variability of relationality evident within so-called relational perspectives. He, for example, argues that the capital-based theorization of class developed by Savage et al. (2013) is an example of an 'individual-attributes' based approach that pays insufficient attention to the way that holding and use of assets by one person can causally connect to those of other people. He identifies more relational perspectives focused around the

Authier JY (1998) Mobilite´s et processus de gentrification dans un quartier re´habilite´ du centre historique de Lyon. In: Grafmeyer Y and Dansereau F (eds) *Trajectoires Familiales et Espaces de Vie en Milieu Urbain*. Lyon: Presses Universitaires de Lyon, pp. 335–352.

Barou J and Prado P (1995) *Les Anglais dans nos Compagnes*. Paris: L'Harmattan.

Bennett T, Savage M, Silva E, et al. (2009) *Culture Class Distinction*. London: Routledge.

Benson M (2011) *The British in Rural France*. Manchester: Manchester University Press.

Berger A, Chevalier P and Dedeire M (2005) *Les Nouveaux Territoires Ruraux*. Montpellier: Université Paul Valéry.

Bernt M (2016) Very particular or rather universal? *City* 20: 637–644.

Betancur J (2014) Gentrification in Latin America. *Urban Studies Research* 2014: 14.

Beyers WB and Nelson PB (2000) Contemporary development forces in the nonmetropolitan West. *Journal of Rural Studies* 16: 459–474.

Bibby P and Brindley P (2016) *Urban and Rural Classifications of English Local Authority Districts and Similar Geographical Units: Methodology (Revised)*. London: Government Statistical Service. Available at: www.gov.uk/government/uploads/system/uploads/attachment_data/file/539130/RUCLAD_Method__Apr_2016_.pdf (accessed 19 January 2018).

Bibby P and Shepherd J (2004) *Developing a New Classification of Urban and Rural Areas for Policy Purposes – The Methodology*. London: Office for National Statistics. Available at: www.gov.uk/government/uploads/system/uploads/attachment_data/file/239084/2001-rural-urban-definition-methodology-technical.pdf (accessed 19 January 2018).

Bidou C (2003) *Retours en ville*. Paris: Descartes et Cie.

Bonerandi E and Deslondes O (2008) Ou' va la géographie rurale? *Géocarrefour* 83: 255–258.

Boucquey N, Campbell L, Cumming G, et al. (2012) Interpreting amenities envisioning the future. *Geo Journal* 77: 83–101.

Bourdieu P (1986) The forms of capital. In: Richardson J (ed) *Handbook of Theory and Research for the Sociology of Education*. New York: Greenwood, pp. 241–258.

Brenner N (2001) World city theory globalization and the comparative-historical method. *Urban Affairs Review* 37: 124–147.

Brenner N, Peck J and Theodore N (2010) Variegated neoliberalization. *Global Networks* 10: 182–222.

Brenner N and Schmid C (2015) Towards a new epistemology of the urban? *City* 19: 151–182.

Bridge G (2001) Bourdieu rational action and the time-space strategy of gentrification. *Transactions Institute of British Geographers* 26: 205–216.

Bridge G (2003) Time-space trajectories in provincial gentrification. *Urban Studies* 40: 2545–2556.

Bridge G (2006) Perspectives on cultural capital and the neighbourhood. *Urban Studies* 43: 719–730.

Brown-Saracino J (2004) Social preservationists and the quest for authentic community. *City and Community* 3: 135–156.

Brown-Saracino J (2007) Virtuous marginality. *Theory and Society* 36: 437–468.

Brown-Saracino J (2009) *A Neighbourhood that Never Changes*. Chicago: University of Chicago Press.

Bryson J and Wyckoff W (2010) Rural gentrification and nature in the Old and New Wests. *Journal of Cultural Geography* 27: 53–75.

Buller H and Hoggart K (1994) *International Counterurbanization*. Aldershot: Avebury.

Bunnell T and Maringanti A (2010) Practising urban and regional research beyond metrocentricity. *International Journal of Urban and Regional Research* 34: 415–420.

Butler T and Lees L (2006) Super-gentrification in Barnsbury London. *Transactions Institute of British Geographers* 31: 467–487.

Butler T and Robson G (2003) *London Calling*. Oxford: Berg.

Cameron S (2003) Gentrification housing redifferentiation and urban regeneration. *Urban Studies* 40: 2367–2382.

Carpenter J and Lees L (1995) Gentrification in New York London and Paris. *International Journal of Urban and Regional Research* 19: 283–303.

Chaney P and Sherwood K (2000) The resale of right to buy dwellings. *Journal of Rural Studies* 16: 79–94.

Clark E (2005) The order and simplicity of gentrification. In: Atkinson R and Bridge G (eds) *Gentrification in a Global Context*. London: Routledge, pp. 256–264.

Clay P (1979) *Neighbourhood Renewal*. Lexington, MA: DC Heath.

Cloke P (1979) *Key Settlements in Rural Areas*. London: Methuen.

Cloke P, Goodwin M, Milbourne P, et al. (1998a) Inside looking out: Outside looking in. In: Boyle M and Halfacree K (eds) *Migration to Rural Areas*. London: Wiley, pp. 134–150.

Cloke P, Phillips M and Rankin R (1991) Middle-class housing choice. In: Champion T and Watkins C (eds) *People in the Countryside*. London: Paul Chapman, pp. 38–51.

Cloke P, Phillips M and Thrift N (1995) The new middle classes and the social constructs of rural living. In: Butler T and Savage M (eds) *Social Change and the Middle Classes*. London: UCL Press, pp. 220–238.

Cloke P, Phillips M and Thrift N (1998b) Class colonisation and lifestyle strategies in Gower. In: Boyle M and Halfacree K (eds) *Migration to Rural Areas*. London: Wiley, pp. 166–185.

Cloke P and Thrift N (1987) Intra-class conflict in rural areas. *Journal of Rural Studies* 3: 321–333.

Cognard F (2006) Le rôle des recompositions sociodémographiques dans les nouvelles dynamiques rurales. *Méditerranée* 107: 5–12.

Darling E (2005) The city in the country. *Environment and Planning A* 37: 1015–1032.

Diry JP (2008) *Les E´trangers Dans les Campagnes*. Clermont-Ferrand: CERAMAC.

Dougherty C (2008) The new American gentry. *Wall Street Journal*. January 19th. Available at: www.wsj.com/articles/SB120069319738001353 (accessed 19 January 2018).

Elden S and Morton A (2016) Thinking past Henri Lefebvre. *Antipode* 48: 57–66.

Erel W (2010) Migrating cultural capital: Bourdieu in migration studies. *Sociology* 44(4): 642–660.

Fielding A (1982) Counterurbanisation in Western Europe. *Progress in Planning* 17: 1–52.

Fijalkow Y and Preteceille E (2006) Gentrification. *Sociétés Contemporaines* 63: 5–13.

Fitchen J (1991) Homelessness in rural places. *Urban Anthropology* 20: 177–210.

Fleming R (2009) Creative economic development sustainability and exclusion in rural areas. *Geographical Review* 99: 61–80.

Friedberger M (1996) Rural gentrification and livestock raising. *Rural History* 7: 53–68.

Friedberger M (1999) Mink and manure. *Southwestern Historical Quarterly* 102: 269–293.

Friedberger M (2000) The rural-urban fringe in the late twentieth century. *Agricultural History* 74: 502–514.

Gale D (1979) Middle class resettlement in older neighbourhoods. *Journal of American Planning Association* 45: 283–304.

Ghertner DA (2015) Why gentrification theory fails in 'much of the world'. *City* 19: 552–563.

Ghose R (2004) Big sky or big sprawl? *Urban Geography* 25: 528–549.

Gkartzios M and Scott M (2012) Gentrifying the rural? *International Planning Studies* 17: 253–276.

Gosnell H and Abrams J (2011) Amenity migration. *Geo-Journal* 76: 303–322.

Gosnell H and Travis WR (2005) Ranchland ownership dynamics in the Rocky Mountain West. *Rangeland Ecology Managment* 58: 191–198.

Guimond L and Simard M (2010) Gentrification and neo-rural populations in the Québec countryside. *Journal of Rural Studies* 26: 449–464.

Hackworth J (2007) *The Neoliberal City*. Ithaca: Cornell University Press.

Hackworth J and Smith N (2001) The changing state of gentrification. *Tidjschrift voor Economische en Sociale Geografie* 29: 464–477.

Halfacree K (2001) Constructing the object. *International Journal of Population Geography* 7: 395–411.

Hedin K, Clark E, Lundholm E, et al. (2012) Neoliberalization of housing in Sweden. *Annals Association of American Geographers* 102: 443–463.

Hervieu B and Hervieu-Léger D (1979) *Retour a' la Nature*. Paris: Editions du Seuil.

Hervieu B and Purseigle F (2008) Troubled pastures, troubled pictures. *Rural Sociology* 73: 660–683.

Hillyard S (2015) Rural putsch. *Sociological Research Online* 20: 5.

Hines JD (2007) The persistent frontier and the rural gentrification of the Rocky Mountain West'. *Journal of the West* 46: 63–73.

Hines JD (2010) Rural gentrification as permanent tourism. *Environment and Planning D* 28: 509–525.

Hines JD (2012) The post-industrial regime of production/consumption and the rural gentrification of the New West archipelago. *Antipode* 44: 74–97.

Hjort S (2009) Rural gentrification as a migration process. *Migration Letters* 6: 91–100.

Hochstenbach C (2015) Stakeholder representations of gentrification in Amsterdam and Berlin. *Housing Studies* 30: 817–838.

Hochstenbach C, Musterd S and Teernstra A (2015) Gentrification in Amsterdam. *Population Space and Place* 21: 754–770.

Housing Assistance Council (2005) *They Paved Paradise Gentrification in Rural Communities*. Washington, DC: Housing Assistance Council.

Hudalah D, Winarso H and Woltjer J (2016) Gentrifying the peri-urban. *Urban Studies* 53: 593–608.

Hurley P and Halfacre A (2011) Dodging alligators rattlesnakes and backyard docks. *GeoJournal* 76: 383–399.

Hurley P, Halfacre A, Levine N, et al. (2008) Finding a 'disappearing' nontimber forest resource. *Professional Geographer* 60: 556–578.

Jean Y and Perigord M (2009) *Géographie Rurale la Ruralité en France*. Paris: Aramand Colin.

Kayser B (1990) *La Renaissance Rurale*. Paris: Aramand Colin.

Kurtz M and Craig V (2009) Constructing rural geographies in publication. *ACME* 8: 376–393.

Lacour C and Puissant S (2007) Re-urbanity. *Environment and Planning A* 39: 728–747.

Lagendijk A, van Melik R, de Haan F, et al. (2014) Comparative approaches to gentrification. *Tijdschrift voor Economische en Sociale Geografie* 105: 358–365.

Lambert C and Boddy M (2002) *Transforming the City. Centre for Neighbourhood Research Paper 6*. Bristol: University of Bristol.

Lamont M (1992) *Money Morals and Manners*. Chicago: University of Chicago Press.

Lamont M (2000) *The Dignity of Working Men*. New York: Russell Sage.

Lapping M, Penfold G and Macpherson S (1983) Right-to-farm laws. *Journal of Soil and Water Conservation* 38: 465–467.

Latour B (1999) *Pandora's Hope*. London: Harvard University Press.

Latour B (2004) *Politics of Nature*. London: Harvard University Press.

Lees L (1994) Gentrification in London and New York: An Atlantic gap. *Housing Studies* 9: 199–217.

Lees L (2003) Super-gentrification: The case of Brooklyn Heights New York City. *Urban Studies* 40: 2487–2509.

Lees L (2006) Gentrifying down the urban hierarchy. In: Bell D and Jayne M (eds) *Small Cities*. London: Routledge, pp. 91–104.

Lees L (2012) The geography of gentrification. *Progress in Human Geography* 36: 144–171.

Lees L, Shin H and López-Morales E (2015a) Conclusion. In: Lees L, Shin H and Lopez-Morales E (eds) *Global Gentrifications and Comparative Urbanisms*. Cambridge: Polity, pp. 441–452.

Lees L, Shin H and López-Morales E (2015b) Introduction. In: Lees L, Shin H and Lopez-Morales E (eds) *Global Gentrifications and Comparative Urbanisms*. Cambridge: Polity, pp. 1–18.

Lees L, Shin H and López-Morales E (2016) *Planetary Gentrification*. Cambridge: Polity.

Lees L, Slater T and Wyly E (2008) *Gentrification*. London: Routledge.

Leitner H and Sheppard E (2016) Provincializing critical urban theory: Extending the ecosystem of possibilities. *International Journal of Urban and Regional Research* 40: 228–235.

Le Jeannic T (1996) Une nouvelle approche territoriale de la ville. *Economie et Statistique* 294–295: 25–46.

Ley D (1986) Alternative explanations for inner city gentrification. *Annals Association of American Geographers* 76: 521–535.

Ley D (1988) Social upgrading in six Canadian inner cities. *Canadian Geographer* 32: 31–45.

Ley D (1996) *The New Middle Classes and the Remaking of the Central City*. Oxford: Oxford University Press.

Ley D (2003) Artists aestheticisation and the field of gentrification. *Urban Studies* 40: 2527–2544.

Ley D and Dobson C (2008) Are there limits to gentrification? *Urban Studies* 45: 2471–2498.

Little J (1987) Rural gentrification and the influence of local-level planning. In: Cloke P (ed) *Rural Planning*. London: Harper and Row, pp. 185–199.

Lobao L (1996) A sociology of the periphery versus a peripheral sociology. *Rural Sociology* 61: 77–102.

López-Morales E (2015) Gentrification in the global South. *City* 19: 564–573.

López-Morales E, Shin H and Lees L (2016) Latin American gentrifications. *Urban Geography*.

Lowe P and Bodiguel M (1990) *Rural studies in Britain and France*. London: Belhaven.

Maloutas T (2012) Contextual diversity in gentrification research. *Critical Sociology* 38: 33–48.

Mathieu N (1990) La notion de rural et les rapports ville campagne en France des années cinquante aux années quatre vingts. *Economie Rurale* 197: 35–41.

Mathieu N (1998) La notion de rural et les rapports ville campagne en France: les années quatre-vingt-dix. *Economie Rurale* 247: 11–20.

McFarlane C (2010) The comparative city. *International Journal of Urban and Regional Research* 34: 725–742.

McFarlane C and Robinson J (2012) Introduction. *Urban Geography* 33: 765–773.

Murdoch J and Pratt A (1993) Rural studies. *Journal of Rural Studies* 9: 411–427.

Musterd S and van Weesep J (1991) European gentrification or gentrification in Europe? In: van Weesep J and Musterd S (eds) *Urban Housing for the Better-Off*. Utrecht: Stedelijke Netwerken, pp. 11–16.

Nelson L and Nelson PB (2010) The global rural. *Progress in Human Geography* 35: 441–459.

Nelson L, Trautman L and Nelson P (2015) Latino immigrants and rural gentrification. *Annals Association of American Geographers* 105: 841–858.

Nelson PB (1999) Quality of life nontraditional income and economic growth. *Rural Development Perspectives* 14: 38–43.

Nelson PB, Oberg A and Nelson L (2010) Rural gentrification and linked migration in the United States. *Journal of Rural Studies* 26: 343–352.

OECD (2016) *National Area Distribution* (indicator), (accessed 5 August 2016). http://doi.org/10.1787/34f4ec4a-en.

Pahl R (1965) *Urbs in Rure*. London: London School of Economics.

Papy F, Mathieu N and Ferault C (2012) *Nouveaux Rapports a' la Nature dans les Campagnes*. Versailles: Editions Quae.

Paris C (2008) Re-positioning second homes within housing studies. *Housing Theory and Society* 26: 292–310.

Parsons D (1980) *Rural Gentrification Geography Research Paper No 3*. Brighton: University of Sussex.

Pattaroni L, Kaufman V and Thomas MP (2012) The dynamics of multifaceted gentrification. *International Journal of Urban and Regional Research* 36: 1223–1241.

Peck J (2015) Cities beyond compare? *Regional Studies* 49: 160–182.

Perrenoud M (2008) Les artisans de la 'gentrification rurale'. *Sociétés Contemporaine* 71: 95–115.

Perrenoud M and Phillips M (forthcoming) The craftsmen of 'rural gentrification'. In: Phillips M (ed) *The Gentrified Countryside*. London: Routledge.

Petersen R (2005) Problems in comparative research. *Poetics* 33: 257–282.

Petersen R and Kern RM (1996) Changing highbrow taste: From snob to omnivore. *American Sociological Review* 61: 900–990.

Phillips M (1993) Rural gentrification and the processes of class colonisation. *Journal of Rural Studies* 9: 123–140.

Phillips M (1998) Rural change: Social perspectives. In: Ilbery B (ed) *The Geography of Rural Change*. Harlow: Longman, pp. 31–54.

Phillips M (2002) The production symbolisation and socialisation of gentrification. *Transactions Institute of British Geographers* 27: 282–308.

Phillips M (2004) Other geographies of gentrification. *Progress in Human Geography* 28: 5–30.

Phillips M (2005) Differential productions of rural gentrification. *Geoforum* 36: 477–494.

Phillips M (2007) Changing class complexions in and on the British countryside. *Journal of Rural Studies* 23: 283–304.

Phillips M (2010) Counterurbanisation and rural gentrification. *Population Space and Place* 16: 539–558.

Phillips M (2011) Material cultural moral and emotional inscriptions of class and gender. In: Pini B and Leach B (eds) *Reshaping Gender and Class in Rural Spaces*. Aldershot: Ashgate, pp. 23–52.

Phillips M (2014) Baroque rurality in an English village. *Journal of Rural Studies* 33: 56–70.

Phillips M (2015) Assets and affect in the study of social capital in rural communities. *Sociologia Ruralis* 56: 220–247.

Phillips M, Fish R and Agg J (2001) Putting together ruralities. *Journal of Rural Studies* 17: 1–27.

Phillips M, Page S, Saratsi E, et al. (2008) Diversity scale and green landscapes in the gentrification process. *Applied Geography* 28: 54–76.

Phillips M and Smith D (forthcoming) Pahl revisited? *Sociologia Ruralis*.

Préteceille E (2007) Is gentrification a useful paradigm to analyse social changes in the Paris metropolis? *Environment and Planning A* 39: 10–31.

Puissant S (2002) Qualitéde vie gentrification rurale et émergence urbaine en Luberon. *Nouvelles Formes d'Urbanité Séminaire-Recontre, Plan Urbanisme Construction Architecture, Paris.* PUCA.

Qian J, He S and Liu L (2013) Aestheticisation rent-seeking and rural gentrification amidst China's rapid urbanisation. *Journal of Rural Studies* 32: 331–345.

Richard F, Dellier J and Tommasi G (2014) Migration environment and rural gentrification in the Limousin mountains. *Journal of Alpine Research* 102-3: 1–15.

Robinson J (2004) In the tracks of comparative urbanism. *Urban Geography* 25: 709–723.

Robinson J (2011) Cities in a world of cities. *International Journal of Urban and Regional Research* 35: 1–23.

Robinson J (2015) Thinking cities through elsewhere. *Progress in Human Geography* 40(1): 3–29.

Robinson J and Roy A (2016) Debate on global urbanisms and the nature of urban theory. *International Journal of Urban and Regional Research* 40: 187–199.

Rofe M (2003) I want to be global. *Urban Studies* 40: 2511–2527.

Rogers S (1995) Natural histories: The rise and fall of French rural studies. *French Historical Studies* 19: 381–397.

Rose D (1984) Rethinking gentrification. *Environment and Planning D* 2: 47–74.

Rousseau M (2009) Re-imaging the city centre for the middle classes. *International Journal of Urban and Regional Research* 33(3): 770–788.

Roy A (2009) The 21st-century metropolis. *Regional Studies* 43: 819–830.

Roy A (2016) Who's afraid of postcolonial theory. *International Journal of Urban and Regional Research* 40: 200–209.

Savage M (2010) *Identities and Social Change in Britain since 1940*. Oxford: Oxford University Press.

Savage M (2015) *Social Class in the 21st Century*. London: Pelican.

Savage M, Barlow J, Dickens P, et al. (1992) *Property Bureaucracy and Culture*. London: Routledge.

Savage M, Devine F, Cunningham N, et al. (2013) A new model of social class? *Sociology* 47: 219–250.

Shin H, Lees L and López-Morales E (2016) Locating gentrification in the Global East. *Urban Studies* 53: 455–470.

Shucksmith M (2011) Exclusive rurality. *Planning Theory and Practice* 12: 605–611.

Slater T (2006) The eviction of criticial perspectives from gentrification research. *International Journal of Urban and Regional Research* 30: 737–757.

Slater T, Curran W and Lees L (2004) Gentrification research. *Environment and Planning A* 36: 1141–1150.

Smith D (2002a) Rural gatekeepers and 'greentrified' Pennine rurality. *Journal of Social and Cultural Geogra-phy* 3: 447–463.

Smith D (2007) The 'buoyancy' of 'other' geographies of gentrification. *Tijdschrift voor Economische en Sociale Geografie* 98: 53–67.

Smith D (2011) What is rural gentrification? *Planning Theory and Practice* 12: 593–605.

Smith D (2013) Reclaiming the 'public' lands: community conflict and rural gentrification. *Journal of Rural and Community Development* 8: 215–227.

Smith D and Holt L (2005) 'Lesbian migrants in the gentrified valley' and 'other' geographies of gentrification. *Journal of Rural Studies* 21: 313–322.

Smith D and Phillips D (2001) Socio-cultural representations of greentrified Pennine rurality. *Journal of Rural Studies* 17: 457–469.

Smith N (1982) Gentrification and uneven development. *Economic Geography* 58: 139–155.

Smith N (1996) *The New Urban Frontier*. London: Routledge.

Smith N (2002b) New globalism new urbanism. *Antipode* 34: 428–450.

Solana-Solana M (2010) Rural gentrification in Catalonia Spain. *Geoforum* 41: 508–517.

Stockdale A (2006) Migration. *Journal of Rural Studies* 22: 354–366.

Stockdale A (2010) The diverse geographies of rural gentrification in Scotland. *Journal of Rural Studies* 26: 31–40.

Stockdale A (2014) Unravelling the migration decision-making process. *Journal of Rural Studies* 34: 161–171.

Sutherland LA (2012) Return of the gentleman farmer?: Conceptualising gentrification in UK agriculture. *Journal of Rural Studies* 28: 568–576.

Thomas A, Lowe B, Fulkerson G, et al. (2011) *Critical Rural Theory*. Lanham: Lexington Books.

Tilly C (1984) *Big Structures Large Processes Huge Comparisons*. New York: Russell Sage.

Van Criekingen M and Decroly JM (2003) Revisiting the diversity of gentrification. *Urban Studies* 40: 2451–2468.

van Gent WPC (2013) Neoliberalization housing institutions and variegated gentrification. *International Journal of Urban and Regional Research* 37: 503–522.

Walker P (2003) Reconsidering 'regional' political ecologies. *Progress in Human Geography* 27: 7–24.

Walker P and Fortmann L (2003) Whose landscape? *Cultural Geographies* 10: 469–491.

Ward K (2010) Towards a relational comparative approach to the study of cities. *Progress in Human Geography* 34: 471–487.

Warde A and Gayo-Cal M (2009) The anatomy of cultural omnivorousness. *Poetics* 37: 119–145.

Woods M (2009) Constructing rural geographies in publication. *ACME* 8: 394–413.

Wright EO (2015) *Understanding Class*. London: Verso.

Wyly E and Hammel D (1998) Modeling the context and contingency of gentrification. *Journal of Urban Affairs* 20: 303–326.

Wyly E and Hammel D (2004) Gentrification segregation and discrimination in the American urban system. *Environment and Planning A* 36: 1215–1241.

BOX 4 MARTIN PHILLIPS REFLECTION

In providing a commentary on the article written by me and Darren Smith, I thought I'd focus on reflecting on some of the influences molding its formation, as this aligns closely with Latour's concept of 'circulating sociologies of translation' as employed in the article.

The origins of the article lie in a research project called International Rural Gentrification (or iRGENT), which Darren Smith and I were involved in leading, along with rural gentrification scholars from France (Frederic Richard, Françoise Cognard, Sylvain Guyot, Julien Dellier, and Pierre Pistre) and the USA (Dwight Hines and Peter Nelson). The bringing together of this number of researchers was in itself something of a landmark experience, given that for the preceding two decades, during which I had been publishing on rural gentrification, most research had been, as mentioned in the article, centered on localized studies, and often been conducted by solitary investigators or small research teams. As discussed in some other writings in this period, the scale and character of gentrification research appeared to differ significantly between rural and urban studies.

The academic arguments presented in the proposal for the iRGENT project[1] included the need to examine some claims in circulation about the 'geography of gentrification', such as gentrification diffused into the countryside from urban areas, gentrification had become a global process, and rural gentrification was a concept most applied and potentially most applicable to the UK. Of particular significance were comments made by Eric Clark about differences between the geographies of the concept and phenomenon of gentrification. Clark (2005: 260) argued that, notwithstanding the rapid growth of studies of gentrification across recent decades, which might be described as a globalization of the concept of gentrification, the geography of gentrification as a phenomenon was still quite 'uncharted'. The starting point of our proposal was very much to agree with the latter argument, particularly in relation to the study of rural gentrification, where, even in the country where use of the concept had been identified as most widespread (Ghose, 2004; Nelson et al., 2010), the number of studies was small, as we document in the article. The article also documented that use of the rural gentrification concept is actually slightly greater in the USA, although in both countries, many more rural-focused studies have addressed phenomena that might be indicative of gentrification but have framed it via other concepts, such as amenity migration, counter-urbanization, or rural restructuring. The number of these studies might suggest that rural gentrification was much more widespread in the UK and the USA

---

1 The project was funded under the Open Research Area collaborative funding scheme, where national funding bodies agree to co-fund a research project. In the case of iRGENT, the funding bodies involved were the Agence Nationale de la Recherche (ANR) in France, the National Science Foundation (NSF) in the USA, and the Economic and Social Research Council in the UK. As outlined in the article, the research in the UK was supported by ESRC grant number ES/L016702/1.

than had been hitherto charted, although the prevalence of other conceptual framings also raised epistemological questions concerning why researchers were not making more use of the gentrification concept.

These other concepts also figured strongly in studies of rural France, along with notions such as neo-ruralism and peri-urbanization, which, while often presented as quite Francophonic concerns, also resemble some aspects of gentrification. This again suggests that rural gentrification is potentially quite widespread in France, although as outlined in the article, the use of the term 'gentrification' in this country has been relatively limited, across both urban and rural studies. This raises the further question of whether the concept of gentrification is actually, as Clark had suggested, global or whether its application is geographically variable, not least between both urban and rural spaces but also between different national contexts. It was to address these questions that iRGENT was born.

The initial proposal for iRGENT was written in 2013, but when Darren and I came to write the article, new studies and debates had risen to prominence, which connected to our initial set of questions. For instance, the long-running debate over the value of gentrification in comparison with other concepts, which had informed some of my own earlier writings about the value of the gentrification concept to rural studies (e.g., Phillips, 2010), was given new impetus by critiques of the concept's cross-contextual application. Authors such as Asher Ghertner and Thomas Maloutas raised questions about whether the widening application of the gentrification concept was to be welcomed or resisted. These arguments were advanced conterminously with the publication of a series of major studies that in effect sought to chart the global reach and dynamics of the phenomenon of gentrification. Notions of planetary gentrification joined the growing number of global studies of gentrification, while calls also emerged for both more contextually specific and for more cross-contextual comparative studies. This last set of calls came to form an explicit focus of the article, which sought to explore how the tensions between them was being addressed within a rapidly growing literature employing the notion of comparative urbanism. As discussed in the article, this literature had been drawn into the study of gentrification, but in ways we felt failed to recognize the diversity of practices of comparison being outlined in discussions of comparative urbanism. This focus of practices was becoming central within the developing iRGENT project because by this stage we were coming to consider how we might connect our studies of gentrification in rural areas in France, the USA, and the UK. However, the literature on comparative urbanism raised issues around the politics and practices of comparison, often drawing on notions of post-colonialism, as well as post-structural strands of thought such as relational and assemblage theory, and as we came to write the article, we began to see that our earlier thoughts about geographies of the concept and phenomenon of gentrification had strong lines of connection to this emerging debate.

This debate was very much urban in focus, although some of the advocates of global and planetary perspectives were making claims about the incorporation of rural spaces into processes of gentrification. These arguments were in some ways simply a more explicit version of a historical geography of gentrification implicitly adopted in many urban studies, which view(ed) it as a process that started in a few cities, which might be characterized as deindustrializing global cities in Europe and North America, but which had extended laterally and down settlement hierarchies to encompass other urban settlements and spaces in what were increasingly viewed as the Global North and Global South. However, some versions of this historical geography now argue that this spread of gentrification was connected to processes of global or planetary urbanization whereby distinctions between the urban and the rural were seen as increasingly irrelevant because they were both part of an urban world.

Such arguments are both highly familiar and challenging to rural researchers. As discussed in a reply to five commentaries on our paper (Phillips and Smith, 2018), rural researchers have long experienced calls to recognize relational connections to the urban and their transformative influence on life and events in the areas they are describing as rural, as well as claims that such connections may undermine the value of any notion of the rural. We argue in our reply that studies of gentrification, including recent work employing notions of planetary urbanization, often enact urbanormativity, whereby the urban, or particular subsets of it, are taken, often implicitly, as being the norm for the operation of social practices and processes, with other locations being '"othered" as spaces of abnormality as spaces of absence or abnormality' (Phillips and Smith, 2018). While studies employing notions of planetary urbanization have raised important questions about a focus on cities, and a particular set of cities and the form that their central areas have taken, or what is described in the article as 'metrocentrity', these studies have tended to avoid explicit reflection on the meaning of the term 'urban' despite this concept being accorded a central ontological position in their objects of study.

Raising questions about the significance of urbanity, and indeed rurality, to gentrification studies has animated much of my writing, including this article on comparative approaches. Being something of an outsider to rural studies, having not been raised in an area I saw as being rural and having received no specific educational training in rural geography, I have long seen the value of transferring concepts and theories from other contexts, be these what might be seen as aspatial social theory and philosophy or from spatialized arenas of study such as urban studies. This willingness to draw on theory from elsewhere very much encompassed gentrification, with one of my earliest publications being an exploration of how themes within urban gentrification studies might be of value to rural studies (Phillips, 1993). Cross-contextual movement of ideas was a practice now quite directly under scrutiny within gentrification studies, although principally in relation to movements of concepts from cities in the Global North to Global South. This paper presented an opportunity to widen the debate about cross-contextual theoretical movements to encompass those of rural and urban space, raising questions not only about the significance of gentrification in spaces taken to be rural but also potentially about the significance, or not, of particular urban spaces to processes of gentrification.

REFERENCES

Clark, E. 2005. The order and simplicity of gentrification – a political challenge. In: Atkinson, R. & Bridge, G. (eds.) *Gentrification in a global context: the new urban colonialism.* London: Routledge, 256–264.

Ghose, R. 2004. Big sky or big sprawl? Rural gentrification and the changing cultural landscape of Missoula, Montana. *Urban Geography*, 25, 528–549.

Nelson, P. B., Oberg, A. & Nelson, L. 2010. Rural gentrification and linked migration in the United States. *Journal of rural studies*, 26, 343–352.

Phillips, M. 1993. Rural gentrification and the processes of class colonisation. *Journal of rural studies*, 9, 123–140.

Phillips, M. 2010. Counterurbanisation and rural gentrification: an exploration of the terms? *Population, space and place*, 16, 539–558.

Phillips, M. & Smith, D. 2018. Comparative ruralism and 'opening new windows' on gentrification. *Dialogues in human geography*, 8, 51–58.

12
Is comparative gentrification possible?
Sceptical voices from Hong Kong

David Ley and Sin Yih Teo

INTRODUCTION

In 2012, Loretta Lees published an essay on the need to marry global gentrification analysis with the programmatic initiative of comparative urbanism. Her message was inclusive and conciliatory: it was necessary to pay full attention to regional contexts outside the global North, to recognize substantive regional variation in the outworking of gentrification processes, and to learn from postcolonial studies how to 'decolonize gentrification' (Lees, 2012). This uses all the right language – local ethnographies, learning through difference, reflexivity – promising the development of comparative gentrification studies. Lees is not an armchair theorist, and she set out to realize her proposal in an ambitious and wide-ranging research programme. The project was launched with workshops in London, UK and Santiago, Chile and resulted in two books: the co-edited *Global Gentrifications* (Lees et al., 2015), which brought together a number of workshop contributors, notably from the global South, and the co-authored *Planetary Gentrification* (Lees et al., 2016).

Perhaps a transition occurred after the conciliatory proposal of 2012, however, specifically between the plural case of *Global Gentrifications* and the singular case of *Planetary Gentrification*. The latter inevitably suggests alignment with *planetary urbanization* (Brenner and Schmid, 2015; Wilson and Jonas, 2018), with its aspiration to a global frame of conceptualization around the urban. While the authors of *Planetary Gentrification* acknowledge the play of comparative urbanism, postcolonialism and political economy in their perspective on gentrification, the dominant explanatory effect is drawn from 'the new economics', a globalizing economic model activated and steered by the state, albeit with a distinction drawn between post-socialist states and others.

Such an aspiration to generalize gentrification has been criticized by several authors, perhaps most astutely by Thomas Maloutas (2012, 2018), who argues for the prevalence of a nuanced regional context that precludes such ambitious efforts. Some critics allude to an imperial, even neo-colonial, ethos behind such a generalization, being diffused from a standard established in the metropolitan cores in advanced societies. Here the current gentrification debate resonates with the wider *contretemps* between supporters of planetary urbanization driven by capitalist political economy and the nay-sayers, who argue for the all-important place of the regional or metropolitan context revealed by grounded ethnography (Peck, 2015; Wilson and Jonas, 2018). The fault lines here are diverse: between abstraction and regional context, between political economy and a more plural approach to interpretation, between a Northern core and a Southern periphery, and in some instances between nomothetic and idiographic perspectives on place. Not all of these divisions are new; nonetheless, they are precipitating considerable agitation which is too often entrenched in a dualistic frame that is both defensive and mutually inattentive.

Our concern is to find a way that lies between this dualism and to give substance to the concept of *comparative gentrification*. Our research interest in Hong Kong, a site which features in earlier transnational research (Ley, 2010), was to examine the relevance of gentrification in a context where it had not been named as such in scholarly work; nor was it a familiar term in public discourse. Was this omission because the processes and features associated with gentrification were not present in Hong Kong, or was there an epistemological obstacle or oversight which had simply disregarded the gentrification problematic? Hong Kong could offer an opportunity for the working out of comparative gentrification. There is only space here to summarize our main arguments (Ley and Teo, 2014); our principal task is to review the responses of critics writing several years later in order to show how difficult reconciliation can be between the regional urbanist approach and comparative efforts which attempt to make conceptual connections between global regions. In this essay we assess these criticisms of our Hong Kong paper as a contribution to pushing forward a larger comparative discussion that seems to have reached an impasse.

GENTRIFICATION IN HONG KONG?

We started with a simple question: is gentrification discernible in Hong Kong? At the time when we were writing the term was not visible in the urban literature on Hong Kong, and from our content analysis of the two newspapers (one English-language and one Chinese-language) regarded as being the most credible by Hong Kong readers, nor did it seem to form part of a wider public discourse. We also interviewed a dozen Hong Kong housing experts who confirmed that gentrification was not part of the local urban conversation.

This was a finding of some surprise, as prior to our fieldwork the concept had already been used in other large cities in the Asia Pacific region, including Seoul, Shanghai and Tokyo (Ha, 2004; He and Wu, 2007; Shin, 2009; Wang and Lau, 2009; Cybriwsky, 2011). Nonetheless there were three clear distinctions between these analyses and the classic mode of gentrification as recognized in Anglo-America in the 1970s. First, in the context of developmental states, gentrification was a process in which the state was heavily implicated. Second, the roles of preservation and renovation, with or without sweat equity, were limited and primarily confined to tourist districts, while new-build apartment buildings were the normal face of gentrification. Third, and most surprising, the term did not necessarily evoke the negativity invariably assigned to it in the Western literature. Under the neutral label of redevelopment, there was indifference concerning a process that was pervasive and taken-for-granted; in some instances, there was even an expectation that public compensation for displacement could lead to improved housing status.

However, largely erasing the first two distinctions, for some years now new-build gentrification in Anglo-America – for example along the River Thames in London – and state-led gentrification – such as the redevelopment of public housing estates – have been common and have narrowed interregional differences. While the actions of the state might not be identical across global regions, today there can be no doubt that the state is a principal actor. The remaining difference, then, is the neutral or even positive perception that gentrification can evoke in East Asia. In Hong Kong the doubling of the homeownership rate to 50% between 1980 and 2001 (Yip et al., 2007), with property price inflation leading to windfall profits up to 1997 and again after 2003 (Forrest and Lee, 2004), strengthened the functional perception of property upgrading as a positive vehicle for creating wealth.

We now faced a question. Was the failure to specify gentrification in Hong Kong the result of ontology, that the phenomenon – gentrification – did not exist, or was it a product of epistemology, of local systems of knowledge that had not identified the role of a nonetheless prevalent urban process? While the urban literature and the newspapers we consulted scarcely referenced gentrification – the term was mentioned on average only once a year in the papers – they nonetheless spoke repeatedly about redevelopment, a term that occurred in the *South China Morning Post* every other day, over 4,700 times in the 26-year period examined. We assembled media stories that mentioned both redevelopment and eviction (and its variants), terms that might be expected to indicate the presence of gentrification. In the heavily urbanized districts of Hong Kong Island and Kowloon, 161 such events were identified. After empirical examination, we concluded that class displacement was indeed occurring in the housing market, and that the change process could be interpreted usefully by the concept of gentrification, albeit gentrification with East Asian characteristics.

Our conclusion was fortified by an important book by a local author, Alice Poon, who had worked for two of Hong Kong's largest property development companies. Disillusioned, she had written *Land and the Ruling Class in Hong Kong* (2006), a stinging rebuke of oligarchic power in the property market and the close collusion with the state. When the Chinese edition of the book appeared in 2010, it became a non-fiction bestseller, reprinted seven times in less than six months. It presented an epistemological awakening to a class analysis of the urban land market. Property tycoons who had been seen as celebrities and role models lost their allure. A local housing expert told us: 'Now people hate the monopoly of developers. They used to be our heroes but no longer. They are now seen as greedy and in collusion with government'. This is rhetoric similar to the class analysis of anti-gentrification activists in the West.

THE CRITICS SPEAK

Our published paper (Ley and Teo, 2014) led to critical responses from some Hong Kong urbanists which were published three years after our paper in this same journal and without any prior interaction. This lack of scholarly contact is unfortunate, especially in view of the injunctions to ethics and responsibility and allusions to collaboration and debate (Cartier, 2017: 470). What is striking about these responses is how closely they follow other objections to pan-regional theory, comprehensively discussed by Jamie Peck (2015). In challenging our comparative gentrification argument, the authors assert the importance of regional context and local knowledge; they homogenize and remove nuance from external theorizing, especially that which is interpreted as Northern political economy; and in downgrading political economy, they also limit the role of market relations and market actors in Hong Kong, instead transferring effective agency to a magisterial state. Gentrification is regarded as an *idée fixe* and shrunk down to its earliest incarnation of young professionals, sweat equity and land rent.

Of course, the commentaries do not speak with a single voice. Anne Haila's (2017) intervention is a largely positive reflection on our idea of a culture of property, informed by her significant research in Singapore (Haila, 2015), which opens the door to a fruitful conversation. Another contribution is concerned not with Hong Kong at all, but with the Chinese city of Shenyang (Tomba, 2017). Contradicting other authors in the forum, Luigi Tomba (2017: 511) writes that, allowing for Asian circumstances, 'many of gentrification's crucial components (displacement, the intervention of capital, the upgrading of the built environment) are there to be observed and experienced'. A particular circumstance in Shenyang (and China at large) is the propelling role of the state, making 'urbanization . . . an extremely large and systematic gentrification *project*' (*ibid*: 515, emphasis in original). The inconsistencies between this assessment and other contributions to the forum are not addressed.

We now briefly review several of the themes raised by the forum contributors as they argue against the existence and relevance of gentrification in Hong Kong.

- Externally-derived urban theory cannot be sufficiently sensitive to the context of East Asia in general and Hong Kong in particular

This has been a constant complaint used to justify the rejection of pan-regional urban theory (Peck, 2015). In this respect it is notable that both Peck (2015) and Lees (2012) endorse the significance of approaches which are sensitive to local contingencies. David Ley's work has also constantly challenged the role of economistic macro-theory, whether in the spatial analysis of the 1970s or the structural Marxism that followed it, preferring a textured local form of study which highlights the interplay of agency and institutions within multiple constraining and facilitating contexts. And a recent paper by two other Hong Kong scholars does discuss gentrification while highlighting the significance of multiple local contexts (La Grange and Pretorius, 2016). Such work forms part of a growing body of scholarship characterized by 'speaking gentrification in the languages of the global East' (Waley, 2016; Lee, 2018). More authors now regard gentrification as a 'critical conceptualization of urban processes in the global East' (Shin et al., 2016: 460).

However, our critics see no place for gentrification theory in Hong Kong. In arguing for 'the complexities of the local' (Lui, 2017: 478), they accuse us of extending gentrification work 'irrespective of context' (Cartier, 2017: 468). The context we have missed, it seems, is the pre-1997 colonial context, highlighted by several critics

(Lui, 2017: 481; Tang, 2017: 489; Smart and Smart, 2017: 522). The critics have less to say about the post-1997 period when Hong Kong continued its transition from an industrial to a post-industrial city (but see Lui, 2017: 485), even though this is the historical context of our paper and where we examine urban socio-spatial change in detail.

Marginalizing capital and culture

The interventions display an aversion to political economy originating in the global North, which one critic describes as 'oversimplification to a single logic' (Tang, 2017: 497) because, he writes, it is 'not the logic of capital' (ibid. 494) that governs the production of space in Hong Kong. And yet the same critic, having dispensed with the role of Northern theorists, appropriates the work of Lefebvre and Gramsci (ibid. 488), although it was Lefebvre who famously declared that there was nothing outside the urban, and that urban capitalism had become a global formation (Wilson and Jonas, 2018). The desire to distance political economy from the critique has disabling consequences. Class relations around neighbourhood change are neglected in favour of the vernacular labels of urban redevelopment or urban renewal (Tang, 2017: 487) – labels that the Hong Kong housing theorist Ray Forrest has dismissed as 'bland euphemisms' (Forrest, 2016: 612). In contrast, it is gentrification that has always presented a 'class-relational perspective on urban change' (López-Morales, 2015: 570). So neither the current displaced tenants nor the powerful property tycoons feature in our critics' accounts. Nor is there any mention by the Hong Kong contributors of Alice Poon's (2006) popular bestseller which articulated for Hong Kongers the class relations around property which had previously been concealed or taken-for-granted. For Hong Kong has an exuberant market orientation that should not be sidelined. As Forrest has noted, 'Hong Kong is perhaps a unique example of a city in which the process of capitalist urban development is starkly and unapologetically exposed' (Forrest, 2016: 610).

There is disagreement among the critics concerning the place of culture and ideology in neighbourhood change. While terms such as the subjectivity of place (Tang, 2017: 497) or the moral discourse of the state (Tomba, 2017: 513) are alluded to, one critic rejects our proposition that there is a widespread culture of property in Hong Kong (Cartier, 2017: 467). However, Carolyn Cartier mis-attributes this criticism to Anne Haila, when Haila in fact identifies the culture of property as 'an interesting concept . . . a good call' (Haila, 2017: 500, 506).

The pre-eminence of the state

Culture and even class relations in the market place are diminished by our critics to make room for the over-riding presence of the state. The state, writes one, is more central than capital or culture (Tomba, 2017: 509). While this author is in fact writing about urbanization in Shenyang in Mainland China, his position is shared by Hong Kong researchers. It is government that 'plays a predominant role in the production of space', writes Wing-Shing Tang (2017: 494). But this is scarcely a critique of gentrification research, since it is the state and state-led gentrification that are the central building blocks of recent research. Loretta Lees' work in London, for example, has emphasized the state's clearance of council housing projects for corporate redevelopment (Lees, 2014), and her Chilean colleague Ernesto López-Morales (2015: 570) finds that the state is 'the principal agent creating gentrification' for the cities he considers in the global South.

According to other Hong Kong scholars, state agencies are 'the key protagonists of gentrification' (La Grange and Pretorius, 2016: 508; see also He, 2019). We likewise argued for the centrality of the developmental state in East Asia in promoting the rapid urbanization that sires gentrification. Hence there is agreement, not disagreement, between authors and critics on this matter, removing one of the building blocks of their critical argument. But unlike them, we wish to consider the role of the state while ensuring we do not undermine other contexts, notably market relations and the cultural interpretation of property.

How nuanced are comparative urbanists?

Comparative urbanists urge sensitivity to context and respect for difference, while aspiring to theory beyond the single case (Robinson, 2016). But is similar respect extended to others? Relevant here is Peck's observation that comparative urbanism tends to privilege local diversity and micro-study while denying equal complexity to the West (Peck, 2015: 171).

A weakness among our critics is some carelessness and over-simplification in their representations of our argument; the opposite of the complexity and nuance they claim for their own understanding of Hong Kong. Categories are frozen and simplified to the point of misrepresentation. Gentrification is limited to its classic form of the 1970s–1980s, when new-build gentrification, often state-led, was not part of the terminology because it was not part of the historical geography. However, in this century, new-build and state-led idioms have become a standard in Anglo-America and here they converge with the gentrification characteristics of East Asia. However, our critics deny such evolutionary complexity in the story of gentrification in Anglo-America, and in limiting the phenomenon to its early classic form, they force an erroneous distinction between Anglo-America and East Asia.

Nor is there any acknowledgement of, let alone engagement with, much of the nuanced empirical work that led to our tentative conclusion – there *is* a question mark in the paper's title. One author shrinks our empirical base to a single newspaper analysis while completely overlooking the second newspaper we examined, the interviews with local housing experts, and our review of Hong Kong's housing and development literature (Tomba, 2017).

The superiority of local knowledge

The casual dismissal of gentrification in Hong Kong is accompanied, indeed justified, by a defensive politics of turf. There is concern about conceptual trespass leading to the 'marginalization of existing critical work' (Cartier, 2017: 476) and the erasure of alternative stories of displacement in Hong Kong (Smart and Smart, 2017). We take the wisdom of local knowledge seriously. The urban or regional scale has commonly been Ley's preferred unit of analysis, while in comparative projects, local cases have been brought to speak to each other to reveal broader generalizations leading to mid-level theory (Hasson and Ley, 1994; Ley, 1996). Indeed, gentrification research has often been conducted in the form of local neighbourhood studies, leading to rich interpretations which go far beyond economic reductionism (see e.g. Zukin, 1982; Lloyd, 2006;

Shaw, 2007). Gentrification, notes López-Morales (2015: 564), 'is also a far richer narrative than simple discussion around conflict over private ownership of land and land value curves'.

There is often a contradiction among comparative urbanists, for while claiming a desire for 'learning from elsewhere' (Robinson, 2016: 188), in practice there may well be a more defensive circling of the wagons, as 'mid-level theorization and process-oriented abstraction is somehow ruled out of bounds' (Peck, 2015: 169). This contradiction is evident among some of our critics. First a normative view is presented that, 'if any framework can help to explain some dimension of urban change, then it is useful, regardless of its origins' (Smart and Smart, 2017: 519), but as the critique is developed, so the tone changes. Gentrification is 'the wrong tool', an 'invasive species' (*ibid*.:524); there is a concern that it sidelines 'local conceptual diversity' (*ibid*.). It need not be so.

We regard gentrification as a theoretical heuristic that directs researchers to such questions as class relations, inequality, involuntary displacement, social redistribution and social justice in the changing urban housing market. Any concept that allows these important relations to cohere has considerable value. Yet, while salient, these relations do not and should not claim to embody the entirety of urban change. Gentrification offers a partial, not a total account, that may overlap with others – so, for example, we include several references to the work of forum participants – but it does not exclude other conceptual entry points that are also fruitful. Some of our critics found a conceptual framework that worked well for them in addressing squatting and resettlement in colonial Hong Kong a generation or more ago. It may be that a different conceptual apparatus – gentrification – works today in a post-industrial context to examine relations in the housing market.

CONCLUSION

In this short essay we have attempted to bring often abstract arguments over regional urbanism and comparative gentrification to focus on the specifics of a single contested case: gentrification in Hong Kong. We have presented the resistance to such a project from regional critics, and have challenged that resistance. While committed to the principle of regional embeddedness in the research process, we are not persuaded by the arguments of critics who dismiss the relevance of gentrification in Hong Kong. Neither, it seems, are other urban scholars, for since 2015 Hong Kong research has increasingly acknowledged the insights permitted by a gentrification problematic in examining urban redevelopment and the housing sector (Ye et al., 2015; Forrest, 2016; La Grange and Pretorius, 2016; Waley, 2016; Ip, 2018; Ng, 2018; Qian and Yin, 2018).

As we hinted earlier, beyond the specifics of comparative gentrification or comparative urbanism lies a series of dualisms, including the fundamental nomothetic-idiographic distinction, debated fiercely in human geography during the 1960s. Like some of today's abstract political economists, William Bunge, a pioneer of theoretical spatial analysis, argued in a research note that 'locations are not unique' and could be assembled together by unbounded spatial theory (Bunge, 1966: 375). However, just eight years later, following his regional grounding in first the Detroit and then the Toronto Geographical Expeditions, Bunge revised his view to the comparative position that 'regions are sort of unique' (Bunge, 1974: 92). While applauding his capacity for adjustment, it seems that, 45 years since, we still have not been able to agree on the bandwidth of this 'sort of' uniqueness.

David Ley, Department of Geography, University of British Columbia, Vancouver, BC V6T 1Z2, Canada

Sin Yih Teo, Department of Geography University of British Columbia, Vancouver, BC V6T 1Z2, Canada

REFERENCES

Brenner, N. and C. Schmid (2015) Towards a new epistemology of the urban? *City* 19.2/3, 151–182.

Bunge, W. (1966) Locations are not unique. *Annals of the Association of American Geographers* 56.3, 375–376.

Bunge, W. (1974) Regions are sort of unique. *Area* 6.1, 92–99.

Cartier, C. (2017) Contextual urban theory and the 'appeal' of gentrification: lost in transposition? *International Journal of Urban and Regional Research* 41.3, 466–477.

Cybriwsky, R. (2011) *Roppongi Crossing: The demise of a Tokyo nightclub district and the reshaping of a global city.* University of Georgia Press, Athens, GA.

Forrest, R. (2016) Variegated gentrification. *Urban Studies* 53.3, 609–614.

Forrest, R. and J. Lee (2004) Cohort effects, differential accumulation and Hong Kong's volatile housing market. *Urban Studies* 41.11, 2181–2196.

Ha, S.K. (2004) Housing renewal and neighbourhood change as a gentrification process in Seoul. *Cities* 21.5, 381–389.

Haila, A. (2015) *Urban land rent: Singapore as a property state.* Wiley-Blackwell, Chichester.

Haila, A. (2017) Institutionalization of the property mind. *International Journal of Urban and Regional Research* 41.3, 500–507.

Hasson, S. and D. Ley (1994) *Neighbourhood organizations and the welfare state.* University of Toronto Press, Toronto.

He, S. (2019) Three waves of state-led gentrification in China. *Tijdschrift voor Economische en Sociale Geographie – Journal of Economic and Social Geography* 110.1, 26–34.

He, S. and F. Wu (2007) Socio-spatial impacts of property-led redevelopment on China's urban neighbourhoods. *Cities* 24.3, 194–208.

Ip, I.C. (2018) State, class and capital: gentrification and new urban developmentalism in Hong Kong. *Critical Sociology* 44.3, 547–562.

La Grange, A. and F. Pretorius (2016) State-led gentrification in Hong Kong. *Urban Studies* 53.3, 506–523.

Lee, S.Y. (2018) Cities for profit: profit-driven gentrification in Seoul, South Korea. *Urban Studies* 55.12, 2603–2617.

Lees, L. (2012) The geography of gentrification: thinking through comparative urbanism. *Progress in Human Geography* 36.2, 155–171.

Lees, L. (2014) The urban injustices of New Labour's 'new urban renewal': the case of the Aylesbury Estate in London. *Antipode* 46.4, 921–947.

Lees, L., H.B. Shin and E. López-Morales (eds.) (2015) *Global gentrifications: Uneven development and displacement.* Policy Press, Bristol.

Lees, L., H.B. Shin and E. López-Morales (2016) *Planetary gentrification.* Polity Press, Cambridge.

Ley, D. (1996) *The new middle class and the remaking of the central city.* Oxford University Press, Oxford.

Ley, D. (2010) *Millionaire migrants: Trans-Pacific life lines*. Wiley-Blackwell, Chichester.

Ley, D. and S.Y. Teo (2014) Gentrification in Hong Kong? Epistemology vs. ontology. *International Journal of Urban and Regional Research* 38.4, 1286–1303.

Lloyd, R. (2006) *Neo-Bohemia: Art and commerce in the post-industrial city*. Routledge, New York.

López-Morales, E. (2015) Gentrification in the global South. *City* 19.4, 564–573.

Lui, T.L. (2017) Beneath the appearance of gentrification: probing local complexities. *International Journal of Urban and Regional Research* 41.3, 478–486.

Maloutas, T. (2012) Contextual diversity in gentrification research. *Critical Sociology* 38.1, 33–48.

Maloutas, T. (2018) Travelling concepts and universal particularisms: A reappraisal of gentrification's global reach. *European Urban and Regional Studies* 25.3, 250–265.

Ng, M.K. (2018) Sustainable community building in the face of state-led gentrification: The story of the Blue House cluster in Hong Kong. *Town Planning Review* 89.5, 495–512.

Peck, J. (2015) Regions beyond compare. *Regional Studies* 49.1, 160–182.

Poon, A. (2006) *Land and the ruling class in Hong Kong*.

Poon, A., B.C. Richmond, X.Y. Qian and C.Z. Yin (2018) From redevelopment to gentrification in Hong Kong: a case study of Kwun Tong town center project. *Open House International* 43.3, 83–93.

Robinson, J. (2016) Comparative urbanism: new geographies and cultures of theorizing the urban. *International Journal of Urban and Regional Research* 40.1, 187–199.

Shaw, W. (2007) *Cities of whiteness*. Blackwell, Oxford.

Shin, H.B. (2009) Property-based redevelopment and gentrification: the case of Seoul, South Korea. *Geoforum* 40.5, 906–917.

Shin, H.B., L. Lees and E. López-Morales (2016) Introduction: locating gentrification in the global East. *Urban Studies* 53.3, 455–470.

Smart, A. and J. Smart (2017) Ain't talkin' 'bout gentrification: the erasure of alternative idioms of displacement resulting from Anglo-American academic hegemony. *International Journal of Urban and Regional Research* 41.3, 518–525.

Tang, W.S. (2017) Beyond gentrification: hegemonic redevelopment in Hong Kong. *International Journal of Urban and Regional Research* 41.3, 487–499.

Tomba, L. (2017) Gentrifying China's urbanization? Why culture and capital are not enough. *International Journal of Urban and Regional Research* 41.3, 508–517.

Waley, P. (2016) Speaking gentrification in the languages of the global East. *Urban Studies* 53.3, 615–625.

Wang, J. and S. Lau (2009) Gentrification and Shanghai's new middle class. *Cities* 26.2, 57–66.

Wilson, D. and A. Jonas (2018) Planetary urbanization: new perspectives on the debate. *Urban Geography* 39.10, 1576–1580.

Ye, M.T., I. Vojnovic and G. Chen (2015) The landscape of gentrification: exploring the diversity of 'upgrading' processes in Hong Kong, 1986–2006. *Urban Geography* 36.4, 471–503.

Yip, N.M., R. Forrest and A. La Grange (2007) Cohort trajectories in Hong Kong's housing system, 1981–2001. *Housing Studies* 22.1, 121–136.

Zukin, S. (1982) *Loft living: Culture and capital in urban change*. Johns Hopkins University Press, Baltimore, MD.

PART FOUR

Gentrifications beyond Anglo-America

'No To Gentrification', in Bo Kaap, Cape Town, South Africa
(photograph: Tom Slater)

INTRODUCTION TO PART FOUR

Up to the mid-2000s, there were few studies of gentrification beyond the 'usual suspects' (Lees, Shin, and Lopez-Morales 2015). Almost everything scholars knew about the process, and the rich body of theory developed to understand it, came from (predominantly large) cities of the Global North, especially from an Anglo-American perspective (both in the US and the UK and in English language contexts). But as we have already explained and seen in the contributions to this *Reader* so far, the scale and pace of urban development (and the extent of displacement) beyond the North have led to fascinating recent empirical and theoretical interventions and changed the landscape of gentrification research in ways that are highly instructive for urban scholars, regardless of where they are located. Does this mean that existing theories need to be abandoned, or do they need to be modified and/or extended? In this *Reader*, our emphasis is very much on the latter, and there is a critical body of work emerging to support this perspective. For example, Marieke Krijnen (2018: 1042) reminds us that the rent gap theory is especially helpful when seeking to 'understand how areas become susceptible to renewed capital investment, i.e. what happens before gentrification occurs' and addresses this question in the context of Beirut, Lebanon. Theoretically, Krijnen demonstrates that calls to make urban theory more cosmopolitan and comparative (e.g., Robinson 2006, 2011) need not necessarily involve jettisoning existing theories formulated in Anglo-American contexts and formulating new theories at ground level, but rather extending existing theories methodologically and conceptually to account for particular political, economic, and institutional contexts. Another example is Melissa Wright's (2014) analysis of the gentrification of the *centro historico* of Ciudad Juarez on the Mexico–United States border in the wake of the carnage and devastation caused there by a transcontinental drug war (2006–2012), instigated by both countries' governments. Wright not only found existing gentrification theory to be highly applicable to explain a situation whereby 'in order to rescue the centro and augment its economic value, the city first needed to be economically and socially destroyed. The formerly vibrant downtown, in short, needed to be killed before it could be rescued' (2014: 2). She then extended it based on the Ciudad Juarez context and brought feminist and Marxist approaches to accumulation by dispossession together to explain a class struggle between, on the one hand, ruling elites intent on a strategy of denigrating the lives and spaces of working-class women and their children living in the *centro* in order to expand the rent gap and ultimately 'clean up' the area and 'reestablish' it as a place for upstanding families and, on the other, activists drawing public attention to the exploitation (in maquiladora factories and in sex work) of working poor women and especially to *feminicidio* (the killing of women with impunity). While gentrification plans were disrupted by activists for some time, this did not last, for those same policy and business elites then targeted young men caught up in the violence of the drug war:

> Rather than refer to the male youth population that dominates the body count as the resident population of the city's poor working-class families, the mayor referred to them as "venomous vermin" who had descended upon the city. . . . Such depictions sought to whitewash the public memory of these young people who were being gunned down on the very streets that had raised them.
>
> (ibid.: 11)

DOI: 10.4324/9781003341239-20

This official 'politics of forgetting' is now working to close the rent gap and extract profits from massively devalorized spaces.

In these two contexts, beyond the usual suspects at least, existing theories of gentrification (especially the rent gap) were helpful but needed contextual modifications and extensions to explain the gentrification unfolding at ground level. However, some urban scholars working with postcolonial theory, not least Ghertner (2015), have taken issue with such an approach. He argued that the term 'gentrification' has been imposed by scholars on places where it doesn't fit or where it makes little sense to struggles occurring at ground level; that it doesn't recognize the diversity of activities taking place where 'public land ownership, common property, mixed tenure, or informality' (p. 552) endure; that it is 'agnostic on the question of extra-economic force' (p. 553); that Western gentrification scholars 'see like capitalists' (p. 553) in their assumption that private land tenure/capitalist urbanization is everywhere; and that those scholars are not alert to forms of displacement that are driven by processes other than gentrification (such as the violent evictions taking place over privatization of nonprivate land tenures). Earlier, we highlighted and agreed with Shin and Lopez-Morales's (2018) critique of Ghertner, and we would add here an important note about the logic of concept formation. Although it is very important to ask theoretical questions about the pertinence of certain concepts and whether they are helpful or not in dissecting urban processes beyond where they were formed, the fact that, for example, the rent gap theory was developed from research in the United States in the 1970s is not by itself a valid reason to dismiss it, ignore it, or indeed unlearn it, in very different contexts, four decades later. The challenge is to take it seriously, and if it turns out not to be useful vis-à-vis a certain geographical context or struggle, then it should not be used.

But at least from the research that is available, and still emerging, it seems to be the case that 'gentrification' still explains what is happening in contexts beyond the usual suspects, and as a term and concept, it is far from 'less than adequate in much of the world' (Ghertner 2015: 554). However, outside the usual suspects, there are of course some very important contextual differences and historical pathways to gentrification that require careful dissection and sensitive analytic scrutiny. In this section, we provide our readers with four articles looking at gentrification in cities outside of the Global North and/or the English-speaking world. A large number of Global South and Global East (note: we are not wedded to these terms but use them for ease here) cities have undergone substantial socio-spatial changes due to intensive state-led and/or private-led investment resulting in the upward and unequal social re-stratification (gentrification) of neighborhoods and communities. In a foundational piece for scholars of gentrification in South Africa, Tanja Winkler investigated the assumptions underpinning the City of Johannesburg's planning policies in the 2000s, which were geared toward encouraging economic competitiveness, private sector investment, real estate (re)development via tax breaks, and public-private partnerships for 'flagship' development. Efforts to create a 'world class African city', Winkler argued, relied on the foreclosure of (mostly poor, mostly informal sector) residents' active political engagement in public decision-making. In planning documents and verbal statements, local state actors saw informal socioeconomic activities as undesirable and unmanageable obstacles in way of urban progress. In Box 5, Winkler updates us on the fast-moving, turbulent political developments affecting urban policies in Johannesburg since 2009 and outlines the sobering realities for people living at the bottom of the class structure in that city today.

In the second article we have chosen for this section, Arnisson Ortega analyses the changes that have taken place in the outer fringes of Manila, Philippines, where vast tracts of agricultural lands have been replaced by gated master-planned residential developments mimicking Western-themed suburban landscapes in the North American context. It might seem strange or even controversial that we have selected an article that does not use the term 'gentrification' to explain these changes, but as Lees, Shin, and Lopez-Morales (2016) argue, even where the processes are not called gentrification locally or where there is no equivalent term, class-driven urban redevelopment is an embedded process in multiple Southern and Eastern contexts. Ortega's analysis points to the growing importance of secondary circuits of accumulation and the planetary shift to rentier extraction and what might be termed the robbery of value rather than the production of value. Asset pursuit and asset stripping (via land grabbing, dispossession, and evictions) is a hallmark of contemporary urbanization and shows little sign of retreating on a planetary scale, and Ortega's study of Manila's fringe is a clear illustration. The third article, by Thaisa Comelli, Isabelle Anguelovski, and Eric Chu, traces the contradictions of the 'upgrading' of two favelas in Rio de Janeiro, Brazil. They demonstrate that these processes not only involve physical constructions of new public spaces and urban infrastructure; they are also attached to concurrent state and private interventions promoting securitization and police control, environmental clean-up, and economic investments in tourism and real estate. The outcome is to stimulate patterns of gentrification that can be understood as what they term 'physical, symbolic, and economic forms of discipline', leading to erasure of long-term socially vulnerable residents through ambivalent experiences of upgrading that affect their livelihoods, behavior, and sense of belonging, in public spaces. The final article in this section, by Lewis Abedi Asante and Richmond Juvenile Ehwi, analyzes the changes that have taken place to dwelling units within compound houses in Bantama, a sub-metro in Ghana's second-largest city, Kumasi. Compound houses are the oldest and most familiar form of housing in West Africa; nevertheless, dwelling units – accommodation or rooms occupied by a single household, with access to shared cooking and bathroom facilities – tend to be poorly maintained, overcrowded, and lacking some basic amenities. In recent years, many private landlords in Ghana have been transforming the ordinary dwelling units in their compound houses into 'apartment dwelling units', where shared facilities become private. Not only has this resulted in the displacement of low-income households in favor of middle- and high-income professionals (reducing the availability of low-income housing during an acute housing shortage), it has led to the erosion of shared courtyard spaces, typically arenas for fostering rich social interactions and crucial social and employment networks. The authors are clear that the rent gap theory is helpful in explaining these changes but also that it needs to be considered alongside local practices, stereotypical tendencies, and cultural factors that play out in how landlords select tenants. In sum, these four papers contribute new insights on how capital-oriented urban (re)development strategies in the Global South and East renew the (negative) role of the state vis-à-vis the informal sector, create new market visibility and discipline, and eventually produce socio-cultural and racial invisibilization and displacement.

REFERENCES AND FURTHER READING

Ghertner, D. A. (2015) "Why Gentrification Theory Fails in 'Much of the World'." *CITY* 19 (4): 552–563.

Janoschka, M., and Sequera, J. (2016) "Gentrification in Latin America: Addressing the Politics and Geographies of Displacement." *Urban Geography* 37 (8): 1175–1194.

Krijnen, M. (2018) "Beirut and the Creation of the Rent Gap." *Urban Geography* 39 (7): 1041–1059.

Lawton, P. (2020) "Unbounding Gentrification Theory: Multidimensional Space, Networks and Relational Approaches." *Regional Studies* 54 (2): 268–279.

Lees, L., Shin, H.B., and Lopez-Morales, E. eds (2015) *Global Gentrifications*: *Uneven Development and Displacement*. Bristol: Policy Press.

Lees, L., Shin, H.B., and Lopez-Morales, E. (2016) *Planetary Gentrification*. Cambridge: Polity Press.

Robinson, J. (2006) *Ordinary Cities: Between Modernity and Development*. London: Routledge.

Robinson, J. (2011) "Cities in a World of Cities: The Comparative Gesture." *International Journal of Urban and Regional Research* 35 (1): 1–23.

Sakizlioğlu, B. (2014) "Inserting Temporality into the Analysis of Displacement: Living under the Threat of Displacement." *Tijdschrift Voor Economische En Sociale Geografie* 105 (2): 206–220.

Shin, H.B., and Lopez-Morales, E. (2018) "Beyond Anglo-American Gentrification Theory." In Lees, L. with Phillips, M. (eds) *Handbook of Gentrification Studies*. London: Edward Elgar, pp. 13–25.

Whitehead, J., and More, N. (2007) "Revanchism in Mumbai? Political Economy of Rent Gaps and Urban Restructuring in a Global City." *Economic and Political Weekly*, June 23, 2428–2434.

Wright, M. (2014) "Gentrification, Assassination and Forgetting in Mexico: A Feminist-Marxist Tale." *Gender, Place & Culture* 21 (1): 1–16.

13
Prolonging the global age of gentrification

Johannesburg's regeneration policies†

Tanja Winkler

INTRODUCTION

It is said that Johannesburg has been built up and torn down no less than five times since it first appeared on the highveld in 1886. And each time it has re-emerged even uglier than before. (Matshikiza, 2004: 481)

At a lecture to the American Planning Association, Sir Peter Hall suggested that many command centre cities of the global North have experienced a 'renaissance'. Hall's (2005) lecture pointed to numerous examples of cities that have witnessed a significant turnabout after decades of decline. This lecture also reiterated the findings of symposium papers presented at the Resurgent City conference hosted by the London School of Economics (LSE). Here, speakers portrayed cities of the global North as 'coming back [due to] globalization, more intense competition, and the rise of the cultural economy' (LSE, 2004: 1). These key requisites, they argued, have restored the economic role of previously degenerated inner city neighbourhoods.

There can be no doubt of the need for capital reinvestment in economically stressed inner city neighbourhoods. A significant number of local authorities are, therefore, engaged in drafting and implementing urban policies that actively seek the economic regeneration of their city centres. However, for a number of planning scholars, contemporary regeneration practices and policies tend to focus on making cities more economically competitive while bypassing issues of social and spatial justice in neighbourhoods earmarked for rejuvenation (Beauregard, 2004; Díaz Orueta, 2007; Fainstein, 2004; Marcuse, 2002; Porter and Shaw, 2009; Roy, 2006). These practices and policies entail pursuing New Urban Policy (Boyle and Rogerson, 2001) and New Conventional Wisdom (Gordon and Buck, 2005) centred on 'economic competitiveness', 'responsive governance', 'social cohesion', and 'social mix' strategies, and the use of such strategies in urban planning frameworks suggests that unemployment, shrinking opportunities, social exclusion, and inner city hardships are a thing of the past (Beauregard, 2004; Catterall, 2004; Marcuse, 2002; Slater, 2006). Rather, street-level spectacles, trendy bars and cafés, social diversity, and funky clothing outlets are deemed necessary regeneration ingredients. Municipalities across the globe are thus rushing to endorse Richard Florida's (2005) celebration of a new 'creative class' in urban centres. In the process, they hope to attract investors, higher income households, the 'creative class', and tourists to occupy the cafés, galleries, sidewalks, and rehabilitated residential stock of formerly disinvested neighbourhoods once lacking in 'creativity' (Slater, 2006; Storper and Manville, 2006). Additionally, while private sector involvement is prioritized in New Urban Policy and New Conventional Wisdom, contemporary regeneration projects are, essentially, facilitated by the state (De Magalhães, 2004). Contemporary regeneration practices and policies are then 'not a sideshow in the city, but a major component of the urban imaginary' (Ley, 2003: 2527), and the City of Johannesburg's policy intent to re-brand Johannesburg as a 'cultural capital' may be added to this globalizing frenzy.

> The City of Johannesburg (CoJ) will work to ensure a successful branding of the Inner City as the Cultural Capital of the country. The title of

DOI: 10.4324/9781003341239-21

'cultural capital' of the country is available and has great potential. In a world where the cultural sector is increasingly prominent in the profiling or branding of cities, this potential strength should be given greater prominence in achieving a world class African city.

(CoJ, ICR Charter, 2007: 22, 23)

Accordingly, New Urban Policy and New Conventional Wisdom are not restricted to command centre cities of the global North, but are being imported by municipalities of the global South as 'best practice', world class enabling precedents to secure a global age of regeneration (Bourdieu and Wacquant, 2001; Smith, 2002). Downtown Johannesburg is thus on the brink of another re-emergence informed by lessons from 'the best run cities in the world' (Mayor Masondo, cited in Davie, 2006). Twenty-five years of capital and white flight from the inner city of Johannesburg recently prompted the City Council to implement a plethora of investor friendly policies to re-attract private capital and middle-class households. However, and contrary to global North experiences, decades of capital and white flight resulted neither in a depopulation of the inner city nor in a vacant, boarded-up landscape. Rather, informal socio-economic activities coupled with a significant inward migration of jobseekers have transformed Johannesburg's downtown. Today, the greater majority of existing inner city residents are poor. Many rely on the informal sector to survive, and many reside in physically dilapidated apartment blocks, or 'bad buildings' as classified by the City Council, while being exploited by slumlords. Informal socioeconomic activities and a doubling of the inner city resident population, in particular, are perceived by municipal officials, policy-makers and politicians as undesirable and unmanageable obstacles in achieving their 'cultural capital' and 'world class African city' vision. As a consequence, local planning policies are seemingly designed to shift undesirable and unmanageable 'obstacles', via exclusionary displacement mechanisms, to 'peripheral locations where they are less of an eyesore and [less of] a threat to the City's renewal process' (Silimela, 2003: 152). This suggests that inner city regeneration in Johannesburg is nothing more than a euphemism for underlying gentrification.

By means of case study research methods and a critical discourse analysis, this article aims to investigate the apparent assumptions underpinning the City of Johannesburg's planning policies to generate a fuller understanding of who stands to benefit, and who does not, economically and spatially, from public sector led regeneration programmes. For the purpose of this study, an in-depth case study of the inner city of Johannesburg will inform research findings, while a discourse analysis will entail a critical examination of the written (in policy documents or in the media) and spoken (during open-ended interviews or at public meetings) language used by municipal officials and politicians. Their standpoint will become apparent, and their argument for private sector reinvestment and intensive urban management, to stimulate the local economy and to curb degeneration trends, will be presented. An understanding of residents' needs and the impact of regeneration policies, in turn, is base on a three-year study with community leaders, local civil society organizations, residents, and informal traders.

For Fainstein (2005), Roy (2006) and Yiftachel (2006), deeper investigations into existing urban policies neither imply a blindness to external political forces nor an assumption that political structures cannot be changed. But investigations also accept that 'existing structures are not changed easily' and that change 'can only be envisaged through collective activity' (Fainstein, 2005: 127). This article will, therefore, proceed by exploring how economic competitiveness, responsive governance, social cohesion, and social mix strategies, found in policy documents across the globe, inform the City of Johannesburg's regeneration practices and policies. It will be structured in three sections. The first will establish a conceptual framework for urban regeneration through which a Johannesburg case study may be evaluated. Here, a more equitable, just, and resident inclusive approach to urban regeneration will be sought. Such an approach is inspired by Fainstein's (1974, 2004, 2005) Just City conceptualizations of planning theory and practice in which the central purpose of planning is to promote social, economic and spatial justice. A Just City position will, therefore, be used as a critical frame of reference in the expository analysis. The second section will establish the origins of Johannesburg's regeneration policies; and both this and the third section will then evaluate the impact of Johannesburg's regeneration practices by responding to Yiftachel's plea to 'reengage planning scholarship with the material basis of urban planning' (2006: 212). In these sections it will become apparent that patterns of access to economic, spatial and political resources are unequally distributed. If such regeneration practices continue to be implemented, then, arguably, the desired 'cultural capital' and 'world class African city' may lead to a gentrified space of social and economic exclusion, and not to a Just City.

ESTABLISHING A CONCEPTUAL FRAMEWORK FOR THIS STUDY

> In 1955, *Time* magazine devoted a cover story to 'The Rebirth of the City'. In 1962, it devoted a similar story to urban rebirth, titled, simply, 'Renaissance'. In 1981, the magazine gave a cover to developer James Rouse, king of the festival marketplace, and titled it 'Cities are Fun!' Six years after that the cover went to 'Bringing the City Back to Life'. The urban comeback has been coming for some time now.
>
> (Storper and Manville, 2006: 1247)

Urban regeneration is performed in different cities under various guises, including, 'renewal', 'rejuvenation', 'reinvestment', 'revitalization', 'renaissance', and, more recently, 'smart growth'. Nearly half a century ago, Jane Jacobs (1961) convincingly demonstrated how state-driven urban renewal programmes destroyed vibrant inner city neighbourhoods. Instead of creating the desired rejuvenation of urban centres, renewal programmes fuelled capital flight, the decentralization of employment to the suburbs, and, what Peterson (1991) terms as, the 'poverty paradox': growing suburban affluence coupled with greater inner city adversity. By the early 1980s, ongoing inner city degeneration became a threat to the competitive market agenda of economically liberal governments. Cities would not become world class entities if the degeneration and under-utilization of blighted urban nodes were allowed to persist. Contemporary regeneration policies, that include concepts such as economic competitiveness, responsive governance, social cohesion, and social mix, thus began to replace former renewal programmes in order to safeguard capitalist production (Boyle and Rogerson, 2001; Gordon and Buck, 2005; Smith, 1996, 2002).

While New Urban Policy (Boyle and Rogerson, 2001) and New Conventional Wisdom (Gordon and Buck, 2005) encompass concepts of social cohesion and responsive governance, the central political and economic imperative for local governments influenced by New Urban Policy and New Conventional Wisdom is to build competitiveness through a search for new opportunities and distinctive sources of advantage. Major regeneration projects are, therefore, justified by local governments as a means towards facilitating the so-called new economy and the differentiated consumption demands of the middle classes (Díaz Orueta, 2007). As a result, since the mid- to late 1980s, a plethora of ambitious inner city regeneration strategies has emerged in various centres across the globe at a scale that far outstrips 1960s urban renewal. The difference between contemporary practices and renewal predecessors is that private sector involvement is now favoured as a platform to establish largescale, multifaceted regeneration. Such partnerships between private capital and the local state have intensified over the past decade resulting in larger, more expensive, more expansive, and more symbolic development projects, from Barcelona's waterfront to Berlin's Potsdamer Platz, from London's Canary Wharf to New York's Battery Park City (Smith, 2002). All have become 'best-practice' precedents, where economic competitiveness, responsive governance, social cohesion, and social mix strategies are in vogue, and where urban regeneration is not perceived as a means of reducing inner city poverty, but as creating economic growth, inflated property values, and higher tax revenues (Beauregard, 2004; Catterall, 2004; Ley, 2003). Many municipalities are thus 'caught within the web of global exchange, and display similarities [in their regeneration policies and outcomes] that are widely shared' (Fainstein, 2004: 4). Many invest in catalytic, or flagship, projects, and many have become consummate agents of the market through the institutionalization of free-market doctrines (Brenner and Theodore, 2005; Smith, 2002). Free-market economic strategies rather than social policies act as catalysts for change, to help create jobs and wealth via a trickle-down philosophy. For this reason, Smith contends that 'urban policy no longer aspires to guide or regulate the direction of economic growth so much as to fit itself to the grooves already established by the market in search of the highest return' (2002: 441).

Public-private partnerships are also forged to establish Business/City Improvement Districts (BIDs/CIDs) and Town Centre Management (TCM) programmes, while zero-tolerance law enforcement, or intensive urban management, is deployed to safeguard capital investments. However, contemporary regeneration practices and policies marginalize and exclude residents in poor inner city neighbourhoods from public decision-making processes regardless of the fact that 'the material legacy of these decisions remain for generations' (Yiftachel, 2006: 213). Concepts such as economic competitiveness, responsive governance, social cohesion, and social mix, embroiled in New Urban Policy and New Conventional Wisdom, serve as excellent examples of how the reality of gentrification is being replaced by a discursive policy language to deflect criticism (Slater, 2006). This will be evidenced in subsequent sections on Johannesburg.

By contrast, resident resistance to New Urban Policy and New Conventional Wisdom is prompting more progressive municipalities in Britain to devise resident inclusive regeneration approaches through the implementation of Social Inclusion Partnerships (SIPs). The aim of SIPs is to target public sector support for specific community development projects in poor neighbourhoods. Similarly, Regional Development Agencies in Britain are in the process of establishing Centres of Excellence for Urban Regeneration to facilitate citizen participation in public decision-making processes (De Magalhães, 2004). Such state-led practices also promote aspects of communicative planning theory. Nonetheless, for some scholars, SIPs and Centres of Excellence evade the multi-dimensionality implicit in the process of urban decline, and they are in conflict with the state's ultimate competitive and urban commodification goals (Amin and Thrift, 1994; Madanipour, 2003). Resident-led approaches to regeneration and planning, such as those facilitated by Community Development Corporations (CDCs) in American cities, may present an alternative to state-led initiatives. These Corporations initiate a broad array of community development project aimed not only at regenerating neighbourhoods but also at strengthening residents' access to political processes (Vidal, 1996). 'CDCs are doing the difficult job of providing services and leadership in communities that need help and that other agencies cannot or will not serve' (Vidal, 1996: 153). Resident-led approaches further support planning for social transformation theories and practices. Still, CDCs rely on state and other grants for their survival, and they are often burdened by internal management problems (Winkler, 2006).

While SIPs, Centres of Excellence, and CDCs have weaknesses and limitations, the purpose of introducing these models is to present actual examples of resident involved as opposed to resident excluded approaches to urban regeneration and planning. A more inclusive approach will, however, require the local state to recognize that there is no, empirically justified, link between economic growth and social equity. Said differently, 'social exclusion and economic exclusion are intertwined' (Fainstein, 2004: 15). Fainstein's conceptualization of the Just City is, therefore, based on an equitable, redistributive, and resident involved approach for planning and regeneration to remedy social and economic exclusion. Such an approach is not blind to the power of the state and of capital in determining who gets what, where and when, but it, nonetheless, subscribes to Friedmann's (1987) theories of social/mutual learning, and to Nussbaum's (2004) argument concerning the development of residents' capacities, in particular their political capacities, for involved and effective public decision-making. Capacitating residents will further require the local state to shift its focus from merely governing the city, and fitting itself into the grooves of the free market, to embracing participatory governance (Campbell and Marshall, 2000). With its roots in social and post-Marxist political economy theory, the Just City model for planning and regeneration is suggestive of aspects of participatory governance. After all, the Just City is a social construct that can only be conceptualized through collective engagement (Fainstein, 2005). Practical solutions to social and economic exclusion are then not the monopoly of municipal officials, politicians, and professional planners, but are collectively formulated through respectful processes of social/mutual learning and residents' active political engagement in public decision-making processes. Additionally, both the substantive (material) content of urban policies and the process of generating urban policies need to be equally judged for their impact on equity (Fainstein, 2005; Yiftachel, 2006). The core task of the Just City is then to understand and critique the substantive and procedural impacts of urban policies to facilitate a platform for transformative intervention (Yiftachel, 2006). It is against this resident involved, equitable, just, and material basis of planning and regeneration that the Johannesburg case study will now be evaluated.

ESTABLISHING THE ORIGINS OF JOHANNESBURG'S REGENERATION POLICIES

After the second democratic municipal elections held in December 2000, 'inner city regeneration' was declared a priority by the newly appointed executive mayor of Johannesburg, Amos Masondo. At the same time, local policy-makers formulated a long-term economic development framework known as the 'Jo'burg 2030 Vision'. By 2030, it was proposed, Johannesburg will be a world class city in compliance with New Urban Policy and New Conventional Wisdom. 'Its economy and labour force will specialize in the service sector so that the economy will operate on a competitive global scale [to] drive up tax revenues, private sector profits, and disposable incomes' (CoJ, 2030 Vision, 2002: 3). The 2030 Vision thus laid the foundation for the first Inner City Regeneration Strategy with an overarching goal 'to raise and sustain private investment leading to a steady rise in property values' (CoJ, ICRS, 2003a: 2). However, the local state failed to recognize that there is no (empirically justified) link between economic growth and social equity. The formulation of these policies also excluded inner city residents, which is contrary to a Just City approach for regeneration. Such findings corroborate Yiftachel's (2006) concern that decision-making in the global South is generally less transparent, and that state actors, and not residents, shape planning practices and policies.

Achieving the Regeneration Strategy's overarching goal required an overt demonstration by the municipality to accommodate investor needs. In addition, the City of Johannesburg began to embrace responsive governance strategies by shifting its role from 'acting merely as an administrator, to becoming an active agent of economic development and growth' (CoJ, 2030 Vision, 2002: 3). Accommodating investor needs and responsive governance strategies, via the adoption of New Urban Policy and New Conventional Wisdom, included establishing public-private partnerships; declaring an 18 km² district in the inner city as an Urban Development Zone (UDZ) so that budding investors could become eligible for substantial tax breaks; stimulating buoyant economic development by supporting 'big business' through the design and implementation of carefully crafted physical interventions; investing in catalytic projects that presuppose a multiplier effect of increased property values through complementary private sector investments; floating municipal bonds to increase investor confidence in the inner city; and facilitating the Better Buildings Programme (BBP) by writing off arrears on identified 'bad buildings' and transferring the ownership of these buildings to private sector developers for rehabilitation.

Investor friendly regeneration policies are, ostensibly, eliciting a financial turnabout in the fortunes of the municipality (Harrison, 2006). '$750 million worth of investment has poured into Johannesburg's inner city over the past four years' (*The Star*, 2008: 6); and an additional $2 billion of public sector money will be allocated to ongoing catalytic, or flagship, projects (*Financial Mail*, 2005) so that 'Johannesburg can be marketed as an exciting Afropolitan city' (Gevisser, 2004: 517) and as the 'cultural capital' of South Africa. City Improvement Districts (CIDs) are also being set-up to facilitate the management of regenerated urban nodes, while 'inner city apartments are being refurbished by private sector developers for up to $800,000 per unit' (*Financial Mail*, 2005: 6). Accordingly, Councillor Tau, a member of the mayoral committee responsible for economic development, is of the opinion that:

> Ten years ago there was severe deterioration in the Inner City. Today it has transformed into a desirable business and residential hub with commercial and residential property prices reflecting this turnaround. Our urban regeneration policies and increased capital investments are critical to competitive economic growth and a property market turnaround despite a global property market slowdown.
>
> (Councillor Tau, cited in *The Star*, 2008: 6)

However, 'this productive engagement between city authorities and private capital [is] also associated with an apparent insensitivity towards poor citizens within the city' (Harrison, 2006: 330). Insensitivities entail implementing intensive urban management policies that comprise, amongst other strategies, tenant evictions from buildings earmarked for the Better Buildings Programme (BBP) and disconnecting the supply of water and electricity to buildings with unpaid municipal bills (*Financial Mail*, 2003; Inner City Community Forum, 2003). If the core task of a Just City conceptualization of planning is to understand and critique the substantive and procedural impacts of urban policy so that transformative interventions may be sought, it then becomes important to ask, what is the City of Johannesburg's regeneration vision?

> Through our regeneration [initiatives], we are going to make millionaires out of a lot of people! What is happening is that a higher calibre of people is now moving in.
> They are taking up the penthouses, and they are creating the world class city that we are talking about.
>
> (Interview, CoJ Director of Inner City Regeneration, 2004)

Explicitly seeking a 'higher calibre of people' to transform the inner city into a world class context presupposes a gentrified vision. While Marcuse (1985) correctly argues that how gentrification is evaluated depends a great deal on how it is defined, this article will not deliberate on a definition for gentrification given the extraordinary depth and progress made by scholars since Glass's (1964) coinage of the term in the mid-1960s. Rather, for the purpose of this study, Hackworth's (2002) succinct definition of gentrification will be used. Accordingly, gentrification is 'the production of space for progressively more affluent users' (Hackworth, 2002: 815). Here, the critical emphasis is on class transformation which has social, economic, and spatial repercussions. Moreover, Slater proposes that 'gentrification is a process directly linked to the injustice of community upheaval and working-class displacement' (2006: 739) which, in turn, undermines the principles of a Just City, as this theoretical model is concerned with the redistributive benefits of urban policies and actions. It is, however, difficult to quantify the extent of community upheaval and resident displacement from Johannesburg's inner city neighbourhoods, because, as sustained by Newman and Wyly:

> It is difficult to find people who have been displaced, particularly if those people are poor . . . By definition, displaced residents have disappeared from the very places where researchers and census-takers go to look for them.
>
> (Newman and Wyly, 2006: 27)

In an economically liberal context where public policy is constructed on a quantitative evidence base, a lack of quantitative evidence regarding the number of displaced residents from the inner city results in a lack of policy to address displacement. It is, therefore, difficult to quantify the exact number of residents displaced from the Drill Hall, Turbine Hall, or the Bus Factory refurbished for the purpose of creating an art gallery, Anglo-Gold Ashanti's new headquarters, and a tourist attraction respectively. Ironically, the City of Johannesburg refers to these resident displaced rehabilitation initiatives as its 'iconic public place projects' (CoJ, ICR Charter, 2007: 19). Furthermore, as already stated, residents are also being displaced from inner city buildings earmarked for the Better Buildings Programme (BBP).

> The nuts and bolts of the BBP is that we identify bad buildings [that] are physically in a shocking state. Those buildings are also in arrears [and] the value of the arrears is much more than the value of the building. This has led to classic market failure. The City then writes-off the debt. [However,] new developers want empty occupation because they can't fix a bad building unless we get rid of the people. For [the City] the big issue is to decant existing tenants to other buildings, because judges often only grant eviction notices [based on] alternative [tenant accommodation].
> And that's a tough one because the City doesn't always have alternatives. I'm a great believer in market forces, and the market is profit-driven. I say to those developers wanting to make a profit: come in, we want you on board; we're trying to create a world class city. So, we need to attract the right people to live here.
>
> (Interview, BBP manager, 2004)

'Bad buildings' are abandoned by their owners, but they are occupied, informally, by residents who are unable to find affordable accommodation through the private housing market. While living conditions in these buildings are abysmal, Wilson and du Plessis argue that 'bad buildings house the poorest and most vulnerable residents of the inner city' (2005: 3). At least 250 'bad buildings' have been identified by the City for its BBP, and 'getting rid' of current occupies means evicting them. 'In doing so, the City exercises its power in terms of the National Building Regulations Act, which empowers a local authority to order the evacuation of a property that poses a threat to the health and safety of those occupying it' (p. 4). However, these buildings are currently occupied by approximately 25,000 residents, and capital investments required to rehabilitate 'bad buildings' exclude many evictees from being able to afford rehabilitated building rentals. Since 2002, 125 inner city buildings have been expropriated, resulting in the eviction of many residents without the City providing suitable alternative accommodation for evictees. 'This is unjust, because it further victimizes poor residents; and it is impractical, because [residents], once evicted, invariably occupy other slum properties in the inner city' (p. 6). It could, therefore, be argued that as many as 25,000 tenants may be displaced from the inner city through the implementation of the BBP. Nonetheless, officials hold on to a belief that:

> For the inner city we want physical [planning] interventions that favour the private sector market. [As such,] we don't need social studies of the inner city. We already know what the community wants. And if we are writing-off $14 million worth of arrears through the BBP, this means $14 million worth of investment is going in.
> That's economic development!
> (Interview, CoJ senior official, 2004)

In accordance then with New Urban Policy and New Conventional Wisdom, economic development entails melding regeneration policies with capital. While the nullification of debts may, theoretically, be viewed as a public investment in the property market, and, as argued by Bénit-Gbaffou (2006), as a type of public subsidy for the private sector, this debt relief policy neither creates secure employment nor shared economic benefits for poor residents as envisaged in a Just City approach for regeneration. Furthermore, informed social studies that embrace principles of social/mutual learning, and that facilitate the development of residents' political capacities for involved and effective public decision-making, are seemingly rejected by municipal officials as they already 'know what residents want'. Spaces for meaningful engagement are thus curbed, thereby diminishing opportunities for participatory governance. Rather, as argued by Smith (2002), Johannesburg's regeneration policies are designed to fit into the grooves of the established market. Of equal concern, the transfer of derelict buildings to private sector developers, without stipulated development controls or an effective land and housing strategy, is simply fuelling the speculative market which may have dire economic, and other, consequences if the 'creative' and middle classes decide not to relocate to and invest in the inner city. Regeneration policies fail to consider these potentially devastating consequences. Instead, local politicians celebrate the fact that 'we are using international models to [facilitate] regeneration: [for now, thanks to a positive property market] occupancy rates are up and investments are increasing' (Councillor Cowan, 2005: 22). The 2030 Vision and the subsequent 2003 Inner City Regeneration Strategy undoubtedly demonstrate a preference for capital accumulation with negligible attention paid to the formulation of social policies.

Legal actions against the City of Johannesburg's eviction policies by a public interest law group, and subsequent court rulings, forced the City to implement more socially responsive policies. A Growth and Development Strategy (GDS), inclusive of a Human Development Strategy (HDS), and a 'new' Regeneration Charter were, therefore, promulgated in 2006 and 2007 respectively.

Both the GDS and the HDS policy documents now make a 'commitment to Johannesburg's poor [by] prioritizing [resident] access to the City's social package' (CoJ, HDS, 2006b: 2, 4). This social package entails a monthly quota of free basic services for some inner city households. Nonetheless, socially responsive policies exclude residents' voices, and, as a consequence, these policies seem simply to be tacked onto the already established economic growth agenda: 'the broad economic growth logic of the 2030 Vision remains intact for the GDS, [so that] Johannesburg may position itself as a world class African city vis-à-vis other cities, nationally and internationally' (CoJ, GDS, 2006a: 2). Socially responsive policies are also perceived as a means of establishing some form of social cohesion in a chaotic and transitional inner city context; and social cohesion as a New Urban Policy is favoured because past governance structures, with clear divisions between public/private and economic/social roles, seem no longer able to secure the necessary conditions for competitive success (Gordon and Buck, 2005).

> Cities in pursuit of world class status need to strike a fine balance between economic growth and social responsibilities. To this end, social cohesion [becomes] an important resource in areas with high levels of mobility [like the inner city]. Creating the means for building social cohesion is crucial to the City's goal of being a world class African city.
> (CoJ, HDS, 2006b: 10; 101; 106)

In May 2007 the City Council launched its most recent regeneration framework, namely the Inner City Regeneration Charter. Through this latest framework, the City hopes to incorporate social policies derived from the Growth and Development and the Human Development Strategies. However, and notwithstanding the inclusion of social policies in the 2007 Charter, the very same regeneration challenges as those identified in the 2030 Vision and in the 2003 Regeneration Strategy continue to emerge, resulting in interventions that hardly differ from those previously formulated. In fact, the Charter is specifically geared towards 'scaling up regeneration operations to ensure rapid results, [as former] City efforts have sometimes been seen as [too] localized, fragmented, and episodic' (CoJ, ICR Charter, 2007: 4). Still, the Charter does go on to stipulate that earlier initiatives 'have been critiqued [for] not [being] sensitive enough to the circumstances of poorer residents and informal businesses' (p. 4). How economically stressed households are accommodated through this new regeneration policy, and how a more sensitive regeneration approach may be facilitated by the state become particularly relevant when we consider the dire circumstances of many inner city residents: 39 percent are formally unemployed (Leggett, 2003); 62 percent earn less than $500 per month (Bénit-Gbaffou, 2006; Winkler, 2006); and at least 10 percent (approximately 11,200 residents) rely exclusively on the informal sector to survive (Leggett, 2003).

ASSESSING THE IMPACT OF THE REGENERATION CHARTER

Social policies identified in the 2007 Charter include the municipality's social package, a suggestion to promote poverty alleviation and community development initiatives, and the implementation of transitional and inclusionary housing projects. An assessment of each of these social policies will, shortly, demonstrate the local government's attempt to address the social responsibility deficiencies of the 2030 Vision and the 2003 Strategy. However, findings will show that these attempts continue to fail existing residents because New Urban Policy and New Conventional Wisdom remain unaltered and are favoured in preference to a Just City.

Accessing the City's social package requires households 'to register themselves with the Council as indigent' (CoJ, ICR Charter, 2007: 55). While this language is in itself problematic, as many residents resent being labelled indigent (participant interviews, 2008), once registered, inner city households are then entitled to receive a quota of free water and electricity. The City's social responsibility here, however, has less to do with supporting economically stressed households and more to do with ensuring that 'if residents are able to access the social package this would significantly add to their ability to pay market rentals' (CoJ, ICR Charter, 2007: 55). Substituting municipal service payments for market rentals is perceived by the City Council as a rent subsidy. But this subsidy is devoid of regulations to curb escalating rentals. Moreover, many inner city households do not hold the rates and utilities accounts for their properties as these are held by landlords. The City Council then places the responsibility on landlords to register individual households as 'indigent', but this rarely happens as absentee landlordism is a common phenomenon in the inner city.

The Charter furthermore abstains from identifying specific poverty alleviation and community development programmes with dedicated budgets. Rather, intensive urban management policies continue to be enforced with the aim of eradicating unmanaged informal trading activities, regardless of the fact that at least 11,200 residents rely exclusively on the informal sector to survive.

> The current disorganized arrangement of many traders presents a key challenge to urban management. The City will [therefore] ensure that there is no more unmanaged trading on the streets of the

Inner City beyond June 2009. Disorganized trading refers to trading without necessary permits, in an area that is not designated as a formalized trading space. A limit will be set on the number of micro-retailers that may trade in the Inner City from approved spaces. This limit will be strictly enforced [and] traders are expected to pay for the right to trade in the Inner City.

(CoJ, ICR Charter, 2007: 28)

Limiting micro-retailing will severely hamper employed livelihood strategies, and informal trading activities typically generate negligible profits rendering the City's expectation to pay for 'the right to trade' in the inner city impossible for most. Traders at designated trading spaces are also bitterly unhappy with municipal permit charges resulting in higher priced goods and fewer shoppers (participant interview, 2002). The municipality's formalization policy remains unrealistic in a context where the formal economy is actually informalizing, and where the informal economy absorbs those who have lost their jobs in the formal sector (Odendaal, 2005). Such findings spotlight the claim made by Fainstein (2004) that social and economic exclusion are intertwined. To make matters worse, the municipality has also officially abdicated its social and welfare service responsibilities, as stipulated in the Regional Spatial Development Framework (CoJ, RSDF, 2003b), thereby giving the local government increased leeway to abandon poor households despite the Charter's 'poverty alleviation' and 'community development' promise. Rather, and in line with New Urban Policy and New Conventional Wisdom, civil society organizations are named in the Charter 'to absorb the poor through their social and welfare programmes' (2007: 36).

The Charter does, however, make provision for '*decant* facilities to enable the relocation of residents from buildings allocated to the BBP' (2007: 52). Nonetheless, only 10 of the 250 buildings identified for the BBP will be redeveloped as 'transitional housing projects in which tenants may reside for a maximum of two years' (CoJ, ICR Charter, 2007: 53). Temporary accommodation curbs security of tenure, and the Charter remains mute on what will happen to tenants after the stipulated two-year period.

At this juncture it is worthwhile turning to Marcuse's (1985) 'exclusionary displacement' argument under gentrification. Exclusionary displacement refers to households that are unable to access affordable housing because neighbourhoods are undergoing gentrification. At a public meeting held in April 2003, the executive mayor of Johannesburg stated that citizens earning less than $500 per month will not be able to afford to live in the inner city (Inner City Community Forum, 2003). As a consequence, the City Council will provide affordable housing for lower income earners on the urban edge. At least 62 percent of the inner city's current residents will, therefore, need to move as a result of exclusionary displacement. This policy of displacement to the urban fringe is corroborated by an inner city ward councillor who is of the opinion that 'location does not matter for the unemployed, so they can be [displaced to] Orange Farm [on the urban fringe]' (participant interview, cited in Bénit-Gbaffou, 2006). Certain strategic city areas are thus gradually taken over and transformed through exclusionary displacement by moving their populaces to other spaces (Díaz Orueta, 2007). Such findings support Marcuse's concerns:

> Displacement from home and neighbourhood can be a shattering experience. At worst it leads to homelessness, at best it impairs a sense of community. Public policy should, by general agreement, minimize displacement. Yet a variety of public policies seem to foster it.
>
> (Marcuse, 1985: 931)

Empirical evidence from a study conducted by the Centre on Housing Rights and Evictions (COHRE) demonstrates that the greater majority of residents interviewed would rather tolerate terrible living conditions than move to the urban edge, as the inner city is perceived to be an easier place to survive without formal employment (COHRE, 2004). This is not to imply that existing and hazardous living conditions do not need to be addressed by the City Council, but rather to highlight residents' identified desire to be centrally located. Regardless of COHRE's research findings, the Charter goes on to state that:

> The City does not wish to move forward on the assumption that the private sector will cater for the middle to upper income market, whereas the public and social sectors will pick up all the responsibilities for housing poorer residents, however logical this may appear at first glance.
>
> (CoJ, ICR Charter, 2007: 53)

This 'logic' revolves around protecting the City Council from 'ending up as a long-term owner and/or manager of social housing when realistic cost recovery cannot be achieved' (p. 53). Policies aimed at cost recovery simply 'ignite market-led growth while glossing over the socially regressive outcomes that are frequent by-products of such initiatives' (Brenner and Theodore, 2005: 103). The City of Johannesburg is thus squandering both an opportunity and its power to ensure the implementation of social policies that are more sensitive to the circumstances of poorer residents because 'private sector providers of medium to high income housing fear that buildings housing the poor in the immediate vicinity of their developments will depress property values and prevent them from securing the right kind of tenants' (CoJ, ICR Charter, 2007: 53).

In the current era of New Urban Policy and New Conventional Wisdom, securing the 'right kind of tenants', together with a drive towards homeownership, privatization, and the break-up of concentrated poverty, further incurs implementing 'social mix' strategies to facilitate the desired 'social cohesion' language found in the Human Development Strategy (CoJ, HDS, 2006b). Based on research findings from an in-depth study of Vancouver's Downtown Eastside, Blomley comments on how 'morally persuasive' social mix policies can be in the face of long-term disinvestment.

> Programs of renewal often seek to encourage home ownership, given its supposed effects on economic self-reliance, entrepreneurship, and community pride.
> Gentrification, on this account, is to be encouraged, because it will mean the replacement of a marginal anti-community (non-property owning and transitory) by an active and responsible population of homeowners.
> (Blomley, 2004: 89)

This 'morally persuasive' argument is also evident in the Johannesburg case:

> Johannesburg will never see the problem of bad buildings addressed unless there is a huge investment in accommodation that provides a judicious mix of options for medium- to high-income earners as well as residents who are at the point in their lives where they cannot afford very much. 75,000 new residential units will be developed by 2015. 20,000 of these units must be affordable if the collective problem of a stressed Inner City residential environment is to be solved. This does not mean that the Inner City is to become a dormitory for the poor. The City envisages the creation of the largest mixed income community in the country, built on the basis of inclusionary housing, and the continued delivery of both medium and high-income ownership options in non-inclusionary buildings.
> (CoJ, ICR Charter, 2007: 50)

Working on the assumption that a socially mixed community will be a socially balanced one, characterized by positive interaction between the classes, less than a third of the City's envisaged units will be earmarked for affordable rental accommodation so that medium and high income homeownership may prevent downtown Johannesburg from becoming a 'dormitory for the poor'. In other words, 'we don't want a whole bunch of indigent people living in the inner city; we want a nice healthy mix' (participant interview, BBP manager, 2004). However, social mix policies invariably involve the movement of the middle class into working-class areas. Advocates of social mix policies seldom, if ever, advocate that middle and upper-middle-class neighbourhoods be balanced by poor or working-class households. Rather, the appeal to bring people back into the inner city is a self-interested appeal that middle and upper-middle classes retake control of the political and cultural economies of inner city neighbourhoods (Smith, 2002). 'Probing the symptomatic silences of who is to be invited back into the city then begins to reveal the class politics involved in urban regeneration' (p. 445). Moreover, such policy optimism rarely translates into an urban context that is spatially, socially, economically and politically just, as envisaged for a Just City. Instead, it leads to Nimbyism, rent increases, exclusionary displacement, socioeconomic segregation, and political isolation (Beauregard, 2004; Blomley, 2004; Slater, 2006).

CONCLUDING REMARKS

To accommodate economic competitiveness, responsive governance, social cohesion, and social mix strategies, local governments across the globe are shifting their roles from acting as mere regulators of the urban context to becoming active agents of the free market (Brenner and Theodore, 2005;

Díaz Orueta, 2007; Gordon and Buck, 2005; Smith, 2002). Case study research methods and a critical discourse analysis of policy documents, media accounts, and interview transcripts demonstrate that this shift is equally evident in the Johannesburg case. Here, policy-makers and politicians are inspired by international, 'best practice' regeneration precedents where market-led redevelopments, tax incentives, public-private partnerships, flagship projects, intensive urban management, middle and high income homeownership, and the disintegration of concentrated poverty are deemed essential for the successful revitalization of urban centres. In Johannesburg, however, an explicit policy link between inner city regeneration and economic growth is, possibly, more blatantly executed than in contexts from where these policies are imported (see Porter and Shaw, 2009). The City of Johannesburg's blind faith in New Urban Policy and New Conventional Wisdom also prevents the local state from recognizing that there is no, empirically justified, link between economic growth and social equity. Instead, New Urban Policy and New Conventional Wisdom usher in emblematic redevelopment undertakings while bypassing unemployment and everyday hardships regardless of the social package, poverty alleviation, community development, transitional accommodation, and inclusionary housing rhetoric found in the 2007 Charter. As such, and in preference to resident inclusive regeneration approaches and redistributive planning actions, local policymakers and politicians remain steadfast in their belief that:

> Regeneration achievements have been realized because private sector players took the lead and established the conditions for further private investment. [This] demonstrates physically what can be done when non-government stakeholders are energized and are enabled to enter into collaboration with government. This has begun to have a dramatic effect, as property owners redevelop their properties and new investors start new developments. The upswing in building refurbishments for middle and upper income accommodation reflects this.
>
> (CoJ, ICR Charter, 2007: 4)

Collaborating with the private sector alone negates possibilities for social/mutual learning between state officials and residents, it forecloses residents' active political engagement in public decision-making, and it diminishes an opportunity to embrace participatory governance. Both the process of generating urban policies and the substantive outcomes of these policies, therefore, fail to meet the needs of Johannesburg's poor inner city residents and the criteria for

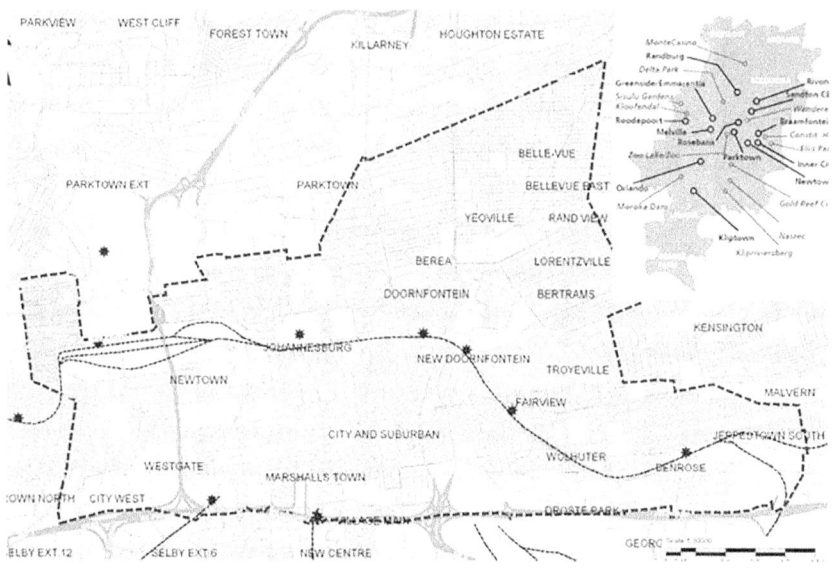

Figure 1 The inner city region of Johannesburg

Source: CoJ, 2008: Map 1. The insert illustrates the City of Johannesburg's entire jurisdiction

Figure 2 A view of downtown Johannesburg
(Photo: author)

Figure 3 Informal trading in the inner city
(Photo: author)

a Just City. Conversely, an inclusive, redistributive, and equitable approach to urban regeneration may generate practical solutions to resident identified problems, for example: residents want to be centrally located; they resent being labelled indigent; the formalization of informal trading activities is crippling employed livelihood strategies; and temporary accommodation curbs security of tenure. Instead, the City Council's overt attempt to repopulate inner city neighbourhoods with the 'right kind' of households will have a devastating impact on existing, but financially strapped, residents. Research findings also demonstrate how a 'cultural capital' and a 'world class African city' vision fails to meet socially progressive objectives, as social policies identified in the 2007 Charter are, essentially, ineffectual, and undermined by the local state. In short, the City of Johannesburg's current regeneration practices and policies stand to benefit only the new urban elite, while prolonging the global age of gentrification.

ACKNOWLEDGEMENTS

This study was financially supported by the National Research Foundation. I am also grateful to Libby Porter and Kate Shaw for their comments on an earlier version of this article, and for facilitating and editing a book that features some of the arguments presented here. Finally, I want to thank all three anonymous referees and Claire Bénit-Gbaffou for their insightful and invaluable suggestions.

NOTE

† Some sections are reused from Winkler, T. (2009) 'Believing in Market Forces in Johannesburg', in L. Porter and K. Shaw (eds) *Whose Urban Renaissance? An International Comparison of Urban Regeneration Strategies*, pp. 25–33.

© 2009 Taylor & Francis Books (UK). By kind permission of the publisher.

REFERENCES

Amin, A. and Thrift, N. (1994) *Globalization, Institutions and Regional Development in Europe*. Oxford: Oxford University Press.

Beauregard, R. (2004) 'Are Cities Resurgent?', *City* 8(3): 421–427.

Bénit-Gbaffou, C. (2006) 'In the Shadow of the 2010 Greater Ellis Park Development: Decision-making and the Poor in Inner City Johannesburg', Paper Presented at the Life of the City Conference, University of the Witwatersrand, Johannesburg, 4–6 September.

Blomley, N. (2004) *Unsettling the City: Urban Land and the Politics of Property*. New York: Routledge.

Bourdieu, P. and Wacquant, L. (2001) 'Neoliberal Newspeak: Notes on the New Planetary Vulgate', *Radical Philosophy* 105: 2–5.

Boyle, M. and Rogerson, R.J. (2001) 'Power Discourses and City Trajectories', in R. Paddison (ed.) *Handbook of Urban Studies*, pp. 402–416. London: SAGE.

Brenner, N. and Theodore, N. (2005) 'Neoliberalism and the Urban Condition', *City* 9(1): 101–107.

Campbell, H. and Marshall, R. (2000) 'Public Involvement and Planning: Looking Beyond the One to the Many', *International Planning Studies* 5(3): 321–344.

Catterall, B. (2004) 'Achieving Resurgent Cities: Community Within/Against/Beyond Empire', *Conference Paper Presented at the Resurgent City Symposium, Leverhulme International Symposium*, 19–21 April, London School of Economics.

Centre on Housing Rights and Evictions (COHRE) (2004) 'Any Room for the Poor?', Unpublished Draft Report, Centre on Housing Rights and Evictions, Johannesburg.

City of Johannesburg (CoJ) (2002) *Jo'burg 2030 Vision*. Johannesburg: City of Johannesburg Publication.

City of Johannesburg (CoJ) (2003a) *Inner City Regeneration Strategy (ICRS)*. Johannesburg: City of Johannesburg Publication.

City of Johannesburg (CoJ) (2003b) *Regional Spatial Development Framework (RSDF)*. Johannesburg: City of Johannesburg Publication.

City of Johannesburg (CoJ) (2006a) *Growth and Development Strategy (GDS)*. Johannesburg: City of Johannesburg Publication.

City of Johannesburg (CoJ) (2006b) *Human Development Strategy (HDS)*. Johannesburg: City of Johannesburg Publication.

City of Johannesburg (CoJ) (2007) *Inner City Regeneration Charter*. Johannesburg: City of Johannesburg Publication.

Councillor Cowan (2005) 'Slumbering Giant Wakes and Flexes its Muscles: The CBD is Poised for a Revival as Years of Planning and Action Start to Bear Fruit', *The Sunday Times*, 6 November, p. 22.

Davie, L. (2006) 'Five Years with Mayor Masondo', *The City of Johannesburg*, Official Website, available online at: [www.joburg.org.za/2006/june/jun30_amosmasondo.stm], accessed 30 June 2006.

De Magalhães, S.C. (2004) 'Centres of Excellence for Urban Regeneration: Promoting Institutional Capacity and Innovation or Reaffirming Old Ideas?', *Planning Theory and Practice* 15(1): 33–47.

Díaz Orueta, F. (2007) 'Madrid: Urban Regeneration Projects and Social Mobilization', *Cities* 24(3): 183–193.

Fainstein, S. (2004) 'Cities and Diversity: Should We Want It? Can We Plan for It?', *Paper Presented at the Leverhulme International Symposium, Resurgent City, London School of Economic*, 19–21 April, London.

Fainstein, S. (2005) 'Planning Theory and the City', *Journal of Planning Education and Research* 25: 121–130.

Fainstein, S. and Fainstein, N. (1974) *Urban Political Movements*. Englewood Cliffs, NJ: Prentice Hall.

Financial Mail (2003) 'A Day in the Life of Oswald Reddy: The Johannesburg Area Police Commissioner', Editorial, 10 October, p. 13.

Financial Mail (2005) 'Life in the City', Editorial, 22 July, p. 6.

Florida, R. (2005) *Cities and the Creative Class*. London: Routledge.

Friedmann, J. (1987) *Planning in the Public Domain: From Knowledge to Action*. Princeton, NJ: Princeton University Press.

Gevisser, M. (2004) 'From the Ruins: The Constitution Hill Project', *Public Culture* 16(3): 507–519.

Glass, R. (1964) *Aspects of Change*. London: Macgibbon and Kee.

Gordon, I. and Buck, N. (2005) 'Cities in the New Conventional Wisdom', in I. Gordon, N. Buck, A. Harding and I. Turok (eds) *Changing Cities: Rethinking Urban Competitiveness, Cohesion and Governance*, pp. 1–21. Basingstoke: Palgrave Macmillan Press.

Hackworth, J. (2002) 'Post-recession Gentrification in New York City', *Urban Affairs Review* 37: 815–843.

Hall, P. (2005) 'The Sustainable City: A Mythical Beast?' *Paper Presented for the L'Enfant Lecture on City Planning and Design, American Planning Association (APA)*, 15 December, National Building Museum, Washington, DC.

Harrison, P. (2006) 'On the Edge of Reason: Planning and Urban Futures in Africa', *Urban Studies* 43(2): 319–335.

Inner-City Community Forum (2003) 'Johannesburg's Better Buildings Programme: A Response', *Interfund Development Update*. Available online at: [www.interfund.org.za/pdf-files/vol5_one/InnerCity.pdf], accessed 3 November 2004.

Jacobs, J. (1961) *The Death and Life of Great American Cities*. London: Penguin Books.

Leggett, T. (2003) 'Rainbow Tenement: Crime and Policing in Inner Johannesburg', *Monograph* 78: 8–33.

Ley, D. (2003) 'Artists, Aestheticization and the Field of Gentrification', *Urban Studies* 40(12): 2527–2544.

London School of Economic (LSE) (2004) 'Symposium Programme', *The Leverhulme International Symposium, Resurgent City*, LSE, 19–21 April, London.

Madanipour, A. (2003) *Public and Private Spaces of the City*. New York: Routledge.

Marcuse, P. (1985) 'Gentrification, Abandonment, and Displacement: Connections, Causes, and Policy Responses in New York City', *Journal of Urban and Contemporary Law* 28: 195–240.

Marcuse, P. (2002) 'Depoliticizing Globalization: From Neo-Marxism to the Network Society of Manuel Castells', in J. Eade and C. Mele (eds) *Understanding the City: Contemporary and Future Perspectives*, pp. 131–158. Oxford: Blackwell.

Matshikiza, J. (2004) 'Instant City', *Public Culture* 16(3): 481–497.

Newman, K. and Wyly, E. (2006) 'The Right to Stay Put, Revisited: Gentrification and Resistance to Displacement in New York City', *Urban Studies* 43(1): 23–57.

Nussbaum, M. (2004) *Women and Human Development*. Cambridge: Cambridge University Press.

Odendaal, N. (2005) '[D]urban Space as the Site of Collective Action', *Paper Presented at the Planning and Natural Resource Management Conference*, eThekwini Municipality, Durban, 24–28 May.

Peterson, P. (1991) 'The Urban Underclass and the Poverty Paradox', in C. Jencks and P. Peterson (eds) *The Urban Underclass*, pp. 3–27. Washington, DC: Brookings Institute.

Porter, E. and Shaw, K. (2000) *Whose Urban Renaissance? An International Comparison of Policy Drivers and Responses to Urban Regeneration Strategies*. London: Routledge.

Roy, A. (2006) 'Praxis in the Time of Empire', *Planning Theory* 5(1): 7–29.

Silimela, Y. (2003) Publishing on the Internet, Johannesburg: Interfund Development Update. Online. 'Urban Renewal and City

Reconstruction: Government Position'. Available at: [www.interfund.org.za/vol5no12004.html], accessed 3 November 2004.

Slater, T. (2006) 'The Eviction of Critical Perspectives from Gentrification Research', *International Journal of Urban and Regional Research* 30(4): 737–757.

Smith, N. (1996) *New Urban Frontier: Gentrification and the Revanchist City*. London: Routledge.

Smith, N. (2002) 'New Globalism, New Urbanism: Gentrification as Global Urban Strategy', *Antipode* 34: 427–450.

The Star (2008) 'The Inner City of Johannesburg Attracts R5,7 Billion in Investment', 16 July, p. 6.

Storper, M. and Manville, M. (2006) 'Behaviour, Preferences and Cities: Urban Theory and Urban Resurgence', *Urban Studies* 43(8): 1247–1274.

Vidal, A. (1996) 'CDCs as Agents of Neighborhood Change: The State of the Art', in D. Keating, N. Krumholz and P. Star (eds) *Revitalizing Urban Neighbourhoods*, pp. 149–163. Kansas: University Press of Kansas.

Wilson, S. and du Plessis, J. (2005) 'Housing and Evictions in Johannesburg's Inner City', *Conference Paper Presented at the Cities and Slums Workshop: The World Housing Congress*, 25 September. Available online at: [www.law.wits.ac.za/cals/WHC%20Cities%20and%20Slums%20Statement%5B1%5D.pdf], accessed 13 February 2008.

Winkler, T. (2006) 'Kwere Kwere Journeys into Strangeness: Reimagining Inner City Regeneration in Hillbrow, Johannesburg', Unpublished PhD thesis, University of British Columbia, Vancouver, Canada.

Yiftachel, O. (2006) 'Re-engaging Planning Theory? Towards South-Eastern Perspectives', *Planning Theory* 5(3): 211–222.

BOX 5 TANJA WINKLER REFLECTION

The political landscape of the city of Johannesburg is much altered since 'Prolonging the global age of gentrification' was published in 2009. No less than six executive mayors have come and gone, leaving in their wake a fragmented policy terrain. The African National Congress's (ANC's) once clear-cut mandate to simultaneously promote economic competitiveness alongside human development was abruptly bridled after the local government elections of 2016 ushered in a coalition government led by the center-right Democratic Alliance (DA). This uncharted political terrain was fractious since the self-identified economic liberalist Herman Mashaba (DA), who was elected as Johannesburg's executive mayor, had to navigate policy directives and budgetary allocations with the left-wing populist party, the Economic Freedom Fighters (EFF). Unsurprisingly, in 2019, Mashaba resigned from his post. The DA was unable to retain confidence in its leadership, and Geoff Makhubo, the ANC candidate, received the councilors' majority vote to replace Mashaba in the intervening years between elections. However, and tragically, both Makhubo and his successor, Jolidee Matongo (ANC), died due to COVID-19-related complications, resulting in Mpho Moerane's (ANC) mayorship for two months prior to the local government elections held in November 2021. The outcome of this election is proving to be equally disorientating. No political party received residents' majority vote. As a result, Mpho Phalatse, the DA's mayoral candidate, is tasked to lead yet another coalition government. But in South Africa's young democracy, coalition governments are, predictably, too unstable to establish broadly favored policies and consensual municipal budgets, thereby impeding their abilities to adequately address the needs of the majority of residents who are still living in abject poverty with minimal opportunities to access the formal economy. Of equal concern, Phalatse is gearing up not only to address Johannesburg's failing and undermaintained urban infrastructure but also to 'establish a dedicated municipal court to prosecute by-law infringements' (Daily Maverick, 2021). Stringent and often violent by-law enforcements – as argued in 'Prolonging the global age of gentrification' – lay waste to collaborative engagements with informal street traders and poor inner-city residents.

The one constant during these politically turbulent years has been the municipality's reliance on the private real estate sector to stimulate an economic turnabout in the inner city. Nevertheless, during the more stable period under Parks Tau's (ANC) (2011–2016) mayorship, seemingly progressive policy directives were promulgated. The 2007 Inner-City Regeneration Charter was replaced, in 2013, by the Inner-City Transformation Road Map, which encompasses not only a need for economic competitiveness but also suggestions for greater citizen involvement in public discission-making processes and access to affordable inner-city housing. Similarly, the 2006 Growth and Development Strategy was replaced, in 2011, by the Joburg 2040 Growth and Development Strategy. This strategy advocates for informal traders while acknowledging that 'affordable rental supply in the inner city remains a challenge' (CoJ, 2040 GDS, 2011: 76). This document even goes as far as to state that 'private developer-led housing projects create islands of exclusion, [thereby] adding another layer to the already fractured and divided Apartheid City' (ibid.). Both policies remain in force.

Yet regardless of these hopeful sentiments, the investor-friendly policies promulgated under Mayor Amos Masondo's (ANC) (2000–2011) watch have remained unaltered, while 'islands of exclusion' have expanded despite political rhetoric and a slow-down in the real estate market. In fact, in October 2013, the municipality embarked on Operation Clean Sweep, which culminated in the eviction of 8,000 informal traders from their place of business for the purpose of 'cleaning up' and re-attracting private capital to the inner city (Bénit-Gbaffou, 2018); in March 2015, 463 residents living in Jeppestown – an inner-city neighborhood abutting the upmarket, developer-driven Maboneng precinct – were served eviction notices (SERI, 2015). Evictions in both cases were justified by the municipality in terms of its outmoded and draconian by-laws that not only contradict sentiments found in the Transformation Road Map (CoJ, 2013) and Joburg 2040, they also spotlight the 'toothless' rhetoric of presumably progressive policies (Bénit-Gbaffou, 2018: 2160). One might then conclude that established policies are mere 'public relations instruments' that are crafted to deflect criticism while knowing that by-laws can be relied on to spearhead insidious gentrification desires (ibid.). Many additional evictions have taken place in the inner city since 'Prolonging the global age of gentrification' was published. But these have failed to make headlines, because these didn't result in litigations (as was the case after Operation Clean Sweep) or mass resident protests (as was the case after the Jeppestown evictions). In the case of the latter example, hundreds of inner-city residents took to the street, chanting "The Constitution enshrines our right to affordable housing" and "We too want to eat sushi in Maboneng!" (Ah Goo, 2018: 108). Furthermore, many additional developers have benefited from the city's subsidization of private capital – via tax incentives and arrears cancelation – thereby allowing them to purchase entire city blocks, and neighboring blocks, for the purpose of creating 24/7 private security colonies for the well-heeled. Maboneng, Victoria Yards, Jewel City, Absa Towers, and much of Braamfontein, may be added to the other 'islands of exclusion' mentioned in the original article. Here, rents have increased more than tenfold since 2009 (Ah Goo, 2018), thereby forever excluding evicted residents who 'had to move' so that the municipality could increase its rates in these precincts. The role of social media has also failed, thus far, to empower grassroots struggles. Rather, platoons of middle-class 'influencers' partake in regular voyeuristic street-walks for the purpose of 'showcasing' – via Instagram and other platforms – the 'sea of inner-city decay' that lies beyond the safety of 'revitalized' zones. But these activities neither contribute to the local economy nor address residents' plight.

Despite an altered political landscape, arguments presented in 'Prolonging the global age of gentrification' are as relevant today as they were in 2009. Private-sector-driven regeneration continues to be favored by the state as a platform to establish wholesale gentrification masquerading as 'transformation'. State actors, not residents, continue to shape public policies, while dedicated budgets and the political will to fulfill responsive governance mandates, street trader support, and affordable rental promises remain elusive. As a result, informal traders and tenure-insecure residents have no other recourse other than to resort to litigation measures and public protests. Such recourses are predicted to intensify as the City Council continues down its fruitless and unjust path of prolonging the global age of gentrification.

By way of a final note, I have not lived in Johannesburg since the original article was published. Arguments presented in this reflection are gleaned from secondary sources. When I was asked by the editors to write this reflection, I hoped to uncover a few stories of hope and *real* transformation (based on known policy reforms). Instead, it is utterly disheartening to learn that inner-city residents and informal traders are worse off than was the case in 2009 (when the situation was already dire).

REFERENCES

Ah Goo, D. (2018). Gentrification in South Africa: The 'Forgotten Voices' of the Displaced in the Inner City of Johannesburg. In: Clark J., Wise N. (eds) *Urban Renewal, Community and Participation*. 89–110. The

Urban Book Series. Springer, Cham. https://doi.org/10.1007/978-3-319-72311-2_5

Bénit-Gbaffou, C. (2018). Beyond the Policy-Implementation Gap: How the City of Johannesburg Manufactured the Ungovernability of Street Trading. *The Journal of Development Studies.* 54(12): 2149–2167. http://doi.org/10.1080/00220388.2018.1460468

City of Johannesburg (CoJ). (2011). *Joburg 2040 Growth and Development Strategy* (2040 GDS). Johannesburg: City of Johannesburg Publication.

City of Johannesburg (CoJ). (2013). *Inner City Transformation Road Map.* Johannesburg: City of Johannesburg Publication.

Daily Maverick. (2021). Local Government: The Hot Seat. DM 168. Official website: daily-maverick.co.za [Accessed: 30 November 2021].

Socio-Economic Rights Institute (SERI). (2015). SERI's Executive Director Publishes Op-ed on Evictions. 15 July 2014. SERI Official website: seri-sa.org. [Accessed: 29 November 2021].

14
Desakota and beyond
Neoliberal production of suburban space in Manila's fringe[1]

Arnisson Andre C. Ortega[2]

Indeed, cityhood is the coming of age of Santa Rosa. Our city has ripened and the people are enjoying the fruits of this ripening.
– Santa Rosa Mayor's State of the City Address (Arcillas-Nazareno, 2008)

In her 2008 State of the City report, Mayor Arlene Arcillas-Nazareno of Santa Rosa, a city 38 kilometers southeast of the Philippine capital city of Manila, enumerated her city's achievements, largely focusing on economic stability provided by the continued influx of foreign investments. Almost five years after achieving official city status, Santa Rosa has been hailed as the "investment capital of Southern Luzon" and a paragon of modern development boasting a staggering annual internal revenue of 1.06 billion pesos (US$ 23.85 million)[3] in 2008 (Cinco, 2009). To ensure this sustained flow of revenue, the city has implemented "effective fiscal management" through multiple local policies, instituted a corporate subsidiary for land-banking, and forged public-private initiatives with the World Bank, private developers, banks, and non-governmental organizations (NGOs) for revenue-generating projects' (Santa Rosa Local Government, 2000). In concert with the Philippine government's continued promotion of global competitiveness, the gold standards of success for local government units (LGUs) like Santa Rosa are industrial development and public-private initiatives, achieving official status as a city, and attracting investors, all of which are legitimized by the prospect of bringing in much needed local revenue and income-generating job provision. I argue that these market-driven developmental narratives and structural adjustments of towns and cities are grounded on a neoliberal rationality strategically entrenched in place-specific conditions.

Situated in Manila's fringe[4] (see Figure 1), a region in the Philippines that has played a significant role in the country's political and economic formation, Santa Rosa's "ripened fruits" are evidenced by an interesting patchwork of industrial complexes, agricultural lands, and residential real estate developments. This land use pattern is arguably reminiscent of Terence McGee's quintessential Southeast Asian urban model *desakota*, characterized by "an intense mixture of agricultural and non-agricultural activities that often stretch along corridors between large city cores" and "dense populations engaged in agriculture" (McGee, 1991, p. 7). In Manila's fringe, vast tracts of agricultural lands have given way to both industrial estates (see Kelly, 1999, 2000; McAndrew, 1994) and gated master-planned residential developments mimicking Western-themed suburban landscapes in the North American context (as described by Jackson, 1985; Fishman, 1987; Kunstler, 1993; Duany et al., 2001; Lindstrom and Bartling, 2003). This paper focuses on the latter as they have become tangible representations of the current Philippine real estate boom. Usually articulated as indicators of "town progress" and enablers of the "Filipino dream" among the new middle class, the remarkable growth of gated residential community developments has indelibly reconfigured everyday life of residents in Manila's fringe.

Using *desakota* as a "hinge concept" and drawing on a rich body of work on critical urban studies, the production of urban space (e.g., Harvey, 1985; Lefebvre, 1991; Smith, 1996; Hackworth, 2007), and (post)colonial urbanism (e.g., Mitchell, 1988; King, 1990; Roy, 2002; Bishop et al., 2003; Legg, 2007), I map a more complex process of rural-urban change, moving beyond a mere consideration of *in situ* integration of agricultural communities into urban economies. In doing so, I identify actual sites of gated community developments, highlighting historical and spatial contingencies in gated community developments, from property transactions to public-private joint ventures to land struggles, and argue for a place-based articulation of neoliberal restructuring. While some urban studies (e.g., Dick and Rimmer, 1998) question the efficacy of *desakota* as an urban model, this paper contends that the discursive resistance that *desakota* presents is particularly useful in situating the unpredictability and instability of neoliberal visions of urban/suburban space. By using the case of the former Canlubang Sugar Estate, a 7,100-hectare property of a landed elite family, I explicate the historical relations of neoliberal restructuring and suburban developments in Manila's fringe and identify market-oriented state plans and policies that legitimated land conversions and the eventual construction of multiple suburban gated

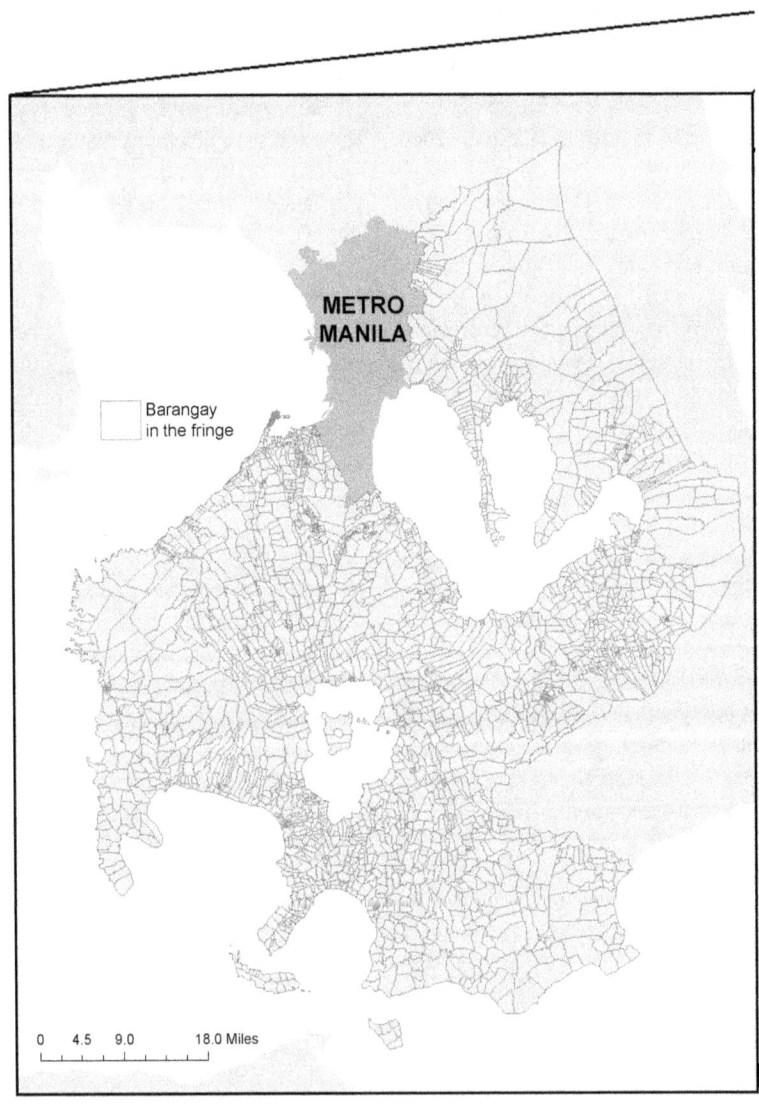

Figure 1 Map of Manila's fringe.

community projects along with other urban and industrial developments. At the same time, I underscore resistance to these developments and the ways these projects impinge on the long-standing land struggles of farmers. The narratives in the paper illustrate how the emergence of suburban gated community developments in Manila's fringe entails the turbulent processes of creative destruction in neoliberal restructuring. Underneath the many suburban developments' projected veneers of wealth, fulfillment of the "Filipino dream," and "sustainability" are the geographies of inequality and resistance based on land struggles of dispossessed farmers and the enduring political-economic dominance of the Philippines' elite.

THEORIZING THE *DESAKOTA* AND THE PRODUCTION OF SPACE

> Could more be done to go beyond the urban-rural dichotomy?
> – Anthony Champion (2004, p. 42)

Urban scholars have critiqued the use of an urban-rural dichotomy in particular contexts due to problems related to its disconnection from material realities on the ground and the varying urban-rural definitions in different countries (see Champion and Hugo, 2004). This is particularly evident in the study of urban processes in the Global South. In the Philippines, for example, James LeRoy observed how the traditional urban and rural dichotomy could not be applied to Philippine towns at the turn of the 19th century:

> There exists no such line of distinction between village and farm as may be found in countries which have reached some degree of industrial development . . . The Filipino town comprises of both town and country in the ordinary sense of these words.
> (LeRoy, 1905, p. 41).

Scholarly attempts to consider new urban forms are not new. One concept that has gained prominence over the years is Terence McGee's *desakota*. Specifically pertaining to Southeast Asian cities, *desakota*[5] refers to "an intense mixture of agricultural and non-agricultural activities that often stretch along corridors between large city cores" and "are characterized by dense populations engaged in agriculture" with increasingly mobile populations integrated into urban economies (McGee, 1991, p. 7). The *desakota*, along with nearby cities and their economic-transport linkages, makes up a functional region known as a mega-urban region (MUR), or extended metropolitan region (EMR) (McGee, 1991; McGee and Robinson, 1995). Throughout his corpora of work, McGee has explained that the mixed urban-rural spatial pattern of *desakota* is hinged on an agriculture and non-agriculture dialectic involving investments that seek to capitalize on cheap labor and land. These unique, or what Cairns (2002) would call "pagan," conditions defy simplistic urban definition and prevent its discursive subjection to a grand urban metanarrative, or in McGee's words, "western bias of urban theory" (McGee, 1995, p. 197).

For certain urban scholars, *desakota* was treated as an urban model from which various settlements and urban agglomerations in Asia were "fitted" or "tested" using spatial analytical techniques such as remote sensing (e.g., Sui and Zeng, 2001; Jones, 2002; Xie et al., 2006). Meanwhile, others have represented desakota's "paganism" as an unsustainable condition eliciting policy-oriented and technocratic projects that advocate for appropriate planning and management schemes (e.g., McGee and Robinson, 1995; Jones, 2002; Laquian, 2005). But such research efforts have fallen prey to a sense of state-rendered spatial fetishism that Agnew (1994) calls "territorial traps."

But *desakota*'s efficacy as a concept was challenged by studies that observed the emergence of "Western"-like built environments such as malls and gated communities across Asian mega-urban regions. The main point of contention involves *desakota*'s supposed transitional nature. Its context-specific conditions, often linked to colonialism, are said to eventually wither away and transform into an urban condition similar to "First World" cities such as Los Angeles (e.g., Webster, 1995; Dick and Rimmer, 1998). I contend that these critiques, while founded on actual observations of built environments, tend to be a-historical and a-spatial, as they render these spaces as naturally following an urban metanarrative, devoid of *in situ* actors, communities, and of agency to resist, while denying the dynamic confluences of political-economic and cultural processes in the production of space. Such assertions not only produce unwanted theoretical tensions between the socalled "local" and "global" scales, but also tend to gloss over historical and spatial contingencies of power, intentions, meanings, shifts, and relations involving urban developments in the Global South, from the roles of transnational transactions involving corporations and governments influencing developmental regimes to the adaptation of dominant urban planning and design ideas. From this theoretical disjuncture, I intervene by using *desakota* as a hinge concept, wherein I invoke its original anti-essentialist, "pagan," resistant, and open character to articulate a production of space that is grounded on empirical understandings of relations and processes. In the case of Manila's fringe, I acknowledge the presence of "suburban" spaces of gated communities that further complicate the production of space in *desakota*. But instead of arguing for a deterministic theoretical trajectory, I argue for framing spaces as relational and open, with planned trajectories hinged on particular development regimes, but with some emergent unintended spatial outcomes. I seek to de-naturalize the seemingly reflexive "suburban" trajectory of urban development in Manila's fringe by uncovering specific project objectives, situating them within urban plans that are guided by a certain political-economic agenda, accounting for historical transactions of properties, and underscoring the resistance of multiple actors.

To do this, I draw from the rich body of work on theorization of space and place. Central to this is Henri Lefebvre's notion of spatial dialectics, the production of space that frames space as both a "product and producer" shaped by class interests, rules of planning and policy experts, resistance groups, and multiple forces, and in turn presents constraints and influences that shape the everyday lives of those involved in its reproduction (Lefebvre, 1991). Related to this is David Harvey's classic effort to extend Marxian thought in understanding space by framing a spatially restless capitalism that, in its quest for maintaining accumulation, is constantly in search of "fixes," operating unpredictably in multiple directions and magnitude and producing volatile spatial forms and contingencies, facilitating capitalism's cyclical crises of boom/bust, accumulation/over-accumulation, and construction/destruction (Harvey, 1985).

But for this paper, I reference recent efforts that interrelate spatial dialectics with cultural, political, and economic processes. In particular, I consider Doreen Massey's (2005) framing of space as complex and open, produced by interrelationships that she terms "power geometries," useful for understanding "localized" processes that are embedded and mutually situated with global relations. Related to this is Gillian Hart's shrewd approach of "multiple trajectories of socio-spatial change" (Hart, 2002) that strategically links Gramscian and Lefebvrian logics in analyzing mutually constitutive notions of space produced by the interlinked cultural and political identities taking place in different contexts.

Such efforts are handy in my attempt to analyze the production of suburban spaces in Manila's fringe using socio-spatial ontology. To do so, instead of viewing urban space as an exogenous entity comprised of territorial units exhibiting socio-demographic and economic characteristics that need mitigating policy interventions, I frame my analysis of urban and suburban spaces as "temporarily fixed structured coherences" intertwining economic, political, and cultural processes and power relations and hierarchies (Lawson, 2010, p. 354). David Harvey elucidates how spaces "structure specific combinations of resources, investments, labor markets, infrastructure, state policies regulating and/or supporting labor, consumption, and cultural systems of reproduction of society" and "are restlessly (re)produced or devalued as other spatial configurations offer greater opportunities for profitability of production" (as cited in Lawson, 2010, p. 354).

I contend that the accelerated emergence of gated community developments, among other built environments in Manila's fringe, are indicative of a neoliberal restructuring in the Philippines. I situate these processes on actual sites in the Philippines but intertwined with global flows and transactions of ideas (e.g., masterplan designs, local governance), labor and target clients (e.g., Overseas Filipino Workers [see below]), and capital (e.g., property investment and transnational network of finance capital). Similar to the pitfalls of "fitting" urban models to places, attempts to understand the spatialities of neoliberalism have a tendency to diagnose places as characteristically "neoliberal" based on a pure end-state form of neoliberalism ideally reminiscent of conditions from the so-called "heartlands" of North America and Western Europe (see these critiques in the works of Brenner and Theodore, 2002; Peck and Tickell, 2002; Larner, 2003; Mitchell, 2004; Castree, 2006; and England and Ward, 2007). Simply put, neoliberalism is an ideology that champions market values and competitive individualism while rejecting forms of institutional or societal forms of solidarity such as state interference in market transactions. For Brown (2005, p. 41), neoliberalism "develops institutional practices and rewards for enacting" market-driven "vision" normatively imposed through discourses and programs in "all spheres." Despite diverse groups, institutions, and multiple interests, the market becomes the "organizing and regulative principle of the state and society," with a dominant market-oriented moral order. Described by Brown (2005, p. 41), "the economy must be directed, buttressed, and protected by law and policy as well as by the dissemination of social norms designed to facilitate competition, free trade, and rational economic action on the part of every member and institution of society."

In spatial terms, neoliberal fantasies envision a global space of unhindered flows, exchange values, and economic integration (e.g., Thomas Friedman's *The World Is Flat* [Friedman, 2005]). But as many geographers have reiterated, neoliberalism cannot be understood as an actualized project over a contained space, as its application on the ground is murky and often contradictory, producing slippages and disjuncture. Rather, scholars have pushed for a processual and path-dependent framing of neoliberalism that is uneven, contradictory, and ongoing (e.g., Brenner and Theodore, 2002; Peck and Tickell, 2002; Castree, 2006; England and Ward, 2007). Gillian Hart excellently describes this process from the vantage point of South Africa, wherein explicitly neoliberal projects "operate on terrains that always exceed them" (Hart, 2008, p. 678). As such, neoliberal projects as they are applied and implemented to actual places, like the Philippines, are contested, negotiated, and adapted, producing spaces of "actually existing neoliberalism" with oftentimes uncanny collusions with political, economic, and social formations. The imposition and acceptance of market rationalities necessarily involve place-specific conditions that legitimize a cross-sectional embrace of neoliberal policies by multiple groups.

Within these uneven and contradictory spaces of "actually existing neoliberalism," cities occupy a strategic role, not just as loci of neoliberal projects but as potent sites for the reproduction of neoliberalism (Brenner and Theodore, 2002). Multiple urban geographers have explored this idea, in particular the dialectical process of "creative destruction," focusing on policy shifts that enable the social, cultural, political, and economic entrenchment of neoliberal projects. This process involves the "destruction" of political and societal formations and institutions that promote egalitarianism, redistribution, or collectivism and the concomitant "creation" of new "shadow-state" organizations, public-private relations, and other institutions that promote market-oriented growth and development (for example, see Mitchell, 2001).

But contingent to these "creative" and "destructive" neoliberal forces transforming cities are multiple urban struggles that contest and resist restructuring, bringing along multiple socio-spatial alternative imageries that re-fashion and re-shape neoliberal trajectories (see Leitner et al., 2007). While multiple issues associated with neoliberalization of cities – from policy shifts to struggles for the right to the city – have been explored in cities in the Global North (e.g., Mitchell, 2001; Keil, 2002; McLeod, 2002; Purcell, 2002; Smith, 2002; Hackworth, 2007), there have also been a number of projects that have interrogated urban processes indicative of neoliberal restructuring in Global South cities. These projects include issues of urban governance (e.g., Xu and Yeh, 2005; Swanson, 2007), gated communities, militarization of the city (e.g., Jürgens and Gnad, 2002; Wu and Webber, 2004; Bolsdorf et al., 2007), and informality and slums (e.g., Shatkin, 2004; Roy, 2005). This paper, meanwhile, discusses the intertwined issues of land use change, property histories, and resistance in Manila's fringe, harkening to earlier works by Kelly (1999, 2000) and McAndrew (1994) on the Cavite Export Processing Zone. However, I focus on the neoliberal production of "suburban" spaces, that of gated community projects and exclusive residential developments physically analogous to suburban landscapes in the North American context (as described by Jackson, 1985; Fishman, 1987; Kunstler, 1993; Duany et al., 2001; Lindstrom and Bartling, 2003; Peck, 2011).

By linking theoretical discussions of *desakota*, production of space, and neoliberal urbanism, this paper intervenes by clarifying the process of *desakotasasi*, focusing on how gated suburban spaces have emerged and the ways these developments are embedded in the uneven and seemingly contradictory geographies of "actually existing" neoliberalism in the Philippines. Further, this paper contributes to an understanding of how neoliberal agendas are mutually constituted in relation to urban transformation and related sociopolitical and economic processes such as overseas Filipino migration, the real estate boom, and dispossession and displacement of farmers. I argue that while *desakota*-like conditions in Manila's fringe hint at trajectories toward suburban and industrial built forms, the processes involved are much more complex, involving transnational flows of capital, populations, and ideas. Linking these processes necessitates a (post) colonial perspective in which I review historical property transactions of the Canlubang Estate and the ways these transactions are embedded in development regimes, from the Spanish-era friar lands to Marcos-era efforts toward industrialization. Further, while these gated suburban spaces are explicit manifestations of market-driven urban development, utopic neoliberal visions of a "single urban discourse" (Dick and Rimmer, 1998) that assume a reflexive transition of *desakota* toward Los Angeles – like conditions suffer from a kind of spatial determinism. Such deterministic assertion loses traction when considering the uneven, mutually constitutive, and sometimes contradictory neoliberal process, as it engages with multiple subjects, institutions, and contestations on the ground. In the following sections I will present accounts illustrating the complexities in the uneven production of suburban space in Manila's fringe, from strategic acquiescence of policies, developments, and interests to staunch ideological resistance and "suburban" projects.

Invoking a reflexive "feminist ethnogeography," where ethnographic research negotiates the role of space, identities, and production of knowledge (see McDowell, 1992; England, 1994; Nagar, 1997), I am "outing" myself as someone who grew up and spent most of my life in Manila and its fringe. Perhaps with simultaneous feelings of embodiment and de-territorialization, similarly and paradoxically invoked by Ananya Roy (2002), I would like to disclaim a "native authenticity" but claim the privileges of navigating everyday life in the "field" for more than two decades and being considered by subjects of my research as a returning "native." This paper is based on almost one year of dissertation field work in the Philippines between 2009 and 2011.

THE BUSINESS OF BUILDING A NATION

With a sense of hope and pride, newly elected Philippine President Benigno Aquino III (2010) began his first term actively reviewing proposals that would lure more foreign investors into the country and that would strengthen public-private partnerships as a means for facilitating economic growth. In his PPP (Public-Private Partnership) framework, Aquino offered multiple incentives to the private sector, from tax cuts to expediting of paperwork, to entice them to engage in joint venture projects with the government. This strategy envisages that economic growth, "with the help of the private sector," will enable the Philippines to "supply for the needs of the global market" and will simultaneously benefit multiple sectors of the economy wherein "every Filipino will be the beneficiary." This narrative that legitimizes explicitly market-oriented and neoliberal policies is not new to the Philippines.

To understand the uneven geographies of neoliberalization in the Philippines, I argue for the need to understand the sociopolitical and economic context that provides the logics of persuasion and legitimization for neoliberal policies and projects. Over the years, neoliberal policies have been legitimized and framed around efforts to build a "globally competitive" nation by attracting foreign investments and by promoting entrepreneurialism, which will in turn provide much-needed jobs. Historically, neoliberal restructuring in the Philippines has been transacted through strategic engagements of the national government with the "unholy trinity" of the World Bank, International Monetary Fund (IMF) and World Trade Organization (WTO) (Peet, 2009). According to Bello (2004), market-oriented policies in the Philippines have gone through a succession of neoliberal regimes, from trade liberalization of the early 1980s to debt repayment from 1986 to 1992 (Bello, 2004). However, the 1986 EDSA Revolution was the critical moment in which social, administrative, and cultural processes shifted. After two decades of highly centralized and authoritarian governance under Ferdinand Marcos, a new government headed by Corazon Aquino faced a huge task of building a nation with a bankrupt economy. The moral order of the time attributed economic stagnation to the highly state-centric and corrupt crony capitalism of the Marcos era. Such a political-economic social setting was an ideal conjunctional moment from which neoliberal restructuring was rationalized and legitimized.

Inspired by "success stories" of the Newly Industrialized Countries of East Asia – the tiger economies – and the experiences of some countries in Latin America, the transnational cadre of the World Bank and its technocrats aggressively advocated a perilous mix of neoliberal free-market policies as effective ways to rebuild the national economy and successfully compete in the global market. These were primarily structural adjustments: privatization, deregulation, liberalization, and debt repayment (Bello, 2004). What has emerged is a national regime of truth that conflates democracy and freedom with free-market capitalism and global competitiveness. It has become the discursive base of an enduring development rhetoric that has promoted "private initiative" and "entrepreneurship" articulated through various policies and programs (Pinches, 1999). From this emergent national "common sense" are seemingly orthogonal and contradictory policies and programs that renovate and negotiate each other based on particular national visions (Gramsci, 2005). To illustrate this process in the Philippine context, I present key policies and programs that are relevant to the emergence of suburban spaces in Manila's fringe.

Salient among explicitly neoliberal projects is the Calabarzon Masterplan, launched in 1990 under President Corazon Aquino. Using a spatial regionalization scheme, Calabarzon aims to transform the "rural" economies of five Southern Tagalog provinces – Cavite, Laguna, Batangas, Rizal, and Quezon – into an industry-based urban area through a combination of multi-million dollar infrastructure projects that include super-highways, railway systems, ports, agro-industrial plantations, export-processing zones (EPZs), and industrial estates (Canlas, 1991). While the concept of regional master planning has been used in Philippine development since the Marcos era, Calabarzon is a distinctively neoliberal rearticulation of master planning, as it relegates state functions into mere facilitators for creating a business-oriented and investment-friendly region catering to the global market. The efforts of Calabarzon were further buttressed by the passage of the Special Economic Zone Act of 1995 (RA 7916), which aimed at facilitating the establishment of special economic zones (SEZs) that provide special privileges to prospective businesses and whose special rights are protected by a government agency, the Philippine Economic Zone Authority (PEZA). With the already existing Calabarzon Masterplan, the region became the location for numerous industrial sites that by 2010 ranked second (approximately 15%) only to the National Capital Region in terms of the number of SEZs in the country. Recent administrations have invoked the Calabarzon project to legitimize development projects in the region, (e.g., former President Gloria Arroyo's efforts to restructure national-regional space into super-regions).[6]

These market-driven programs serve as the logical base from which social justice – oriented programs are embedded through strategic slippages and loopholes. For instance, the implementation of the Comprehensive Agrarian Reform Program,[7] one of several incarnations of land reform in the Philippines that aims to redistribute agricultural lands to landless farmers, is filled with numerous documented cases of land conversion and other forms of redistributive evasion, such as cancellations of Certification of Landownership and land reversals, revocation of emancipation patents, and actual landlord resistance to redistribution (e.g., Antonio, 1994; Bello, 2004). Walden Bello (2004, p. 33) contends that the law behind the program was a "compromised result of congressional haggling between lawmaker-landowners and the advocates of reform" and was thus permeated with gaping loopholes and avenues for redistributive circumvention by landlords. Among several loop-holes that facilitate redistributive circumvention, one of the most controversial and perhaps the most relevant to suburban development in Manila's fringe, is land conversion. While the program stipulates a general prohibition against conversion of prime agricultural lands to urban-industrial use, the Department of Agrarian Reform (DAR) has set up policy conditions to allow applications for conversion, such as:

... requirements of people for housing to respond to the growing housing needs of the people; Industrialization – some agricultural lands need to be developed for non-agricultural purposes as not to hinder industrialization in urban and rural areas; Agricultural lands already devoted to non-agricultural uses prior to land reform; Land Resources Maximization – there are programs that need to be implemented in agricultural but marginal areas.

(Department of Agrarian Reform, 2007)

As local governments in Manila's fringe bear the burden of finding their own source of revenue, as stipulated by the Local Government Code of 1991, allowing the conversion of "idle" and "unproductive" agricultural and forest lands into more profitable land uses and developments has become a logical practice. This propinquity is further bolstered by pro-market programs, such as Calabarzon, put in place by the national government. Thus, planning officers in fringe communities tend to consider land conversion as an inevitable reality, as expressed by an official:

Those fields [*bukid*] are not anymore being used for planting. Converting them to housing developments will benefit the municipality. We have to go with the "flow of time" (*agos ng panahon*).

(Personal interview with a city planning officer, August 2009)

These pro-market plans are impelled through multiple modes of persuasion, from provincial meetings and training seminar to drafting of comprehensive land use plans (CLUPs). As one city planner related,

We have to make sure that the city plans follow the (*super*) regional plan set by the national government. We communicate with other city offices to make sure this happens.

(Personal interview with a city planning officer, August 2009)

But it is in the Comprehensive Land Use Plans (CLUPs) of local governments where the discursive space of neoliberalization and its persuasive mechanisms are mapped by a transnational cadre of public-private individuals, technocrats, bureaucrats, planners, and politicians. In Manila's fringe, CLUPs of local governments textually enshrine not just their explicitly market-based development but also their corporate metamorphosis. For instance, the World Bank and National Economic Development Authority along with a private consultancy planning firm collaborated with a select group of local government units in drafting their town CLUPs toward a market-delimited functional region dubbed as "Metro CALA" (Cavite and Laguna). Santa Rosa is one of the component towns which has a CLUP that is analogous to other Metro CALA town plans. According to Santa Rosa's CLUP, the local government ought to focus its efforts on "revenue-generating" projects, suggested to be funded by loans from government financial institutions, commercial banks, and international institutions such as the World Bank, Japan International Cooperating Agency, Office of Economic Cooperation and Development, and Asian Development Bank. Further, Santa Rosa is encouraged to organize a corporate subsidiary that would perform "land banking, land development and housing functions" and from which the local government could engage in public-private partnerships and joint venture agreements with land owners, private developers, and international NGOs, such as Habitat for Humanity and World Vision (Santa Rosa City Planning Office, 2000). Such pronouncements became the textual referent that facilitated conversion of both privately owned prime agricultural lands – such as the Santa Rosa section of the Canlubang Estate – and the use of state-owned lands in engaging with public-private joint venture projects. Over the years, these plans have yielded an ideal financial situation for Santa Rosa: a sustained flow of capital with total revenue reaching over a billion pesos and official status as a city, which renders increased autonomy to the local government.

BOOMING REAL ESTATE

Our real estate industry is proving strong and we thank the government, particularly Madam President, for keeping the fundamentals strong in the financial sector and generally keeping a business-friendly economy.

– Philippine Real Estate Festival (PREF) Chairperson Rosemarie Basa, *3rd Philippine Real Estate Festival in Manila*

For three consecutive years, the Philippine Real Estate Festival (PREF) has successfully brought together the "who's who" among the Philippines' political-economic elite and real estate agents working for big development corporations. Both industry insiders like PREF Chairperson Rosemarie Basa and government officials are jubilant and bullish about the Philippine property market as they mutually support each other to maintain the boom. The current real estate boom has become the serendipitous structural product of neoliberal reforms that continue to legitimize land-banking, land conversion, and construction of gated residential developments in Manila's fringe.

For landowners, in particular political-economic elites that navigate the spaces of government and business, explicitly neoliberal programs promoted by the state have enabled them to "liberate" their landed estates from the potential for redistribution through land reform and deliver these properties into the "profitable" hands of the market. Since the 1990s, vast tracts of land on Manila's fringe, from small parcels to large former agricultural estates, have been converted and transacted with banks and real estate developers. As many properties become part of extensive land banks of real estate developers, with the entry of Filipino-Chinese taipans that tap East Asian capital investment linkages into the property market, combined with sustained demand from Overseas Filipinos and continued government support, a new cycle of the real estate boom emerged beginning around the early to mid-2000 (Lucas, 2007; Magno, 2008). Overseas demand has sustained the market while housing loans from the government-owned Pag-ibig fund posted an average growth of 47% from 2007 to 2009 (Pag-ibig, 2009). While housing markets have crumbled in various parts of the world, the current boom in the Philippines has become the much-needed moral boost to celebrate a "resilient" national economy and thus to continue neoliberal restructuring (PREF, 2010).

Signs of this boom can be seen on the ground, from the large highway billboards featuring the latest posh villages to mall lobbies packed with real estate sales stalls. Vast tracts of agricultural land in Manila's fringe have given way to pre-packaged gated community projects,[8] several of which are comprised of prefabricated houses, community clubhouses, basketball courts, swimming pools, and other amenities. Many development projects carry eclectic Anglo-American/European names such as Cambridge Village and Grand Riviera, and are marketed as spaces that reflect American suburban life, conjuring what Fishman (1987) describes as a culture of leisure and family life based on the principles of exclusion from the city and low-class workers and of inclusion of middle-class residents.

These recent gated housing projects have become "*balikbayan* attractions," as their development has been sustained by a steady overseas demand and remittance monies from Overseas Filipinos (see Francisco, 2008; Lucas, 2007; Dumlao, 2008). For instance, 40% of property buyers in the high-end Timberland Heights of San Mateo, Rizal were U.S. based professionals (Salazar, 2008). To maintain this overseas demand for properties in the Philippines, the government-owned Pag-ibig fund established an Overseas Filipino Workers Financing Program that makes it easier for Overseas Filipinos to make their mortgage payments from abroad (Pag-ibig, 2009). Meanwhile, private developers have followed the transnational geographies of the OFW market by effectively instituting overseas marketing operations with affiliated agents in Filipino communities abroad, and regularly holding overseas property caravans that showcase the latest property developments in the Philippines.

From the perspective of the government, maintaining the boom is important to keep the national economy "resilient." Cognizant of the "essential role of the private sector in housing," the state's role, since the administration of Corazon Aquino, has become a mere "enabler" or "facilitator" of private ventures by providing incentives for developers to engage in public-private housing projects with national agencies and local governments (Housing and Urban Coordinating Council, 2011). Meanwhile, two landmark real estate laws were passed in recent years to capitalize on the boom: the Real Estate Investment Trust (REIT) Bill and the Real Estate Service Act (RESA) Bill.

For local government units, the financial impacts of the boom are undeniably significant. When mapping the internal revenue generated by LGUs in Manila's fringe, an interesting geography of capital accumulation emerges (Figure 2): towns with barangays[9] having an above median number of non-socialized housing developments ($n > 2$) tend to exhibit annual internal revenues of

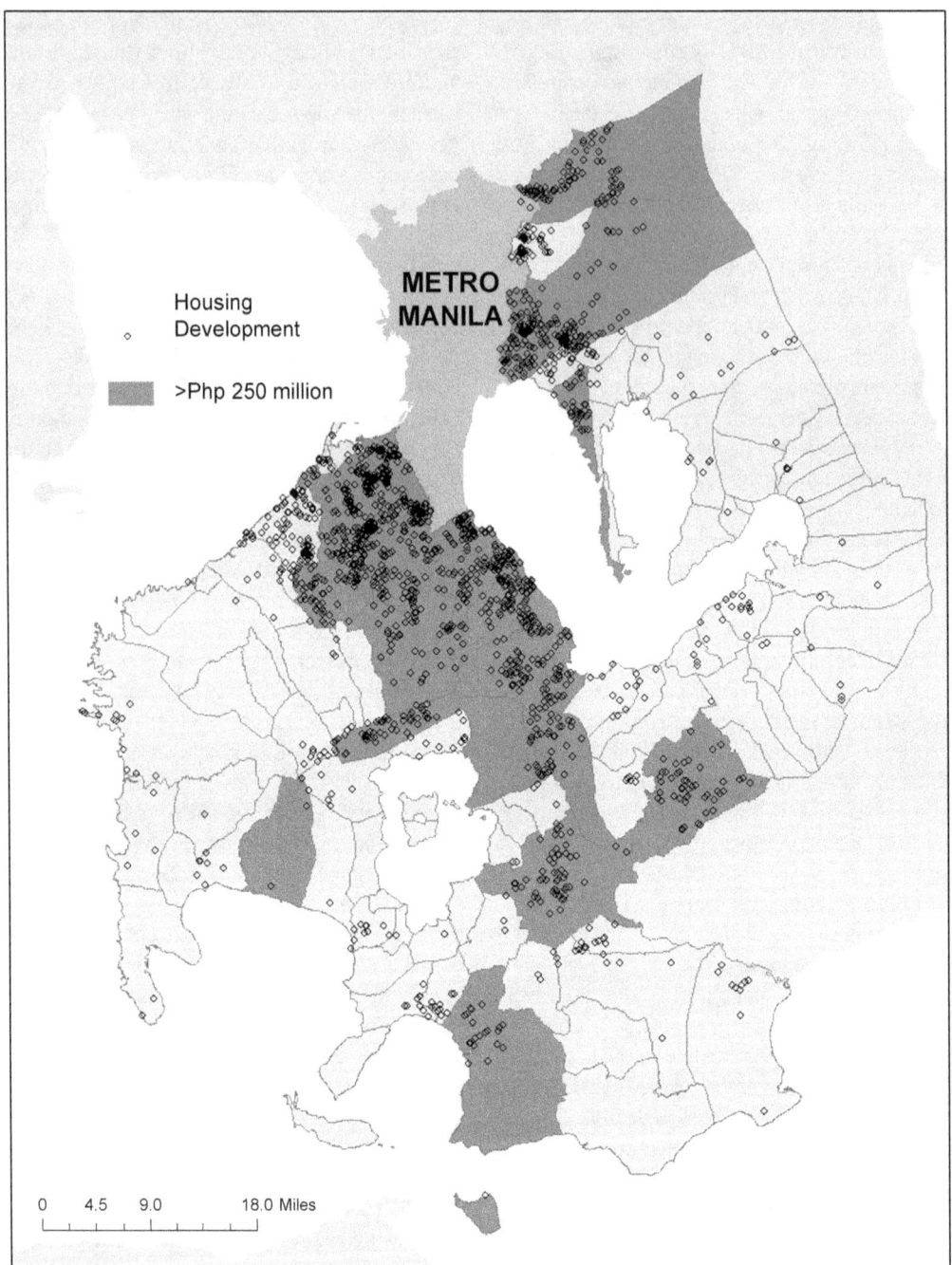

Figure 2 Map of housing developments and LGUs with annual internal revenue of more than 250 million pesos in Manila's fringe, 2008.

Source: Housing and Land Use Regulatory Board (2010) and Commission on Audit (2008).

more than a quarter of a billion pesos (US$5.63 million). Some of these towns include Santa Rosa, Calamba, Biñan, and Cabuyao in Laguna province; Tagaytay, Imus, Silang, Carmona, Trece Martires and Dasmariñas, in Cavite province; and Antipolo, Cainta, and Rodriguez in Rizal province. This spatial pattern illustrates the propensity of the local governments' core *habitus* toward land conversion and urban development.

PRODUCING GATED SUBURBIA IN CANLUBANG

A typical bus ride along the South Superhighway, the main thoroughfare that connects Metro Manila to the provinces of Laguna and Batangas, requires passing through the material evidence of the real estate boom in Manila's fringe: multiple gated master-planned community developments juxtaposed with industrial and commercial establishments amidst smaller parcels of cultivated land. Along the highway are large billboards advertising the latest high-end gated community projects in the region, using utopic visions of the "world-class city," "suburban living," and the "Filipino dream." But underlying these "new" spaces of wealth and modernity are political-economic transactions and relations that need to be exposed.

I focus on the case of the Canlubang Estate to show the "placed" acquiescence of processes and historical relations that have emerged in recent years surrounding property and development of gated communities. Canlubang is one of the largest landed estates in the country, occupying 7,100 hectares of property straddling four towns in Laguna Province, including Santa Rosa. Canlubang previously formed the controversial Calamba *Friar Estate*, considered as the "crux, if not the casus belli, of the Philippine Revolution of 1896" (United States Congress, 1911, p. 1132). Table 1 shows the historical property transfers of the estate. The estate was originally developed by Chinese residents prior to its confiscation by Spanish colonizers (Cushner, 1976). From then on, it has been transacted from Spanish religious orders to American capitalists and eventually to powerful Filipino landed elites. In particular, two prominent Filipino families were directly involved in the estate's transactions, the Madrigals and the Yulos. In 1948, the whole estate was "sold" to former Speaker of the House and Justice Secretary, Jose Yulo. Canlubang became Yulo's showcase, a sociospatial laboratory where he attempted to build a "model agro-industrial complex" that showed how "management and labor can work together and share in the profits of a free enterprise system" (Philippine Enterprise Magazine,

Year	Transaction
1678	Spanish Don Tomas de Andaya purchases the estate in a public auction
1759	Jesuit order Society of Jesus acquires property
1802	Spanish government confiscates the property from the Jesuits and sells to Don Jose Clemente Azanza in a public auction
1831	Dominican order Province of the Most Holy Rosary of the Philippines purchases the property
1896	Philippine Revolution
1905	American colonial government acquires friar land
1912	John Switzer of Pacific Commercial Company and Alfred Ehrman purchase the Calamba Friar estate and establish the Canlubang Sugar Estate
1940	Don Vicente Madrigal purchases Canlubang from the Switzer-Ehrman conglomerate
1941—1945	Japanese occupation of the Philippines
1948	Jose Yulo acquires the property from Madrigal

Table 1 Canlubang Estate Property Transfers
Sources: Cushner, 1976; Olivera, 1981; Larkin, 1993.

January – February, 1975, pp. 44–50) and which should be "copied throughout the land if agrarian unrest was to be solved" (Olivera, 1981, p. 206). To quell brewing resistance from farmers, Yulo used this "Canlubang formula" of abolishing land tenure and concomitantly converting farmers into plantation workers with standardized salaries. In the sugar central, his wife helped establish schools, a hospital, theaters and dance halls, and a parish church. In addition, the Yulo family provided free education to children of employees, free hospitalization and other medical services, free housing, electricity, and water, and sold cheap rations of prime commodities. Thus, plantation workers and their families considered Canlubang as the "*hawlang ginto*" (golden cage).

In the 1970s, President Ferdinand Marcos instituted the National Industrial Estates Program that necessitated the creation of a prohibitive development zone encompassing a 50-kilometer radius from Manila with the intention of deflecting investments and other industrial projects to other parts of the country (Caoili, 1988). As a result, industrial developments clustered just along the fringes of this radius. Canlubang, with its strategic location, significantly benefited from this program. After the death of Jose Yulo in 1976, the estate was subdivided among his "entrepreneurial" children who conscripted regional planners to concoct the Canlubang Urban Development Project that aimed at converting the estate into a mixed-use "new Philippine city" for the "New Filipino" (Olivera, 1981, p. 224).

With the political-economic ties of the Yulos, the Plan was easily appended into the CLUPs of affected local government units, formally legitimizing the theoretical land use conversion of the entire estate. Because the Plan rendered the whole estate as "non-agricultural" and the farmers tilling the land designated "plantation workers" and not tenant farmers, the estate was exempted from CARP. this exemption gave the Yulo family the lee-way to actualize the conversion of the estate and push forward with the Plan.

Over the years, the implementation of this "Urban Development Plan" was done in piecemeal fashion. Along with the subdivision and disbursement of the estate to Jose Yulo's children was the emergence of multiple development corporations that were assigned sections of Canlubang, embarking on distinct residential and industrial development projects. In succeeding years, many of these development projects involved joint venture agreements with more established real estate developers. Notable of these were the multiple agreements with Ayala Land Corporation, which yielded the Laguna Technopark and several exclusive gated communities in the northern section of Canlubang. After the effective closure of the Canlubang Sugar Estate in 1996, more joint venture agreements were forged with other real estate developers that include well-established companies such as Senator Manuel Villar's Vistaland Corporation (e.g., Santa Elena City, Valenza, La Vecina Dos Rios), Moldex Realty (e.g., Alegria Dos Rios), and new taipan property developers such as the Lucio Tan-owned Eton Properties (e.g., Eton City project).

But among all the recent development projects in Canlubang, the largest and perhaps the most controversial is Nuvali. A joint venture project between several Yulo companies and real estate giant Ayala Land Incorporated,[10] Nuvali spans 1,600 hectares of gently rolling hills formerly devoted to sugar plantations. The project was master-planned by the California-based consultancy firms Community Design, and Architecture and Calthorpe Associates, and adopted one of urban planning's recent innovations that offers an alternative design to "suburbia": new urbanism (Calthorpe Associates, 2010; CD+A, 2010). In 2007, Ayala Land Corporation started its marketing campaign for Nuvali by claiming it to be the "Philippines' first city of the future" and by using "green" and "sustainable" mantras such as "*evoliving* – the harmonious integration of nature" (AyalaLand, 2008). This ambitious mixed-use "new city" is comprised of a commercial center and business district (e.g., Evozone and Solenad), self-sustaining exclusive gated communities (e.g., Abrio, Avida Settings, Venare, Elano, Montecito) and schools (e.g., Xavier School), with environmentally sound and LEED-approved amenities, such as parks, open spaces, wake-boarding facilities, manmade lakes, and a bird sanctuary.

For the four local government units which Canlubang straddles, Nuvali, Eton City, and other residential and industrial developments are all hallmarks of city progress and symbolic capital of local economic growth. Its northern section, which is part of Santa Rosa, is used by the local government in its promotional and tourism campaigns as the material proof of its booming economy. For the national government, the

PEZA-accredited special economic zones in the northern section that house Business Processing Outsourcing offices and other businesses are important nodes that support a globally competitive national economy by attracting foreign capital and providing jobs. For the real estate industry, Nuvali is seen as the paragon of property developments as it shrewdly incorporates sustainability and environmental consciousness with "progress."

SPACES OF "DESTRUCTION" AND RESISTANCE

The "creative" processes that generate public-private agreements, market-oriented developments, and that shape industrial and suburban spaces in Canlubang also entail "destructive" processes that erode and/or prohibit old relations and practices in everyday life. The everyday geographies of the new residents of gated-community developments in Nuvali and other gated communities in Canlubang, grounded on posh mansions, shopping complexes, parks and office buildings, are in stark contrast to their upland neighbors in Buntog and other indigenous farming communities that have thus far remained in Canlubang. Since the closure of the sugar plantation, residents of these farming communities are contending with a different kind of gate, a sociospatial boundary that demarcates ideology and everyday lives.

During my visit to Buntog, the most populated *sitio* in the upland region of Canlubang, I met Jose, one of the activist farmers of the community. Jose offered to guide me on a tour of the steep upland region, identifying actual locations of intimidation and harassment by the military and security personnel. While discussing the history of the estate, he pointed toward areas where suburban developments are currently being built and the possible locations of new gated-community and condominium developments. His portrayal painted a grim spatial picture of Canlubang, wherein Buntog and other upland communities lay dangerously within the proposed new developments (see Figure 3, showing Jose pointing at the encroaching developments in Canlubang).

Figure 3 Jose pointing at Nuvali and nearby suburban gated developments in Canlubang.
Photo by author (2010).

The settlement history of Buntog residents in Canlubang describes a classic case of land-grabbing, seen in many (post)colonial states of the Global South (see Li, 2010). According to the Buntog farmers, their ancestors moved to the area at the turn of the 20th century, cleared the forest and cultivated a mixture of crops (see Kuyek and Skinner, 2003). By the time Jose Yulo acquired the estate, including Buntog, and re-established the sugar plantation, Buntog farmers were coerced into limiting cultivation of certain crops while planting coconut trees and Arabica

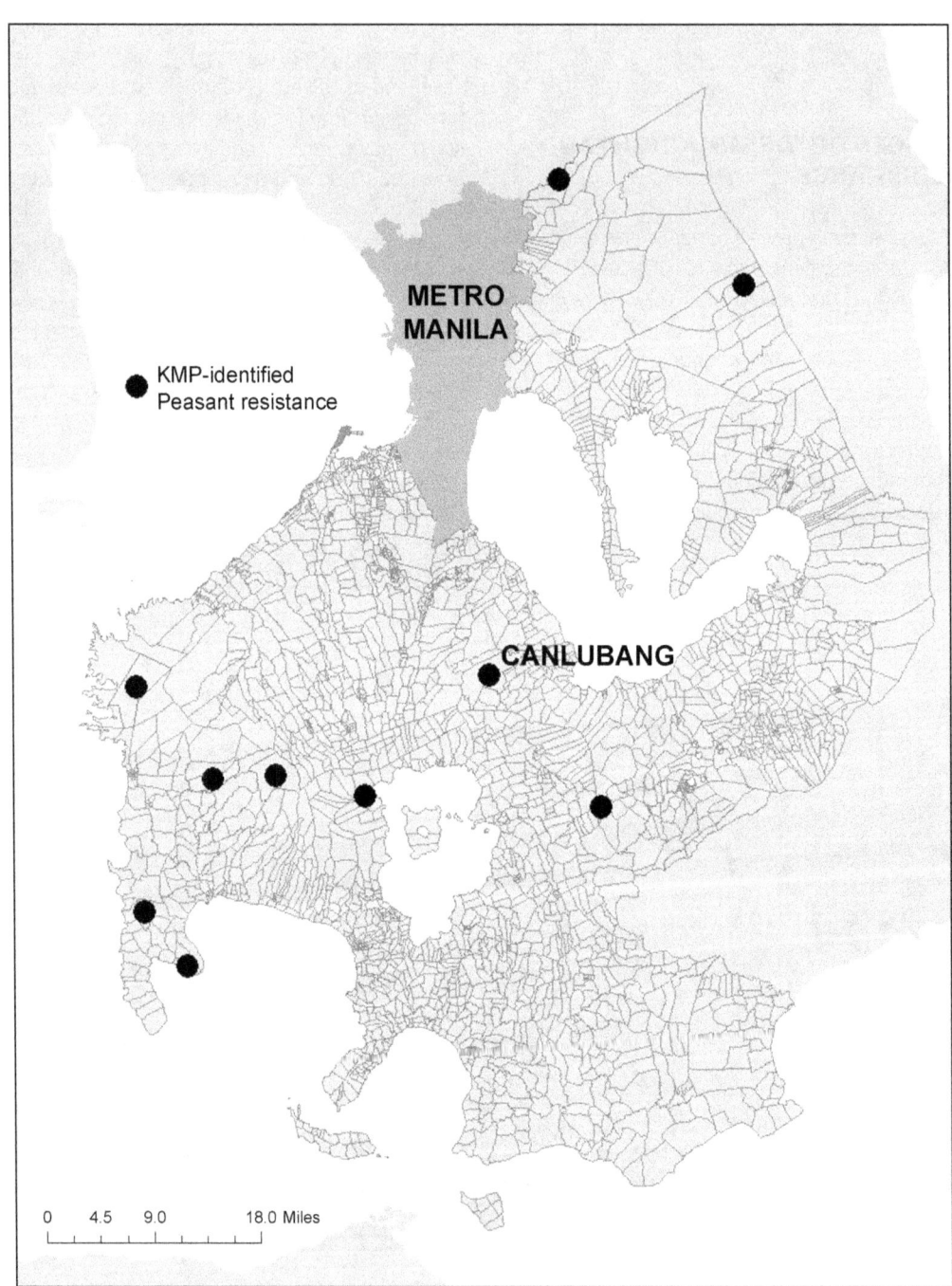

Figure 4 Map of KMP-identified peasant struggles in Manila's fringe.

Source: Kilusang Mambubukid ng Pilipinas (KMP).

coffee to supply the plantation (Olivera, 1981; Kuyek and Skinner, 2003). Over the years, Buntog farmers worked as paid laborers on the plantation, working multiple jobs in the lowland and/or cultivating particular crops. During the heyday of sugar production, Canlubang workers, including the Buntog farmers, were relatively well compensated, enjoying competitive wages and virtually free basic services and amenities. Thus, minority clamor for land redistribution was easily dissipated by the majority.

But by the 1970s, things started to turn sour for residents. As peripheral sections of the sugar estate were converted to golf courses, residents of communities were compelled to "self-demolish" and/or be evicted. But this practice of "self-demolition" eventually evolved into more forceful eviction as more parcels of land in Canlubang were developed into industrial and residential developments. Several years before the sugar mill's closure in 1996, the seemingly harmonious interrelationships among various Canlubang residents, former plantation employees, and the Yulo family had almost entirely faded following widespread unrest and acts of resistance. When the CARP was implemented, farmer groups initiated attempts to claim parcels of the estate, despite Canlubang's exemption due to its previous "theoretical" land use conversion. Eventually, security personnel were deployed to prevent farmers from planting crops in certain sections of the estate, leading to multiple accounts of harassment against the resident farmers.

Despite the euphoric and celebratory depiction of Nuvali, its development is ridden with controversial incidents of political-economic collusion, violence, and evictions. Even before securing a development permit from the local government units concerned, the development and construction process commenced following the closure of the plantation with the securing of the area by security personnel, effectively prohibiting the planting of rice and other crops. During this period, the pacification of farmers and their practices entailed the use of force and violence, as evidenced by documented accounts of farmers who attempted to plant in the area. As the project commenced, four lowland communities in the southern section, which is within the jurisdiction of the local government of Calamba, were demolished despite legal challenges to the project by organized farmers in the area. Currently, the development of the southern section of Nuvali is still in contention, with the city mayor, developers, and other individuals facing a court case (Calamba Business Directory, 2010). Nonetheless, pre-selling of Nuvali properties and actual construction of gated communities are on-going and, according to some Canlubang residents, the remaining lowland communities of Canlubang will most likely be demolished in 2012. While the Nuvali project continues in the lowlands of Canlubang, farmers in the nearby upland community of Buntog are contending with similar issues. Plans are being made to develop a series of mixed-use leisure projects in the uplands of Canlubang that will connect the lowlands with the Tagaytay highlands. In recent years, surveyors and architects from Yulo companies have been surveying the area while negotiating with upland communities about their "inevitable" eviction and relocation. However, these "negotiations" thus far have failed, as Buntog farmers remain steadfast with their intent to remain in the area. By 2010, Buntog had become a "hotspot" for violence and unrest between local residents and the collective force of the police, military, and private security of the Yulo corporations (Ellao, 2010). Ever since these clashes, a special action group from the Philippine military have been deployed in the area, setting up makeshift outposts at strategic locations in Buntog and conducting regular patrols of the area to ensure "peace and order" while purging the community of NPA (New People's Army) communist rebels. To effectively spatially contain and purge Buntog, several restrictive policies have been in force: prohibition of the large-scale transport of harvested crops and construction materials, imposition of curfews, cutting off of electricity and water supplies, and the strategic installation of several security posts along established paths into the community.

Despite these abuses, the struggle of the Buntog farmers continue. Among all the indigenous communities in the Canlubang estate, Buntog has stood its ground over the years and is thus the material and symbolic space of resistance to "new urban" developments in Canlubang. For Jose, there is no other alternative but to fight for "land and life." Buntog farmers have organized and aligned themselves with a militant national peasant organization, Kilusang Mambubukid ng Pilipinas – KMP (Peasant Movement of the Philippines). Through this organization, they have actively organized with other farmers in the

Philippines and participated in multiple actions to resist development projects that would eject farmers from their lands.

Amidst the continuing developments in Manila's fringe, spaces of peasant resistance continue to emerge. Figure 4 shows locations of KMP-identified farming communities that are resisting development. These spaces, where the "creative-destructive" processes are being questioned and contested, act as sociospatial fulcrums that mire the future trajectories of "urban" and/or "suburban" developments.

CONCLUSION

In this paper, I have argued how *desakota*'s "pagan" (Cairns, 2002) and anti-essentialist character are useful theoretical hinges in explicating the production of suburban spaces in Manila's fringe. By using a sociospatial ontology, I have detailed how gated master-planned community developments are grounded on neoliberal restructuring in the Philippines. But as geographers have constantly reiterated, the place-based articulation of market-oriented neoliberal projects in the Philippines that envisions a globally competitive and investment-reliant national economy involves the strategic acquiescence of groups, relations, and policies, such as the transnational mobilities of Overseas Filipinos, agrarian reform, land use conversion, and local government decentralization as well as the concomitant preservation and tightening of the political-economic grip of landed elites. This acquiescence has resulted in a real estate boom, with its perceived contribution to economic growth, and has provided the much-needed outcome for earlier neoliberal restructuring in the Philippines, legitimizing continued market-oriented programs.

This boom is expressed within actual sites in Manila's fringe through the emergence of numerous master-planned gated "suburban" communities. Using the case of Canlubang, I employ a sociospatial ontology in exposing enduring land issues underlying the much-celebrated landscapes of wealth expressed in the estate. Through development projects that invoke neoliberal mantras, the landowning elite family of Canlubang was able to accumulate land and evade redistribution. These development projects in Canlubang are illustrative of the creative (property market, gated developments, public-private joint ventures) and destructive (practices and relations, attachment to land) processes of neoliberalization. The "destruction" does not just involve the "roll-back" of the welfare-like sugar estate, but also entails practices of brute force in evicting indigenous residents from the estate.

Faced with violence and an impending eviction, Buntog residents in Canlubang have remained steadfastly resisted developments in the area. In other parts of Manila's fringe, farming communities have aligned themselves with the KMP and are standing up together to oppose multiple mixed-use leisure- and gated-community projects. These accounts are instructive in reflecting on *desakota*'s "pagan" and resistant character. Contrary to deterministic pronouncements of an all-out Southeast Asian transition into "First World" urban conditions, I argue that the persistence of *desakota*-like spaces is hinged on resistant communities and actors that mire the timing, magnitude, and direction of the urban trajectories of Manila's fringe. Instead of situating the region within a historically linear rendition of urban transition, I invoke Massey's (2005) imagining of space as dynamic, complex, processual, relational, and open to multiple trajectories of the future. This framing opens up the analysis to temporal processes of the past and future, such as the property transactions forged during the colonial era, land struggles of dispossessed farmers, and the transnational circuits of capital transacted through OFW homebuyers. This also leads to some possible questions about future spatial scenarios. What kinds of spaces will eventually emerge from Manila's fringe? What social and political-economic processes will shape these spaces?

I end this paper with a call for more critical urban studies. As Philippine real estate continues to boom and new developments are built, generating a seemingly doxic euphoria, I call for projects that uncover processes of "accumulation by dispossession," which thrust "the costs of devaluation of surplus capitals upon the weakest and most vulnerable territories and populations" (Harvey, 2005, p. 185). Studies that challenge and expose the pitfalls of market-oriented developments are crucial in exploring alternative developments and in expanding the range of questions and solutions to inequalities.

NOTES

1. I would like to thank Victoria Lawson, Katharyne Mitchell, and Suzanne Davies Withers for their suggestions. I also thank Elvin Wyly and the anonymous reviewers who gave constructive comments.
2. Correspondence concerning this article should be addressed to Arnisson Andre Ortega, Palma Hall 336, Population Institute, College of Social Sciences & Philosophy, University of the Philippines, Diliman, Quezon City, 1101 Philippines; telephone: +63-2-494-6677; fax: +63-2-920-5402; email: arnisson@gmail.com
3. Based on the 2008 average exchange rate of US$1 = Php 44.439 (Bangko Sentral ng Pilipinas, 2010).
4. "Manila's fringe" is a loose spatial construct that alludes to the historical political-economic ties of the surrounding area to Manila, the capital city of the Philippines. I concur with the idea that the spatial extent of Manila has been produced by multiple institutions and key individuals over time, from the demarcation of colonial Manila's *intramuros* versus the *extramuros* (de Lemps, 2000) to the establishment of Metropolitan Manila as an administrative unit (Caoili, 1988). Operationally, I consider Metropolitan Manila's adjacent provinces of Batangas, Cavite, Laguna, and Rizal as the component parts of Manila's fringe, which is analogous to the subregion identified as the Manila Mega-Urban Region by Jones (2002) and Laquian (2005).
5. Based on his extensive field work in Indonesia, McGee coined *desakota* after the Bahasa Indonesian words, *desa*, meaning "city" and *kota*, meaning "village."
6. The establishment of the "super-regions" is part of the Medium Term Public Investment Program (MTPIP) of the Arroyo Administration (Executive Number 561). The partitioning of the Philippines into these super-regions and the specific developmental goals assigned to each region represents an all-out production of neoliberal space that aims to meet global market demands.
7. The CARP officially ended in 2008, but a new expanded version, CARPER (Expanded Comprehensive Agrarian Reform Program), was enacted in 2009. For many of its critics, CARP has failed in redistributing lands to farmers. The landowning elite, most of whom occupy national government posts, are able to circumvent CARP through various tactics and practices that capitalize on their socioeconomic and political power and networks. Some of these tactics involve stock distribution options, land conversion and re-classification, and voluntary transfer options for farmers. Numerous and extensive studies have focused on pitfalls of the Philippine CARP experience, in particular, the abuses experienced by tenant farmers and political-economic collusions of landlords and politicians (see Putzel, 1992; Riedinger, 1995; Kerkvliet, 2002; Borras, 2007).
8. According to the Housing and Land Use Regulatory Board (2007), residential subdivisions account for 85% of all projects (1,587 Open Market, Medium Cost, Economic, Simple Subdivision projects out of 1,870 total projects) approved by the agency in 2007. The majority of these developments are on Manila's fringe.
9. A baranguay is the smallest administrative unit in the Philippines, analogous to a village.
10. The Ayala Land Corporation is credited for developing the country's first high-end master-planned gated community projects inspired by the architecture of Palo Alto, California, such as Forbes Park in 1948, San Lorenzo in 1952, Bel Air in 1954, Urdaneta in 1957, San Miguel in 1960, Magallanes in 1962, and Dasmariñas in 1962 (Lachica, 1984).

REFERENCES

Agnew, J., 1994, The territorial trap: The geographical assumptions of international relations theory. *Review of International Political Economy*, Vol. 1, 53–80.

Antonio, M. N., 1994, Land scam: Agrarian "reform," Ramos style. *Multinational Monitor*, January 1. Retrieved November 12, 2010 from www.allbusiness.com/specialty-businesses/435151-1.html

Aquino, B., III, 2010, State of the nation address of his excellency Benigno C. Aquino III. *Official Gazette of the Office of the President of the Philippines*, July 26. Retrieved August 1, 2010 from www.gov.ph/2010/07/26/state-of-the nation-address-2010

Arcillas-Nazareno, A., 2008, *State of the City Address*. Mayor Arlene Arcillas-Nazareno's website, July 10. Retrieved January 5, 2010 from http://arlene-arcillasnazareno.com/09/news2.php?ID=49

AyalaLand, 2008, *Evoliving at NUVALI: A Vision of Sustainability*. Ayala Land Incorporated website. Retrieved August 2, 2009 from www.ayalaland.com.ph/article/evoliving_at_nuvali_a_vision_of_sustainability.

Bangko Sentral ng Pilipinas, 2010, *Exchange Rates*. Bangko Sentral ng Pilipinas website. Retrieved May 4, 2010 from www.bsp.gov.ph/statistics/sdds/exchrate.htm

Bello, W., 2004, *The Anti-development State: The Political Economy of Permanent Crisis in the Philippines*. Quezon City, Philippines: Focus on the Global South and University of the Philippines Sociology Department.

Bishop, R., Phillips, J., and Yeo, W. W., 2003, *Postcolonial Urbanism: Southeast Asian Cities and Global Processes*. London: Routledge.

Bolsdorf, A., Hidalgo, R., and Sanchez, R., 2007, A new model of urban development in Latin America: Gated communities and fenced cities in the metropolitan areas of Santiago de Chile and Valparaiso. *Cities*, Vol. 24, 365–378.

Borras, S., 2007, *Pro-poor Land Reform: A Critique*. Ottawa, Canada: University of Ottawa Press.

Brenner, N. and Theodore, N., 2002, Cities and the geographies of "actually existing neo-liberalisms". *Antipode*, Vol. 34, 349–379.

Brown, W., 2005, *Edgework: Critical Essays on Knowledge and Politics*. Princeton, NJ: Princeton University Press.

Cairns, S., 2002, Troubling real estate: Reflecting on urban form in Southeast Asia. In T. Bunnell, L. Drummond, and K. C. Ho, editors, *Critical Reflections on Cities in Southeast Asia*. Singapore: Times Academic Press, 101–123.

Calamba Business Directory, 2010, *Mayor Chipeco Kinasuhanngmgataga-Canlubang*. Calamba Business Directory website, December 26. Retrieved December 28, 2010 from www.calamba.ph/news-and-events/230-mayor-chipeco-kinasuhan-ng-mga-taga-canlubang

Calthorpe Associates, 2010, *Green City Metro Manila*. Calthorpe Associates website. Retrieved March 1, 2010 from www.calthorpe.com/metro-manila

Canlas, C., 1991, *Calabarzon Project: The Peasants' Scourge*. Manila, Philippines: Philippine Peasant Institute.

Caoili, M., 1988, *The Origins of Metropolitan Manila: A Political and Social Analysis*. Quezon City, Philippines: New Day Publishers.

Castree, N., 2006, From neoliberalism to neoliberalisation: Consolations, confusions, and necessary illusions. *Environment and Planning A*, Vol. 38, 1–6.

CD+A, 2010, *Canlubang Estate New Town Master Plan*. CD+A website. Retrieved March 1, 2010 from www.community-design.com/projects/city/canlubang.php

Champion, A., 2004, Lest we re-invent the wheel: Lessons from previous experience. In A. Champion and G. Hugo, editors, *New Forms of Urbanization: Beyond the Urban-Rural Dichotomy*. Aldershot: Ashgate, 25–42.

Champion, A. and Hugo, G., editors, 2004, *New Forms of Urbanization: Beyond the Urban-Rural Dichotomy*. Aldershot: Ashgate.

Cinco, M., 2009, Santa Rosa now part of billionaire's club. *Philippine Daily Inquirer*, August 21. Retrieved September 12, 2009 from http://newsinfo.inquirer.net/inquirerheadlines/regions/view/20090821-221294/Sta-Rosa-now-part-of-billionaires-club

Commission on Audit, 2008, *Bureau of Internal Revenue Zonal Values*. Retrieved February 10, 2009 from www.coa.gov.ph/Financial_Reports.htm

Cushner, N., 1976, *Landed Estates in the Colonial Philippines*. New Haven, CT: Yale University Press.

de Lemps, X. H., 2000, Shifts in meaning of "Manila" in the nineteenth century. In C. Macdonald and G. Mangubat Pesigan, editors, *Old Ties and New Solidarities: Studies on Philippine Communities*. Manila, Philippines: Ateneo De Manila University Press, 219–233.

Department of Agrarian Reform, 2007, *Primer on Land Conversion Series of 2007*. Retrieved November 12, 2007 from www.dar.gov.ph/pdf_files/publications/land_conversion.pdf

Dick, H. and Rimmer, P., 1998, Beyond the Third World City: The new urban geography in Southeast Asia. *Urban Studies*, Vol. 35, 2303–2320.

Duany, A., Plater-Zyberk, E., and Speck, J., 2001, *Suburban Nation: The Rise of Sprawl and the Decline of the American Dream*. New York, NY: New Point Press.

Dumlao, D., 2008, Despite strong peso, OFWs still buying houses. *Philippine Daily Inquirer*, February

10. Retrieved October 15, 2008 from http://globalnation.inquirer.net/news/breakingnews/view/20080210-118004/Despite-strong-peso-OFWs-still-buying-houses

Ellao, J. A., 2010, Peasants in Hacienda Yulo vow to continue fighting for the land they till. *Bulatlat*, June 11. Retrieved November 5, 2010 from www.bulatlat.com/main/2010/06/11/peasants-in-hacienda-yulo-vow-to-continue-fighting-for-the-land-they-till

England, K., 1994, Getting personal: Reflexivity, positionality, and feminist research. *The Professional Geographer*, Vol. 46, 80–89.

England, K. and Ward, K., editors, 2007, *Neoliberalization: States, Networks, Peoples*. Malden, MA: Blackwell Publishing.

Fishman, R., 1987, *Bourgeois Utopias: The Rise and Fall of Suburbia*. New York, NY: Basic Books.

Francisco, R., 2008, RP property firms look closer to home for sales. *Philippine Daily Inquirer*, April 14. Retrieved October 13, 2010 from http://blogs.inquirer.net/househunter/2008/04/14/rp-property-firms-look-closer-to-home-for-sales/

Friedman, T. L., 2005, *The World Is Flat: A Brief History of the Twenty-First Century*. New York, NY: Farrar, Strauss, & Giroux.

Gramsci, A., 2005, *Selections from the Prison Notebooks* (15th ed.; Q. Hoare and G. N. Smith, ed. and transl.). London: Lawrence and Wishart.

Hackworth, J., 2007, *The Neoliberal City: Governance, Ideology, and Development in American Urbanism*. Ithaca, NY: Cornell University Press.

Hart, G., 2002, *Disabling Globalization: Places of Power in Post-apartheid South Africa*. Berkeley, CA: University of California Press.

Hart, G., 2008, The provocations of neoliberalism: Contesting the nation and liberation after apartheid. *Antipode*, Vol. 40, 678–705.

Harvey, D., 1985, The geopolitics of capitalism. In D. Gregory and J. Urry, editors, *Social Relations and Spatial Structure*. Houndsmill and London: Macmillan, 128–163.

Harvey, D., 2005, *The New Imperialism*. Oxford: Oxford University Press.

Housing and Land Use Regulatory Board, 2007, *HLURB Accomplishment Report*. Retrieved January 29, 2010 from http://hlurb.gov.ph/uploads/agency-profile/2007AccomplishmentReport.pdf

Housing and Land Use Regulatory Board, 2010, *Housing and Land Use Regulatory Board Online Inquiry Database*. Retrieved from http://hlurb.gov.ph/online-inquiries/

Housing and Urban Development Coordinating Council, 2011, *Brief History*. Retrieved June 15, 2011 from www.hudc.gov.ph/index.php?p=52

Jackson, K., 1985, *Crabgrass Frontier: The Suburbanization of the United States*. New York: Oxford University Press.

Jones, G., 2002, Southeast Asian urbanization and the growth of mega-urban regions. *Journal of Population Research*, Vol. 19, 119–136.

Jürgens, U. and Gnad, M., 2002, Gated communities in South Africa – experiences from Johannesburg. *Environment and Planning B: Planning and Design*, Vol. 29, 337–353.

Keil, R., 2002, "Common – sense" neoliberalism: Progressive conservative urbanism in Toronto, Canada. *Antipode*, Vol. 34, 578–601.

Kelly, P., 1999, Everyday urbanization: The social dynamics of development in Manila's extended metropolitan region. *International Journal of Urban and Regional Research*, Vol. 23, 283–303.

Kelly, P., 2000, *Landscapes of Globalization: Human Geographies of Economic Change in the Philippines*. London and New York: Routledge.

Kerkvliet, B., 2002, *The Huk Rebellion: A Study of Peasant Revolt in the Philippines*. New York: Rowman & Littlefield Publishers.

King, A., 1990, *Urbanism, Colonialism, and the World Economy*. New York: Routledge.

Kunstler, J. H., 1993, *The Geography of Nowhere: The Rise and Decline of America's Man-Made Landscape*. New York: Touchstone.

Kuyek, D. and Skinner, A., 2003, Tales from Tagalog. *New Internationalist*. Retrieved February 12, 2010 from www.newint.org/issue363/tagalog.htm

Lachica, E., 1984, *Ayala, the Philippines's Oldest Business House*. Makati, Philippines: Filipinas Foundation.

Laquian, A., 2005, *Beyond Metropolis: The Planning and Governance of Asia's Mega-urban Regions*. Baltimore, MD: Johns Hopkins University Press.

Larkin, J. A., 1993, *Sugar and the Origins of Modern Philippine Society*. Berkeley, CA: University of California Press.

Larner, W., 2003, Neoliberalism? *Environment and Planning D: Society and Space*, Vol. 21, 509–512.

Lawson, V., 2010, Reshaping economic geography? Producing spaces of inclusive development. *Economic Geography*, Vol. 86, 351–360.

Lefebvre, H., 1991, *The Production of Space* (D. Nicholson-Smith, trans.). Malden, MA: Blackwell (original work published in 1974).

Legg, S., 2007, *Spaces of Colonialism: Delhi's Urban Governmentalities*. London: Blackwell Publishing.

Leitner, H., Peck, J., and Sheppard, E., 2007, *Contesting Neoliberalism: Urban Frontiers*. New York: Guilford Press.

LeRoy, J., 1905, *Philippine Life in Town and Country*. New York: Knickerbocker Press.

Li, T., 2010, Indigeneity, capitalism, and the management of dispossession. *Current Anthropology*, Vol. 51, 385–414.

Lindstrom, M. and Bartling, H., 2003, *Suburban Sprawl: Culture, Theory, and Politics*. Lanham, MD: Rowman & Littlefield.

Lucas, D., 2007, OFW remittances fueling growth in real estate. *Philippine Daily Inquirer*, May 20, 2007. Retrieved October 15, 2008 from http://globalnation.inquirer.net/news/breakingnews/view_article.php?article_id=6700

Magno, R., 2008, *Fundamentals of Real Estate Development*. University of the Philippines SURP website, February 18. Retrieved May 10, 2009 from www.upd.edu.ph/~surp/news/news_magno%20lecture.PDF

Massey, D., 2005, *For Space*. Thousand Oaks, CA: Sage.

McAndrew, J., 1994, *Urban Usurpation – From Friar Estates to Industrial Estates in a Philippine Hinterland*. Quezon City, Philippines: Ateneo De Manila University.

McDowell, L., 1992, Doing gender: Feminisms, feminists, and research methods in human geography. *Transactions of the Institute of British Geographers*, Vol. 17, 399–416.

McGee, T. G., 1991, The emergence of desakota regions in Asia: Expanding a hypothesis. In N. Ginsburg, B. Koppel, and T. G. McGee, editors, *The Extended Metropolis: Settlement Transition in Asia*. Honolulu: University of Hawaii Press, 3–26.

McGee, T. G., 1995, Eurocentrism and geography: Reflections on Asian urbanization. In J. Crush, editor, *Power of Development*. London: Routledge, 187–204.

McGee, T. G. and Robinson, I., editors, 1995, *The Mega-urban Regions of Southeast Asia*. Vancouver, Canada: University of British Columbia Press.

McLeod, G., 2002, From urban enterpreneurialism to a "revanchist city"? On the spatial injustices of Glasgow's renaissance. *Antipode*, Vol. 34, 602–624.

Mitchell, K., 2001, Transnationalism, neo-liberalism, and the rise of the shadow state. *Economy and Society*, Vol. 30, 165–189.

Mitchell, K., 2004, *Crossing the Neoliberal Line: Pacific Rim Migration and the Metropolis*. Philadelphia, PA: Temple University Press.

Mitchell, T., 1988, *Colonising Egypt*. Cambridge: Cambridge University Press.

Nagar, R., 1997, Exploring methodological borderlands through oral narratives. In J. P. Jones, H. J. Nast, and S. Roberts, editors, *Thresholds in Feminist Geography*. New York: Rowman and Littlefield, 203–224.

Olivera, B., 1981, *Jose Yulo, the Selfless Statesman*. Quezon City, Philippines: University of the Philippines, Filipiniana Research Center.

Pag-Ibig, 2009, *Pag-Ibig Fund Corporate Profile and History*. Pag-Ibig website. Retrieved August 2, 2009 from www.pagibigfund.gov.ph/history.htm

Peck, J. 2011, Neoliberal suburbanism: Frontier space. *Urban Geography*, Vol. 32, 884–919.

Peck, J. and Tickell, A., 2002, Neoliberalizing space. *Antipode*, Vol. 34, 380–404.

Peet, R., 2009, *Unholy Trinity: The IMF, World Bank, and WTO* (2nd ed). London: Zed Books.

Philippine Enterprise Magazine, 1975, The man behind Canlubang Sugar Estate, January–February.

Pinches, M., 1999, Entrepreneurship, consumption, ethnicity, and national identity in the making of the Philippines' new rich. In M. Pinches, editor, *Culture and Privilege in Capitalist Asia*. New York: Routledge, 275–301.

PREF, 2010, *About Us – Philippine Real Estate Festival*. Retrieved July 31, 2010 from www.philrealestatefestival.com/aboutus.html

Purcell, M., 2002, Excavating Lefebvre: The right to the city and its urban politics of the inhabitant. *Geojournal*, Vol. 58, Nos. 2–3, 99–108.

Putzel, J., 1992, *A Captive Land: The Politics of Agrarian Reform in the Philippines*. Quezon City, Philippines: Ateneo de Manila University Press.

Riedinger, J., 1995, *Agrarian Reform in the Philippines: Democratic Transitions and Redistributive Reform*. Palo Alto, CA: Stanford University Press.

Roy, A., 2002, *City Requiem, Calcutta: Gender and the Politics of Poverty*. Minneapolis, MN: University of Minnesota Press.

Roy, A., 2005, Urban informality: Towards an epistemology of planning. *Journal of the American Planning Association*, Vol. 71, 147–158.

Salazar, T., 2008, 40% of Filinvest's mountain suburb buyers from overseas. *Philippine Daily Inquirer*, September 6. Retrieved October 15, 2008 from http://services.inquirer.net/print/print.php?article_id=20080906-158970

Santa Rosa City Planning Office, 2000, Santa Rosa comprehensive land use plan. *Senate of the Philippines*, February 25, 2009, Senate approves proposed Real Estate Service Act on third reading. Senate of the Philippines website. Retrieved August 2, 2009 from www.senate.gov.ph/press_release/2009/0225_enrile1.asp

Shatkin, G., 2004, Planning to forget: Informal settlements as "forgotten places" in globalising Metro Manila. *Urban Studies*, Vol. 41, 2469–2484.

Smith, N., 1996, *The New Urban Frontier: Gentrification and the Revanchist City*. London and New York: Routledge.

Smith, N., 2002, New globalism, new urbanism: Gentrification as urban strategy. *Antipode*, Vol. 34, 427–450.

Sui, D. and Zeng, H., 2001, Modeling the dynamics of landscape structure in Asia's emerging desakota regions: A case study in Shenzhen. *Landscape and Urban Planning*, Vol. 53, 37–52.

Swanson, K., 2007, Revanchist urbanism heads south: The regulation of indigenous beggars and street vendors in Ecuador. *Antipode*, Vol. 39, 708–728.

United States Congress, 1911, *Administration of the Philippine Islands*, Vol. 1. Washington, DC: United States Congress.

Webster, D., 1995, Mega-urbanization in ASEAN: New phenomenon or transitional phase to the "Los Angeles World City"? In T. G. McGee and I. Robinson, editors, *The Mega-urban Regions of Southeast Asia*. Vancouver, Canada: University of British Columbia Press, 27–44.

Wu, F. and Webber, K., 2004, The rise of "foreign gated communities" in Beijing: Between economic globalization and local institutions. *Cities*, Vol. 21, 203–213.

Xie, Y., Yu, M., Bai, Y., and Xing, X., 2006, Ecological analysis of an emerging urban landscape pattern – desakota: A case study in Suzhou, China. *Landscape Ecology*, Vol. 21, 1297–1309.

Xu, J. and Yeh, A., 2005, City repositioning and competitiveness building in regional development: New development strategies in Guangzhou, China. *International Journal of Urban and Regional Research*, Vol. 29, 283–308.

15
Socio-spatial legibility, discipline, and gentrification through favela upgrading in Rio de Janeiro

Thaisa Comelli, Isabelle Anguelovski, and Eric Chu

INTRODUCTION

Urbanization in the global South is often characterized by spatial fragmentation and the unequal distribution and allocation of urban infrastructure, public spaces, and environmental amenities (McConnachie and Shackleton 2010; WHO 2010). Among megacities, so-called 'informal settlements'[1] are often emblematic symbols of over-urbanization (Davis 2006), where social inequalities are reflected in the physical organization of space. While informal settlements traditionally convey images of overcrowding, poor facilities, lack of basic services, and informality (Kuffer and Barrosb 2011; UN-Habitat 2013, 85), they are also increasingly relevant examples of how capital attraction policies and mega-events are shaping urban redevelopment and growth, employing discourses of development and progress, welfare, and security whilst silently excluding the voices and practices of historically marginalized communities (Leitner, Peck, and Sheppard 2007; Sánchez and Broudehoux 2013; Mascarenhas 2014; Maharaj 2015).

In slums all over the world, traditional explicit removal and demolition policies have recently shifted towards more in situ upgrading through private and public investments. While informal settlements continue to experience prejudice, marginality, and forced removals, the current intervention paradigm is couched within a lexicon of state-led urban integration, development, and modernization (Conde and Magalhaes 2004; Blanco and Kobayashi 2009). Such trends – along with growing 'poverty fetishism', where wealthier classes associate poverty with a nostalgic notion of authenticity (Benz 2016) – reveal the extent to which informal settlements are becoming politically, socially, and economically attractive, a dynamic which opens up new opportunities for market revaluation and re-branding (Cummings 2015; Lees, Shin, and López-Morales 2015).

This article contributes to the epistemology of urban (in)formality and processes of legibility through analyzing the transformation of informal settlements – or favelas in Portuguese – in the South Zone of Rio de Janeiro, Brazil, before, during, and after the World Cup and Olympic Games that took place in 2014 and 2016. We respond to calls for revisiting research on urban redevelopment and socio-spatial change in the global South using the lens of gentrification and urban upgrading (see Janoschka, Sequera, and Salinas 2014). We shift away from the traditional scholarly attention on conflicts surrounding housing evictions and displacement (see Silvestre and de Oliveira 2012; Freeman and Burgos 2017) to focus on much needed research on conflicts within (or created by) public spaces.[2] We examine the discourses, practices, and contradictions of upgrading and regeneration in favelas in Rio de Janeiro by asking: To what extent do concurrent processes of favela securitization and public space upgrading catalyze new forms of legibility and discipline, and how do long-time residents navigate them?

Our research finds that favela upgrading in Rio not only involves physical constructions of new public spaces and urban infrastructure, it is also attached to concurrent state and private interventions promoting securitization and police control, environmental clean-up, and economic investments in tourism and real estate. We argue that, when combined with favela pacification, upgrading projects not only contribute to the socio-spatial legibility of these settlements, they also stimulate patterns of gentrification that can be understood as physical, symbolic, and economic forms of discipline. Through these intersecting processes, we observe class- and race-based social change that lead to the erasure of long-term socially vulnerable residents through ambivalent experiences of upgrading that affect their livelihoods, behavior, and sense of belonging in public spaces. More broadly, our study contributes new insights on how capital-oriented urban planning strategies in the global South renew the role of the state inside self-built settlements, create new market visibility, and eventually produce socio-cultural and racial invisibilization and displacement.

URBAN GOVERNANCE RESTRUCTURING, LEGIBILITY, AND GENTRIFICATION IN THE GLOBAL SOUTH

Our conceptual approach is premised on the idea that urban governance restructuring in the global South is a double-edged sword. While promulgating democracy, participatory governance, and security (as in the case of Brazil), gentrification also leads to increased state presence in historically marginalized neighborhoods, especially by creating 'legible' spaces for capital through coercion and socio-spatial control of low income residents. In Rio, favela residents tend to be the targets of such strategies and often experience them within the context of urban regeneration, thus resulting in heightened contradictions in their experiences of socio-spatial change.

Theories of governance decentralization received attention in the 1990s due to a renewed optimism over the opportunities brought on by re-democratization (Gwynne and Kay 2004; Grindle 2009). Through municipal schemes such as participatory budgeting, citizens gained increased control over public finance, service provision, environmental quality, and other development priorities (Heller 2001; Baiocchi 2003). Brazil is often referred to as having some of the most successful examples of participation in local governance (see Wampler and Avritzer 2004; Wampler 2010; Baiocchi et al. 2011). However, re-democratization did not yield benefits for all social and economic sectors, as the poorest, especially favelas residents, continued to experience lack of property rights, access to public services, as well as increasing violent conflicts (Walton 1998; Davis 2009; Rodgers 2012; Moncada 2013).

Urban public space provision is one arena upon which the intersecting dynamics between governance decentralization, privatization of public services and/or infrastructure, and urban violence are represented and practiced by public, private, and civil society actors. As these actors come together within one urban space – for instance in neighborhoods of self-built settlements – they competitively claim ownership of it, thereby reconfiguring the uses of streets, plazas, and other open areas (Alves and Evanson 2011; Bodnar 2015). In the case of Brazil's favelas, the state and its affiliated organs have increasingly deployed securitization tactics to maintain the rule-of-law in light of violent conflicts within public spaces. This point draws on theories of urban security and pacification (Samara 2010; Graham 2012; Willis 2015), which note that cities are increasingly relying on policing and other military tactics in public spaces and streets that disproportionately target low-income and minority neighborhoods. At the same time, public spaces are also appropriated and reconfigured by 'parallel governments', 'multiple sovereignties' or 'hybrid' institutions – such as local private militia, gangs, or drug traffic factions – whose practices increase the complexity of competition and disputes within these settlements (Alsayyad and Roy 2009; Colona and Jaffe 2016).

In parallel to securitization policies, there is a desire from the state and market to render informal neighborhoods more 'legible' by legitimizing and exerting control over people, artifacts, and symbols (Scott 1999; Taylor and Broeders 2015). The concept of legibility here is fundamental since it provides symbolic and spatial interpretations of public spaces. For example, in environmental psychology, legibility is considered to be a 'physical and spatial quality of the surroundings' (Ramadier and Moser 1998). In Lynch's *The Image of the City* (1960), legibility is also related to urban morphology and the ability of individuals to orient themselves in a city or a specific urban environment. This concept also relates to social and cultural aspects, as inhabitants from different cultural backgrounds can experience a certain space in different ways (Ramadier and Moser 1998). Therefore, during processes of transformation (both morphological and symbolic) in favelas, the urban environment of those spaces becomes part of the cognitive lexicon of dominant classes; that is, they become more readable (and consequently less intimidating) and more appealing to outsiders for different investments and social practices.

Many of the securitization tactics and legibility interventions experienced in Brazilian favelas emerged from the economic restructuring of cities and the growing influence of globalized economic flows and the need to secure or optimize them. In Southern cities, the growing influence of globalized trade and investment promoted private capital as the primary driving force behind recent municipal politics, planning action, and spatial development (Harvey 1989; Lefebvre 1991; Fainstein 2010). Yet in many cases, the shift from manufacturing to a service sector, technology, finance, and real-estate investment driven economy created powerful urban regimes and special interest groups that prevented municipal governments from effectively accounting for collective interests and benefits (Pierre 1999; Kearns and Paddison 2000;

Atkinson and Bridge 2005; Sassen 2018). Such processes often took place in the context of a transition to democracy, or a shift from 'local government' to 'local governance,' and entailed more democratic power, accountability, and transparency (Cheema and Rondinelli 2007). However, in some cases, they also coexisted with populist politics couched in subtler neoliberal policies (Weyland 1999; Nuijten, Koster, and de Vries 2012). As a result, cities in the global South became hamstrung by capacity and governance deficits symptomatic of the post-colonial condition (Watson 2009; Robinson 2011; Roy 2011a). They also saw the consolidation of decision-making powers amongst elite groups (Swyngedouw 2005) and the reinforcement of rent capture practices (Smith 2002).

Discourses and practices of neighborhood regeneration arose from this backdrop of structural biases towards decentralized network governance approaches, a persistent unraveling of public sector planning and decision-making authorities, and concentrated power amongst urban elites. In the early 2000s, urban geography and development scholars took interest in urban regeneration and started to examine concurrent socio-spatial changes within self-built settlements and other low-income neighborhoods together with nascent gentrification trends. In their views, gentrification is a strategy of the global international elite who are in search of capital accumulation (Smith 2002; Atkinson and Bridge 2005) but that it required 'elastic yet targeted' definitions (Clark 2005). Yet today, the extension of the term to the global South is facing a backlash for its overstretching (Maloutas 2012) and for extending Western-derived urban theory onto the rest of the world through path dependent processes (Ghertner 2015).

Despite this debate, urban scholars continue to refer to gentrification to examine urban restructuring and socio-spatial change in Southern cities (Ley and Teo 2014; Lees, Shin, and López-Morales 2015, 2016; López-Morales 2015). In this paper, we consider gentrification in the global South – through our research in Rio – to be an adaptable process and concept with certain assumptions that need to be carefully scrutinized and empirically tested, something which has been increasingly adopted beyond academic circles. In that sense, we assume that gentrification can experience transformation through time and space.

Gentrification in Rio does not necessarily involve what Lees describes as 'intensive and uneven processes of capital-led restructuring with significant influxes of upper- and middle-income people and large doses of class-led displacement from deprived urban areas' as uneven and combined development takes place (Slater 2009; Lees, Shin, and López-Morales 2015, 441). When studying gentrification in the global South, one must consider that cities such as Rio encompass diverse types of land tenure, informal economies, and alliances between elites and marginalized groups, which forces us to move beyond the concepts of rent gap and rent-seeking, commodification of housing, private property rights and profit accumulation, or working-class neighborhoods (Ghertner 2015; Bernt 2016; Anguelovski, Irazabal, and Connolly in press). Others claim the need to even alter gentrification theory to account for new dynamics of exclusion and new examples of how they take place (e.g. Lees, Shin, and López-Morales 2016; Waley 2016). Furthermore, studying gentrification in the South requires moving beyond victimization and caricaturization of the urban poor as subjects deprived of resources or agency (Roy 2011b) and adopting postcolonial and subaltern urbanism approaches (Roy 2011b; Lees, Shin, and López-Morales 2015).

In the case of slums and informal settlements, their historical illegal status and unique morphology made them especially *illegible* to market forces and the state, which then prompted new urban codes and legislation to describe favelas as 'subnormal settlements' framed as 'Zones of Special Urbanistic Interest.' Instead of adapting the urban lexicon to favelas, Brazilian legislation has made them 'zones of exception' (Roy 2011b) that need to be rendered *legible*. Yet, once formerly residual urban spaces in trendy zones (i.e. spaces of exception) start to receive investments and economic and symbolic value, the state will then attempt to make such spaces more *legible* to its interests and those of private investors (Handzic 2010). Locally, we observed that this process ultimately affects the ways in which residents experience their neighborhood spaces, including public spaces.

In our study, we hypothesize that gentrification is taking place in Rio's favelas in a unique way. We treated gentrification as an assumption – or like the 'urban society' of Henri Lefebvre, a virtual object (Lefebvre [1970] 2003, 3) – which manifests solid signs and could generate epistemology through a transduction methodology. We do not have conclusive proof that, overtime, an entire class (and racial group) would be replaced by another. It is definitely an ongoing process, affected by some specific conditions, but one whose signs are being strongly felt and voiced by long-term residents. To inductively illustrate these signs, we examine how sources of state/market sponsored upgrading promulgate particular forms of legibility. In our case, formal state-led urbanization, land tenure provision, investments in tourism, enclosure, and policing in favelas increase legibility, which then lead to displacement and the slow erasure of local residents through the imposition of new disciplines. From this, we note how the agents of socio-spatial change in neoliberal cities can select from a myriad of disciplinary pathways (e.g. through policing/securitization, environmental upgrading, and neighborhood investments) to further particular and pre-defined forms of urban legibility.

METHODOLOGY

This paper uses an emblematic and critical case study approach of slum upgrading through public space enhancement and increased pacification in the connected favelas of Babilônia and Chapeu Mangueira in Rio de Janeiro, Brazil. These two communities are situated in the district of Leme, one of the wealthiest districts of the South Zone of Rio. Since both favelas are located on the same hill – also called Babilônia – we only refer to 'Babilônia' in our analysis. Babilônia and Chapeu Mangueira were selected because they are smaller and less dense compared to other favelas in Rio (and even the South Zone). Both also have attractive ocean views and a high concentration of green space, which makes them more livable while also more vulnerable to gentrification pressures. We considered that favelas in Rio are not only some of the most emblematic slums in the world, but they also illustrate current examples of state-led regeneration and upgrading in the context of external investments and mega-events.

Our fieldwork included three different stages: first in March 2015 (immediately after the World Cup and before the Olympic Games), second in July 2016 (during the Olympic Games), and finally in February – March 2018 (after the mega-events and the financial crisis). We consider this a critical period for favela communities in Rio, not only because real estate fluctuated intensely but also because it shows that the structure of the Pacification Police (UPP) was fragile and became destabilized soon after the Olympic Games. As of early 2018, Rio is also experiencing one of the city's worst security crisis in history, which has again boosted prejudice against favelas and heightened security, control, and discipline.

In the first phase of our research, we used a snowball sampling approach to conduct semi-structured interviews with key informants. This included developing interview instruments for long-established residents – including the president and members of the neighborhood association – new residents, planners/architects, and officers from the Rio Pacification Police (UPP). We combined these interviews with numerous field observations in new public spaces and other upgraded areas of Babilônia. Later, in July 2016, we followed these communities during the preparation for the Olympic Games. Our goal was to understand social changes and the evolution of local rules and norms from the beginning of the upgrading process until the completion of two mega-events that profoundly transformed Rio's urban space and redevelopment.

During the interviews, we asked respondents about their personal experience of public spaces, the diversity of activities practiced in those spaces, important changes inside the community and interactions between residents from different backgrounds, and about the evolving role of government agents and planning professionals. We also asked about the interactions between tourists and locals and about their perceptions of changes within the community after real estate prices started to increase. In particular, we asked about residents' perceptions of public and private investment in environmental improvements, their changing use of upgraded public (and green) spaces, and their experiences with police patrol, profiling practices, and community resistance strategies in the favelas. Architects and planners were also consulted about their criteria and priorities for each upgrading project, challenges that appeared along the way, interactions between them, the residents, and the government, and their perception of the impact of gentrification in these favelas. Finally, questions to the UPP focused on the role of the police inside the community, the process of regulating public spaces, and possible community conflicts. Here it is important to mention that in 2016, Babilônia elected a new neighborhood association president, which led to a different discourse towards changes inside the community. Finally, in February and March 2018, we reinterviewed some key neighborhood actors to update some of our earlier data with more community experiences since the mega events. It is also important to mention that, in contrast to our field research in 2015 and 2016, during our last visits in the community in 2018, UPP officers did not want to respond to any interviews and neighborhood association members advised us not to visit the favela unaccompanied.

MARGINALITY AND URBAN UPGRADING IN SOUTH ZONE FAVELAS

Within Rio de Janeiro, 'hill' (*morro* in Portuguese) and 'asphalt' (*asfalto* in Portuguese) have long been symbols of two different societies (Gonçalves 2013). Due to Rio's unique topography, residual areas in the city were located throughout the hills, where many favelas were built. Over the years, a mixture of financial constraints, lack of land tenure, and the constant threat of removals led favela dwellers to refrain from investing in their own housing. During much of the 20th century, consecutive municipal administrations ignored or tried to eradicate land occupation on the hills (Conde and Magalhaes 2004). For most of this period, the urban middle class was reluctant to expand upwards into the favelas due to violence and the 'myths of marginality' (Perlman 1977), which referred to negative stereotypes and preconceptions about favelas and their residents. For favela residents, however, the lack of investment interest shielded them from the most intense real estate pressures facing the city.

Beginning in the 1990s, as part of (re)democratization and the introduction of new governance processes, the government began to openly express the intention to integrate the favelas into the 'formal' city. Early experiences of favela upgrading culminated in the most well-known program, the *Favela Bairro* (1994), which facilitated massive investments into regenerating medium-sized favelas (between 500 and 2500 households) through financial support from the Inter-American Development Bank (Perlman 2010). Considered an international success, *Favela Bairro* represents one of the largest upgrading programs of its kind in Brazil and has since served as an exemplar for similar programs across Latin America.

For Rio, the legacy of *Favela Bairro* meant that removal policies have been less commonly adopted and deployed. Current policy paradigms focus on improving favelas' environment instead of promoting its cleansing. For favelas in Rio's South Zone in particular, which have some of the best views over the ocean, areas that were once considered an urban problem are now seen as a valuable asset. In 2009, a unit of the Pacification Police (UPP) was installed in Babilônia after being deployed in other neighborhoods as soon as 2007 (See Table 1). Developed by the municipal Department of Security (*Secretaria de Seguranç,a*), the UPP's goal is to reinforce the presence of the state, permanently remove drug traffic from favela communities, and foster a closer relationship between citizens and the government. Although data show that UPP presence has contributed to lower violence rates in Rio in

Year	Key Events	Related Developments and Implications
2007	The Government of Rio launches the UPPs, pacification police stations aimed at bringing an arm of the state into the favelas.	
2007–2009	Brazil is selected to host the 2014 World Cup and Rio de Janeiro is selected to host the 2016 Olympic Games. UPPs brought a general sense of safety to Rio's residents and tourists, boosting tourism and commercial initiatives focused on outsiders. Private value capture combined with growing investments led to skyrocketing real estate speculation in subsequent years. The South Zone was one of the most affected areas.	
2010	*Morar Carioca* program is launched in Rio.	Favelas participating in *Morar Carioca* received investments in infrastructure, housing, and public spaces, making them more appealing. Frequent media coverage related to such improvements highlighted the peaceful status of some favela communities. Tourism and real estate prices continued to rise, bringing new symbolic values to favelas.
2016	New political scandals began to emerge during one of the largest economic recessions in Brazilian history. In October, right after the Olympic Games, Rio's Security Secretary, José Mariano Beltrame, resigns. Beltrame was in office for 10 years during which he introduced UPP units across the city.	
2017	Wars between rival drug gangs intensify in Rio and across Brazil.	
2018	The Brazilian Senate approves federal intervention to improve Rio's security, leading to the presence of army forces inside the city and favela communities. The governor of Rio de Janeiro announced an austerity package to balance public accounts and mitigate public deficit. This led to late payments to state employees, including the military police. Many security specialists affirm that UPPs are failing (including Beltrame) and must be rethought. Real estate prices plummeted due to the recession.	

Table 1 Summary of recent key events for favela's transformation in Rio

Year	Key Events	Related Developments and Implications
		Conditions of violence again emerge from within favelas across Rio. Commercial activities in touristic favelas suffer from a slight loss of customers.
		The city is again considered to be in a state of war. Gentrification in touristic favelas of the South Zone decelerate but persists in the South Zone neighborhoods.

Table 1 (Continued)

general (Cano 2012), we note that strategic planning policies in the city have been accompanied by 'states of exceptions' regimes (Vainer 2011) and by street normalization through discipline, punishment, and state control (Rubino 2005). Thus, we argue that the municipality has pacified historically stigmatized favelas using discourses of the 'city of fear' (*phobolosis* as defined by de Souza 2008).

In 2010, the municipality launched a new program, *Morar Carioca*, to completely and permanently integrate favelas into Rio's urban fabric by 2020 as a part of the legacy of the 2016 Olympic Games.[3] In this process, Babilônia and Chapeu Mangueira were selected as pilot sites. At the time, *Morar Carioca* was designed to be the most comprehensive program of favela rehabilitation in Rio's history, with a budget of R$8 billion (approximately US$4.5 billion at the time) (Leitão and Delecave 2013). In contrast to *Favela Bairro*, *Morar Carioca* focused on favela de-densification and the enforcement of stricter rules for new building constructions in a more coercive model of growth control (Magalhães 2013). Not only focusing on infrastructure and housing,[4] *Morar Carioca* promised new public spaces and sustainable public facilities along with participatory planning processes.

This combined process of favela consolidation, upgrading, and pacification has opened up opportunities for both local entrepreneurs and outside investors to channel money into previously inaccessible parts of the city and transforming the neighborhoods' built environment (Gonçalves 2005; Cavalcanti 2009). Concurrently, since the early 2000s, real estate pressures have increased dramatically in Rio de Janeiro (see Figure 1). Thus, favelas in the South Zone – such as Vidigal, Rocinha, and Babilônia – are particularly vulnerable since they are built in prime locations close to beaches and coastlines.

Before the World Cup and Olympic Games, some critics considered that investments in favela upgrades, coupled with states of exception and the creation of new growth and investment coalitions, were jeopardizing social inclusion, urban rights, and democratic gains attributed to the different urban reform agendas (Gaffney 2010; Hérnandez-Medina 2010; Rolnik 2011). Like Vidigal and Rocinha, Babilônia is similarly vulnerable to gentrification pressures (see Figures 2 and 3). The favela is inhabited by around 4000 residents benefiting from a large amount of preserved vegetation and an ecological trail, which is unusual for favelas in Rio, where massive densification generally erases any environmental amenities. Babilônia is therefore highly attractive to outsiders. Furthermore, *Morar Carioca* projects brought new eco-friendly constructions, the revitalization of major pathways, and the urbanization of access and leisure areas (see Figure 4). New plazas and viewpoints – wooden decks attached to the main pathways – sprung up across the neighborhood. Such amenities are easily accessible by revitalized staircases and benefit from new paved slopes (see Figure 5). This increasingly peaceful and green environment, privileged location, recent upgrading, and attractive views have boosted tourism and the arrival of new middle or upper-class residents and visitors. Many local bars with English menus have been opened, and some of them offer two-course lunch menus for US$30, far beyond the reach of local residents. A new upscale art gallery with a view of the ocean has also recently opened. Besides that, in 2016, there were 18 hostels in Babilonia, but only eight of them were managed by locals (Fagerlande 2018).

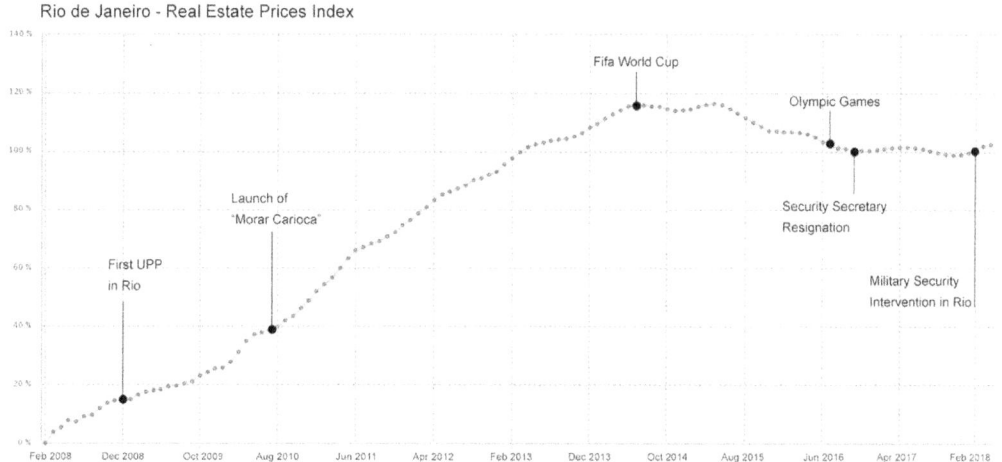

Figure 1 Real estate prices related to key events from Table 1.
Source: FIPE-Zap BR, modified by authors.

Increasing local real estate prices are reflected in local studies. A 2012 report by the Getulio Vargas Foundation (FGV) showed that after the arrival of the UPPs in Babilônia, the rent of two-bedroom apartments in Leme increased by 80% and their sale price by 138% (FGV 2012). During our 2016 fieldwork, we identified one-bedroom apartments in Babilônia renting for more than US$400 a month, in a context where local residents' average wage is US$460 a month. Still, in 2018, almost two years after the Olympic Games, apartments in Babilônia show a sale price of R$700,000 or R$7950 per square meter (approximately US$190,000 or US$2160 per square meter).[5] However, it is challenging to evaluate gentrification through property or rental prices within favelas in Rio due to the widespread reported presence of informal transactions taking place in the selling and renting of properties (Pearlman 2016). Even in Rio's more formal neighborhoods, the local government does not provide systematic real estate data and most information is held by private agencies or associations. We also observed that, during the past years, real estate prices swelled throughout the city in general,[6] encompassing almost all neighborhoods and making it harder to evaluate the degree to which the UPPs, upgrading projects, or mega-events played a role in particular favela communities. However, since the Olympic Games in 2016, the combination of political scandals, economic recessions, and security crisis have contributed to lower prices[7] and slowed down tourism. In Babilônia, our fieldwork reveals that from the eighteen hostels that existed in 2010, only eight remain. In this changing context of public-private securitization, investment, and tourism development, the next section examines how concurrent processes of favela securitization and public space upgrading and greening have facilitated new forms of control and discipline in Babilônia, as well as how residents have been confronting them.

PARADOXICAL EXPERIENCES OF FAVELA PACIFICATION AND UPGRADING

This section shows that the attempt to achieve socio-spatial legibility in Babilônia's spaces – i.e. more recognizable and symbolically accessible environments – is leading to different forms of physical, symbolic, and economic discipline that catalyze gentrification and produce contradictory experiences for favela residents. Here, capital-oriented urban planning strategies renew the role of the state inside favelas to create new market visibility for outside visitors and investors and eventually produce social invisibilization and displacement. Figure 6 shows the main roles of the actors involved in the upgrading programs and pacification policies, along with the results of such policies for long-time residents and their relation with public spaces.

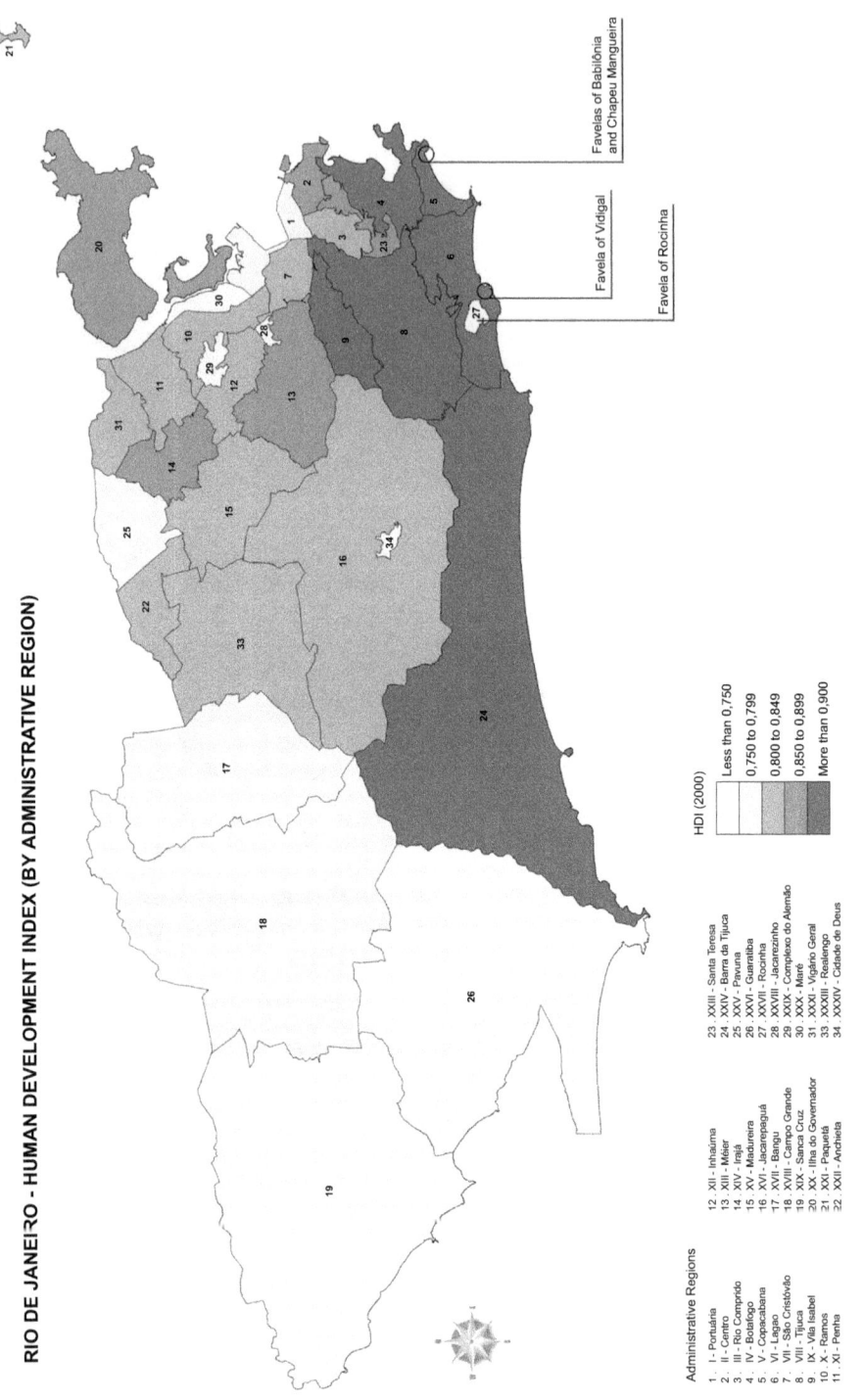

Figure 2 Three emblematic favelas of Rio (Rocinha, Vidigal, and Babilônia) amidst prime locations – wealthier zones with high HDI.
Data retrieved from Rio's Municipality, modified by authors.

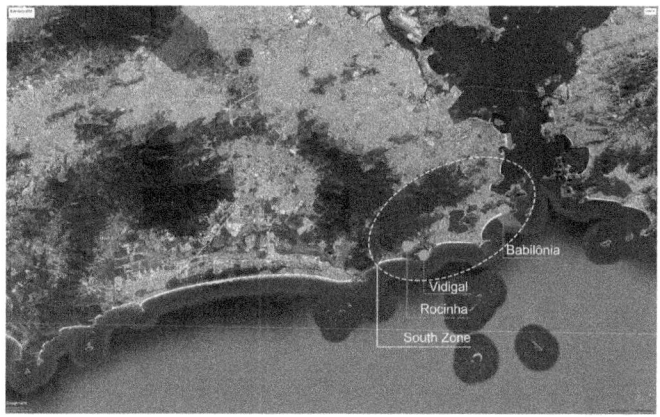

Figure 3 Aerial view of Rio de Janeiro. We highlight the South Zone and favelas with privileged views to the ocean and access to centers of interest.

Source: Google Earth 2017, modified by authors.

Figure 4 Remodeled slopes and stairways
(Photo: Thaisa Comelli, 2015).

Figure 5 New 'plazas': wooden decks attached to the hills to create additional space
(Photo: Thaisa Comelli, 2015).

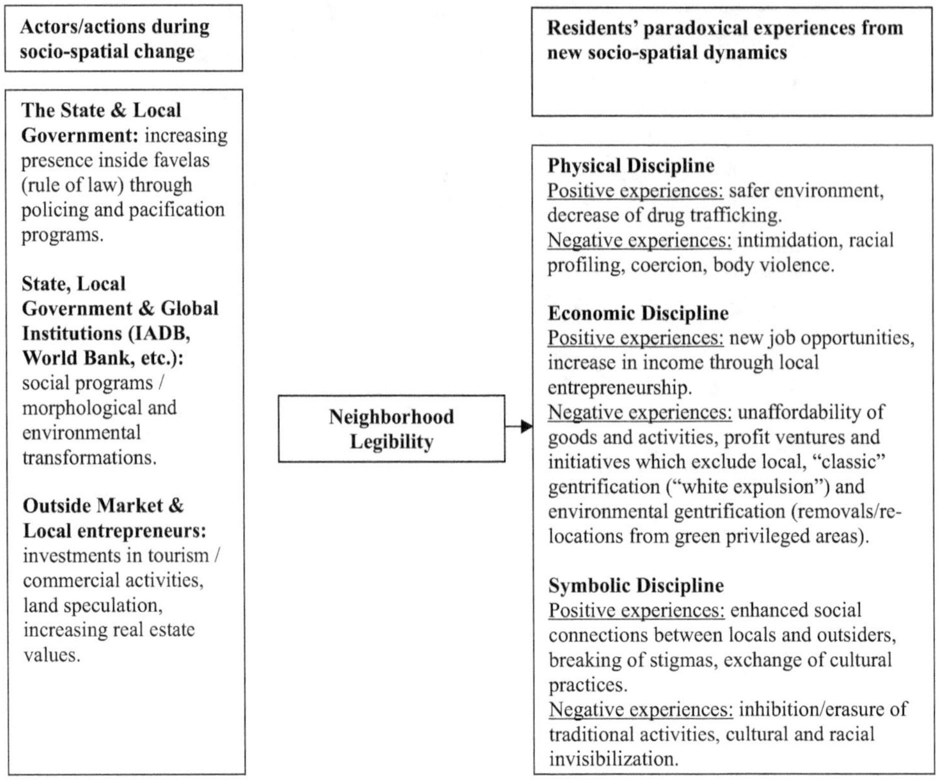

Figure 6

Actors/actions during socio-spatial change	Residents' paradoxical experiences from new socio-spatial dynamics
The State & Local Government: increasing presence inside favelas (rule of law) through policing and pacification programs. **State, Local Government & Global Institutions (IADB, World Bank, etc.):** social programs / morphological and environmental transformations. **Outside Market & Local entrepreneurs:** investments in tourism / commercial activities, land speculation, increasing real estate values.	**Physical Discipline** Positive experiences: safer environment, decrease of drug trafficking. Negative experiences: intimidation, racial profiling, coercion, body violence. **Economic Discipline** Positive experiences: new job opportunities, increase in income through local entrepreneurship. Negative experiences: unaffordability of goods and activities, profit ventures and initiatives which exclude local, "classic" gentrification ("white expulsion") and environmental gentrification (removals/re-locations from green privileged areas). **Symbolic Discipline** Positive experiences: enhanced social connections between locals and outsiders, breaking of stigmas, exchange of cultural practices. Negative experiences: inhibition/erasure of traditional activities, cultural and racial invisibilization.

(Connected via: **Neighborhood Legibility**)

Figure 6 Social-spatial favela changes and new forms of discipline.

PHYSICAL DISCIPLINE

The relationship between the residents of Babilônia and UPP agents has been uneasy since their initial arrival, which has strongly affected the local public environment and residents' use of public spaces. Although it is beyond the scope of this paper to examine security policies in greater depth, our field observations and interviews reveal that the physical constraints imposed by the UPP in communal areas cannot be ignored. Even during the community's most prosperous and peaceful times, many residents expressed a perception of being coerced and controlled in public spaces, noting how police presence is a way to make favelas more attractive for outsiders (interview 2015).

Historically, pervasive crime, violence, and drug-trafficking in Rio's informal settlements created long-lasting territorial stigma towards poor neighborhoods. Favela residents were traditionally imagined and portrayed by politicians and by the media as potential bandits and drug dealers. Although waves of crime come and go for decades, and disputes for territory in the city can be traced back to the first half of the 20th century (mostly due to illegal gambling practices), it was in the 1980s that criminality became highly associated with drug trafficking and favelas (Misse 2007). During the 1990s, for instance, Rio was described as a city at war, which contributed to boost many major investments in favelas (Leite 2000).

Amidst that context, the promise of a permanent presence of the state inside favelas generated optimism within many stigmatized residents. Therefore, during our first research phase in Babilônia in 2015, when asked about the recent opening of the community to the outside and their more recent appeal to outsiders, residents were mostly unanimous in reporting this as a positive trend. They highlighted how the presence of outsiders reflected and further helped to break down former patterns of socio-spatial stigmatization and negative preconceived views about residents and favelas more generally. One long-time resident also stressed how media and arts have helped to re-legitimate and revalue favelas during this process:

'When did a long-established resident ever imagine that a movie or a soap opera would be recorded here? When I was younger and a TV reporter came to a favela community, it was only to announce a gunfire shooting.'
> Young female resident, born and raised in Babilônia (2015)

As a consequence of the neighborhood opening up, residents and outsiders have had greater contacts and social interactions with each other. When outsiders come to visit or live in the favela, they are able to move beyond preconceived views and appreciate their experience of the place. As a member of the Neighborhood Association highlighted:

'I like it because our community learns to cohabit with them [outsiders] and they learn to cohabit with us. And for them, they imagine that they will find a dirty place, houses falling apart. But then they arrive here and see a different thing. And that's why they fall in love. They don't want to leave here. They come and want to stay.'
> Neighborhood Association worker, born and raised in Babilônia (2015)

Here, visitors break down negative stereotypes through social and physical contacts within the neighborhood.

However, this opening has come with a price. Favelas have been secured through the Pacification Police (UPPs), which are permanently stationed up and downhill from Babilônia and are controlled by the military police. As typical across favelas in Rio, UPP officers holding semi-automatic rifles and machine guns guard the entrance of the neighborhood. UPP officers are also regularly circulating inside community streets and squares. Officially, the role of the UPP is to maintain a safer environment inside the favelas, avoid the further spread of the drug traffic, and protect residents from violence. According to UPP officers, their intervention ensures greater peace in the community and helps keep drug trafficking at controlled and unorganized levels (interview 2015). They also argue that, at least in Babilônia, most of the time drugs are sold within the community in private spaces and drug consumption is internal.

Resident perceptions and experiences seem more mixed. Even though many of them recognize the fact that heavy drug-trafficking has decreased since the arrival of the UPP, others complain that their community was always peaceful and that the UPP was not necessary, at least compared to other favelas in Rio (interview 2015). Besides, community leaders argue that the UPP by itself does not address the need for structural social changes in Rio and in favelas more specifically; instead, what is needed is the elimination of racial segregation and stigma (interview 2016). Some interviewees further argued that the UPP program is a state-orchestrated strategy to control residents' behavior, and not only those involved in drug trafficking:

'Nothing changed for black people in Brazil. Before, *senzalas*;[8] today, favela. One of the biggest lies about the UPP project is that it deters the sale of narcotics and the presence of drug dealers. Here, there are no traffickers. Traffickers are the ones who sell drugs on a large scale, and there are no traffickers here ... We experience a police state, in which the only branch of the state that acts here inside is the institution of the Military Police.'
> Neighborhood Leader (2016)

Police militarization target not only drug dealers but also racially-profiled residents with no connection to local organized crime. In fact, many residents perceive the UPP presence as discriminatory and racist way to control specific subgroups within the community, namely Afro-Brazilians. Community leaders point to officers' behavior as 'aggressive' and 'disrespectful' and accuse them of treating residents as 'dogs,' forcing people to remain quiet in fear of arrests (interview 2016).

By our final fieldwork phase in the community in early 2018, the situation had significantly worsened. The renewed and widespread drug war between dealing factions has dramatically affected penitentiaries and favelas throughout the country. In February 2018, army forces entered Rio allegedly to reinforce security until the municipality recovers enough financial and logistical capacity to address the crisis. Even though Babilônia has always been one of the calmest favelas in Rio, such incidents severely affected local tourism and livelihoods (Fagerlande 2018). One resident noted this towards outsiders and researchers:

'Don't come up here. The climate is not very good these days. Wait a few weeks ... If you find

a resident who takes responsibility for you, you can come, but it is at your own risk.'
Neighborhood Association worker (March 2018)

In sum, the unsafe environment favelas have experienced most recently again has affected the lives of Babilônia residents and has been used by the government to build upon previous efforts and justify more explicit and renewed physical discipline – what Willis (2015) calls the 'Right to Kill' inside the community. Normalized profiling and violence further legitimizes arrests and killings.

SYMBOLIC DISCIPLINE

In addition to explicit forms of physical discipline, a militarized presence of the state in Babilônia is used to achieve neighborhood legibility through regulating and disciplining consumption and cultural practices – a form of more symbolic control of residents.

As the UPP is responsible for approving activities and events organized in public areas, especially those in the newly upgraded wooden decks constructed through *Morar Carioca* investments, police officers are also helping to reshape Babilônia to fit the consumption tastes of white Brazilian middle class and foreigners. Before the arrival of the UPP in 2009, local authorities had little control over the social practices and traditions of favela residents. During interviews, residents claimed to have routinely organized outdoor barbecues and celebrations in different public spaces across the communities, negotiating the terms and rules of such events among themselves (interview 2015). In contrast, the police now act as a regulator of events in public spaces, prompting some residents to argue that officers are abusing their power and depriving residents of their socio-cultural rights (interview 2015). Also, long-time residents (and even some foreign private investors) argue that the UPP tend to favor events promoted by gentrifiers and newcomers in the newly built plazas, with authorized events focused on attracting tourists. One of the strongest sources of conflict is the deck of a touristic bar called *Estrelas da Babilônia* (Babilônia Stars). Residents claim that the bar owner has appropriated this public space for commercial use, preventing locals from carrying out their own recreational activities:

'Before [. . .] a resident could party in the streets, everyone gathered together. Nowadays all o\f this is forbidden. To be able to organize an event there, I had to ask the UPPs, but they vetoed the event. [. . .] So, we don't have public spaces in the community anymore. I don't know what happens, because [the bar owner] just arrived. Every weekend there is Latino Music there. The UPP allows it every weekend. [ ] The truth is that his bar is for tourists. [ ] I think that the officers want us – little by little – to leave the community and have fun in other places, so this place can turn into a tourism venue.'
Local bar owner (2015)

In sum, the local police is protecting, legitimizing, and even (in)directly promoting the economic activities of newcomers.

In response to community complaints, the UPP notes that officers do not discriminate when they regulate events or individuals in the community (interview 2015). What they call 'peaceful' events are not prohibited. However, officers argue that events such as *Baile Funk* (traditional Afro-Brazilian music) have long been associated with drug trafficking and orgies, and that they are more dangerous social events that need to be regulated or prohibited (interview 2015). Despite claims about non-discrimination, the UPP's descriptions of the process for authorizing local events show an inclination towards gentrifiers:

'We have an art gallery here. If you are organizing a *vernissage* there, there's no way that we will deny it. But not if in the same gallery you are organizing a *Baile Funk*. *Baile Funk* does not only require our authorization, it requires the authorization of the Department of Security and the Fire Station. Before the UPP, *Baile Funk* parties were a huge "market of drugs". Everyone knows that – drugs, orgy, everything [. . .] But there's no discrimination for any kind of event.'
UPP Officer (2015)

Foreigners who have invested in Babilônia confirm UPP discriminatory practices, though some of them attempt to organize Afro-Brazilian events (which the UPP often authorizes) as a way to revisibilize local cultural practices, encourage residents to mobilize and reoccupy public spaces (interview 2016), and build counter-narratives about Afro-Brazilian celebrations as vibrant, locally-embedded, and inclusive socio-cultural practices.

The restrictions towards *Baile Funk* celebrations are raising community concerns over racial stigmas and profiling against the cultural traits of some favela residents – Afro-Brazilians in particular – thus contributing to the elimination of such practices from the community's daily life. Such transformations are illustrative of symbolic forms of invisibilization, gentrification, and concurrent processes of both racial dispossession (of Afro-Brazilians) and racial privilege (of white middle-class gentrifiers and visitors) produced by contemporary capitalism and transnational investment in Latin American cities. As Janoschka, Sequera, and Salinas (2014) argue, the implementation of neoliberal policies tends to restrict possibilities for poor and excluded populations to appropriate space for their social and economic reproduction, and it privileges the consumption taste and behavior of newcomers. Even though *Baile Funk* was culturally produced mostly in the favelas, this celebration has spread to private enclosed middle- and high-class clubs visited mostly by white Brazilians.[9] Therefore, community leaders and local non-profits regret the criminalization of Afro-Brazilian cultural practices, their elimination from public spaces, and their displacement, appropriation, and commodification in exclusive social clubs for the pleasure of tourists and upper classes (interview 2016). As Harvey (2004) notes, this represents a form of black cultural dispossession by white appropriation and exploitation.

From the residents' point of view, the criminalization and prohibition of *Baile Funk* parties in Babilônia is an emblematic example of how the local government invisibilizes favela culture and controls residents' socio-spatial right to public space and local traditions. Even though public and green spaces have become more abundant, beautified, and formalized, residents feel removed from their neighborhoods and compelled to leave the neighborhood to carry out activities that have always been common inside the community, which might prove to be unsafe in other favelas:

> 'If I want to go to a *Baile Funk* party, I have to go to other communities and put myself at risk. Because when you go to a *Baile Funk* party you don't come back early, so it is dangerous. I don't go anymore. I prefer to stay at home.'
> Chapeu Mangueira resident (2015)

In doing so, residents therefore face a double risk – one of losing their culture and another of losing their lives as they enter other (and maybe rival) favelas to access traditional cultural identity and practices.

Besides conflicts due to cultural events and celebrations, our study also shows that symbolic discipline can be seen through the practices of tourists who visit the community via organized tours. Although residents mostly note that the presence of tourists can break stigmas and provide fruitful exchanges between people from different cultural backgrounds (interview 2015), many residents critique the way in which community tours are being handled and codified by the government and private initiatives as a form of slum tourism[10] (see Frenzel and Koens 2012). When criticizing tourism carried by outside companies, residents argue that the contact between tourists and long-time residents may be superficial and actually prevent the meaningful exchange of knowledge on the community's past and current struggles (interview 2015). Interviewees further complain that tourists sometimes only visit beautified and upgraded areas that create a manicured image of favelas:

> 'The municipality only puts make-up in some places, especially where the tourists go. I do not have anything against the tourists, everyone is a human being, but they do not say hello. They pass by you and they want to see the landscape. They do not want to know about the origins of those living here. They use the same places that we do. The difference is that they only go to the places where there was any kind of intervention.'
> Babilônia Resident who participated in public space revitalization projects (2015)

Even though brief visits to Babilônia might make outsiders more sympathetic towards residents, they do not provide enough impact or knowledge to further their understanding of local life experiences or to make visitors rethink issues of poverty and inequality (Jones and Sanyal 2015).

In sum, even though the relations between the formal and informal city are now more intense and frequent in Rio, social exchanges in upgraded public spaces are still weak and superficial. Symbolic discipline inside the community does not seem to compensate for the damage to a community's loss of socio-cultural habits, traditions, and experienced racism.

ECONOMIC DISCIPLINE

So far, we considered physical and symbolic forms of discipline as attached to gentrification in South Zone favelas. However, the most classic forms of gentrification in Babilônia are taking place through economic means. State-led urban upgrading programs are reclaiming and rebranding the city for businesses, middle classes, and market forces more generally (Hackworth 2002; Smith 2002; Davidson 2008; Rousseau 2009; Lees 2012), while applying what Ghertner (2015) identifies as extra-economic force and state violence.

During our first visit in Babilônia in 2015, hostels, bars, and art galleries had been sprouting up all over the community. Even though some residents did not know the formal concept of gentrification, all of them associate these new investments to externally driven rising real estate prices and land and property speculation. In response, according to the former President of the Neighborhood Association, some mobilization emerged early on against speculation and the risk of land formalization in the community. Residents feared that new real estate transactions benefited outsiders, either middle class Rio residents who come to invest in the favelas or foreigners, resulting in possible coerced displacements:

> 'The proposal was to initiate the process of regularizing land ownership [when *Morar Carioca* started]. But I alerted the residents of the danger of land ownership regularization after the UPP. If land ownership regularization had come before the UPP, I would look at it with other eyes, but coming after the UPP, it is very dangerous because you will increase and amplify the desire for speculation . . . [Regularization] is also included in this 'package' of removal.'
> Neighborhood Association President (2015)

As these words illustrate, residents started to see land tenure regularization and/or land titling in Rio with an eye of concern and have subsequently moved away from demanding a formalization of their land occupation – a departure from what previous studies have considered as tools for securing sustainable livelihoods and erasing poverty (Minnery et al. 2013).

However, in contrast to many gentrifying neighborhoods in the global North, Babilônia and Chapeu Mangueira residents are not yet collectively organizing or participating in formal resistance movements against gentrification. Within embryonic forms of economic gentrification, many residents see possible benefits, such as a chance to grow financially and achieve social mobility (interviews 2015). Some interviewees revealed their enrollment in state-sponsored training programs and their interest in the new job opportunities and courses for tourism professionals that have accompanied the upgrades (interviews 2015). Small business owners interviewed also see such opportunities as a chance to achieve greater decision-making power over their housing situation and to benefit from the economic development of their community, so that leaving or staying in the community can be a choice and not an issue of survival (interviews 2015).

Some long-term residents are also becoming small entrepreneurs by renting parts of their property to visitors and becoming informal real estate professionals. Some new bars geared toward tourists are being established as residents, immediately after the arrival of the UPP, anticipated new capital inflows and investments to open new or rehabilitate former establishments (interviews 2015). In other cases, they participate in a reforestation cooperative and become tourist guides of the green reserve at the top of the Babilônia hill. In these specific cases, instead of being replaced by new middle-class residents, established inhabitants are empowering themselves to become the new local middleclass:

> 'It's progress, but progress is complicated. People have to adapt to the new way and to interact with what the government is proposing for this place. We cannot stay like it was before. We cannot stay stopped in time, and you have to enjoy the opportunities to start something new . . . It is pulling everyone. I come with the bar, and then other person comes with another bar, and then other person comes with handicrafts, others with a nice project . . . So, it's a good thing.'
> Bar Owner (2015)

In the views of these new business owners, being entrepreneurial and catering to visitors will give long term residents new opportunities to grow.

Residents' attempt to profit from the growing interest of outsiders and reinvent themselves instead of being slowly evicted might help to slow down class-based displacement inside the community. Still, those who are not property owners particularly suffer from higher rental prices. Even those who do own properties conclude that besides eating and sleeping, leisure or other activities are no longer affordable (interviews 2015). Moreover, even though the government has implemented social rental or discounts to gas and light bills to subsidize the poorest families and residents displaced by upgrading programs, these forms of assistance seem too basic to address the complex pressures and processes of gentrification and eviction.

Finally, representatives of the local government (through *Morar Carioca* projects) along with private investors have played a role in the physical eviction of residents living in green areas in Babilônia through a new type of economic discipline. While long-term residents initiated green space protection in the uphill areas of the community in the 2000s, a commercial shopping center in the South Zone now helps to finance its protection, maintenance, and promotion (interview 2015). Furthermore, the creation of this green space also included the eviction and relocation of some of the oldest residents and their homes that were labeled as being located in 'high risk' or 'protected areas,' which coincidently were the areas with the most attractive views in the community. While some residents relocated without much resistance, others lament the small size of new apartments and their loss of access to green space as they were moved downhill (interview 2016). This can be interpreted as environmental gentrification (Checker 2011; Anguelovski 2016) and 'white cleaning,' and reveals the role of private capital in ensuring the legibility of public and open spaces in the favela and in becoming a primary driving force behind municipal planning. In other words, the physical removal of uphill residents has allowed the privatization and enclosure of the green space for the benefit of investors and outside visitors, while previous residents have born the environmental costs. Green and open spaces have thus become landscapes of pleasure and privilege (Chu, Anguelovski, and Roberts 2017; Anguelovski, Irazabal, and Connolly in press) for visitors and newcomers through processes of securitization, privatization, and eviction. Today, aside from the abovementioned assistance for evicted residents or discounts in utility, no specific action – or even discussion – has been taken to address gentrification in Babilônia. Architects and members of the Neighborhood Association regret the lack of municipal action about exclusion and displacement, yet they consider the changes brought on by gentrification as inevitable:

> 'Our goal is to guarantee this favela has the right to turn the community into a neighborhood. Once we try to do it with more rationality, more quality, in the best way we can, it will attract others. We cannot do something with quality to be repulsive. It is not our job; it is contradictory. We want to improve the situation, and once we do it, gentrification happens. There must be government supervision in this process.'
>
> Architect working on upgrading projects in Babilônia and Chapeu Mangueira (2015)

Urban redevelopment in Rio illustrates sociospatial tensions present in many revitalized or revitalizing neighborhoods, where physical and environmental improvements can be captured by elites and reinforced by decisions made by urban designers and architects.

In early 2018, despite increasing confrontations between drug dealers and police forces, economic gentrification pressures have dissipated though not fully disappeared.

Residents highlight that this slowdown is only temporary until new developers return to the most appealing areas of Rio, which include favela communities in the hill of the South Zone. The current President of the Neighborhood Association highlights this readjustment in a longer process of neighborhood reevaluation and private value capture:

> 'The recent confrontations [violent events between alleged drug dealers and the police in 2018] – it's obvious, they interrupted the process of gentrification a bit . . . The UPP is now like a mirage [referring to the recent dismantling of the pacification project]. But of course, it's not over yet. We know that all over Europe, people who live "on the hill" are rich. Even more in prime areas. Only in Brazil is this the opposite. It's important to highlight that.'
>
> Neighborhood Association President (2018)

Over the long term, pressures from external capital seem to be much stronger than the ability of residents to resist real estate speculation and price increases, even if some of them participate in the new economy as small entrepreneurs. Our analysis reveals that only external entrepreneurs and a few residents are able to harness benefits from new economic opportunities. The current governance regime in Rio far from guarantees the implementation of a redistributive agenda, thus facilitating silent and more acute forms of spatial segregation and social exclusion.

DISCUSSION: PRODUCING DISPOSSESSION, INVISIBILIZATION, AND SEGREGATION THROUGH LEGIBILITY

Our study of public space upgrading in Babilônia contributes new insights on how capital-oriented urban planning strategies in the global South renew the role of the state inside self-built settlements, create new market visibility, and eventually produce social and cultural invisibilization and displacement. Since the 1990s and into the recent World Cup (2014) and Olympic Games (2016), government agents in Rio preached progressive urban governance paradigms such as transparency, equality, inclusion, and participation. However, our research shows that through informal settlement upgrading projects and pacification policies, such new paradigms mask policies that ultimately make spaces more legible to economic and social actors outside of the favela. Socio-spatial legibility is thus creating a very peculiar process of gentrification: one based on intersecting forms of physical, symbolic, and economic discipline.

In short, the concurrent processes of revitalization, enclosure, and policing of open spaces in favelas increase socio-spatial legibility, which then lead to displacement and erasure of local residents. The agents of legibility – which include the UPP (an organ of the state), outside investors, and tourists – can exert discipline according to myriad pathways to further particular and predefined forms of urban socio-spatiality and gentrification that residents, in turn, experience in ambiguous ways. State-led, top-down urban upgrading in Rio's favelas illustrates the key role played by state and private investors in boosting gentrification (Hackworth 2002; Smith 2002; Davidson 2008; Rousseau 2009; Lees 2012) and in molding and securing informal communities for the consumption behavior of outsiders. Such efforts are a means to reclaim and rebrand the city for businesses, middle classes, and market forces more generally, with important impacts on long-term residents, many of them Afro-Brazilian residents.

From a theoretical standpoint, contemporary approaches to favela public space upgrading entail a double process of co-creating securitization and segregation through environmental clean-up, upgrades and enclosure, and police violence in which the most socially and racially fragile residents are slowly being re-criminalized and dispossessed. First, upgrades in public spaces, along with a militarized permanent police presence in the community, have played a major role in coercing and oppressing residents to create a more legible community. Investments in environmental protection and the removal of residents from green spaces are accelerating this process. Although Babilônia is not traditionally marked by violent conflicts, recent events show that the environment inside Rio's favelas is unstable and that physical tensions are increasingly acute. In October 2016, for instance, immediately after the Olympic Games, local newspapers announced that conflicts between the police and locals ended in two deaths in Chapeu Mangueira. In 2017, many newspapers in the city alleged that rival criminal factions were already disputing the territory. In April 2018, confrontations between criminals led to a Special Operations Command action inside the hill of Babilônia. Even if many residents first experienced increased security in the favelas and outside acceptance due to the UPP pacification programs, they have also witnessed or lived through discriminatory practices and race-based persecution, which indicates a practice of state revanchism (see Smith 2005) towards Afro-Brazilian and low-income residents. The early presence of the UPP combined with upgrading interventions helped secure the path for gentrification and direct physical eviction from and militarized control of restored public and green spaces.

Second, physical upgrades to public space through UPP actions and upgrading programs like *Morar Carioca* are reshaping community life in subtler ways, interfering with endogenous cultural and traditional manifestations – such as *Baile Funk* – through processes of securitization, control, and order. Our findings indicate that UPP officers tend to symbolically discipline residents and their practices by favoring events and parties organized by gentrifiers or for tourists, while more local events (far from the touristic path created by the upgrading programs) often do not receive approval. As a result, socio-cultural practices of Afro-Brazilian residents, in particular, become invisibilized, erased, or dispossessed. Finally, alliances between the state and market have created new types of economic discipline, a more visible manifestation of gentrification that is rapidly increasing rent and real estate prices throughout the community. While several residents have become entrepreneurs, changes from within the community may be occurring faster than a majority of the residents can adapt to, and such changes have subsequently shifted community activism away from land tenure demands.

Our analysis helps to theorize how capital-oriented slum upgrading and socio-spatial control in favelas can enable a revanchist city through a dialectic process of creation (of new public spaces and new legibility) and destruction (of practices, of symbols, and of local values). The apparent integration of the formal and informal city, of the rich and the poor, and of the 'asphalt' and the 'hill' is producing a new form of separation and fragmentation between them, either through public space use and police control in the short-term or through longer-term affordability threats. These experiences have brought on new socio-spatial and racial tensions that are in turn obliterating traditional socio-cultural manifestations in favelas. New regulations – together with sanitized and green images of favelas – are slowly threatening residents' right to their own neighborhoods by controlling residents' daily behavior and movement through the space, undermining established social and cultural practices, and debilitating their ability to resist land speculation.

From a policy standpoint, our study reveals that pacification, reinvestment, and gentrification can result in the bifurcation of space into the 'marginal' and into the 'gentrified', where in fact the two can exist simultaneously and in the same militarized space. The various manifestations of gentrification are reconfiguring the meanings, uses, and controls of public space while producing state/market legibility, environmental privilege, physical control, social cleansing, and economic restructuring. As the UPP secures gentrification and protects middle-class and/or white gentrifiers, they sanitize, repress, and exclude the most marginalized residents and then reshape a green, clean, and secure landscape for outsiders and their leisure practices.

In other words, rendering the natural and social environment of the favela more legible to state and market control has transformed them into an object of discourse remaking, discipline, and control in which gentrification plays a central role.

In that context, future research on gentrification in the global South must further unpack how a combination of improvements to the built and natural environment in self-built settlements come together to produce contested values upon which groups are competing in local spaces – within and across neighborhoods. It should explore how residents navigate, re-appropriate, or contest the converging public and private interests in redeveloping, formalizing, and (re)racializing informal settlements. Last, new theoretical and empirical lenses are needed to understand how the re-militarization of self-built/informal settlements is transforming and shifting capital accumulation while avoiding important questions at the intersection of social redistribution, economic empowerment, and cultural and racial reparation.

ACKNOWLEDGEMENTS

The authors would like to thank all the residents and activists from various Babilônia communities for sharing their time and lived experiences with us. We also thank staff members from RioOnWatch for their guidance, expertise, and support offered during our field research. We also acknowledge the Universitat Internacional de Catalunya for supporting the original Master's thesis fieldwork upon which the initial part of this paper was based.

DISCLOSURE STATEMENT

No potential conflict of interest was reported by the authors.

FUNDING

This research contributes to the Maria de Maetzu Unit of Excellence grant (MDM-2015–0552) at the Institute for Environmental Science and Technology (ICTA) within the Universitat Auto'noma de Barcelona (UAB). Isabelle Anguelovski acknowledges the support of the Ramon y Cajal fellowship (RYC-2014–15870) and the

ERC Starting Grant GREENLULUS (GA678034). Eric Chu acknowledges research travel support from the Department of Geography, Planning and International Development Studies at the University of Amsterdam. Thaisa Comelli acknowledges the support of CAPES (Coordination for the Improvement of Higher Level Education Personnel – Brazil) and CNPq (Brazilian National Council for Scientific and Technological Development).

NOTES

1. In this article, we use the generic terms 'slums' and 'informal settlements' because of their strong presence in the international popular and academic literature. However, we recognize the prejudice that may come attached to such words, and also to the fact that they encompass a variety of different urban settlements (with different degrees of informality, construction quality, or even economic status). We also used the word 'favela' since it is the local term in Brazil, where the case study is located.
2. Our understanding of public spaces for this study is broad, encompassing more traditional public spaces (which are less common in favelas) such as plazas, decks, streets, stairways, and even private spaces for public use.
3. See official government webpage dedicated to the legacy of the 2016 Olympic Games: www.brasil2016.gov.br/pt-br/legado/morar-carioca. Last accessed on 16 May 2018.
4. Although *Morar Carioca* provided some new housing developments, it was not the focus of the program. To address housing deficit in Brazil, the federal government launched the program *Minha Casa Minha Vida* (My House My Life) in 2009, one year before *Morar Carioca*.
5. Information sourced from local real estate websites (www.zapimoveis.com.br and www.nestoria.com.br).
6. See: https://riotimesonline.com/brazil-news/rioreal-estate/brazils-real-estate-sales-rise-9-4-in-2017/.
7. See https://riotimesonline.com/brazil-news/rio-real-estate/brazil-real-estate-prices-down-for-8th-consecutive-month-in-august/.
8. During the period of slavery in Brazil, *senzalas* were the places where slaves were housed.
9. Traditional funk parties such as *Baile da Favorita* used to take place in the favela of Rocinha, but now have special editions in private clubs in Monte L´ıbano, a wealthy recreation area in Leblon.
10. During our first visit, tours were held by community-based associations and private companies. Recently, even community-based touristic activities have ceased.

REFERENCES

Alsayyad, N., and A. Roy. 2009. "Modernidade medieval: cidadania e urbanismo na era global." *Novos Estudos – CEBRAP* 85: 105–128.

Alves, M., and P. Evanson. 2011. *Living in the Crossfire: Favela Residents, Drug Dealers, and Police Violence in Rio de Janeiro*. Philadelphia: Temple University Press.

Anguelovski, I. 2016. "From Toxic Sites to Parks as (Green) LULUs? New Challenges of Inequity, Privilege, Gentrification, and Exclusion for Urban Environmental Justice." *Journal of Planning Literature* 31 (1): 23–36.

Anguelovski, I., C. Irazabal, and J. J. Connolly. in press. "Grabbed Urban Landscapes: Sociospatial Tensions in Green Infrastructure Planning in Medellín." *International Journal of Urban and Regional Research*.

Atkinson, R., and G. Bridge. 2005. *Gentrification in a Global Context*. New York: Routledge.

Baiocchi, G. 2003. "Emergent Public Spheres: Talking Politics in Participatory Governance." *American Sociological Review* 68 (1): 52–74.

Baiocchi, G., P. Heller, M. K. Silva, and M. Silva. 2011. *Bootstrapping Democracy: Transforming Local Governance and Civil Society in Brazil*. Stanford: Stanford University Press.

Benz, T. 2016. "Urban Mascots and Poverty Fetishism: Authenticity in the Postindustrial City." *Sociological Perspectives* 59 (2): 460–478.

Bernt, M. 2016. "Very Particular, or Rather Universal? Gentrification Through the Lenses of Ghertner and López-Morales." *City* 20 (4): 637–644.

Blanco, C., and H. Kobayashi. 2009. "Urban Transformation in Slum Districts through Public Space Generation and Cable Transportation at Northeastern Area: Medellin, Colombia." *Journal of International Social Research* 2 (8): 75–90.

Bodnar, J. 2015. "Reclaiming Public Space." *Urban Studies* 52 (12): 2090–2104.

Cano, I. 2012. *Os donos do morro: Uma avaliac¸a˜o exploratœria do impacto das Unidades de Pol´ıtica Pacificadora (UPPs) no Rio de Janeiro*. Rio de Janeiro: FBSP/Lav-UERJ.

Cavalcanti, M. 2009. "Do barraco a' casa: tempo, espac¸o e valor(es) em uma favela consolidada." [From Shanty to House: Time, Space and Value(s) in a Consolidated Favela.] *Revista Brasileira de Cieˆncias Sociais* 24: 69–80.

Checker, M. 2011. "Wiped Out by the 'Greenwave': Environmental Gentrification and the Paradoxical Politics of Urban Sustainability." *City & Society* 23 (2): 210–229.

Cheema, G. S., and D. A. Rondinelli. 2007. *Decentralizing Governance: Emerging Concepts and Practices*. Washington, DC: Brookings Institution Press.

Chu, E., I. Anguelovski, and D. Roberts. 2017. "Climate Adaptation as Strategic Urbanism: Assessing Opportunities and Uncertainties for Equity and Inclusive Development in Cities." *Cities* 60: 378–387.

Clark, E. 2005. "The Order and Simplicity of Gentrification: A Political Challenge." In *Gentrification in a Global Context*, 256–264. London: Routledge.

Colona, F., and R. Jaffe. 2016. "Hybrid Governance Arrangements." *The European Journal of Development Research* 28 (2): 175–183.

Conde, L. P., and S. Magalhaes. 2004. *Favela-Bairro: uma outra história da cidade do Rio de Janeiro*. Vol. 1. Rio de Janeiro: ViverCidades.

Cummings, J. 2015. "Confronting Favela Chic: The Gentrification of Informal Settlements in Rio de Janeiro, Brazil." In *Global Gentrifications: Uneven Development and Displacement*, edited by L. Lees, H. Shin, and E. López-Morales, 81–99. Bristol: Policy Press.

Davidson, M. 2008. "Spoiled Mixture: Where Does Stateled 'Positive' Gentrification End?" *Urban Studies* 45 (12): 2385–2405.

Davis, D. E. 2009. "Non-state Armed Actors, New Imagined Communities, and Shifting Patterns of Sovereignty and Insecurity in the Modern World." *Contemporary Security Policy* 30 (2): 221–245.

Davis, M. 2006. *Planet of Slums*. London and New York: Verso.

de Souza, L. 2008. *Fobópole: o medo generalizado e a militarizaçãoda questão urbana*. Rio de Janeiro: Bertrand Brasil.

Fagerlande, S. 2018. "Grandes eventos esportivos: impactos nas favelas do Rio de Janeiro." *Bitácora Urbano Territorial* 28 (2): 143–151.

Fainstein, S. 2010. *The Just City*. Ithaca: Cornell University Press.

FGV (FundaçãoGetúlio Vargas). 2012. *Indicadores socioeconómicos nas UPPs do Estado do Rio de Janeiro*. Rio de Janeiro: FGV.

Freeman, J., and M. Burgos. 2017. "Accumulation by Forced Removal: The Thinning of Rio de Janeiro's Favelas in Preparation for the Games." *Journal of Latin American Studies* 49 (3): 549–577.

Frenzel, F., and K. Koens. 2012. "Slum Tourism: Developments in a Young Field of Interdisciplinary Tourism Research." *Tourism Geographies* 14 (2): 195–212.

Gaffney, C. 2010. "Mega-events and Socio-Spatial Dynamics in Rio de Janeiro, 1919–2016." *Journal of Latin American Geography* 9: 7–29.

Ghertner, D. A. 2015. "Why Gentrification Theory Fails in 'Much of the World'." *City* 19: 552–563.

Gonçalves, R. 2005. "O mercado de aluguel nas favelas cariocas e sua regularizaçãonuma perspectiva histórica." [The Rent Market in Rio de Janeiro's Favelas and Their Regulation from a Historical Perspective]. *GEOgraphia* 13 (26): 114–135.

Gonçalves, R. 2013. *Favelas do Rio de Janeiro: história e direito*. Rio de Janeiro: Pallas/PUC-Rio.

Graham, S. 2012. "The New Military Urbanism." In *The New Blackwell Companion to the City*, 121–133. Oxford: Wiley-Blackwell.

Grindle, M. S. 2009. *Going Local: Decentralization, Democratization, and the Promise of Good Governance*. Princeton: Princeton University Press.

Gwynne, R. N., and C. Kay, eds. 2004. *Latin America Transformed: Globalization and Modernity*. London: Hodder Education.

Hackworth, J. 2002. "Postrecession Gentrification in New York City." *Urban Affairs Review* 37 (6): 815–843.

Handzic, K. 2010. "Is Legalized Land Tenure Necessary in Slum Upgrading? Learning From Rio's Land Tenure Policies in the Favela Bairro Program." *Habitat International* 34 (1): 11–17.

Harvey, D. 1989. "From Managerialism to Entrepreneurialism: The Transformation in Urban Governance in Late Capitalism." *Geografiska Annaler: Series B, Human Geography* 71 (1): 3–17.

Harvey, D. 2004. "The 'New Imperialism': Accumulation by Dispossession." *Actuel Marx* 35 (1): 71–90.

Heller, P. 2001. "Moving the State: The Politics of Democratic Decentralization in Kerala, South Africa, and Porto Alegre." *Politics & Society* 29 (1): 131–163.

Hérnandez-Medina, E. 2010. "Social Inclusion through Participation: The Case of the Participatory Budget in São Paulo." *International Journal of Urban and Regional Research* 34: 512–532.

Janoschka, M., J. Sequera, and L. Salinas. 2014. "Gentrification in Spain and Latin America – A Critical Dialogue." *International Journal of Urban and Regional Research* 38: 1234–1265.

Jones, G. A., and R. Sanyal. 2015. "Spectacle and Suffering: The Mumbai Slum as a Worlded Space." *Geoforum* 65: 431–439.

Kearns, A., and R. Paddison. 2000. "New Challenges for Urban Governance." *Urban Studies* 37 (5–6): 845–850.

Kuffer, M., and J. Barrosb. 2011. "Urban Morphology of Unplanned Settlements: The Use of Spatial Metrics in VHR Remotely Sensed Images." *Procedia Environmental Sciences* 7: 152–157.

Lees, L. 2012. "The Geography of Gentrification. Thinking Through Comparative Urbanism." *Progress in Human Geography* 36 (2): 155–171.

Lees, L., H. B. Shin, and E. López-Morales, eds. 2015. *Global Gentrifications: Uneven Development and Displacement.* Bristol: Policy Press.

Lees, L., H. B. Shin, and E. López-Morales. 2016. *Plane-tary Gentrification.* Malden: John Wiley & Sons.

Lefebvre, H. 1991. *The Production of Space.* Oxford: Wiley-Blackwell.

Lefebvre, H. [1970] 2003. *The Urban Revolution.* Minneapolis: University of Minnesota Press.

Leitão, G., and J. Delecave. 2013. "O programa Morar Carioca: novos rumos na urbanizac͵aõdas favelas cariocas?" *O Social em Questão* 1 (29): 265–284.

Leite, M. P. 2000. "Entre o individualismo e a solidariedade: dilemas da pol´ıtica e da cidadania no Rio de Janeiro." *Revista Brasileira de Cieˆncias Sociais* 15: 73–90.

Leitner, H., J. Peck, and E. S. Sheppard, eds. 2007. *Contesting Neoliberalism: Urban Frontiers.* New York: Guilford Press.

Ley, D., and S. Y. Teo. 2014. "Gentrification in Hong Kong? Epistemology vs. Ontology." *International Journal of Urban and Regional Research* 38 (4): 1286–1303.

López-Morales, E. 2015. "Gentrification in the Global South." *City* 19 (4): 564–573.

Lynch, K. 1960. *The Image of the City.* Cambridge, MA: MIT Press.

Magalhães, A. 2013. "O 'legado' dos megaeventos esportivos: a reatualizac͵aõda remoc͵aõde favelas no Rio de Janeiro." *Horizontes Antropológicos* 19: 89–118.

Maharaj, B. 2015. "The Turn of the South? Social and Economic Impacts of Mega-Events in India, Brazil and South Africa." *Local Economy* 30 (8): 983–999.

Maloutas, T. 2012. "Contextual Diversity in Gentrification Research." *Critical Sociology* 38 (1): 33–48.

Mascarenhas, G. 2014. "Cidade mercadoria, cidade-vitrine, cidade turística: a espetacularizac͵aõdo urbano nos megaeventos esportivos." *Caderno Virtual de Turismo* 14 (1): 52–65.

McConnachie, M. M., and C. M. Shackleton. 2010. "Public Green Space Inequality in Small Towns in South Africa." *Habitat International* 34: 244–248.

Minnery, J., T. Argo, H. Winarso, D. Hau, C. C. Veneracion, D. Forbes, and I. Childs. 2013. "Slum Upgrading and Urban Governance: Case Studies in Three South East Asian Cities." *Habitat International* 39: 162–169.

Misse, M. 2007. "Mercados ilegais, redes de protec͵aõe organizac͵aõlocal do crime no Rio de Janeiro." *Estudos Avanc͵ados* 21 (61): 139–157.

Moncada, E. 2013. "The Politics of Urban Violence: Challenges for Development in the Global South." *Studies in Comparative International Development* 48 (3): 217–239.

Nuijten, M., M. Koster, and P. de Vries. 2012. "Regimes of Spatial Ordering in Brazil: Neoliberalism, Leftist Populism and Modernist Aesthetics in Slum Upgrading in Recife." *Singapore Journal of Tropical Geography* 33 (2): 157–170.

Perlman, J. 1977. *O mito da marginalidade: favelas e polı́ca no Rio de Janeiro.* Rio de Janeiro: Paz e Terra.

Perlman, J. 2010. *Favela: Four Decades of Living on the Edge in Rio de Janeiro.* Oxford: Oxford University Press.

Pearlman, J. 2016. "The Formalization of Informal Real Estate Transactions in Rio's Favelas." In *Slums: How Informal Real Estate Markets Work*, edited by E. Birch, S. Chattaraj, and S. Wachter, 58–82. Philadelphia: University of Pennsylvania Press.

Pierre, J. 1999. "Models of Urban Governance: The Institutional Dimension of Urban Politics." *Urban Affairs Review* 34 (3): 372–396.

Ramadier, T., and G. Moser. 1998. "Social Legibility, the Cognitive Map and Urban Behaviour." *Journal of Environmental Psychology* 18 (3): 307–319.

Robinson, J. 2011. "Cities in a World of Cities: The Comparative Gesture." *International Journal of Urban and Regional Research* 35: 1–23.

Rodgers, D. 2012. "Haussmannization in the Tropics: Abject Urbanism and Infrastructural Violence in Nicaragua." *Ethnography* 13 (4): 413–438.

Rolnik, R. 2011. "Democracy on the Edge: Limits and Possibilities in the Implementation of an Urban Reform Agenda in Brazil." *International Journal of Urban and Regional Research* 35: 239–255.

Rousseau, M. 2009. "Re-imaging the City Centre for the Middle Classes: Regeneration, Gentrification and Symbolic Policies in 'Loser Cities'." *International Journal of Urban and Regional Research* 33 (3): 770–788.

Roy, A. 2011a. "Urbanisms, Worlding Practices and the Theory of Planning." *Planning Theory* 10 (1): 6–15.

Roy, A. 2011b. "Slumdog Cities: Rethinking Subaltern Urbanism." *International Journal of Urban and Regional Research* 35: 223–238.

Rubino, S. 2005. "A Curious Blend? City Revitalization, Gentrification and Commodification in Brazil." In *Gentrification in a Global Context: The New Urban Colonialism*, edited by R. Atkinson and G. Bridge, 225–240. London: Routledge.

Samara, T. R. 2010. "Policing Development: Urban Renewal as Neo-Liberal Security Strategy." *Urban Studies* 47 (1): 197–214.

Sánchez, F., and A. Broudehoux. 2013. "Mega-events and Urban Regeneration in Rio de Janeiro: Planning in a State of Emergency." *International Journal of Urban Sustainable Development* 5 (2): 132–153.

Sassen, S. 2018. *Cities in a World Economy*. London: Sage Publications.

Scott, J. C. 1999. *Seeing Like a State: How Certain Schemes to Improve the Human Condition Have Failed*. New Haven, CT: Yale University Press.

Silvestre, G., and N. de Oliveira. 2012. "The Revanchist Logic of Mega-Events: Community Displacement in Rio de Janeiro's West End." *Visual Studies* 27 (2): 204–210.

Slater, T. 2009. "Missing Marcuse: On Gentrification and Displacement." *City* 13 (2–3): 292–311.

Smith, N. 2002. "New Globalism, New Urbanism: Gentrification as Global Urban Strategy." *Antipode* 34: 427–450.

Smith, N. 2005. *The New Urban Frontier: Gentrification and the Revanchist City*. London: Routledge.

Swyngedouw, E. 2005. "Governance Innovation and the Citizen: The Janus Face of Governance-Beyond-the-State." *Urban Studies* 42 (11): 1991–2006.

Taylor, L., and D. Broeders. 2015. "In the Name of Development: Power, Profit and the Datafication of the Global South." *Geoforum* 64: 229–237.

UN-Habitat. 2013. *Streets as Public Spaces and Drivers of Urban Prosperity*. Nairobi: United Nations Human Settlements Programme.

Vainer, C. 2011. "Cidade de Exceçaõ: reflexões a partir do Rio de Janeiro." [City of Exception: Reflections from Rio de Janeiro]. *Anais do Encontro Nacional da ANPUR* 14.

Waley, P. 2016. "Speaking Gentrification in the Languages of the Global East." *Urban Studies* 53 (3): 615–625.

Walton, J. 1998. "Urban Conflict and Social Movements in Poor Countries: Theory and Evidence of Collective Action." *International Journal of Urban and Regional Research* 22 (3): 460–481.

Wampler, B. 2010. *Participatory Budgeting in Brazil: Contestation, Cooperation, and Accountability*. Philadelphia: Penn State Press.

Wampler, B., and L. Avritzer. 2004. "Participatory Publics: Civil Society and New Institutions in Democratic Brazil." *Comparative Politics* 36: 291–312.

Watson, V. 2009. "Seeing From the South: Refocusing Urban Planning on the Globe's Central Urban Issues." *Urban Studies* 46 (11): 2259–2275.

Weyland, K. 1999. "Neoliberal Populism in Latin America and Eastern Europe." *Comparative Politics* 31: 379–401.

WHO. 2010. *Hidden Cities: Unmasking and Overcoming Health Inequities in Urban Settings*. Geneva and Kobe: World Health Organization.

Willis, G. D. 2015. *The Killing Consensus: Police, Organized Crime, and the Regulation of Life and Death in Urban Brazil*. Berkeley: University of California Press.

16
Housing transformation, rent gap and gentrification in Ghana's traditional houses

Insight from compound houses in Bantama, Kumasi

Lewis Abedi Asante and Richmond Juvenile Ehwi

INTRODUCTION

Housing is one of the most basic human needs and can have a profound impact on the happiness, lifestyle, self-esteem, and productivity of an individual (Alagbe & Aduwo, 2014). This notwithstanding, the delivery of adequate housing to urban dwellers has been a considerable challenge for national governments in many developing countries (Addo, 2013). In Africa, state withdrawal from direct housing provision coupled with a growing urban population has created a substantial housing shortfall (Arku, 2006; Asante et al., 2018). For instance, Ghana's housing gap is estimated to be between 70,000 to 120,000 units annually (World Bank, 2014). This high housing gap has compelled most urban dwellers to live in multi-habited compound houses provided by private landlords (Addo, 2016; Obeng-Odoom & Amedzro, 2011).

The compound house is the oldest and most familiar form of housing in West Africa (Afram, 2007). In the 1960s, most low income Ghanaians lived in compound houses (Korboe, 1992). Recently, compound houses accounted for 51.5 percent of all houses in Ghana (Ghana Statistical Service, 2012) and have recorded the highest annual growth of all house types, at 5.5 percent between 2000 and 2010 (Ghana Statistical Service, 2014b). Nevertheless, studies have described dwelling units – accommodation or rooms occupied by a single household – in compound houses as inadequate because they tend to be poorly maintained, overcrowded, and lack some basic amenities (Addo, 2013). Moreover, access to shared facilities such as standpipes, toilets, kitchens, and bathrooms in compound houses has been associated with numerous problems, including long queues and squabbles (Adu-Gyamfi et al., 2020).

In tackling these problems, many private landlords in Ghana have recently been transforming the ordinary dwelling units in their compound houses into apartment dwelling units. This transformation has largely focused on providing exclusive access to toilet, bathroom and kitchen facilities for tenants, thereby reducing the sharing of facilities. A new large-scale study has shown a marked housing transformation in urban and rural Sub-Saharan Africa between 2000 and 2015, doubling the prevalence of improved housing (Tusting et al., 2019). Tipple (1996) argues that housing transformation contributes to urban environments in ways that are beneficial to the aims of sustainable development. He indicates that housing transformation is an effective mechanism of housing supply; makes efficient use of existing finite resources; improves the social, economic, and environmental quality of the living environment; adds value to existing buildings and increases the potential property tax base (Tipple, 1996). Furthermore, housing transformation has

DOI: 10.4324/9781003341239-24

also been identified as an important intervention in achieving the United Nations Sustainable Development Goal 11, which aims for universal access to adequate, safe, and affordable housing by 2030.

The primary objective of this study is to scrutinize how the transformation of dwelling units is changing the characteristics of compound houses in Bantama. Furthermore, the study examines the rent gap that is realized through the transformation of dwelling units in compound houses in Bantama's residential market. Lastly, the article analyzes the consequences of the local practice of advance rent – a lumpsum rental payment – and socio-cultural norms for rent gap and gentrification in compound houses in Bantama.

This paper fills a critical knowledge gap in housing and urban studies literature in two crucial ways. Firstly, most of the existing literature in developing countries has focused on the transformation of public housing or government estates (Alagbe & Aduwo, 2014; Avogo et al., 2017; Tipple et al., 2004). These studies argue that transformation in public housing is driven by residents' dissatisfaction with the spaces within their dwelling units (Avogo et al., 2017). Therefore, transformation takes place by improving housing conditions and providing accommodations for family members to live rent-free and for outsiders to rent (Tipple, 1999; Tipple et al., 2004). Housing transformation in traditional compound houses has yet to be explored, as the literature has tended to focus on the design and physical characteristics of compound houses (Korboe, 1992), the tenure dynamics and support networks of households (Acheampong, 2016), and the monopolistic behaviour of private landlords demanding long periods of advance rent (Adu-Gyamfi et al., 2020; Arku et al., 2012; Ehwi et al., 2020).

Secondly, recent studies have drawn attention to how increasing land values in the city centre of Kumasi is driving the conversion of compound houses from residential to commercial use and hence causing gentrification (Cobbinah et al., 2019; Twumasi-Ampofo & Oppong, 2016). These studies, however, do not empirically focus on the transformation that takes place in compound houses without a change of use, and the factors that drive such transformation. The closest study to this paper is by Awanyo et al. (2016) who analyzed the social relations of production and consumption of houses and rooms within the capitalist housing market in the Greater Accra region and identified the beneficiaries of housing transformation. They argue that housing transformation is an integral part of the broader processes of the urban housing market in the Greater Accra region, which are fueled by the growing prominence of the middle-class.

Drawing on empirical insights from Bantama in Kumasi, this paper focuses on the transformation taking place in traditional compound housing. It argues that this transformation is altering some of the known characteristics of compound houses, namely the dwelling unit, the sharing arrangements regarding communal amenities, and the social composition of households. It further examines the huge rent gap that emerges following the transformation and how it impacts the household composition in such transformed dwellings. We argue that the ongoing transformation in traditional compound houses in Bantama is consistent with the gentrification of Ghana's low-cost rental housing, as the transformed houses become attractive to higher-income groups, who outbid lower-income groups in terms of their ability to pay higher land rent.

The rest of the article is organized as follows. The next section reviews the characteristics of compound houses in West Africa. This is followed in Section three by a conceptualization of the nexus between housing transformation, rent gap, and gentrification. In Section four, we describe the study area and outline the research methods. Section five discusses the findings. The study is concluded in Section six.

THE CHARACTERISTICS OF COMPOUND HOUSES IN WEST AFRICA

Several studies have demonstrated that compound houses in West African cities and towns have three key features, namely, the types of accommodation, the shared space and facilities, and the housing class (Afram, 2007; Okeyinka, 2014). Firstly, the accommodations in compound houses are, conventionally, ordinary dwelling units of single rooms and/or chamber and hall[1] (Tipple et al., 1994). In terms of design, these dwelling units are arranged in a series of either single-banked or double-banked rooms in single or multi-storey compound houses. Single-banked implies that the courtyard is surrounded by all the dwelling units in the compound house (see Figure 1). Double-banked, also known as '*face me I face you*', means that all the dwelling units in the compound house are on both sides of a common lobby while the courtyard is at the rear of the building (see Figure 2). The open courtyards in most compound houses are square, rectangular or circular. However, it is also possible to find compound houses in West Africa without a courtyard. These different variations of compound houses can be found in many West African cities, particularly Accra, Kumasi and Lagos (Okeyinka, 2014; Tipple *et al.*, 1997).

Secondly, apart from the exclusive occupation of a dwelling unit, all households in the compound house share common facilities and space such as a toilet, kitchen, drying lines, water, and electricity meters and the open courtyard. The courtyard – conceptualized as the spatial arena where social interactions and inter-household activities are nurtured – is of particular importance to sociologists (Korboe, 1992). Owing to this design and living arrangement, compound houses foster a sense of community and support networks, which sharply contrasts with the more individualized lifestyles and associated living arrangements more typical in Western countries (Addo, 2013; Korboe, 1992). However, over the years, the sharing of common spaces and facilities has been at the centre of many problems in compound houses in urban Ghana. A study by Afram and Owusu (2006) is a case in point. The authors found that most tenants had a problem with the principle of equal sharing of electricity bills, especially when there are perceptions that some households use more electrical gadgets than others (See also Adu-Gyamfi *et al.*, 2020; Yankson, 2012a). The study further revealed tenants' frustrations with the long morning queues

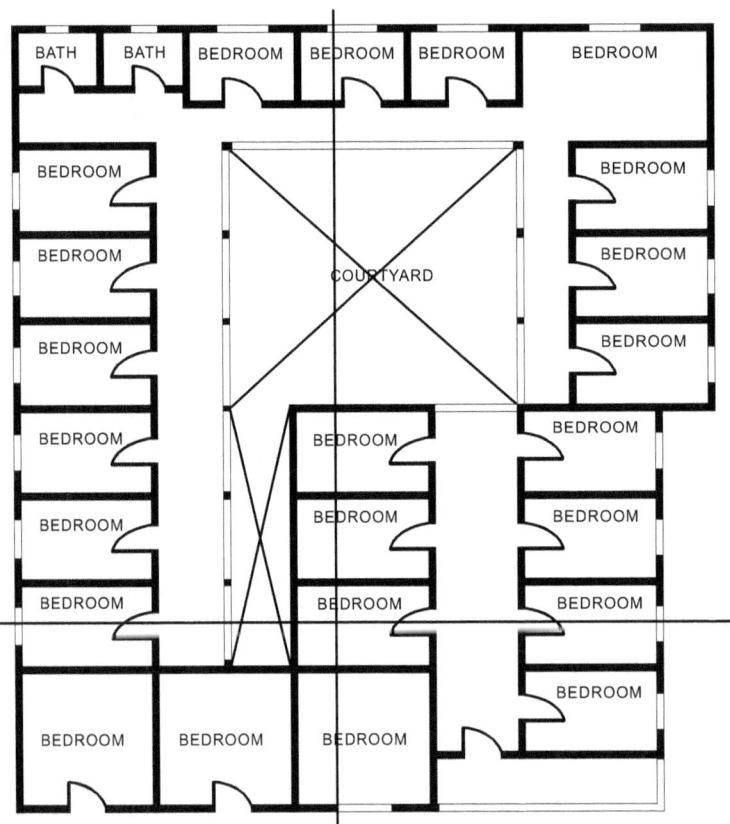

Figure 1 Floor Plan of a Double-Banked Compound House.

Source: Okeyinka (2014)

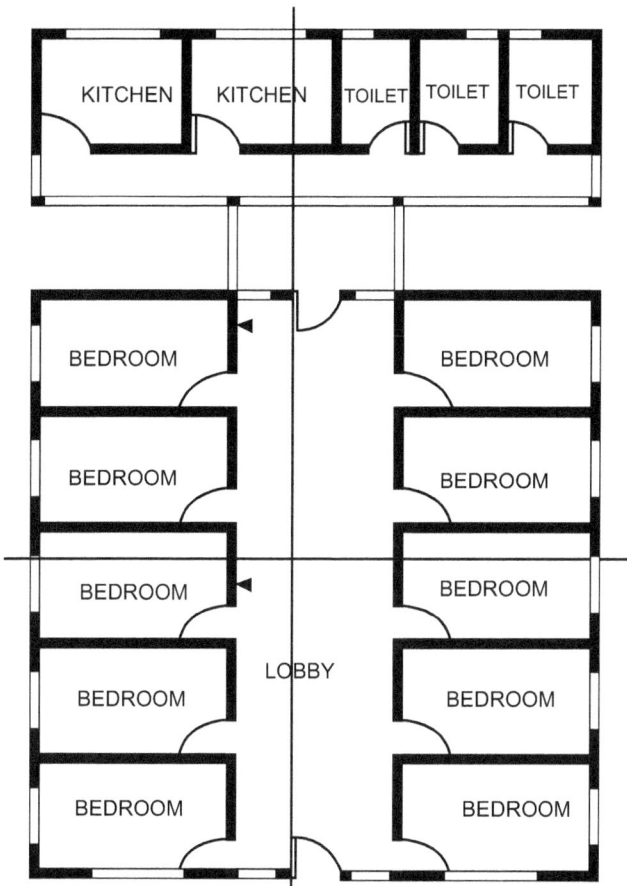

Figure 2 Floor Plan of a Single-Banked Compound House.
Source: Okeyinka (2014)

to use toilet and bathroom facilities, and the compulsion to do laundry on weekdays to avoid competition over the drying lines on weekends. While Addo (2013, 2016) acknowledges that the characteristics of dwelling units in compound houses have a negative impact on residential satisfaction of households, she also points out that households derived the most satisfaction from community support and neighbourhood characteristics, explaining why many households may wish to stay on in such dwelling units.

Lastly, compound houses, according to Addo (2013), provide accommodation for members of an extended family or persons who do not have any blood relations. She categorizes multi-habitation in compound houses into three groups, namely, sole occupation by members of an extended family, mixed habitation of both family members and non-family members, and shared houses exclusively occupied by non-related tenants (Addo, 2013). This article is concerned with the latter two household types. There is consensus in the literature that the compound house is the most familiar form of housing for low-income and less educated Ghanaians, most of whom work in the informal sector (Awanyo, 2009; Cobbinah *et al.*, 2019). Rents of dwelling units in compound houses are low because they are usually found in poor neighbourhoods characterized by deteriorating buildings, poor building plans, poor sanitation and drainage and inadequate maintenance, among others. However, Arku *et al.* (2012) indicate that compound houses are recently becoming the primary source of housing for all income groups due to the limited housing supply. Similarly, Owusu (2011) believes that the effect of economic liberalisation and globalisation have re-configured the housing supply and demand dynamics to the extent that rising rents are pushing middle-income earners

Income range	Income per month (in US$)	Maximum monthly rent levels affordable at rent to income ratio of 10%
No wage	0–9.02	–
Very Low	9.03–18.05	1.81
Low	18.06–90.25	9.03
Moderate	90.26–180.50	18.05
Middle	180.51–360.99	36.10
Mid-high	361–541.49	54.15
High	541.50–721.98	72.20
Very High	Above 721.98	90.25

Table 1 Income ranges and the levels of affordable rents in Ghana.
Source: World Bank (2014).

to settle for dwelling units in compound houses in urban areas. However, both Arku *et al.* (2012) and Owusu (2011) did not provide empirical data to support this assertion. Table 1 shows the different income groups in Ghana and the maximum monthly rents they can afford.[2] The paper argues that, conceptually, the transformation of dwelling units is changing the traditional characteristics of compound houses in Bantama.

CONCEPTUALIZING THE NEXUS BETWEEN HOUSING TRANSFORMATION, RENT GAP AND GENTRIFICATION

This paper situates the research problem within land economics theoretical perspectives of the processes and characteristics of housing redevelopment in cities around the world (Haila, 1990; Luque, 2015). From the 1960s to the 1990s, neoclassical and Marxist land economists differed on the relationship between housing transformation, rent increment and resultant gentrification. On the one hand, neoclassical economists argued that the industrial restructure from manufacturing to service-based industries in many cities around the world has changed the occupational class structure from one dominated by large manual working-class to white-collar managers and professionals (Hamnett, 2003; Ley, 1981). They argued that the consumption and lifestyle patterns of the young and middle-class professionals determined land-use decisions and the patterns of production in inner-cities (Butler, 1997). Consequently, the increment in the rental values of renovated and new houses and its associated gentrification reflect attempts by developers to meet the taste of high-income professionals and managers (Eduful & Hooper, 2015).

On the other hand, Marxist land economists argued that the mediating force between housing transformation and gentrification is not the new middle class but the widening rent gap between property and land values in the inner-city (Clark, 1988; Slater, 2017; Smith, 1987). This informed the development of the rent gap theory by Neil Smith, who argued that the movement of manufacturing industries from inner-cities to the suburbs was accompanied by a corresponding flight in investment as well as working-class abandonment of the core (Smith, 1979, 1987). The depreciation of housing capital in inner-cities led to a divergence between the capitalized ground rent (which is the amount of ground rent realized from the house in its current state) and the potential ground rent (which is the maximum amount of ground rent appropriated under highest and best use) (Slater, 2017; Smith, 1979). Therefore, the capital investment in housing transformation by property developers and its consequent displacement of low-income tenants in inner-cities should be understood as a strategy to exploit and close the rent gap. Following this revelation, Smith (1979, p. 538) argues that gentrification represents 'a back to city movement by capital and not people'.

Analysing both the consumption and production-driven explanations, Lees (1994, p. 148) asserted that the views of both neoclassical and Marxist land economists are valid and should be regarded as part of the same process. She further argues that 'juxtaposing a Marxist analysis with a cultural analysis allows political economy, culture and society to be considered together, enabling a more sensitive [and comprehensive] illustration of the gentrification process' (ibid). It is therefore not surprising that more recent analysis has observed both production-side and consumption-side theories of gentrification arising from housing redevelopment in cities (Eduful & Hooper, 2015). It is important to note that, while we draw

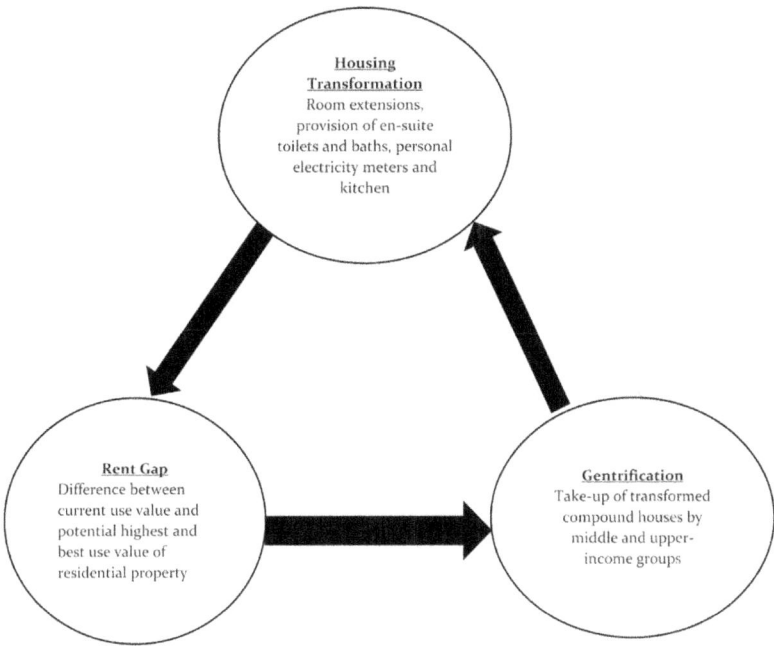

Figure 3 Conceptual framework.

insights from both camps to analyze the relationship between housing transformation, rent gap, and gentrification in Bantama (see Figure 3), we are more inclined towards Marxist theories as they offer important theoretical insights into the agencies of different social classes in the production and consumption of housing.

Like most concepts in housing studies, much of the discussion on housing transformation, rent gap, and gentrification has taken place in the Global North; but there is an emerging interest in these concepts in the Global South (Lees, 2012; Lemanski, 2014). The challenge, however, is that they have typically explored how housing transformation, rent gap, and gentrification has travelled from the Global North to the South (Eduful & Hooper, 2015; Lees et al., 2015, 2016). Scholars have criticized this kind of approach and analysis that seeks to project housing transformation, the rent gap and gentrification as global concepts, with the same characteristics everywhere in the world (Maloutas, 2012, 2018). Lemanski (2014) has argued that theories rooted in particular empirical locations should be enriched with contextual analysis elsewhere. Combining analysis of gentrification and downward raiding, she developed the concept of hybrid gentrification (Lemanski, 2014) and implores scholars working in the Global South to pay attention to the unique characteristics of their case studies, where they are located and how local exigencies contribute to the existing knowledge on housing transformation, the rent gap and gentrification. This article and the arguments it develops in subsequent sections is a response to this charge.

The historical analysis of housing transformation in most parts of Africa follows the concept of 'housing career' (Avogo et al., 2017; Tipple et al., 2004). Scholars argue that families continually evaluate their housing situation based on cultural (societal) and familial (personal) norms (Morris & Winter, 1975). When their housing situation does not meet these norms or desires, it creates dissatisfaction which produces a propensity to reduce the normative deficit (Avogo et al., 2017; Morris & Winter, 1975). Both landlords and tenants adopt various mechanisms to cope with these changing housing circumstances (Yankson, 2012b). Housing transformation is not only limited to landlords' extension or alteration of an existing building but also to tenants' adjustment of their housing needs. Therefore, housing transformation has both supply and demand dimensions.

Housing extension is one of the supply-side modes of transformation that landlords adopt to reduce the deficit. Initially, they undertake internal and external alterations to improve their housing circumstances, both in terms of the services they provide and the available space (Arku *et al.*, 2012; Asiama, 1984). This is mostly done to accommodate an increase in family size. As Adu-Gyamfi (2018) notes, individuals adjust housing foremost to accommodate their expanding families. Over time, landlords accommodate tenants when some family members move out due to marriage, employment and education, among other factors. Consequently, scholars argue that housing transformation could serve as an income-generating activity achieved through renting and home-based enterprises (Asiama, 1984; Avogo *et al.*, 2017). On the demand side, households begin their housing career by renting relatively small accommodations (Asante *et al.*, 2018). Initially, they are less concerned about living in sub-standard or overcrowded compound houses with shared facilities and spaces (Yankson, 2012b). However, as their income increases, they move upward along their housing careers by relocating from ordinary dwelling units with shared facilities to nearly self-contained apartments.

Consequently, the production behaviour of landlords and the consumption pattern of tenants influence the rents of dwelling units in cities. On the one hand, many landlords in inner-city neighbourhoods in West Africa own or occupy dwelling units whose latent values remain unrealized (Slater, 2017), partly because of disinvestment in the dwelling units and in the surrounding neighbourhood. This disinvestment is often attributed to the inadequacy of the rents landlords receive from low-income tenants, a proportion of which is used for their upkeep (Arku *et al.*, 2012; Slater, 2017). This has created a wide rent gap between the current rental value and the potential rental value, should transformation occur. Of late, some landlords are transforming their rental dwelling units to close the rent gap and to extract higher rent from prospective tenants (Eduful & Hooper, 2015). Following public choice theory, Owusu-Ansah *et al.* (2018) liken landlords' extraction of rents from tenants to how capitalists exploit workers. They note, however, that, while capitalists re-invest their profits in the capital accumulation process, landlords tend not to re-invest the rents extracted from tenants in the transformation of their houses. Therefore, landlords possess excessive rental power, which emerges from the nature of rent they extract from tenants. From the location of their property (differential rent 1), landlords obtain rental power from merely owning land in a location of superior quality; and from investment in location (differential rent 2), they acquire rental power which is often not proportionate with the amount they have invested (Hallett, 1979; Owusu-Ansah *et al.*, 2018).

On the other hand, tenants' preference to live a particular lifestyle is increasing the demand for improved housing. For instance, Addo (2013) note that the changing socio-economic conditions in African urban centres have resulted in the individualization of family systems in the twenty-first century. The individualized lifestyle increases the demand for housing transformation. Also, young professionals with relatively high disposable income and service-oriented jobs in urban areas are more likely to seek transformed rental properties than less educated and low-income households (Adarkwa & Oppong, 2005; Tusting *et al.*, 2019).

Transformed dwelling units usually command rent increases. This increment reflects how much tenants are willing and able to pay for transformed housing units and whether landlords will be motivated to invest in housing extensions in order to close the gap. As we will show in our findings, where the rent gap is big enough, gentrification will occur (Helbrecht, 2018; Lees *et al.*, 2015), implying that an increase in rent following housing transformation will force out low-income groups to make way for middle and high-income groups (Adarkwa & Oppong, 2005; Lees *et al.*, 2015).

A further issue worth mentioning is the practice of long advance rent payment. While rent in Ghana are mostly advertised per calendar months, private landlords require tenants to pay an initial lump-sum equivalent to two to five years rent (Ehwi *et al.*, 2020). Upon expiration of the first lease, tenants have to pay to another lump-sum for subsequent renewals, making rent a series of capital payments (Asante *et al.*, 2018). We argue that this local practice does not only increase rent on transformed dwelling units beyond what low-income tenants can afford, but also create competition among higher-income groups for the available transformed housing units.

Moreover, in the gentrification literature, it has been argued that 'so long as a tenant is capable of paying the rent on his room he is not prevented from taking up residence by other obstacles'

(Asiama, 1984, p. 182). However, we will learn in this paper that in a typical Kumasi setting, some landlords may prioritize societal values and cultural norms over the ability to pay advance rent. In a nutshell, this paper argues that the relationship between housing transformation, the rent gap and gentrification can be conceptualized as cyclical (see Figure 3). The case study of compound houses in Bantama, Kumasi provides insight into this relationship.

STUDY AREA

Kumasi is the second-largest city in Ghana and is located about 270 kilometres away from Accra, the national capital of Ghana. It doubles as the capital of the Kumasi Metropolitan Assembly and the Ashanti Region of Ghana. Kumasi has a population of about 1.8 million people and occupies a total land area of 254 square kilometres (Ghana Statistical Service, 2014a). Kumasi was chosen for this study for several reasons. The housing deficit in Kumasi alone constitutes 72 per cent of the entire housing deficit in the Ashanti region, implying that Kumasi is one of the cities in Ghana with the highest demand for housing (World Bank, 2014). Also, 54.9 per cent of all houses in Kumasi are compound houses (Ghana Statistical Service, 2014a). These compound houses are evenly spread across the ten sub-metropolitan areas in the city, namely Subin, Suame, Bantama, Tafo, Manhyia, Asawase, Oforikrom, Asokwa, Nhyiaeso and Kwadaso (Ghana Statistical Service, 2014a). However, the Bantama submetro was selected for this research due to the high density of compound houses in the community. Interestingly, Kumasi has been the case study site of numerous past studies on compound houses (Afram, 2007; Korboe, 1992) but none has explored housing transformation and its attendant rent gap and gentrification in the city. Figure 4 is a map of Kumasi metropolis showing Bantama.

Bantama has a total population of 35,294. It has 9,716 households who live in 2964 houses (Ghana Statistical Service, 2014a). Bantama is a residential and commercial area (see Figure 5). The Komfo Anokye Teaching Hospital, the biggest hospital in Kumasi, is in Bantama. It is approximately 1.65 km and about 14 minutes from Adum, the central business district of Kumasi in the north-western direction. Therefore, economic activities in the city centre have spilled over onto Bantama High Street, which extends from the Komfo Anokye Teaching Hospital to the western bypass over a distance of 1.9 km (Cobbinah *et al.*, 2019). A recent study by Cobbinah *et al.* (2019) has shown that many compound houses along Bantama High Street have been converted into commercial uses due to the flourishing economic activities along that stretch. We argue in the subsequent sections of the paper that dwelling units in compound houses in the residential neighbourhoods of Bantama are also being transformed into apartments.

METHODS

This research was conducted between November 2019 and January 2020. It adopted a qualitative research design to answer the three research questions posed. The research participants comprised three main groups who were purposively sampled because there is no systematic way of mapping compound houses that have undergone a transformation given that most of this transformation take place without recourse to formal planning processes. The first group of participants comprised estate agents in the Bantama sub-metro area who specialize in the rental and sale of properties. Only estate agents with at least five years of experience of working in Bantama's rental housing market were recruited, as they could draw on their local knowledge of Bantama and networks to help us identify specific compound houses that have recently undergone a transformation. Following their lead, 30 compound houses were identified, and the respective landlords of those properties alongside 34 tenants were recruited for this research.

We engaged with landlords because the research sought to understand the factors that led them to transform their compound houses into apartment complexes. For each compound house, we asked landlords about the total number of units in the property and how many have been transformed into self-contained apartments. We also inquired about the ownership structure of compound houses and how it shapes the transformation of dwelling units. We noticed that, in cases where the original owner of the compound house was alive, the rooms tended to be

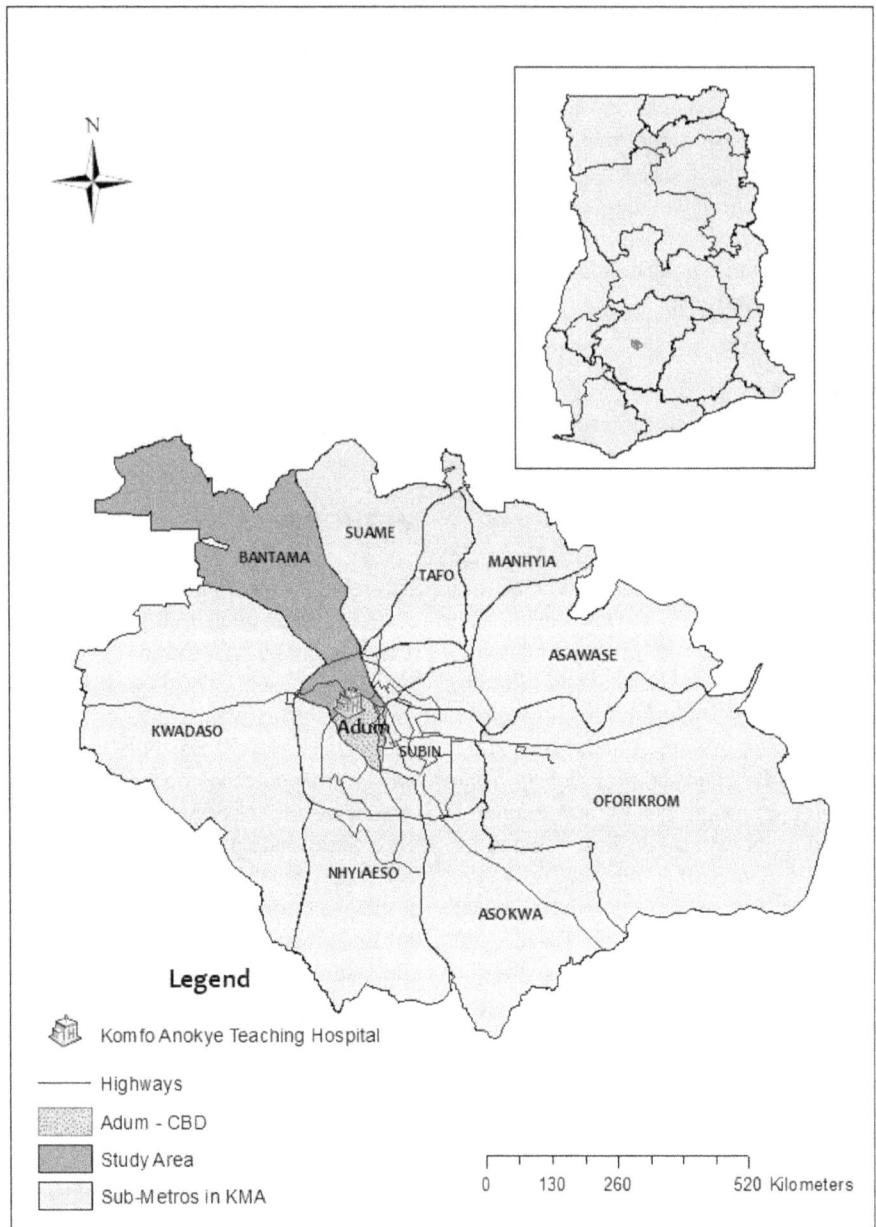

Figure 4 Map of Kumasi Metropolis showing the Bantama Sub-Metro.

transformed after the older children have moved out. In a situation where the original owner had passed away, each of the surviving children had generally been allocated rooms in the house through inheritance, although the collective right of ownership to the house fell to the head of the family, known in local parlance as *abusua panin* (Abubakari *et al.*, 2019a; Amole *et al.*, 1993).

Therefore, references to landlords within this article not only refer to people who hold the right of ownership of the whole compound house, but also to those who hold the right of ownership of a dwelling unit in the compound house. This point is important because some landlords participated in our research in the capacity of coowner of the compound house. We found, in some compound houses, that where a surviving child had been allocated two or more rooms, they lived in one (sometimes an ordinary dwelling unit) and transformed the other(s) for rental. It was also evident

A view of the Bantama High Street from the Komfo Anokye Teaching Hospital

A view of the residential neighourhoods in Bantama

Figure 5 An image of the commercial and residential precincts in Bantama.

in some cases that surviving children moved out of the house completely, and either transformed their allocated unit or left it in its ordinary state for rental.

We also sought to understand how tenants are grappling with the financial obligations that come with living in a transformed rental dwelling. All interviews were conducted on weekends and evenings, and each lasted between 30 to 45 minutes. Interviews were also audio-taped with respondents' consent. The audiotapes were transcribed and analyzed thematically. The interviews were complemented by participant observation of the housing situation within the compound houses and some photographs were taken as evidence. The analysis followed a 5-stage process of transcript analysis outlined by Morris (2015), which entails the following: firstly, a careful review of all transcripts and note-taking. Secondly, noting all the important quotes in the transcripts. Thirdly, coding and identification of the major themes, and fourthly, selecting the main themes for the write-up. Finally, the findings were interpreted, analysed and discussed. In discussing our findings, respondents were identified with the following pseudonyms: EA for Estate Agent, PL for Private Landlord, MT for Male Tenant and FT for Female Tenant.

Our tenant respondents comprised 26 males and eight females. The majority (78 per cent) of the tenants were aged between 23 to 45 years while the remaining were either below 23 years or above 45 years. Furthermore, 22 of the tenant respondents were married, whereas the remaining eight were either single, divorced or widowed. The average household size was three.

Concerning the landlords, they comprised 19 males and 11 females. Three landlords were single while the rest were either married, divorced or widowed. Nine landlords were aged between 31 to 38 years, having become landlords through inheritance. The remaining 21 were aged 48 years and above. The average age of the landlords is 52 years. It was found that the younger landlords were more educated than the older ones: of the younger landlords, 5 were educated up to senior secondary school and three up to tertiary level, while 14 of the older landlords had only primary education and a further 7 had no formal education. As a result, the elderly landlords who are in the majority were either engaged in low-income generating activities (specifically home-based petty trading) or were unemployed while their younger counterparts were involved in teaching, craft and administrative activities.

TRANSFORMATION IN COMPOUND HOUSES IN BANTAMA

Exclusive access to facilities

Bantama has a good mix of single-banked, double-banked, single and multi-storey compound houses, just like in other sub-metros in Kumasi. There was a total of 265 dwelling units in the selected 30 compound houses in Bantama, representing an average of 9 dwelling units per house. Of the total number of dwelling units, 173 representing 65.28% have been transformed into apartment units while the remaining 34.72% are ordinary units. Ordinary dwelling units in compound houses in Bantama are characterized by exclusive access to only bedroom units. Other facilities, such as the toilet, bathroom and kitchen, are shared. In contrast, households living in the apartment dwelling units in Bantama have exclusive access to a bedroom and either a toilet, bathroom or kitchen facility. There were twice as many apartment dwelling units in our sample as there were ordinary dwelling units, signifying growing transformation of compound dwelling units, as it is currently happening in government estates (Avogo et al., 2017). We found that the transformation in compound houses in the central parts of Kumasi are not only conversions from residential to commercial use as some studies (See Cobbinah et al., 2019; Twumasi-Ampofo & Oppong, 2016) suggest, but also from one residential use to another.

Generally, the transformation in the compound houses involved providing households with exclusive access to bathrooms, toilets, kitchens and electricity meters. When bathrooms were added to an existing dwelling unit, they were mostly accompanied by the addition of a toilet. Like most en-suite apartments around the world, the most basic facilities that define transformed dwelling units in Bantama are the bathroom and toilet. Therefore, they are usually the first extensions made when the decision is taken to transform a dwelling unit in a compound house. We found that, where there was no exclusive access to bathroom and toilet facilities in a transformed dwelling unit, some tenants declined to rent. Furthermore, findings showed that there were more single-room self-contained (51.08%) and chamber and hall self-contained (38.15%) dwelling units than two-bedroom apartment (10.98%) dwelling units in compound houses in Bantama. This finding is not particularly surprising because most compound houses, as shown in Figures 1 and 2, are originally designed to accommodate single rooms and chamber and hall dwelling units, and hence there is limited space for other uses like dining (Okeyinka, 2014). Importantly, the study found that landlords were more inclined to add facilities, as opposed to additional rooms, to existing dwelling units in compound houses in Bantama. In most cases, this was due to space constraints. Those who did not have space constraints converted some existing dwelling units into two-bedroom apartments.

More than half of the transformed dwelling units had exclusive access to a kitchen. Where a household did not have exclusive access to a kitchen, they shared the kitchen with an adjoining neighbour. It was found that, although all tenants preferred a kitchen for their exclusive use, this was not possible, and negotiated sharing arrangements between close neighbours therefore became imperative. Additionally, the study found that the majority of the transformed dwelling units (86%) had separate electricity meters installed by the Electricity Company of Ghana (ECG), some of which were funded by the tenants (63%) and the others by the landlord (37%). In most cases, tenants sought the approval of landlords to install the electricity meters. We also found that some landlords encouraged tenants to acquire separate meters. Where tenants finance the installation of the prepaid meters, they deduct their expenses from the rent payable, or they ask their landlords to reimburse them.

Limited sharing of facilities and space

Compound houses are noted for their shared spaces and facilities, including courtyards and standpipes, among others (Korboe, 1992; Obeng-Odoom & Amedzro, 2011). However, our findings suggest that there is reduced sharing in the selected compound houses in Bantama due to the increasing number of apartment dwelling units. For example, it was found that water was the only facility commonly shared by all households, irrespective of whether they lived in an ordinary or transformed dwelling unit in a compound house. Unlike the Electricity Company of Ghana, the Ghana Water Company Limited does not have an arrangement for tenant households to acquire personal water meters. Interviews revealed that tenant households adopted a points system in sharing the water bills. The points per household are determined by the number of people in the household. Thus, the total bill is first divided by the total number of people in the whole compound house. As shown in Figure 6, the average is then multiplied by the points per household. Adu-Gyamfi and his colleagues also observed the points system in sharing utility bills in their study on homeownership aspirations of households living in compound houses in Kumasi

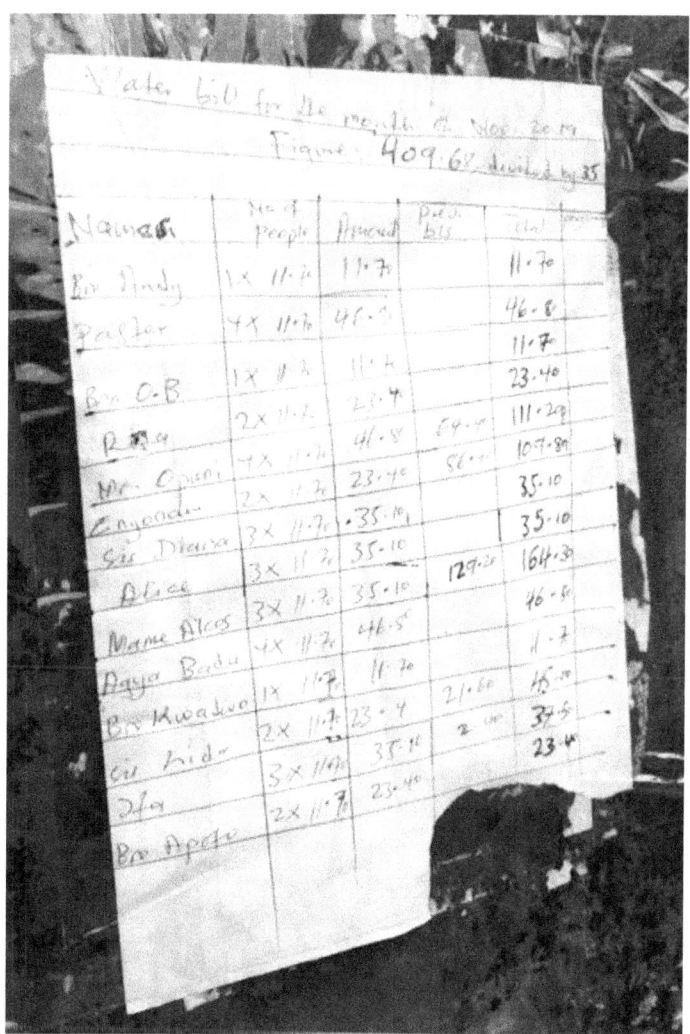

Figure 6 An example of points system of water bill sharing in a compound house in Bantama.

(Adu-Gyamfi, 2018; Adu-Gyamfi et al., 2020). In Bantama, we found that a household with four people attains four points. Children and visitors were usually only counted after 14 days of joining a household, but in some houses, they were not counted until after three months. A tenant deemed trustworthy would usually volunteer to collect and pay the water bills. Tenants emphasized the importance of trustworthiness due to perceptions that some landlords who live on the same premises might persuade an untrustworthy volunteer to allow them to evade the payment of water and other utility bills (Adu-Gyamfi et al., 2020).

Furthermore, the courtyard is still a shared space in most compound houses. In terms of sanitation, sweeping the courtyard is the sole responsibility of the women in each of the households. The sweeping tasks are assigned to the households using a rota. Women are exempted from their sweeping duties if they are over six months pregnant or if they are sick. Men who live alone are also exempted from the sweeping task. In the Ghanaian society, patriarchy still dominates in most domestic affairs (Abubakari et al., 2019b) and hence it is unusual for men to perform some domestic chores like sweeping when there are women in a house. This patriarchal dominance is, however, more prevalent in low-income indigenous suburbs. In compound houses with a common corridor, lobby or balcony, each household sweeps and cleans the frontage of their dwelling unit. The courtyard also serves as space where most households do their laundry and dry their clothes, as washing machines and dryers remain uncommon in compound houses in Kumasi and nationally. While in some compound houses tenants can use any available drying line, others share the drying lines equally among the households. Moreover, since middle-income households have increasingly moved into compound houses, the courtyard has assumed another function – parking space for vehicles given the absence of parking lot in compound houses (See Figure 7). We found that, in single storey compound houses, tenants park their vehicles in a space close to their dwelling units. However, in multi-storey compound houses, tenants who live on the upper floors park in a place that does not obstruct the mobility of other renters.

In short, while the transformation of dwelling units has limited sharing of facilities and spaces in compound houses in Bantama, sharing has not been totally eliminated. Therefore, some of the problems associated with sharing facilities identified by Afram and Owusu (2006), Yankson (2012b) and Addo (2013, 2016), namely the long

Figure 7 An image showing vehicles of some tenants in Bantama.

morning queue to use shared facilities and the misunderstanding which arise from sharing utility bills may persist in compound houses. Also, the current additional use of the courtyard as a parking lot means that new forms of space-sharing arrangements must be negotiated to avoid squabbles and disenchantment, particularly among non-car-owning households who might feel their spaces have been unfairly encroached upon.

It is worth pointing out that, while the use of courtyards in ordinary compound houses remains unchanged except for weekends when women come out to do laundry, the arrival of middle-income car-owning households has meant that the courtyard would remain unencumbered during the weekdays when these relatively well-off tenants drive off to work. This allows all households to use the courtyards as they please during the day. However, in the evening, when the car-owners arrive, the courtyard loses its publicness to the exclusive use of the car owners. It is clear, therefore, that shared spaces in transformed dwelling units have changed in ways that are consistent with the lifestyle of the new middle-class while subjugating the needs of all others.

Changing social class

There is a stereotypical view of occupants of compound houses in previous studies. They are portrayed as less or un-educated, under-employed or low-income earners and informal sector workers (Acheampong & Anokye, 2015; Addo, 2016; Yankson, 2012a; Yeboah, 2005). However, juxtaposing respondents' monthly incomes with the World Bank's (2014) income classification bands paints a different picture of their social class. For example, Table 2 shows that no low-income earner lives in the transformed dwelling units in Bantama. The majority of the respondents fall within the middle and mid-high-income brackets. A few high and very high-income earners are also living in apartment compound houses. This suggests that compound houses in Bantama predominantly cater for the housing needs of the middle (41.18%) and high-income earners (14.71%). This finding strongly supports the claims by Arku *et al.* (2012) and Owusu (2011) that an increasing number of high-income households are now living in informal rental dwelling units in compound houses.

Income range	Income per month (in US$)	Number and percentage of respondents (N ¼ 34)
From 'no wages to low wages'	(0 9.02) – (18.06 90.25)	0 (0)
Moderate	90.26–180.50	1 (2.94)
Middle	180.51–360.99	14 (41.18)
Mid-high	361–541.49	13 (38.24)
High	541.50–721.98	5 (14.71)
Very high	Above 721.98	1 (2.94)

Table 2 Income of tenants in transformed units in compound houses in Kumasi.

Note: Percentages are in parenthesis.

Source: Field data (January 2020).

Occupation of household heads	Number and percentage of respondents
Nurses	4 (11.76)
Teachers	3 (8.82)
Bankers	3 (8.82)
Medical doctors	3 (8.82)
Students	2 (5.88)
Engineers	2 (5.88)
Others	18 (52.94)
Total	34 (100)

Table 3 Occupation of tenant respondents in Bantama.

Source: Field data (January 2020).

Furthermore, the findings indicate that the dominance of respondents within the middle to very-high-income bracket may be linked to the nature of their educational attainment. For instance, 31 out of 34 respondents, representing 91.2% had completed tertiary education while the remaining respondents had completed senior secondary school. Regarding their employment backgrounds, Table 3 indicates that respondents were mostly professionals from 22 distinct professions within the formal sector. For example, they comprised nurses (11.76%), teachers (8.82%), bankers (8.82%), medical doctors (8.82%), students

Year in which tenancy was agreed	Average rent for apartment units (in US$)	
	Single room self-contained	Chamber and hall self-contained
2000	14.44–18.05	18.05–27.07
2004	18.05–21.66	27.07–30.68
2008	21.66–27.07	30.68–36.10
2012	27.07–32.49	36.10–45.12
2016	32.49–45.12	45.12–54.15
2019	45.12–54.15	54.15–72.20

Table 4 Monthly rent of some apartment units in compound houses in Bantama.

Source: Field data (January 2020).

(5.88%), IT-consultants, accountants, architects, engineers, laboratory technicians and pharmacists. The dominance of health-related professionals may be attributed to the proximity of most dwellings to the Komfo Anokye Teaching Hospital. It could be argued that the professional profile of these tenants strongly support the view that transformed housing units appeal to professionals who earn relatively high-incomes from their white-collar jobs in urban areas (Awanyo et al., 2016).

RENT GAP AND GENTRIFICATION IN BANTAMA

In Bantama, we found that there is a direct relationship between housing transformation and the rent gap, as conceptualized by Smith (1979) and more recently by Slater (2017). The findings showed that rent increased by at least 100 per cent after the housing transformation. This increment confirms Marxist differential rent theories, as landlords in Bantama obtained the rental power to increase rent by at least two-fold after the transformation of their compound houses, although their investment towards improving the dwelling units may not be commensurate with the rent increment (Owusu-Ansah et al., 2018).

Regarding tendencies towards gentrification, some landlords and estate agents confirmed during the interview that low-income households who could no longer afford the rent increment moved out. A few months prior to the expiry of an existing tenancy, landlords inflate the rent of dwelling units such that tenants who cannot afford the new rent are forced out. This vacancy subsequently allowed landlords to transform their ordinary dwelling units into apartments to take advantage of the uplift in rental values following the transformation. Below was one landlord's submission:

> I did not ask them to move out. It was one of the options they had, in addition to staying on. Unfortunately, they moved out. Since this property is my primary source of livelihood, I did the extensions and increased the price
> (Interview, PL2, Male, 3/12/2020).

While the above assertion suggests that the decision taken by low-income households to move out is purely voluntary rather than an eviction, there is no gainsaying that it has allowed landlords to undertake improvements that are appealing to middle-and-high-income households. For the majority of landlords in Bantama, the preoccupation is to realize at least twice the rent of an ordinary dwelling unit through housing transformation. They indicated that this premium is attractive and big enough to motivate them to transform the housing units in their compound houses. One landlord hinted at this when he said:

> I gain twice as much when I make an extension to every unit in my house. I think this is very good. I still have a few more ordinary units to modify. People like self-contained units. One tenant will pay me his rent next month, and once he pays, I will start work. As long as the rent is doubled, I am fine.
> (Interview, PL12, Female, 12/12/2019)

This confirms the rent gap theory, which argues that investment in housing transformation is largely influenced by landlords' attempts to extract the maximum possible rent from their property and thus close the rent gap (Eduful & Hooper, 2015; Smith, 1987). Therefore, it may be justifiable to argue that potential accrual of economic gains by landlords following housing transformation is spurring gentrification in Bantama. As argued by Slater (2017), closing the rent gap requires the displacement of persons obtaining use-value from the present land use in order to capitalize the land to the perceived optimal or highest and best use. Thus, the rent gap highlights specific social class interests where the quest for shelter is undermined for the quest for profit (Slater, 2017). Also, weak tenant protection and non-enforcement of the Rent Act in Ghana (Adu-Gyamfi et al., 2020) serves to empower landlords to vary rents payable *suo motu*, akin to how Marx conceptualizes capitalist exploitation of their workers (Owusu-Ansah et al., 2018).

Furthermore, our findings sharply contrast those of Awanyo et al. (2016), whose work on housing transformation in the Madina-Adenta concluded that increasing property income was not a reason for housing transformation but rather attributed the drive to transform housing to an attempt to provide comfort and to meet the needs of family members. It further became evident that landlords in our study seemed less concerned about the possibility of displacing low-income households in favour for the middle- and high-income earners consequent to the transformation. They were generally unwilling to negotiate fixed monthly rents with prospective and current tenants due to the high demand for apartment units in compound houses. As shown in Table 4, landlords reviewed the monthly rents upward every 2 to 4 years, when the next advance rent was due.

Landlords' insistence on 2 to 5-year lump sum advance rent is not limited to West African nations but is also common in some East African countries, including Tanzania (Cadstedt, 2010). Unfortunately, the majority of the landlords in Bantama indicated that they demanded between 2 to 5 years of advance rent. This has been identified as one of the significant reasons why many renters cannot retain their properties, and why prospective first-time renters may struggle to take-up rental accommodation (Arku et al., 2012; Asante et al., 2018). The practice contradicts the provisions in Ghana's Rent Act, 1960 (Act 220), which only permits landlords to charge advance rent for six months for longer tenancies, with subsequent payment due semi-annually (Arku et al., 2012). While the rent for the apartment dwelling units may not be extremely high, even from the standpoint of the low-income tenant, they are perceived to be quite high for virtually all income groups because of the extended periods over which the advance rent is charged.

Surprisingly, there was one landlord who permitted her tenant to pay rents monthly. The tenant in question was appreciative of the relief that paying monthly rent has brought to his household:

> I have been paying rent of 300 cedis (US$54.15) for my chamber and hall self-contained. I pay monthly. It has been beneficial. I feel so lucky. If every landlord was like mine, many low-income households would have been able to rent self-contained units. If I had to pay an advance rent of about 2 to 3 years . . . I would not have been able to rent this accommodation. Even if she increases my monthly rent, it wouldn't be a burden
>
> (Interview, MT, 35 years, 27/11/2019).

The comment above goes to show that, although the monthly rents of apartment dwelling units in compound houses were affordable to most middle- and high-income households, some of them struggled to pay the advance rent. Regarding how they financed the lump-sum payment of advance rent, some tenants indicated that they relied on their savings while others borrowed from financial institutions to pay their advance rent. Some tenants bemoaned how servicing the bank loans used in paying the advance rent has compounded their financial burden. A tenant remarked the following:

> In 2017, when I saw this accommodation, the landlord asked for a monthly rent of 300 cedis (US$54.15) and advance rent of 4 years. So, I had to raise an amount of 14,400 cedis (US$2,599.14). My bank gave me a personal loan of 15,000 cedis (US$2707.43) at an interest rate of about 30 per cent payable in 2 years. Since then, I have been paying a loan instalment of about 850 cedis (US$153.42), higher than the monthly rent of 300 cedis (US$54.15) I had to pay. This advance rent thing is frustrating for some of us who even have higher incomes
>
> (Interview, MT, 45 years, 3/12/2019).

The above extract means that the ability to continue living in a transformed dwelling is not only a function of one's income but also the availability of support from banks, employers, friends and family members in paying the lump sum advance rent that landlords demand. This implies that both the poor and rich are made financially worse off due to the practice of advance rent, and suggests that the rent gap theory alone is not sufficient to explain the dynamics of gentrification taking place in Bantama. Hence, a more nuanced conceptualisation that integrates the rent gap and the payment of advance rent is imperative.

This point is instructive because the rent gap theory was developed following empirical realities of housing market operations in the Global North, where rents are often paid per calendar month. This makes the theory not entirely applicable in a Ghanaian city context if the localized practice of upfront payment of 2 to 5-years' rent is not considered. Another localized practice which departs from the imperative of gentrification following conceptions from the Global North is that, in Bantama, the socio-cultural characteristics of prospective tenants sometimes take precedence over their ability to pay the advance rent of a transformed dwelling unit. These characteristics often include one's profession, physical appearance[3] and household composition: some landlords prefer to let their dwelling units to medical doctors, nurses and other health professionals because their expertise would be handy when medical attention is needed. Commenting on the kinds of tenants that landlords prefer, an estate agent remarked that:

> Sometimes, landlords will specifically inform you that they need a particular class of people. So, when a tenant approaches us for accommodation, we quickly ask their profession. If they fit the landlord's specification, we go with them to see the accommodation. If not, we do not take the person there [to the landlord's premise]
> (Interview, PL6, Male, 4/12/2019)

From the above statement, one could argue that estate agents also play a crucial role in shaping the form of gentrification taking place in Bantama as their subjective preferences and inherent biases could mediate who is ultimately taken to meet the landlord. This represents a classic case of principal-agent problem (Anglin & Arnott, 1991).

Elaborating on the kinds of tenant they expected, a landlord said:

> I do not just rent out my property to tenants because they have the money to pay the advance rent. I look at their appearance too. If your hairstyle is 'rasta' (a vernacular for having dreadlocks), I will not give it to you. Also, if you are in tattered jeans, I would not give it to you
> (Interview, PL16, Male, 20/12/2019).

It is evident from the above assertion that landlords stereotype tenants, although this is not to undermine the African cultural understanding of decency and responsibility. This biased profiling has the potential to deny a prospective tenant the opportunity to gain access to housing simply because they do not fit such biased profiling. Similarly, relying on such stereotypes can cause landlords to admit a tenant who might fit the desired profile but may, in reality, be a worse tenant in other crucial respects. Some landlords also preferred renting to married couples who have children because they perceive such tenants to be more responsible and relatively less mobile.

It is however unclear whether tenants' gender or marital status influence landlords' decision to let out their transformed rental dwelling units. We can speculate this might be a factor, especially in patriarchal societies where it is common for single mothers to be branded as promiscuous or for older unmarried men to be viewed as irresponsible. All these local stereotypes and agency problems play into the extent to which landlords can take full advantage of the uplift in rent that housing transformation brings, and the characteristics of middle-class tenants who take up residence in the transformed rental dwellings. One can thus argue that a combined analysis of the rent gap, the practice of advance rent payment and the socio-cultural norms sought by landlords is crucial to understanding the dynamics of gentrification in compound houses in Bantama. This is consistent with the argument by Lees (1994) that a juxta-position of Marxist and cultural analysis deepens our understanding of the gentrification process.

CONCLUDING REMARKS

This article sought to shed light on the ongoing transformation in traditional compound houses in developing countries and how this is altering the conventional physical features of compound houses, the use of their common areas and the social composition of their tenants. We drew empirical insights from interviews with estate agents, landlords and tenants in Bantama, a sub-metro in Ghana's second-largest city, Kumasi. The paper finds evidence that the transformation of compound houses is taking place in Bantama. However, contrary to findings in previous studies (Cobbinah et al., 2019) that the transformation is reflected in landlords' conversion of residential spaces in their compound houses to commercial properties, we found that the transformation did not only involve a change in the use of properties as earlier suggested. We have argued that there is also conversion of ordinary dwelling units with shared facilities and open courtyards to largely self-contained apartment dwelling units. Such transformation is intended to take advantage of the two-fold increase in rent brought about by growing housing demand from highly educated and middle-and high-income professionals. Responding to this growing demand, landlords have substantially altered the conventional features of compound houses. Physically, most transformed units now have exclusive access to bathrooms, toilets, kitchens and electricity meters. This just leaves water and the open courtyards as the only common utility and shared space, respectively, for inter-household interactions. The courtyard, however, is gradually losing its characteristic as the arena for fostering rich social interactions owing to the retreat lifestyle of the affluent new residents. The transformation is also changing the social composition of tenants in compound houses as low-income households are being pushed out in favour of high-income households. Housing transformation has invariably increased rents in compound houses to levels that are affordable only to higher-class groups, making the prospect of gentrification more immanent.

Furthermore, the findings uncovered in this study lead us to question the generalization of axioms associated with the rent gap theory and gentrification beyond Western contexts. Indeed, the insights from this article suggest that analysis of the nexus between housing transformation and potential gentrification in parts of sub-Saharan Africa must necessarily account for rent gaps in addition to local practices, stereotypical tendencies and cultural factors that play out in tenant selection. Arriving at such insights requires that debates regarding housing transformation be made more nuanced to reflect realities prevailing in other contexts, namely, advance rent, renters' appearance and socio-cultural factors to gain an in-depth appreciation of the dynamics of the private rental housing market. Thus, contrary to one of the key canons of rent gap and gentrification theories – ability to pay – the study demonstrates that, at least in Bantama, ability to pay the contract rent is not sufficient to make even higher-income households secure or retain their apartments. It is also evident that advance rent inflates cost of securing a tenancy not just beyond the financial reach of low-income households but also high-income households, creating a phenomenon of super-gentrification (Butler & Lees, 2006), even though compound houses are not necessarily the best form of housing in African and international comparative terms. Existing social networks and relief packages provided by banks and employers such as personal loans play a crucial role in helping tenants retain their transformed rental properties. The availability of these interventions means that renters can have access to loans to pre-finance the payment of the advance rent while repaying their debt in monthly instalments. This means, in reality, the financial burden of paying higher rent either as a lump-sum to landlords or in the form instalment to employers is always present.

Furthermore, landlords unfettered right to transform their dwelling units and subsequently review the rent upward is symptomatic of a dysfunctional institutional and regulatory regime in the rental housing market in Ghana, as previous studies have extensively highlighted (Arku et al., 2012; Obeng-Odoom, 2011). Our findings thus add to calls for swift governmental intervention in terms of enforcing the relevant 6-month advance rent provision in Section 25(5) of the Rent Act, 1963 as well as modifying and repealing provisions that are incongruous with contemporary realities of both landlords and tenants (Adu-Gyamfi et al., 2020; Arku et al., 2012; Owusu-Ansah et al., 2018). The urgency of this call lies in the fact that there is a growing number of landlords who are currently transforming their compound houses, against a back-drop of widening housing deficit. We would thus suggest that any review of the Rent Act should include a provision that specifies that the determination of rents in transformed dwelling units should be informed by a professional valuer's advice, rather than the current arbitrary decisions taken by landlords which unfairly disadvantage low-income tenants. If nothing is done, then displacement of low-income households in favour of middle- and high-income professionals will continue apace and worsen housing affordability for low-income households. Further research is needed to explore the following issues at depth: the extent to which estate agents shape gentrification from a principal-agent perspective; how landlords' socio-demographic characteristics and perceptions influence the gentrifiers they let their properties to; the social relations between tenants living in ordinary dwelling units and transformed apartments, particularly how they negotiate the use of the remaining shared facilities such as the courtyard; and whether surviving children and spouses of deceased owners of compound houses can privatize their interests through title registration.

NOTES

1. A local term which refers to accommodation with a bedroom and a hall
2. Rates were originally in Ghana Cedis. We adopted Bank of Ghana Daily Interbank FX Rates of US$1¼ 5.5403, as of 18 December, 2019. These rates are used in subsequent conversions.
3. This included but not limited to one's hairstyle, facial make-up, clothing labels, sense of fashion. One's appearance could easily send a wrong message to the landlords, which may be contrary to reality.

REFERENCES

Abubakari, Z., Richter, C. & Zevenbergen, J. A. (2019a) Plural inheritance laws, practices and emergent types of property: Implications for updating the land register, *Sustainability*, *11*, pp. 6087–6017.

Abubakari, Z., Richter, C. & Zevenbergen, J. A. (2019b) A tripartite normative interaction in land registration: Inheritance and land information updating, in: *20th Annual World Bank Conference on Land and Poverty: Catalysing Innovation*, pp. 1–23, Washington, DC, March 25–29, 2019.

Acheampong, R. A. (2016) The family housing sector in urban Ghana: Exploring the dynamics of tenure arrangements and the nature of family support networks, *International Development Planning Review*, *38*(3), pp. 297–316.

Acheampong, R. A. & Anokye, P. A. (2015) Housing for the urban poor: Towards alternative financing strategies for low-income housing development in Ghana, *International Development Planning Review*, *37*, pp. 445–465.

Adarkwa, K. K. & Oppong, R. A. (2005) Gentrification, use conversion and traditional architecture in Kumasi's central business district: Case study of Odum Precinct, *Journal of Science and Technology*, *25*, pp. 80–90.

Addo, I. A. (2013) Perceptions and acceptability of multihabitation as an urban low income housing strategy in greater Accra metropolitan area, Ghana. *Urban Forum*, *24*, pp. 543–571.

Addo, I. A. (2016) Assessing residential satisfaction among low income households in multihabited dwellings in selected low income communities in Accra, *Urban Studies*, *53*, pp. 631–650.

Adu-Gyamfi, A. (2018) A house for the nuclear family: The case of Ghana, *Housing and Society*, *45*, pp. 157–185.

Adu-Gyamfi, A., Poku-Boansi, M. & Cobbinah, P. B. (2020) Homeownership aspirations: Drawing on the experiences of renters and landlords in a deregulated private rental sector, *International Journal of Housing Policy*, *20*, pp. 417–430.

Afram, S. O. (2007) The traditional Ashanti compound house: A forgotten resource for home ownership of the urban poor, in: *Conference on African Architecture Today, Kwame Nkrumah University of Science and Technology*, Kumasi, Ghana, June 5–7, Kumasi. Available at www.mudonline.org/aat/2007_documents/AAT_Afram_paper-web-based-publication.pdf (accessed 10 December 2019).

Afram, S. O. & Owusu, S. E. (2006) Design innovations towards enhancing the quality of living in multi-storey compound housing for low-income households in Kumasi, Ghana. *Journal of Science and Technology*, *26*, pp. 89–101.

Alagbe, O. A. & Aduwo, E. B. (2014) The impact of housing transformation on residents' quality of life: A case study of low-income, *Covenant Journal of Research in the Built Enviornment*, *2*, pp. 134–147.

Amole, B., Korboe, D. & Tipple, G. (1993) The family house in West Africa: A forgotten resource for policy makers?, *Third World Planning Review*, *15*, pp. 355–372.

Anglin, P. M. & Arnott, R. (1991) Residential real estate brokerage as a principal-agent problem, *The Journal of Real Estate Finance and Economics, 4*, pp. 99–125.

Arku, G. (2006) Housing and development strategies in Ghana, 1945–2000, *International Development Planning Review, 28*, pp. 333–358.

Arku, G., Luginaah, I. & Mkandawire, P. (2012) You either pay more advance rent or you move out: Landlords/ladies' and tenants' dilemmas in the low-income housing market in Accra, *Urban Studies, 49*, pp. 3177–3193.

Asante, L. A., Gavu, E. K., Quansah, D. P. O. & Osei Tutu, D. (2018) The difficult combination of renting and building a house in Urban Ghana: Analysing the perception of low and middle income earners in Accra, *GeoJournal, 83*, pp. 1223–1237.

Asiama, S. O. (1984) The land factor in housing for low income urban settlers: The example of Madina, *Third World Planning Review, 6*, pp. 171–184.

Avogo, F. A., Wedam, E. A. & Opoku, S. M. (2017) Housing transformation and livelihood outcomes in Accra, Ghana, *Cities, 68*, pp. 92–103.

Awanyo, L. (2009) Meeting housing-space demand through in situ housing adjustments in the greater Accra Metropolitan Area, Ghana, *Environment and Planning C: Government and Policy, 27*, pp. 302–318.

Awanyo, L., Mccarron, M. & Attua, E. M. (2016) Affordable housing options for all in a context of developing capitalism: Can housing transformations play a role in the greater Accra Region, *African Geographical Review, 35*, pp. 35–52.

Butler, T. (1997) *Gentrification and the Middle Classes* (Ashford: Ashgate Publishing Limited).

Butler, T. & Lees, L. (2006) Super-gentrification in Barnsbury, London: Globalization and gentrifying global elites at the neighbourhood level, *Transactions of the Institute of British Geographers, 31*, pp. 467–487.

Cadstedt, J. (2010) Private rental housing in Tanzania – A private matter? *Habitat International, 34*, pp. 46–52.

Clark, E. (1988) The rent gap and transformation of the built environment: Case studies in Malmö 1860–1985, *Geografiska Annaler, Series B: Human Geography, 70*, pp. 241–254.

Cobbinah, P. B., Amoako, C. & Osei Asibey, M. (2019) The changing face of Kumasi Central, *Geoforum, 101*, pp. 49–61.

Eduful, A. & Hooper, M. (2015) Urban impacts of resource booms: The emergence of oil-led gentrification in Sekondi-Takoradi, Ghana, *Urban Forum, 26*, pp. 283–302.

Ehwi, R. J., Asante, L. A. & Morrison, N. (2020) Exploring the financial implications of advance rent payment and induced furnishing of rental housing in Sub-Saharan African cities: The case of Dansoman, Accra-Ghana, *Housing Policy Debate*, pp. 1–23. https://doi.org/10.1080/10511482.2020.1782451

Ghana Statistical Service. (2012). *2010 Population and Housing Census* (Accra: Ghana Statistical Service).

Ghana Statistical Service. (2014a). *2010 Population and Housing Census: District Analytical Report* (Accra: Ghana Statistical Service).

Ghana Statistical Service. (2014b). *2010 Population and Housing Census: Housing in Ghana* (Accra: Ghana Statistical Service).

Haila, A. (1990) The theory of land rent at the crossroads, *Environment and Planning D: Society and Space, 8*, pp. 275–296.

Hallett, G. (1979) *Urban and Land Economics: Principles and Policy* (London: The Macmillan Press Ltd.).

Hamnett, C. (2003) Gentrification and the middle-class remaking of inner London, 1961–2001, *Urban Studies, 40*, pp. 2401–2426.

Helbrecht, I. (2018) Gentrification and Displacement, in: I. Helbrecht (Ed.) *Gentrification and Resistance: Researching Displacement Processes and Adaptation Strategies*, pp. 1–8 (Wiesbaden: Springer Fachmedien Wiesbaden GmbH).

Korboe, D. (1992) Family-houses in Ghanaian cities: To be or not to be? *Urban Studie, Urban Studies, 29*(7), pp. 1159–1171.

Lees, L. (1994) Rethinking gentrification: Beyond the positions of economics or culture, *Progress in Human Geography, 18*, pp. 137–150.

Lees, L. (2012) The geography of gentrification: Thinking through comparative urbanism. *Progress of, Progress in Human Geography, 36*, pp. 155–171.

Lees, L., Shin, H.B. & Lopez-Morales, E. (2015) *Global Gentrifications: Uneven development and Displacement* (L. Lees, H. B. Shin, & E. Lopez-Morales, Eds.). Bristol: Policy Press.

Lees, L., Shin, I.I.D. & Lopez-Morales, E. (2016) *Planetary Gentrification*. Cambridge: Polity Press.

Lemanski, C. (2014) Hybrid Gentrification in South Africa: Theorising across Southern and Northern Cities, *Urban Studies*, *51*, pp. 2943–2960.

Ley, D. (1981) Inner-city revitalisation in Canada: A Vancouver case study, *The Canadian Geographer/Le Géographe Canadien*, *25*, pp. 124–148.

Luque, J. (2015) *Urban Land Economics* (Cham: Springer).

Maloutas, T. (2012) Contextual diversity in gentrification research, *Critical Sociology*, *38*, pp. 33–48.

Maloutas, T. (2018) Travelling concepts and universal particularisms: A reappraisal of gentrification's global reach, *European Urban and Regional Studies*, *25*, pp. 250–216.

Morris, A. (2015) *A Practical Introduction to In-depth Interviewing* (London: SAGE Publications Ltd.).

Morris, E. W. & Winter, M. (1975) A theory of family housing adjustment, *Journal of Marriage and the Family*, *37*, pp. 79–88.

Obeng-Odoom, F. (2011) Private rental housing in Ghana: Reform or renounce? *Journal of International Real Estate and Construction Studies*, *1*, pp. 71–90.

Obeng-Odoom, F. & Amedzro, L. (2011) Inadequate housing in Ghana, *Urbani Izziv*, *22*, pp. 127–137.

Okeyinka, Y. (2014) Multi – habitation: A form of housing in African urban environments, *IOSR Journal of Environmental Science, Toxicology and Food Technology*, *8*, pp. 21–25.

Owusu, G. (2011) Urban growth, globalization and access to housing in Ghana's largest metropolitan area, Accra, in: *4th European Conference on African Studies*, Uppsala. Available at: www.aegis-eu.org/archive/ecas4/ecas-4/panels/81-100/panel-90/ECAS-FULL-PAPER-GEORGE-OWUSU.pdf (accessed 22 November 2019).

Owusu-Ansah, A., Ohemeng-Mensah, D., Abdulai, R.T. & Obeng-Odoom, F. (2018) Public choice theory and rental housing: An examination of rental housing contracts in Ghana, *Housing Studies*, *33*, pp. 938–959.

Slater, T. (2017) Planetary rent gaps, *Antipode*, *49*, pp. 114–137.

Smith, N. (1979) Toward a theory of gentrification: A back to the city movement by capital, not people, *Journal of the American Planning Association*, *45*, pp. 538–548.

Smith, N. (1987) Gentrification and the rent gap, *Annals of the Association of American Geographers*, *77*, pp. 462–465.

Tipple, A. G., Korboe, D. & Garrod, G. (1997) Income and wealth in house ownership studies in urban Ghana, *Housing Studies*, *12*, pp. 111–126.

Tipple, G. A. (1996) Housing extensions as sustainable development, *Habitat International*, *20*, pp. 367–376.

Tipple, G. A. (1999) User-initiated transformations of government-built housing stocks: Lessons from developing countries, *Journal of Urban Technology*, *6*, pp. 17–35.

Tipple, G. A., Amole, B., Korboe, D. & Onyeacholem, H. (1994) House and dwelling, family and household: Towards defining housing units in West African Cities, *Third World Planning Review*, *16*, pp. 429–450.

Tipple, G. A., Owusu, S. E. & Pritchard, C. (2004) User-initiated extensions in government-built estates in Ghana and Zimbabwe: Unconventional but effective housing supply, *Africa Today*, *51*, pp. 79–105.

Tusting, L. S., Bisanzio, D., Alabaster, G., Cameron, E., Cibulskis, R., Davies, M., Flaxman, S., Gibson, H. S., Knudsen, J., Mbogo, C., Okumu, F. O., von Seidlein, L., Weiss, D. J., Lindsay, S. W., Gething, P. W. & Bhatt, S. (2019) Mapping changes in housing in Sub-Saharan Africa from 2000 to 2015, *Nature*, *568*, pp. 391–394.

Twumasi-Ampofo, K. & Oppong, R. A. (2016) Traditional architecture and gentrification in Kumasi revisited, *African Journal of Applied Research*, *2*, pp. 97–109.

World Bank. (2014). *Rising Through Cities in Ghana: Ghana Urbanization Review Overview Report* (Washington, DC: World Bank). Retrieved from http://documents.worldbank.org/curated/en/613251468182958526/pdf/96449-WP-PUBLIC-GhanaRisingThroughCities-Overview-full.pdf (accessed 22 November 2019).

Yankson, P. W. K. (2012a) Landlordism and housing production in greater Accra metropolitan area, in: E. Ardayfio-Schandorf, P. W. K. Yankson & M. Bertrand (Eds), *The Mobile City of Accra: Urban Families, Housing and Residential Practices, (First)*, pp. 163–182 (Dakar: Council for the Development of Social Science Research in Africa).

Yankson, P. W. K. (2012b) Rental housing and tenancy dynamics with particular focus on low-income households in Greater Accra metropolitan area, in E. Ardayfio-Schandorf, P. W. K. Yankson & M. Bertrand (Eds), *The Mobile*

City of Accra: Urban Families, HOUSING and Residential Practices, pp. 183–206 (Dakar: Council for the Development of Social Science Research in Africa (Codesria)).

Yeboah, I. E. A. (2005) Housing the urban poor in twenty-first century sub-Saharan Africa: Policy mismatch and a way forward for Ghana, *GeoJournal, 62*, pp. 147–161.

PART FIVE

■ Planetary gentrification and digital transformations

Opponents of Digital Gentrification in New York City, USA
(photograph: Shannon Stapleton, permission: Reuters)

INTRODUCTION TO PART FIVE

As we stated in our introduction to this *Reader*, new configurations of gentrification present challenges to gentrification studies, theories, and concepts as they evolve. Neil Smith (1996: 68) was rather prescient in updating his rent gap theory, in the mid-1990s, when he pointed out that

> it is also possible to conceive of a situation in which, rather than the capitalized ground rent being pushed down through devalorization, the potential ground rent is suddenly pushed higher, opening up a rent gap in a different manner. This might be the case, for example, when there is rapid and sustained inflation, or where strict regulation of a land market keeps potential ground rent low, but is then repealed.

Dissecting these words in a study of the privatization and financialization of a rent-regulated multifamily housing complex in Manhattan, Ben Teresa (2019: 1401) has pointed out, 'We no longer have to only conceive of such a situation, but we can observe this process in motion.' He demonstrates that privatization involves 'the reorganization of state power from managing social goods to ensuring the private profitability of those assets' and that financialization (the integration of finance and real estate markets) 'introduces new actors and practices that reorder the scale for establishing potential rent and increases expectations about profitability and risk' (p. 1405). The intensity and magnitude of capital flows in New York City are such that *sustained disinvestment is no longer a precondition for gentrification*. Along these lines, and especially relevant to this section of the *Reader*, Wachsmuth and Weisler (2018: 1152) examined the explosion of Airbnb rentals in New York City and argued that 'across certain neighborhood types (primarily still-gentrifying areas and now-affluent, formerly gentrifying areas), the new, technologically-enabled possibility of short-term rentals systematically raises potential ground rents – and thus creates rent gaps even where there has been little or no devalorization of existing housing.' Short-term rentals, they demonstrate, have massively widened the scope for land and real estate speculation – and the scope for displacement. And as Rozena and Lees (2021) demonstrate with respect to 'Airbnbification' in London, the displacements are varied and complex.

In this section, we include four articles that explore these issues in depth, by focusing on the ramifications of digital platforms and technological advancements on urban space and, especially, on housing markets. The pace of change since we edited the *Gentrification Reader* in 2010 has been extraordinary. Airbnb has gone from being a small enterprise in San Francisco to a global phenomenon with offices in cities all over the world, yet its astonishing impact on cities is far from positive for people who most urgently require affordable housing. The articles we have chosen are not just about Airbnb, however; they are fundamentally about the lack of regulation occurring in multiple urban contexts, which has allowed municipalities and business elites to prioritize the interests of tourists over those of (often vulnerable) residents. Three of the four articles focus on cities in southern Europe, which have been on the frontlines of both the housing market consequences of short-term rentals and organized resistance to them.

In one of the earliest and still most important contributions to a fast-growing literature, Agustin Cocola-Gant analyzes the explosive growth of short-term rentals in Barcelona, Spain – a city with a housing market that has almost become synonymous with Airbnb and its displacement effects. Cocola-Gant's paper is notable not only for its documentation of the increasing conversion of housing into accommodation for visitors and the Marcusian forms of displacement that occur but also for its argument that what happens on a grand scale is the "substitution of residential life by tourism" when residents move out, as the only buyers tend to be tourist investors. In Box 6, Cocola-Gant revisits his paper and reflects on some of the theoretical lessons and the debates his work ignited. In the next paper in this section, Alberto Amore, Cecilia de Bernardi, and Pavlos Arvanitis assess the impacts of Airbnb in Athens, Lisbon, and Milan. Despite some important differences between (and within) these three contexts, they share a common pattern in that short-term renting platforms exploded in the context of post–global financial crisis urban governance, where private development and foreign investment were two main ingredients in what was considered a quick-fix solution for the economic problems brought by the crisis. The outcome is that short-term rental platforms have been closing the rent gap and extracting massive profits for the owners of capital at a faster rate than in conventional or traditional gentrification processes of the past. In the third article we have chosen, by Alvaro Ardura Urquiaga, Iñigo Lorente-Riverola, and Javier Ruiz Sanchez, similar patterns are observed in Madrid. They analyze the holiday rental supply in Madrid over three years (2015–2018), verifying a strong association between the growth in tourist arrivals, the settlement of new residents from wealthy economic backgrounds, and increasing rental prices. This has been occurring in the context of the massive deregulation of local rental contracts and the growth of transnational real estate investment trusts, with strong potential to produce displacement of some of the most vulnerable residents in the metropolis. The final article in the section is by Erin McElroy, who has gained international attention via her 2013 co-founding of the Anti-Eviction Mapping Project, a data-driven cartography and oral history project documenting the dispossession and resistance surrounding the Tech Boom 2.0 in the Bay Area of California. In a historical-materialist analysis of several waves of technological innovation and dispossession in this region, McElroy frames Bay Area technologies of dispossession through what she terms 'postsocialist analytics', studying Silicon Valley's earlier racialized Cold War histories of space, as well as the impact of postsocialist transition upon the temporality of both global capital and anti-capitalist imaginaries.

REFERENCES AND FURTHER READING

Ferreri, M. and Sanyal, R. (2018) "Platform economies and urban planning: Airbnb and regulated deregulation in London" *Urban Studies* 55 (15): 3353–3368.
Fields, D. and Rogers, D. (2021) "Towards a critical housing studies research agenda on platform Real Estate" *Housing, Theory and Society* 38 (1): 72–94.
Gurran, N. and Phibbs, P. (2017) "When tourists move in: How should urban planners respond to airbnb?" *Journal of the American Planning Association* 83 (1): 80–92.
Nasreen, Z. and Ruming, K. (2021) "Struggles and opportunities at the platform interface: Tenants' experiences of navigating shared room housing using digital platforms in Sydney" *Journal of Housing and the Built Environment*, forthcoming.
Rozena, S. and Lees, L. (2021) "The everyday lived experiences of Airbnbification in London" *Social and Cultural Geography* (Online early: https://www.tandfonline.com/doi/full/10.1080/14649365.2021.1939124)
Smith, N. (1996) *The New Urban Frontier: Gentrification and the Revanchist City*. New York: Routledge.
Teresa, B. F. (2019) "New dynamics of rent gap formation in New York city rent-regulated housing: Privatization, financialization, and uneven development" *Urban Geography* 40 (10): 1399–1421.
Wachsmuth, D. and Weisler, A. (2018) "Airbnb and the Rent Gap: Gentrification through the sharing economy." *Environment and Planning A* 50 (6): 1147–1170.

17
Holiday rentals
The new gentrification battlefront

Agustín Cocola-Gant

INTRODUCTION

1.1 The phenomenon of holiday rentals is becoming a central gentrification battlefront in several cities in both the North and the South. A look at the internet shows how residents and activists in different places are expressing concerns about the impacts that vacation flats have in their neighbourhoods, especially after the spread of portals such as Airbnb. Research about the impacts of vacation rentals and how they are contested, however, remains in its infancy. Some authors reveal that behind the rhetoric of the sharing economy there is simply another opportunity for capital accumulation (Arias-Sans and Quaglieri-Domínguez 2016). The suppliers, far from being single families that occasionally rent the homes in which they live, tend to be the same investors and landlords that were fuelling previous rounds of gentrification. Other authors note that short-term rentals are a central element in the context of growing protests and campaigns that point to tourism as a factor in urban inequality (Colomb and Novy 2016; Füller and Michel 2014; Peters 2016; Opillard 2016). Despite these initial steps, there are no empirical studies that assess the way in which holiday rentals transform communities and, consequently, reveal why they are being resisted and by whom.

1.2 By gentrification, I refer to a process of capital investment in the built environment that caters to the demands of affluent users and, along the way, displaces the indigenous population (Lees et al. 2016). I show that the growth of vacation rentals fuels housing rehabilitation and that this increasing conversion of housing into accommodation for visitors entails different forms of displacement. The phenomenon, then, needs to be regarded as an example of tourism gentrification. Also, the conversion of housing into accommodation for visitors is a consequence of the liberalisation of the housing market and the change from housing as shelter towards housing as an investment vehicle (Bone 2014; Cole et al. 2016). To understand why vacation rentals represent the new gentrification battlefront, I focus on the impacts of the process. I explore how displacement takes place and who is affected by it. It is worth noting that although in classical gentrification the middle-classes displace low income residents (Butler 2002), in this case both middle and working class residents are being displaced by the pressure of tourist investors. Indeed, the process has an impact on both tenants and owners, which contradicts the liberal rhetoric of home ownership as a protection against displacement. In the next section, I describe the forms of displacement noted by gentrification research. In the following sections I present my methodology and my empirical findings. Finally, I discuss my results and I relate them with the literature on displacement.

FORMS OF DISPLACEMENT

2.1 I draw on the conceptualisation of residential displacement advanced by Marcuse (1985) and other authors (Newman and Wyly 2006; DeVerteuil 2011; Slater 2009; Davidson and Lees 2010). The most visible form of displacement is usually 'direct displacement', which refers to an involuntary out-migration from a place. While direct displacement is the most visible form of displacement, Marcuse (1985) also noted that an important but hidden impact of gentrification is 'exclusionary displacement': the

DOI: 10.4324/9781003341239-27

difficulties in finding affordable accommodation in gentrifying areas. Marcuse added a final category – 'displacement pressure' – which refers to changes at the neighbourhood scale such as loss of social networks, stores or public facilities that are central to everyday life. Marcuse stated that as the area becomes 'less and less livable, then the pressure of displacement already is severe. Its actuality is only a matter of time' (1985: 207). As Davidson and Lees (2010) suggest, displacement means a lot more than simply the moment of eviction. The pressure of displacement has long-term implications that makes it progressively difficult for low-income residents to remain over time.

METHODOLOGY AND CASE STUDY

3.1 This paper is the result of a mixed method research approach that took place in Barcelona between February and October 2015. The case study was the so-called Gòtic neighbourhood in Barcelona's historic centre (Cócola Gant 2014a, 2014b). The area is a middle class neighbourhood that had been experiencing a process of classical gentrification since the early 1990s. A survey of 220 households was conducted with the aim of gathering data about housing conditions and to estimate the supply of holiday rentals. For this purpose, other secondary sources were also used, in particular Airbnb and Inside Airbnb. However, the research emphasised the qualitative approach as the main goal of the project was to give voice to long-term residents in order to examine how the growth of holiday apartments affects them on a daily basis. In this regard, 42 in-depth interviews were conducted as well as participant observation. Community contestation against vacation rentals is a visible practice in Barcelona's city centre (Figure 1). However, I was more concerned with the hidden impacts that holiday apartments have on the everyday lives of residents. I did not ask residents about how they organise their political actions against the growth of tourist accommodation, but instead I asked why such a growth is seen by many as the main cause of tension in the neighbourhood. Importantly, 40 out of the 42 interviewees stated that holiday rentals displace residents. They talked about expulsions, harassment, rent increase, affordability problems, the pressure of tourist investors, daily disruptions and so on. In other words, they reflected different forms of displacement.

Figure 1 Protests against holiday rentals. Barcelona, August 2014.
Photograph by Ernest Cañada.

3.2 The question of positionality and how academics get involved in gentrification issues was present in all phases of the research. I believe that gentrification research is a political activity and, consequently, we should make our work more relevant to those people who are at risk of displacement. However, rather than emphasising the spectacular or resistance practices (DeVerteuil 2015), I argue that revealing how displacement takes place is a necessary political tool in confronting the rhetoric of success and growth and in showing the actual conditions in which people experience urban inequalities. In his research in Brooklyn, Slater (2006: 748) depicts how he was told by a community organiser that the best way he could help with local efforts in resisting gentrification was to 'come up with some numbers to show us how many people have been and are being displaced'. As social injustices are visible if only the facts are placed in evidence, making efforts to show how inequalities take place is a central tool for political action, especially to confront the hegemony of city leaders who believe that tourism growth is in the interest of all.

HOLIDAY RENTALS: SUPPLY AND IMPACTS

4.1 In this section, I describe my empirical results, which are organised in three sub-sections. First, I provide a general introduction to holiday rentals in Barcelona. Second, I analyse the supply of holiday rentals, in particular the extent to which housing has been converted into accommodation for visitors. Finally, I analyse my qualitative findings and show the way in which holiday rentals lead to different forms of displacement.

An approximation to holiday rentals in Barcelona

4.2 The phenomenon of holiday rentals has been documented in Barcelona since the late 1990s. In a period when tourism began to be the main industry in the city, some residents depict how young Americans left flyers in postboxes with the sentence 'you live in a goldmine'. At this stage it was sporadic, involved middle class guests from North Europe and America and hosts tended to be childless families or young professionals. In the early 2000s, the phenomenon grew. Investors and hotel companies bought entire apartment buildings and transformed them into vacation flats. Some landlords gradually stopped renting to traditional tenants. Lifestyle migrants also bought second homes in Barcelona and rented them to visitors while they are away. Although the number of single families who actually rented the homes in which they lived also grew, in this period holiday rentals became an investment opportunity for many. The important point is that the activity fuelled housing rehabilitation and this involved an increasing conversion of housing into tourist accommodation. It is at this moment when residents experienced community tension and neighbourhood organisations started to complain, a fact that was noted by some scholars (Degen 2004; García and Claver 2003). It is worth stressing, therefore, that the pressure of vacation flats was already a fact prior to the creation of Airbnb in 2008. What Airbnb has done is to expand the situation that existed before: more business opportunities for investors, tourist companies and landlords, and more visibility for those who rent rooms in their homes.

The supply of holiday rentals

Nowadays, an exploration of the supply of vacation flats shows the extent to which housing has been converted into accommodation for visitors. Airbnb does not reveal how many apartments they list or how many 'hosts' use the portal. By checking the website, one can only see the number of apartments listed at that moment but it does not show the apartments that have been booked. Therefore, the total number of apartments taken out from the housing stock will always be larger than the apartments listed on Airbnb during any specific day. In any case, data gathered from Airbnb is useful in terms of understanding the phenomenon and in comparing the supply in different areas. The project 'Inside Airbnb' captures such a supply in several cities every few months, including Barcelona. I use the listing captured by Inside Airbnb on 2nd October, 2015, which produces the following distribution:

Figure 2 Flats listed in Airbnb Barcelona. 2 October, 2015.
Source: compiled from Inside Airbnb.

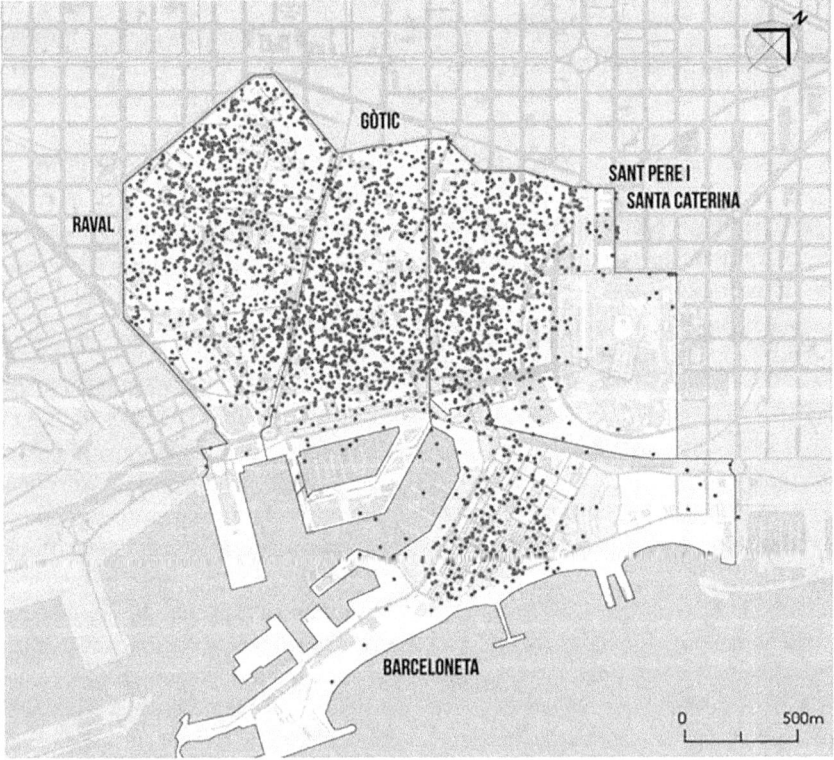

Figure 3 Flats listed in the historic centre of Barcelona (Ciutat Vella). 2 October, 2015.
Source: compiled from Inside Airbnb.

4.3 In Barcelona, there were 14,539 flats listed on Airbnb. Interestingly, those flats represent 2.2% of existing households. However, the phenomenon is uneven and there is a strong concentration in central areas. In the historic centre (the district called Ciutat Vella) the proportion is 9.6%. Ciutat Vella has four neighbourhoods, of which the Gòtic has a proportion of 16.8%. Therefore, in the Gòtic neighbourhood, 1 out of 6 apartments were listed on Airbnb on 2nd October, 2015. These proportions can be seen in the following table:

2015	Airbnb listings	Households	Airbnb/Households
Barcelona	14,539	655,175	2.2
Ciutat Vella	3,845	39,926	9.6
Raval	1,340	16,776	7.9
Gótic	1,091	6,461	16.8
S Pere, S Cat., Ribera	1,111	9,869	11.2
Barceloneta	303	6,821	4.4

Table 1 Airbnb listings on 2 October, 2015 and existing households. Source: Inside Airbnb and Barcelona City Council, Statistics.

Qualitative results: holiday rentals and displacement

4.4 This sub-section explores how the conversion of housing into tourist accommodation is experienced by residents. The aim is to better understand the impacts that vacation flats cause on communities and, by so doing, to comprehend why they are being resisted. Put simply, as short-term rentals are an appealing business opportunity, long-term residents represent a barrier to capital accumulation. Notwithstanding, the displacement process is not so straight forward and actually takes several forms. The empirical work confirms the occurrence of the different types of displacement conceptualised by Marcuse (1985): direct displacement, exclusionary displacement and displacement pressures.

4.5 Direct displacement. Processes of direct displacement are a central concern within the community. Ultimately, the 1,191 vacation flats that exist in the Gòtic area once provided accommodation for long-term residents. There are cases in which tenants are economically compensated if they agree to leave prior to the end of the agreement. In other cases, the landlord simply does not renew the contract. Despite the fact that for tenants it is never easy to move out involuntarily, there are several cases in which the eviction process has been more dramatic and violent, especially for lifetime tenants. Harassment and deliberate degradation is being used to force tenants to leave.

4.6 Exclusionary displacement. Although direct displacement is more visible, I argue that exclusionary displacement affects a larger number of residents as they are excluded from the possibility of accessing housing. This exclusion is caused by two interrelated issues. Firstly, the fact that 16.8% of flats have been taken out of the housing stock means that several landlords and companies do not even consider the idea of renting to residents as they can make higher profits from short-term rentals. Secondly, the latter intensifies the rise in rent prices which in Ciutat Vella is now 9% higher than the average in Barcelona, despite the fact that in 2007 it was 3% lower. As a resident states, 'it took me ages simply to find a flat available to long-term residents. But they are so expensive that you cannot afford them on local wages'. The difficulties in finding affordable accommodation accelerates 'classical' gentrification as only middle- and upper-class groups can afford to move to the area. At the same time, exclusionary displacement is at the origin of several strategies implemented by residents who want to remain in the area but for which 'staying put' involves accepting poor living conditions, overcrowding or spending more than 50% of their income on rent.

4.7 Displacement pressures. On the one hand, the fact that apartment buildings combine residential and tourist uses is the cause of daily cohabitation troubles that have been for many the main reason to move out of the property. There are several types of disruption that affect the private lives of residents. The most frequent is noise and the growing difficulties encountered in resting and sleeping during night time. Several interviewees explained that sometimes visitors do not even know which flat to go and so they try to open residents' doors. These pressures affect all residents and not only tenants. I interviewed a couple who decided to sell their flat and move to a different neighbourhood: 'in the building 14 out of 20 flats were holiday apartments. Some of them were actually youth hostels. And they radically changed our lives (...)'. The coexistence of residential and tourist uses also produces an economic pressure in which residents cannot afford the upkeep of a building increasingly used by visitors. On the other hand, the pressure of tourist investors is on the increase. As a resident explains, 'it is not a coincidence that every week I find in my post-box an offer to buy my flat saying "great opportunity!". The thing is that I feel I am trying to resist against something that ultimately says that I am a leftover here. That says: what are you doing here? This place is for tourists'.

DISCUSSION: TOWARDS A CONCEPTUALISATION OF COLLECTIVE DISPLACEMENT

5.1 The description of the way in which holiday rentals are experienced by residents shows that the moment of eviction is not the only form of displacement (Marcuse 1985; Davidson and Lees 2010). Although direct displacement is an important consequence, the process causes indirect impacts that are crucial to understanding community opposition to tourism. From this point of view, understanding displacement pressures involves understanding the lived experiences of residents before direct displacement takes place. But also, I want to stress the importance of exclusionary displacement. The growth of the phenomenon excludes residents from the possibility of accessing housing while also provoking mounting affordability pressures. The current loss of housing stock also means that residents that have suffered direct displacement are unable to find accommodation in the neighbourhood. This point is crucial as it makes it increasingly difficult to reproduce the local community that, instead, is replaced by transient consumers.

5.2 I suggest that the growth of tourism and the consequent conversion of housing into accommodation for visitors results in a process of social change that I call 'collective displacement'. Collective displacement needs to be seen as the final consequence of a process in which all forms of displacement come together. First, the growth of tourism causes a progressive out-migration of residents via direct displacement. Second, it is at the origin of housing shortage and price increase, which excludes other residents from the possibility of moving into the area. Third, this exclusion is accelerated by the daily disruptions and economic pressures caused by vacation flats. Finally, such disruptions and the pressure of tourist investors 'force' residents to sell their flats. In such a context, the only buyers tend to be tourist investors, which further intensifies and reproduces the displacement process. In conclusion, the growth of the phenomenon results in a vicious circle that solely enables the reproduction of further accommodation for visitors rather than for long-term residential use. It is a snowball process in which the area loses residents and excludes potential ones from the possibility of moving in. It leads to a form of collective displacement never seen in classical gentrification, that is to say, to a substitution of residential life by tourism.

FINAL REMARKS

6.1 Tourism-driven displacement is central to understanding why vacation flats are resisted. As stressed by Slater (2015), it is important to note that displacement is actively produced and has nothing to do with a supposedly natural functioning of the free market. The process is fuelled by investors, tourist companies and individual landlords for whom the conversion of residential buildings into accommodation for visitors is a new business opportunity. It is also facilitated by the state via the liberalisation of the housing market as it allows such a conversion. By way of contrast, for residents and for those who need a place to live holiday rentals represent the new gentrification battlefront. The phenomenon threatens their right to stay put while making it increasingly difficult for residents to find affordable accommodation. The example of vacation rentals shows the extent to which tourism can be a displacing process and, as such, a process that leads to urban inequalities. This fact opens new questions for gentrification research, but especially for public policy, as it challenges the assumption that the growth of tourism is inherently positive.

6.2 I have suggested that the growth of the phenomenon could lead to a substitution of residential life by tourism. Although further research is needed, this outcome is confirmed by early demographic studies in Barcelona (López-Gay and Cócola Gant 2016) as well as in other tourist destinations (Kesar et al. 2015) that links the growth of vacation rentals to a progressive population decrease. I suggest that this snowball process also needs to be related with changes in the entire character of the place. The mutation of places into spaces of tourism consumption makes everyday life increasingly difficult (Cócola Gant 2015). In this regard, we need empirical studies to explore the extent to which the growth of the tourism industry undermines the use value of neighborhoods as places for social reproduction.

ACKNOWLEDGEMENTS

This research is supported by the Portuguese National Funding Agency for Science, Research and Technology (SFRH/BPD/93008/2013) and by the School of Geography and Planning, University of Cardiff. The author is grateful to Geoffrey DeVerteuil and Peter Mackie for their support and supervision and to the anonymous reviewers for their useful comments and suggestions.

REFERENCES

Arias-Sans, A & Quaglieri-Domínguez, A (2016) Unravelling Airbnb. Urban Perspectives from Barcelona. In Russo, P & Richards, G (eds.) *Reinventing the Local in Tourism: Travel Communities and Peer-produced Place Experiences*. London: Channel View.

Bone, J (2014) Neoliberal Nomads: Housing Insecurity and the Revival of Private Renting in the UK. *Sociological Research Online* Vol. 19, No 4, www.socresonline.org.uk/19/4/1.html.

Butler, T (2002) Thinking Global But Acting Local: The Middle Classes in the City. *Sociological Research Online* Vol. 7, No 3, www.socresonline.org.uk/7/3/timbutler.html. [doi:10.5153/sro.740]

Cócola Gant, A (2014a) *El Barrio Gótico de Barcelona. Planificación del pasado e imagen de marca*. Barcelona: Madroño.

Cócola Gant, A (2014b) The Invention of the Barcelona Gothic Quarter. *Journal of Heritage Tourism*, Vol. 9, No 1, pp. 18–34 [doi:10.1080/1743873X.2013.815760].

Cócola Gant, A (2015) Tourism and Commercial Gentrification. In *The Ideal City. Between Myth and Reality*. RC21 Conference. Urbino: ISA, pp. 1–25.

Cole, I, Powell, R & Sanderson, E (2016) Putting the Squeeze on "Generation Rent": Housing Benefit Claimants in the Private Rented Sector-Transitions, Marginality and Stigmatisation. *Sociological Research Online*, Vol. 21, No 2, www.socresonline.org.uk/21/2/9.html [doi:10.5153/sro.3909]

Colomb, C & Novy, J (2016) Urban Tourism and its Discontents: An Introduction. In Colomb, C & Novy, J (eds.) *Protest and Resistance in the Tourist City*. London: Routledge, pp. 1–30.

Davidson, M & Lees, L (2010) New-build Gentrification: Its Histories, Trajectories, and Critical Geographies. *Population, Space and Place*, Vol. 16, No 5, pp. 395–411.

Degen, M (2004) Barcelona's Games: The Olympics, Urban Design, and Global Tourism. In Sheller, M & Urry, J (eds.) *Tourism Mobilities: Places to Play, Places in Play*. London: Routledge, pp. 131–142.

Deverteuil, G (2011) Evidence of Gentrification-induced Displacement Among Social Services in London and Los Angeles. *Urban Studies*, Vol. 48, No 8, pp. 1563–1580 [doi:10.1177/0042098010379277].

Deverteuil, G (2015) *Resilience in the Post-Welfare Inner City: Voluntary Sector Geographies in London, Los Angeles and Sydney*. Bristol: Policy Press [http://doi.org/10.1332/policypress/9781447316558.001.0001].

Füller, H & Michel, B (2014) Stop Being a Tourist! New Dynamics of Urban Tourism in Berlin-Kreuzberg. *International Journal of Urban and Regional Research*, Vol. 38, No 4, pp. 1304–1318 [doi:10.1111/1468-2427.12124].

García, M & Claver, N (2003) Barcelona: Governing Coalitions, Visitors and the Changing City Center. In Hoffman, L, Fainstein, S & Judd, D (eds.) *Cities and Visitors: Regulating People, Markets, and City Space*. Oxford: Blackwell, pp. 113–125 [doi:10.1002/9780470773673.ch6]

Kesar, O, Dezeljin, R & Bienenfeld, M (2015) Tourism Gentrification in the City of Zagreb: Time for a Debate? *Interdisciplinary Management Research*, Vol. 11, pp. 657–668.

Lees, L, Shin, HB & López-Morales, E (2016) *Planetary Gentrification*. Cambridge: Polity Press.

López-Gay, A & Cócola Gant, A (2016) Cambios demográficos en entornos urbanos bajo presión turística: el caso del barri Gòtic de Barcelona. In Domínguez-Mújica, J & Díaz-Hernández, R (eds.) *XV Congreso Nacional de la Población Española*. Fuerteventura: Asociación de Geógrafos Españoles, pp. 399–413.

Marcuse, P (1985) Gentrification, Abandonment, and Displacement: Connections, Causes, and Policy Responses in New York City. *Journal of Urban and Contemporary Law*, Vol. 28, pp. 195–240.

Newman, K & Wyly, EK (2006) The Right to Stay Put, Revisited: Gentrification and Resistance to Displacement in New York City. *Urban studies*, Vol. 43, No 1, pp. 23–57 [doi:10.1080/00420980500388710]

Opillard, F (2016) From San Francisco's "Tech Boom 2.0" to Valparaíso's UNESCO World Heritage Site: Resistance to Tourism Gentrification in a Comparative Political Perspective. In Colomb, C & Novy, J (eds.) *Protest and Resistance in the Tourist City*. London: Routledge, pp. 129–151.

Peters, D (2016) Density Wars in Silicon Beach: The Struggle to Mix New Spaces for Toil, Stay and Play in Santa Monica, California. In Colomb, C & Novy, J (eds.) *Protest and Resistance in the Tourist City*. London: Routledge, pp. 90–108.

Slater, T (2006) The Eviction of Critical Perspectives from Gentrification Research. *International Journal of Urban and Regional Research*, Vol. 30, No. 4, pp. 737–757. [doi:10.1111/j.1468-2427.2006.00689.x].

Slater, T (2009) Missing Marcuse: On Gentrification and Displacement. *City*, Vol. 13, No 2–3, pp. 292–311 [doi:10.1080/13604810902982250].

Slater, T (2015) Planetary Rent Gaps. *Antipode*, online.

BOX 6 AGUSTÍN COCOLA-GANT REFLECTION

The paper was based on a qualitative analysis of a mature destination such as Barcelona and described forms of displacement caused by short-term rentals (STRs). It also anticipated that Airbnb had nothing to do with the sharing economy. Context is important because being in Barcelona gave me somehow a 'privileged' position to study how tourism was driving neighborhood change. In Barcelona, community associations started to condemn the excesses of tourism in the late 1990s, and holiday rentals appeared in the city in the early 2000s. In 2005, before the creation of Airbnb, the city council approved a regulation to license STRs, and by 2011, there were almost 3,000 authorized holiday apartments. The license implied a change in the use of the unit from residential to commercial use. These STRs were entire apartments available all year round for visitors and managed by professional operators. In May 2011, the *Indignados* movement occupied squares around Spain for several weeks. In such gatherings, people discussed all types of socio-political issues, and the urban question was an important one. In Barcelona, community groups were created in each neighborhood, and in the city center, the main concern was tourism in general and holiday rentals in particular. Back then, one of their actions was to print stickers with the sentence 'Homes for people, not tourists', and organized walking tours to mark STRs around the city center. The point is that since the early 2000s, property owners rehabilitated buildings to be converted into STRs, and the process implied the displacement of elderly and working-class residents living in centrally located run-down blocks who usually suffered from harassment and deliberated degradation. The extra-local demand brought by tourism was opening up new investment opportunities in the built environment, triggering a sort of first-wave gentrification in areas that had historically suffered abandonment from capital. In addition, tourism growth was seen as a neoliberal solution to recovery from the 2008 financial crisis, and the increase in the number of visitors, hotels, and STRs was exponential between 2010 and 2019, intensifying the dynamics of tourism-led neighborhood change. The evidence in Barcelona was that tourism was driving gentrification, and when I started studying the phenomenon and reading about gentrification theory, this evidence was showing a geography of gentrification that questioned some of the theories to explain the process; in particular, that gentrification was the effect of new middle-class professionals replacing blue-collar workers due to changes in occupational structures of the post-industrial city. In Barcelona, however, rent gaps have been closed when the state and the real estate sector marketed places for tourism, attracting transient consumers from more advanced economies. Therefore, in the explanation of gentrification, tourism and the unequal division of labor were key points in this case. But if the attraction of an extra-local demand has been seen by developers to be necessary to stimulate local property markets, STR digital platforms took this to another level. Digital technology increases the ability of producers to effectively reach ever-more distant consumers, and in this case, platforms such as Airbnb intensified tourism-led gentrification as property owners can now list their properties online and reach a potential global demand. The private rental market increasingly caters to transient populations who are willing to pay high rent for short stays.

Among the forms of displacement showed in the paper, the most visible one was that landlords were replacing tenants with tourists. There was an increasing conversion of housing into accommodation for visitors and long-term residents were seen as a barrier to capital accumulation. The second one was that as housing was lost to Airbnb, STRs reduced housing alternatives for residents due to both price increase and lack of stock available in the long-term rental market. Finally, findings showed that the sharing of apartment buildings with tourists was a dramatic disruption for residents, causing mental health issues. The loss of neighbors and their substitution with unknown visitors break community ties and are the causes of fears and concerns that affect the lives of several people, especially the elderly. The result is an exclusionary process in which residential areas increasingly become leisure spaces for transient and mobile populations, becoming less attractive for more permanent residents to live in. The expansion of STRs and the type of neighborhood change that it entails have been driving a sort of change in land use from residential to touristic, and in many cases the process leads to population loss.

At the conceptual level, the conversion of some areas in tourist-only places led some authors to define the process as touristification, suggesting further that it is something essentially incompatible with gentrification as it may be at odds with the arrival of new middle-class residents in these areas. It is clear that tourism-led neighborhood change differs in many ways of classical examples of gentrification. However, I do think that touristification and gentrification feed, rather than clash with, each other. In terms of population change, touristification is never complete, and there are not cases of a total substitution of residential life by tourism. While population losses take place, we need to see migration flows in these areas, exploring inflow and outflow profiles. In this sense, it has been shown that spatial dislocation affects the most vulnerable population, and the incomers are young professionals who reside for a short- or mid-term period of time. There is social upgrading of the population residing in touristified areas. This is also related to another point, which is the supposed dichotomy between permanent residents versus visitors. For me, this argument seems an oversimplification of a more complex population change process driven by flows of different profiles of people in which the line between stable resident and weekend visitors have blurred. For instance, the STR market during the pandemic has survived by way of adapting it to mid-term rentals for floating young professionals, and new mixed-use developments have been flourishing that combine residential units for middle- and upper-class people with STRs and leisure spaces, signaling a convergence of tourism and high-end residential uses. Notwithstanding, the touristification/gentrification debate cannot be reduced to a population change analysis. From a production-side perspective, tourism and STRs accelerate gentrification as they open rent gaps and consequently are seen by landlords and developers as key elements to extract profits from property markets while displacing indigenous populations. Here, the geography of STRs is important. For instance, Mediterranean cities, such as Naples and Porto, did not experience classical gentrification in previous decades, and central areas were inhabited by working-class populations living in degraded built environments. The proliferation of STRs has opened the rent gap, and capital started to flow in. In a very short period, these places moved from a phase of 'decline' to a new phase of physical upgrading, escalating property prices, and social change.

18
The impacts of Airbnb in Athens, Lisbon and Milan

A rent gap theory perspective

Alberto Amore, Cecilia de Bernardi and Pavlos Arvanitis

INTRODUCTION

The 2007–2008 Global Financial Crisis had serious consequences for the economy of the so-called PIGS countries. (Halverson, 2016). While the implication of the crisis for state and government restructuring is acknowledged in tourism studies (see Amore & Hall, 2017 for a review), the implications for the housing market and temporary accommodations are currently overlooked. This is somehow bizarre given the significant relationship between the stock market and the real estate market in these countries (Lou, 2017). A phenomenon deserving much attention in the current global urban housing market is that of short-term rentals within the context of the so-called sharing economy (Aguilera et al., 2021). In tourism literature, the establishment of temporary renting platforms is often defined in contrast with the hospitality sector (Dogru et al., 2019; Guttentag & Smith, 2017) or demographic trends in visitor consumer behavior (Liang et al., 2018; Lu & Tabari, 2019). To date, however, the implications of sharing economy and temporary accommodations in the urban housing market has had a limited appraisal, with the few works of the kind being predominantly from geography and urban studies.

One of the dominant organizations on the sharing economy stage is Airbnb. Airbnb was founded in 2008 and represents nowadays the channel for booking 'millions of room nights for tourists around the globe' (Guttentag, 2015, p. 1193). According to the most recent estimates, Airbnb has had more than 500 million guest arrivals all-time, with an average of more than 2 million guests per night (Airbnb, 2020). The Airbnb phenomenon is global, with more than 100,000 cities in 220 countries and regions offering a temporary facility to tourists, with millennials representing the largest share of users (Airbnb, 2020; Oskam, 2019). Given the influence Airbnb has had in the accommodation sector over the last ten years, there have been scholars referring to it as a 'disruptive innovation' in the contexts where it operates (Guttentag, 2015; Guttentag & Smith, 2017). On the one hand, there are studies showing how Airbnb affects the conventional long-term rental market (Horn & Merante, 2017; Mermet, 2017). On the other hand, studies suggest that the interaction of Airbnb with the housing market is more complex and needs to be framed within the broader process of urban change (Aguilera et al., 2021; Oskam, 2019). However, the impact of Airbnb in prime urban tourism areas is big enough to not be disregarded (Mermet, 2017; Oskam, 2019). As Oskam (2019) observes, temporary letting providers use Airbnb to list apartments and homes to overcome financial strives and make available properties that would be otherwise vacant. However, it also influences the rental market by inducing a switch from long-term to short-term renting.

Scholars acknowledge both positive and negative aspects of Airbnb. On the one hand, Airbnb represents an important source of income that appeals renters as well as a more convenient accommodation service for customers (Oskam, 2019). Other effects include employment opportunities (Romão et al., 2018) and a higher volume of visitors to secondary tourist cities (Ioannides et al., 2018). On the other hand, platforms like Airbnb call for regulations and policies to overcome socio-economic drawbacks at the urban level (Nieuwland

& van Melik, 2018) and in the hospitality sector in particular (Fang et al., 2016). Moreover, critics stress on the consistent tax leakage of Airbnb and other platforms of the kind (Murillo et al., 2017). Overall, the effects of Airbnb in the society and the environment of cities are mostly uncharted (Frenken & Schor, 2017).

The opposition against Airbnb is much emphasized in mainstream media and grassroot initiatives (Hickey & Cookney, 2016). In a recent report on the impacts of Airbnb in Edinburgh, United Kingdom, critics raised 'concerns that the stock of available and affordable housing is being reduced, and that the character of the Old Town in particular is being changed' (Cockburn Association, 2018, p. 2). Ultimately, destination management organizations and local authorities acknowledged the need to regulate the sharing economy market for temporary properties. In Palma de Mallorca, Spain, the renting of vacations homes is prohibited and subject to a hefty sanction (Martín-Martín et al., 2019). Similarly, the introduction of a new legislation for short-term rentals in Barcelona now sets a limit of licenced providers within the city (Aguilera et al., 2021).

The aim of the present paper is to ascertain the relationship between temporary accommodation platforms such as Airbnb and trends in the urban housing market in Portugal, Italy and Greece in the aftermath of the 2007–2008 Global Financial Crisis. Building upon the rent gap theory (Smith, 1979) and the Lukesian notion of power (Lukes, 2005), it shows how Airbnb has been fostering the process of gentrification in Athens, Lisbon and Milan. The objective of this paper is threefold. First, it illustrates the spatial distribution of Airbnb in the selected cities and how these overlap with prime urban tourist areas. Second, it looks at overt forms of power and lobbying in key episodes of governance. Finally, it compares the regulatory framework for temporary accommodations in the aforementioned cities to ascertain relevant similarities.

LITERATURE

The literature widely addresses the nexus between the housing market and the 2007–2008 Global Financial Crisis (Lou, 2017; Martin, 2011). As Martin (2011, p. 597) observes, global financial fluctuation and speculative bubbles in the United States and the United Kingdom had 'geographically differentiated' impacts on housing markets at the local level. Looking at the European Union, evidence suggests that the financial crisis was particularly strong in urban and metropolitan areas with a dominant housing market (Dijkstra et al., 2015). Focusing on the PIGS countries (Portugal, Italy, Greece and Spain), the nexus between housing and finance is even stronger. As Lou (2017, p. 736) explains, this 'interdependence implies that investors are unable to hedge the risk across the real estate and stock markets when they are extremely volatile', with negative repercussions at the macro-economic level.

Research on the repercussions of the 2007–2008 Global Financial Crisis in urban tourism literature is limited in geographical range and policy focus. According to Amore and Hall (2017, p. 6), the 2007–2008 Global Financial Crisis has triggered 'a new frontier of hyperneoliberal development agenda that harshens the competition for the attraction of visitors and capitals on a global-local scale'. Particularly with cities in Southern Europe, the financial crisis and the austerity politics reinforced the economic relevance of tourism a panacea to economic revitalization (Cócola-Gant, 2018; Mendes, 2018; Souliotis, 2013). Yet, these cities had been embracing a tourism-driven urban development agenda in the years before the crisis. As Russo and Scarnato (2018, p. 455) recently observed, 'the tourism development agenda has been given full leeway to drive recovery, despite the fact that the real estate bubble linked to tourism had been in the first place one of the determinants of the extraordinary dimensions of that slump'.

The phenomenon of Airbnb in PIGS countries following the 2007–2008 Global Financial Crisis is gaining momentum. Relevant for the purpose of this study are the works of Cócola-Gant and Gago (2019) in Lisbon and Aguilera et al. (2021) in Milan. On the one hand, the evidence from Lisbon suggests the pervasive nature of sharing economy platforms in the displacement of existing residents out of the *Alfama* historic neighbourhood (Cócola-Gant & Gago, 2019). On the other hand, regulatory frameworks promoting sharing economy and tourism in Milan are legitimized 'in the context of a political consensus around the desirable growth of the visitor economy' (Aguilera et al., 2021, p. 11). However, both studies marginally acknowledge or overlook the phenomenon of Airbnb through a theoretical framework that combines insights from Smith's rent gap theory and the Lukesian analysis of power.

Gentrification and the rent gap theory

Gentrification refers to the process of urban change encompassing global and regional capital cities around the world in which 'disinvested inner-city neighbourhoods are upgraded by pioneer gentrifiers and the indigenous residents are displaced' (Lees et al., 2008, p. 10). The process of classical gentrification usually consists of four waves. Properties in inner-city areas are first occupied by owners, but when the latter relocate elsewhere, the real estate market enters a new phase with predominantly rented properties to lower-income residents. In the long run, properties progressively lose value and become appealing to both small and large developers who purchase and refurbish the housing stock to bring back more affluent middle-upper class residents.

The rent gap theory was first introduced by Neil Smith in 1979 to explain the decline and regrowth of cities in North America between the 1970s and the 1980s (Lees et al., 2008). Building on evidence from neighbourhoods in Philadelphia and New York, he concluded that contemporary urban development and regeneration were 'all part of the differentiation of geographical space at the urban scale' (Smith, 1986, p. 18). The circulation of capital outside the city as part of the process of gentrification contributed to the creation of 'the economic opportunity for restructuring the central and inner cities' (Smith, 1986, p. 2). In Smith's words, the resulting rent gap was 'the disparity between the potential ground rent level and the actual ground rent capitalized under the present land use' (Smith, 1979, p. 545).

Building from the work of Smith, Harvey (1989, p. 9) observed that 'investments to attract the consumer dollar have paradoxically grown a-pace as a response to generalised recession', with city authorities in North America and Europe embarking on large-scale revitalization projects in retail, sports, entertainment, leisure and tourism (Amore, 2019). The resulting shift towards urban entrepreneurialism came with a drastic reframing of urban governance, as observed in the cases of Budapest, Hungary (Olt et al., 2019) and Auckland, New Zealand (Nel, 2015) among others. In contrast, Badcock's (1989) concluded that post-recession capital circulation back to the city was not as straightforward in Adelaide, Australia, where the intervention of state and local authorities in concert provided a 'much potent agent of gentrification' (Badcock, 1989, p. 125).

The application of the rent gap theory in the study of tourism gentrification is addressed particularly in the context of US urban redevelopment. Evidence from New Orleans shows how retail and residential displacement is 'largely driven by mega-sized financial firms and entertainment corporations who have formed new institutional connections with traditional city boosters (chambers of commerce, city governments, service industries) to market cities' (Gotham, 2005, p. 1115). Research outside of the US also provides a rent gap appraisal of urban redevelopment from a tourism perspective, with a focus on real estate market trends, land use planning and residential displacement (Clark & Mahmoud, 2016; Liang & Bao, 2015). The emphasis on commercial and residential uses is mainstream in tourism gentrification literature, with findings from, among others, heritage sites (Amore, 2016), regeneration projects (Lestegás et al., 2019), rapid urbanization (Liang, 2017) and post-disaster recovery (Gotham & Greenberg, 2014).

Research connecting the implications Airbnb to the framework of the rent gap theory is limited (Yrigoy, 2019; Wachsmuth & Weisler, 2018). Research from Reykjavik, Iceland, shows how the impact of Airbnb in the housing market contributed to the soaring of house prices, with unfair competition between locals and tourists for accommodation in the centre of the city (Mermet, 2017). Similarly, evidence from New York, United States, shows how Airbnb has contributed to a new form of rent gap and induced gentrification in residential areas (Wachsmuth & Weisler, 2018). As Wachsmuth and Weisler (2018, p. 1153) further observe, 'Airbnb is in effect shifting the "highest and best use" of residential housing in neighbourhoods with sufficient extra-local tourist interest, and the result is a rent gap'. Finally, research conducted in Palma de Mallorca, Spain, shows how Airbnb contributes to a vicious cycle in which the viral spreading of tourist rental accommodation has repercussions both in terms of residential letting and tourist accommodation prices (Yrigoy, 2019).

Power: a radical view

Lukes (2005) notion of power distinguishes between overt, covert and hegemonic forms of coercion, coalitions, manipulation and non-decision-making mechanisms. As Hall (2011, p. 43) explains, Lukes identifies 'three different approaches, or dimensions, in the analysis of power, each focusing on different aspects of the decision-making process'. The first dimension of power refers to the implementation of policies and overt action of key stakeholders in imposing their vision to other subjects. The second dimension of power refers to the 'interface between the political system and the socio-cultural environment' (Farmaki et al., 2015, p. 186) and its legitimization through regulations, legislation and allegedly neutral guidelines (Lascoumes & Le Galès, 2007; Le Galès, 2011). Finally, the third dimension refers to the 'prevailing political ideology' (Farmaki et al., 2015, p. 186), which also frames 'how the tourism production system markets and packages places and people' (Britton, 1991, p. 476).

Following previous research in the field, we can identify a range of first-dimension forms of power in decision-making and planning in tourist cities. For example, stakeholders 'can coalesce around issues other than economic growth' (Bahaire & Elliott-White, 1999, p. 254) and agree on supporting a given policy decision (Bryson & Crosby, 1993). Conversely, stakeholders can object on decisions and matters that may undermine their personal gain, as in the case of the hotel and tourism industry in Cyprus (Farmaki et al., 2015). The second dimension of power is less visible, yet it is much decisive in urban planning. The focus on policy documents, laws and regulations 'is a fruitful avenue to demonstrate and interpret changing forms of governance' (Le Galès, 2011, p. 143). Documents like white papers and reports are far from being neutral; rather, 'they produce specific effects, independently of the objective pursued . . . which structure public policy according to their own logic' (Lascoumes & Le Galès, 2007, p. 3). Finally, the third dimension of power concerns the current hyperneoliberal shift in the contemporary city (Amore & Hall, 2017). Scholars stressed on market-driven and market-obeying urban development agendas over the last thirty years (Gotham & Greenberg, 2014; Harvey, 1989), including the rise of Airbnb and of sharing economy platforms (Oskam, 2019).

As Amore (2019, p. 55) puts it, 'the rhetoric regarding the economic benefits of tourism to urban development permeates the logics and decisions of all relevant stakeholders'.

The literature addresses episodes of governance regarding Airbnb through either one of Lukes' three dimensions. Looking at the overt forms of power, Airbnb has spent considerable resources in lobbying efforts, especially in objecting regulations that could inhibit or set a cap on short-term rentals (Gurran & Phibbs, 2017; Guttantag, 2015). In the case of Singapore, the Airbnb legal team lobbied against the strict regulations in the state, arguing that the platform simply enhances visibility and reachability of the Singaporean housing market (Koh & King, 2017). Focusing on the use and manipulation of information, evidence from the United States suggests that Airbnb has been actively concealing data about users' operations (Sans & Quaglieri, 2016; Wegmann & Jiao, 2017). Similarly, there have been cases where Airbnb intentionally manipulated data on multi-listers while emphasizing on the listing from single primary homeowners (Oskam, 2019). Finally, the hegemonic rhetoric on the economic benefits of Airbnb permeates current urban tourism debates among local authorities and neighbourhood associations, as in the cases of Barcelona and Lisbon (Amore, 2019).

METHODOLOGY

Based on the work of Smith, the authors collected statistical information on the housing market in Athens, Lisbon and Milan to identify spatial patterns between the concentration of Airbnb listed properties and the property value fluctuations. Data was collected from European and national government databases in Greece, Italy and Portugal. Given the reluctancy of Airbnb with the release of anonymised data for research purposes and public awareness, the authors opted to use data from consultancy firm AirDNA and from the independent website Inside Airbnb. The use of AirDNA is mainstream in academic research and studies in hospitality (Kwok & Xie, 2019) and the data provided are 'known as one of the best sources possible for academic research on Airbnb' (Kwok & Xie, 2019, p. 258). Moreover, this study deploys a qualitative research design, with archival data collection from national government, local government, media releases and reports focusing on Airbnb and its impact in Athens, Lisbon and Milan. This approach resembles that of Aguilera et al. (2019), which adopted 'a sociological approach to public policy to analyse the processes of politicization and collective action around, and different regulations' of Airbnb and other short-term rental platforms (Aguilera et al., 2019, p. 3). In this case, the authors opted to use Lukes' theory to analyse episodes of urban governance, policy regulations and rhetoric and regarding Airbnb and the sprawl of short-term rentals in the observed cities.

For the purpose of this study, the authors convened to deploy a longitudinal analysis for the period between 2011 and 2018. to provide a longitudinal appraisal of the long-term repercussions of the 2007–2008 Global Financial Crisis in the housing market. The choice of Athens, Lisbon and Milan for this study is fourfold. First, it provides a comparative appraisal from different PIGS countries. Second, it frames the recent shift in urban redevelopment in Greece, Italy and Portugal in light of the reforms and the agreements set in place with supranational authorities like the European Central Bank, the European Commission and the International Monetary Fund. Third, it looks at the phenomenon of Airbnb in the three main metropolitan areas and economic hubs in Greece, Italy and Portugal. Finally, the surge of Airbnb in these three countries occurred around the same time, with Airbnb opening a branch for Southeast Europe and the Mediterranean in 2017.

CONTEXT

Table 1 provides an overview of relevant housing, hospitality and short-term rental platform data for the three cities. Looking at Athens, there were at total of 9122 active short listings in 2019, making the Greek capital the biggest city by listing nationwide. Around 88% of the listings are for entire flats or houses, with 32.1% concentrated in the city centre. According to Inside Airbnb (2020a), 50.8% of listings were from multiple homeowners, with a peak of nearly 70% of multiple listings in *Plaka*. The repercussions of the 2007–2008 Global Financial Crisis were severe for Greece and the housing market in Athens, with property value index plummeting 40% between 2007 and 2018 (Delmendo, 2019; GlobalPropertyGuide, 2019). Similarly, Lisbon is the largest city by listings in Portugal, with 16,230 listed properties in 2019. Of these, 74.8% are for entire houses and flats, with 53% of listings concentrated in the central city area and a peak of 75.7% multiple listings in the *Baixa*. Just like Greece, the financial crisis and the regime of austerity under the *Troika* had a severe impact in the Lisbon housing market, with a 52% contraction of the house market in the metropolitan area and a 11% depreciation between 2010 and 2012 (INE, 2020a).

Conversely, Milan is the second-largest city by listings in Italy, with 17,659 registered properties in 2019, 60% of which were single listings. Around 73% of listings are for entire flats or houses, with 23.6% concentrated within the central city area (*Cerchia dei Bastioni*) (Inside Airbnb, 2020b). The presence of Airbnb in Milan mitigated the effects of the financial crisis on the housing market of the city. Regional and local authorities viewed Airbnb as a win-win solution to support 'new public and private sharing services and products in a more sustainable and inclusive economy' (Aguilera et al., 2019, p. 12) and to reposition the city of Milan as a leading tourist destination. However, this has led to early signs of tourism gentrification.

FINDINGS

Athens

The case of Athens resembles the crisis-driven urbanization model of Gotham and Greenberg (2014), with the 2007–2008 Global Financial Crisis acting as an artificial market trigger. Before the crisis, the housing market of Athens and Greece was estimated at €1 trillion, with nearly 9 out of 10 Greek families owning a house (Bank of Greece, 2014). Since then, the property value in Athens dropped by nearly 40%, with the internal housing market put under severe strife due to strict austerity policies and higher taxation on homeowners. House sales across the country decreased by 80% since 2007 (Bank of Greece, 2019), with renting prices decreasing between 41% and 50% at the neighbourhood level. The property market particularly in Athens, has been characterized by a stagnating demand, limited cash flow and finance access, capital controls, lack of financial incentives to renovate dated properties and lack of foreign investments. Moreover, property auctioning from banks and financial institutions have become a widespread practice, with nearly 20,000 auctions in 2018, 25,000 in 2019 and an

	Athens	Lisbon	Milan
Population[1]			
City	664,046	506,088	1,366,180
Metropolitan Area	2,622,404	1,851,077	4,106,356
GDP (€ millions)[2]	79,807	66,956	200,116
% national	45.2%	35.9%	11.8%
Housing Price Index[3,4,5]	60.9e	123.7	84.9
Visitor Expenditure (€ millions)[6,7,8]	2,000	3,917	2,633
Tourist Density (% estimate)	2.3%	2.9%	1.5%
Total Bed nights[9,10]	6,764,777	10,758,765	12,428,655
Number of hotels establishments[11,12,13]	239	213	473
Hotel occupancy rate[14,15]	81%	78%	72%
Active short-term rentals[16]	9,122	16,230	17,659

Table 1 Key indicators for the observed cities.

Sources:

1 Eurostat Urban Audit (2019), estimates at December 31st 2018
2 Eurostat (2019), 2016 data
3 Bank of Greece (2019), 2016 data (estimated base year 2010 = 100)
4 INE (2019), 2016 data (base year 2010 = 100)
5 ISTAT (2019), 2016 data (base year 2010 = 100)
6 Institute of the Greek Tourism Confederation and Bank of Greece (2018), 2017 data estimates
7 WTTC (2018), 2017 data
8 MasterCard Report (2018), 2017 data
9 Office for National Statistics and Insete Intelligence (2019), 2018 data
10 ECM Benchmarking Report (2019), 2018 data
11 Athens Chamber of Hotels and Insete Intelligence (2019), 2018 data
12 Camara Municipal de Lisboa (2018)
13 ISTAT (2019), 2018 data
14 GBR Consulting (2018)
15 Statista (2019), 2018 data
16 Inside Airbnb, 2020

estimated 35,000 in 2020, for a combined value of over € 6.4 billion. In this context, property investors purchased empty houses popular tourist spots and rent them out on Airbnb and other platforms (Bateman, 2019).

In terms of overt forms of power and stakeholder agency, property owners in Athens welcomed the introduction of Airbnb as an opportunity to cover the increasing housing taxes costs. Moreover, Airbnb granted an additional source of income that enabled property owners to pay the mortgages. The Hellenic Property Federation (POMIDA) also welcomed the breakthrough of the gridlock by stating that Airbnb enabled homeowners to lease their properties for short periods and thus supplement a further source of income (POMIDA, 2019). From an entrepreneurial perspective, the rise of Airbnb in Athens favoured the rise of small complementary activities like property management, cleaning and laundry services. In a joint statement issued in May 2019, the Athens Chamber of Commerce and POMIDA noted that properties listed on Airbnb accounted for 5.3% of the whole housing stock in the capital and that short-term rental provided through sharing economy platforms were an important vehicle for income generation (Athens Chamber of Tradesmen, 2019). The benefit of Airbnb to the national economy is currently estimated at USD$ 1.4 billion (Athens Chamber of Tradesmen, 2019), with relevant implications for the development of sharing economy platforms in the city. However, there is rising opposition from local residents who expressed their complaints about the change of land use and increased noise levels by holidaymakers. Similarly, hotel owners and tourism associations raised concerns over the questionable level of service offered by unprofessional property owners. The Hellenic Chamber of Commerce, in particular, has been highlighting the negative impacts of Airbnb to the Athens hospitality industry over the last years as well as the social implications of uncontrolled and unregulated short-term rental market for the city (Hellenic Chamber of Hotels, 2019). The inflated housing market is also affecting the temporary student population, with a 10% increase of average rent between 2018 and 2019 only (Spitogatos.gr, 2019).

Airbnb and other short-term rental platforms took advantage of the regulatory vacuum in the Greek legislation on private vacation homes and shared accommodations. The legislative framework on Airbnb and sharing economy platforms was first introduced in 2016 (Law 4446/2016) clearly stating that short-term leases are a special category of residential lease which can be provided by the owner of the property both to a legal or physical entity (the lessee). These leases are different from room rental leases which fall under a different category and are considered a business activity liable to VAT, whereas short-term leases are exempt from VAT. The legislation was further enhanced in 2017 with the promulgation of Law 4465/2017 and Law 4472/2017 which clarified areas that were still vague regarding short-term rentals. The latest addition in the legislation came in the form of a Ministerial Decree (MD 1059/2018) which stated that anyone could use their properties for short-term letting for up to 90 days a year without having to report their properties in the national registry. Anyone seeking to rent their property through sharing economy platforms for periods exceeding 90 days now has to register the property and report their activity as property traders.

With reference to the hegemonic dimension of power, the rhetoric of Airbnb as the panacea to overcome the financial crisis and the harsh regime of austerity reinforced the belief among Athenians on short-term rentals as a solution to their financial strives. The investments on property renovations underpinned the idea of Airbnb being a win-win solution for homeowners. The Airbnb reports on the social and economic impacts of short-term renting in Athens reiterates the narrative of the benefits of the platform among Athenians (Airbnb, 2015). However, the resulting rise in rent prices puts the student population under fierce rental competition for rooms and apartments, with mounting protests against the activity Airbnb in the city (Kathimerini, 2019; Roussanoglou, 2018, 2019).

Lisbon

The rise of Airbnb in Lisbon and its impact in the housing market has been recently referred to as buy-to-let investment (Cócola-Gant & Gago, 2019), with a concentration of listed houses particularly in the old part of the city. The 2010 bailout and the *Troika* led to a major shift on leisure-led urban revitalization policies aiming at attracting foreign investors and tourists in order to reduce the trade deficit (Mendes, 2018; Santos Pereira, 2011). The conjunctural rise of Airbnb in Lisbon favoured international competition for housing market in the Portuguese capital, with the soaring of the housing index in key tourist areas of the city. According to the *Instituto Nacional de Estatística* (INE), the value of properties in key tourist areas is significantly above the average house price, with peaks of +43% and +52.4% in the *Baixa* and *Avenida da Liberdade* respectively (INE, 2020b). In comparison, the ratio between the average Lisbon house value and the properties in the aforementioned neighbourhoods in 2011 were of +2.6% and +21.8% (INE, 2020c). Over the same period, the number of apartments listed in Lisbon soared from 20 to nearly 17,000, with 90% of the properties listed on Airbnb (AirDna, 2020).

In contrast to Athens, the *Troika* found the housing market of Lisbon, and Portugal more broadly, to be excessively regulated and included the removal of the rent cap as part of the conditions for the bailout. Focusing on the overt dimension of power, the National Government regarded tourism as the ideal flywheel for the relaunch of the Portuguese economy. In the words of the then Minister for the Economy, Alvaro Santos Pereira, Portugal and its capital could become the Florida of Europe (Santos Pereira, 2011). Airbnb prospered in such climate of market deregulation and leisure-led policymaking. Similarly, owners of multiple properties in Lisbon benefited from Airbnb. According to a recent study, the ratio between short-term rental homes and owners is 2-to-1, with companies that administer whole apartments buildings through Airbnb in key areas of the historic city centre (Reis Ribeiro, 2018). A second study suggests that each of the top 25 homeowners listed at least 60 properties on Airbnb in the last year, with a personal gain of nearly € 25 million (Rio Fernandes et al., 2019). The resulting gentrification of the Lisbon historic centre has put low-income residents and the elderly under real estate pressure, with increasing cases of eviction and discontinuation of rental agreements (Lourenço, 2018).

With regards to the second dimension of power, special regulations and legislation legitimized the market-obeying regime of buy-to-let tourism gentrification in Lisbon. On the one hand, the introduction of the Golden Visa programme in 2012 attracted foreign residents who had the capital to purchase properties and invest resources in the refurbishment of houses (SEF, 2019). On the other hand, the introduction of the new urban lease law in 2012 deregulated the private rental market by providing landowners and renters more freedom in the stipulation of urban rental agreements (Lei n° 31/2012). The legislation, in particular, created a dedicated scheme for the resolution of existing subsidized rentals, thus enabling landowners to quickly relocate properties in the market (Lei n° 31/2012). With regards to short-term rentals, the legislation on *alojamento local* (2012 and 2018) gives local authorities the power to define containment areas and set a limit on the number of listings a single owner can advertise. Under the new legislation, the Lisbon city council was able to suspend new licences in key historic neighbourhoods for a year and temporarily contain the sprawl of short-term rentals in these areas (Bratley, 2018). The latter clause, however, does not apply to pre-existing listings in these areas.

The hegemonic dimension of power in the rise of Airbnb in Lisbon can be seen in the statements of local residents, the Lisbon city council and real estate agents. On the one hand, residents protested with the surge of Airbnb in Lisbon, but they also acknowledged how foreign tourism spending is important for the economy of the city (Mancini & Gomes, 2017). Conversely, the current Lisbon Mayor, Fernando Medina argues that Airbnb, the sharing economy and the rise short-term rentals bring dynamic to underpopulated areas of Lisbon and reduce the number of empty properties in the city centre (Hickey & Cookney, 2016). Similarly, London-based real estate group Athena Advisers encourage investors to purchase properties in Lisbon and list them on Airbnb as the 'rich cultural offering and upbeat atmosphere stemming from a city that's undergoing continued regeneration is elevating its position as a European tourism heavyweight' (Athena Advisers, 2016, p. 2). The Athena Advisers report stresses on the economic output of Airbnb in Lisbon and the spillover effect to the wider tourism industry of the city. In doing so, they reiterate the positive outlook of property investment in Lisbon, regardless of clear signs of market saturation in prime urban tourism areas.

Milan

From a rent gap theory perspective, the drop of housing prices in Milan as a result of the 2007–2008 Global Financial Crisis can be assimilated to the classical process of capital flight away from the city. The development policies in Milan over the last decade enhanced the urban entrepreneurial agenda, favouring private development and real estate rather than affordable housing in the city centre and in the inner-city areas (Costa et al., 2016). New building permits and the refurbishment of existing facilities boosted the housing market in Milan, with Airbnb contributing to the rise of house prices in the central city area. The housing price index in Milan oscillated between 2010 and 2017, with the lowest house price registered in 2015 (ISTAT, 2018a, 2018b). However, the housing market in the city centre is currently growing (Agenzia delle Entrate, 2019; ISTAT, 2019), a trend which underpins the exponential growth of house listings on Airbnb in the prime urban tourism areas of the city. Evidence from Milan shows how influential private and corporate stakeholders initially favoured a *lasseiz-faire* approach on short-term rentals regulation that much favoured Airbnb. In particular, the absence of an explicit cap on short-term house listings in key areas of the city reflect a market-driven approach aiming at quick return on investment. This was strikingly evident during the 2015 Expo, with Airbnb local households earning nearly 70% of the revenues during the event (Statista, 2018). The lobbying from the Italian Hotel Association against the many grey areas in the existing legislation (FederAlberghi, 2018) and the boost of listings following 2015 led the regional legislator to promulgate a stricter regulation for Airbnb and other platforms. The legislation foresaw homeowners to adopt a special reference code for property listings and compulsory registration in the *Comune* (L.R. 27/2015 Art. 38 § 8, 8 bis, 8 ter). Both Airbnb and homeowners publicly objected the legislation, stating that the new regulations were unconstitutional (Dell'Oste, 2019). The lobbying of Airbnb even persuaded the national government to appeal to the Constitutional Court (FederAlberghi Varese, 2018), but the verdict in favour of the region and the more recent promulgation of a nationally binding regulatory framework in 2019 now force Airbnb listings to include a code (*Codice Identifica-tivo di Riferimento – CIR*) for all listed properties.

Focusing on the second dimension of power, the special legislation for the 2015 Expo created the ideal regulatory vacuum for the growth of Airbnb and similar providers in Milan. It is worth noting that the 2015 Expo had to be realized in a time in which the local government was being restricted by austerity measures and the promulgation of the Fiscal Compact. In this context, Airbnb became a rather quick-fix solution to meet the hospitality requirements and the 20 million visitor projections for the event. The conjunctural crisis in the housing market, the highly parcelled home ownership and the opportunity of the 2015 Expo provided the ideal context to the legitimization of Airbnb and sharing economy practices.

In addition, research evidence from two Milanese universities and sharing economy gurus were included to reinforce the positive image of Airbnb in the Sharexpo Report. The latter provided economic and social indicators depicting the multiple benefits of sharing economy and stressed on the positive attitude among local residents in favour of Airbnb and similar platforms (Sharexpo, 2014). Following the event, the initial regulatory vacuum was partially addressed, with the introduction of the CIR, yet the enforcement scheme put in place is objectively limited in resources and scope to implement the regulations (Aguilera et al., 2019).

Evidence of the hegemonic dimension of power is most visible in the discourses on Airbnb and its growth in Milan. The initial legislations of 2014 and 2015 underpinned the rhetoric of Airbnb as a positive driver for change that favoured 'the integration and interoperability between the public and private digital platforms in the tourism sector' (L.R. 27/2015 Art. 2, § k). Similarly, the emphasis on entrepreneurship, digital marketing and smart cities was used to support regulations and stakeholders who were favourable to the introduction of Airbnb as short-term rental platform in a city seeking to position itself as an all-year round destination. In December 2014 the *Comune* of Milan launched the Milano Sharing City initiative, with local universities and intellectuals enhancing the positive rhetoric of Airbnb and the sharing economy. This was the case, again, of the Sharexpo report, which exhorted in experimenting sharing economy services for the benefits to the city of Milan and its community (Manieri, 2015; Sharexpo, 2014). The discourse focused emphatically on the possibility to 'cooperate' and to 'participate' in the regulatory process and the economic gains of participating in the sharing economy (Sharexpo, 2014, pp. 40–43). More importantly, it depicted the supportive function of Airbnb for low-income homeowners (Sharexpo, 2014, p. 60) which, as it turned out, was far from reflecting the reality.

DISCUSSION AND CONCLUSION

As this study shows, the three cities can be quite heterogenous in their basic characteristics, even though the number of bed nights, tourist density and hotel occupancy rates are rather similar. Furthermore, the three cases all share a common pattern in post-Global Financial Crisis urban governance, with rentals and housing market deregulation and the widespread of short-term renting platforms. Private development and foreign investment were two main ingredients in what was considered a quick-fix solution for the economic problems brought by the crisis. The three cities have also in common the discourses surrounding Airbnb as one-size-fit-all tool to support local residents. The issues created by Airbnb have also resulted in policy developments. Both Athens and Milan have sharpened the legislation surrounding short-term rentals such as Airbnb, enforcing the registration of the hosts. Lisbon has instead opted for empowering the city council to contain the development in certain areas, but this does not apply for the rentals that already exist.

The findings of this study underpin research carried in New York (Wachsmuth & Weisler, 2018), with Airbnb and similar short-term rental platforms reducing the rent gap at a faster rate than with conventional housing gentrification processes. However, the evidence from Athens, Lisbon and Milan does not suggest manifest episodes of gentrification in areas off the beaten track as illustrated in the work of Wachsmuth and Weisler (2018). This is probably due to the different relevance of these cities within the global urban hierarchy (Amore, 2019). Looking at previous research on Airbnb, this study agrees with Ioannides et al. (2018) on the concentration of Airbnb listings in key urban tourist areas and attractions. This study concurs with the findings of Ioannides et al. (2018) and Mermet (2017), whose work analysed the long-term implications of Airbnb for the housing market in Utrecht and Reykjavik respectively. Focusing on current research carried in Lisbon, this study reinforces the findings of Cócola-Gant and Gago (2019) on the speculative nature of Airbnb and the housing market in the city. In particular, the quick rental turnaround observed in the *Alfama-Mouraria* is reflection of the surge in property values observed in main urban tourist neighbourhoods of *Baixa* and *Avenida da Liberdade*. With regards to Milan, the evidence of this study underpins the findings of Aguilera et al. (2019) on the lobbying from Airbnb legal team and homeowners' associations against stricter regulation and monitoring of short-term listings.

A series of preliminary policy advises can be drawn from this study. Airbnb and similar sharing economy platforms prosper in contexts of strong market deregulation and international tourism growth. Policies that regarded Airbnb as a flywheel to overcome austerity or boost rooms capacity for mega-events are short-sighted and overlook the socio-economic disparities that emerge between existing residents and tourists. In light of recent comments and concerns on the phenomenon of overtourism and tourismphobia, sustainable urban tourism planning represents the only viable solution. It is up to local, national and European authorities to enhance regulation by introducing quotas and limiting listing periods to reduce uncontrolled tourism density during the high season.

This study sheds light on the phenomenon of Airbnb and short-term rentals in three urban areas where the 2007–2008 Global Financial Crisis profoundly affected the real estate market in PIGS countries. This is the first study of the kind that addresses property-led tourism gentrification with an appraisal of overt, covert and hegemonic forms of power. The evidence provided in this work shows that Airbnb is a means to foster a steady change in the visitor economy in Athens, Lisbon and Milan. Additionally, this work shows how Airbnb listings expedited the process of capital circulation outside and back to cities addressed in the rent gap theory applications in relation to urban tourism (Liang, 2017; Liang & Bao, 2015; Mermet, 2017).

There are at least two shortcomings in the current study. From a methodological perspective, this study only focusses on one city for each of the observed PIGS countries. Further research including other cities to the study (e.g. Porto, Rome and Thessaloniki) will provide more empirical evidence to what reported in this work. From a proxy data collection perspective, instead, the authors acknowledge the fragmented nature of housing prices currently available for Athens, Lisbon and Milan. In particular, there is very limited statistical data aggregated at neighbourhood level for the years 2008-2018. Direct data collection at neighbourhood level is therefore encouraged to provide further empirical underpinning to this research.

REFERENCES

Agenzia delle Entrate. (2019). *Banca dati delle quotazioni immobiliari*. wwwt.agenziaentrate.gov.it/servizi/Consultazione/ricerca

Aguilera, T., Artioli, F., & Colomb, C. (2021). Explaining the diversity of policy responses to platform-mediated short-term rentals in European cities: A comparison of Barcelona, Paris and Milan. *Environment and Planning A: Economy and Space, 53*(7), 1689–1712.

Airbnb. (2015). *Airbnb positive impact in athens* [Blog post]. https://blog.atairbnb.com/airbnbs-positive-impact-in-athens/

Airbnb. (2020). *Fast facts.* https://press.airbnb.com/fast-facts/

AirDna. (2020). *Lisbon data.* www.airdna.co/vacation-rental-data/app/pt/lisboa/lisbon/overview

Amore, A. (2016). I do (not) want you back! (Re)gentrification of the arts centre, Christchurch. In C. M. Hall, S. Malinen, R. Vosslamber, & R. Wordsworth (Eds.), *Business and post-disaster management: Business, organisational and consumer resilience and the Christchurch Earthquakes* (pp. 79–96). Routledge.

Amore, A. (2019). *Tourism and urban regeneration: Processes compressed in time and space.* Routledge.

Amore, A., & Hall, C. M. (2017). National and urban public policy in tourism. Towards the emergence of a hyperneoliberal script? *International Journal of Tourism Policy, 7*(1), 4–22. https://doi.org/10.1504/IJTP.2017.082761

Athena Advisers. (2016). *Airbnb market report Lisbon – August 2016.*

Athens Chamber of Tradesmen. (2019). *USD 1.4 bn the estimated benefit to the national economy from Airbnb.* www.eea.gr/arthra-eea/se-14-disekatommiria-dolaria-ipologizete-to-ofelos-tis-ellinikis-ikonomias-apo-to-airbnb/

Badcock, B. (1989). An Australian view of the rent gap hypothesis. *Annals of the Association of American Geographers, 79*(1), 125–145. https://doi.org/10.1111/j.1467-8306.1989.tb00254.x

Bahaire, T., & Elliott-White, M. (1999). Community participation in tourism planning and development in the historic city of York, England. *Current Issues in Tourism, 2*(2), 243–276. https://doi.org/10.1080/13683509908667854

Bank of Greece. (2014). *Study on real estate agencies.* www.bankofgreece.gr/RelatedDocuments/TE_EREVNA_KTIMATOMESITON.pdf

Bank of Greece. (2019). *Indices of residential property prices: Q2 2019* [Press Release]. www.bankofgreece.gr/en/news-and-media/press-office/news-list/news?announcement=e53ada32-e98d-49c8-b173-6032f7263e8d

Bateman, J. (2019, February 18). Athens property boom: Greeks left out as prices rise. *BBC News.* www.bbc.co.uk/news/world-europe-47237923

Bratley, C. M. (2018, October 25). New Alojamento local rules come into effect. *The Portugal News.* www.theportugalnews.com/news/new-alojamento-local-rules-come-into-effect/47267

Britton, S. (1991). Tourism, capital, and place: Towards a critical geography of tourism. *Environment and Planning D: Society and Space, 9*(4), 451–478. https://doi.org/10.1068/d090451

Bryson, J. M., & Crosby, B. C. (1993). Policy planning and the design and use of forums, arenas, and courts. *Environment and Planning B: Planning and Design, 20*(2), 175–194. https://doi.org/10.1068/b200175

Clark, E., & Mahmoud, Y. (2016). Rent gaps in the Spanish crisis. In M. Blàzquez, M. MirGual, I. Murray, & G. X. Pons (Eds.), *Turismo y crisis, turismo colaborativo y ecoturismo* (pp. 31–42). Societat d'Història Natural de les Balears.

Cockburn Association. (2018). *The Airbnb phenomenon: Impact and opportunities of the collaborative economy and disruptive technologies: How should Edinburgh respond to short-term letting?.*

Cócola-Gant, A. (2018). Tourism gentrification. In L. Lees & M. Phillips (Eds.), *Handbook of gentrification studies* (pp. 281–293). Edward Elgar.

Cócola-Gant, A., & Gago, A. (2019). Airbnb, buy-to-let investment and tourism-driven displacement: A case study in Lisbon. *Environment & Planning A: Economy and Space.* https://doi.org/10.1177/0308518X19869012

Costa, G., Cucca, R., & Torri, R. (2016). Milan: A city lost in the transition from the growth machine paradigm towards a social innovation approach. In T. Brandsen, S. Cattacin, A. Evers, & A. Zimmer (Eds.), *Social innovations in the urban context* (pp. 125–142). Springer.

Dell'Oste, C. (2019, April 11). Affitti Airbnb in Lombardia, negli annunci serve il codice. *Il Sole 24 Ore.* www.ilsole24ore.com/art/affitti-airbnb-lombardia-annunci-serve-codice-ABWOEYnB

Delmendo, L. C. (2019, February 2). Greek house prices are rising again, as economy continues to recovery. *GlobalPropertyGuide* [Press release]. www.globalpropertyguide.com/Europe/Greece/Price-History

Dijkstra, L., Garcilazo, E., & McCann, P. (2015). The effects of the global financial crisis on European regions and cities. *Journal of Economic Geography, 15*(5), 935–949. https://doi.org/10.1093/jeg/lbv032

Dogru, T., Mody, M., & Suess, C. (2019). Adding evidence to the debate: Quantifying Airbnb's disruptive impact on ten key hotel markets. *Tourism Management, 72*, 27–38. https://doi.org/10.1016/j.tourman.2018.11.008

Fang, B., Ye, Q., & Law, R. (2016). Effect of sharing economy on tourism industry employment. *Annals of Tourism Research, 57*(3), 264–267. https://doi.org/10.1016/j.annals.2015.11.018

Farmaki, A., Altinay, L., Botterill, D., & Hilke, S. (2015). Politics and sustainable tourism: The case of Cyprus. *Tourism Management, 47*, 178–190. https://doi.org/10.1016/j.tourman.2014.09.019

FederAlberghi. (2018). *Turismo e shadow economy: Tutela del consumatore, concorrenza leale ed equità fiscale al tempo del turismo 4.0*. www.federalberghi.it/UploadFile/2018/09/turismo%20e%20shadow%20economy%20-%20ediz ione%20settembre%202018.pdf

FederAlberghi Varese. (2018, March 26). *Codice identificativo per gli appartamenti turistici: il Governo contro la legge di Regione Lombardia* [Press Release]. www.federalberghivarese.it/new/comunicati-stampa/904-comunicato-stampa-a-codice-identificativo-per-gli-appartamenti-turistici-il-governo-contro-la-legge-di-regione-lombardia

Frenken, K., & Schor, J. (2017). Putting the sharing economy into perspective. *Environmental Innovation and Societal Transitions, 23*, 3–10. https://doi.org/10.1016/j.eist.2017.01.003

GoblalPropertyGuide. (2019a). *Greece: Market in depth*. www.globalpropertyguide.com/Europe/Greece#market-in-depth

Gotham, K. F. (2005). Tourism gentrification: The case of New Orleans' Vieux Carre (French Quarter). *Urban Studies, 42*(7), 1099–1121. https://doi.org/10.1080/00420980500120881

Gotham, K. F., & Greenberg, M. (2014). *Crisis cities: Disaster and redevelopment in New York and New Orleans*. Oxford University Press.

Gurran, N., & Phibbs, P. (2017). When tourists move in: How should urban planners respond to Airbnb? *Journal of the American Planning Association, 83*(1), 80–92. https://doi.org/10.1080/01944363.2016.1249011

Guttentag, D. A. (2015). Airbnb: Disruptive innovation and the rise of an informal tourism accommodation sector. *Current Issues in Tourism, 18*(12), 1192–1217. https://doi.org/10.1080/13683500.2013.827159

Guttentag, D. A., & Smith, S. L. (2017). Assessing Airbnb as a disruptive innovation relative to hotels: Substitution and comparative performance expectations. *International Journal of Hospitality Management, 64*, 1–10. https://doi.org/10.1016/j.ijhm.2017.02.003

Hall, C. M. (2011). Researching the political in tourism: Where knowledge meets power. In C. M. Hall (Ed.), *Fieldwork in tourism: Methods, issues and reflections* (pp. 39–54). Routledge.

Halvorsen, K. (2016). Economic, financial, and political crisis and well-being in the PIGS-countries. *Sage Open, 6*(4), 1–13. https://doi.org/10.1177/2158244016675198

Harvey, D. (1989). From managerialism to entrepreneurialism: The transformation in urban governance in late capitalism. *Geografiska Annaler: Series B. Human Geography, 71*(1), 3–17. https://doi.org/10.1080/04353684.1989.11879583

Hellenic Chamber of Hotels. (2019). *Overtaxation does not solve social issues* [Press Release]. www.grhotels.gr/GR/BussinessInfo/News/Lists/List/ItemView.aspx?ID=693

Hickey, S., & Cookney, F. (2016, 29 October). Airbnb faces worldwide opposition. It plans a movement to rise up in its defence. *The Guardian*. www.theguardian.com/technology/2016/oct/29/airbnb-backlash-customers-fight-back-london

Horn, K., & Merante, M. (2017). Is home sharing driving up rents? Evidence from Airbnb in Boston. *Journal of Housing Economics, 38*, 14–24. https://doi.org/10.1016/j.jhe.2017.08.002

Inside Airbnb. (2020a). *Athens*. http://insideairbnb.com/athens/?neighbourhood=&filterEntireHomes=false&filterHighlyAvailable=false&filterRecentReviews=false&filterMultiListings=false

Inside Airbnb. (2020b). *Milan*. http://insideairbnb.com/milan/

Instituto Nacional de Estatistica (INE). (2020a). *Valor e número de vendas de alojamentos familiares*. INE.

Instituto Nacional de Estatistica (INE). (2020b). *Preços da Habitação nas Cidades*. https://geohab.ine.pt/index.html?locale=Pt-pt

Instituto Nacional de Estatistica (INE). (2020c). *Valor médio mensal das rendas dos alojamentos familiares clássicos arren- dados (€) por Localização geográfica*. INE.

Ioannides, D., Röslmaier, M., & van der Zee, E. (2018). Airbnb as an instigator of 'tourism bubble' expansion in Utrecht's Lombok neighbourhood. *Tourism Geographies*, 1–19. https://doi.org/10.1080/14616688.2017.1409261

ISTAT. (2018a). *Prezzi delle abitazioni – II trimestre 2018*. www.istat.it/it/files//2018/10/CS-abitazioni-provv-Q22018.pdf

ISTAT. (2018b). *Prezzi delle abitazioni – IV trimestre 2018*. www.istat.it/it/files//2019/03/CS-abitazioni-provv-Q42018.pdf

ISTAT. (2019). *Prezzi delle abitazioni – II trimestre 2019*. www.istat.it/it/files//2019/09/CS-abitazioni-Q22019.pdf

Kathimerini. (2019). *Rising rents for students in Athens this fall*. www.ekathimerini.com/243927/article/ekathimerini/business/rising-rents-for-students-in-athens-this-fall

Koh, E., & King, B. (2017). Accommodating the sharing revolution: A qualitative evaluation of the impact of Airbnb on Singapore's budget hotels. *Tourism Recreation Research*, *42*(4), 409–421. https://doi.org/10.1080/02508281.2017.1314413

Kwok, L., & Xie, K. L. (2019). Pricing strategies on Airbnb: Are multi-unit hosts revenue pros? *International Journal of Hospitality Management*, *82*, 252–259. https://doi.org/10.1016/j.ijhm.2018.09.013

Lascoumes, P., & Le Galès, P. (2007). Introduction: Understanding public policy through its instruments – from the nature of instruments to the sociology of public policy instrumentation. *Governance*, *20*(1), 1–21. https://doi.org/10.1111/j.1468-0491.2007.00342.x

Le Galès, P. (2011). Policy instruments and governance. In M. Bevir (Ed.), *The Sage handbook of governance* (pp. 142–159). Sage.

Lees, L., Slater, T., & Wyly, E. (2008). *Gentrification*. Routledge.

Lestegás, I., Seixas, J., & Lois-González, R. C. (2019). Commodifying Lisbon: A study on the spatial concentration of short-term rentals. *Social Sciences*, *8*(2), 33–47. https://doi.org/10.3390/socsci8020033

Liang, L. J., Choi, H. C., & Joppe, M. (2018). Understanding repurchase intention of Airbnb consumers: Perceived authenticity, electronic word-of-mouth, and price sensitivity. *Journal of Travel & Tourism Marketing*, *35*(1), 73–89. https://doi.org/10.1080/10548408.2016.1224750

Liang, Z. X. (2017). The rent gap re-examined: Tourism gentrification in the context of rapid urbanization in China. In M. Gravari-Barbas, & S. Guinand (Eds.), *Tourism and gentrification in contemporary metropolises* (pp. 276–298). Routledge.

Liang, Z. X., & Bao, J. G. (2015). Tourism gentrification in Shenzhen, China: Causes and socio-spatial consequences. *Tourism Geographies*, *17*(3), 461–481. https://doi.org/10.1080/14616688.2014.1000954

Lou, T. (2017). Nonlinear causality relationship between stock and real-estate returns in PIGS countries: Wealth effect or credit-price effect. *Applied Economics Letters*, *24*(11), 736–741. https://doi.org/10.1080/13504851.2016.1226480

Lourenço, P. (2018, April 18). "Bullying" imobiliário esvazia bairros de Lisboa. *Jornal de Notícias*. www.jn.pt/nacional/especial/bullying-imobiliario-esvazia-bairros-de-lisboa-9267961.html

Lu, L., & Tabari, S. (2019). Impact of Airbnb on customers' behavior in the UK hotel industry. *Tourism Analysis*, *24*(1), 13–26. https://doi.org/10.3727/108354219X15458295631891

Lukes, S. (2005). *Power: A radical view*. Palgrave Macmillan.

Mancini, D., & Gomes, C. (2017, September 19). The dark side of tourism: Lisbon's 'terramotourism'. *Euronews*. www.euronews.com/2017/09/19/lisbon-s-tourism-magnet-is-kicking-out-local-residents

Manieri, M. (2015). Ecco come la città di Milano ha favorito la sharing economy durante Expo [Blog post]. http://collaboriamo.org/ecco-come-la-citta-di-milano-ha-favorito-la-sharing-economy-durante-expo/

Martin, R. (2011). The local geographies of the financial crisis: From the housing bubble to economic recession and beyond. *Journal of Economic Geography*, *11*(4), 587–618. https://doi.org/10.1093/jeg/lbq024

Martín-Martín, J. M., Ostos-Rey, M. S., & Salinas-Fernández, J. A. (2019). Why regulation is needed in emerging markets in the tourism sector. *American Journal of Economics and Sociology*, *78*(1), 225–254. https://doi.org/10.1111/ajes.12263

Mendes, L. (2018). Tourism gentrification in Lisbon: Neoliberal turn and financialisation of real state in a scenario of austerity urbanism. In I. David (Ed.), *Crisis, austerity and transformation: How disciplining neoliberalism is changing Portugal* (pp. 25–46). Lexington.

Mermet, A. C. (2017). Airbnb and tourism gentrification: Critical insights from the exploratory analysis of the 'Airbnb syndrome' in Reykjavik. In M. Gravari-Barbas & S. Guinand (Eds.), *Tourism and gentrification in contemporary metropolises* (pp. 52–74). Routledge.

Murillo, D., Buckland, H., & Val, E. (2017). When the sharing economy becomes neoliberalism on steroids: Unravelling the controversies. *Technological Forecasting and Social Change, 125*, 66–76. https://doi.org/10.1016/j.techfore.2017.05.024

Nel, E. (2015). Evolving regional and local economic development in New Zealand. *Local Economy, 30*(1), 67–77. https://doi.org/10.1177/0269094214564833

Nieuwland, S., & van Melik, R. (2018). Regulating Airbnb: How cities deal with perceived negative externalities of short-term rentals. *Current Issues in Tourism*. https://doi.org/10.1080/13683500.2018.1504899

Olt, G., Smith, M. K., Csizmady, A., & Sziva, I. (2019). Gentrification, tourism and the nighttime economy in Budapest's district VII – the role of regulation in a post-socialist context. *Journal of Policy Research in Tourism, Leisure and Events, 11*(3), 394–406. https://doi.org/10.1080/19407963.2019.1604531

Oskam, J. A. (2019). *The future of Airbnb and the 'sharing economy': The collaborative consumption of our cities*. Channel View Publications.

POMIDA (Hellenic Property Federation). (2019). *Short term leases*. www.pomida.gr/touristikes_misthoseis.php

Reis Ribeiro, L. (2018, July 23). Portugal é líder europeu no emprego em plataformas como Uber e Airbnb. *Diario de Noticias*. www.dn.pt/edicao-do-dia/23-jul-2018/portugal-e-lider-europeu-no-emprego-em-plataformas-online-como-uber-e-airbnb-9624324.html

Rio Fernandes, J. A., Carvalho, L., Chamusca, P., Gago, A., & Mendes, T. (2019). *Lisboa e a Airbnb*. Book Cover Editora.

Romão, J., Kourtit, K., Neuts, B., & Nijkamp, P. (2018). The smart city as a common place for tourists and residents: A structural analysis of the determinants of urban attractiveness. *Cities, 78*, 67–75. https://doi.org/10.1016/j.cities.2017.11.007

Roussanoglou, N. (2018, August 28). Airbnb market booming in Athens. *Kathimerini*. www.ekathimerini.com/232072/article/ekathimerini/business/airbnb-market-booming-in-athens

Roussanoglou, N. (2019, January 20). Property owners doubling rent revenues thanks to homesharing. *Kathimerini*. www.ekathimerini.com/236813/article/ekathimerini/business/property-owners-doubling-rent-revenues-thanks-to-homesharing

Russo, A. P., & Scarnato, A. (2018). Barcelona in common: A new urban regime for the 21st-century tourist city? *Journal of Urban Affairs, 40*(4), 455–474. https://doi.org/10.1080/07352166.2017.1373023

Sans, A. A., & Quaglieri, A. (2016). Unravelling Airbnb: Urban perspectives from Barcelona. In A. P. Russo & G. Richards (Eds.), *Reinventing the local in tourism: Producing, consuming and negotiating place* (pp. 209–228). Channel View Publications.

Santos Pereira, A. (2011). *Portugal na Hora da Verdade O que fazer para vencermos a crise nacional*. Gradiva.

Serviço de Estrangeiros e Fronteiras (SEF). (2019). *Applying for a residence permit for investment activity*. Lisbon: SEF. www.sef.pt/en/Documents/FICHA_ARI_PDF3_Pedido_EN.pdf

Sharexpo. (2014). *Documento d'Indirizzo Sharexpo: Milano città condivisa per Expo 2015*. https://issuu.com/sharexpo/docs/documento_d_indirizzo_sharexpo/7

Smith, N. (1979). Toward a theory of gentrification, a back to the city movement by capital, not people. *Journal of the American Planning Association, 45*(4), 538–548. https://doi.org/10.1080/01944367908977002

Smith, N. (1986). Gentrification, the frontier and the restructuring of urban space. In N. Smith & P. Williams (Eds.), *Gentrification of the city* (pp. 15–34). Allen & Unwin.

Souliotis, N. (2013). Athens and the politics of the sovereign debt crisis. In K. Fujita (Ed.), *Cities and crisis: New critical urban theory* (pp. 236–269). Sage.

Spitogatos.gr. (2019). Ποιες είναι οι τιμές ενοικίασης στα φοιτητικά σπίτια. www.spitogatos.gr/articles/agora_akiniton/poies-einai-oi-times-enoikiasis-sta-foititika-spitia/

Statista. (2018). *Number of Airbnb inbound guests in the Italian city of Milan in 2015 and during the Milan Expo 2015*. www.statista.com/

Wachsmuth, D., & Weisler, A. (2018). Airbnb and the rent gap: Gentrification through the sharing economy. *Environment and Planning A: Economy and Space*, *50*(6), 1147–1170. https://doi.org/10.1177/0308518X18778038

Wegmann, J., & Jiao, J. (2017). Taming Airbnb: Toward guiding principles for local regulation of urban vacation rentals based on empirical results from five US cities. *Land Use Policy*, *69*, 494–501. https://doi.org/10.1016/j.landusepol.2017.09.025

Yrigoy, I. (2019). Rent gap reloaded: Airbnb and the shift from residential to touristic rental housing in the Palma Old Quarter in Mallorca Spain. *Urban Studies*, *56*(13), 2709–2726. https://doi.org/10.1177/0042098018803261

19
Platform-mediated short-term rentals and gentrification in Madrid

Alvaro Ardura Urquiaga, Iñigo Lorente-Riverola and Javier Ruiz Sanchez

INTRODUCTION

'Classical gentrification' (Lees et al., 2008: 10) can be understood as a substitution of the resident population in some areas of cities by higher-income classes following periods of social and economic decline. Its most relevant characteristic is the rise in the cost of living according to the newcomers' standards, which eventually may force lower-income residents to find new areas in which to live. In recent years, the middle class's growing access to tourism, the globalisation of real estate operations that take advantage of planetary rent gaps and the emergence of new platforms providing access to short-term accommodation in private residences are broadening the spectrum of locations and circumstances under which gentrification can take place. Madrid is an example and an appropriate case study for this phenomenon.

For the last 40 years, the Centro district of Madrid has undergone significant transformations that have evinced classical gentrification. After a period of decline (Leal, 2004), the reputation, activity, demography and household size of some of its six administrative quarters have changed significantly – especially after the 2008 financial crisis (Table 1). In particular, the transnational residential relocations from higher-income countries – both in the longer and shorter term – to the city have drastically changed the gentrification landscape of Madrid. Its urban amenities and cultural collections (acquired over a long history of transcontinental empire), coupled with its lower housing costs (relative to Northern Europe) and easy accessibility for short-stay tourists, have contributed to an influx of new, mobile workers and visitors, who have partially displaced lower-income populations from the city's centre, including those of lower-status mobile workers from the Global South. Madrid is an illustrative case of these new processes of transnational gentrification because of its semi-peripheral status, where, like Lisbon (Sequera and Nofre, 2020) and Barcelona (Arias Sans and Quaglieri, 2016; Cocola-Gant and López-Gay, 2020, this issue), housing stock has been transformed from longer-term stock to short-term tourist uses. From a visitor's perspective, short-term residential accommodation can provide a more 'authentic' local experience than a hotel, at an overall more affordable price (Füller and Michel, 2014; Novy, 2019). For landlords, either renting complete apartments or monetising unused housing capacity can be a more profitable alternative to the conventional real estate market (López García, 2018; Pérez et al., 2015; Red2Red Consultores, 2017). This situation changes the classical landscape of gentrification, as contributors to this Special Issue argue.

The aim of this paper is to provide empirical evidence of a new 'transnational gentrification' (the arrival of wealthy migrants who change the socio-economic character of certain areas of Madrid), neighbourhood upgrading that correlates with the rapid increase since 2013 in platform-mediated, short-term rental supply and rising rental costs. Madrid offers an empirical site for thinking about key concepts and theories of gentrification in light of contemporary, global forces of real estate accumulation and population

DOI: 10.4324/9781003341239-29

	2006–2008					2009–2012					2013–2017				
	D Population /%	D Households /%	D Household size (ppl)/%	D Rental price (e/m2)/%		D Population/%	D Households /%	D Household size (ppl)/%	D Rental price (e/m²)/%		D Population /%	D Households /%	D Household size (ppl)/%	D Rental price (e/m2)/%	
Palacio	21088 / 24.39 %	210 / 20.09%	20.09 / 22.04%	–		2721 / 23.04%	2109 / 20.04%	20.05 / 21.18%	–		2398 / 21.75%	+ 224 / 2.04%	20.07 / 21.72%	+ 4.80 / 37.80%	
Embajadores	21934 / 23.75 %	+ 95 / 0.44%	20.1 / 22.12%	–		21.719 / 23.42%	+ 145 / 2.36%	20.1 / 22.19	–		22.840 / 25.98%	+ 44 / 0.20%	20.13 / 23.07%	+ 6.00 / 47.24%	
(Lavapie´s)															
Cortes	2713 / 26.15%	27 / 20.14%	20.14 / 25.21%	–		2108 / 20.98%	+ 40 / 1.43%	20.04 / 20.95%	–		2367 / 23.37%	+ 143 / 2.72%	20.1 / 22.50%	+ 6.10 / 44.85%	
Justicia (Chueca)	2642 / 23.63%	+ 54 / 0.69%	20.1 / 22.27%	–		2125 / 20.73%	+ 160 / 1.49%	20.06 / 21.43%	–		2622 / 23.66%	+ 73 / 0.88%	20.09 / 22.24%	+ 5.50 / 37.16%	
Universidad (Malasan~a)	22383 / 26.74%	2117 / 20.76%	20.14 / 23.13%	–		2783 / 22.34%	+ 132 / 2.24%	20.07 / 21.63%	–		21.759 / 25.42%	+ 96 / 0.61%	20.11 / 22.73%	+ 5.50 / 40.44%	
Sol	2688 / 27.88%	224 / 20.65%	20.17 / 23.70%	–		2266 / 23.27%	+ 71 / 2.24%	20.11 / 22.56%	–		2486 / 26.21%	229 / 20.76%	20.11 / 22.74%	+ 5.00 / 38.17%	
District's total	27448 / 25.42%	29 / 20.09%	20.12 / 22.64%	20.89 avg / 25.01% avg		23.722 / 22.30%	+ 439 / 1.62%	20.07 / 21.61%	21.83 avg / 211.6% avg		26.472 / 24.40%	+ 551 / 0.95%	20.11 / 22.69%	+ 5.48 avg / + 37.80%	
Madrid's total (exc. Centro)	+ 40,322 / 1.32%	+ 35,074 / 3.20%	20.052 avg / 20.93% avg	+ 0.32 avg / + 2.60% avg		231,347 / 21.00%	+ 22,266 / 1.94%	20.081 avg / 21.45% avg	21.24 avg / 210.28% avg		226.986 / 20.88%	26.204 / 2.23%	20.072 avg / 21.40% avg	+ 2.78 avg / + 26.47% avg	

Table 1 Variations of population, number of households, and listing price for homes from 2006 to 2008, from 2009 to 2012, and from 2013 to 2017 in the Centro district and the city of Madrid.

Source: Municipal Population Register of Madrid, and Idealista.com (www.idealista.com/informes-precio-vivienda).

mobility. It challenges the prism of non-overlapping waves of gentrification that scholars have used to describe the phenomenon in the Anglo-American context (Aalbers, 2019; Hackworth and Smith, 2001; Lees et al., 2008), broadening the empirical framework of transnational gentrification linked to new forms of hybrid real estate and short-term accommodation. Moreover, it shows how the transformation of housing stock from long-term single use to shorter-term, multiple use, challenges the meaning of cities, potentially disrupting communities based on place-based ties and shared daily understandings of place. The paper is organised into five sections. The first section provides context for contemporary transformations, fitting Madrid's contemporary gentrification within a longer historical timeline. The second reviews the recent theoretical contributions on the mutation of gentrification processes, such as the concepts of transnational gentrification, planetary rent gaps and recent updates to the wave model theory. The subsequent two sections provide details of the methodology and the results of our study of Madrid. Finally, we conclude that transnational gentrification is a characteristic of fifth wave gentrification processes in Southern Europe.

FROM CLASSICAL TO TRANSNATIONAL GENTRIFICATION IN MADRID

Madrid's first gentrification processes can be traced back to the late 1970s and 1980s (Figure 1). Chueca (in the Justicia administrative quarter) evolved from being one of the main drug-dealing areas in the city to becoming the LGBT + neighbourhood of Madrid, constituting the city's first great urban success story. Malasan˜a having been the centre of 'la Movida' (Götte, 2014; Lechado and García, 2005),[1] state-led regeneration initiatives turned it (Universidad quarter) into a so-called 'hipster' area (Davidson, 2008). In order to renew obsolete urban infrastructure, improve public space, promote local commerce and revitalise a declining neighbourhood in the central district, which had lost 14.6% of its population between 1986 and 1996 (Justo, 2011), the municipal government established a special *Area de Rehabilitacio´n Preferente* (ARP, or in English, 'preferential rehabilitation area') around Dos de Mayo square in Malasan˜a in 1994. A year later, it extended it to the South (López de Lucio et al., 2016). The plan also incentivised building restoration to attract developer interest in properties. In the same fashion, the municipality launched a programme in 2006 to renovate the southern part of the neighbourhood ('ARI Pez-Luna', in English 'integrated rehabilitation area'). In 2008, a private operator attempted to rebrand the south-eastern part of Malasan˜a, largely known as the red-light district, with the acronym TriBall (*Tria´ngulo Ballesta*, following the examples of names such as SoHo or NoLIta in New York) to create a leisure area focused on art, culture and design. This was the paradigmatic case of private, commercially induced neighbourhood gentrification in Madrid (Janoschka et al., 2014; Sequera and Janoschka, 2015). In 1998, the municipality launched a regeneration programme for Lavapie´s (in the Embajadores quarter). The neighbourhood is well known as Madrid's 'melting pot', as it has traditionally received a significant share of foreign-born residents.[2] Just as in Malasan˜a, the ARP was managed by the local authority with contributions from national and regional administrations, providing public funds for refurbishment of private buildings with no oversight of their effect on real estate prices. Similarly, the social composition of the neighbourhood was changing, as it drew more members of the so-called 'creative classes' (Florida, 2002) or, more critically, members of Lavapie´s retain its active social movement networks (Sequera, 2013), es an intellectual bourgeoisie (Garnier, 2017; Ley, 1996) as well as some left-wing municipal social movements.

The spatial peculiarities of each area give the illusion of a graduated gentrification, with different degrees of urban transformation that vary from a mature stage in the more 'noble' Chueca to a partially concluded, ongoing process in Lavapiés, where building quality is lower and residential units smaller (García Pérez, 2014: 76). These characteristics have helped especially the anti-eviction movement. At present (2018), Malasan˜a is considered to be in an intermediate stage, with renovations for the private market rather than for the public interest leading the transformation of the neighbourhood. In these areas, where a higher degree of housing stigmatisation was used as a political alibi for privatised urban regeneration in the 1990s, first stage gentrification in Chueca and Malasan˜a coincided

Figure 1 Map of the Centro district and its surrounding administrative quarters. The thick dashed line represents its best-connected surrounding neighbourhoods.

with the speculative expansion of the Spanish economy, which accelerated displacement of lower-income groups. Later urban regeneration projects (Lavapié's and the southern part of Malasaña) coincided with the end of the expansionist economic cycle, mitigating some displacement (Sorando and Ardura, 2018).

The 2008 global real estate crisis led to a 40% drop in housing prices on a national level, both in sale and rental markets, from a peak in 2007 Q3 to a trough in 2014 Q1.[3] Despite that, Centro's population remained stable until 2011 and, due to pre-crisis gentrification, some of its residents may already have been economically less vulnerable. During the crisis, however, housing prices in the district fell for five consecutive years, until they began to bounce in 2013 (up 26% over 2011), and population in Centro began to fall (6% over 2011 data). Although some other districts experienced larger decreases in the cost of real estate after the crisis, Centro offered better conditions for realising potential rent increases, as is characteristic in gentrified areas (Hammel, 1999). Despite the loss of population, most neighbourhoods grew slightly in the number of households during the 2011–2017 period. The combination of factors – skyrocketing housing prices, loss of population but stabilisation in the number of households as additional units are brought onto the market – allows us to make the initial assumption that Centro may have become attractive for a new group of residents with higher incomes or fewer economic restraints. It also leads us to question the population data used by the Municipal Population Register. The main reason for the residents to put themselves on the Register is the possibility of accessing certain services – traffic and parking permissions and, above all, public health assistance, of particular importance in Spain. As the duration of stay of short-term visitors is not comparable with renters and owners, there is no need for them to have access to these public services. Short-term foreign residents – often neither traditional tourists nor neighbours in the conventional sense – may not be in the Register. This has led to suggestions that the population data may over-estimate population loss (Sorando and Ardura, 2018).

Of course, digital platforms greatly facilitate increased spatial mobility and, as these emerged after 2012 – especially Airbnb – Madrid's value as a tourist hub drastically shifted the real estate market. This created a rent gap – but not for the local real estate market, since there was little additional higher-income demand from Spanish workers. Instead, on a European and even global scale, the relatively low cost of Spanish real estate and the existence of a higher-income, mobile population of consumers of urban spaces incentivised speculative investments based on flexible access to housing via digital platforms. Three significant policy decisions shaped this process in relation to the rental market in Madrid after the financial crisis. First, the new *Ley de Arrendamientos Urbanos* (Urban Rental Act) (2013) reduced the minimum duration of rental contracts from 5 to 3 years and consequently made the rotation of tenants easier; second, was the creation of real estate investment trusts, or *Sociedades Ano´nimas Cotizadas de Inversio´n Inmobiliaria* (SOCIMIs by its Spanish acronym) (Ley, 16/2012); and third, the establishment of the 'golden visa' programme aimed to attract foreign investors to the Spanish real estate sector (which accounted for 6% of sales in 2018, according to Estadística Regional Inmobiliaria (2018: 80)). Thus, the arrival of international corporate landlords and digital platforms for holiday renting seems to have played an important role in a new surge of gentrification, helping to transform the housing market of Madrid. As an example, the investment fund Blackstone through its SOCIMI (Fidere) has acquired 1860 houses for e128.5M from the *Empresa Municipal de Vivienda y Suelo* (Madrid's public housing authority) (Simón Ruiz, 2019; Vidal, 2018). Madrid has consequently climbed to the top of the league tables of international luxury housing investments (López Letón, 2019).

Although these processes of gentrification have been thoroughly studied from the perspective of the increase in housing prices and the settlement of new, higher class groups (Echaves García, 2017; Idealista.com, 2018; López García, 2018; Rodríguez López, 2017), the implementation of new regulations for the real estate market, in combination with the emergence of 'P2P tourism', 'home-sharing', 'holiday' or 'short-term rentals' sharply changed this situation (Ardura, 2017; Gil, 2018), increasing the presence of tourists and lifestyle immigrants from higher-income countries and thus accelerating the rise of real estate prices and increasing economic speculation in Centro and beyond.

LITERATURE REVIEW

The transnational character of real estate speculation and demand in Madrid leads to a new type of gentrification that has not yet been fully accounted for. This section examines these changes through the lens of the recent academic contributions regarding the mutation of gentrification processes. We examine the 'wave model' introduced by Hackworth and Smith (2001), later updated by Lees et al. (2008: 179) – as it permits the evaluation of the degree of maturation of gentrification processes through time by depicting their canonical stages. This model relates the different mutations of the gentrification processes to the global economic crisis. A more recent contribution to this wave model identifies a fifth wave of gentrification that can be considered as the transnational 'urban materialization of financialized or finance-led capitalism' (Aalbers, 2019: 1) – where, as Aalbers puts it, 'corporate landlords and platform capitalism' play a significant role. Earlier processes of gentrification in Madrid can be characterised as first and second wave. They affected central areas of the city, with later sporadic state-led processes, and involved local real estate actors. Meanwhile, the more recent processes are more akin to Aalbers' fifth wave. Despite the clarity of this qualitative frame and its obvious applicability to cities in the 'Global North', gentrification waves were essentially defined in an Anglo-American context. Therefore, they are not entirely transferable to other social, economic and political situations. The shift to the fourth wave – explained in the model by the reconfiguration after the dot.com crisis, that is, the massive 'switch' of capital to real estate – barely affected a Spanish economy propelled by its own national real estate bubble, which burst simultaneously with the global financial crisis.

However, wave theories should also incorporate not just the temporal modifications of 'rent gaps' (Smith, 1979) and localised 'uneven development' (Smith, 1982) in relation to a changing political economy. They should also consider how markets for local real estate can be globalised by space – time compression (Harvey, 1989).

As Smith (2010: 19) has pointed out, cities now 'find themselves competing economically with each other across national borders in a way that would have been inconceivable in the 1970s'. Slater (2017) uses the term 'planetary rent gap', in which global financial agents, real estate promoters, public administrations and local populations interact in a very uneven way depending on the context to produce the optimal conditions for accumulation. From the vantage point of real estate capital, this competition extends to attracting globally mobile, higher-income real estate consumers to the spaces of the city – cities whose amenities are also embellished by state institutions or public programmes for art and culture, yet another way in which the state 'leads' gentrification processes in Southern Europe. Furthermore, Spain's place as a main tourism destination also facilitates the exploitation of housing as a tourist asset (Janoschka et al., 2014). As Cocola-Gant (2018: 7–8) explains, in lower-income economies, such as in South-western Europe, where tourism is an important economic sector, 'the consumption power of the middle-classes is smaller than in advanced economies, [and] tourism comes to supplant the lack of local demand that real estate capital needs for the realization of surplus value'.

In this context, the proliferation of short-term rentals managed on digital platforms appears to be playing a significant role in transforming housing investment and markets (Barron et al., 2018; see also Sequera and Nofre, 2020). Although tourism gentrification has been described before in the case of cities such as New Orleans (Gotham, 2005) or Barcelona, in the case of Madrid it was not on the public agenda until the rise of digitally mediated holiday rentals, as residents began to see how the activity of these platforms 'threaten[ed] their right to stay put while making it increasingly difficult for residents to find affordable accommodation' (Cocola-Gant, 2016). Madrid's urban transformation helps us to better understand the particularities of gentrification in Southern Europe, where foreign real estate investment and mobile tourists are changing cities.

METHODOLOGY

Many high-income foreigners come to the city as tourists, for short stays. We focus here on this aspect of transnational gentrification – specifically, its relation to tourism. Access to short-term rentals provides tourists with cheaper alternatives to hotels, which are also more flexible[4] and apparently more 'authentic' (e.g. 'live like a local') than traditional short-term residential rentals (Füller and Michel, 2014; Novy, 2019; Zervas et al., 2017). Our main hypothesis is that the proliferation of short-term rentals produces higher prices than the average traditional rent, potentially inducing transnational gentrification in some areas of Madrid – that is, an unaffordable rise in the cost of living compared with the local residents' disposable incomes, accompanied by a substitution of the resident population by wealthier international settlers. Despite the intuitiveness of this hypothesis, its verification is debated given the externalities that affect the housing market: overall housing demand, seasonality of tourism, density of touristic venues, supply distribution, accessibility by public transport, the approval of municipal ordinances regarding short-term rentals (Ardura-Urquiaga et al., 2019). The most recent and comprehensive studies agree that the highest price increases in Barcelona have occurred in the most touristic areas of the city. However, the rise in prices cannot be exclusively attributed to Airbnb (García-López et al., 2019). To verify this hypothesis, we analysed some key indicators related to transnational gentrification: the growth of the number of residents from wealthy economic regions, the purchasing power of the local population and the dynamics of the real estate market based on empirical data from short-term accommodation platforms as well as traditional, long-term ones. Analysing these variables, we identify (1) areas where monthly rental prices have grown alongside the increase of short-term rentals on Airbnb; (2) areas where monthly rental prices have grown faster than the available income per capita; and (3) areas where the substitution of working-class immigrant populations occurred during and after the economic crisis of 2008.

First, we use local census data to identify international residents and areas that have experienced a decline in local population. Second, these data are contrasted with data from Inside Airbnb and Airdna to see which areas of the city have seen higher than average growth in short-term rental supply (Airdna.co, 2018; Cox, 2015).[5] Next, we study the evolution of rental prices listed on traditional real estate platforms, using data from

Idealista.com (one of Spain's most popular real estate websites), correlating it with the emergence of short-term rentals in some specific areas of the city (Hernández and Grasso, 2017; Idealista.com, 2018; López García, 2018; Sanz, 2018). At this point, some short-term rentals may be reflected in the statistics as empty houses – therefore, they would not be substituting traditional rentals. This fact has been considered by comparing the number of empty houses with the increments of short-term rentals to avoid obtaining skewed results. Finally, the hypothesis can be confirmed by studying the population's income in the identified areas. This way we may conclude that the local emergence of short-term rentals in areas with small numbers of empty apartments, correlate with housing prices increasing above the disposable income of residents[6] (Ayuntamiento de Madrid, 2015; ESNE, 2018; Vivus Finance, 2017) and verify the substitution of working-class immigrant residents with people from higher-income countries. All this provides a clearer picture of the key aspects of transnational gentrification which lead to potential displacement of residents. It must be stated, however, that the implicit complexity of gentrification processes and the level of aggregation of the analysed data can only show us the potential vulnerability of some areas of the city to population displacement. Further residential mobility data from the Madrid census would complement this research in the future.

RESULTS

Wealthier immigration

As noted above, the Spanish recession accelerated population loss in the central district of Madrid. However, the district attracted international residents, who helped boost the total immigrant population by 5% from 2015 through January 2018. New immigrants settling in the area, however, have a new socio-economic profile. According to data from the yearly census, the number of people from wealthy geo-economic regions is still growing – in 2008, residents from EU15 or OECD countries barely reached 25% of the immigrant population in the city centre. Now these countries represent almost half of the foreigners living in the area. By contrast, the size of Latin American and especially African communities shrank dramatically.

This new composition of the immigrant resident community reflects a shift in the model of immigration (Figure 2). Whilst in the past, the central district was a preferred destination for people coming from under-privileged geo-economic regions searching for a conveniently located space within the urban system, today the area has become the popular choice for immigrants from wealthier countries. This shift is especially remarkable in the neighbourhoods where the most important tourist amenities are located – such as Palacio, Cortes and Sol – or where there have recently

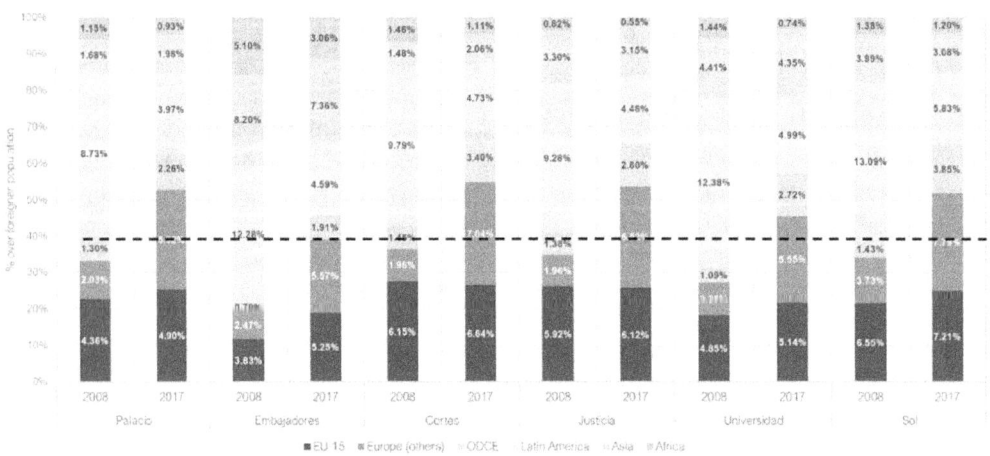

Figure 2 Composition of the immigrant population before and after the Spanish economic crisis by Madrid central district neighbourhoods.

Source: Authors. Data from Ayuntamiento de Madrid (2018a).

been patterns of gentrification made evident by the settlement of local 'creative classes' (Sorando and Ardura, 2016, 2018). In some neighbourhoods, residents from wealthier OECD countries reach and exceed 60% of the immigrant population, having represented on average less than 40% before the crisis. Given that the data presented in this section have been gathered from the population census, the registered population has met the requirement of providing proof of residence in the area for more than three months. Therefore, it indicates a trend of residents coming from high-income countries and gaining access to housing, thus supporting the hypothesis that the city centre has become an emerging destination for lifestyle migrants, that is, relatively privileged social classes from higher-income countries, who may relocate for lifestyle and leisure reasons above labour market reasons (Benson and O'Reilly, 2014). However, many of these international residents from higher-income countries no doubt also work.

Digital platforms and the touristic specialisation of the centre

In conjunction with the settlement of new, higher-income migrants, Madrid has gained favour in recent years as a destination for short-stay visitors from the Global North. The data from the recently started 'Frontur' and 'Egatur' initiatives, carried out by the National Institute of Statistics, show that the city has recently experienced significant changes in the origin of incoming tourists, from being an established destination for national tourism to becoming an attractive option for short international visits. International arrivals by plane dropped between 2011 and 2013 but then grew by 38.5% – or 29.3% over 2008 arrivals (Ministerio de Transportes, Movilidad y Agenda Urbana, 2017; Rodríguez, 2016). Overnight hotel stays grew in a similar proportion after 2013 (Bacon and Garcia, 2018). However, the supply of hotel rooms has remained stable since 2013 (Ayuntamiento de Madrid, 2018b; Bacon and Garcia, 2018). This could be explained by the short duration of stays, in combination with a high stock of rooms and balanced demand throughout the year that translates into hotel occupancy rates below 70%. However, the number of incoming international tourists has grown at a faster rate than the supply of hotel rooms and the occupancy rates of hotels and hostels. Whilst occupancy rates grew 5% between 2015 and 2017, international visitors increased by 15% and national tourism decreased by 3%. Over this period, the number of listings offered on Airbnb doubled (Figure 3). It stands to reason that short-term rental platforms are accommodating an important part of the increased number of visitors.

As the data reflect, the growth in international visitors corresponds with the skyrocketing growth of listings on Airbnb, which began in 2014. According to Airdna.co (July 2018) there were 29,588 listings in Madrid, 26,925 present on Airbnb – 91% of the total. According to Insideairbnb.com, the total number of listings in Madrid on Airbnb in July 2018 was 18,362.[7] Some hosts rent a spare room in their home periodically, while others use properties as full-time speculative investments and manage them through specialised holiday rent management companies 41% of the listings are available all year round, 59% are managed either by professionals or by owners of more than one apartment (Airdna.co, July 2018).

Over the 2015–2018 period, Embajadores (Lavapié's) and Universidad (Malasan͂a) were the locations where vacation rental platforms initially became more popular, coinciding with areas with the fastest growing rates of immigration from high-income countries and declining numbers of residents from lower-income countries. Meanwhile, the supply increased exponentially in the city centre, almost doubling the number of listings in the central neighbourhoods. In a location pattern that differs from that of hotels, vacation apartments have grown around a North – South axis across the district, where a large number of shopping franchises and souvenir stores are concentrated.[8] Our findings show that the effect of short-term rentals on the traditional housing market may be considerable. Using the data available on Insideairbnb.com (July 2018), considering only listings available more than 90 days a year and differentiating how those listings are managed, we observed that only half of the filtered 11,224 listings in Madrid appeared to be offered under the terms of the sharing economy – hosting visitors in spare rooms during short periods of time or using an entire empty home for that purpose. There are 5264 offerings for 'complete apartments'[9] managed by professional hosts who manage more than two listings on the

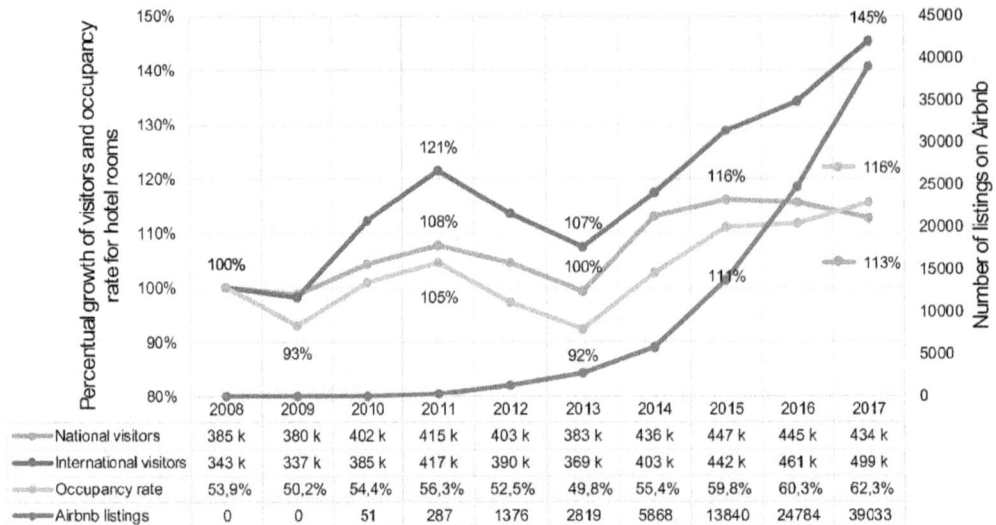

Figure 3 Number of visitors in Madrid compared with hotel occupancy rates and number of listings on Airbnb.
Source: Authors. Data from Ayuntamiento de Madrid (2018b) and Airdna.co (2018).

Figure 4 Airbnb listing density by census sections, 2015–2019.
Source: Authors. Data from Insideairbnb.com.

platform – which were most likely to have been removed from the traditional rental market. Centro accounts for more than 67% of them – 3530 apartments of the total 70,505 units in the district, including 27,885 rental units and 11,190 empty ones (INE, 2011).

The centre is where the Airbnb phenomenon has intensified (Figure 4) – presenting the highest density of short-term rentals in a short period of time. The concentration of tourist attractions in the district, the past gentrification of several areas, in combination with the new regulations for rentals, constituted an optimal setting for the adoption of the new rental technologies and the consequent transformation of the rental supply to host international newcomers. It is not surprising that Chueca, Malasan˜a and Lavapie´s had the densest clusters of short-term rentals since their implementation took place. From that moment, the residential fabric of the district became more and more appealing to landlords and real estate investors, causing the expansion of the compact cluster of holiday rentals running through the district's North – South axis.

Short-term rentals beyond the central district

Meanwhile, the supply of vacation rentals grew in the vicinity of Centro: to the West, the neighbourhood of Puerta del A´ngel; to the North, Chamberı´ and Tetua´n; to the East, Barrio de Salamanca and Retiro (in the more affordable areas of these districts, traditionally the wealthiest bastions of Madrid); to the South, Arganzuela, Carabanchel and Usera. All these areas saw significant growth in the number of listings between 2015 and 2018 (Airbnb, 2016). Given the lack of tourist attractions in these areas in comparison with the city centre, the presence of outliers of growth in some sectors of these districts is remarkable, indicating the emergence of new clusters of short-term rentals. However, the potential impact of the proliferation of short-term rentals in these districts is different, given their significant differences compared with Centro. Whilst all of them are well connected with the centre by public transport, residents' incomes and purchasing power vary considerably.

The southern, western and northern limits of the M-30 ring road provide access to significant housing supply that traditionally has responded to the needs of the working classes and lower-income immigrants. The housing prices in these areas plummeted during the economic crisis – thus maximising the possible benefits of new investment in devalued real estate. To give a concrete example, the areas closest to public transport – or to the central district in the case of Puerta del A´ngel – have experienced the highest levels of growth, around three times the average number of listings of their districts. By contrast, the eastern and northern boundaries of the centre are home to the city's highest-income earners. There, the number of Airbnb listings has risen in proportion with that in lower-income neighbourhoods of the city centre – but the increase is concentrated in the lower-cost areas of these wealthy neighbourhoods, enabling them to garner much higher rents. Although the central district represents the vast majority of listed properties, its nearest neighbours are also providing opportunities for turning traditional rental units into short-term rental properties.

Income and rent affordability

As housing prices are expected to increase, the hypothesis of potential displacement of the local population is supported if the rise in rental prices is related to the increase in speculative investments in properties listed on short-term rental platforms, and if the proportion of the local residents' disposable income spent on housing increases as a result. To test this hypothesis, we considered the growth of holiday rentals, traditional rent prices and the population's income together. Given that homeowners are less likely to be displaced by the emergence of short-term rentals, only the rise of the cost of the rent over renters' incomes has been considered to evaluate the possibility of residential displacement. As noted above, the central district is receiving visitors from countries with higher income levels who have on average, therefore, greater purchasing power compared with both the local and immigrant communities living in the central district before the economic crisis started in 2008. It can be observed (Figure 6) that the overall foreign population (including migrants from the Global South) fell by 34% in the area between 2010 and 2014, the hardest times of the economic crisis. In the centre of Madrid the traditional housing rentals' price shrank 24% from 2007 to 2014. The income in the area also decreased by 13% up until 2014.

This was the same year Airbnb began to take off in the city of Madrid, experiencing exponential growth until 2017. By that time, the Municipality had drafted an action plan to establish restrictive conditions for new short-term rentals within the most affected districts, which was to be approved in 2018 with the main goal of controlling the pressure of Airbnb on the housing market. However, the proposal was suspended. In parallel, the long-term rental price in the district grew by 33% after 2014, situating the cost of rent at levels never seen before, even when compared with pre-crisis prices. During that period, the number of migrants living in Centro began to recover but at a much slower pace than housing prices, given the settlement of migrants from First World economies.

The correlation between the growth in rental prices and the emergence of short-term rentals in Centro is clear. On average, a listing on the digital platform is expected to produce 100% more benefits and earnings than a traditional rental if it maintains an occupancy rate above 65% throughout the year (Ayuntamiento de Madrid, 2017). This may have subsequently led landlords to raise the price of rents according to these expected benefits, given that the market allows them to choose between either renting the property through the digital platform or traditionally renting it in an increased price bracket.

Beyond Centro, the growth of short-term rentals also coincides with the increase in the cost of rent in some areas, especially those best located and with better transport links with the centre. However, the increase in the number of listings is significantly lower. Despite that, the surge in rental prices is faster than what residents' purchasing power can keep up with. Given that the recession negatively affected income from 2009 until 2014 – and this income had not recovered by 2018, the end of the time frame considered in this study – and that rental prices grew by 39% between 2014 and 2018, and 9% over prices in 2008, it is possible that lower-income groups were displaced from Centro and its inner suburbs when trying to renew rental contracts. Also, the fall in

Figure 5 Madrid; income per capita in the 2014 census sections.

Source: Authors. Data from Ayuntamiento de Madrid (2015).

income could lead lower-income homeowners to list spare rooms to complement their wages, making some of the increase in short-term rentals an indicator of precariousness rather than tourism gentrification (Semi and Tonetta, 2019). Using income data (Figure 5), the evolution of long-term rental prices (Hernández and Grasso, 2017) and the monthly price for complete apartments[10] listed on Airbnb, we estimated the areas where the rising cost of rent could potentially lead to displacement because of unaffordable living expenses for the average resident.

First, we considered the case of an individual paying the full cost of rent, earning the average income for the area, and living in a 50 m^2 single room apartment. Before 2014, the cost of renting in the central district represented between 38.3% (Justicia) and 61% (Embajadores) of the average net income. Assuming the average growth of income and rental prices described above, the expansion of short-term rental platforms (Figure 6) coincided with rental price increases on long-term rentals that now take up 49.1% (Justicia) and 78.3% (Embajadores) of disposable income. Even as the traditional rental market bit in to residents' disposable income (from 10.8% in Justicia to 17.3% in Embajadores), the average monthly rent of an equivalent apartment through short-term rental platforms represents between 62.1% (Justicia) and 97% (Sol) of the locals' net income (Table 2).

These significant increases in housing prices make the average resident especially vulnerable to displacement during this new wave of tourist gentrification. As prices increased, renters saw their purchasing power reduced, even though data suggest their economic situation improved after the recession – though it is important to note that observed economic improvements in the data might reflect the arrival of wealthier residents in an area rather than increased income for the existing population. The reduction of purchasing power might force them to either move to a different neighbourhood – confirming the hypothesis of gentrification – or to share the cost of the rent with others in order to afford it – another form of displacement.

If we performed an equivalent analysis to assess the effects of digital short-term rental platforms on those rentals paid by more than one person, the data show how this alternative could mitigate the potential displacement of population. In those cases of shared rents, the loss of purchasing power ranged between 7.3% (Justicia) and 11.6% (Embajadores), deduced from rental prices which would represent between 32.8% (Justicia) and 52.2% (Embajadores) of the average disposable income.

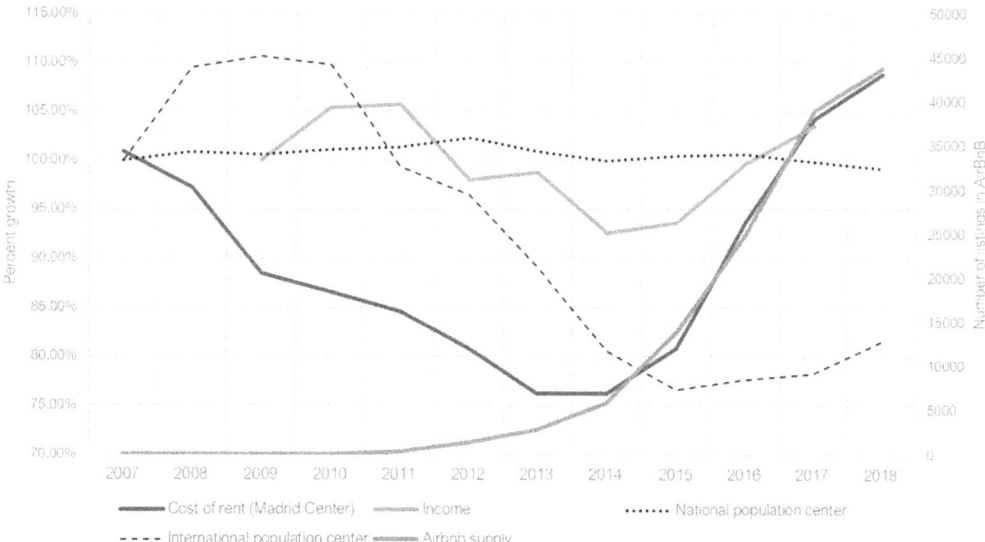

Figure 6 Evolution of international population, cost of the rent, income per capita and supply of short-term rentals on Airbnb.

Source: Data from Ayuntamiento de Madrid (2018a) and Airdna.co (2018).

Neighbourhood	Monthly income 2014	Monthly income 2017	50 m² rental price 2014	50 m² rental price 2017	50 m² rental price Airbnb 2017
Cortes	1519.42 e	1621.33 e	664.05e (43.7%)	910.0 e (56.1%)	1276.5e (78.7%)
Embajadores	1052.59 e	1123.19 e	642.16e (61.0%)	880.0 e (78.3%)	967.5e (86.1%)
Justicia	1803.58 e	1924.55 e	690.81e (38.3%)	946.7 e (49.2%)	1196.5e (62.2%)
Palacio	1567.22 e	1672.34 e	625.14e (40.0%)	856.7 e (51.2%)	1244.8e (74.4%)
Sol	1296.77 e	1383.74 e	678.65 (52.3%)	930.0 e (67.2%)	1342.9e (97.0%)
Universidad	1348.18 e	1438.60 e	654.32e (48.5%)	896.6e (62.3%)	1057.7e (73.5%)

Table 2 Available income and cost for individually paid 50 m² rents in 2014 and 2017 in the Central district of Madrid.
Sources: Ayuntamiento de Madrid (2018a), Idealista.com (2018) and Airdna.co (July 2018).

As seen in Table 2, the areas where short-term rental services grew the most coincide with the lowest registered income. It is worth noting the case of Embajadores – the lowest-income area of the Centro district, where the share of low-income migration dramatically diminished during the recession. Airbnb has grown the most in this sector and the increase in cost of housing represents the highest losses of purchasing power in the city, validating the hypothesis of gentrification.

However, this phenomenon has not been exclusive to Embajadores-Lavapié's. Whilst people living in the wealthy north-east neighbourhoods (e.g. Almagro, Castellana, Salamanca) can afford rising rental prices, traditional working-class neighbourhoods such as Puerta del Ángel and Valdeacederas, both located next to the M-30 ring-road and well connected to Centro, have experienced a similar pattern of falling non-housing-related purchasing power resulting from increasing rental costs.

CONCLUSION

Although Madrid ranks amongst the world's 'alpha' cities[11] it had experienced only medium range gentrification processes until 2013 – milder than those in Barcelona – that can be classified within the two first waves of gentrification processes (Hackworth and Smith, 2001), thus arguably in tension with the idea of gentrification as a global strategy formulated by Smith (2002), since urban processes in Madrid at this point did not look at all like the gentrification experienced in paradigmatic Anglo-American examples. However, since 2013 we can argue that Madrid has been undergoing 'transnational gentrification' that 'connects redevelopment capital to housing demand not within a single city-region but transnationally, and thus creates new possibilities for profitable housing reinvestment – and new threats of displacement – in markets where such possibilities would not have existed on the basis of local demand alone' (Sigler and Wachsmuth, 2016: 2). This can be seen in the demographic statistics of new people arriving to live in Madrid. While visits from lower-income economies in the Global South have been in decline since the 2008 recession began, tourists and immigrants from higher-income economies such as the EU 15 and OECD – especially the USA – have outstripped even national tourism in Madrid.

Given the fact that those countries are benefiting from being on the wealthy side of the global rent gap (Lees et al., 2015) in relation to the Spanish economy, their citizens can, on average, afford to pay higher prices for shorter stays, as long as the accommodation market is flexible and secure enough to access. This situation makes visitors from wealthy countries the main target of P2P accommodation services (Wachsmuth and Weisler, 2018). Therefore, it is not surprising that the most touristic areas of the city as well as either the closest or best-connected surrounding areas have witnessed the highest increases in short-term rentals through digital 'homesharing' platforms – amongst which Airbnb stands out.

This paper emphasises the hypothesis of gentrification as a cause of potential displacement of the local population given the unaffordable rise in housing expenses in some areas. The rapid increase in the holiday rental supply from 2013 onwards coincides in time with the arrival of wealthy immigration, tourism and the escalation of prices for traditional rentals. Moreover, as Cocola-Gant (2016) suggested as a general pattern, the Madrid neighbourhoods that lost the most residents (Sol and Embajadores) between 2013 and 2017 also saw the greatest growth of holiday rentals, although the loss of population began earlier than the consolidation of the short-term rental market.

This emergence of digital platform-mediated short-term rentals has intensified the previously initiated processes of gentrification in the district of Centro, and it has broadened the phenomenon to its most immediate surroundings although to a lesser degree, regardless of the income levels of the areas in question. Despite the disparity in income, the densification of the vacation rental supply in Puerta del A´ngel (Western periphery), Tetua´n (Northern periphery), Arganzuela (South end) and Barrio de Salamanca (East end, in its less expensive areas) has been similar. However, residents living in the first three of these neighbourhoods are more vulnerable to higher costs of living, given their significantly lower incomes. The data show how they may have either more limited access to housing or difficulty moving within the area after the consolidation of the vacation rental market.

To summarise, the gentrification processes in the case of Madrid Centro and the surrounding districts may be the result of the settlement of new residents arriving from countries on the positive side of the rent gap with Spain, in combination with an intensification of tourism that has made the holiday rental sector into 'the new battlefront' (Cocola-Gant, 2016), especially in Southern Europe. This new wave of transnational gentrification shows a strong presence of international real estate actors making use of platform-mediated short-term home rentals and turning them into one of their principal investments. This would make Madrid a prototypical case for Hackworth and Smith's theoretical frame, updated by Aalbers. The flexibilisation of the real estate market made possible by short-term rental platforms has intensified the commodification of housing in and beyond the city centre, rather than enhancing its use value through sharing.

ACKNOWLEDGEMENTS

We would like to thank Matthew Hayes, editor of this *Special Issue*, for his guidance and support through the publishing process. Added to the reviewers', his suggestions helped us to improve the overall structure and style of the article.

FUNDING

The author(s) received no financial support for the research, authorship, and/or publication of this article.

NOTES

1. A movement of counter-cultural renaissance in Madrid during the post-Franco era, based in the underground pop music scene.
2. Currently large communities from Senegal and Bangladesh coexistent with a strong Chinese commercial activity and a significant Moroccan population.
3. The average for the EU was only around 7.5% according to Eurostat (available at: http://ec.europa.eu/eurostat/product?code=prc_hpi&mode=view).
4. The 'Law for Urban Rentals' (*Ley de Arrendamientos Urbanos*) of Madrid covers yearly renting contracts, forcing their extension up to 3 years from the date of signing at the renter's demand.
5. These web pages study the supply of rooms and apartments in the city of Madrid by scraping and cleaning the data shown on Airbnb, making this information and other relevant insights available for download.
6. The disposable income has been calculated by subtracting the income per capita from the estimated cost of living in Madrid.
7. The data source, airdna.co, uses different filtering protocols than Insideairbnb.com. Also, airdna.co added the listings served on homeaway.com since June 2017. Consequently, different counts among platforms can be expected.
8. A graphic representation of this can be found at http://datos.elespanol.com/proyec-tos/airbnb/.
9. This is a conservative approach, which acknowledges that a significant number of users may, in fact, be sharing their apartments' spare capacity. However, as some municipalities are passing ordinances to control the professionalisation of the short-term rentals, the type of listings may change (Shatford, 2017).

10. On average, an apartment rented by month through Airbnb has a 30% discount over its nightly price – increasing its competitivity with the traditional rental market.
11 According to the Global City Network classification, available at: www.lboro.ac.uk/gawc/gawcworlds.html.

REFERENCES

Aalbers M (2019) Revisiting 'The changing state of gentrification' – Introduction to the Forum: From third to fifth-wave gentrification. *Tijdschrift voor Economische en Sociale Geografie* 110(1): 1–11.

Airbnb (2016) *17 Neighborhoods to watch in 2017: Airbnb data reveals trending neighborhoods for travel*. Available at: https://press.atairbnb.com/17-neighborhoods-to-watch-in-2017-airbnb-data-reveals-trending-neighborhoods-for-travel/ (accessed 1 July 2018).

Airdna.co (2018) *Madrid, Spain*. Available at: www.airdna.co/market-data/app/es/madrid/madrid/overview (accessed 1 July 2018).

Ardura A (2017) La incidencia de la proliferación del alojamiento turístico en viviendas en el centro de Madrid. In: 3er encuentro europeo Vivre la ville. Available at: www.vivre-la-ville.fr/wp-content/uploads/2017/03/Vivre-La-Ville-Madrid-2017_PonenciaTurismo-ES.pdf (accessed 1 July 2018).

Ardura-Urquiaga A, Lorente-Riverola I, Mohíno-Sanz I, et al. (2019) 'No estamos tan mal como Barcelona': Análisis de la proliferación y regulación de las viviendas de uso turístico en Madrid y Barcelona. *Boletín de La Asociación de Geógrafos Españoles* 83: 1–47.

Arias Sans A and Quaglieri A (2016) Unravelling airbnb: Urban perspectives from Barcelona. *Reinventing the Local in Tourism: Producing, Consuming and Negotiating Place* 73: 209.

Ayuntamiento de Madrid (2015) *Renta neta media de los hogares (Urban Audit)*. Available at: www.madrid.es/portales/munimadrid/es/Inicio/El-Ayuntamiento/Estadistica/Areas-de-informacion-estadistica/Econo mia/Renta/Renta-neta-media-de-los-hogares-Urban-Audit-/?vgnextfmt=default&vgnextoi d=65e0c19a1666a510VgnVCM1000001d4a900aRCRD&vgnextchannel=ef863636b44b4210VgnVCM2000000c205a0aRCRD (accessed April 2018).

Ayuntamiento de Madrid (2017) *La Oferta de Alojamiento Turístico en Madrid: Características y Distribución Territorial*. Report by Red2Red consultants for Area de Desarrollo Urbano Sostenible.

Ayuntamiento de Madrid (2018a) Ayuntamiento de Madrid. *Banco de datos*. Available at: www-2.munimadrid.es/CSE6/jsps/menuBancoDatos.jsp (accessed April 2018).

Ayuntamiento de Madrid (2018b) *Encuesta de Ocupación hotelera*. Available at: www2.munimadrid.es/CSE6/jsps/menuBancoDatos.jsp (accessed April 2018).

Bacon P and Garcia C (2018) Market report: Madrid, Spain. *Horwath HTL: Hotel, Tourism and Leisure*, 5 February. Available at: http://horwathhtl.com/wp-content/uploads/sites/2//2018/02/HHTL_MR-SPAIN_Feb.pdf (accessed 1 July 2018).

Barron K, Kung E and Proserpio D (2018) The sharing economy and housing affordability: Evidence from Airbnb. *SSRN Electronic Journal*. http://doi.org/10.2139/ssrn.3006832 (accessed 1 July 2018).

Benson M and O'Reilly K (2014) New horizons in lifestyle migration research: Theorising movement, settlement and the search for a better way of life. In: Benson M and Osbaldiston N (eds) *Understanding Lifestyle Migration: Theoretical Approaches to Migration and the Quest for a Better Way Of Life*. Basingstoke: Palgrave Macmillan, pp. 1–26.

Cocola-Gant A (2016) Holiday rentals: The new gentrification battlefront. *Sociological Research Online* 21(3). Available at: https://journals.sagepub.com/doi/10.5153/sro.4071 (accessed 1 July 2018).

Cocola-Gant A (2018) Tourism gentrification. In: Lees L and Phillips M (eds) *Handbook of Gentrification Studies*. Cheltenham and Northampton: Edward Elgar, pp. 281–293.

Cocola-Gant A and López-Gay A (2020) Transnational gentrification, tourism and the formation of 'foreign only' enclaves in Barcelona. *Urban Studies* 57(15): 3025–3043.

Cox M (2015) Adding data to the debate. *Inside Airbnb*. Avaliable at: http://insideairbnb.com/ (accessed 1 July 2018).

Davidson M (2008) Spoiled mixture – Where does state-led 'positive' gentrification end? *Urban Studies* 45(12): 2385–2405.

Echaves García A (2017) El difícil acceso de los jó´venes al mercado de vivienda en España: Precios, regímenes de tenencia y esfuerzos. *Cuadernos de relaciones laborales* 35(1): 127–149.

ESNE (2018) *Coste de vida en Madrid*. Available at: www.esne.es/servicios/welcome-eras-mus/coste-de-vida-en-madrid/ (accessed 1 July 2018).

Esradística Registral Inmobiliaria (ERI) (2018) *Anuario 2018*. Registradores de Espana.

Florida R (2002) *The Rise of the Creative Class. And How It's Transforming Work, Leisure and Everyday Life*. New York: Basic Books.

Füller H and Michel B (2014) 'Stop being a tourist!' New dynamics of urban tourism in Berlin-Kreuzberg. *International Journal of Urban and Regional Research* 38(4): 1304–1318.

Garcia-López M-A, Jofre-Monseny J, Martínez Mazza R, et al. (2019) Do short-term rental platforms affect housing markets? Evidence from Airbnb in Barcelona. *SSRN Electronic Journal*. Available at: https://papers.ssrn.com/sol3/papers.cfm?abstract_id=3428237 (accessed 1 July 2018).

García Pérez E (2014) Gentrificación en Madrid: De la burbuja a la crisis. *Revista de Geografía Norte Grande* 58(5–6): 71–91.

Garnier JP (2017) El espacio urbano, el Estado y la pequeña burguesía intelectual: La radicalidad crítica en cuestión. In: Tello R (ed.) *Jean-Pierre Garnier: Un sociólogo urbano a contra-corriente*. Barcelona: Ed. Icaria, pp. 189–202.

Gil J (2018) El conflicto de Airbnb aterriza sobre Madrid. *Diario Público*, 11 January. Available at: http://blogs.publico.es/contraparte/2018/01/11/el-conflicto-de-airbnb-aterriza-sobre-madrid-2a-parte/ (accessed 1 July 2018).

Götte D (2014) *De la transición española a la movida madrileña*. Munich: GRIN Verlag.

Hackworth J and Smith N (2001) The changing state of gentrification. *Tijdschrift voor economische en sociale geografie* 92(4): 464–477.

Hammel DJ (1999) Gentrification and land rent: A historical view of the rent gap in Minneapolis. *Urban Geography* 20(2): 116–145.

Harvey D (1989) *The Condition of Postmodernity: An Enquiry into the Origins of Cultural Change*. Cambridge, MA: Blackwell.

Hernández A and Grasso D (2017) ¿Buscas alquiler en Madrid o Barcelona? Este mapa muestra dónde te lo puedes permitir. *El Confidencial*, 1 September. Available at: www.elconfidencial.com/vivienda/2017-09-01/alquiler-precio-barrios-madrid-barcelona_1435196/ (accessed 1 July 2018).

Idealista.com (2018) *Housing prices report 2018*. Available at: www.idealista.com/informes-precio-vivienda (accessed 1 July 2018).

Instituto Nacional de Estadística (INE) (2011) *Censo de Población y Vivienda*. Available at: www.ine.es/censos2011_datos/cen11_datos_inicio.htm (accessed 1 July 2018).

Janoschka M, Sequera J and Salinas L (2014) Gentrification in Spain and Latin America – A critical dialogue. *International Journal of Urban and Regional Research* 38(4): 1234–1265.

Justo A (2011) Transformaciones en el barrio de Malasaña. Hacia la gentrificación. *Viento Sur* 116: 73–79.

Leal J (2004) Segregation and social change in Madrid metropolitan region. *The Greek Review of Social Research* 113: 81–104.

Lechado JM and García JML (2005) *La movida: Una crónica de los 80*. Madrid: EDAF.

Lees L, Shin HB and López-Morales E (2015) *Global Gentrifications: Uneven Development and Displacement*. Bristol: Policy Press.

Lees L, Slater T and Wyly E (2008) *Gentrification*. London: Routledge.

Ley 16/2012, de 27 de diciembre, por la que se adoptan diversas medidas tributarias dirigidas a la consolidación de las finanzas públicas y al impulso de la actividad económica. BOE. Boletín Oficial del Estado, pp. 88, 097–88, 155.

Ley D (1996) *The New Middle Class and the Remaking of the Central City*. Oxford: Oxford University Press.

López de Lucio R, et al. (2016) *Madrid 1900–2010. Guía de Planeamiento y diseño urbano (Madrid 1900–2010. Urbanism and Urban Design Guide)*. Madrid: Ayuntamiento de Madrid.

López García A (2018) Radiografía del Mercado de la vivienda 2017–2018. *Fotocasa*. Available at: http://prensa.fotocasa.es/wp-content/uploads/2018/05/Radiograf%C3%ADa-del-mercado-de-la-vivienda-2017–2018-BAJA.pdf (accessed 1 July 2018).

López Letón S (2019) Madrid es la tercera ciudad del mundo donde más casas de lujo se buscarán este año. *El País*, 22 March. Available at: https://elpais.com/economia/2019/03/20/vivienda/1553099878_898631.html (accessed 1 July 2018).

Ministerio de Transportes, Movilidad y Agenda Urbana (2017) Tráfico comercial por aeropuertos. *Aeropuerto de Adolfo Suarez-Madrid-Barajas*. Available at: www.fomento.gob.es/BE/?nivel=2&orden=03000000 (accessed 1 July 2018).

Novy J (2019) Urban tourism as a bone of contention: Four explanatory hypotheses and a caveat. *International Journal of Tourism Cities* 5(1): 63–74.

Pérez N, González M, Sevillano L, et al. (2015) Dormir en el limbo: Radiografía de Airbnb. *El Español*, 21 November. Available at: http://datos.elespanol.com/proyectos/airbnb/ (accessed 1 July 2018).

Red2Red Consultores (2017) *Análisis del Impacto de las Viviendas de Uso Turístico en el Distrito Centro*. Madrid. Available at: www.ma-drid.es/UnidadesDescentralizadas/UDCMedios/noticias/2017/05Mayo/05viernes/Notasprensa/ficheros/Informe_final_5_mayo-viviendas-uso-turístico(1).pdf (accessed 1 July 2018).

Rodríguez P (2016) Sorprendente evolución del turismo en Madrid. *Mind the Blog Universidad Europea*. Available at: https://blog.universidadeuropea.es/es/turismo/viajes-y-turismo/sor-prendente-evolucion-del-turismo-en-madrid (accessed 1 July 2018).

Rodríguez López J (2017) Las viviendas que pudieron hundir la economía espan~ola. La caída del mercado de vivienda y sus consecuencias. *Cuadernos de relaciones laborales* 35(1): 71–99.

Sanz E (2018) *Alquileres: ¿Alquiler turístico vs tradicional? Solo es ma´s rentable a partir del 60% de ocupación*, 27 June. Available at: www.elconfidencial.com/vivienda/2018-06-27/alquiler-turistico-rentabilidad-alquiler-tradi-cional-precios_1584220/ (accessed 1 July 2018).

Semi G and Tonetta M (2019) Plateformes locatives en ligne et rente urbaine a' Turin: Les classes moyennes face a' l'austérité. *Annales de Géographie* 727(3): 40.

Sequera J (2013) *Las políticas de gentrificación en la ciudad neoliberal. Nuevas clases medias, producción cultural y gestión del espacio público. El caso de Lavapie´s en el centro histórico de Madrid*. PhD Thesis, Universidad Autónoma de Madrid, Spain.

Sequera J and Janoschka M (2015) Gentrification dispositifs in the historic centre of Madrid: A re-consideration of urban governmentality and state-led urban reconfiguration. In: Lees L, Shin HB and López-Morales E (eds) *Global Gentrifications: Uneven Development and Displacement*. Bristol: Policy Press, pp. 375–394.

Sequera J and Nofre J (2020) Touristification, transnational gentrification and urban change in Lisbon: The neighbourhood of Alfama. *Urban Studies* 57(15): 3169–3189.

Shatford S (2017) Is Airbnb regulation impacting short-term rental growth? *AIRDNA*. Available at: www.airdna.co/blog/effects-airbnb-regulation (accessed 1 July 2018).

Sigler T and Wachsmuth D (2016) Transnational gentrification: Globalisation and neighbourhood change in Panama's Casco Antiguo. *Urban Studies* 53(4): 705–722.

Simón Ruiz A (2019) *Blackstone abre la puerta a la venta de pisos sociales comprados en Madrid*. Available at: https://cincodias.elpais.com/cincodias/2019/04/23/companias/1556045-344_333951.html (accessed 1 July 2018).

Slater T (2017) Planetary rent gaps. *Antipode* 49: 114–137.

Smith N (1979) Toward a theory of gentrification: A back to the city movement by capital, not people. *Journal of the American Planning Association* 45(4): 538–548.

Smith N (1982) Gentrification and uneven development. *Economic Geography* 58(2): 139.

Smith N (2002) New globalism, new urbanism: Gentrification as global urban strategy. *Antipode* 34(3): 427–450.

Smith N (2010) *Uneven Development: Nature, Capital, and the Production of Space*. University of Georgia Press.

Sorando D and Ardura A (2016) *First we Take Manhattan. La destrucción creativa de las ciudades*. Madrid: Catarata.

Sorando D and Ardura A (2018) Procesos y diná– micas de gentrificación en las ciudades españolas. *Papers. Regió Metropolitana de Barcelona* 60: 34–47.

Vidal L (2018) 'Los "fondos buitre" en la ciudad, una cuestión de soberanía?' Opinión. *Barcelona: CiDOB*. Available at: www.cidob.org/en/publications/publication_series/opinion/ciudades_globales/els_fons_vol_tor_a_la_ciutat_una_queestio_de_sobirania/(language)/cat-ES (accessed 1 July 2018).

Vivus Finance (2017) *¿Cuánto cuesta vivir en Madrid? Principales Gastos*. Available at: www.vivus.es/blog/economia-de-hoy/cuanto-cuesta-vivir-en-madrid/ (accessed 1 July 2018).

Wachsmuth D and Weisler A (2018) Airbnb and the rent gap: Gentrification through the sharing economy. *Environment and Planning A: Economy and Space* 50(6): 1147–1170.

Zervas G, Proserpio D and Byers JW (2017) The rise of the sharing economy: Estimating the impact of Airbnb on the hotel industry. *Journal of Marketing Research* 54(5): 687–705.

20
Postsocialism and the Tech Boom 2.0
Techno-utopics of racial/spatial dispossession

Erin McElroy

I could barely see the punches being thrown in front of me. The backyard of the East Bay Rats motorcycle club arena was beyond its saturation point with eager witnesses of the 'Nihilists vs. Marxists' boxing match slowly unfolding, a complementary event to the annual East Bay Anarchist Book Fair. Another Saturday evening in West Oakland, emblazoned with rickety spotlights, tattered ropes, sweat, black leather, and cigarettes. Some moaned and others cheered as opponents were knocked to the ground in repetitive blows, indicating the ideological rise or fall of some semblance of a strategic futurity, of some mutation of an older logic intended to encapsulate and make sense of the contradictions, struggles, and sinkholes of a landscape entangled in broad strokes of disinvestment, reinvestment, deterritorialization, and reterritorialization, popularly discoursed today as 'gentrification', but also bearing other names and analytics.

It was just months before, in an outburst of actions intended to highlight violences of Silicon Valley Tech Boom-induced dispossession, that many in the crowd set to task the blockading of 'Google Buses' in San Francisco and Oakland, private shuttles from multiple tech corporations viscerally understood as agential in eviction and rental increases. Some protestors 'weaponized vomit' upon the buses in repugnance. Since 2011, Silicon Valley has penetrated both cities in new though differential ways, as high-tech corporations such as Facebook, Google, and Apple have unleashed private luxury shuttle buses that enable the reverse commuting of high-paid workers to Silicon Valley headquarters. While numerous technology companies themselves have existed in San Francisco since the postsocialist Dot Com Boom, it has only been during the 'Tech Boom 2.0' that Valley technology corporations have facilitated urban dwelling for suburban campus workers. And, disproportionately, this workforce composed of young, white men, colloquially reified as 'tech-bros'. In 2014, real estate speculator Jennifer Rosdail mapped this newly venerated human as a 'quadster', or those 'under forty [who] like to hang in the sun with their friends', and prefer to live in 'The Quad' – an emergent real estate geometry covering much of San Francisco's Mission District. Allegedly, quadsters 'work very hard – mostly in high tech – and make a lot of money' (Paragon, 2014).

While the labor performed by this new techno-human is imagined to exist immaterially, there are material effects, effects highly racialized and spatialized. As work by the Anti-Eviction Mapping Project – a data-driven cartography and oral history project that I cofounded in 2013 to document the dispossession and resistance surrounding the Tech Boom 2.0 – has shown, 69% of San Francisco's evictions have occurred within four blocks of tech bus stops, as speculators capitalize on property that can be advertised as adjacent, thereby increasing value (McElroy, 2016). Further, per census data, Black populations, along with Black and Latinx household income levels, have been shrinking in both San Francisco and Oakland, demographics largely non-represented in Silicon Valley technology corporations outside of service worker positions. Denigrating Silicon Valley's decomposition and recomposition of

DOI: 10.4324/9781003341239-30

Bay Area social/political worlds, members of the anarchist collective Defend the Bay pleaded during the bus protests,

> We encourage all Bay Area residents to take action against the tech takeover's many manifestations: increased rents, exclusive access to transportation, and the intensified police repression that accompanies gentrification, which is literally killing Black and brown residents in their own neighborhoods.
>
> (as cited in Tiku, 2014)

Increased police violence was further linked to imbrications between high-tech companies with military surveillance partnerships bearing global impact, from Google's with the military robotics group Boston Dynamics, to Facebook's facial recognition software being utilizing by Oakland's Domain Awareness Center to surveil and suppress illiberal 'threat'.

Yet while Google does contribute to military robotics designed to kill racialized collectives of people 'elsewhere', it is also now working to 'cure death' for others, celebrating of a transhumanist acceleration into cyborgian immortality. As Google's former CEO Eric Schmidt triumphantly proclaimed in 2010, Google's actual goal is to engineer the 'age of augmented humanity' (Gannes, 2010). Accordingly, the boxing ring punches thrown to the rhythm of the insurrectionist band Death Drive were partly bemoaning impositions of local and global dispossessions draped under the shiny veneer of techno-utopics.

While acknowledging heterogeneous histories of Bay Area racialized dispossession, this paper situates the contemporary spatial, racial, and temporal transformations constitutive of (and constituting) the Tech Boom 2.0 through a postsocialist lens, focusing upon the material impact of the Cold War and postsocialist transition. After all, it was during the Cold War that Silicon Valley was birthed as a military/educational hybridity designed to engineer the 'free world'. As it attempted to craft the ideal scientific hero of the pastoral suburbs, it positioned the Valley landscape as antithetical to that of San Francisco and Oakland, the latter home to anti-capitalist dissent, racialized urban immigration, and grey, industrial density. It was post-1989 that the suburban geography of the Valley techno-hero shifted towards urban peripheries as IT began catering towards consumer use, inciting new forms of labour and liberalism, as well as mobility. It was the bleeding of Silicon Valley into postsocialist urbanity that cemented conditions of contemporary tech-driven racialized dispossession. Arguably, urban sublation was laboratory practice for global spatial incorporation, producing what J.A. English-Lueck (2002) nominates as 'silicon places'.

Additionally, post-Cold War conditions of increased Silicon Valley mobility into formerly impenetrable space, set in place with the Dot Com Boom and actualized with the Tech Boom 2.0, are made possible through emergent postsocialist technologies of time. While postsocialist techno-utopics fantasize the elimination of both space and time, enabling the 'real-time' global reach of Silicon Valley, such utopics bear material racial/spatial residues, along with attendant forms of protest. Such protests call for alternative futures, some past, some yet-to-come, as well as differential frameworks with which to conceptualize the present.

Postsocialist analytics are therefore tools with which we can better conceptualize the Bay Area Tech Boom 2.0 present, as they facilitate a particular unearthing of spatial, racial, and temporal technologies of dispossession in modes that traditional Marxist and neoliberal scholarship alike on gentrification largely does not. Such a utilization of post-socialist analytics, in the words of Neda Atanasoski and Kalindi Vora in their astute introduction to this volume, inherently must 'dehomogenize the "socialism" in postsocialism', while concurrently unmooring '(post)socialism from a particular geographic location' (2017, p. 5). Further, applying postsocialist analytics in theorizing Bay Area formations of dispossession and resistance unmoors the Bay Area present from the increasingly well-rehearsed debates of gentrification studies,[1] offering supplementary temporal and spatial frameworks. Reading the constitution, materiality, and affective worlds of Silicon Valley through a postsocialist lens then reveals that postsocialism is far from only a global condition; of its multifarious chronotopics, it endures irreducibly in the Bay Area.

It is both the spatial and temporal contours of the postsocialist Bay Area condition that I dwell on here, questioning how theorizations of postsocialism might help articulate conflicts around the futurity of Silicon Valley's local and global backyard. Through postsocialist analysis, we can perceive the Nihilist and Marxist boxers sunken into the drunken, dirty backyard stage as, in David Scott's words, stranded in the present, bereft of future hope amidst a 'melancholic silence' and paresis, yet also clinging on to some*thing*, some futures past, worth fighting for (2013, p. 116). Accordingly, we might consider their punches as responsive to the dominance of neo/liberal horizons routed into what Scott describes as the 'ruin of time and the accompanying loss of futures' (2013, p. 125). Yet, haunting their punches also endure what Derrida conjures as 'ghosts chained to ghosts', refusing to vanquish, dwelling in the spaces of riot, rot, and irreverence (1994, p. 3). And these two conditions – that of nihilistic despair and that of being haunted with some semblance of hope for revolutionary futures past – when compounded upon local and global theaters of dispossession, fashion something new. This paper proceeds to frame Bay Area technologies of dispossession through postsocialist analytics, studying Silicon Valley Cold War racialized histories of space, as well as the impact of postsocialist transition upon the temporality of both global capital and anti-capitalist futurities. As such, it progresses from the Cold War through the Dot Com Boom and into the present.

SILICON VALLEY AND THE COLD WAR

Silicon Valley and early informatics bear well-established roots in Cold War technological infrastructure. Following the Second World War, the US set to task employing scientists and psychologists to study possibilities of global dissemination of the democratic mind, merging science and politics to script new notions of a universal humanism. For instance, MIT mathematician Norbert Wiener, theorist of human – machine interaction who coined the term *cybernetics*, and Columbia professor Lyman Bryson, a champion of what he described as a 'scientific humanism', argued that democratic nations must utilize science and technology to construct social spaces in which individuals could obtain maximum freedom (Turner, 2013, pp. 159–160). This would allegedly ensure global peace by 'containing' Communism. In the words of Katherine Hayles, 'Deeply connected to the military, bound to high technology for its very existence and a virtual icon for capitalism, the cyborg was contaminated to the core, making it exquisitely appropriate as a provocation' (2006, p. 159). While cyborgs are not my focus here, the same assemblage of force that gave birth to the cyborg gave rise to early Silicon Valley technologies, along with the romanticized techno-human of whom such modernization both reflected (and to whom it benefited).

Although relationships between the science and military developed during World War II, it was as the Cold War came into fruition presaged by the 1947 National Security Act, along with the actual US wars in Korea and Vietnam intended to prevent Communist growth, that US science gained increased federal funding and freedom, strengthening relationships between higher education, military defense, and scientific research. While the Cold War demanded a strong state to fight the structural 'enemy', American political traditions demanded a weak one. To reconcile such contradictions, universities and scientific industries were effectively empowered as federal agents, redefined to engineer national and economic security. While East Coast universities such as MIT could make short lobbying trips to Washington, DC, geographically distant Stanford University realized that setting up a DC office would be expeditious, and so they did; Stanford's own geographic distance incited its governmental centrality (O'Mara, 2015, p. 27).

Also during this time, US pro-development urban planners began advocating to decentralize post-industrial urbanities, denigrating the social unrest accompanying what planner Tracey Augur pathologized as 'near-slum environments' (1948, p. 312). In San Francisco, these ideas were intimately linked to the racialization of Filipinx and Black migration, facilitating 'white flight' to suburban spaces like Silicon Valley while redlining segregation landscapes. Simultaneously, city centers such as San Francisco were scripted as Soviet atomic targets, and so ideas of dispersal saturated the public imaginary, an imago welcomed by Stanford. Thus, it was both Bay Area racialized geographies and Cold War spatial imaginaries that impelled millions of dollars to be funneled into military defense research on suburban high-tech firms, surrounded by prefabricated US Army-erected houses. As Brian Chung argues, these contexts led to the heightened status of the scientist as the ideal suburban resident (2011, p. 39). Valorizing this new Cold War hero, Stanford University built its campus-adjacent research park, solidifying what Paul Edwards nominated the 'iron triangle', or the triangular partnership between the Pentagon, top rank research universities, and defense industries (1977, p. 44). Government support for scientific freedom and the 'Cold War multiversity' only bolstered post-Sputnik as the Eisenhower administration endeavored to not fall behind in the great space race.

Silicon Valley, which after the Gold Rush had emerged as the orchard capital of California, or the 'Valley of Heart's Delight', mutated with the settlement of technology companies. In 1956, inventor William Shockley established the first semiconductor laboratory in Mountain View, and the next year, Lockheed Missile and Space moved to Sunnyvale. And with them came IBM, FMC, and other Cold War military defense industries. In 1971, the Valley of Heart's Delight was reconstituted as 'Silicon Valley', referencing the mineral relied upon by semiconductor companies. Stanford's first dean of engineering, Frederick Terman, or the 'Father of Silicon Valley', pushed to transform the research behemoth into a regional high-tech corporate magnet, for instance, convincing his former students William Hewlett and David Parker to start their own company (Leslie, 2000; Rosenberg, 2002, p. 15). This era saw the emergence of what Nick Dyer-Witheford describes as 'futuristic accumulation', or 'the commodification of publicly created scientific knowledge, which via copyright and patent, becomes privatized as intellectual property for the extraction of monopolistic technological rents' (2010, pp. 487–88). In other words, iron triangle formation utilized extractive mechanisms of technological rent to speculate upon the future.

While the 'Valley of Hearts Delight' relied upon immigrant labor, building racialized geographies, such landscapes further transformed as silicon chips replaced prune trees. New high-tech companies heralded an imaginary of a cleaner, lighter, post-agricultural utopia – one racialized, classed, and gendered. Stanford's Board of Trustees proclaimed the post-Fordist emergence of a 'light industry of a non-nuisance type' that would 'create a demand for technical employees of a high salary class that will be in a financial position to live in this area,' or in other words, 'a better class of workers' (as cited in Findlay, 1992, p. 132). 'Anti-factory' pastoral parks and residential worlds became poised against San Francisco and Oakland and their largely POC-led social/political movements, such as the Black Panther Party, the Brown Berets, La Raza Unida, and the San Francisco State strike of 1968.

Of course, this is not to say that San Francisco was not also being developed into a global city throughout the Cold War, even if ultimate scientific achievements were slated to occur further south. Development projects of the era were intended to 'Manhattanize' the urban scape, as well as redline certain neighborhoods to maintain whiteness (McGovern, 1998; Schafran, 2013). Meanwhile, throughout the Cold War, Oakland became the first of six sites tested by the Ford Foundation's Grey Areas program. Aimed to disrupt social unrest, the program discursively abdicated 'race' with 'poverty' to mitigate 'juvenile delinquency', gang violence, and 'human problems in the city' through assimilatory projects of 'human engineering' (Roy, Schrader, & Crane, 2015, p. 294). What such grammar elided was that social unrest was quelling in Oakland not because of juvenile delinquency, but because white homeowners grew racialized anxieties about the rise of Black homeownership. Domestic pacification, the program proffered, was a means of what Robert McNamara would later describe to the World Bank as 'defensive modernization' (Ayres, 1983). These Cold War technologies were first tested in the Valley's own racialized backyard before being employed elsewhere.

Woven into histories of race and racism within the Valley are also those of Cold War-driven assimilation. It was Cold War conditions that inspired the region's white communities to win the hearts and minds of Cold War Asia, abating postwar patterns of racial segregation for some Asian American collectives differentially than other racialized minorities (Cavin, 2012). This era saw the Cold War suburb mutate into what Chung describes as a 'trans-Pacific hub of Chinese high-tech business', in which it is commonly ridiculed that '"Silicon Valley is built on ICs" – not integrated circuits but Indian and Chinese engineers' (2011, pp. 4, 45). Of course, this elides differential experiences of heterogeneous Asian collectives impacted by varying racist, colonial, socialist, and national contexts. Nevertheless, it has been upon a backdrop of Cold War geopolitics that Asian American subjectivities have differentially crystallized.

Perhaps such contexts of Cold War subjectivity helped fuel myths of Silicon Valley culture as one of meritocracy, multiculturalism, and postraciality towards the end of the Cold War and into the postsocialist era. As Apple's former CEO and visionary Steve Jobs suggested in 1997, while racial difference does not matter in Silicon Valley, 'what matters is how smart you are' (cited in Reinhardt, 1997). In 1997, *Business Week* asserted that Silicon Valley was the 'immigrant gateway', or 'the quintessence of the American Dream', where 'any good idea in a garage can turn into a gold mine' with 'no pedigree required' (Reinhardt, 1997). Of course, such imago endured in myth form only throughout the Cold War and its aftermath. When Iron Curtain disintegration led to job cuts at defense divisions of tech firms, regional press suggested that with layoffs of white suburbanites, Asian domination saturated the 'doomed' future. Articles titled 'No More Mr. White Guy' and 'War Surplus Job-Market Misfits' index such fears, pointing to conditions of postsocialist racialization in the Valley (Chung, 2011, p. 31). Silicon Valley Cold War-era racial liberalism therefore can be read as constitutive of, yet distinct from, the era that followed.

POSTSOCIALISM AND THE DOT COM BOOM

With defense cutbacks following 1989, questions arose as to the direction Silicon Valley would take in the now postsocialist era. When the Internet developed in 1993, proceeded by the creation of the Web, it became clear that their commercialization by consumer-based technology companies would impel Silicon Valley forward. Companies such as Netscape, Cisco, Hewlett-Packard, 3Com, and Intel exploded software job growth, leading to the Dot Com Boom (Hughes & Cosier, 2001). This is the era from which Michael Hardt and Antonio Negri wrote their seminal *Empire* (2000), describing the replacement of local territorial rule with global flows, decentering and deterritorializing, effacing the tripartite geography of 'second' and 'third world' divisions. The Web and Silicon Valley were theorized as intricately part of this new social order, constituting the US's 'soft power', led by the internet business sphere – the offspring of Cold War informatics.

The internet was supposed to be, as William Mitchell suggested, 'anti-spatial', comprised of a 'negative geometry' (1996). However, as evidenced in the spatial/racial infrastructural transformations that accompanied postsocialist technologic growth, utopian dreams of immateriality themselves dematerialize. During the last quarter of the twentieth century, the Valley's housing prices rose more rapidly than anywhere else in the US, totaling a 936% increase (Cavin, 2012, p. 12). Not only did Dot Com Boom employment favor upper-class and white workers within the Valley, leading to racialized real estate geographies, but further, racism within Silicon Valley prevented implementation of IT unions (Cooper, 1996).

The financialization of the technology realm excited real estate developers upon the Valley's urban borders as well, inciting what Stephen Graham and Simon Guy described as the '"dot-com invasion" of IT entrepreneurs and internet industries to downtown San Francisco', an invasion clearly classed and racialized (2002, p. 372). As Richard Walker chronicled,

> Obscure little South Park (near the foot of the Bay Bridge), once a refuge for a small black residential block, is now a popular eating spot for the denizens of Virtual valley, the new hot spot for multimedia electronics and computer magazine publishers.
>
> (1995, p. 39)

During this time, evictions grew by 400%, and as Nancy Mirabal described, displacement was linked to the preservation of whiteness (2009). And, as Graham and Guy elaborate, 'renewal' was also gendered: 'Ideologically driven and utopian discourses of corporeal, territorial and urban transcendence, based on the fantasy of perfect IT systems, can thus be understood as a series of (largely masculinized) "omnipotence fantasies"' (2002, p. 369).

Yet, it was pre-1989 that these omnipotence fantasies first coalesced. For instance, during the Cold War that Steve Jobs first visited the Soviet Union, desirous of breaking through the Iron Curtain. Along these lines, a caption below a 1977 photojournalistic piece on Intel, the world's largest producer of semiconductor computer chips, reads, 'The Sun Never Sets on Intel', indexing early Silicon global desire (as cited in Marez, 2013, p. 87). Yet, these early desires of dissemination proved difficult to realize until after the Cold War, when cluster cloning Silicon

Valley became viable, and increasingly normalized (Rosenberg, 2002). This post-1989 era has been one in which neoliberalism, or what Scott describes as 'smugly confident liberalism', has accumulated momentum by 're-territorializing power to roll back what was now perceived as the "moral evil" of communism' (2013, p. 4). While early liberal conceptions of the internet growing out of non-consumer-based networks imagined the internet as a freedom vehicle to those from repressive regimes, Communist or otherwise, this imaginary largely became muddied through Dot Com corporatization. Furthermore, these liberal imaginaries themselves were often Cold War figments, tethered to one conception of freedom while eliding others, for instance, early Romanian hacking cultures that instead drew upon Communist-era opposition to Western neoliberal imperialism (Dunne, 2016; Țichindeleanu, 2010).

Of course, the Boom busted shortly after it began, largely due to overconfident investment. While the ensuing crash led a drop in rental and home prices in the Bay Area, it also incited the restructuring of surviving companies into more robust capitalist machines, constituting the emergence of mega-tech companies such as Apple, Cisco, and Intel. These laid the foundation for the sharing economy and app-based industries that constitute the Tech Boom 2.0, in which racialized spatial and temporal IT materializations are haunted by those of the Dot Com Boom era. Today, heralding the imaginary of clean, light industry, and imbricated in the grammar of liberal democracy, Silicon Valley corporations now penetrate the former Second World, often exploiting a technologically inclined labor force and cheaper rental and production costs. Silicon Valley-like places globally percolate, for instance, Cluj-Napoca, Romania, which has in recent years been nominated the 'Silicon Valley of Europe'. Postsocialist Valley geography therefore has not only sublated local urbanities such as San Francisco and Oakland through new technologies of transit, but also former socialist landscapes, signaling new imperial spatiality endemic to the age of global techno-capitalism. The phenomenon of producing Silicon space beyond Valley confines is thus one of postsocialist spatiality, mobility, and global liquidity. This is not simply because prestidigitation has outgrown Silicon Valley space; postsocialist relations inhere globality.

POSTSOCIALIST TECHNOLOGIC TIME

The logics of post-1989 Silicon Valley constitute and are constituted by accelerated logics of mobility, techno-utopics, and freedom, but also a solidification of postsocialist temporality. As Silicon Valley itself temporally changed form and consciousness after 1989, post-socialist temporal analysis is requisite. The Cold War's collapse solidified a new global order of time in which, in the words of Susan Buck-Morss, '"we" . . . may have nothing more nor less in common than sharing *this* time' (2002, p. 68). As Buck-Morss illuminates, while the capitalist project has long been one in which land has been acquired and exploited as quickly as possible, the socialist one aspired to accelerate time in contained space per a Marxian evolutionism. Extrapolating upon this logic, we can observe two ratios simultaneously emerging: capitalist space/time, and socialist time/space.[2] With the disintegration of the Cold War came the imposition of time/space into the triumphalism the of space/time, forging the figment of a new, in the words of Anita Starosta, 'common time' (2014). This incorporation required translation, or 'a process of never-finished synchronization among multiple temporalities – and by the same token, the process of forging the only possible authentic "we"' (2014, p. 205). Silicon Valley Time, having abdicated that of Greenwich, was first made possible with Dot Com Boom. Now, via Tech 2.0, it has even more robustly centralized itself, governing the virtual and material means through which information is absorbed. Returning to time and space ratios, if postsocialist time/space indeed has been incorporated into capitalist space/time, in other words, space/time over time/space, all that remains are capitalism squared. Time has been reduced to nothing, so that accumulation of space and/through capital can transpire in absolutely no time at all.

This new postsocialist Silicon Valley temporality and its fantasies of immaterial temporality augment under the rubric of what I describe as *techno-utopic liberalism*. Technoutopic liberalism disseminates the imaginary that digital technology can and will remedy the world's maladies, spread real-time freedom of information to all, and telescope the 'backwards' and 'uninformed' parts of the globe into techno-utopic futurity. For instance, in 2014, a lengthy article in *Time* featured a story detailing Facebook CEO Mark Zuckerberg's new project, Internet.org, designed to supply even the most 'remote' spaces of the planet with internet. The cover image of the article depicted a tall, white Zuckerberg surrounded by grave-looking children from the rural town of Chandauli, India. The cover, along with the mission of the project, received much critique for its overt coloniality, and as Kentaro Toyama chastised, 'Internet.org is a form of colonialism that whitewashes Facebook's techno-imperialism under a cloak of doing good' (2014). As a form and extension of capitalism, techno-utopic liberalism protracts both race and racism into new domains in the name of future freedom. Reliant upon the racial and the spatial, it disseminates the imaginary of spatial difference now antiquated and immaterial.

Within techno-utopic logics, on-demand mobility is now desired over private property ownership, so long as it is paired with access to capital and space. For instance, both Eastern European and Bay Area urban landscapes are now peppered with 'digital nomads', avatars of ultimate techno-utopic freedom, accruing capital for Silicon Valley corporations through remote labor and sharing economy lifestyles, largely made possible by San Francisco's own Airbnb and Uber. Consequently, the mobility of capital and information, fiber-optically transmitted in real time, facilitates and is facilitated by the proliferation of highly paid Valley technology workers into global space. For instance, anytime an Airbnb host or guest (digital nomad or not) interfaces with Airbnb in any of its 190 operable countries, the startup gains capital. Yet, Airbnb is one of the leading causes of evictions in both San Francisco and Oakland, as long-time tenants are displaced to create more profitable short-term housing. Thus, as techno-utopic liberalism superficially dissolves longstanding Lockean intimacies of freedom with private property and the hetero-normative household, it still relies upon capitalist systems of value, facilitating real displacement. But through the logics of Tech 2.0, value is rendered abstract in novel ways.

Despite fantasies of omnipotence in which spatial difference disintegrates in real time, space still exists, unevenly penetrated by postsocialist techno-utopic ontologies. And despite the post-1989 absorption of formerly unobtainable spaces into Silicon Valley (from Eastern European to Bay Area cities), there also remain, in Starosta's words, 'perverse tongues' that defy the logics of universality in unlikely places, sometimes in backyard Marxist/Nihilist boxing rings, sometimes elsewhere (2014). These perverse tongues cry out against the spatial and temporal magnetism of Silicon Valley across the globe, and against its authorial place in the creation of local cartographies. Repudiating the authority of postsocialist Silicon Valley Time, their obdurate voices call for futures other than those being rendered by techno-utopic liberalism, while also demanding other analytics with which to theorize the present.

Yet, it is liberalism and the politics of rights that are dominantly galvanized in the Bay Area as antidote to conditions of gentrification, particularly by non-profit and reform-based visionaries under the aegis of 'housing is a human right'. Upholding the inclusive genre of the rights deserving human, these formations understand rights as universally applicable given the collapse of the Iron Curtain. However, as Sylvia Wynter's work teaches us, throughout modernity, the 'mono-humanist' universal 'Man' of humankind has claimed universality while utilizing race to script the elision of the racialized into the domains of the non-human, or not-quite human (Wynter & McKittrick, 2015). This pattern makes suspect human rights-based calls for universal application. While the mono-humanist Man attempts to absorb everything possible into his domain, asserting that those not recognizable as him assimilate, there remain cultural and political formations outside of his world, offering alternative versions of humanity, whether we think of this as Wynter's 'demonic grounds' (1994), the perversion of tongues, or a vomit-splattered tech bus. As Alexander Weheliye questions, 'What different modalities of the human come to light if we not take the liberal humanist figure of Man as the master-subject but focus on how humanity has been imagined and lived by those subjects excluded from this domain?' (2014, p. 8). The rancor of Marxist vs. Nihilist boxing match therefore emerges as one of countless responses to such a question, indexing a desire for not only alternative futures than those ascribed by both the invisible hand of global capital doing its thing and reifications rights-based universalisms, but also differential epistemologies with which to theorize dispossessions of the present. In the words of Atanasoski and Vora,

The dominance of present-day liberal politics, which collapse political notions of freedom with the unrestricted spread of free markets, and justice with liberal rights-based outcomes, beg for an extended exploration of the aftermaths of the social, political, and cultural disappearance and subsequent reconfiguration of a socialist political imaginary.

(2017, p. 14)

Such explorations, through a postsocialist theoretical approach, are needed to disinter the spatial/racial/temporal ramifications of techno-utopics as they subsume the political. While Silicon Valley liberalism extends Man's domain locally and globally, it also protracts libertarian ontologies that understand tech corporations as more effective than lethargic government. Accordingly, techno-utopian liberalism seeks to vaccinate against the sluggishness of regulatory liberal democracy, ultimately offering techno-freedom to all. For instance, San Francisco's current mayor Edwin Lee's election campaign was bankrolled by Silicon Valley venture capitalist Ron Conway, one of the primary investors of numerous IT companies, from Google to Airbnb. It was Lee who established the 'Twitter Tax Break Zone' in 2011 to encourage tech to relocate from the Valley to San Francisco tax-free, inciting heightened eviction rates within its geography. Meanwhile, Conway's public-private hybrid companies such as sf.citi's attempt to override public decision-making bodies to benefit tech and tech-friendly politicians, privileging anti-regulatory legislation. This structure invokes what Paul Carr describes as a 'cult of disruption', or the disruption of non-Silicon Valley space/time with techno-utopics (2012). As a 2016 signage campaign by the San Francisco datacenter Digital Reality promulgated in Bay Area Rapid Transit (BART) trains, 'Your Next Stop, West Oakland Station. The New Edge of Silicon Valley: Disrupt Your Industry from our Data Center.' Below its text was a streamline map of the Bay Area, pointing out West Oakland's proximity to both San Francisco and the Valley. In response, stickers manifested upon signs, proclaiming', Keep Hoods Yours: By Any Means Necessary', invoking Cold War-era Panther resistances to racialized technologies of dispossession. Nevertheless, the datacenter was erected, now visible from the BART train in West Oakland, appropriatively adorned with its new motto: 'Hella connected'.

The disruptive cult of Silicon Valley has been made famous through events such as 'Disrupt SF', in which startups compete for the 'Disrupt Cup' and the $50,000 accompanying cash prize. The 2014 champion of Disrupt SF went to the makers of 'Alfred', a sharing economy application that manages other on-demand apps, and further, comes equipped with a human being – one's very own Alfred – who delivers products and laundered clothing, and who even cleans houses, performing duties such as replenishing paper towel on paper towel holders, all for $99/month. The idea is not only 'to cut into the 30 average hours/week that people spend on household chores, but to relieve some of the mental strain of dealing with multiple apps and services, and coordinating them together' (Crook, 2014). Alfred serves as an allegory for the contradictions between techno-utopic fantasy and racialized/gendered materiality constitutive of Silicon Valley disruptions. Who becomes an Alfred, conscripted to exploitative service labor, and who wins $50,000, or has the luxury of paying for the surplus labor that Alfred performs? This was what the Anti-Eviction Mapping Project questioned in 2014 as we held a protest outside of Alfred's ceremonious awarding in San Francisco. But before we could disrupt the event for long, we were shoved out by a private security firm determined that the event was 'undisruptable'. In a global economy in which time remains valuable, yet in which capital circulates timelessly, some lack the time to perform the drudgery of service labor, or to be disrupted by protest for that matter, yet others have no option but to replace paper towel rolls upon a sharpened backdrop of increased rental prices and income disparity, draped in the vernacular facade of 'hella connected'.

NIHILISMS

Protests enacted outside of the Disrupt Cup and Google buses are frequently critiqued as neo-Luddite, 'anti-tech', and out-of-joint. However, such disapprobation assumes that postsocialist Silicon Valley techno-utopics are both the unavoidable future, and that they are entirely new. Not only are Silicon Valley disruptions dependent upon Cold War spatial/racial/temporal logics and their postsocialist turn, but beyond that, they hinge upon capitalism, itself an older technology predicated upon reducing every 'thing' into the spectral abstraction known as money, dissolving diverse ontologies into value form. As was once written in the *Community Manifesto*, 'All that is solid melts into air' (Marx & Engels, 1967, p. 3). Thus, it would be an unjust assertion that 'anti-tech' demonstrations have been simply directed towards the novelty of new technologies abdicating older ones, for instance, in the case of Alfred, servitude. Rather, protests pivot against a moment in which all that is assumed to be air, to be immaterial, calcifies into solidity, into the shrapnel and debris left in the wake of a new iteration of capitalism on steroids. Weaponized vomit and boxing ring punches can instead be read as perverse tongues calling for something other than the presumed common time of postsocialism, yet paralyzed by the gravity of its dispossessive weight. These tongues critique racialized forms of eviction, surveillance, and consciousness that have newly drawn Silicon Valley into urban and global space.

This contradictory despair and hope, mired within the sinkholes of the leading global industry, can be understood as both reflective and productive of a postsocialist condition. Silicon Valley renegotiations of space are only made possible through post-Cold War circuits of capital, knowledge, and fantasy. Silicon Valley globality can be theorized as a world-historical conjuncture which, in Gary Wilder's words, produces a 'politicotemporal paralysis' whereby imaginaries of freedom have been collapsed with those of markets, diffused across a global space in which alternatives to liberal capitalist democracy appear foreclosed (2015, p. 196). And this collapse has been abetted by the very technologies that it creates. Therefore, arguably, postsocialism, as an analytic, is prerequisite in indexing not only epistemologies surrounding the phenomenon today discoursed as Tech Boom-induced gentrification and its global condition, but also, of the social worlds emerging to combat it. For it is those social worlds, those bodies ensconced within boxing rings, bruised in supernova, perhaps bloody, perhaps not, that the hegemony of Francis Fukuyama's celebrated telos of liberal progress falls short, becoming, to summon Derrida, 'only gospel' (1994, p. 56).

Throughout the summer of 2014, the San Francisco Mime Troupe toured the Bay Area region with its satirical musical comedy, 'Ripple Effect', written by Eugenie Chan, Tanya Shaffer, and Michael Gene Sullivan. The performance stewed with familiar tensions upon the Bay Area tech-driven gentrifying landscape, allegorizing a world in which revolutionary potential is swallowed by Silicon Valley surveillance infrastructures, inciting economies of gentrification and loss. But during its enactment, something else transpired too.

Much of the Mime Troupe's performance takes place aboard a small vessel called the Distant Horizon, traversing the waters surrounding San Francisco. The captain/tour guide, Deborah, played by Velina Brown, enacts recursive paranoia, illuminating that she does not trust anything invented before 1988, the year before the end of the Cold War that, she makes clear, also witnessed the birth of both Prozac and cell phones. Onboard her ship sits two passengers. Jeanine (Lisa Hori-Garcia) is an app developer from Nebraska working for a tech giant, Octopus. Anxious and over-stimulated, Jeanine explains that she has trouble focusing when beyond the confines of her office cubicle. And then there is Sunny (Keiko Shimosato Carreiro), a Vietnamese immigrant and defender of the American dream, yet simultaneously traumatized by the US invasion of Vietnam, now overprotectively raising her daughter and running a beauty salon in the predominantly Black neighborhood of San Francisco's Bayview. As it turns out, Sunny is monitoring her daughter with a surveillance app invented by the uneasy Jeanine, who had originally conceived of the technology to oversee her disabled grandmother who was prone to wandering. Further, Sunny is facing eviction because Jeanine's company is acquiring new office space in the gentrifying neighborhood. But the plot does not end here.

As the story unfolds, we learn that the distrustful captain Deborah had been an active member of the Black Panther Party, and that since the 1960s, she has been searching for a lost partner seemingly disappeared by COINTELPRO operations. Seamlessly, it unravels that her partner was not actually disappeared, but instead went underground, only to reemerge as the CEO of Octopus, Jeanine's boss, now a staunch defender of capitalism. The play reaches its apex as the women realize that the only way to dismantle the Octopus and its various tentacles surveilling all intimate space while controlling information flows, is for all three women to collaborate, dismantling Octopus's technology through a backdoor that Jeanine had coded into the surveillance app. At first Jeanine is reticent, complaining to the adamant Deborah that she is not political, and that she does not know how to fight the new technocratic empire. To this, Deborah dramatically retorts, 'There is no such thing as not political!' much to the crowd's delight. In other moments, Deborah undoes Sunny's identification as being middle-class, vehemently shouting, 'There is no middle-class; there is only the working-class!', and the rich. As Sullivan later explained, the performance intentionally hinted that the conjoining of different working classes is integral to fight a common enemy: that of the gentrifying tech giant empire (cited in Schiffman, 2014). The performance concluded with the women acknowledging that together, though direct action in the streets, they could keep Sunny and her daughter in their home.

Months before the performance, I was asked by the Mime Troupe to participate in their 2014 debut in Dolores Park in San Francisco by rallying the audience after the protest. Just a block away from the performance was the site of a seven-unit household fighting an eviction notice issued by Google's then head of e-Security. The Mime Troupe had envisioned that following the uplifting performance and rallying cry, that audience members would be inspired to join tenants and march to their home in an act of solidarity. But following the performance, upon the park sprinkled with artisanal picnics, tiny gatherings, and a partially exhausted crowd, few people joined our minute picket as we crawled up Dolores Street.

While larger and more successful anti-eviction protests have occurred since then, the inability to rally even a dozen people in a crowd over 500 seemed indicative of postsocialist post-protest despair. Is the Distant Horizon approaching a new working-class collectivity in which the defeat of the high-tech empire and its global penetrations is possible? Or, does it harken to something else, some other horizon haunted by, to conjure Scott's work, 'a wound that will not heal', a wound that takes over, disrupting the linearity of historical time (2014, p. 13)? A wound scarred upon global imaginaries following the supposed evacuation of socialist alterity. A wound that suggests, by the anonymous author of the anarchist text *Desert*, 'the world will not be "saved"' (Anonymous 2011, p. 6). As the author offers, the revolutionary time of protest, of romance, is of the same making as global capitalism – ideologies of universality conscripted through Marxist-Hegelian timelines of global overcoming. Fighting a universal, that of postsocialist techno-utopic globality and its attendant forms of racial/spatial dispossession, will only result in failure if another universal is applied to dismantle it, leading to recurrent catastrophes and paralysis. In the case of such universal application, perhaps failure, following the work of Jack Halberstam, is revolutionary. To disrupt the gentrifying forces of techno-utopics and correlative technologies of racialized dispossession, we do not need one perversion of tongue to triumph; neither the Nihilists nor Marxists need emerge victorious. To disrupt the disruption, it would take, hypothetically, the endurance of multiple and incongruous perversions, visceralities, and failures. It would take revolutionary imaginaries unscripted through liberal teleologies, unbound by the common time of techno-utopics, yet irrevocably tethered to a postsocialist condition. As such, it seems that postsocialism is one of many necessary analytics needed to theorize the present, the past, and the heterogeneity of futures both already here, and yet-to-come.

DISCLOSURE STATEMENT

No potential conflict of interest was reported by the author.

NOTES

1. Since its 1960s nomination, gentrification, as an analytic, has been widely contested and studied, though disproportionately in Western urban studies scholarship, largely drawing on the disciplines of sociology and geography. Debates have saturated this scholarship as to gentrification's definition, its causality, and its universality (Hackworth, 2002; Lees, Shin, & López-Morales, 2015; Smith, 2010). While these conversations are important, disciplinary constraints and geographies have stymied possibilities of intersecting with other frameworks and analytics, for instance, those coming out of the humanities, or, for instance, those that provincialize Western urban studies, methods, and temporalities.
2. There have been debates as to whether the Soviet Union can be theorized as an empire in its

move to expand, as Moore (2001) and Lazarus (2012) well argue, and therefore we cannot elide the importance of space when theorizing Soviet socialism. Neither can we ignore the importance of time under capitalism. Rather, I draw upon these ratio formations to stress differential structures of spaciotemporal valorization.

REFERENCES

Anonymous. (2011). Desert. *The Anarchist Library*. Retrieved from http://theanarchistlibrary.org/library/anonymous-desert

Atanasoski, N., & Vora, K. (2017). Introduction: Postsocialist politics and the ends of revolution. *Social Identities*, 1–16. doi:10.1080/13504630.2017.1321712

Augur, T. (1948). The dispersal of cities: A feasible program. *The Bulletin of the Atomic Scientists*, 4(10), 312–315. doi:10.1080/00963402.1948.11460257

Ayres, R. (1983). Arms production as a form of import-substituting industrialization: The Turkish case. *World Development*, 11(1), 813–823.

Carr, P. (2012, October 24). Travis shrugged: The creepy, dangerous ideology behind Silicon Valley's cult of disruption. *Pando Daily*. Retrieved from https://pando.com/2012/10/24/travis-shrugged/

Cavin, A. (2012). *The borders of citizenship: The politics of race and metropolitan space in Silicon Valley* (Unpublished doctoral dissertation). University of Michigan, Ann Arbor, MI.

Chakravartty, P., & Da Silva, D. (2012). Accumulation, dispossession, and debt: The racial logic of global capitalism – an introduction. *American Quarterly*, 64(3), 361–385. doi:10.1353/aq.2012.0033

Chung, B. (2011). *Exceptional visions: Chineseness, citizenship, and the architectures of community in Silicon Valley* (Unpublished doctoral dissertation). University of Michigan, Ann Arbor, MI.

Cooper, M. (1996, May 27). Class war @ Silicon Valley: Disposable workers in the new economy. *The Nation*. Retrieved from www.highbeam.com/doc/1G1-18344305.html

Crook, J. (2014, September 9). Alfred club, because automatic is better than on-demand. *Tech Crunch*. Retrieved from http://techcrunch.com/2014/09/09/alfred-club-because-automatic-is-better-than-on-demand/

Derrida, J. (1994). *Specters of Marx: The state of the debt, the new work of mourning, and the new international* (P. Kamuf, Trans.). New York, NY: Routledge.

Dunne, S. (2016). *In search of the most dangerous town on the internet*. Mountain View: Norton. Retrieved from https://us.norton.com/mostdangeroustown/index.html#!/en-US

Dyer-Witheford, N. (2010). Digital labour, species-becoming and the global worker. *Ephemera: Theory & Politics in Organization*, 10(3), 484–503.

English-Lueck, J. A. (2002). *Cultures@Silicon Valley*. Stanford: Stanford University Press.

Findlay, J. (1992). *Magic lands: Western cityscapes and American culture after 1940*. Berkeley: University of California Press.

Gannes, L. (2010, September 7). Eric Schmidt: Welcome to the "age of augmented humanity". *Gigaom*. Retrieved from https://gigaom.com/2010/09/07/eric-schmidt-welcome-to-the-age-of-augmented-humanity/

Gilmore, R. W. (2002). Fatal couplings of power and difference: Notes on racism and geography. *The Professional Geographer*, 54(1), 15–24. doi:10.1111/0033-0124.00310

Graham, S., & Guy, S. (2002). Digital space meets urban place: Sociotechnologies of urban restructuring in downtown San Francisco. *City*, 6(3), 369–382. doi:10.1080/1360481022000037788

Hackworth, J. (2002). Postrecession gentrification in New York City. *Urban Affairs Review*, 37(6), 815–843. doi:10.1177/107874037006003

Halberstam, J. (2011). *The queer art of failure*. Durham, NC: Duke University Press.

Hardt, M., & Negri, A. (2000). *Empire*. Cambridge, MA: Harvard University Press.

Hayles, N. K. (2006). Unfinished work from cyborg to cognisphere. *Theory, Culture & Society*, 23(7/8), 159–166. doi:10.1177/0263276406069229

Hughes, P., & Cosier, G. (2001). What makes a revolution? Disruptive technology and social change. *BT Technology Journal*, 19(4), 24–28. doi:10.1023/A:1013718227208

Lazarus, N. (2012). Spectres haunting: Postcommunism and postcolonialism. *Journal of Postcolonial Writing*, 48(2), 117–129. doi:10.1080/17449855.2012.658243

Lees, L., Shin, H. B., & López-Morales, E. (Eds.). (2015). *Global gentrifications: Uneven development and displacement*. Bristol: Policy Press.

Leslie, S. (2000) The biggest "angel" of them all: The military and the making. In M. Kenney

(Eds.), *Understanding Silicon Valley: The anatomy of an entrepreneurial region* (pp. 48–70). Stanford: Stanford University Press.

Marez, C. (2013). Cesar Chavez, the united farm workers, and the history of star wars. In Nakamura & Peter A. Chow-White (Eds.), *Race after the internet* (pp. 85–108). New York: Routledge.

Marx, K., & Engels, F. (1967). *The communist manifesto* [1848]. (A. Taylor, Trans.). London: Penguin.

McElroy, E. (2016). San Francisco tech bus stops, displacement, and architectures of racial capitalism. *Arcade, 34*(2), 26–26.

McGovern, S. (1998). *The politics of downtown development: Dynamic political cultures in San Francisco and Washington DC*. Lexington: University Press of Kentucky.

McKittrick, K. (2006). *Demonic grounds: Black women and the cartographies of struggle*. Minneapolis: University of Minnesota Press.

Mirabal, N. (2009). Geographies of displacement: Latina/os, oral history, and the politics of gentrification in San Francisco's mission district. *The Public Historian, 31*(2), 7–31. doi:10/1525/tph.2009.31.2.7

Mitchell, W. (1996). *City of bits: Space, place and the infobahn*. Cambridge, MA: MIT Press.

Moore, D. C. (2001). Is the post-in postcolonial the post-in post-soviet? Toward a global postcolonial critique. *PMLA, 116*(1), 111–128.

O'Mara, M. (2015). *Cities of knowledge: Cold war science and the search for the next Silicon Valley*. Princeton, NJ: Princeton University Press.

Paragon Real Estate Group. (2014). *The hottest SF neighborhood for young high tech*. Retrieved from www.paragonre.com/Hottest_SF_Neighborhood_for_Young_High_Tech

Park, L., & Pellow, D. (2004). Racial formation, environmental racism, and the emergence of Silicon Valley. *Ethnicities, 4*(3), 403–424. doi:10.1177/1468796804045241

Reinhardt, A. (1997, August 7). What matters is how smart you are. *Business Week*. Retrieved from www.businessweek.com/1997/34/b35414.htm

Rosenberg, D. (2002). *Cloning Silicon Valley: The next generation high-tech hotspots*. New York, NY: Reuters.

Roy, A., Schrader, S., & Crane, E. (2015). Gray areas: The war on poverty at home and abroad. In A. Roy & E. Crane (Eds.), *Territories of poverty: Rethinking North and South* (pp. 289–314). Athens: University of Georgia Press.

Schafran, A. (2013). Origins of an urban crisis: The restructuring of the San Francisco Bay area and the geography of foreclosure. *International Journal of Urban and Regional Research, 37*(2), 663–688. doi:10.1111/j.1468-2427.2012.01150.x

Schiffman, J. (2014, July 3). SF Mime Troupe takes to the Bay in 'Ripple effect'. *The San Francisco Examiner*. Retrieved from http://archives.sfexaminer.com/sanfrancisco/sf-mime-troupe-takes-to-the-bay-in-ripple-effect/Content?oid=2841263

Scott, D. (2013). *Omens of adversity: Tragedy, time, memory, justice*. Durham, NC: Duke University Press.

Simpson, A. (2014). *Mohawk interruptus: Political life across the borders of settler states*. Durham, NC: Duke University Press.

Smith, N. (2010). *Uneven development: Nature, capital, and the production of space*. Athens: University of Georgia Press.

Starosta, A. (2014). Perverse tongues, postsocialist translations. *Boundary 2, 41*(1), 1–15. doi:10.1215/01903659-2409730

Tadiar, N. (2013). Life-times of disposability within global neoliberalism. *Social Text, 31*(2), 19–48. doi:10.1215/01642472-2081112

Țichindeleanu, O. (2010). Towards a critical theory of postcommunism: Beyond anticommunism in Romania. *Radical Philosophy, 159*, 26–31.

Tiku, N. (2014, April 2). Oakland rebels so sickened by techie scum, they barfed on a Yahoo Bus. *Valley Way*. Retrieved from http://valleywag.gawker.com/youll-probably-believe-what-these-oakland-rebels-did-t-1557036480

Toyama, K. (2014, December 15). The problem with the plan to give internet access to the whole world. *The Atlantic*. Retrieved from www.theatlantic.com/technology/archive/2014/12/the-problem-with-the-plan-to-give-internet-to-the-whole-world/383744/

Turner, F. (2013). *The democratic surround: Multimedia & American liberalism from World War II to the psychedelic Sixties*. Chicago: University of Chicago Press.

Voyles, T. (2015). *Wastelanding: Legacies of uranium mining in Navajo country*. Minneapolis: University of Minnesota Press.

Walker, R. (1995). Landscape and city life: Four ecologies of residence in the San Francisco

Bay area. *Ecumene*, *2*(1), 33–57. doi:10.1177/147447409500200103

Weheliye, A. (2014). *Habeas viscus: Racializing assemblages, biopolitics, and black feminist theory of the human*. Durham, NC: Duke University Press.

Wilder, G. (2015). Review of the book: Omens of adversity: Tragedy, time, memory, justice, by D. Scott. *The Journal of Latin American and Caribbean Anthropology*, *20*(1), 189–200. doi:10.1111/jlca.12120

Wynter, S. (1994). Afterword: Beyond Miranda's meaning: Un/silencing the "demonic ground" of "Caliban's woman". In C. Boyce & E. Fido (Eds.), *Out of the Kumbla: Caribbean women and literature* (pp. 355–366). Trenton, NJ: Africa World Press.

Wynter, S., & McKittrick, K. (2015). Unparalleled catastrophe for our species? Or, to give humanness a different future: Conversations. In K. McKittrick (Ed.), *Sylvia Winter: On being human as praxis* (pp. 9–89). Durham, NC: Duke University Press.

PART SIX

Resisting planetary gentrification

Resistance to gentrification, Okmeydani, Istanbul, Turkey (photograph: Clara Rivas-Alonso)

INTRODUCTION TO PART SIX

In the now huge scholarly literature on gentrification, resistance to gentrification always seems to take a back seat to explanations and case studies of its causes and effects. It would take a (much-needed) whole book to analyze the varied struggles against gentrification that have taken place in different cities at different times and to dissect the links between those struggles, the lessons learned, and the gains made. As gentrification has become a leading edge of the neoliberal imagination in countless contexts, 'resistance to neoliberal urbanism necessarily means resistance to gentrification' (Benach and Albet 2018, p. 290), so it is important to note that what might not be specifically an anti-gentrification strategy may have important consequences in the fight for affordable housing and protecting people from eviction. As Mayer (2013) explains, anti-gentrification struggles are just one element of the variegated, fragmented field of urban social movements that deal with a very diverse set of practices, such as squatting, autonomous social centers, and commoning campaigns. Especially effective in contexts where gentrification is occurring have been campaigns for policy action beyond the urban scale, such as living wage campaigns. The high cost of housing in so many nations is consigning the poor to great financial strain, so the work of living wage activists is absolutely crucial to the right to housing. Policy interventions and even some social movements are too often 'area based', when the differences that could be made at the level of the welfare state and labor market are substantial.

Unfortunately, attacks on welfare states are happening in multiple contexts because these remnants of a Keynesian-Fordist political economy are viewed by the political classes as dangerous impediments to the advancement of financialization. To continue the relentless pace of expanding global accumulation, more and more of those human needs that have not been commodified in previous rounds of financialization have been monitored and monetized. Pensions, health care, education, and especially housing have become much more aggressively appropriated, colonized, and financialized (Aalbers 2016; Rolnik 2019). Anti-gentrification struggles should be – and usually are – part of broader struggles to protect the legacies of the welfare state against predatory attacks by this generation's vulture capitalists. As important as it is to explain the dirty process of gentrification, supported by accounts of destroyed lives, evictions, homelessness, loss of jobs, loss of community, loss of place, and so on, it is just as important to monitor and understand how gentrification has been resisted and with what outcomes.

A superb starting point for identifying and analyzing the myriad ways in which gentrification is resisted is the essay we reprint here by Sandra Annunziata and Clara Rivas-Alonso (2018), which offers a really helpful classification of anti-gentrification practices. As these authors argue, 'difficulties arise when individual everyday actions that allow dwellers to stay put, or to find other options in the face of brutal evictions, are not considered part of traditional forms of organized resistance' (p. 409). Therefore, they call for an approach to understanding resistance that takes account of the broad spectrum of political practices from institutional, structural, and collective action to micro-scale actions and interactions in neighborhoods, streets, and households. In Box 7, Clara Rivas-Alonso reflects on this essay in tribute to her co-author, who tragically passed away in early 2019. The next article we include is by Florian Opillard, who reports on the anti-displacement movement in San Francisco that emerged in response to the Tech Boom 2.0 (see the article by Erin McElroy in the previous section). He traces what he terms the 'structuring mosaic' of individuals, anti-eviction direct action groups, artistic and mapping collectives, and non-profits that gradually built up political power and visibility, and particularly striking are the 'repertoires of contention' (a concept initially put forward by Charles Tilly) that came together across different movements to fight a common cause: the loss of affordable housing and the racial banishment of people from the city. The third article in this section, by Maria Carla Rodríguez and María Mercedes Di Virgilio, is a refreshing intervention in the debate on gentrification in Latin American cities, for it focuses on resistance rather than on conceptual squabbles over whether 'gentrification' is an appropriate term. Focusing on the class struggles taking place in three neighborhoods on the south side of Buenos Aires, Argentina, they explain the rise and success of territorially based social movements that, facing displacement and unaffordable living costs, redirected their actions and relationships with the local government in order to mitigate the negative effects of gentrification on their constituent groups. Interestingly, these movements did not arise in specific reaction to gentrification, but collective action within and across these neighborhoods built an effective response against its most damaging consequences. The final paper in this section, by Seon Young Lee and Yoonai Han, explores the evolution of art activism against gentrification and its potential in South Korea. By examining the case of *Takeout Drawing* – a café and art gallery in Seoul – it explores how art activists responded to the increasingly exclusive urban changes brought about by commercial gentrification and how the grounded practices of art activism forged an interaction with institutionalized politics. When the café was threatened with eviction by its owner, artists squatted in the café and remained there for about one year from 2015 to 2016, generating significant public attention by holding several different types of cultural activities, drawing sustained support from artists and citizens, and ultimately triggering a larger mobilization against rapacious property speculation. Taken together, these four essays provide an indication of the rich variety of tactics and strategies deployed by those fighting for social and housing justice in cities in multiple contexts, which should continue to be analyzed in the detail and rigor they deserve.

In our next (third) *Reader*, a decade from now, we hope to be able to republish work on alternatives to gentrification; as Steele (2018) rightly laments, such writing in gentrification studies is very limited to date.

REFERENCES AND FURTHER READING

Aalbers, M. (2016) *The Financialization of Housing: A Political Economy Approach*. London: Routledge.

Annunziata, S. and Lees, L. (2016) "Resisting 'Austerity Gentrification' and Displacement in Southern Europe." *Sociological Research Online*, 21 (3), 148–155.

Annunziata, Sandra and Clara Rivas-Alonso. (2018) "Resisting Gentrification." In *Handbook of Gentrification Studies*, edited by Loretta Lees and Martin Phillips, 393–412. Cheltenham, UK: Edward Elgar Publishing Limited.

Benach, N. and Albet, A. (2018) "Gentrification and the Urban Struggle: Neil Smith and Beyond," In *Gentrification as a Global Strategy. Neil Smith and Beyond*, edited by Abel Albet and Nuria Benach, 282–296. London: Routledge.

Crossa, V. (2013) "Play for Protest, Protest for Play: Artisan and Vendors' Resistance to Displacement in Mexico City." *Antipode*, 45 (4), 826–843.

Gillespie, T. (2016) "Accumulation by Urban Dispossession: Struggles Over Urban Space in Accra, Ghana." *Transactions of the Institute of British Geographers*, 41 (1), 66–77.

Lees, L. and Ferreri, M. (2016) "Resisting Gentrification on Its Final Frontiers: Learning from the Heygate Estate in London (1974–2013)." *Cities*, 57, 14–24.

Mayer, M. (2013) "First-World Urban Activism: Beyond Austerity Urbanism and Creative City Politics." *CITY*, 17 (1), 5–19.

Rolnik, R. (2019) *Urban Warfare: Housing under the Empire of Finance*. London: Verso.

Steele, J. (2018) "Self-renovating Neighbourhoods as an Alternative to Gentrification or Decline." In *Handbook of Gentrification Studies*, edited by L. Lees with M. Phillips. Cheltenham, UK: Edward Elgar Publishing Limited.

21
Resisting gentrification

Sandra Annunziata and Clara Rivas-Alonso

INTRODUCTION

Currently processes of urban destitution are gripping the vast majority of cities across the world. We believe that understanding the responses to these attacks on the most vulnerable holds the key to unlocking present and future struggles. This chapter challenges the conceptualization of resistance in gentrification theory and seeks to foster debate about the analytical framework for studying resistance to gentrification. We begin by discussing what resistance is and what we mean by resistance in the field of gentrification studies. We argue that we need to go beyond the current state of affairs in the literature given the acuteness of gentrification at the present time – a time characterized by economic breakdown and political upheaval, a global financial crisis, austerity measures, and a crisis of democracy.

Rather than assuming a given definition of what it means to resist gentrification, we seek to open up the notion of resistance to gentrification asking: which specific set of practices can be catalogued under the label of 'gentrification resistance' today? Under which circumstances does it overtly and covertly unfold? What if the 'appeal' and visibility of resistance is not that useful after all and invisibility is the best strategy to resist gentrification pressures? Moreover, could resistance to displacement be a reactionary concept? In other words, are we referring to the creation of alternatives or simply to oppositional, defensive practices?

International comparisons of gentrification have framed some of the regularities as the 'state-led class restructuring of urban space' (Lees et al. 2015: 443). However, can we also talk about global regularities and tactics in the way urban populations, both organized or individually, resist? As post-colonial conceptualizations challenge Anglo-Saxon hegemony in knowledge production, new geographies of gentrification contribute to the understanding of the global regularities of class restructuring processes intertwined with unresolved colonial histories and racial fault lines. As Mbembé and Nuttall point out, the question needs to be posed whilst complicating 'the center of gravity of traditional forms of analysis' (2004: 351). Thus we argue here that looking at different forms of resistances explicitly self-defined as anti-gentrification or implicitly addressing this issue (anti-speculation, anti-system, anti-privatization) can strengthen our collective repertoire and social imaginaries regarding the potential and limits of what we know (and do) to counter processes of gentrification. But in doing so we open up the tricky question of what counts (and what does not) as resistance to gentrification.

We start from the assumption that resistance to gentrification is a set of complex practices that should be pluralized and problematized in relation to its scope, its agents and its intentionality. We attempt to foster much-needed conversations across scales, going from the micro to the macro (and everything in between). Furthermore, we do so by focusing on both strengths and weaknesses, in order to understand the limits and potential of resistance to the acute and generalized phase of gentrification and its global dimension, acknowledging the fact that gentrification processes might have long taken place in other places under different labels (see Maloutas 2012; Janoschka and Sequera 2016).

In the following section we will frame the way resistance to gentrification and displacement is conceptualized in the gentrification literature, underlining what is missing and what has been less explored. In the first section, which draws on classical studies and political economy approaches, we will frame resistance as the right to stay put and as a conscious opposition to the structural forces that result in the current regimes of expulsion. We then go on to offer a classification of resistance practices, followed by an attempt to enrich the conceptualization of resistance: we problematize the way resistance has been conceptualized in gentrification studies drawing on post-structuralist theories, relational approaches, and other disciplines that have addressed its complexity.

Exploring the heterogeneity of practices that seek to counter displacement (in its direct, indirect, symbolic and exclusionary forms) has allowed us to argue that politically conscious, overtly oppositional, intentional and visible practices of resistance are not the only way to counteract gentrification-induced displacement. While interesting regularities and convergences among different practices of resistance are on the horizon, we argue that the field of resistances is also characterized by non-politicized, covert, unintentional, informal, and deliberately invisible practices of everyday life that draw on different perceptions of time and survival, the negotiation of ambiguity and mobilization of invisibility. We argue that the visibility of resistance and counter collective knowledge production, central in anti-gentrification practices, might not be that useful after all in spaces where informality, ambiguity and invisibility have become some of the best strategies through which to resist the assault of displacement.

THEORIZING RESISTANCE IN GENTRIFICATION STUDIES

Resistance is a recurrent theme in gentrification studies. Most critical gentrification scholars agree that after having explored processes of gentrification, their geographies, causes and effects, it is high time that we shift our attention to resistance (Lees et al. 2008). However, exploration of those strategies and tactics that seek to counter the violence of gentrification remains very limited. As Lees and Ferreri (2016) point out, through their direct involvement in resistance to state-led gentrification practices in London, '(r)esistance to gentrification still deserves renewed attention in gentrification studies and beyond' (p. 3).

Knowledge of gentrification resistance, however, benefits from going beyond the field of gentrification studies. Acknowledging that resistance can encompass everything from revolution to hairstyle, Hollander and Einwohner (2004) argue that practices of resistance have in common a system (or a target) they seek to oppose and they imply action (or a set of actions). More specifically in gentrification studies the most commonly defined practice of resistance is the Right to Stay Put. It is described by Hartman (1984) as a long life right of tenure for tenants. It has become a political slogan and a resistance practice; it implies recognition of the forces that produce displacement (e.g. Marcuse 1985a; Janoschka 2016); forces induced by gentrification and for the production of gentrification.[1] It involves an action of opposition to the mode of urban development that generates displacement of the most vulnerable. In gentrification studies resistance has a very specific, social scientific, meaning: it is the practices of individuals and groups who attempt to stay put in the face of exclusionary, neoliberalizing forces. In this respect we can say that resistance to gentrification 'seeks to occupy, deploy and create alternative spatialities from those defined through oppression and exploitation' (Pile, in Rose 2002: 3). However, this is, we argue, a rather 'minimal definition' (ibid) of resistance as a 'common sense' reaction to the regimes of expulsion taking place both in the so-called global South and North.[2]

Under the current regimes of expulsion, practices that counter gentrification are also identity-based and have much more micro, less visible dimensions. As much as resistance to gentrification can be collective, politically organized and visible, it can also be highly heterogeneous, somehow contradictory and incoherent, reflecting the intimate conflicting feelings of individuals, deliberately invisible, unconscious and practised in solitude. We have to learn how to explore the different forms that resistance to gentrification takes, as well as the cultural politics of agency (Rankin 2009), and to navigate outside of what we see and can decipher as an anti-gentrification resistance if we are to enrich the notion. As Rankin (ibid) argues in regards to planning theory, gentrification theory can be informed by Scott's (1985) observation of the 'hidden transcripts' and the 'infra-politics' in reference to the everyday practices of resistance mobilized by peasants in South Asian rural areas. They are described as 'weapons of the weak', in the sense that they constitute the root of a collective social mobilization.

In her reconceptualization of resistance, Hynes (2013) refers to Collins and Munro (2010: 550), and calls for a 'micro politics of everyday life' to suggest an exploration of resistance in between macro-political analyses of visible, collective struggles against structures of power (e.g. urban social movements and squatting practices) and micro-sociological analyses, which take seriously the smaller-scale dynamics of power and resistance as they affect individuals in the context of everyday life. In this sense we must consider that resistance to gentrification is intrinsically related to scale, and the possibility of jumping scales: from the body, to the home, to the neighbourhood up to the national and global (Smith 1992).

Assessments of valuable and practical alternatives that go beyond resistance as an oppositional (contradictory and paradoxical) practice have been, to date, a marginal part of gentrification studies. In fact, even if we use a 'strategic' concept with 'political' value (Lees et al. 2016), such as gentrification-induced displacement, we argue that we still lack understanding of resistance in gentrifying contexts, besides institutional measures or housing cooperatives (ibid: 221–224), radical policy incrementalism (see Gallaher's 2016 interpretation of condo conversion and right to buy as a practice of staying put in Washington DC) and the building of local strategic alliances (as in the Traditional Retail Markets Networks discussed in Dawson and Gonzales 2016). Alongside the now classic work of Chester Hartman (1984), anti-gentrification studies and progressive policies have been developed in the Anglo-American context such as: Peter Marcuse's (1985b: 922) 'floating zone': 'a set of policies and procedures capable to reverse the negative effect of gentrification: provision and maintenance of decent, secure and affordable housing in stable and non-discriminatory neighbourhoods for all city residents'; the anti-growth machine movement and the preservation of a single occupancy hotel in the Tenderloin, San Francisco (Robinson 1995); and the battle for Tompkins Square Park in New York City (Smith 1996). These are cases that remain key reference points in the gentrification literature but they do not help us much when faced with a new, acute and predatory phase of capitalist accumulation in cities around the globe. As Lees and Ferreri (2016) argue, such classic US-centric studies must not remain dominant in a properly cosmopolitan gentrification studies.

A more multidisciplinary approach to resistance can be found in urban social movement theory. In fact, for urban social movement theorists, practices of resistance at the urban scale are often in relation to gentrification processes. According to Mayer (2013) anti-gentrification struggles are part of the fragmented, variegated, and deeply impacted by the neoliberal order, field of urban social movements, and stand against the commodification of urban space, 'scandalizing' the new regime of accumulation. Activists today deal with a diverse set of practices: squatting, social centres and autonomous spaces, citizen organizations claiming the urban commons or spontaneous movements with a poetic perception of social reality (Petropoulou 2014) that can be grouped under the umbrella of 'the right to the city' (Mayer 2009, 2013). They encompass different 'forms of alliances across towns and across issues, between housing activists and artists, leftist groups and cultural workers, small business owners and the new precarious groups – as all of them feel threatened by contemporary forms of development entailing gentrification, mega projects, and displacement' (Mayer and Boudreau 2011: 281). They are overtly oppositional and clearly visible. Making the invisible and the unspoken dimension of injustice visible is one of the core issues of urban social movements that deliberately use anti-gentrification (and anti-systemic) discourses. In fact, visibility makes a collective claim easily recognizable and recognition is a fundamental component of resistance (Hollander and Einwohner 2004).

Besides these academic debates, we should also acknowledge that the most effective (and interesting) work on resistance to gentrification is not academic. It comes from activist-scholars who position themselves halfway between community engagement and academic reflection (Routledge and Derickson 2015). This body of work assumes the form of handbooks, blogs, passionate writing, documentaries/movies and artist-activist works. These types of material are accessible, easy to read, reduce complexity and clearly offer possible solutions. They are written for and with communities, and imply the participation of those directly affected by gentrification. The first handbook of this type was *Displacement, How to Fight It?* by Hartman et al. (1982). They argued that 'each variation of the basic profiteering assault on housing requires different sort of responses from anti-displacement groups' (1982: 28) and they provided a whole set of place-specific, cause-related and community-based ways to fight displacement. More recently, new anti-gentrification handbooks have been produced in relation to the distinctiveness of displacement in context. Among them the struggle against a new gentrification, that of council estates, as seen in *Staying Put: An Anti-Gentrification Handbook for Council Estates in London* (2014), the result of a collaboration between the London Tenants Federation, gentrification scholar-activist Loretta Lees, Just Space and Southwark Notes Archive Group. In Spain, a passionate biographical account of the struggle against eviction for mortgage arrears *Vida Hipotecada* [Mortgaged Lives] written by Colau and Alemany (2012) as a result of the work of the *Plataforma de los Afectados por la Hipoteca* (PAH), can also be seen as an anti-displacement manifesto.

A CLASSIFICATION OF ANTI-GENTRIFICATION PRACTICES

While acknowledging that anti-gentrification practices must be contextualized, we also think that the existing anti-gentrification literature allows us to establish a set of regularities. We have classified the literature in Table 1 into the following categories: prevention, institution-based measures: e.g. fostering public housing policies, tenants protection, and alternative planning tools to prevent and mitigate displacement; mitigation and legal bricolage: e.g. delay, negotiation, compensation practices, anti-eviction, re-housing, buyout practices that can only postpone the problem or move it somewhere else; building alternatives: e.g. community planning, squats, occupations, protests and urban commons; counter narratives, building awareness and strategic mobilization of (collective) identities: e.g. collective constructions of sense of belonging and alternative narratives mobilized against mainstream discourses. We discuss each group referring to the literature listed in the table. Although we have tried to be as comprehensive as possible the table will no doubt have gaps, it is however a fair reflection of the kinds of resistances to gentrification happening around the world.

Prevention

A lot of the measures that prevent gentrification-induced displacement are directly dependent on land and housing regimes, namely public housing policies, tenants' protection and rent regulation. Publicly subsidized housing plays a crucial role in the prevention of gentrification. It is described as a 'barrier to gentrification' (Ley and Dobson 2008) and a fundamental part of spatial justice based on rights that have spatial implications (Brenner et al. 2011). The role played by housing policies as a barrier to gentrification was explored by Newman and Wyly (2006), who asked what the tipping point was in terms of low-income residents staying in a gentrifying neighbourhood. The decline of tenants' protection under neoliberal regimes is due to the erosion of low income housing stock as a collective asset (via demolition or privatization) and the weakening of regulations that protect tenants (such as the abolition of rent control, the introduction of express eviction measures and property-oriented taxation regimes). The critique of the demolition and privatization of public housing is the premise and the core of any anti-displacement discourse applicable also to the clearing of informal housing (Ascensao 2015; İslam and Sakızlıoğlu 2015). However, the success in banning privatization depends on the strength of solidarities among tenants. Their desire to become property owners or achieve acceptable compensation can become a divisive force.

Rent regulation, a fundamental anti-gentrification measure, is under threat or has been completely abandoned under certain neoliberal-oriented regimes. After decades of housing deregulation, rent control, which brought housing law reforms, has been subject to revisionism (Arnott 1995). The first generation of rent control, the 'nominal rent freeze system' (ibid) has been substituted in some cases by a new, more flexible second generation of rent control described as 'highly beneficial' for tenants' protection (Lind 2001). This type of rent cap can be seen in cases such as Berlin, where low income tenants were protected in areas targeted by cautious urban renewal programmes and upgrading (Holm et al. 2013). The regulation of condo conversions into luxury apartments can also prevent gentrification to a great extent. For instance, the Berlin North-Neukölln Tenants' Alliance achieved the enforcement of a pre-existing anti-speculative measure, *milieuschutz* (social environmental protection), to ban the luxury conversion of historical and former low-income apartments in

Focus	Prevention, institution-based measures	Mitigation and legal bricolage: delay, negotiation, compensation	Building alternatives: community planning, squats, occupations, protests and urban commons	Enhancing visibility, counter narratives, building awareness and strategic mobilization of (collective) identities
Eviction / Housing privatization / Building conversion / Demolition	*Publicly subsidized housing as a 'barrier to gentrification'*: Vancouver: Ley and Dobson (2008); Buenos Aires: Rodríguez and Di Virgilio (2016) *Tenants protections, rent control and regulations*: New York: Newman and Wyly (2006); USA: Hartman (1984); Berlin: Holm et al. (2013), Connolly (2016) *Urban renewal without evictions*: Lima, Perù: Betancur (2014); Belgium: Uitermark and Loopmans (2013)	*Zoning regulations (encouragement and discouragement zones)*: New York: Marcuse (1985) *Anti-eviction practices*: Spain: Colau and Alemany (2012); Rome, Athens, Madrid: Annunziata and Lees (2016); Rome: Mudu (2015), De Feliciantonio (2016) *Displacement Free Zones*: Park Slope, New York City: Lees et al. (2008: 250–255); USA: Kolodney (1991); Puerto Rico, Morales-Cruz (2012)	*Community organization, grassroots movements and alternative planning*: USA: Hartman, Keating and LeGates (1982), DeFilippis (2004); London Tenants Federation et al. (2014); Istanbul: Erman and Coşkun-Yıldar (2007); Caracas, Venezuela: Velásquez-Atehortúa (2014); Sweden: Rätt att bo kvar (n.d.)	

Table 1 A classification of practices used to resist gentrification

Building conversion regulations: Barcelona: Assemblea de Barris per un Turisme Sostenible (ABTS) (2016); Berlin: Holm, Brendt, Britta (2014)	*Community land trusts*: New York: Hartman et al. (1982); London: London Tenants Federation, Lees, Just Space and SNAG (2014)	*Resistance via legal action and legal struggle*: Puerto Rico: Morales-Cruz (2012); London: Lees and Ferreri (2016); Lima, Perú: Betancur (2014)	*Anti-gentrification protests*: Tompkins Square Park in New York City (see Smith 1996); Gezi Park, Istanbul: Gül and Cünük (2014); Accra, Ghana: Gillespie (2016)	*Counter narratives of mainstream urban governance*
Anti-privatization struggles: London, Berlin, Amsterdam: Holm (2007); Berlin: Mayer (2013)	*Vacancy control, confiscation/acquisition of abandoned property*: New York: Hartman, Keating and LeGates (1982)	*Resistance by tenants and tactics of negotiation*: Rome: Herzfeld (2009)	*Political housing squats*: European cities: Martinez and Cattaneo (2016); Europe: Squatting Collective (2015); Rome:	• *Blogs and media activism*: Berlin: GentrificationBlog; UK: Slater (2014)
Single occupancy hotels: San Francisco: Robinson (1995)		*Court cases against master plans*: Santiago, Chile, in Lees, Shin and López-Morales (2016)	Mudu (2015); Berlin: Holm and Kuhn (2011); New York: Maeckelbergh (2012); Amsterdam: Pruijt (2013), Uitermark (2004)	• *Arts*: Mexico City: Crossa (2013); Lisbon: LefthandRotation; Berlin, Hamburg: Novy and Colomb (2013)
Street vendors' resistance: Mexico City, Mexico: Betancur (2014), Crossa (2013)		*Compensation, in the case of condo conversion*: Washington DC: Gallaher (2015)	*Critical resilience and the reproduction of the commons*: London, Los Angeles, Sydney: DeVerteuil (2016); Athens: Stavrides (2016)	• *'visioning workshop' and alternative design competitions*: London, UK: Lees and Ferreri (2016); Barcelona: Portelli (2015)
Historical centre preservation	*Grassroots movements' legal controls over urban renewal policy*: San Francisco: Hartman (1974), Robinson (1995)		*Informal occupation and land squatting*: Santiago: Casgrain and Janoschka (2013); South Africa: Cabannes et al. (2010); Lisbon: Ascensao (2015); India: Slum Dwellers International, McFarlane (2010)	
Urban renewal/regeneration plans	*Environmental legal struggle*: Pearsall (2014)			
Retail changes				
Slum improvement				

(Continued)

Focus	Prevention, institution-based measures	Mitigation and legal bricolage: delay, negotiation, compensation	Building alternatives: community planning, squats, occupations, protests and urban commons	Enhancing visibility, counter narratives, building awareness and strategic mobilization of (collective) identities
Environmental planning		*Anti-speculation ordinance*: San Francisco: Hartman (1974)	*Armed conflict*: Turkey (this chapter); South America: Janoschka and Sequera (2016)	Antievictionmappingprojecj.or – *Poetry*: Mexico and Greece: Petropoulou (2014)
Criminalization of informality and squatting		*Land value extraction policies*: Puerto Rico: Lees, Shin and López-Morales (2016)		*Alternative culture and social centre*: Hamburg: Noeger (2012)
Militarization of urban spaces		*Retail resistance*: Mexico City: Lefthandrotation (2015), *Defend Traditional Retail Markets Networks*, London: Dawson and Gonzales (2016)		*Mutual support for threatened groups (evicted, minorities, street vendors, specific guilds)*: Spain: Colau and Alemany (2012), Crossa (2013)
Symbolic changes				
Otherization of minority groups				*Informal networks of support*: Jakarta, Dakar: Simone (2009)
				Invisible forms of resistance (collective and individual): South East Asia: Scott (1985); Egypt, Iran: Bayat (2000); Israel/Palestine: Yiftachel (2009)

Table 1 (Continued)

the area (Connolly 2016). Similar requests come from organizations advocating for the de-growth of tourism and regulation of building conversions for temporary and touristic uses (such as *Assemblea Barris Turisme Sostenible* [Assembly of Districts for Sustainable Tourism] n.d., in Barcelona).

In the case of redevelopment, rehabilitation and land use transformation, alternative community planning has proven effective for neighbourhood stability. The self-hab program proposed in New York City in the 1980s is still relevant for the new housing crisis. This practice sought the recovery and self-renovation of abandoned property, given to tenants' cooperatives by the city after a process of confiscation.[3] This type of practice has been linked to vacancy control guaranteed by a juridical system that implies that abandoned or empty property can be taken over by the city and converted into social housing. However, vacancy control is not implemented in all situations. For this reason, critical planning practices attempt to foster community engagement and participation as a strategy to mitigate top-down planning decisions before it negatively impacts residents (Taylor and Edwards 2016; Novy and Colomb 2013; Uitermark and Loopmans 2013). This type of work challenges the responsibility and reflexivity of planning professionals in the face of an urbanism that is reproducing injustice. Even if highly heterogeneous (see a comparison of anti-privatization movements in Europe by Holm 2007), critical planning practices advocate for alternative forms of urban development. They are oriented towards a long-term goal such as radical egalitarian access to the city as well as a more short-term set of claims such as the preservation of urban heritage of the built environment (Mayer 2013), banning renewal projects and asking for a more cautious type of intervention (see Holm and Kuhn 2011) or stopping eviction (see the case of Kotti and Co, in Berlin, in Mayer 2013). As for North America and London, practices of community organizing can inform the most appropriate forms of solidarity, collective ownership when desired (see DeFilippis 2004), as well as sustainable economy and alternative city plans.[4]

Delaying, compensation and re-housing

When preventative measures are not in place (the norm nowadays) resistance practices can easily take the form of compensation, re-housing and delaying strategies. One delaying strategy is the request for an eviction free zone (EFZ). This tool was described by Kolodney (1991: 513) as a 'legal bricolage in an era of political limited expectation'. An EFZ can be place-based, applied directly onto an entire neighbourhood, or people-based, helping vulnerable residents. It must be accompanied by a whole set of legal services, where lawyers work together with community groups on tenants' rights to delay or stop evictions. The core of an anti-eviction zone is a 'vigorous (and participated by the community) legal defence against eviction' (ibid: 518). EFZs have never properly existed; however, moratoria on anti-eviction practices were extensively implemented city-wide for vulnerable groups in Rome until the advent of the crisis which represented a real turning point for anti-eviction practices (Annunziata and Lees 2016). When the attempt to stop or delay eviction fails and eviction becomes unavoidable, resistance practices call for one-to-one replacement (from the previous home to a new home, for everyone). The re-housing process must consider a possible relocation near the previous home, to allow continuity in everyday life (such as school for children and other facilities regularly used by residents). This is for instance one of the core claims of the anti-eviction manifesto of the European Coalition for the Right to Housing (see https://housingnotprofit.org/en) and the claim of the housing movements in Rome: '*Ogni sfratto sarà una barricata*' [each eviction will be a barricade] (Mudu, in Martínez and Cattaneo 2016).

Recently Gallaher (2016) drawing on the case of Washington DC argued that the tenants' right to buy in cases of condo conversion and related forms of compensation can be seen as a way to enable residents to stay put. Explaining how challenging and contradictory the practices can be, she argues that compensation may result in a new opportunity in the life of indebted tenants. Drawing from Roy (2009), Karaman (2014: 290) has further complicated the picture by problematizing resistance in the context of a '"politics of compensation" that is simultaneously, and paradoxically, communitarian and market-centered'. However, considering the severity of displacement, the literature also considers compensation or buying someone out a very divisive practice which limits solidarity and undermines the possibility of staying put for the most fragile residents.

Critical counter-narratives, awareness campaigns, collective identities

When the production of gentrification implies spatial, semantic and social cleansing to accommodate new uses and meanings (the subtlest and most pervasive form of displacement) resistance is very challenging. Exclusionary and symbolic displacement (see Blomley 2004; Janoschka 2016) permeates everyday life and calls for a different type of conceptualization and related forms of resistance. Here the production of critical counter-narratives and awareness campaigns which aim to delegitimize planning practices and rent extraction are crucial. Collective knowledge production has taken the form of open platforms, blogs, websites, public lectures, art and media work, all done with the specific goal of framing counter narratives, and/or a critical and ironic understanding of gentrification. A variety of methods have been used such as the artist interventions of the collective Left Hand Rotation (n.d): *Gentrificación no es un Nombre de Señora, Museo de los Desplazados, Ficción Inmobiliaria*, the Creative Charlois Control; the Swedish version of LTF et al's (2014) The Right to Stay Put, *Rätt att bo kvar* (n.d.), in council estates which used reggae to spread its message; Italian hip hop in the case of the lake struggle in Rome, *'IL LAGO CHE COMBATTE'* – *Assalti frontali & Il Muro del Canto* (2014); Turkish hip hop denouncing Roma cleansing through so-called urban renewal (*Sulukuleli Roman Rap Grubu Tahribad-ı İsyan – TOKİ KAFALAR*, 2015); Berlin anti-tourist actions, 'Berlin Doesn't Love You', that seeks to build awareness of the pervasive multiple forms of gentrification happening in Berlin. A critical political economy approach regarding urban transformation in Berlin is at the core of the detailed Berlin Gentrification Blog (n.d.) edited by Andrej Holm, as well as systematic, prompt and full responses to the mainstream, acritical interpretation of housing unaffordability in the media.[5]

Another practice that builds awareness about the effects of gentrification is critical mapping and data analysis. The Anti-Eviction Mapping Project (n.d.) in the San Francisco Bay Area makes visible the nexus between urban displacement and more contemporary (self)entrepreneurial, touristic and high-tech related urban development. The eviction maps in Madrid (*Madrid Desahuciado* 2015) by VIC in collaboration with the *Plataforma de los Afectados por la Hipoteca* (PAH) show the effects of the debt-induced housing crisis in Madrid.

These works have in common an attempt to challenge consolidated social imaginaries and define a counter narrative to the hegemonic idea of urban living. Irony, creativity and rhetoric are used to counter the mainstream discourses and legitimacy surrounding the kind of urban development that implies financial burden and displacement for local residents. These practices of resistance, have however, been documented as internally contradictory, at risk of being hijacked by new forms of economic development such as 'the creative city' (Mayer 2013) or falling into the trap of the 'commodification of the culture of resistance' as documented by Noeger (2012: 157) in the case of anti-gentrification practices in Hamburg, which became incorporated into the processes of gentrification they originally meant to defend against.

Methods of urban mobilization and resistance draw, in some situations, on the strategic mobilization of (collective) identity and cultural practices. For example, in the case of *Ripensar Bon Pastor*, a collective in Barcelona who developed an engaged anthropology and considered the character and culture of the neighbourhood as an important tool for resistance. In this particular case, as can happen in other neighbourhoods with a strong historical (and political) identity, collective memory was mobilized in order to construct belonging in the present, thus rooting their lives and strengthening ties to their neighbourhood under threat (Portelli 2015). In other contexts, the strategic mobilization of collective identities includes the militarization of neighbourhoods (Janoschka and Sequera 2016), or the work of neighbourhood associations that organize struggles (or alliances) with gentrifying forces (e.g. Erman and Coşkun-Yıldar 2007). Practices of mobilization of identity that are not necessarily deemed overtly antagonist can easily escape epistemological exercises that attempt to recognize them as resistance. However, these could pave the way for further conceptualizations of innovative ways of escaping the physically and symbolically destructive character of gentrification.

Organized and informal squatting

Squatting is considered the quintessential practice of staying put (Martínez and Cattaneo 2016). Social movement theorists have contributed extensively towards exploring the varieties and heterogeneity of squatting practices (Uitermark

2004; Mudu 2015). The 'political squatting movement' as a direct answer to housing and the loci of an alternative to capitalism is the assumption of the Squatting European Kollective (Martínez and Cattaneo 2016). However, we can say that today squatting does not necessarily relate to a consciously political and oppositional choice by individuals in search of a counter culture or alternative to capitalism. Deprivation-based squatting, one of the configurations of squatting described by Pruijt (2004), is back as a visible manifestation of a time characterized by multiple crises: economic breakdown and political upheaval, a global financial crisis connected to housing, austerity measures and the shrinkage of citizenship rights. McFarlane (2010) sees squatting as a global phenomenon and links it with squatted settlements and informal housing. In the context of the so-called Global South, organizations such as Slum Dwellers International and the achievement of legal title deeds through legalization of informality contribute to an 'entrepreneurial image of urban squatters as skilled and capable' (ibid: 772). These initiatives carry an anti-poverty discourse that can be seen as a right to stay put. However, even if informal settlements can be considered a form of do-it-yourself strategy, their legalization and inclusion in formal market dynamics carries the risk of rising land and housing prices 'to the point where the original inhabitants are priced out' (ibid: 771).

Besides the organized forms of squatting and the newly emerging anti-eviction platforms, we also find a large number of fragmented 'residents survival' tactics as documented by Herzfeld in Rome (2009). In some cases, they are capable to act as a bounded community. However, when it comes to displacement, social ties get broken and solidarity erodes, which has an intimate and irredeemable effect on displaced people. Contrary to the mobilization of visibility, irony and thought-provoking anti-gentrification practices, 'resident survival' remains largely invisible. We will argue in the following section that mobilizing invisibility rooted in everyday practices becomes a tactic of survival.

TOWARDS MORE INCLUSIVE GEOGRAPHIES OF RESISTANCE

As said earlier the above classification has its limits. It is dominated by the Anglo-Saxon conceptualizations of resistance within gentrification studies. It contains then, the 'shortcomings that both post-colonial and post-structuralist theory have identified' (Lees et al. 2015: 9), this cannot be ignored and it pushes us to consider the real complexity and variants of a given moment of resistance, something that might allow us to identify the opening up of possibilities (Cerulo 2009; Farías 2011; McFarlane 2011a). We recognize the need to go beyond the idea of a homogeneous hegemonic force, namely capitalism, in its globalized form (Roy 2011), as the main factor behind urban processes of destitution in order to account for the complexity and indeed possible successes of practices of resistance. In an attempt to respond to Roy's (2016) 'Who's afraid of postcolonial theory?' we recognize the urgent need to unpack understandings of resistance rooted in Western theorizations, not by simply choosing to focus on cases located in the so-called Global South, but by also trying to theorize away from the 'master narrative that is Europe' (2016: 205). As argued by Ley and Teo (2014) the epistemological absence of gentrification as a term to explain the phenomena does not necessarily imply the absence of the process itself; in the same vein, we argue that the absence of theorization of resistance to gentrification does not imply its absence either.

New and recently conceptualized types of gentrification continue to affect the everyday life of urban citizens. Moving away from a political economy approach in the study of gentrification, we find the micro-politics of everyday life to be a starting point in challenging the conceptualization of resistance in gentrification studies. We see everyday life as the 'quiet encroachment of the ordinary' (Bayat 2000: 545), the struggle of 'thousands of small movements in spaces of survival and stealth' (Yiftachel 2009: 250). The experience of the everyday is a breeding ground for non-normative ways of associating. In this field, Bebbington (2007) draws on Habermas to identify the links between mobilization and everyday practices, as the latter are being colonized by 'modern capitalism and welfare statism'. Merrifield (2013) advocates 'encounter' as an inspiration to conceive another way of political engagement. It is 'a more free-floating, dynamic, and relational militancy, to be sure, "horizontal" in its reach and organization' (p. xvii). Subsequently he presents us with a key question: 'How to ensure that this encounter in everyday life – this spontaneous lived moment – assumes a mutation of world-historical significance?' (Merrifield 2013: 92). Similarly, we ask if these practices can be seen as resistance to gentrification and whether they are in fact reactionary.

It is through these new critical openings within the literature that struggle and resistance in everyday practices of urban living might be understood better. In particular, the notion of urban assemblage as developed by Farías (2011) 'allows us to think about spatial formations as products that must be constantly defended, held together, maintained and repaired' (Farías 2011: 370); McFarlane (2011a) also sees in urban assemblage a key to unlock the complexity of becoming urban: 'Assemblage is a latent possibility of new politics and movements based on desire and becoming that can both emerge through and exceed capitalism' (p. 211). Urban assemblage theory thus compels us to seek the processes rather than the structures, radically opening up the meaning of urban resistance, which might translate into the different ways dwellers perform the 'right to be' (drawing from Merrifield 2013) or into 'everyday practices of emergence' as described by Ong (2011) when referring to the worlding of cities.

Considering this critique and the gaps identified in the literature we are opening up the notion of resistance to its (yet) non-politicized forms, its covert dimensions, to informality and invisibility. Besides the different types of anti-gentrification measures identified in the literature, we propose here four aspects, deeply rooted in the everyday urban experience, under which we could further analyse different practices of resistance: temporalities, negotiating ambiguity (and limits of solidarity), invisibility, and informality.

Temporalities

Different temporalities of practices of resistance depend on strategic positioning in respect to gentrification pressures. 'In dwelling the city people draw upon previous experience or memories, and the multiple temporalities and rhythms of the city itself help to shape the possibilities of learning through dwelling' (McFarlane 2011b: 23). There are practices that seek a long-term solution for staying put or short-term steps for solving urgent need (such as re-housing of evictees or temporary shelter). They might be oriented towards the strategic reframing of the long-term strategic view for city development (such as counter-narratives) or be limited to the short-term improvement of a neighbourhood resulting in neighbourhood-based practices.

Time is also a crucial variable for understanding the dynamics of resistance, since it does not have the same value and is not perceived in the same way by those involved in the process. For a household under threat, time is a matter of survival. For the city administration, a financial organization, a real estate broker, it is just a matter of postponement of financial gains, a practice of power-relations. At the same time, how past and future are conceptualized within the implementation of gentrification projects is essential in order to understand the positions different actors take and the narratives they draw from. The memory of a completed project or a gentrified neighbourhood can be mobilized by those resisting in order to remind the public and institutions how these projects do not work for the benefit of all. At the same time, and once a project has started, agents act on their guesses of the different future outcomes of the gentrifying landscape: some will decide to organize themselves (more often than not, the more precarious the position the less they are likely to get involved); others will decide that the struggle is not for them, and will try to find an escape route (normally trying to find housing nearby, if affordable); other dwellers will actually act on the possibility of taking advantage of the changes. It is thus that aspirations, desires and conceptualizations of past and future have a direct impact on how dwellers decide to take different positions in the present. The different meanings of time stress the need to clearly understand different threats or fears, intentionality and positionality of the agents involved in the struggle against gentrification.

Negotiating ambiguity

The need to be flexible in searching for alternatives sheds light on the limits of solidarity when dealing with material needs and the negotiation of ambiguity. The austerity and violent urbanizing practices which characterize the global financial crisis around the world result in highly visible solidarity in the face of displacement (see the growing anti-eviction platforms in Chicago, Spain, Ireland, to name a few). The real burden for the success of these resistance practices comes from a culturally rooted, internal contradiction within the anti-displacement movement. In a proprietary society anti-gentrification practices have to face a consolidated (and culturally rooted) preference for homeownership as a means of wealth, welfare and social reproduction. The landscape of resistance is full of contradictions as far as the challenge posed by homeownership and lack of tenure alternatives is not resolved. For instance, the collective struggle against the privatization of public housing in Rome can result in a de-facto anti-eviction zone or in negotiations with the institution for the most convenient sale price. Those willing to negotiate in this climate are mainly organized tenants willing to buy. However, negotiation can be contradictory when proprietary aspirations are prioritized against the need of tenants or other groups severely affected by housing vulnerability (those forced to pay prohibitive rent at market prices, unable to buy or access public housing due to a chronic shortage, already evicted from previous houses and living in temporary accommodation). There are notable exceptions, where homeownership concerns can become a force of further solidarity actions that include tenants and informal dwellers. In cases where informal housing is historically rooted, applying for and receiving homeownership certificates or regularization might be the main objective for the fulfilment of citizenship rights. And yet, this move works as a strategy to improve informal dwellers' position at the possible negotiating table, thus forming and strengthening a collective that cares for the neighbourhood as a whole, as much as their own personal homeownership situations.

Moreover, both negotiating with the local authorities whilst building an anti-institution narrative can go hand in hand. Local authorities might be the only point of information in regards to a possible urban renewal plan, and thus become a possible key ally in the struggle. This allows us to break down the idea of the state or institutions as homogeneous constructions (in fact, there are civil servants within the institutions that consider their work to serve and protect dwellers, whilst dealing with political interests, top-down questionable decisions and nepotism). This inherent complexity of the (corrupted) institutional apparatus can work both in favour of and against those affected residents. On the one hand, dwellers need to carry out a certain amount of research (with the help of city-wide voluntary organizations and activists) to improve their position. On the other hand, that same complexity also translates into sometimes institutional incompetence, which gives room for informed resistance to intervene and can lead to delays in the implementation of urban plans (when no one really knows exactly what is going on – especially if the legal framework changes rapidly). The ambiguity of the positions different actors take in regards to urban transformation depending on the circumstances and what is to be gained, are key in the processes.

Mobilizing invisibility and informal networks

We would like to draw attention to a growing number of practices of resistance which do not fit the classification of formal/visible practices. Contrary to the mobilization of visibility, irony and thought-provoking anti-gentrification practices can remain invisible. Not everyone is willing to negotiate overtly with those responsible for their displacement. In these cases, we argue that people tend to find solutions informally and outside of institutional regimes, especially when they start failing them. The majority of practices of resistance are in fact outside the classic/institutional/normative approach in which progressive policies have been formulated. Invisibility and informality play a key role in those cases. McFarlane's (2012: 105) conceptualization of informality/formality is particularly helpful when addressing their possible politicization: 'They co-constitute and dissolve spaces, becoming politicized or depoliticized at different moments, and they both enable and restrict urban life.' Furthermore, Simone's (2004) account of informality and notion of 'people as infrastructure' is particularly relevant: 'These intersections, [. . .], have depended on the ability of residents to engage complex combinations of objects, spaces, persons, and practices. These conjunctions become an infrastructure – a platform providing for and reproducing life in the city' (2004: 408). Informality can be applied to ambiguous homeownership situations, whereby dwellers who have built their own houses mobilize this identity to organize themselves. Another way informality works is through networks whereby family and neighbours get together to support whoever is in need. These radical forms of solidarity could strategically mobilize (in)visibility (drawing on Papadopoulos and Tsianos 2007) to hide from (or block) the relentless path of urban restructuring in its various forms. Remaining institutionally invisible is a key tool in order to stay put: if you become too visible, too noisy, you risk being stigmatized or excluded from a normative way of living.

We have created a working table (Figure 1) where we present what we have seen as practices of resistance to gentrification so far in the tension between visibility and invisibility/formality and informality. We argue that using the different conceptual threads described above as points of reference allows us to anchor highly diffuse and unstable concepts for detailed exploration. We hope this will trigger further conversations about different ways of resisting gentrifying forces.

CONCLUSION

We initially identified four sets of practices that have sought to mitigate gentrification from the gentrification literature, as summarized in Table 1. This body of work allows us to say that practices of resistance and possible alternatives can only be site-specific. If we see them all together they constitute an attempt to contextualize and define place-specific anti-displacement agendas and localized action plans as suggested by Lees et al. (2016: 224).

However, the achievements of these practices in the face of the acuteness assumed by gentrification at the current conjuncture are limited. In some cases, those limits are not only the lack of institutional attempts to prevent displacement but also internal contradictions within the resistance practices themselves. In order to problematize the way resistances have been conceptualized in gentrification studies to date we drew on post-structuralist theories and relational approaches. These angles have allowed us to see that politically conscious, overtly oppositional, intentional and visible practices of resistance are not the only way to counteract gentrification-induced displacement. We have argued that the field of resistances is also characterized by non-politicized, covert, unintentional, informal, and deliberately invisible practices of everyday life that draw on different perceptions of time and survival, negotiations of ambiguity and mobilization of invisibility.

We have witnessed the growth of collective practices aimed at amplifying the possibilities of a future where dwellers retain as much agency as possible within a landscape of urban displacement and dispossession. There are certain regularities in resistance practices that enrich our repertoire: informality mobilized whenever necessary, informal networks of support where precious knowledge is shared (that might include neighbours, acquaintances in local municipalities, practices of situated solidarity), and differences between homeowners and tenants' aspirations that at first might seem insolvable, but that finally might help organize a neighbourhood better against gentrification pressures. In order to further understand what the possibilities are in the face of dispossession and eviction, we have tried to unpack the concept of resistance, unburdening it from more structural narratives and further incorporating all those aspects that enrich the concept ontologically. Resistance is far from a uni-dimensional, linear storyline of collective action: in fact, resistance happens at different levels of engagement and in constant relation to other processes (what today is resistance tomorrow can be compliance), from the forces it seeks to overcome to multi-scalar hegemonic fault lines. In this sense, the meaning of resistance needs to be constantly negotiated according to an ever-changing landscape of circumstances.

Negotiating ambivalences and ambiguities (or refusing to negotiate) with institutional and private actors demonstrates how resistance itself is a deeply complex concept, relative and adapted to the context precisely by those who carry it out, and consider themselves part of it. Further difficulties arise when individual everyday actions that allow dwellers to stay put, or to find other options in the face of brutal evictions, are not considered part of traditional forms of organized resistance. We have tried here to find a balance on what counts as formal anti-gentrification practices and individual, non-organized, (and sometimes) incoherent behaviour, whilst staying away from romanticizing the precarious lives of the resisting 'urban poor'.

NOTES

1. This concept is borrowed from the idea of displacement by and for development explored by Penz et al. (2011). On the need to strengthen

the nexus between development studies and gentrification studies see Lees et al. (2016).
2. We say so-called as we follow Comaroff and Comaroff's (2012) remark (quoted in Roy 2016: 207) of the South being a 'relation, not a thing in and of itself'.
3. A similar scheme was introduced in Italy as a result of the claims of the housing squatting movement and became regulated by a regional law for Self-Rehab (*autorecupero*) in 1998.
4. See for example 'Towards a community-led plan for London: policy directions and proposals' (2013), which was a proposal for the next London Plan by Just Space in London.
5. Among them see Tom Slater's (2014) response to the *Guardian* newspaper.

REFERENCES

Annunziata, S. and Lees, L. (2016) 'Resisting austerity gentrification in Southern European cities', *Sociological Research Online*, 21(3), np, [Online]. Available at: www.socresonline.org.uk/21/3/5.html (accessed 14 November 2016).

The Anti-Eviction Mapping Project (n.d.) [Online]. Available at: www.antievictionmappingproject.net/narratives.html (accessed 14 November 2016).

Arnott, R. (1995) 'Time for revisionism on rent control?', *The Journal of Economic Perspectives*, 9(1), 99–120.

Ascensao, E. (2015) 'Slum gentrification in Lisbon, Portugal. Displacement and the imagined future of an informal settlement', in Lees, L., Shin, H. and López-Morales, E. (eds) *Global Gentrifications: Uneven Development and Displacement*, Bristol: Policy Press.

Assemblea de Barris per un Turisme Sostenible (ABTS) (n.d.), [Online]. Available at: assembleabarris.wordpress.com (accessed 14 November 2016).

Bayat, A. (2000) 'From "dangerous classes" to "quiet rebels": politics of the urban subaltern in the global south', *International Sociology*, 15(3), 533–557.

Bebbington, A. (2007) 'Social movements and the politicization of chronic poverty', *Development and Change*, 38, 793–818.

Betancur, J. (2014) 'Gentrification in Latin America: overview and critical analysis', *Urban Studies Research* [Online]. http://doi.org/10.1155/2014/986961 (accessed 30 November 2016).

Blomley, N. (2004) *Unsettling the City: Urban Land and the Politics of Property*, New York: Routledge.

Brenner, N., Marcuse, P. and Mayer, M. (2011) *Cities for People, Not for Profit: Critical Urban Theory and the Right to the City*, New York: Routledge.

Cabannes, Y., Yafai, S. and Johnson, C. (2010) *How People Face Evictions*, London: Development Planning Unit, University College London.

Casgrain, A. and Janoschka, M. (2013) 'Gentrificación y resistencia en las ciudades latinoamericanas El ejemplo de Santiago de Chile', *Andamios*, 10(22), 19–44.

Cerulo, K. (2009) 'Nonhumans in social interaction', *Annual Review of Sociology*, 35, 531–552.

Colau, A. and Alemany, A. (2012) 'Mortgaged lives. From the housing bubble to the right to housing', *Journal of Aesthetics & Protest Press* [Online]. Available at: www.joaap.org/press/pah/mortgagedlives.pdf (accessed 14 November 2016).

Collins, R. and Munro, R. (2010) 'Exploring the sociological re-imagining of politics: a conversation', *Sociological Review*, 58(4), 548–562.

Connolly, K. (2016) '"No bling in the hood . . ." Does Berlin's anti-gentrification law really work?', *The Guardian*, 4 October [Online]. Available at: www.theguardian.com/cities/2016/oct/04/does-berlin-anti-gentrification-law-really-work-neukolln (accessed 14 November 2016).

Crossa, V. (2013) 'Play for protest, protest for play: artisan and vendors' resistance to displacement in Mexico City', *Antipode*, 45(4), 826–843.

DeFilippis, J. (2004) *Unmaking Goliath: Community Control in the Face of Global Capital*, New York, NY: Routledge.

Di Feliciantonio, C. (2016) 'The reactions of neighbourhoods to the eviction of squatters in Rome: an account of the making of precarious investor subjects', *European Urban and Regional Studies*, first published on 8 August 2016. http://doi.org/10.1177/0969776416662110.

Erman, T. and Coşkun-Yıldar, M. (2007) 'Emergent local initiative and the city: the case of neighbourhood associations of the better-off classes in post-1990 urban Turkey', *Urban Studies*, 44(13), 2547–2566.

Farías, I. (2011) 'The politics of urban assemblages', *City*, 15(3–4), 365–374.

Gallaher, C. (2016) *The Politics of Staying Put, Condo Conversion and Tenant Right-to-Buy in Washington DC*, Philadelphia: Temple University Press.

Gentrification Blog (n.d.), [Online]. Available at: gentrificationblog.wordpress.com (accessed 14 November 2016).

Gillespie, T. (2016) 'Accumulation by urban dispossession: struggles over urban space in Accra, Ghana', *Transactions of the Institute of British Geographers*, 41(1), 66–77.

Gül, M., Dee, J. and Cünük, C. (2014) 'Istanbul's Taksim Square and Gezi Park: the place of protest and the ideology of place', *Journal of Architecture and Urbanism*, 38(1), 63–72.

Hartman, C. (1984) 'The right to stay put', in Lees, L., Slater, T. and Wyly, E. (2010) (eds) *The Gentrification Reader*, New York: Routledge, pp. 531–541.

Hartman, C., Keating, D. and LeGates, R. (1982) *Displacement: How to Fight It*, Washington, DC: National Housing Law Project.

Herzfeld, M. (2009) *Evicted from Eternity: The Restructuring of Modern Rome*, Chicago: University of Chicago Press.

Hollander, J. and Einwohner, R. (2004) 'Conceptualizing resistance', *Sociological Forum*, 19(4), 533–554.

Holm, A. (2007) 'Housing privatisation in London, Berlin and Amsterdam comparison of procedures, driving forces, and resistance', *PRESOM*, Newsletter 3, 1–9.

Holm, A., Grell, B. and Bernt, M. (eds) (2013) *The Berlin Reader. A Compendium on Urban Change and Activism*, Bielefeld: Transcript-Verlag.

Holm, A. and Kuhn, A. (2011) 'Squatting and urban renewal: the interaction of squatter movements and strategies of urban restructuring in Berlin', *International Journal of Urban and Regional Research*, 35(3), 644–658.

Hynes, M. (2013) 'Reconceptualizing resistance: sociology and the affective dimension of resistance', *TheBritish Journal of Sociology*, 64(4), 559–577.

'IL LAGO CHE COMBATTE' – Assalti frontali & Il Muro del Canto (2014) YouTube video, added by Marcello Saurino, [Online]. Available at www.youtube.com/watch?v=Dcb_Thrq2P8 (accessed 14 November 2016).

İslam, T. and Sakızlıoğlu, B. (2015) 'The making of, and resistance to, state-led gentrification in Istanbul, Turkey', in Lees, L., Shin, H. and López-Morales, E. (eds) *Global Gentrifications: Uneven Development and Displacement*, Bristol: Policy Press, pp. 249–269.

Janoschka, M. (2016) 'Gentrification displacement dispossession: key urban processes within the Latin American context', *INVI*, 31(88), 17–58.

Janoschka, M. and Sequera, J. (2016) 'Gentrification in Latin America: addressing the politics of the geography of displacement', *Urban Geography*, 37(8), 1175–1194.

Just Space (2013) Towards a Community-Led Plan for London: policy directions and proposals. [Online]. Available at: justspacelondon.files.wordpress.com/2013/09/just-space-a4-community-led-london-plan.pdf (accessed 14 November 2016).

Karaman, O. (2014) 'Resisting urban renewal in Istanbul', *Urban Geography*, 35(2), 290–310.

Kolodney, L. (1991) 'Eviction free zones: the economics of legal bricolage in the fight against displacement', *Fordham Urban Law Journal*, 18(3), 507–544.

Lees, L. and Ferreri, M. (2016) 'Resisting gentrification on its final frontiers: learning from the Heygate Estate in London (1974–2013)', *Cities*, 57, 14–24 [Online]. http://dx.doi.org/10.1016/j.cities.2015.12.005 (accessed 13 November 2016).

Lees, L., Shin, H. and López-Morales, E. (eds) (2015) *Global Gentrifications: Uneven Development and Displacement*, Bristol: Policy Press.

Lees, L., Shin, H. and López-Morales, E. (2016) *Planetary Gentrification*, Cambridge: Polity Press.

Lees, L., Slater, T. and Wyly, E. (2008) *Gentrification*, New York: Routledge.

Left Hand Rotation (n.d.) [Online]. Available at: www.lefthandrotation.com/home/index.htm (accessed 14 November 2016).

Ley, D. and Dobson, C. (2008) 'Are there limits to gentrification? The contexts of impeded gentrification in Vancouver', *Urban Studies*, 45(12), 2471–2498.

Ley, D. and Teo, S. (2014) 'Gentrification in Hong-Kong? Epistemology vs. ontology', *International Journal of Urban and Regional Research*, 38(4), 1286–1303.

Lind, H. (2001) 'Rent regulation: a conceptual comparative analysis', *International Journal of Housing Policy*, 1(1), 41–57.

London Tenants Federation, Lees L., Just Space and SNAG (2014) *Staying Put: An Anti-Gentrification Handbook for Council Estates in London* [Online]. Available at: southwarknotes.files.wordpress.com/2014/06/staying-put-web-version-low.pdf (accessed 10 September 2016).

Madrid Desahuciado (2015) *viveroiniciativasciudadanas.net*, 10 March [Online]. Available at: viveroiniciativasciud adanas.net/2015/03/10/madrid-desahuciado (accessed 14 November 2016).

Maeckelbergh, M. (2012) 'Mobilizing to stay put: housing struggles in New York City', *International Journal of Urban and Regional Research*, 36(4), 655–673.

Maloutas, T. (2012) 'Contextual diversity in gentrification research', *Critical Sociology*, 38(1), 33–48.

Marcuse, P. (1985a) 'Gentrification, abandonment and displacement: connection, causes and policy responses in New York City', *Journal of Urban and Contemporary Law*, 28(1–4), 195–240.

Marcuse, P. (1985b) 'To control gentrification: anti-displacement zoning and planning for stable residential districts', *New York University Review of Law & Social Change*, 13(4), 931–952.

Martínez, M. and Cattaneo, P. (eds) (2016) *The Squatters' Movement in Europe: Commons and Autonomy as Alternatives to Capitalism, Squatting Europe Kollective*, London: Pluto Press.

Mayer, M. (2009) 'The "right to the city" in the context of shifting mottos of urban social movements', *City*, 13(2), 262–374.

Mayer, M. (2013) 'First world urban activism: beyond austerity urbanism and creative city politics', *City*, 71(1), 5–19.

Mayer, M. and Boudreau, J.-A. (2011) 'Social movements in urban politics: trends in research and practice', in Mossberger, K., Clarke, S.E. and John, P. (eds), *Oxford Handbook on Urban Politics*, Oxford: Oxford University Press, pp. 273–291.

Mbembé, J.-A. and Nuttall, S. (2004) 'Writing the world from an African metropolis', *Public Culture*, 16(3), 347–372.

McFarlane, C. (2010) 'Squatting movement', in Hutchison, R. (ed), *Encyclopedia of Urban Studies*, Thousand Oaks, CA: SAGE Publications, Inc, pp. 771–774.

McFarlane, C. (2011a) 'Assemblage and critical urbanism', *City*, 15(2), 204–224.

McFarlane, C. (2011b) *Learning the City: Knowledge and Translocal Assemblage*, Hoboken, NJ: Wiley-Blackwell.

McFarlane, C. (2012) 'Rethinking informality: politics, crisis, and the city', *Planning Theory & Practice*, 13(1), 89–108 [Online]: http://doi.org/10.1080/14649357.2012.649951 (accessed 15 September 2016).

Merrifield, A. (2013) *The Politics of the Encounter: Urban Theory and Protest Under Planetary Urbanisation*, Athens, GA: University of Georgia Press.

Morales-Cruz, M. (2012) *Lawyers and 'Social' Movements: A Story About the Puerto Rico 'Zero Evictions' Coalition* [Online]. Available at: www.law.yale.edu/documents/pdf/sela/SELA12_Morales-Cruz_CV_Eng_20 120508.pdf (accessed 30 November 2016)

Mudu, P. (2015) 'Housing and homelessness in contemporary Rome', in Clough Marinaro, I. and Thomassen, B. (eds), *Global Rome: Changing Faces of the Eternal City*, Bloomington, IN: Indiana University Press, pp. 62–80.

Newman, K. and Wyly, E. (2006) 'The right to stay put, revisited: gentrification and resistance to displacement in New York City', *Urban Studies*, 43(1), 23–57.

Noeger, L. (2012) *Gentrification and Resistance*, Munich: Lit Verlag.

Novy, J. and Colomb, C. (2013) 'Struggling for the right to the (creative) city in Berlin and Hamburg: new urban social movements, new "spaces of hope"?', *International Journal of Urban and Regional Research*, 37(5), 1816–1838.

Ong, A. (2011) 'Introduction: worlding cities, or the art of being global', in Roy, A. and Ong, A. (eds), *Worlding Cities: Asian Experiments and the Art of Being Global*, Malden, Oxford: Wiley-Blackwell, pp. 1–26.

Papadopoulos, D. and Tsianos, V. (2007) 'How to do sovereignty without people? The subjectless condition of postliberal power', *boundary 2*, 34(1), 135–172.

Pearsall, H. (2014) 'Superfund me: a study of resistance to gentrification in New York City', *Urban Studies*, 50(11), 2293–2310.

Penz, P., Drydyk, J. and Bose, P. (2011) *Displacement by Development. Ethics, Rights and Responsibility*, Cambridge: Cambridge University Press.

Petropoulou, C. (2014) 'Crisis, Right to the City movements and the question of spontaneity: athens and Mexico City', *City*, 18(4–5), 563–572.

Portelli, S. (2015) *La ciudad horizontal. Urbanismo y resistencia en un barrio de casas baratas de Barcelona*, Barcelona: Ediciones Bellaterra.

Pruijt, H. (2004) 'Okupar en Europa' [Squatting in Europe], in Martínez Lopez, M. and Adell, R. (eds), *¿Dónde están las llaves? El movimiento okupa: prácticas y contextos sociales*, Madrid: La Catarata, pp. 35–60.

Rankin, K. (2009) 'Critical development studies and the praxis of planning', *City*, 13(2), 262–374.

Rätt att bo kvar (n.d.), [Online]. Available at: koloni.info/Ratt_att_bo_kvar_2016.pdf (accessed 14 November 2016).

Robinson, T. (1995) 'Gentrification and grassroots resistance in San Francisco's Tenderloin', *Urban Affairs Review*, 30, 483–513.

Rodríguez, M. and Di Virgilio, M. (2016) 'A city for all? Public policy and resistance to gentrification in the southern neighborhoods of Buenos Aires', *Urban Geography*, 37(8) [Online]. http://doi.org/10.1080/02723638.2016.1 152844 (accessed 30 November 2016).

Rose, M. (2002) 'The seductions of resistance: power, politics, and a performative style of systems', *Environment and Planning D-Society & Space*, 20(4), 383–400.

Routledge, P. and Derickson, K. (2015) 'Situated solidarities and the practice of scholar activism', *Environment and Planning D: Society and Space*, 33(3), 391–407.

Roy, A. (2009) 'The 21st century metropolis: new geographies of theory', *Regional Studies*, 43(6), 819–830.

Roy, A. (2011) 'Slumdog cities: rethinking subaltern urbanism', *International Journal of Urban and Regional Research*, 35(2), 223–238.

Roy, A. (2016) 'Who's afraid of postcolonial theory?', *International Journal of Urban and Regional Research*, 40, 200–209.

Scott, J.C. (1985) *Weapons of the Weak: Everyday Forms of Peasant Resistance*, New Haven, CT: Yale University Press.

Simone, A. (2004) 'People as infrastructure: intersecting fragments in Johannesburg', *Public Culture*, 16, 407–429.

Slater, T. (2014) 'There is nothing natural about gentrification', *Newleftproject.org*, 24 November [Online]. Available at: www.newleftproject.org/index.php/site/article_comments/there_is_nothing_natural_about_gent rification (accessed 14 November 2016).

Smith, N. (1992) 'Contours of a spatialized politics: homeless vehicles and the production of geographical scale', *Social Text*, 33, 54–81.

Smith, N. (1996) *The New Urban Frontier: Gentrification and the Revanchist City*, New York: Routledge.

Stavrides, S. (2016) *Common Space: The City as Commons (In Common)*, London: Zed Books.

Sulukuleli Roman Rap Grubu Tahribad-ı İsyan – TOKİ KAFALAR (2015) YouTube video, added by Eşitlik Özgürlük Emek [Online]. Available at: www.youtube.com/watch?v=wddJgQDslrE (accessed 14 November 2016).

Taylor, M. and Edwards, M. (2016) 'Just space economy and planning: opening up debates on London's economy through participating in strategic planning', in Beebejaun, Y. (ed), *The Participatory City*, Berlin: Jovis, pp. 76–86.

Uitermark, J. (2004) 'Framing urban injustices: the case of the Amsterdam squatter movement', *Space and Polity*, 8(2), 227–244.

Uitermark, J. and Loopmans, M. (2013) 'Urban renewal without displacement? Belgium's "housing contract experiment" and the risks of gentrification', *Journal of Housing and the Built Environment*, 28(1), 157–166.

Velásquez-Atehortúa, J. (2014) 'Barrio women's invited and invented spaces against urban elitisation in Chacao, Venezuela', *Antipode*, 46(3), 835–856.

Yiftachel, O. (2009) 'Critical theory and "gray space": mobilization of the colonized', *City*, 13(2–3), 246–263.

BOX 7 CLARA RIVAS-ALONSO REFLECTION

'Resisting gentrification' is the result of a collaboration between Sandra Annunziata (then a post-doctoral research fellow researching resistance to gentrification in three Southern European cities) and me (then a PhD student researching resistance to gentrification in Istanbul). Sandra became a dear friend, but she sadly passed away prematurely, far too soon, not too long after this piece of writing was completed (see https://aesopyoungacademics.wordpress.com/2019/04/11/sandra-annunziata-in-memoriam/; www.acme-journal.org/index.php/acme/article/view/2018/1528). This commentary reflects on the journey we embarked on as writing partners, which is inherently connected to our friendship, and it is also another way to honor her and her precious work.

Beginning in the autumn of 2014, a group of urban researchers – PhD students, visiting PhD students, and post-doctoral research fellows (Sandra, Chris, Nastassia, Dicle, Bahar, Stefano, Alvaro, and I), all working on different projects about gentrification around the globe, came together over a period of time in the geography department at Leicester University under the tutelage of Loretta Lees. Even if we were all approaching gentrification through different lenses, the elasticity of gentrification studies meant we had a lot of shared interests, especially theoretically but also as scholar-activists committed to fighting gentrification. Our coming together was not predestined; rather, it was facilitated by our co-presence at that time in Leicester working with Loretta. It was an amazing learning experience with and through like-minded people with different competences. There was a critical mass of us that enabled our successful coming together as a study group every week or so to discuss/critique key texts in gentrification studies. Each time we chose different themes for our sessions (whether planetary rent gap theory, a post-colonial framework on gentrification, gendered experiences of gentrification, an interdisciplinary gentrification studies, religion and gentrification, and so on). We would meet at university, in each other's homes or in cafes and pubs where, unnoticed to us, we were simultaneously forging friendships and *becoming* fully-fledged gentrification scholars. At the end of the 2015 academic year, to celebrate these new friendships, I invited Sandra and Nastassia to my hometown of Badajoz, a historically poor border city in southwest Spain, where they would be welcomed by my family and a pretty unbearable heat, and where late-night eating habits would be the hinge to many controversial conversations about gentrification, among other topics. It was a spirit of intellectual exchange that grew out of us being brought together at Leicester at a moment in time that pushed us to be curious about not just gentrification but also each other and solidified our commitment to our collective engagement with gentrification studies.

The gentrification research group in Leicester kept growing, as PhDs, visiting academics, and new post-docs, came in and out. Even though we were all carrying out fieldwork in different corners of the world, we still found time to work together. We also went to various conferences and workshops with Loretta and with each other, bringing ideas there and back to Leicester. To mention just some, Loretta, Sandra, and Bahar went to Berlin to the Kosmos workshop called 'Universal gentrification? Conceptual challenges of comparative urbanism', organized by Andrej Holm, where Loretta also did a book presentation at the Pro qm bookshop, in Berlin, on her new *Planetary Gentrification* book with Hyun Bang Shin and Ernesto Lopez-Morales. Loretta and I went to the Netherlands, where she gave the Alexander von Humboldt lecture, and we participated in several gentrification seminars and also a gentrification fieldtrip in Nijmegen. Most of us attended the presentation of *Staying Put: An Anti-gentrification Handbook for Southern European Cities* organized by Sandra in Rome (see www.city-analysis.net/2017/02/10/philipp-katsinas-reviews-anti-gentrification-workshop-staying-put/). The latter involved a series of workshops with those being directly affected by gentrification, activists from across Europe, other gentrification researchers, and policy makers. Sandra and I also presented our work on resistance at the Contested Cities conference in Madrid; feedback there helped inform our co-authored chapter. And pretty much all of us went to Lisbon in 2018 for the Planetary Apartheid Conference – slowly but surely the Leicester "gang" of gentrification studies (as Simone Tulumello affectionately called us) was making itself known in the academic milieu.

In the relationship that Sandra and I developed, it was clear that our shared interest in practices of resistance to gentrification could potentially be very productive. We were able to identify the connecting lines between Sandra's work and mine. Her focus was on the different ways resistance to gentrification could offer viable successful alternatives. Her invaluable work on Italy, Spain, and Greece materialized in the *Anti-gentrification Handbook for Southern European Cities* mentioned earlier, an organic document that allows for further editing and intervention (and which Alvaro Ardura Urquiaga and I helped translate into Spanish). And my own PhD research on practices of resistance to state-led gentrification in Istanbul reverberated with her work: we were both interested in the macro and micro (everyday) practices of resistance in different contexts that shared the violence of gentrification induced displacement and destitution.

Sandra and I started, fairly early on, to have conversations (plenty of them during late-night working sessions at Leicester University, or over red wine and pasta at her flat) about how theorizations of resistance to gentrification in the literature did not capture many of the more messy, invisible, and perhaps more-difficult-to-codify practices of resistance to processes that were (still are) affecting urban (and rural) spaces globally with different intensities and dis/guises. At that time, around 2014–2016, we observed how the gentrification literature had focused primarily on 'processes of gentrification' and had mainly identified macro urban social movements as the resisting forces against such processes. This, we felt, neglected the more intimate, strategically hidden, everyday actions whose mere existence in the face of (physical and/or symbolic) displacement constituted insurrection or unwillingness to be captured within the logics of gentrification and other urban capitalist processes. We sought to complement academic work on resistance to gentrification (which at the time was actually quite dated and limited) with activist/civil society initiatives (and Sandra's own activism and experience with ETICity [see https://radicalhousingjournal.org/2021/sandra-her-research-and-doing-together/], amongst others, was key here), which, as we argued, was the most effective (and actually also the most interesting) work on resistance to gentrification. Our goal to include non-academic work on resistance to gentrification into the fold of academic work on resistance to gentrification (and actually vice versa) made us draft a table of anti-gentrification resistance practices, one that we felt might fill some of the gaps in the literature. Doing so also allowed us to offer our own theoretical analysis of these said practices, which we summarized using the categories of temporalities, negotiating ambiguities, mobilizing invisibility, and informal networks. The non-academic practices of resistance to gentrification we researched also set the tone of our collaboration: we engaged with critical perspectives, adding our own healthy doses of curiosity, enthusiasm, and eagerness, to see what knowledge production could actually do, and change, when focusing on social and urban injustices. We didn't know it at the time, but that initial coming together in Leicester, the subsequent meetings and discussions and learning in Madrid, Lisbon, and beyond, and countless WhatsApp and Skype conversations (both juggling the tasks of new motherhood and academic deadlines) were instrumental in the coming together of our ideas, finally wrapped together in our chapter 'Resisting gentrification', written for Loretta's (with Martin Phillips) new *Handbook of Gentrification Studies*.

Our geographical focus in the chapter was planetary – we wanted to move beyond just Northern (Western, European, Anglo-American) focused cases, beyond North-South comparativism, or the single case study. We found threads in realities historically linked through the Mediterranean, or a Southern European culture of sorts, opening up the concept of Europe to include the ultimate border country, Turkey, where so much of the so-called East and West (or North and South) is reworked and reproduced. In this sense, we were able to enrich readings of practices of resistances in Southern European cities with perspectives that stemmed from each case and served as an angle to approach the rest of the cases, bearing in mind that there were also differences that not only needed to be taken into account but also were essential analytical nodes through which our approach could be fostered.

If our aim was to offer an imperfect and work-in-progress analysis of resistance practices that could be easily adaptable and altered to reflect further developments on practices of resistance to gentrification, personally and significantly this chapter also set the tone of/for our collaborative work. We set out to find the right questions to ask and found ourselves excitedly mobilizing our own work in ways that supported innovative takes on resistance; in apparent hopelessness, we were able to find hope. Our collaboration also allowed me to identify time and temporalities as a key focus in my PhD thesis, topics long overshadowed by space in geographical accounts of gentrification.

Of course, things have changed dramatically since we wrote and worked together: mainly, Sandra is painfully no longer with us. Still, the chapter we wrote together can help gentrification scholars understand that resistances are multiple, varied, and ever-changing. Moreover, it calls for more research (and activism) on resisting gentrification, this is much needed in a post-COVID-19 world as gentrification itself adapts and even exploits new challenges.

This chapter (and indeed my reflection on writing it here) is part of Sandra Annunziata's legacy and her vision of the world; it is also precious proof of Sandra's huge potential and how it was cut short way too soon. The questions we came up with are still hugely relevant, part of ongoing, collaborative conversations on how to make urban spaces more equitable and just and how to connect places through their processes of urban reproduction, beyond their similarities and differences. I will always be eternally grateful for the time that Sandra and I had together (and how intellectually engaging it was), and I will always find her in my/our attempts at answering questions of urban justice and pushing the conversation forward.

22 Resisting the politics of displacement in the San Francisco Bay Area

Anti-gentrification activism in the Tech Boom 2.0

Florian Opillard

1 Since Neil Smith's works on the Lower East Side as "New Urban Frontier"[1] much has been said on gentrification processes and their contextual variations. The wide range of scholars who draw on the concept to refer to processes of social change, displacement, and dispossession, attests to its gains in legitimacy and applicability far beyond the American academic field.[2] Yet we need to point to the issues which this increased use of gentrification as a lens for the study of urban processes tends to provoke. As Anne Clerval puts it, "the voices that defend a 'positive' interpretation of gentrification are in reality contributing to a depoliticization of the analyses of urban transformations, in favor of an interpretation in moral terms."[3] Is it possible then to remain critical of gentrification without washing the concept out of its contentious and political content? How can critical geography produce knowledge that does not end up being instrumentalized by the institutions it indeed denounces?

2 Along with its extended use, the word "gentrification" has become so related to San Francisco that it has become rare to read about one without the other: San Francisco is precisely one of the places that contributed to the spread of gentrification's scope. Being one of the most gentrified cities in the United States and the most expensive to live in right before New York City,[4] San Francisco is also well known today for facing a crisis often named a "tech boom 2.0." The recent developments, which occurred in the past three years, mostly concern the structuring of an "anti-displacement movement" in the city, supposedly driven by an unprecedented surge of capital through the installation of well paid "tech workers" from the Silicon Valley. The activists who have already fought the "first tech boom" in the late 1990's appear today as a structuring mosaic of individuals, anti-eviction direct action groups, artistic and mapping collectives, and non-profits slowly building up political power and visibility.

3 It is precisely the building of that collective cohesion in the recent San Francisco Anti-Displacement Coalition (SFADC) that this research seeks to explore, drawing from both San Francisco's hyper-gentrification context[5] and its boiling political activism milieu.[6] It advocates for an analysis of the city's gentrification processes displacing the researcher himself or herself from a distant observer to a participant observer, from a producer of abstract and objective knowledge to a co-producer of situated and contextual savoir-faire.[7] This shift in the researcher's position as an actor of social movements allows this analysis to reconstruct the process of gentrification and resistance to it from a day-to-day perspective. Therefore, gentrification and resistance are not seen as distinct and isolated social phenomena that develop independently. In the case of San Francisco, although they are often depicted as the two sides of a Class War 2.0, they both shape one another through complex relations of power, including domination, domestication or dissension,[8] that materialize in both public spaces and

the public sphere. These relations of power are the battlefields that this study of resistance to loss and displacement analyzes, concentrating on the recent emergence of a citywide coalition.[9]

4 This article first describes the way in which the current entanglement of the city-scale neoliberal policies and a strong influx of capital from the tech industry is building up San Francisco's Tech Boom 2.0. This context is secondly approached through the lens of ethnographic work among two of the most active and recent activist groups in the Tenants Movement, from their meetings to their actions in public spaces. Finally, this article attempts to offer an overview of the movement's political outcome along with its scale shift from San Francisco to the Bay Area.

1. IS SAN FRANCISCO'S GENTRIFICATION A TECH BOOM 2.0?

5 San Francisco's social movement has made quite a lot of noise these past months in the local and national media. The "anti-tech" movement, as many activists and reporters called it, seems to have gained visibility since activists started blocking Google and Facebook private shuttles, among others. The debate over the goal of the movement – to fight the "tech takeover" or to stop displacement – has been focused on the role that tech corporations play in the city's hyper gentrification. From this debate emerged the name of the current phase of gentrification: the Tech Boom 2.0. In this section of the article, I will first try to contextualize the debate over the role of the tech industry in the process of gentrification in San Francisco. The first tech boom in the years 2000 will serve as a precedent for both displacement and the organizing against the tech industry. I will then draw attention to the differences between these two episodes and point out the material and symbolic changes that the city is currently experiencing. I will finally account for the politics that fuel such a process, focusing on the question of the memory of the displacees.

1.1 A Tech Boom 2.0?

6 In many discussions between activists in meetings, around a coffee or even in the documents written by their organizations, references to the dot-com boom in the year 2000 are very common. Not only is the dot com boom the last crisis that is still remembered by the many who were displaced and who fought displacement, but it is also a common reference called upon to measure today's social crisis in the city. It is thus very important to understand this first crisis as a measurement standard that orientates the debates over the magnitude of today's tech boom. The famous speculative bubble that grew at the end of the 1990's fueled much investment in the Bay Area, and more particularly in the city of San Francisco. At the time, entrepreneurs and computer software designers rushed to the city with the goal of making easy money by starting an Internet company. In a city where more than 60% of housing is renter occupied and where districts like the Mission and Chinatown concentrate low and very low income populations,[10] the sociology of these workers was quite homogeneous and often differed from that of the people already living in the city: young white and single entrepreneurs with no children, what the acronym Yuppies, for young urban professionals, summed-up at the time. According to the activists' narratives, the anger against the Yuppies grew, as the rush for easy money became a rush for commercial space. Mostly, this space was found in the South of Market (SOMA) district and in the Mission District, two of the remaining working-class districts of the city. Finding space there was accomplished by a phenomenal rise in evictions of Latino and working-class tenants who did not seem to be as profitable for landlords as the young entrepreneurs would be. The cohabitation between old and new residents became harder as spatial proximity highlighted the social, cultural, and economic gap. Regardless of the actual solidarities within the existing communities, new residents often saw the possibility of moving into the Mission as both daring and risky as they confronted the city's new urban frontier.[11] The community's response to these waves of evictions is still exemplary today for its strength and visibility. In the Mission, the building of a strong coalition called the Mission Anti-Displacement Coalition is still taken as an example of vigorous community organizing against gentrification, as it brought together a wide variety of actors and revealed strong ties between community organizers, local activists and artists.[12]

7 What, then, do the dot-com boom and the current tech boom have in common? The 1996

election of Mayor Willie Brown – a powerful businessman and free market advocate – resonates with the election of Edwin Lee, the current Mayor, often referred to by local activists as "one of the most pro-tech mayors that the city's ever had." The parallel can also be made for the Board of Supervisors, whose political orientation was contested in 2000 by the progressive coalition in the ballot. One of the best examples of the current pro-tech policy of the mayor and Board of Supervisors is, undoubtedly, the Twitter tax-break approved in 2011. It exempts Twitter from paying about 22 million dollars payroll tax over six years[13] on the condition that the corporation settles its office space in Mid-Market. As a result, the Mid-Market and the SOMA districts experienced dramatic changes over the past 3 years. The rapid accumulation of capital and the installation of a residential economy around new offices forced the already distressed, existing communities out, along with the rush of engineers brought to the city center by their company's private shuttle service.[14] Yet, comparable as it may be to the one in the 2000s, the current social crisis seems to differ widely when it comes to fighting back. According to a local activist who fought the first boom:

> During the first boom, things were pretty clear and straightforward: evictions intended to find office space for a given startup using the Ellis Act, everything was on the table. Today, we're not only facing Ellis Act evictions, but the number of buyouts and the strategies employed by obscure companies make it way harder to fight back![15]

8 Resulting from an unprecedented capital influx, the rapid gentrification of the city seems a lot harder to grasp for activists slowly building power on a local scale: tenants simply cannot afford the time to mobilize. Another reason is the complexity of the speculation process itself. The following sections will attempt to deconstruct this process as well as its political implications.

1.2 The politics of displacement, spatial reinvention and forgetting

9 There is a misinterpretation in the way that the media spread the "anti-tech" discourse. This leads the reader to think that the gentrification process mainly sets its origins in the rush of tech workers in the city, hence accusing them of displacing "real San Franciscans" and implying that tech workers do not belong in the category. This debate misleads us on both the gentrification process and the communication strategy that the social movement produces. In San Francisco, real estate developers take advantage of the rent gap that the surge of rich engineers participates in creating, making a "quick buck"[16] out of rent controlled housing. Instated for the apartments built before 1979, rent control is a non-renewable resource that is often bypassed by developers through the use of the Ellis Act, a state law that allows the owner of a building to get out of the rental market, on the condition that they take out all of their properties of the same building at once. The loophole in the Ellis Act – no justification is needed to use the Ellis Act – allows corporations to buy entire buildings, Ellis Act all the tenants, remodel and sell each apartment piece by piece as luxury "condos," thus exempting them from rent control. Taking advantage of the legislation, some real estate developers have made the use of the Ellis Act their business model, entering and exiting the rental market several times. The case of Elba Borgen, one of what the Anti-Eviction Mapping Project calls the "dirty speculators" lightens the speculation process through the use of the Ellis Act (Figure 1). Elba Borgen is accused, by the Anti-Eviction Mapping Project to have used the Ellis Act 27 times under her name and under the name of a Real Estate company to evict tenants from apartments she previously bought since 2001.[17]

10 "The Speculator Loophole: Ellis Act Evictions in San Francisco," a report released by the non-profit Tenants Together and the Anti-Eviction Mapping Project, stresses that 79% of the Ellis Act evictions in 2013 concerned properties that were bought 5 years earlier or less (Figure 2).[18]

11 The analysis of the speculation processes through the Ellis Act, which leads only a small part of the total number of evictions, is nevertheless only the tip of the iceberg. The number of owners proposing buyouts to their tenants is both harder to evaluate and much higher, and that is a notable difference between the years 2000 and today. Buyouts are said to have skyrocketed since

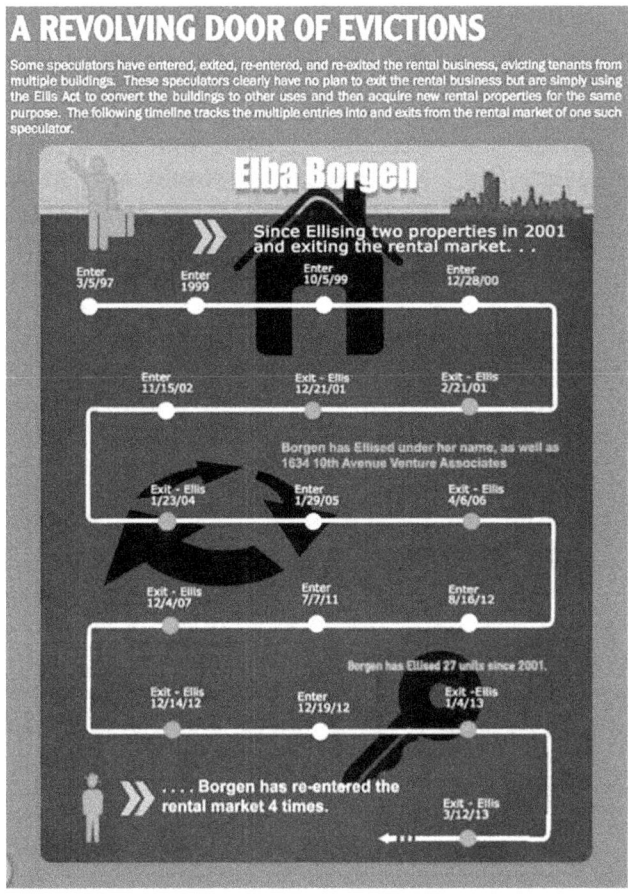

Figure 1 "A Revolving Door of Evictions." The Anti-Eviction Mapping Project's visual of Elba Borgen's itinerary on San Francisco's rental market.

Source: http://tenantstogether.org/downloads/Ellis%20Act%20Report.pdf

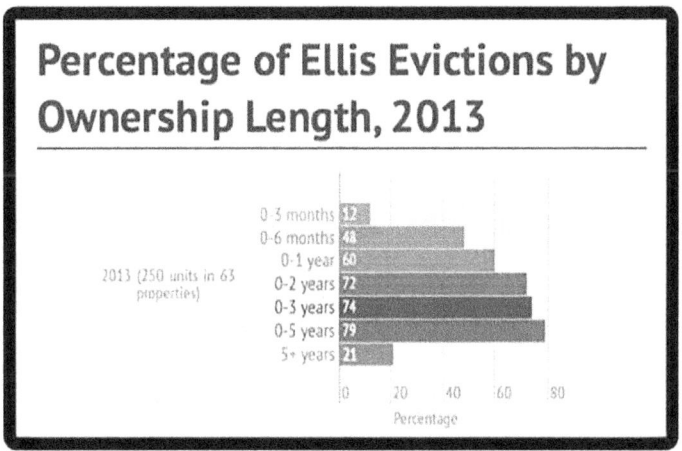

Figure 2 "Percentage of Ellis Evictions by Ownership Length, 2013"

Source: http://tenantstogether.org/downloads/Ellis%20Act%20Report.pdf

2006 with the city's attempt to regulate the condominium conversions following an Ellis Act. As the Anti-Eviction Mapping puts it:

> Since [2006, buyouts] have skyrocketed, with landlords using the threat of an Ellis eviction as a club to coerce tenants into taking a buyout. In addition, by threatening and Ellis eviction and bullying the tenant into a buyout, landlords can also avoid the restrictions on re-rental which are attached to Ellis evictions and re-rent the apartment at a much higher rent.[19]

12 In this current context, gentrification is harder to objectify and therefore much easier to depict as immanent to an uncontrollable market economy. On the contrary, and as Smith puts it, "gentrification is not random; developers do not just plunge into the heart of slum opportunity, but tend to take it piece by piece." Smith describes how these developers have a "vivid block-by-block sense of where the frontier lies,"[20] making them well aware strategists for the bleaching of the city. Cleaner and whiter, cleaner because whiter, whiter therefore cleaner, "bleaching" designates the fact that, as Nancy Raquel Mirabal puts it referring to Chester Hartman, "urban renewal and the politics of space are connected to the preservation of whiteness. When it comes to gentrification, whiteness holds currency. [. . .] In other words, creating spaces where white bodies and desires and, most importantly, consumption, dominate and shape the neighborhood."[21] These politics of space are well known in San Francisco as most of the African American migrants have already been displaced out of the city, and as the Latino community has been experiencing displacement with much violence since the 1970s. Yet, the process by which space can be made available for consumption by white bodies is not natural either. Rather, "[f]or the collective memory of space to be reconstituted, there needs to be a mutual forgetting of what came before the constructions of new buildings, restaurants, and businesses."[22] These politics of forgetting are systematically accompanied by politics of "spatial reinvention" along with the promotion of the "new" over existing communities of color. In San Francisco, the examples of spatial reinvention are very common, from the social cleansing operation "Clean up the Plaza" in the heart of the Mission[23] to the renaming of the Mission as "The Quad – A Newly Defined Metahood" by a real estate agent.[24]

1.3 Old and new landscapes of power: the material and symbolic shifts in gentrifying San Francisco

13 Drawing on Sharon Zukin's notion of "Landscapes of Power,"[25] this part will insist on the way in which changes affect every dimension of everyday life in a context of hyper gentrification. The example of the Mission District will be used to analyze the dramatic changes that illustrate the tensions at play in the city between local cultural capital (the Latino community), the influx of capital through urban motilities (the surge of engineers) and global financial capital (real estate speculation strategies). These elements contribute to shifts that can be witnessed in the landscape which embodies the struggles over the material and symbolic appropriation and control over space.

14 There is a striking dichotomy in the Mission District that reveals at multiple scales the progressive shift that the district is experiencing. Walking along Valencia Street, one can point out the contrasts with Mission Street, the parallel street 50 meters away. Valencia street is dotted with small vibrant businesses: curiosities shops, minimalist style coffee shops,[26] clothing stores that make holding a PhD a requirement for their models,[27] modern design sound system stores and concept stores. The co-owner of the said sound system store, a young binational French-US citizen entrepreneur described his work as "an ephemeral project. I just decided to help a friend rebuild this place for the store to function. [. . .] I don't really know what I'll be doing in 3 months: the project's almost over and . . . you know, you gotta move on." When asked about the kind of people who buy devices in the store, he described the clients as "mainly rich locals, young entrepreneurs that can afford it. Tourists just stop by and take a peak, but that's it."[28] In this whole part of the Mission, white bodies are wandering, buying, relaxing or bicycling. Fifty meters from there, on Mission Street and towards the south of the Mission, one enters the Latino Mission with its taquerias, its murals glorifying the community's struggles for social justice, its Latino community centers, and most importantly its dwellers' brown bodies.

15 The making of this socio-spatial fracture happens both in an insidious and a sudden way that punctuates everyday life. Insidious is the constant condo-conversion process that is transforming the landscape of Victorian facades into luxury six-story secure live-work buildings, as well as the progressive rarefaction of warehouses and working class jobs. Along with this background noise of social shift, the rhythm of the Private Shuttles, endlessly stopping at public stops or jamming traffic is a constant reminder of tenants' evictions in the making.[29] Finally, the evictions,[30] the controversial killing of Alex Nieto by the SFPD in Bernal Heights on March 21, 2014,[31] the arrest of activists on the fringes of marches are the sudden cymbal crashes that shake or mobilize both the activists and their communities. They are pieces that add up to the progressive social cleansing and criminalization of poverty in the city, of which the current fight over Plaza 16 is the most striking. This Plaza is located in the north of the Mission, at the intersection of Mission, 16th Street and the BART. It is today subject to a debate over the campaign to "Clean up the Plaza," started by a coalition of merchants, business owners and neighbors fed up with "the blight of this corner," advocating for a "better access to safe, clean and walkable transportation corridors." This group came along with a ten-story condo development project allowed by the Planning Commission. This development is seen as a means for the city to support the displacement of poverty along with its ugliness – i.e. the "junkies, 'smash and grab' thieves who prey on parked cars, prostitutes, the mentally ill, the substance addicted, and assorted other criminals and lost souls,"[32] – which the 24/7 presence of a police car right next to the plaza has already started doing.

2. FROM CHATS TO DISCOURSES, FROM MEETINGS TO MARCHES, FROM BODIES TO PERFORMANCES: ENTERING THE ACTIVISM MILIEU

16 How can one resist to such a hyper-gentrification context?[33] The following developments borrow from fieldwork interviews and participant observation done with two specific collectives that intend to fight the processes of gentrification: Eviction Free San Francisco and the Anti-Eviction Mapping Project. While some of their members participate in both groups, their functions seem distinct but complementary and coherent with the structuring of a growing Tenants Movement.

2.1 Two cases of group styles

17 The study of activism in the context of neoliberal urban policies appears key to understanding the frames of a social movement in the making. One of these frames – the definition, function and actions of the groups in which activism is shaped – can be investigated through the lens of "group styles." As defined by Nina Eliasoph and Paul Lichterman, group styles are "recurrent patterns of interaction that arise from a group's shared assumptions about what constitutes good or adequate participation in the group setting,"[34] they participate in shaping individual activist trajectories, they ground the Tenants Movement in the day to day embeddedness of capitalist patterns of domination.

18 Eviction Free San Francisco (EFSF) is a mutual help and direct action group that seeks to "hold accountable and to confront real estate speculators and landlords that are displacing our communities for profit."[35] The meetings usually gather twenty to thirty people. The backbone of the group is composed of five people, who created the collective in the summer of 2013; they prepare the meeting agendas, take stacks[36] in meetings and debate on the propositions to submit to a vote. Most of them have known each other for some time now and participate in several activist collectives and projects. Some of them are professional organizers (e.g. working for the Housing Rights Committee) while others are participating as volunteers. Many of them are tenants fighting their own eviction or having fought it in the past and who are willing to give back. The collective is open to anyone who wants to participate, and everyone attending the meeting gets to vote on the propositions made, with the condition that the discussions occurring during the meeting cannot be made public. Journalists are therefore kindly asked to manifest themselves and leave.

19 At the beginning of each meeting, the facilitator enunciates the "meeting culture (ground rules)," which everyone is invited to follow (Figure 3).

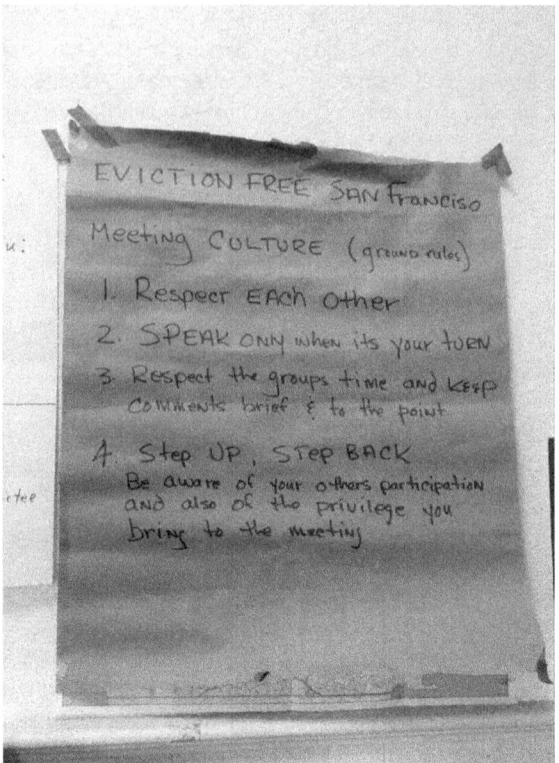

Figure 3 Eviction Free San Francisco's meeting Ground Rules and Meeting Culture, April 2014. Credits: Florian Opillard.

20 These rules specifically show the group's preoccupation with the reproduction of society's intersectional structures of domination (race, sex, and class) within the group. They invite structurally dominated and silent minorities to step up. The willingness to challenge structures of domination within the group itself makes it necessary to clearly define the meeting agenda, the time devoted to each item and to take stacks. Such a structure creates a safe and designated space for structurally oppressed and silenced minorities to take up their own right to speech. It is not rare to witness harassed tenants both describe the symbolic violence which they face every day and express their gratitude towards the group. Unlike Eliasoph and Lichterman, who point to the existence of "Language of Expressive Individualism" and "Active Disaffiliation" in civic groups,[37] I argue that the EFSF is best characterized by the language of individual restraint and group celebration, along with a discrete but active affiliation. In each meeting, group celebration is expressed on two occasions: at the beginning of each meeting when the group comments on the past actions, and at the end of the meeting, when each participant gets to express their own feelings about the group. For that matter, while this moment could be the peak of individual expression, people tend to shirk their own interest and declare their willingness to help for the benefit of the group.

21 The second group that this research focuses on differs in its organization and its aims. The Anti-Eviction Mapping Project (AMP) is a "data-visualization, data analysis, and digital storytelling collective documenting the dispossession of San Francisco Bay Area residents. The project seeks to de-isolate those displaced and act as a tool for collective resistance."[38]

22 The collective rarely gathers all of its members in one place. It is composed of approximately sixty people in total, many of whom occasionally give a hand, grant an interview, help encoding or organizing the collected data. The bonds between the participants are therefore difficult to capture, and often maintain blurry as a strategy. The group and its activities revolve largely around its

main figure, Erin McElroy, an experienced activist close to the anarchist circles who dedicates her time and energy to the cohesion of the collective's branches and communication with universities,[39] city institutions or the press. The division of labor is, therefore, fairly easy to read: while "the tech guys" encode the website or make the maps at the SudoRoom[40] in Oakland, another group generally meets in the Tenants Union's building to discuss ongoing projects. While the EFSF is composed of many tenants with low economic capital, the AMP comprises mostly highly educated and politicized young activists, all of them aware of both the part they play in the gentrification process and the ways to fight it.

23 Unlike the EFSF, the meeting culture in the AMP is not stated at the beginning of each meeting. Once again, it is very rare to witness people putting their individual interests before the ones of the group: people are invited to propose their skills to the group, be it encoding, networking, mapping, distributing surveys. Yet, "negative experiences"[41] are not unheard of: during a meeting, a 45-year-old white man who expected to be given some interesting work to do as a cameraman explained: "I just want to say right away that I feel like this project is not going the way I think would be profitable for me, because some people are calling dibs. I don't want to have to deal with the leftovers." By expressing his frustration, this person put himself before the group and felt the pressure of the others, all agreeing on the fact that both the primary frame (conducting a meeting) and the secondary frame (building political tools and raising awareness) were broken: this "white privileged male who has a high idea of himself and of his work," as described by a member of the meeting, interrupted it by transgressing the speech norms.

2.2. Repertoires of contention

24 Along with the analysis of group styles, the analysis of the repertoires of contention[42] of the two organizations reveals the groups' complementarity: while the AMP blows the whistle on "dirty landlords and serial evictors," the EFSF focuses on their direct targeting and "public shaming." The circulations of activists in both groups and their close relationships might explain their working together. Yet, it seems that, although six people are consistently participating in the work of both collectives, they belong to distinct activism patterns and traditions.

25 As a direct action group, the EFSF exemplifies anti-capitalistic community activism, which is deeply rooted in the city's political history since the 1950s.[43] Rebecca Gourevitch, an activist working for the Tenants Union and the EFSF, explained the influence of the Occupy movement, from which many of the current collectives in the Bay Area derive. The EFSF "first meetings started just like Occupy," in 2013, as the Anti-Displacement Coalition fought the eviction of Mrs. Lee's family a 74-year-old Chinese-speaking lady, who became the very icon of the movement.[44] The fight over cases of evictions mostly revolves around three modes of action: protesting in public spaces, rallying, and publicly denouncing "greedy" landlords and speculators. Protesting is probably the most common and the least specific action that the EFSF implements. The group holds several meetings prior to the protest in the Tenants Union's house on Capp Street, setting date and time, banners and signs, itinerary and speakers. The march organized on April 12, 2014, "To End Displacement of San Francisco's Educators"[45] is a great example of the logistics of such a protest. Noting that more and more teachers were coming to the group to report their own eviction, the group decided to combine a Google Bus blockade with a march making several stops to highlight cases of eviction in the Mission. In this case, the activists employed spatial strategies to direct the media attention to the bus blockade and the march. The discussions in the preparation meetings insisted on space as both a frame and a strategic tool for the activists to master: the knowledge of the streets, the limitation of their visibility prior to the blockade and the necessary occupation of space with enough bodies to block the street revealed a necessary control over public space. Along with protests, the EFSF's more specific mode of action consists in launching campaigns to publicly discredit "greedy landlords" responsible for the eviction of tenants by giving out their names, addresses, phone and fax numbers, and encouraging activists to drive out to their home and talk them out of evicting. This mode of action is often considered radical by the local media, since the publication of names and addresses points fingers at individuals who are

not considered responsible for their company's policies.

26 Despite its actions, the group has not so far dealt with significant police pressure,[46] although the protests in public spaces are never made official. Rather, the itineraries are often negotiated on site with police officers in charge, making it possible for the 300 people to protest and block the streets.

27 The Anti-Eviction Mapping Project's modes of action correspond to the pattern of tech activism, specific to the Bay Area, and most of its activities are implemented by the activist milieu of the East Bay. Using technology as a tool to implement and empower community activism, the group makes maps, using both their own collected data and the available data on evictions and housing ownership. The first and most visible project that the group implemented was the No-Fault Evictions and the Ellis Act Evictions Maps.[47] Erin McElroy insists on the use of maps as tools to "show a chronology and an accumulation of evictions [,] to be able to say: 'what does this represent over time in terms of the destruction of our neighborhood.'"[48] In fact, the two maps below have had a great resonance in the Tenants Movement. They identify areas that are being struck the most by the displacement of tenants (Figure 4).

28 Along with the mapping, the group investigates landlords who "make evictions their business models," as claimed repeatedly during the protests. The group has edited three main lists of "dirty landlords": the Dirty Dozen – Worst Evictors, Dirty Thirty – Evicting the Disabled and Elderly and the Dirty 2.0 – Tech Evictors. These lists mobilize the volunteers to research the practices of landlords and companies that evict for profit, collecting personal and professional information and spreading their photos in the media. Giving a face to the processes of evictions – a tactic shared by the EFSF – contributes to deconstructing the anonymity of the state and corporate apparatuses, which dissolve and fragment political responsibility. Lastly, the group distributed more than two hundred surveys

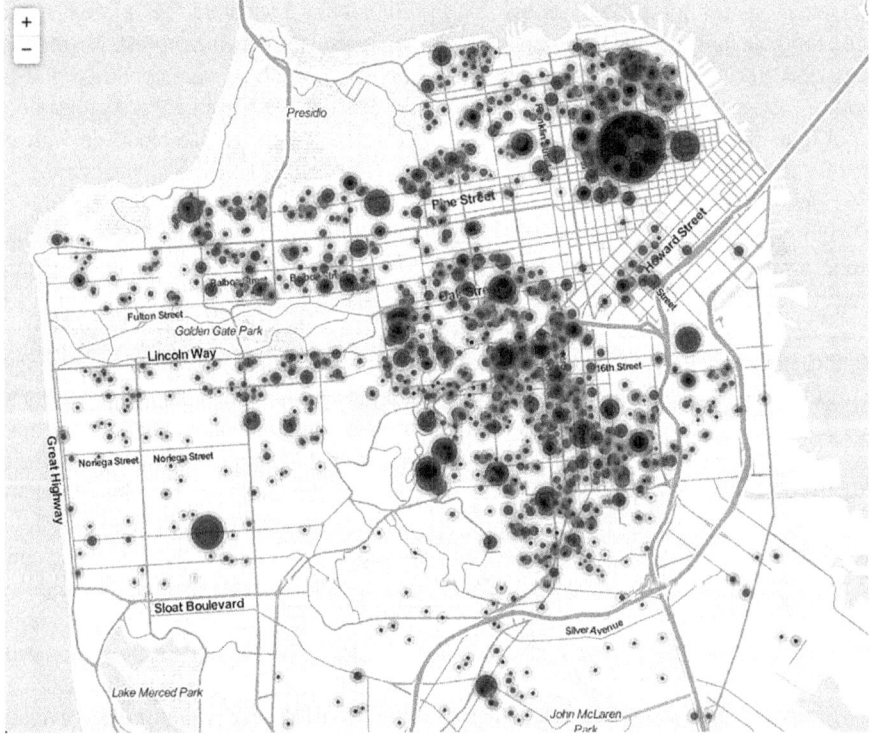

Figure 4 San Francisco Ellis Act Evictions map by the Anti-Eviction Mapping Project.
Source: www.antievictionmappingproject.net/ellis.html.

to get in touch with displaced tenants and build the Oral History Project. Those who were willing to go further were contacted to tell more about their eviction and be recorded. Prior to the interviews, the volunteers in the group attended a workshop on oral history held by an activist and trained oral historian from the CUNY Graduate Center. The "Narratives of Displacement and Loss" map collects and geolocalizes oral stories of evictions; it aims to grasp the emotional and memorial thickness of space and place,[49] and to fight the politics of renaming evoked earlier.[50]

29 Both collectives appear as two components that bring their own activist culture and their group style to the growing San Francisco Anti-Displacement Coalition. They bring small victories and participate in building a common political discourse over spatially fragmented fights. In the last section of this article, the analysis of the structuring of this coalition will lead to a scale shift from San Francisco to the Bay Area.

3. POLITICAL OUTCOME OF A GROWING POLITICAL COALITION

30 In what ways can the above description of two of the most recent and dynamic groups of the forming coalition shed light on both the recent turns in the gentrification processes and the local communities' responses? According to Rachel Brahinsky, "The "Google bus," which is what people in the Bay Area call the mass of private, tech commuter buses that fill the rush-hour streets, is not essentially the problem. In fact, it may be the seed of the solution."[51] Precisely because it is provocative, Brahinsky's assertion might be the key to an analysis of the current situation: the community response to the political, material and symbolic processes of dispossession that tenants are facing, despite its micro-scale fights, has gained significant power and coverage in the latest months.

3.1 The building of the San Francisco anti-displacement coalition

31 On February 7, 2014, after a series of Neighborhood Tenants Conventions, the Tenderloin Community School hosted the biggest Citywide Tenants Convention that the city had seen in years. Many important figures of the now official "Tenants Movement" spoke on the microphone, some of them obviously at ease in front of such a big audience, like Erin McElroy, or Ted Gullicksen, director of the Tenants Union. After some organizers spoke about the importance of continuing the fight to stay in their homes, came Mrs. Lee's time to speak, who claimed that she would not go away and would rather be taken out of her home by the sheriff in person. Six of the eleven city supervisors were present: Calvin Welsh, a famous figure of the tenants' fights since the 70's; Randy Shaw, the director of the Tenderloin Housing Clinic; and other political figures and journalists, including a French and a British team. The outcomes of this convention were discussed through the vote on the propositions that the Anti-Displacement Coalition could pass on to the Board of Supervisors. One of them, called the Real Estate Sales Tax, was likely to gain support among the activists in the forthcoming months, "and if the board doesn't vote it, then we'll pass it through the ballot in November!" said Sara Shorts, the executive director of the Housing Rights Committee. This convention appears to have laid the first stone of a complex and hierarchized structure, the San Francisco Anti-Displacement Coalition, which gathered tenants on many occasions: it rallied to Sacramento to push Mark Leno's bill in State Assembly (February 18), pushed David Campos' Relocation Bill for victims of the Ellis Act (March 17), marched to denounce the police murder of Alex Nieto in Bernal Heights (March 29), or marched in the Mission to fight Benito Santiago's eviction (April 2nd). This coalition, although it benefits from the experience accumulated by both the organizing and the activism milieu, is not per se a territorial organization. It is rather composed of distinct groups which converged in the political fight for Proposition G (real estate sales tax) in the ballot initiative, and which are planning to do so on November 2015's ballot.

32 The Anti-Eviction Mapping Project and Eviction Free San Francisco are a part of this coalition; both are based in the Mission district, where the fight against loss and displacement is historically strong. The Tenants Union, whose famous fighter for tenants rights and former Director Ted Gullicksen passed away in November 2014, acts as one of the main territorial resources of many gravitating groups: it offers a workspace, material and technical support (mainly to the EFSF and the

AMP) in the Mission district, legal resources by editing the Tenants Handbook and volunteer tenants counseling. The Housing Rights Committee, another "housing clinic," provides space for direct action meetings, sign making and tenants' legal support, backs the Tenants Union in its missions. More than that, these two organizations appear as a crucible for young housing activists and organizers who learn from years of fighting experience and political fights by gravitating in these sociability circles. Other organizations like Our Mission No Eviction and Causa Justa: Just Cause handle work that is more specifically directed towards and led by black and Latino residents, while the Chinatown Community Development Corporation actively supports the Chinese community. Before the campaign for Proposition G on the Ballot, the coalition rarely appeared as a united front on punctual marches or rallies. Rather, each organization would individually take on their own part and coordinate with each other, making the coalition a communicational and juridical entity heading the fight in City Hall and on the Board of Supervisors.

3.2 From public spaces to the public sphere: debates in the media through the political agenda

33 The tenants' fight in City Hall, on the Board of Supervisors and in the streets is precisely what has been drawing so much media and political attention in the past year. Starting with the Occupy movement in 2011, from which many of today's activist sociability networks emanate, the fight over loss and displacement continually grew as both the number of evictions, buyouts and tenant harassment cases exploded, and as the tech shuttles became a crystallizing fight. The first bus blockades in November 2013, organized by Heart of the City Collective, rapidly spread the word of transnational corporations such as Google or Facebook targeting the Bay Area. They also contributed to the construction of an "anti-tech" discourse along with the spreading of the icon of the "techie," an image of the self-centered libertarian tech employee making the Bay Area their playground. This term has nevertheless been challenged for its lack of complexity, a reproach some of the members of the movement have acknowledged by participating in encounters[52] between employees of tech companies and the main organizations described here. These encounters were at first rarely mentioned in the media,[53] since the need for a loud and clear political message fuels the construction of reified categories. It is only after some of leading activists started publishing pieces in the media that the discourse started to complexify,[54] and, along with it, the political fights at the city and state level.

34 In San Francisco, David Campos, supervisor of the Mission district, is at the front of the fight for tenants' rights. Through the support of Tenants Organizations, he introduced a bill at the Board of Supervisors in April 2014 that proposed to increase the relocation fee for any tenant evicted through the use of the Ellis Act. The board voted on this proposition after Scott Weiner, supervisor of the Castro, insisted on making sure that the fee would not have a dissuasive effect on what he called "mom and pop" landlords. In fact, this measure is meant to help tenants who are being evicted with a short-term notice face the cost of eviction, although Campos clearly states that Limited Liability Corporations which use the Ellis Act as a tool for speculation would not have a hard time bypassing the measure.

35 The November 2014's Ballot Initiative is another example of the political outcome of the SFADC's organizing. Proposition G emerged after a series of Tenants Conventions held in 2014. This proposition intended to dissuade speculators from flipping properties by taxing the profits of each real estate sale,[55] a measure that Harvey Milk had already introduced in 1978. Although the proposition was defeated in the Ballot (No: 53.91%; Yes: 46.09%), a much bigger fight the fight over proposition G gave a clear image of the political forces battling over San Francisco's housing crisis as it crystallized progressive forces in the city. Maria Zamudio, organizer at Causa Justa: Just Cause and strong advocate for Proposition G, states that "While it did not win this year, Prop G was a part of a larger progressive narrative that did win."[56] This movement may actually have achieved more than simply the creation of a progressive narrative, or maybe the narrative itself has material effects that activists are currently witnessing. Gen Fujioka, in the online journal 48Hills, released on January 5, 2015, provides an analysis[57] of the Ellis Act evictions showing that while the number of evictions had been increasing dramatically from 2010 to 2013, the number of units withdrawn from the rental

Figure 5 Annual rate of rental units officially withdrawn under Ellis Act – 2010–2013.
Source: http://48hillsonline.org/2015/01/04/facing-eviction-threat-tenants-push-back-slow-ellis-evictions-2014/

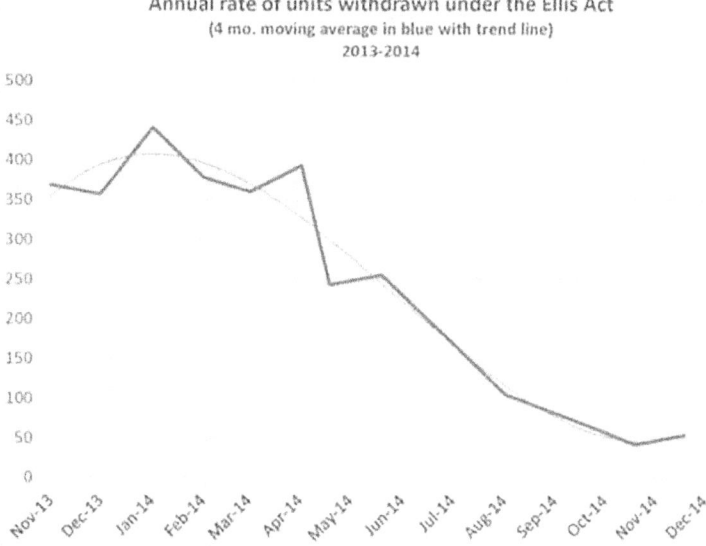

Figure 6 Annual rate of rental units officially withdrawn under Ellis Act – 2013–14.
Source: http://48hillsonline.org/2015/01/04/facing-eviction-threat-tenants-push-back-slow-ellis-evictions-2014/

marked through the use of the Ellis Act significantly slowed down during the last months of 2014 (Figures 5 and 6).

3.3 From San Francisco to the Bay Area

36 The fight against the Ellis Act, and more generally against displacement in San Francisco, is nevertheless not limited to the city itself, and through the year 2014, a series of political fights crystallized progressive forces and indicated a scale shift in their organizing from the city of San Francisco to the Bay Area and the State of California. Two of the fights that put San Francisco on the state scene are the fight over California's seventeenth state assembly district and Mark Leno's bill to reform the Ellis Act in State assembly. Although both fights ended up as defeats for progressives, they both indicate the importance of the recent organizing and activism pushed by what James Tracy called "organizations [. . .] that resuscitated the art of disruptive action in confronting displacement,"[58] among which are the Anti-Eviction Mapping Project and Eviction Free San Francisco. In the fight over a State Assembly's seat, another democrat joined David Campos in the race: David Chiu, President of the Board of Supervisors. Whereas David Campos was largely supported by labor organizations (second source of donations after small Real Estate developers), the AMP has shown that David Chiu received 26% of his donations from "large Real Estate developers" and "problematic donors"[59] and raised twice as much in campaign donations. The fight was, therefore, presented as the one of David against Goliath. The maps drawn by Professor Corey Cook from the University of San Francisco[60] reveal the territorial dimension of the vote (Figures 7 and 8):

37 Along with the clear orientation of the endorsers, the geography of the vote reveals that the stakes of this battle over State Senate are clearly marked between real estate developers in downtown San Francisco and the housing advocates voters in the Mission, the Haight and

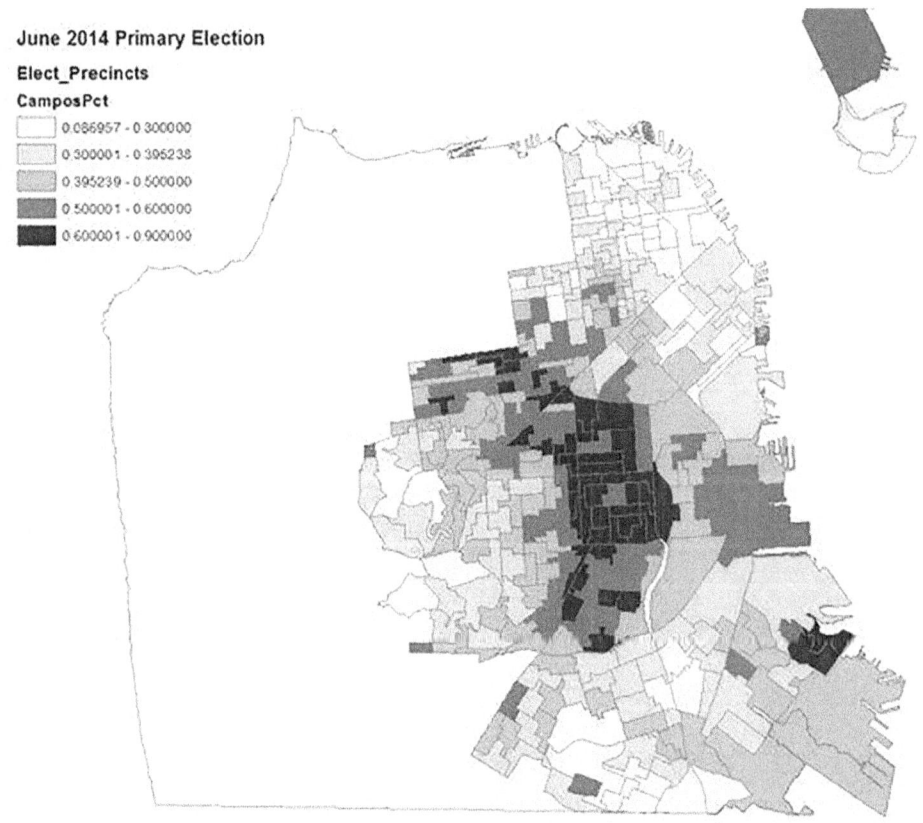

Figure 7 June 2014 Primary Election map – David Campos

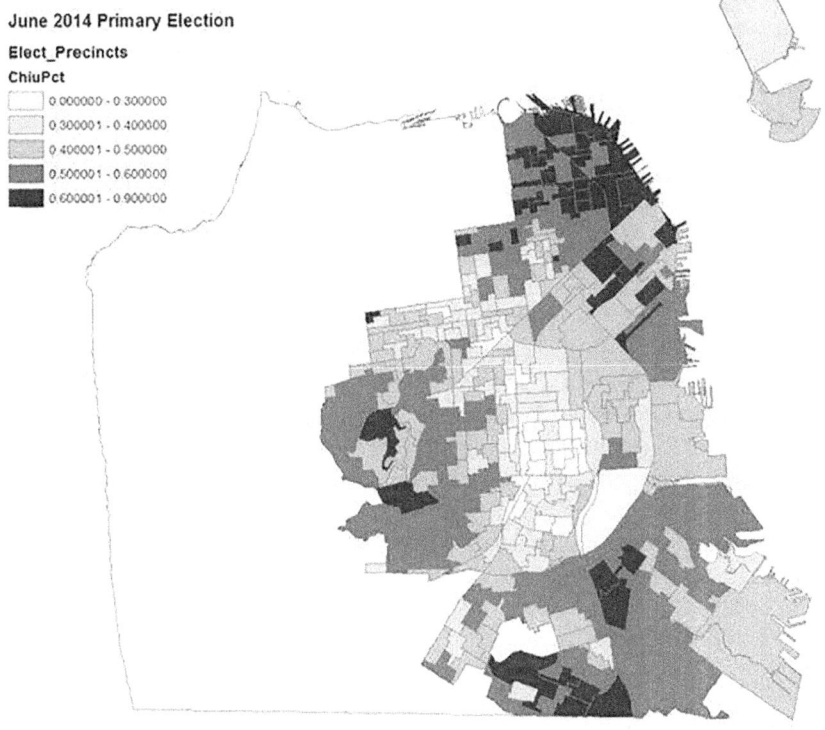

Figure 8 June 2014 Primary Election map – David Chiu

the Tenderloin. The same goes for the fight in the State Senate for Mark Leno's Bill that intended to allow the city of San Francisco to locally reform the Ellis Act, making it impossible for landlords to evict tenants through the use of the Ellis Act in the 5 years following the purchase of a given property. An important local campaign allowed Mark Leno's bill to go to the State Senate, mobilizing many organizing and activist groups, along with statewide organizations such as Tenants Together or the Alliance of Californians for Community Empowerment (ACCE). One of the big points of this campaign was certainly the Renters day of Action on February 19, 2014, a rally that brought more than 500 tenants to State Capitol in Sacramento, including renters from "Merced, Fresno, Sacramento, Concord and Oakland."[61] Although this piece of legislation concerned San Francisco, the regional aspect of this fight confirmed San Francisco as the political showcase for progressive politics. It seems clear that housing issues in San Francisco cannot be limited to the city itself. Rather, as Brahinsky puts it, "We need to stop talking about San Francisco and start talking about the San Francisco Bay Region."

38 To start talking about the San Francisco Bay Region implies a major change in the analysis of embedded patterns of racial and class segregation, "This means that [. . .] the region needs to be respected. Oakland is not a playground, a new frontier, or a place of last resort; it is a place with a history and a present."[62] As a matter of fact, this scale shift can already be observed in local activism. For example, Causa Justa: Just Cause is an influent non-profit which focuses specifically on the racial processes at stake in gentrification, while its members are for the most part Latino or black. Its actions mostly take place in Oakland, where the fight over racial and class discrimination is strong in the context of the emergence of Oakland as the new frontier for gentrified San Franciscans. In terms of organizing, a growing part of the work is now being done outside of San Francisco, and the relocation of 2014 and 2015's Anarchist Book Fairs at the Crucible in Oakland where a panel on gentrification reunited activists from the whole urban

region, or the creation of an activist group called Defend the Bay Area in March 2014, including activists mostly from Oakland and San Francisco, prove that social scientists are missing the reality of gentrification, displacement and the resistance to it by only focusing on San Francisco. That weakness is common and simple to enunciate: research on gentrification generally deals with urban change rather than with the displacees, urban policy rather than the process of displacement, gentrified areas (San Francisco) rather than the displaced people. Thus, those who are pushed out disappear from the social landscape; they simply do not fit in the new symbolic and political landscapes of power that replace them. Social science research does play a role in this odd silence: many researchers, usually white and middle-class, feel much more comfortable dealing with, for example, young white middle class couples than with the recently arrived illegal immigrants who barely speak the language.

CONCLUSION

39 In the past year, activism in San Francisco has proved particularly dynamic. Private Shuttle blockades, street protests or strong pieces of legislation passed by the Board of Supervisors evoked some of the most active years of city scale coalitions like the Mission Anti-Displacement Coalition in the years 2000. The "techies" seem to have replaced the "yuppies," the dot-com 2.0 replaced the first wave of gentrification. Nevertheless, the ethnographic lens advocates for a more complex and detailed analysis of the construction of these artificial categories. A closer look at the two collectives, which highly contributed to the surge of media attention, allows us to better situate both historically and geographically this moment as the yet un-institutionalized response to almost entirely institutionalized speculation practices on housing. Focusing on these groups provides a better understanding of how the activism context not only disrupts tech buses from working, it also contributes to the design of legislation within the realm of political opportunities that, despite being rejected by a majority of the 200,000 voters, compose strong moments of cohesion and construction of local and statewide progressive politics.

NOTES

1. Neil Smith, *The New Urban Frontier: Gentrification and the Revanchist City* (New York: Routledge, 1996), 288. In his book, Neil Smith describes the way in which Manhattan's Lower East Side is being fought over and seen by real estate developers as an urban territory to take back from the working class. In these struggles over land occupation, the image of the "frontier" is often conveyed, making the Lower East Side the new frontier to be conquered and civilized.
2. Loretta Lees, Tom Slater and Elvin Wyly, *The Gentrification Reader* (New York: Routledge, 2010), 648; Anne Clerval, "La gentrification à Paris intra muros: dynamiques spatiales, rapports sociaux et politiques publiques," Thèse de doctorat (Université Paris 1 – Panthéon Sorbonne, 2008), 602.
3. Anne Clerval, "'Gentrification or Ghetto': Making Sense of an Intellectual Impasse," *Métropolitiques*, 29/01/2015, www.metropolitiques.eu/Gentrification-or-ghetto-making.html.
4. Tracy Elsen, Tuesday, "For the Fourth Month Straight, SF's Median Rent Tops NY's," *Curbed San Francisco*, http://sf.curbed.com/archives/2014/12/02/for_the_fourth_month_straight_sfs_median_rent_tops_nys.php, last accessed December 2, 2014.
5. Loretta Lees defined super-gentrification in the *Journal of Urban Studies* in 2003 as the "transformation of already gentrified, prosperous and solidly upper-middle-class neighborhoods into much more exclusive and expensive enclaves," For more see L. Lees, "Super-gentrification: The Case of Brooklyn Heights, New York City," *Urban Studies* 40, no. 12 (November 2003): 2487–2509. Hyper-gentrification is a term used to describe the widespread gentrification of already gentrified urban areas as an equivalent to Neil Smith's "gentrification generalized" or "third-wave gentrification." The blog Vanishing New York published an article describing this process: Jeremiah Moss, "On Spike Lee & Hyper-Gentrification, the Monster that Ate New York," *Jeremiah's Vanishing New York*, 3 March 2014.
6. Setting its reality into published words may appear as a form of betrayal of the constantly evolving, multi-layered and not yet enfolded reality of what a social movement can be. This paper is not to be understood as

7. Michael Burawoy, "The Extended Case Method," *Sociological Theory* 16, no. 1 (March 1998): 4–33.
8. Catherine Neveu, "Démocratie participative et mouvements sociaux: entre domestication et ensauvagement?," *Participations*, De Boeck Supérieur, no. 1 (2011/1): 186–209.
9. This article borrows from the author's PhD in the making: "A Comparative Ethnography of Anti-gentrification Activism in Two Neoliberal Urban Contexts (San Francisco, United-States – Valparaíso, Chile)," School for Advanced Studies in Social Sciences, 2013–2016, Paris.
10. The city of San Francisco started releasing in 2009 data through the Housing Elements, revealing that in districts like the Mission in 2014, 80% of the inhabitants were renters, while the average rent for a two bedroom apartment was approximately four times higher than what a very low income (VLI) family makes per month. Very Low Income families make between 0 to 50% of the Area Median Income, whereas Low Income Families make 51 to 80% of the Area Median Income. Housing Elements can be found here: www.sf-planning.org/index.aspx?page=3899, last accessed June 8, 2015.
11. Smith, *The New Urban Frontier*, 288.
12. Karl Beitel, *Local Protest, Global Movements: Capital, Community, and State in San Francisco* (Philadelphia: Temple University Press, 2013), 220.
13. See the tax-break by the numbers at Eve Batey in News on Jun 24, 2014 (10:53 am), "San Francisco's Mid-Market Tax Break by the Numbers," *Sfist*, http://sfist.com/2014/06/24/san_franciscos_mid-market_tax_break.php.
14. The debate over the political decision regarding the Private Shuttle Program would also exemplify the power of the tech industry over local politics. More about this debate in this article: Tim Redmond, "Investigation: SF Gave the Google buses a 'Handshake' Pass for Years. Now Will the Violators Finally Get Tickets?," *48hillsonline*, http://48hillsonline.org/2014/02/20/investigation-sf-gave-the-google-buses-a-handshake-pass-for-years-now-will-the-violators-finally-get-tickets/, last accessed February 20, 2014, and in this one: Joshua Sabatini, "Emails Show 'Handshake Agreement' for Tech Buses Using SF Transit Stops," *The Examiner*, www.sfexaminer.com/sanfrancisco/emails-show-handshake-agreement-for-tech-buses-using-sf-transit-stops/Content?oid=2715002, last accessed February 25, 2014.
15. Anti-eviction Mapping Project's meeting, San Francisco Tenants Union, February 2014.
16. Description of the group Eviction Free San Francisco on their Facebook page: www.facebook.com/EvictionFreeSummer/info?tab=page_info.
17. Ellis Act Report by the San Francisco Tenants Union. http://tenantstogether.org/downloads/Ellis%20Act%20Report.pdf.
18. Ellis Act Report.
19. See also the map that accompanies this explanation at www.antievictionmappingproject.net/buyouts.html.
20. Smith, *The New Urban Frontier*, 23.
21. Nancy Raquel Mirabal, "Geographies of Displacement: Latina/os, Oral History, and the Politics of Gentrification in San Francisco's Mission District," *The Public Historian* 31, no. 2 (May 2009): 7–31.
22. Ibid., 17.
23. See the Internet website: http://cleanuptheplaza.com/, accessed June 8, 2015.
24. See Jennifer Rosdail's website for a description of the "quadsters" at Jennifer Rosdail, "The Quad – A Newly Defined Metahood," accessed June 8, 2015 http://jenniferrosdail.com/the-quad-is-born/.
25. Sharon Zukin, *Landscapes of Power: From Detroit to Disney World* (Oakland: University of California Press, 1993), 338.
26. The coffee shop Four Barrel is one of the only coffee shops to benefit from so much space facing its front door, allowing it to have seats and bike racks on the sidewalk. You do not need to be a consumer to sit. In other words, everyone can theoretically wander in front of it. Paradoxically enough, the mostly black population living in the projects facing Four Barrel does not wander; they generally do not even walk on the same side of the street.
27. Betabrand, on 780 Valencia Street: www.bizjournals.com/sanfrancisco/blog/2014/03/san-francisco-clothing-retailer-betabrand-makes.html.
28. Interview, Valencia Street, February 21, 2014.
29. A Berkeley study by Alexandra Goldman analyses that rents have gone up 20%

around bus stops: Alexandra Goldman, *The "Google-Shuttle Effect": Gentrification and San Francisco's Dot Com Boom 2.0*, Professional Report, Master of City Planning (Berkeley: University of California, Spring 2014). The Anti-eviction Mapping Project has revealed that evictions have risen by 69% within four blocks of the bus stops between 2011 and 2013: www.antievictionmappingproject.net/techbusevictions.html.
30. To carry the metaphor further, see the movie *Boom, the Sound of Evictions*, available online at www.youtube.com/watch?v=9FfOHVu_noY&list=PLOEIqpRJkeOB5EPygX6Y6d5z_Cx11RkUq, last accessed June 8, 2015.
31. This website gathers information about Alex Nieto's murder: http://justice4alexnieto.org/, last accessed June 8, 2015.
32. Julia Carrie Wong, "The Battle of 16th and Mission: Inside the Campaign to "Clean up" the Plaza and Build Luxury Housing," *48hillsonline*, http://48hillsonline.org/2014/03/18/battle-16th-mission-inside-campaign-clean-plaza-build-luxury-housing/, last accessed March 18, 2014.
33. Lees, Slater, and Wyly, *Gentrification*, 344.
34. Nina Eliasoph and Paul Lichterman, "Culture in Interaction," *American Journal of Sociology* 18, no. 4 (2003): 735–794.
35. See the group's website: https://evictionfreesf.org/?page_id=5, last accessed June 8, 2015.
36. This expression is used in meetings to designate the list of speakers created to facilitate the meeting. See "Taking Stacks (Meeting Facilitation Technique)," *Cultivate.coop*, http://cultivate.coop/wiki/Taking_Stack_%28Meeting_Facilitation_Technique%29, last accessed June 8, 2015.
37. Eliasoph and Lichterman, "Culture in Interaction," 735.
38. See the group's website: https://antievictionmap.squarespace.com/about/, last accessed June 8, 2015.
39. Stanford students made a San Francisco Eviction Story Map with the collaboration of Erin McElroy: www.arcgis.com/apps/MapTour/?appid=0c0a337c534146c2bf6f2fab1932eaef, last accessed June 8, 2015.
40. This group defines itself as an "open membership hackerspace interested in and working toward positive social change." See their website: https://sudoroom.org/wiki/Welcome, last accessed June 8, 2015.
41. Erving Goffman, *Frame Analysis: An Essay on the Organization of Experience* (New York: Harper and Row, 1974), 586.
42. Tilly's "repertoires of contention" refer to a set of contextual tools that groups and individuals use within social movements. Charles Tilly, *From Mobilization to Revolution* (New York: Addison-Wesley, 1978), 349.
43. Beitel, *Local Protest*, 220.
44. Interview with Rebecca Gourevitch, March 22, 2014.
45. For a complete description of the event, see the group's website: https://evictionfreesf.org/?p=1531, last accessed June 8, 2015.
46. Although a significant increase in police presence was felt during the march after the police murder of Alex Nieto, on March 21, 2014.
47. All the maps referred to are available on their website, at https://antievictionmap.squarespace.com/.
48. Interview with Erin McElroy, February 18, 2014.
49. Yi-Fu Tuan, "The City and Human Speech," *Geographical Review* 84, no. 2 (April 1994): 144–151.
50. The interactive map was released in May, 2015, www.antievictionmappingproject.net/narratives.html, last accessed June 8, 2015.
51. Rachel Brahinsky, "The Death of the City? Reports of San Francisco's Demise Have Been Greatly Exaggerated," *Boom: A Journal of California* 4, no. 2, Issue title: "San Francisco Matters" (Summer 2014): 43.
52. A description of one of them can be found in SF Gate's report: www.sfgate.com/technology/article/Tech-workers-housing-activists-clash-at-happy-5270076.php.
53. Reports are often twisted and focus on the issues rather than the bridges that already exist between the tech world and activism in San Francisco: Ellen Huet, "S.F. Tech Workers, Housing Activists Clash at Happy Hour," *SF Gate*, Updated 8:45 pm, Wednesday, February 26, 2014, www.huffingtonpost.com/rolla-selbak/sf-tech-worker-and-an-act_b_4870767.html.
54. See Erin McElroy's publications: Erin McElroy and Kelsey Gilmore Innis, "Tech Workers and the Eviction Crisis," *Model View Culture*, https://modelviewculture.com/pieces/tech-workers-and-the-eviction-crisis, last accessed February 25, 2014 and Jim Edwards, "Meet the Woman at the Heart of San Francisco's Anti-tech Gentrification Protests," *Business Insider*,

www.businessinsider.com/erin-mcelroy-and-san-francisco-anti-tech-gentrification-protests-2014–5?IR=T, last accessed May 25, 2014. For a straightforward deconstruction of the anti-tech dimension of this movement, read Erin McElroy and Tim Redmond, "There Was Never an Anti-tech Movement in SF," *48hillsonline*, http://48hillsonline.org/2015/02/17/never-anti-tech-movement-sf/, last accessed February 17, 2014.
55. See description of the proposition here: http://ballotpedia.org/City_of_San_Francisco_Transfer_Tax_on_Residential_Property_Re-Sold_in_Five_Years,_Proposition_G_%28November_2014%29, last accessed June 8, 2015
56. Gen Fujioka, "Who Really Won the SF Election?" *48hillsonline*, http://48hillsonline.org/2014/11/11/real-winners-losers-nov-4-election/, last accessed November 11, 2014.
57. Gen Fujioka, "Facing the Eviction Threat: Tenants Push Back and Slow Ellis Evictions in 2014," *48hillsonline*, http://48hillsonline.org/2015/01/04/facing-eviction-threat-tenants-push-back-slow-ellis-evictions-2014/, last accessed January 4, 2015.
58. James Tracy, *Dispatches against Displacement: Field Notes from San Francisco's Housing Wars* (Oakland: AK Press, 2014), 150.
59. Anti-Eviction Mapping Project's website, www.antievictionmappingproject.net/chiu.html, last accessed June 8, 2015.
60. See Professor Corey Cook's Twitter account: https://twitter.com/CoreyCookUSF/media, last accessed June 8, 2015.
61. Randy Shaw, "Rally at State Capitol Ignites Ellis Act Teform," *Beyond Chronicle*, www.beyondchron.org/rally-at-state-capitol-ignites-ellis-act-reform/, last accessed February 19, 2015.
62. Brahinsky, "The Death of the City?," 50.

23
A city for all?
Public policy and resistance to gentrification in the southern neighborhoods of Buenos Aires

María Carla Rodríguez and María Mercedes Di Virgilio

INTRODUCTION

In the past several years, many scholars have investigated gentrification processes in Latin American cities (Contreras Gatica, 2011; Herzer, Virgilio, María, & Rodríguez, 2015; Inzulza-Contardo, 2012; Janoschka, Sequera, & Salinas, 2014; Lopez-Morales, 2011; Nobre, 2002; Ospina, 2012; Salinas Arreortua, 2013; Sanfelici, 2007). Some papers go so far as to question the appropriateness of gentrification as a concept to explain the socioeconomic transformations seen in these cities (e.g. Jaramillo, 2007). Few papers, however, analyze the experiences of *resistance to gentrification* that Lees, Slater, and Wyly (2008) discuss in their formative textbook on the concept. The present paper examines the case of Buenos Aires, Argentina to highlight anti-gentrification actions in the Latin American context; these actions, we find, are inspired by broader urban social movements and class struggles.

We first review gentrification's limitations in accounting for contemporary transformations in Latin American cities. We also review the connection between gentrification processes and social class. Without considering this relationship, it is difficult to understand why gentrification processes are often strongly resisted by existing neighborhood residents and why such resistance must be taken seriously, rather than conceived of as "futile" (c.f. Zukin, 2010). Our analysis also accounts for the role of the state in the promotion of gentrification processes.

We focus on three neighborhoods on the South side of Buenos Aires: La Boca, Barracas, and Parque Patricios. The changes in these pericentral neighborhoods are reviewed with attention to two facets of state intervention: (1) the persistent promotion of neoliberal urban renewal policies over the last few decades and (2) the genesis and development of Law 341 and the PROGRAMA de Autogestion de la Vivienda (PAV) (Self-Managed Housing Program).

This paper draws on two lines of research developed at the Gino Germani Institute at the University of Buenos Aires. The first is a longitudinal study of urban transformations in the southern area of Buenos Aires beginning in the mid-1990s. The second is drawn from data collection on urban living conditions in the same area. Both lines of inquiry involve four dimensions: changes in the characteristics and structure of the local population, transformations in the built environment, effects of urban public policies, and shifting social dynamics (Herzer, 2010). Our approach to data collection is based on these two lines of research. The first phase of research for the present paper involved a review of official statistical information and household surveys conducted in target neighborhoods. The second phase used open and semi-structured interviews with a number of neighborhood actors (including civil servants, organization leaders and cadres, real estate agents, and employees of various state institutions). A critical mass of interviewees was

DOI: 10.4324/9781003341239-35

recruited according to the following criteria: territorial embeddedness within and actions related to their neighborhood, visibility and scope of actions within the neighborhood, and involvement in public policies – particularly the implementation of Law 341. The interview data were complemented with the ideas and reflections that emerged from activist participation in the political leadership of the Movimiento de Ocupantes e Inquilinos (MOI; Occupiers and Tenants Movement) and in cooperation with a range of community-based organizations and public agencies.

The paper is structured as follows: in the first part, gentrification is addressed as a conceptual framework, paying particular attention to the Latin American context and to understandings of resistance. Next, the paper presents an overview of the pericentral southern area of Buenos Aires, focusing on contemporary restructuring processes within these neighborhoods. The subsequent section analyses specific urban renewal policies that have contributed to gentrification processes – here we pay particular attention to conflicts around displacement. We conclude our arguments with some reflections on the nature of social movements that resist gentrification in Buenos Aires and the political possibilities they might unlock.

CONCEPTUAL UNDERSTANDINGS OF GENTRIFICATION AND ITS RESISTANCE

As Janoschka et al. (2014) point out, new regional debates on gentrification are emerging within the field of urban studies. In this field, urban renewal, revitalization, and rehabilitation are key components of conceptual understandings gentrification processes. Some authors, on the other hand, have dismissed the concept of gentrification as inadequate in certain urban and regional contexts (e.g. Jaramillo, 2007). Janoschka et al. (2014) identify four major lines of gentrification studies currently being explored in Latin America. The first deals with the symbolic dimensions of gentrification in urban spaces (e.g. commercial and tourist-driven or cultural gentrification, the renovation of historic centers, and the resignifying of cultural heritage sites; all are accompanied by special regulatory mechanisms). The second is policy-centered, highlighting the relationship between tourism promotion, revitalization actions, and gentrification. The third focuses on local real estate market dynamics, including the study of declining and gentrifying areas both in central and peripheral areas of the city and in informal, self-built, low-income neighborhoods. The fourth approach considers resistance to gentrification and the role of counter-hegemonic social urban movements, which are an important influence in many Latin American cities. This paper follows the fourth line of research, examining how the actions and strategies of grassroots organizations have limited the development and reduced the effects of gentrification in the South of Buenos Aires.

Before analyzing this resistance, we first summarize the uses and appropriations of the concept of gentrification in the Latin American context. Latin American gentrification has been associated with a wide range of urban restructuring processes and sites, namely: (1) so-called "revitalization" of cultural heritage sites in historical urban centers (Carrión, 2010; Marcadet, 2007; Paquette, 2006; Redondo & Zunino Singh, 2010); (2) transformations in pericentral residential areas where working class families and the declining industrial sector have been displaced due to rising real estate prices and the commodification of social housing (Bidou-Zacharrriasen, Hiernaux, & Rivière, 2003; Contreras Gatica, 2011; Herzer, 2012; Muñoz, 2008; Talesnik & Gutiérrez, 2002); (3) the conversion of informal settlements to suburban development in peripheral areas where policies promoting home ownership and the formalization of the rental market have led to land-title regularization and infrastructure development (Ward, Jiménez, & Di Virgilio, 2015); and (4) the growth of slums, particularly those located within consolidated urban areas (e.g. Favela Barrio in Rio de Janeiro; see Baena, 2011; Cummings, 2013, 2015). This diverse range of urban processes suggests that "gentrification is more than the colonization of housing assets by residents who own a high cultural and economic capital" (Casgrain & Janoschka, 2013, p. 24).

Glass (1964) coined the term gentrification in London during the rise of the welfare state, which was accompanied by improved living standards for large swathes of the British population but also displacement related to neighborhood upgrading. In Latin America, gentrification processes have historically been linked to the varied and conflicting spatialities of neoliberal urbanism (see Brenner, Peck, & Theodore, 2010). Our understanding of Latin American gentrification is associated with material and symbolic urban changes that have occurred since neoliberalism began in the late 1970s. In our view, the concept of gentrification cannot be applied without attention to the changes experienced by the working class in Latin America (and Argentina in particular) precipitated by global processes of neoliberalization. The effects on the Latin American working class were exacerbated by structural adjustment policies in the 1980s and 1990s. This is particularly the case in Buenos Aires, where gentrification developed in parallel to processes of economic and social restructuring.[1] In Casgrain and Janoschka's (2013, p. 23) observation:

> Neoliberal urban policies [had and] have as an objective to reestablish class controls by introducing extensive processes of *accumulation through dispossession*. At a neighborhood level, such dispossession, as well as the consolidation of class inequalities, is often materialized in gentrification processes.

Thus, in order to unpack the concept of gentrification we emphasize that the class dimension constitutes the real core of the phenomenon (Bridge, 1995, 2001; Glass, 1964; Herzer, 2010; Janoschka et al., 2014; Wacquant, 2008) and that the gentrification processes, which have resulted in the spatial eclipse of working class areas by middle- and upper-middle class people, are wrapped up in broader socio-spatial and economic transformations affecting the working class. These processes are all expressed through territorial and political disputes (Bourdieu, 2000). From the standpoint of class struggle, then, we understand gentrification in Latin America as an effect of neoliberal socio-spatial dynamics supported by variegated forms of symbolic and/or material displacement of low-income people, coupled with their exclusion from political decision-making about the future of the city (Casgrain & Janoschka, 2013).

The role of the state is prominent in the segregation and displacement of low-income people and their resources, activities, and institutions (Davidson, 2008; Díaz Orueta, 2013; Herzer, 2010; Rousseau, 2009). The state does not merely facilitate and legalize the dispossession of low-income working families, it also advances state-supported redevelopment actions through an aggressive discourse of revanchist ideology, that of "reconquering" particular urban areas for the middle classes and of revalorizing land and real estate in working class neighborhoods. The relationships between class, space, and the state constitute the wider conceptual framework within which gentrification unfolds in cities like Buenos Aires.

It is also necessary to analyze the flip side of gentrification-related state intervention: under what conditions does the state act in order to mitigate or curb gentrification's harmful effects? During the past few decades, at the height of gentrification, strong resistance has developed in many cities (Leite, 2010). Resistance has tended to revolve around the struggle for access to and control of urban spaces, as well as the uneven power dynamics among the social classes. The emergence of resistance in cities like Buenos Aires may act as a crack in neoliberal urbanism (Holloway, 2011). These emancipatory experiences include both organized struggles and many forms of micro-resistance in everyday life (see Newman and Wyly (2006) for New York; De la Garza (2014) for Barcelona; Gledhill and Hita (2014) for Salvador Bahía (Brazil); Casgrain and Janoschka (2013) for Santiago de Chile; Delgadillo (2009) for México City). Within this political climate, local governments have been forced to launch strategies to reduce gentrification-related displacement. Territorially based social movements (at least in the case of Buenos Aires) seem to play an important role in local efforts to counteract displacement.

It is important to highlight the study carried out by Newman and Wyly (2006, p. 28), which enables us to understand the geographies of anti-displacement activities. These authors sought to explain why gentrified neighborhoods in New York City do not always produce displacement, finding that "after two generations of intense gentrification, any low- and moderate-income renters who have managed to avoid displacement are likely to be those people who have found ways to adapt and survive in an increasingly competitive housing market." This is linked specifically to actions individual residents take to adapt to spikes in housing prices.

On the basis of more recent literature, it is possible to identify several types of resistance strategies:

(1) Actions driven by relatively organized grassroots collectives (De la Garza, 2014; Drissel, 2011; Gledhill & Hita, 2014; Rodríguez, 2014). In the case of Buenos Aires, as we point out later on, collectives have promoted cooperative housing management and production strategies.
(2) Presence of social services targeting vulnerable groups (DeVerteuil, 2012; Herzer, Rodriguez, Redondo, Di Virgilio, & Ostuni, 2005; Thomasz, 2010). These services include community kitchens, transit centers for homeless people, and other social centers (Finchett-Maddock, 2010), all of which tend to operate in non-commercialized buildings (i.e. public, nonprofit, and/or state-owned buildings).
(3) A variety of individual residents' strategies (Newman & Wyly, 2006), such as overcrowding, enduring high housing costs and poor housing quality, and owner-occupation. In some places, residents have organized anti-gentrification campaigns, lobbying elected officers and, in extreme cases, resorting to private property destruction. These actions constitute what we might call everyday, micro-scale resistance.
(4) Public housing initiatives to counter the effects of gentrification (Delgadillo, 2009; Guevara, 2010; Levy, Comey, & Padilla, 2006; Newman & Wyly, 2006). For example, regulating rents can be an important form of public intervention. Subsidized housing in various forms (e.g. public subsidy, federal public housing, housing vouchers, etc.) falls into this category. Inclusive zoning is also a strategy for the production of low-cost units.

Obviously, these different forms of resistance to gentrification are not exclusive of one another. On the contrary, as we shall see later, they can occur in combined and/or symbiotic ways. They may also develop at different times and scales; everyday micro-scale resistance strategies can give way to territorially based forms of organization, which may in turn precipitate state intervention in a gentrifying neighborhood.

CHARACTERISTICS OF OUR THREE CASE STUDY NEIGHBORHOODS IN BUENOS AIRES

Our observations and analysis are centered on three neighborhoods in Southern Buenos Aires: La Boca, Barracas, and Parque Patricios. La Boca is a neighborhood emblematic of the historical process through which the working class in Argentina was formed. This area developed as a working class neighborhood of European immigrants who brought to Argentina a rich history of political organizing. This influence was evident during the great Tenants' Strike in 1907. Over time, the immigrants integrated into local society, moved to other neighborhoods, and nourished the city's middle-income class consciousness. At first, La Boca's neighborhood development was strongly linked to activities of the Riachuelo Port, the center of the local economy. Between 1947 and 1991, however, La Boca lost 40% of its population; these losses accelerated during the 1970s when the port was deactivated and many local factories closed.

Barracas was also a formerly dynamic industrial neighborhood, but successive crises and the city's industrial eviction policies during the dictatorship in the late 1970s and early 1980s led to neighborhood decline. In these years, three clearly differentiated areas emerged: one is predominantly residential, the second is an industrial and services area, and the third includes the slums of Villa 21 and Zavaleta. Over the last two decades these two poor neighborhoods have experienced the fastest population growth in Barracas. Barracas is a fragmented and discontinuous urban zone, crossed by highways and railways, precarious settlements, and a complex of public hospitals that occupy approximately 17 hectares. It is here that the current city government has begun work on a new civic center.

Parque Patricios has historically been a working class area. Its economy was structured around the municipal slaughterhouses, which begun operations at the end of the 1860s and were active until the end of the nineteenth century when they moved West. A large number of subsidiary small industries accompanied the growth of slaughtering businesses (e.g. tallow factories, candles, sacks, tanneries, etc.), consolidating the neighborhood's industrial working class profile. From 7 to 14 January 1919, a general strike known as "La Semana Trágica" (The Tragic Week) took place, ending with a brutal massacre of hundreds of workers. At present, industrial activities have largely disappeared and empty warehouses are part of the landscape. The closure of the Caseros Prison toward the end of the 1990s also left several plots of land vacant – their fate remains uncertain.

These three neighborhoods comprise most of the political-administrative city area called Commune 4, which is located in the Southeast of Buenos Aires. The neighborhoods are part of the southern fringe of Buenos Aires and are adjacent to Commune 1, sharing a partial border with Commune 8 in the Southwest (see Figure 1 and Table 1). Commune 4 has 218,245 inhabitants (7.55% of the city's total population) and has seen an increase (1.3%) in the size of population between 2001(INDEC, 2001) and 2010 (INDEC, 2010). This growth has mainly resulted from an increase in the number of families who lived in slums located in Barracas and in La Boca.

According to the 2010 Census, 10.4% of the population in Commune 4 was unemployed and 10.7% was underemployed, meaning that 21.1% of its inhabitants found it difficult to integrate into the labor market (INDEC, 2010). The unemployment rate exceeds the urban average, which is 14.7%. The most significant economic activities in Commune 4 are those related to industry (tannery, road freight transportation, and chemical industries), construction and commercial activities; however, employment in services is not as great as that in other communes (GCBA, 2011). In October 2013, salaried workers in Commune 4 earned an average salary of USD $329, which is 32% less than the metropolitan area's average. Among Commune 4's workers, however, the income of 41.1% (almost double the city's average) was not sufficient to cover a basic basket of goods and services (Consejo Económico y Social de la Ciudad de Buenos Aires, 2013). The population in Commune 4 skews relatively young: 45.47% are under 29 years old, has relatively low educational levels compared to the rest of the city, and has a relatively high number of

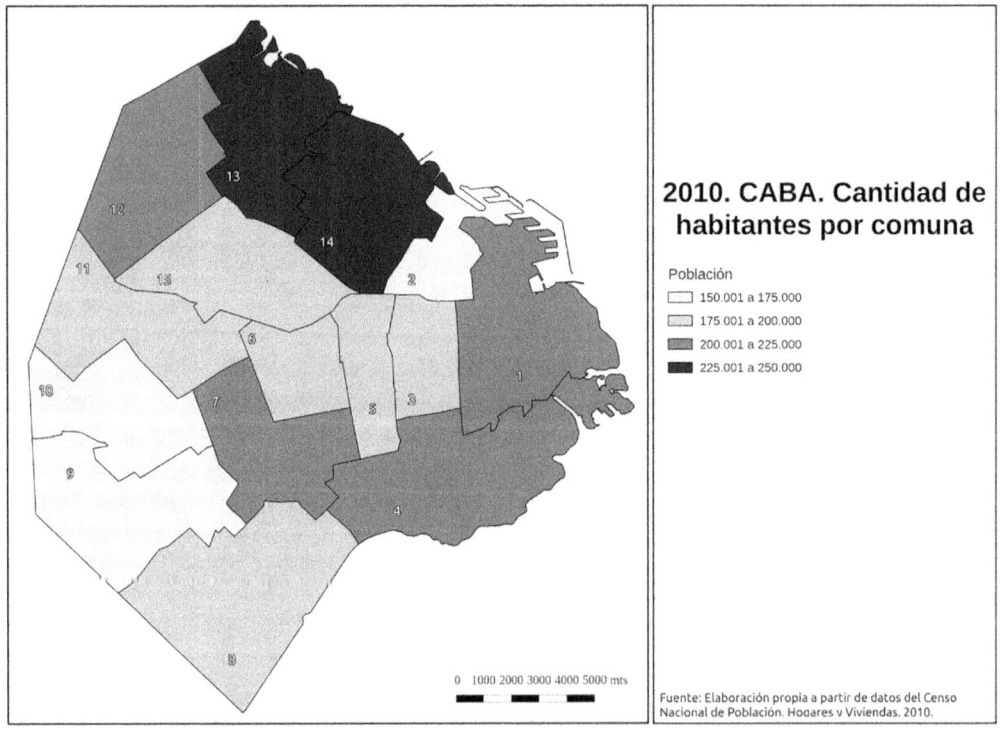

Figure 1 City of Buenos Aires by population and communes, 2013.

Source: Consejo Económico y Social de la Ciudad de Buenos Aires (2013).

Living conditions	Commune 1	Commune 4	Commune 8	CABA
Unemployment rate	7.40%	10.40%	9.60%	6.20%
Underemployment rate	9%	10.70%	8.60%	8.50%
Average middle income (in USD)	$430	$329	$317	$484
Average total household income (THI) (in USD)	$625	$628	$597	$828
Average per capita family income (PCFI) (in USD)	$400	$258	$210	$407
Income under TB	33.30%	41.10%	45.30%	23.30%
Unregistered workers	32.10%	33.50%	36.60%	26.70%
Deficitary dwelling typologies	8%	7.50%	4%	6.20%
Illegal dwelling possession regime	13.12%	14.62%	18.77%	11.67%
Overcrowding per room	18.79%	19%	23.26%	10.20%
Overcrowded dwellings due to cohabitation	4.80%	5.70%	11%	3.90%
Households with UBN	15.90%	12.66%	11.31%	6%
Dwellings with insufficient building quality	11%	8.79%	10.90%	3.36%
Households with no sewers	2.08%	3.45%	4.56%	0.99%
Households with no drinking water supply system	1.28%	0.67%	0.94%	0.41%
Households with no gas networks	17.02%	22.09%	36.37%	7.82%

Table 1 Selected living condition indicators in the more vulnerable communes of Buenos Aires, 2010.
Source: Censo Nacional de Población, Hogares y Viviendas 2010, and Encuesta Anual de Hogares 2012.

female-headed households (44%, the second largest value in the whole city) (Consejo Económico y Social de la Ciudad de Buenos Aires, 2013). These indicators illustrate that this area's working population is highly vulnerable to spikes in real estate values and to pro-gentrification urban policy implemented in these neighborhoods.

Regarding housing conditions in Commune 4, the urban layout has an elongated shape from East to West. Residential dwellings are distributed throughout all the neighborhoods. Sixteen per cent of residential buildings are abandoned (this is actually below the city's average) (Consejo Económico y Social de la ciudad de Buenos Aires, 2013). The three neighborhoods also comprise a significant stock of warehouses and factory installations, both occupied and abandoned, with a rate of 33.5% of inactive stores (2,647 buildings). In addition, 5,234 dwellings in the commune are rooms in boarding houses or tenements representing 7.51% of the commune's total dwellings, one of the highest proportions in the whole city (Consejo Económico y Social de la ciudad de Buenos Aires, 2013).

The majority of Commune 4's slums are located in Barracas. Tenement rooms define the characteristic informal habitat in La Boca, and boarding houses and squatter houses are found in all three neighborhoods. Furthermore, in Commune 4, 7.5% of households live in housing that is classified as "deficient," with 14.62% under "irregular" (non-permanent) forms of tenure, 19% in overcrowded rooms (nearly 10 percentage points over the city's mean values), and 5.7% sharing dwellings (Consejo Económico y Social de la Ciudad de Buenos Aires, 2013). A large number of households in the commune still lack basic services and, in addition, this population has been a victim of forced eviction processes that are territorially concentrated in these locations. It is estimated that during the last 4 years (2010–2014) more than 20,000 families have been evicted (Consejo Económico y Social de la Ciudad de Buenos Aires, 2013).

VULNERABILITY, GENTRIFICATION AND DISPLACEMENT THE SOUTHERN NEIGHBORHOODS OF BUENOS AIRES

Since the beginning of the 1990s, La Boca, Barracas, and Parque Patricios have been subject to urban renewal and gentrification. The transformation of the built environment in the three neighborhoods has taken place through public and, to a lesser degree, private investments (Herzer, 2010). Low-income workers are being replaced by higher-income residents; many low-income households also persist on the verge of displacement as property prices and rents continue to rise.[2]

Neoliberal urbanism has progressed in three waves: (1) a series of urban changes fostered by measures adopted by the dictatorship in the mid-1970s (forced and massive evictions from slums, liberalization of the rental market, building of motorways, and the creation of a historical conservation area); (2) urbanization beginning in the 1990s, supported by public – private projects, changes in planning and building codes, and investments in infrastructure and; (3) urban renewal during the 1990s and early 2000s in the city's southern neighborhoods. Between 1988 and 2005, successive local governments concentrated municipal construction investments in the southern area. Between 1988 and 1997, city infrastructure spending in this area increased from 6% to 15% of the total municipal budget (GCBA, 1998). In 2004, soon after the 2001 national crisis, 37.63% of the infrastructure investment of the whole city – now managed by the Centros de Gestión y Participación (Management and Participation Centres)[3] – took place in the southern area, compared with 11.61% in the northern area. By 2005 this trend had become more pronounced, as the southern area received 51.24% of the total infrastructure investment, in stark contrast with 8.25% invested in the northern area (GCBA, 2005).

Urban renewal in the southern neighborhoods was catalyzed by historical preservation projects in the city's center, the San Telmo neighborhood. The renewal work began in 1980 and continued in the urbanization plan for the coastal areas of the Río de la Plata and Riachuelo rivers during the first half of the 1990s. The 1993 restructuring of Puerto Madero into an urban area, led by a public – private corporation and supported by the national government, propelled the urban development of the coastal areas as a whole. These transformations enabled the development of new commercial uses, services, and housing for high-income groups.

In 1993, the city government of Buenos Aires launched a renewal project in La Boca centered around construction of coastal barriers. The area had been subject to recurring storm-related flooding, which curtailed the use of its coastal areas. For this project the government obtained a loan (USD$120 million) from the International Development Bank (Herzer, 2010). Coastal construction was followed by other improvements, including investments in neighborhood beautification and tourism promotion (Rodríguez et al., 2011).

In Barracas, 1990s urban renewal was driven by private firms purchasing underused industrial plots to build luxury housing complexes. More recent public investments have been similar. The administration of Mayor Anibal Ibarra, as the chief of government (1999–2007), set the basis for the neighborhood's transformation: the creation of a Metropolitan Design Centre where the Fish Market once stood, coupled with renovations of Colonia Sola, a historical social housing compound. State projects intensified during the term of Mayor Mauricio Macri, who (from 2007 onwards) promoted the transformation of several plots located under the 9 de Julio South motorways. Works carried out included installing public street lights, paving streets and sidewalks, moving fences and perimeter walls, creating bicycle lanes and ramps for the disabled, building skate ramps, installing waste receptacles, planting trees and bushes, finishing the renovation of the Music Palace (begun by Mayor Ibarra), and approving the Design District (with special tax clauses designed to attract private investment). The decision to move the civic center in 2012 and to begin works for the new city government offices were also enforced under Mayor Macri; however, his government did not complete the renovation of Colonia Sola. Private investment has grown in the middle-income and luxury rental markets, increasing density in areas such as Montes de Oca Avenue, the neighborhood's main street (Herzer et al., 2015).

Neighborhood transformation is more recent in Parque Patricios. The first state act in this direction was deactivation of the Caseros Prison in 2001. Between 2000 and 2010, a series of social services aimed at poor people, as well as other public services, were established in the neighborhood. Measures taken to promote the district's expansion include tax benefits and preferential credit rates for firms, academic organizations, and employees moving into the neighborhood (Law 2972, 2008). Changes in the local-level planning code promoted construction of high-rise buildings with exceptions to FOT (total occupancy factor) for technology-based enterprises. Future planned interventions involve promoting real estate and infrastructure ventures: offices for the private Banco Ciudad, a new Metropolitan Technology Centre, a new police station, and extensions of the Underground Line H and Metrobus toward Parque Patricios. The city government has also intervened through more cosmetic initiatives, such as the remodeling of the local park (Parque de los Patricios) and the repair of street surfaces and street lights. A new safety plan for the area, part of the strategy to attract private investment (currently USD $250 million), led to installation of surveillance cameras in public spaces. Together these projects have increased the price of land per square meter by 25% between 2008 and 2011 (GCBA, 2011).

The abovementioned changes involve the private- or state-driven substitution of previous land uses with more lucrative activities. In addition, the government's decision to relocate the city's civic center contributed to socioeconomic polarization in the southern areas of Buenos Aires. On one hand, as these renovated areas have been consolidated, the more vulnerable resident population has suffered displacement through evictions and the pressure of higher rents.[4] On the other hand, life in the nonrenovated areas has become more precarious.

RESISTANCE TO GENTRIFICATION AND DISPUTES OVER URBAN SPACE

Law 341 as housing policy

Law 341, passed in December 2000, provides soft loans from the Instituto de Vivienda de la Ciudad (IVC) (City Housing Institute) to facilitate low-income households' access to housing in the city. As a central feature, the law classifies social organizations as subjects who can receive loans; these organizations act as project-executing agencies and can receive loans to start new projects or rehabilitate and improve existing projects. The law also provides loans up to 30 years to individuals for purchase of housing. Interest rates are subsidized and range from 0% to 4%, while repayment installments for individual households cannot surpass 20% of the family income. The law does not establish minimum restrictions for loan recipients' income and does not require previous savings.

Law 341's origins are linked to social organizations and grassroots initiatives that emerged during the 1980s to lobby for low-income housing. Several grassroots social organizations played a key role in the design and implementation of this policy, namely the Movimiento de Ocupantes e Inquilinos (MOI-CTA) and the Mutual de Desalojados de La Boca (La Boca Evicted Mutual Society). Based on Article 31 of the Constitution of the Autonomous City, these organizations promoted self-managed housing plans for lower income populations. A multiactor board was founded in 1999, which included the MOI, the Mutual de Desalojados de La Boca, and the first Housing Commission of the legislature of the autonomous city of Buenos Aires. This board took up MOI's mission of cooperation, self-management, collective ownership, mutual aid, and the use of local assistance including loans to individual households. Organizations such as Comedor Los Pibes also joined this fight early on. The passage of Law 341, then, was the result of the political mobilization of low-income people at risk of eviction due to the urban renewal process that had started in La Boca (Rodríguez, 2009; Zapata, 2013).

The anti-eviction movement expanded after the 2001 crisis, bringing in a large range of organizations, social movements (including the unemployed workers movement Movimiento Territorial de Leberacion – MTL-CTA), political parties, and hundreds of squatting and tenant families. During this stage many cooperatives were organized among families living in tenements and or squatting in abandoned buildings. More recently, a network of coalitions and alliances have raised the profile of these movements, involving public university activists and intellectuals and religious organizations. Movements like MOI and MTL have formally integrated with the Argentine Workers' Central Union (CTA) and Los Pibes, which are also allied with sectors of the Workers General Confederation.

According to the Instituto de Vivienda de la Ciudad (IVC), between the passage of Law 341 and March 2012, 519 registered organizations comprising 10,101 families have been registered in the new housing programs (Zapata, 2013). By the same date 110 cooperatives (involving 2,474 families) had been able to purchase plots inside the metropolitan area (Zapata, 2013).[5] This trend indicates an effective "capture" of urban land for low-income housing within gentrifying areas. Organizations composed of low-income families were able to take advantage of the dip in real estate prices during the 2001/2002 crisis.

By the end of 2012, out of the 110 social organizations that managed to purchase plots, 15% (17 cooperatives with 565 families) finished their work, 37.2% (41 cooperatives with 902 families) reported "good" progress on their buildings, and 47% had not been able to begin renovations or construction for various reasons (Zapata, 2013) (see Table 2). Even so, the number of buildings started or completed is significant. Approximately 60% of these housing projects are located in our three case study neighborhoods (see Figure 2) and are managed by social organizations based in these areas. The most common style is small complexes of 20 to 25 units; three high-rise buildings have also been organized by MOI and MTL (Territorial Liberation Movement). The construction of this housing illustrates how Law 341 and the Self-Management Housing Program have bolstered low-income populations' ability to exercise their right to the city (Zapata, 2013).

State of works	Projects	Number of dwellings
Finished	17	565
Underway	41	902
To be started	52	1,007
Total projects	110	2,474
Dwellings with public deeds	110	2,474
Registered cooperatives	519	10,101

Table 2 Rate of progress of the Programa de Autogestión para la Vivienda (Self-Managed Housing Program), March 2012.
Source: Cecilia Zapata (2013)

Figure 2 PAV/Law 341 plots and works.
Source: Guevara (2010).

Disputes and struggles over urban space

In La Boca, Law 341 is the culmination of a long cycle of organizing stemming from the emergence of democratic political movements in 1983. During the 1980s, a neighborhood-based initiative pushed for the local government to purchase 21 tenements for low-income housing.[6] However, this initiative lacked adequate political and financial support and remained unfulfilled in 2014.

When the La Boca riverside coastal defenses were built in 1997 – a public investment designed to mitigate recurrent flooding in the area – tenement rents soared. Landlords from a number of low-income residential buildings in La Boca evicted their tenants and placed the properties up for sale. The city government, under pressure from neighborhood activists like Asamblea de Desalojados de La Boca, implemented several policies to forestall further evictions. The Asamblea families managed to purchase property in tenements and squatting buildings for use by households facing eviction. This initial action catalyzed further public investment in social housing, which eventually totaled around 130 condominiums (Guevara, 2010).

These investments expanded public housing in the area and curtailed the displacement effects of gentrification. From a political and community perspective, public investment in housing supported the fragmented, yet extensive, network of households fighting eviction (see Guevara, 2010 for a detailed account of this). Municipal property managed by the city's Housing Initiative has also provided a source of land to be used for low- and middle-income housing. It is estimated that approximately 2,500 dwellings can be built in these municipal plots (Guevara, 2010). This is quite significant in relation to the neighborhood's real estate market as a whole (approximately 11,000 dwellings in 2001) and in relation to the neighborhood's housing deficit (approximately 3,400 dwellings) (see Figure 3, Guevara, 2010).

In the Barracas neighborhood, an urban renewal zone where most residential construction is now loft-style housing for middle – high income sectors, industrial land uses coexist with housing developments managed by housing cooperatives within the framework of Law 341 (e.g. the La Fábrica, Yatay, and Los Vecinos Luchadores projects). These self-managed complexes (see Figure 4) are at present produced at a cost of USD $500/m^2; their quality and design easily compete with privately-led renovation projects. This coexistence shows that it is possible to "renew" a neighborhood without sacrificing its socially mixed composition. The plot occupied by the Pitaluga historical textile factory is a material and symbolic example of this complexity. Part of it has been renovated into the Complejo Barracas Central, a luxury complex of loft-style dwellings. The other part is occupied by the Cooperativa Autogestionaria de Viviendas La Fábrica (Self-Managed Housing Cooperative La Fábrica), of the Movimiento de Ocupantes e Inquilinos of the Central de Trabajadores de la Argentina (MOI-CTA).

The CTA MTL began its activities in Parque Patricios in 2003. With resources provided by

Figure 3 Caminito Cooperative. La Boca. Law 341. Dolmen Technical Team.

Source: Photographic survey produced by Lazarini Kaya and Cecilia Zapata in Zapata M,C, (2015)

Figure 4 Law 341. Cooperative La Fabrica – MOI. Pasaje Icalma. Barracas.
Source. Pablo Jeifetz. EPI MOI. 2015.

Figure 5 Panoramic picture of Cooperative Emetele (MTL) (Monteagudo 592, Parque Patricios).
Source: Photographic survey produced by Lanarini Kaya and Cecilia Zapata in Zapata M.C. (2015).

Law 341, a cooperative of 320 families developed housing in Barrio Monteagudo (see Figures 4 and 5). This new housing complex is a landmark for social heterogeneity, with a radio station (whose signal covers the whole city), commercial businesses, and community neighborhood programs. A paradox lies in the fact that, initially, this investment was intended to improve real estate values in the area. Disputes over the mission (i.e. focused on growth or social housing) of public investments continues. The government's allegiances can be derived from this simple fact:

while new firms moving to the neighborhood are exempt from payment of the ABL tax (public lighting and cleaning tax) for 10 years, its social housing residents have been subject to large payment increases – up to 700% – for the same tax in 2012.

CONCLUSIONS

The cases discussed in this article illustrate how conflicts over the right to the city in Buenos Aires are rooted in territorial and class struggles against the detrimental effects of gentrification. Analyzing these cases enables us to highlight the complexity and diversity of anti-gentrification social movements and alliances and conflicts among many class actors operating within constantly changing urban landscapes. Our cases document the political and material actions that have enabled low-income citizens to effectively resist displacement. Thus, we argue that class conflicts are at the root of gentrification, not only because displacement predominantly affects lower and middle-income groups, but also because resistance is carried out via collective actions by these groups.

We have described key social groups – MOI, MTL, Asamblea de Desalojados de La Boca, CTA, etc. – that carry out actions in our case study neighborhoods. These are not necessarily movements against gentrification as a phenomenon but territorially-based social movements that, facing displacement and unaffordable living costs, have redirected their actions and relationships with the local government in order to mitigate the negative effects of gentrification on their constituent groups. In short, these organizations build responses against gentrification but did not arise in reaction to gentrification. In this sense, they diverge from anti-gentrification collective action observed in places like Berlin, Barcelona, or Mexico City.

This paper highlights the effects of collaborations between local government and neighborhood-based social movements. In this sense, it contributes to understandings of the transformative possibilities of such collaborations. Our analysis of Law 341 gives a detailed account of the mechanics of resistance to gentrification-based displacement in our case study neighborhoods. Cooperative-based construction and management of social housing is a key factor in this resistance. Neighborhood-based and more universal forms of organizing against gentrification are both parts of a multilevel strategy that involves actions and alliances within Argentina and also with other Latin American populations adversely affected by neoliberal urbanism.

Our analysis has led us to agree with one of Wacquant's (2008, p. 198) key arguments:

> To build better models of the changing nexus of class and space in the neoliberal city, we need to relocate gentrification in a broader and sturdier analytic framework by revising class analysis to capture the (de)formation of the post-industrial proletariat, resisting the seductions of the prefabricated problems of policy, and giving pride of place to the state as producer of socio-spatial inequality.

To this, however, we add the following consideration about the characteristics of the urban social movements' collective and political actions and their consequences.

In Buenos Aires, the state has in the last three decades promoted neoliberal urban renewal policies in our three case study neighborhoods. Each set of policies has its own form and context, but they share an underlying theme of displacement and exclusion of low-income groups. In La Boca, this process has unfolded through the development of a tourist-oriented enclave accompanied by "historical preservation" strategies that replace residential uses with commercial ones and exclude original residents. In Barracas and Parque Patricios, the push to shift the local economy toward design industries, information technologies, communications, and logistic activities means that a new class of workers linked to these activities is moving to live and work in these neighborhoods, displacing previous residents. In our case study areas we found eviction processes with various characteristics: forced evictions (Hotel Sur in Parque Patricios), market-based evictions (people unable to afford rent increases or new residential units built for middle – high income populations or solely for investment purposes), "accidents" (fires in slums in La Boca), and, more recently, public work-based displacements (a towpath being laid in Villa 21–24).

Public – private redevelopment actions are displacing existing residents in some neighborhoods while simultaneously increasing social fragmentation in other areas in which, for the time being, development is on hold. In Barracas, this process is very important in Villa 21–24 where the population has increased due to the development of an informal rental market. In La Boca, residential buildings are highly deteriorated along the Necochea axis and the South zone of Avenida Almirante Brown. In Parque Patricios, the South – Southwest sector has followed the same path.

What is new in relation to earlier periods when nobody was talking about gentrification in Latin America? Our research shows that, in the case of Buenos Aires, resistance actions have reshaped state actions and policies (this has taken place in a democratic context radically different from evictions during the 1976–1983 dictatorship) and have operationalized social power in an organized way, sustained under a logic that is permeated with participatory democratic ideals. Urban social movements have demanded solutions through public debates that link specific policy demands to city-wide democratic ideals – for example, framing housing as a universal right for urban residents. These linkages provide our case with a distinctive character when compared with most other places; during the latest wave of global gentrification, resistance actions have declined in many cities (see for instance Lees & Ley, 2008).

Thus, on the one hand, the nature of gentrification and its resistance in Buenos Aires constitute a contradiction whose study provides for a complex analysis of contemporary neoliberalism. On the other hand, the emergence of a new form of class relations is rooted in a changing urban geography of gentrification: urban renewal, neighborhood "upgrading," evictions, and various groups' capacities to stay put coexist uneasily in one neighborhood and are rooted in common processes. Our findings contribute to a better understanding of the possibilities for – and contradictions inherent in – the development of counter-gentrification movements.

Finally, in order to context contemporary neoliberal urbanism (in macrostructural and symbolic terms) it seems more necessary than ever to counteract neoliberal forces with a struggle for the rights to the city and demands for universal access to basic goods. Regarding the latter, we do not simply mean local, universal access to a set of resources and benefits, but rather to something linked to both individual and collective subjectivities – popular, collective sovereignty over the material, and symbolic aspects that constitute urban life.

Disclosure statement

No potential conflict of interest was reported by the authors.

NOTES

1. For a detailed analysis of these issues and of their spatial impact see Kessler and Di Virgilio (2008, 2010).
2. Herzer (2012) sampled 431 low-income dwellings in La Boca between 2000 and 2008. 1.2% had changed use, 3.7% had been demolished, and 5.6% were uninhabited. In total, 54.5% of the households sampled in 2000 no longer lived on the same premises by 2008. Given the nature of the sample, it is possible to know with certainty why those families decided to migrate and where they went. Taking into account the characteristics of those who replaced them, it is clear that population displacement in La Boca is ongoing.
3. The "Centros de Gestión y Participación" (Management and Participation Centres) are local management units that have been decentralized throughout the communes in accordance with the city's constitution, which was approved in 1996. These units have elected authorities but provide only a few social and civil services.
4. Although there are no official statistics available, we estimate that 20,000 people are evicted every year in the city of Buenos Aires. This number is derived from data from the Statistics Bureau of the Civil National Court of Appeals. According to the National Court of Appeals, between 2006 and 2008, 12,661 eviction orders were started. In this period there were also increasing numbers of criminal proceedings for the offence of usurpation or squatting, in which offenders are required to vacate the premises. The Criminal and Correctional National Court of Appeals of the Federal Capital has

estimated that 1,362 such proceedings began between 2006 and 2008, and at the same time the Federal Criminal and Correctional National Court of Appeals registered 248 proceedings (Arcidiácono & Royo, 2009).
5. Even with Law 341 in place, 409 cooperatives that applied (78.8% of the total) could not advance with the purchase of plots. This illustrates the need to implement further state policies to help low-income communities gain access to urban land.
6. This was called RECUP La Boca and was a policy initiative linked to the action of professional city planners related to government spheres and with capability for the management of additional resources from international cooperation.

REFERENCES

Arcidiácono, Pilar, & Royo, Laura. (2009). Déficit habitacional y desalojos forzosos en la Ciudad de Buenos Aires: Apuntes sobre una política de expulsión y desresponsabilización. In CELS (Eds.), *Informe 2009 Derechos humanos en la Argentina* (pp. 303–331). Buenos Aires: CELS.

Baena, Victoria. (2011). Favelas in the spotlight: Transforming the slums of Rio de Janeiro. *Harvard International Review*, *33*(1), 34.

Bidou-Zacharrriasen, Catherine, Hiernaux, Nicolas D., & Rivière, Helene. (2003). *Retours en ville: Des processus de "gentrification" urbaine aux politiques de "revitalisation" des centres*. Paris: Descartes.

Bourdieu, Pierre. (2000). Efectos de Lugar. In P. Bourdieu (Director), *La miseria del mundo*. Buenos Aires: Fondo de Cultura Económica.

Brenner, Neil, Peck, Jamie, & Theodore, Nik. (2010). Variegated neoliberalization: Geographies, modalities, pathways. *Global Networks*, *10*(2), 182–222.

Bridge, Garry. (1995). The space for class? On class analysis in the study of gentrification. *Transactions*, *20*(2), 236.

Bridge, Gary. (2001). Bourdieu, rational action and the time-space strategy of gentrification. *Transactions of the Institute of British Geographers*, *26*(2), 205–216.

Carrión, Fernando. (2010). *El laberinto de las centralidades históricas en América Latina*. Quito: Ministerio de Cultura del Ecuador.

Casgrain, Antoine, & Janoschka, Michael. (2013). Gentrificación y resistencia en las ciudades latinoamericanas el ejemplo de santiago de chile. *Andamios*, *10*(22), 19–44.

Consejo Económico y Social de la Ciudad de Buenos Aires. (2013). *Diagnóstico sociohabitacional de la ciudad de Buenos Aires* [Socio-housing diagnosis of the city of Buenos Aires]. Buenos Aires: CES.

Contreras Gatica, Yasna. (2011). La recuperación urbana y residencial del centro de Santiago: Nuevos habitantes, cambios socioespaciales significativos. *EURE (Santiago)*, *37*(112), 89–113.

Cummings, Jason. (2013). *Confronting the Favela Chic* (Unpublished doctoral dissertation). Cambridge, MA: Harvard University.

Cummings, Jason. (2015). Confronting Favela Chic: The gentrification of informal settlements in Rio de Janeiro, Brazil. In Loretta Lees, Hyun Bang Shin, & Ernesto López-Morales (Eds.), *Global Gentrifications uneven development and displacement*. Bristol: Policy Press.

Davidson, Mark. (2008). Spoiled mixture: Where does state-led 'positive' gentrification end? *Urban Studies*, *45*(12), 2385–2405.

De la Garza, Muna M. (2014). *Gentrificación, resistencias y desplazamiento en España: Propuestas analíticas*. Documento de Trabajo: Contested City. Retrieved from http://contested-cities.net/workingpapers/2014/transformaciones-urbanas-y-procesos-de-gentrificacion-desde-la-resistencia-aproximaciones-un-movimiento-vecinal-en-la-barceloneta-barcelona/

Delgadillo, Victor M. (2009). Patrimonio urbano y turismo cultural en la ciudad de México. Las Chinampas de Xochimilco y el Centro Histórico. *Andamios*, *6*(12), 69–94.

DeVerteuil, Gilles. (2012). Resisting gentrification-induced displacement: Advantages and disadvantages to "staying put" among non-profit social services in London and Los Angeles. *Area*, *44*(2), 208–216.

Díaz Orueta, Fernando. (2013). Sociedad, espacio y crisis en la ciudad neoliberal. In Josepa Cucó (Ed.), *Metamorfosis urbanas. ciudades españolas en la dinámica global*. Barcelona: Icaria.

Drissel, David. (2011). Anarchist punks resisting gentrification: Countercultural contestations of space in the New Berlin. *International Journal of the Humanities*, *8*(10), 19–44.

Finchett-Maddock, Lucy. (2010). Finding space for resistance through legal pluralism: The hidden legality of the UK Social Centre Movement. *The Journal of Legal Pluralism and Unofficial Law, 42*(61), 31–52.

GCBA. (1998). *Plan urbano ambiental de la ciudad de Buenos Aires. Elementos de diagnóstico. Documento de Trabajo*. Buenos Aires: Gobierno de la Ciudad de Buenos Aires, Secretaría de Planeamiento Urbano y Medio Ambiente.

GCBA. (2005). *Programa general de acción de gobierno 2005–2007*. Buenos Aires: Gobierno de la Ciudad de Buenos Aires.

GCBA. (2011). *Informe territorial comuna 4* (Territorial report for commune 4). Buenos Aires: Gobierno de la Ciudad de Buenos Aires.

Glass, Ruth. (1964). *London: Aspects of change*. London: Mac Gibbon & Kee.

Gledhill, John, & Hita, María G. (2014). Las redes de organización popular aún pueden cambiar la ciudad? El caso de Salvador, Bahía, Brasil. In M Di Virgilio & M Perelman (Eds.), *Ciudades Latinoamericanas: Desigualdad, Segregación y Tolerancia*. Buenos Aires: CLACSO. Retrieved from www.clacso.org.ar/libreria-latinoamericana/buscar_libro_resultado.php?campo=titulo&texto=Ciudades±Latinoamericanas&imageField.x=26&imageField.y=14

Guevara, Tomás. (2010). *Políticas habitacionales y procesos de producción de hábitat en la ciudad de Buenos Aires. El caso de La Boca* (Unpublished master's thesis). Buenos Aires: Facultad de Ciencias Sociales, Universidad de Buenos Aires.

Herzer, Hilda. (2010). *Con el corazón mirando al sur: Transformaciones en el sur de la ciudad de Buenos Aires*. Buenos Aires: Espacio Editorial.

Herzer, Hilda (comp.). (2012). *Barrios al sur: Renovación y pobreza en la ciudad de Buenos Aires*. Buenos Aires: Café de las Ciudades.

Herzer, Hilda, Rodriguez, C., Redondo, A., Di Virgilio, M.M., & Ostuni, F. (2005). Organizaciones sociales en el barrio de La Boca: Cambios y permanencias en un contexto de crisis. *Estudios Demográficos y Urbanos, 20*(2), 269–308.

Herzer, Hilda, Virgilio, Di, María, M., & Rodríguez, María C. (2015). Gentrification in the city of Buenos Aires: Global trends and local features. In L. Lees, H.B. Shin, & E López-Morales (Eds.), *Global gentrifications uneven development and displacement*. Bristol: Policy Press.

Holloway, John. (2011). *Agrietar el capitalismo, el hacer contra el trabajo*. Buenos Aires: Ediciones Herramienta.

INDEC. (2001). *Censo nacional de población, hogares y viviendas*. Argentina: Instituto Nacional de Estadísticas y Censos.

INDEC. (2010). *Censo nacional de población, hogares y viviendas*. Argentina: Instituto Nacional de Estadísticas y Censos.

Inzulza-Contardo, Jorge. (2012). 'Latino gentrification'?: Focusing on physical and socioeconomic patterns of change in Latin American inner cities. *Urban Studies, 49*(10), 2085–2107.

Janoschka, Michael, Sequera, Jorge, & Salinas, Luis. (2014). Gentrification in Spain and Latin America. A critical dialogue. *International Journal of Urban and Regional Research, 38*(4), 1234–1265.

Jaramillo, Samuel. (2007). *Reflexiones sobre las políticas de recuperación del centro (y del centro histórico) de Bogotá* (Documento CEDE, 2006–40). Bogota: Universidad de los Andes.

Kessler, Gabriel, & Di Virgilio, María M. (2008). The new urban poverty: Global, regional and Argentine dynamics during the last two decades. *Cepal Review, 95*, 31–50.

Kessler, Gabriel, & Di Virgilio, María M. (2010). Impoverishment of the middle class in Argentina: "New Poors" in Latin America. *Laboratorium: Russian Review of Social Research, 2*, 200–220.

Lees, Loretta, & Ley, David. (2008). Introduction to special issue on gentrification and public policy. *Urban Studies, 45*(12), 2379–2384.

Lees, Loretta, Slater, Tom, & Wyly, Elvin. (2008). *Gentrification*. London: Routledge.

Leite, Rogerio. (2010). A exaustão das cidades: Antienobrecimento e intervenções urbanas em cidades brasileiras e portuguesas. *Revista Brasileira de Ciências Sociais, 25*(72), 73–175.

Levy, Diane K., Comey, Jennifer, & Padilla, Sandra. (2006). *In the face of gentrification: Case studies of local efforts to mitigate displacement*. Washington, DC: Urban Institute.

Lopez-Morales, Ernesto. (2011). Gentrification by ground rent dispossession: The shadows cast by large-scale urban renewal in Santiago de Chile. *International Journal of Urban and Regional Research, 35*(2), 330–357.

Marcadet, Yann. (2007). Habitar en el centro de la ciudad de México: Prácticas espaciales en la

Santa María La Ribera. *Alteridades*, *17*(34), 39–55.

Muñoz, Francisco. (2008). *Urbanalización. Paisajes comunes, lugares globales*. Barcelona: Gustavo Gilia.

Newman, Kathe, & Wyly, Elvin. (2006). The right to stay put, revisited: Gentrification and resistance to displacement in New York City. *Urban Studies*, *43*, 23–57.

Nobre, Eduardo A. (2002). Urban regeneration experiences in Brazil: Historical preservation, tourism development and gentrification in Salvador da Bahia. *Urban Design International*, *7*(2), 109–124.

Ospina, Natalia. (2012). *A quién pertenece el centro histórico de Santa Marta? Análisis sobre la recuperación del centro histórico*. Entre los Discursos Hegemónicos y las Desigualdades Sociales (Unpublished master's thesis). Buenos Aires: Facultad de Arquitectura y Urbanismo, Universidad de Buenos Aires.

Paquette, Catherine. (2006). Des habitants pour le centre historique? Mexico face à i'un des défis majeurs de la réhabilitation. In H. Rivière d'Arc & M. Memoli (Eds.), *Vivre dans le centre des villes, un pari urbain en Amérique Latine*. París: Armand Colin.

Redondo, Adriana, & Zunino Singh, Dhan. (2010). El Entorno Barrial. La Boca, Barracas y San Telmo. Breve Reseña Histórica. In Hilda Herzer (Org.), *Con el Corazón Mirando al Sur. Transformaciones en el Sur de la Ciudad de Buenos Aires* (pp. 97–117). Buenos Aires: Espacio Editorial.

Rodríguez, María C. (2009). *Autogestión, políticas del hábitat y transformación social*. Buenos Aires: Espacio Editorial.

Rodríguez, María C. (2014, April). *Estado, clases y gentrificación. La política urbana como campo de disputa en Tres Barrios de ciudad de Buenos Aires*. Coloquio Internacional: Perspectivas del Estudio de la Gentrificación en México y América Latina, Instituto de Geografía, UNAM, México, DF.

Rodríguez, María C., Mejica, Arqueros, Soledad, Rodríguez, María, F., Gómez Schettini, Mariana, & Zapata, María C. (2011). La política urbana "PRO": Continuidades y cambios en contextos de renovación en la ciudad de Buenos Aires. *Cuaderno Urbano*, *1*(1), 81–101.

Rousseau, María. (2009). Re-imaging the city centre for the middle classes: Regeneration, gentrification and symbolic policies in "Loser Cities". *International Journal of Urban and Regional Research*, *33*(3), 770–788.

Salinas Arreortua, Luis A. (2013). Gentrificación en la ciudad Latinoamericana. El caso de Buenos Aires y ciudad de México. *Geographos*, *4*(44), 281–305.

Sanfelici, Daniel de Mello. (2007). Urbanismo neoliberal e gentrificação: As políticas de revitalização do centro de Porto Alegre/RS. *Ciência Let*, *41*, 188–203.

Talesnik, Daniel, & Gutiérrez, Alejandro. (2002). Transformaciones de frentes de agua: La forma urbana como producto estándar. *Eure*, *28*(84), 21–31.

Thomasz, Ana G. (2010). Debajo de la alfombra de los Barrios del sur. Derecho a la ciudad o nuevas formas de higienismo. *Intersecciones En Antropología*, *11*(1), 15–27.

Wacquant, Loic. (2008). Relocating gentrification: The working class, science and the state in recent urban research. *International Journal of Urban and Regional Research*, *32*(1), 198–205.

Ward, P. M., Jiménez, H. E., & Di Virgilio, M. M. (2015). *Housing policy in Latin American cities: A new generation of strategies and approaches for 2016 UN-Habitat III*. New York: Routledge.

Zapata, María C. (2013). *El programa de autogestión para la vivienda: El ciclo de vida de una política habitacional habilitante a la participación social y del derecho al hábitat y a la ciudad* (Documentos de Jóvenes Investigadores, 36). Buenos Aires: Instituto de Investigaciones Gino Germani. Retrieved from http://webiigg.sociales.uba.ar/iigg/textos/documentos/dji36.pdf

Zapata, M. Cecilia. (2015). *De los programas 'llave en mano' a los programas por autogestión. Un análisis de los modos de producción de vivienda de interés social en la Ciudad de Buenos Aires* (Tesis doctoral). Buenos Aires: Facultad de Ciencias Sociales, Universidad de Buenos Aires.

Zukin, Sharon. (2010). *Naked city: The death and life of authentic urban places*. Oxford: Oxford University Press.

24
When art meets monsters

Mapping art activism and anti-gentrification movements in Seoul

Seon Young Lee and Yoonai Han

1. INTRODUCTION

Commercial gentrification, which is "the gentrification of commercial premises or commercial streets or areas" (Lees, Slater, & Wyly, 2008, p. 131), has become a social issue over the last couple of years in South Korea (hereafter Korea). Commercial gentrification is closely connected with residential gentrification, since commercial gentrification takes place to cater to the newcomers' tastes and preferences (Bridge & Dowling, 2001; Ley, 1996; Zukin et al., 2009). The phenomenon defined as commercial gentrification in Korea seems rather different from that in the West, since the term has emerged in Korea as a buzzword to describe the deepening social conflicts between tenants and landlords surrounding the Commercial Building Lease Protection Act (Lee, 2016). Commercial gentrification in Korea has been shaped by the social and spatial transformations whereby neighbourhoods serving local needs become hotspots for shopping, dining, and art, and the pioneers (who play a crucial role in the initial transformations), as well as residents, are displaced by franchised shops armed with big capital because of the extreme commercialisation and rising rent (Lee, 2016). As the impact of commercial gentrification has grown extensive, the social conflict surrounding displacement is being intensified.

In comparison with the previous anti-gentrification movements in Korea (mainly concerning residential gentrification), more recent actions have seen the use of creative resistance strategies, since many artists take part in them. Anti-gentrification movements led by artists have become stronger and have been pushing the state to come up with solutions and preventative measures. In particular, Takeout Drawing's (hereafter TOD) anti-gentrification movement has become a beacon for later anti-gentrification movements. TOD was both an art gallery and a café in Hannam, Seoul. It has provided an exhibition and working space to artists, including those in early careers, attracting many visitors.

However, TOD received considerable attention after it started protesting against the property owner – a well-known K-pop singer PSY – who wanted to evict it (Kirk, 2015). TOD squatted in the café and remained there for about one year from 2015 to 2016, ultimately succeeding in its large mobilisation of activists and public attention by practising novel forms of activism. Many artists took part in the TOD protest, holding several different types of cultural activities, drawing sustained support from artists and citizens. The success of TOD may be considered an atypical case in the Korean urban context, where desires for redevelopment backed up by speculative capital often override the rights to stay put. Even after TOD's success, many people in gentrifying areas still struggle to maintain the right to stay put. Many of them are likely to fail in their fights against gentrification. However, TOD's struggle has contributed to the expansion of the anti-gentrification movements, by framing the growing displacement of commercial tenants in Seoul as a legacy of historically exploitive gentrification. This small but powerful shift in urban politics brought by TOD shows how persistent pressure from the grassroots level has brought about social change, as Logan and Molotch (1987, p. 296) emphasised:

People can capture control over the places in which they live and critically judge the value of what they make and the community conditions under which they produce it by doing this consistently over time and place, diverse urban people can together build better lives.

Since creative resistance with social collaboration makes a difference to how cities are produced and consumed (Pinder, 2008), the importance of culture in social movements has been explored in the West (Baumgarten, Daphi, & Ullrich, 2014). More specifically, social and artistic practices have been studied under the names of cultural activism (Buser, Bonura, Fannin, & Boyer, 2013; Verson, 2007), artivism (Poposki, 2011), art activism (Groys, 2014) and creative resistance (Novy & Colomb, 2013). Also, substantial literature examines the artistic forms of resistance and their effects on urban politics in East Asia (e.g. Krischer, 2012; Kee, Kim, & Lee, 2014; Chang, 2016; Luger, 2016, 2017).

Upon reflecting on ongoing discussion into the relationship between art and the city, this paper sheds light on the evolution of art activism against gentrification and its potential in Korea. This paper raises two questions: how are the art activists responding to the increasingly exclusive urban changes brought be commercial gentrification? And how are the grounded practices of art activism are forging an interaction with institutionalised politics? The TOD protest in Seoul is used to investigate the questions.

The methodological approach to study the case of TOD's art activism includes 1.5-year ethnographic observation and in-depth interviews with major actors in the movement. Ethnographic observation from late 2015 to early 2017 allowed us to fly in and out of the boundary among researchers, activists and local residents. By staying rooted at the site of struggle, we could explore how the concepts in urban social movement and gentrification take shape from concrete spaces and everyday practices. Participatory observation in art performances, film festivals, researchers residency, and weekly breakfast meetings where recent issues were discussed allowed a nuanced understanding of the potentials and limitations of the activism. One experimental form of participatory observation we attempted was 'Disaster Lab' formed in January 2016 at the site of struggle. Disaster Lab was formed by a group of artists, cultural activists, journalists and researchers, who gathered to archive the neighbourhood changes, to draw public and media attention to the issue and to seek resolution of the dispute. This platform enabled us to carefully examine the various participants' responses to gentrification, a commonly perceived threat to TOD and their own lives. Interviewees were selected after the ethnographic observation and the resolution of the conflict. Mapping how the protests grew, we identified 12 key informants who significantly contributed to the movement's outreach: 3 musicians, 1 filmmaker, 1 cultural activist, 1 play writer, 1 novelist, 1 visual artist, 1 performing artist, 1 photographer, 1 designer and 1 community activist. These informants provided vivid accounts on how they experienced and responded to gentrification throughout TOD struggle.

To achieve the research aim, the next section discusses contestation regarding urban space and artists. The third section explores the formation and mobilisation of anti-gentrification coalitions by TOD, paying attention to how the activism expanded beyond the reach of conventional urban social movement. The fourth section examines the transformation process of TOD as an unfortunate tenant into an active subject of anti-gentrification movement. It then shows the shifting political landscape of public and policy discourses on gentrification and art activism in Korea. The final section summarises the research findings with regard to the research questions. Lastly, it discusses the meaning and implications of creative resistance by TOD, and outlines this paper's contribution to wider research.

2. SHIFTING SPATIALITIES OF ANTI-GENTRIFICATION MOVEMENT IN KOREA

Lloyd and Clark (2000) defined a city as an entertainment machine, where culture, art and the creative industry are increasingly becoming more crucial to urban economic growth. Cultural consumption and production are especially vital in the post-Fordist economy and it is spatialised as a "neo-bohemia" (Lloyd, 2002, p. 518). Culture and art have succeeded in developing a creative industry that transforms cities into hotspots that attract more people. As this industry has positively rebuilt cities' image and facilitated investment, governments have acknowledged that artists and culture are essential catalysts for urban regeneration (Mathews, 2010). As a result of the policy solution (Rossi, 2019), culture-led and art-led urban regeneration have become important in public policies. However, this often causes gentrification, which is "a key aspect of the entertainment machine, creating amenity-rich neighborhoods for affluent urban residence" (Lloyd & Clark, 2000, p. 16). Artists and entrepreneurs with distinctive cultural tastes seeking cheap rent and spacious living and working quarters are viewed positively since new galleries and shops are a sign of regeneration (Zukin et al., 2009). However, they are criticised for eroding the cultural authenticity and identity of the neighbourhood (Peck, 2005), and for the "commodification of cultural milieu" (Zukin, 1989). In this process, artists and cultural producers play a role as gentrifiers in the beginning, but they are then displaced by a more affluent "creative class" later on (Florida, 2003), as criticised by critical academics and activists (Rossi, 2019).

Likewise, gentrification represents how urban conflict can be triggered by changes to the socio-spatial structure, as only a few people gain wealth and power, while the majority of people are excluded from their workplaces and homes. Therefore, displacement galvanises people into action and citizens are mobilised to react to social conflicts through partaking in protests in the hope that a solution to their problem will be found. This grassroots mobilisation is a form of urban social movement (Castells, 1983) – a crucial challenger to urban politics when its ability to meet citizens' demands has been lost. To make USMs successful, it is crucial to obtain support from the wider society. The intersection between art and activism can make a difference to how a society and its individuals respond to displacement, eviction and gentrification through an unconventional form of resistance. Art activism reveals the roots of people's socio-spatial problems through its more radical approach to addressing them and enables us to imagine solutions. It seems minor, but results in significant changes via the butterfly effect (Verson, 2007, p. 177).

Locating art activism in the shifting urban politics of Seoul's gentrification allows a contextualised understanding of the coalition of business tenants and artists as emerging subjects of resistance. Residential displacement resulting from large-scale housing (re)development was dominant mode gentrification took in Korea during the 1980s–1990s (Lee, 2018; Shin & Kim, 2016). Housing tenant evictees were, therefore, major actors in anti-gentrification movement, despite that the use of the term gentrification arrived much later. Business tenants became pivotal actors when the profit rate of housing (re)development decreased, leading speculative capital to turn to commercial redevelopment in city centre (Lee, 2016). In this vein, gentrification in Korea is less a single product of public policy recipes that mobilise art and culture for urban regeneration, than a historical construct of a rising form of gentrification centred on commercial redevelopment. The conflict between business tenants and landlords in city centre Seoul can be thus understood as a geographic manifestation of transforming urbanisation process of Korea.

Commercial gentrification became a new nexus of speculative capital and urban social movement. Yongsan incident, where 5 evictees and 1 police were dead during the forced eviction in 2009 (Kim, 2010), marked the symbolic moment. A business tenants association (Business Owners Association for Doing Business with Peace of Mind) was created in 2013 to resolve the problems resulting from unequal lease agreement and organise the struggle of commercial tenant. Expressing commercial tenants' concerns in an organised fashion unlike in the past, the association gained public recognition. Legitimacy and authenticity of struggles for business tenants right are often questioned even by some progressive activists because business tenants are imagined to be 'middle class' and therefore not as vulnerable as housing tenants. However, the vulnerability of business tenants (Tamura, 2014) is deepening by the flux of speculative capital into low-rise, low-density, old housing areas (Kim, 2010) and affected commercial areas in city centre.

Displacement occurs at a faster pace in commercial gentrification due to the relatively small size of units displaced and costs for forced evictions when needed, giving less space for tenants to respond. Collective action is difficult when displacement results from an individual dispute between a tenant and a landlord, despite that eviction became rampant in the city. Moreover, unlike the law and policy improvement, albeit incomplete, housing tenants made through protests over the last decades (Lee, 2019; Shin, 2018), commercial tenants right has gained less attention in public and policy discourse since the severity was widely recognised in the late 2000s. Since the business tenants do not have many alternatives and access to compensation packages[1] (Lee, 2014). In sum, business tenants struggle from huge rent increase and tenure insecurity in spite of sparse academic and political attention.

The unlikely coalition of business tenants and artists in USM points to the most vulnerable class in commercial gentrification. A brief reflection of Duriban protest in 2010 helps understand how business tenants and artists together recognised rent increase and forced eviction as threats to life, and formed a coalition. Duriban protest became a reference point and motive for many art activists partaking in TOD's resistance in 2015. An attempt to evict Duriban, a noodle restaurant run by a novelist in Hongdae, Seoul, prompted musicians' resistance against the controversial redevelopment[2] (Kee et al., 2014; Ok & Kim, 2013). Independent musicians whose culture prospered in the Hongdae area during the late 1990s and 2000s joined the protest to support Duriban. Frustrated musicians participated, identifying themselves as the same victims of displacement in Hongdae, where the neighbourhood's vivid live music culture and local restaurants were fading away in favour of consumption space for tourists in the mid-to late-2000s. Movements in TOD and Duriban are paradigmatic of emerging anti-gentrification art activism in Seoul in that protesters at the two sites shared a collective identity: in both cases, the participants were both artists and business evictees, whose fate was shaped largely due to urban redevelopment.

Accordingly, USMs, where artists influenced or were influenced by gentrification, will be examined closely. We suggest art activism can offer a new way to understand anti-gentrification movement in Korea, as they are calling into question the fundamental democracy and growing injustice in urban (re)development process. Democracy and justice have been arduously defended over decades, taking different spatialities throughout Korean urbanisation and industrialisation. We use this case study to explore the spatiality activism has taken in the deepening gentrification in city centre Seoul. In doing so, TOD's resistance is located in the historical path of art activism in Seoul not only for its use of art practices as a mode of protest, but also for its political concerns for rights to urban spaces.

3. RISE OF ARTISTS AS POLITICAL SUBJECTS IN TAKEOUT DRAWING ACTIVISM

This section examines how TOD prompted a city-wide mobilisation of various art activists to the resistance. Then it identifies who were involved, and suggests how the overarching framing of gentrification as a threat to 'self-generation', crucial to sustaining life as independent artists prompted the activism. By 'self-generation' threatened by rising rent, TOD activists meant the status of being able to produce art without relying on capitals in art market or financial support of the government, a particularly challenging task for emerging artists. Despite challenges, in 2010 the longstanding commitment of TOD to create a self-generated art space reached a viable of model a café and an art space combined. In this way, TOD could provide working space for emerging and established artists and nurturing escape from public subsidy and giant capital. TOD seemed to carry out the self-generation project successfully only until when the tenancy contract was put to an end by the landlord in 2015. The more visitors TOD attracted, the faster the rent increased and the landlord soon asked to vacate the property. The building was sold twice after TOD opened its space in 2010, when the first landlord guaranteed prolonging of the tenancy contract for at least 15 years. Later a new landlord bought the building in 2012 and attempted to evict TOD to contract with a chain café. The attempted eviction, which mobilised hired private security, caused public anxiety and brought together activists from across the city. The termination of tenancy and eviction attempts imposed substantial limitations to sustaining the project, resonating among artists who were exposed to the same threat in other places in the city.

Regarding the growing presence of art activism in urban politics, the location of TOD, Hannam, fell outside the conventional spatiality of USM. It was neither a public square where conventional protests take place, nor the most distressed neighbourhood where mega construction projects come in and followingly traditional anti-eviction protests take place. It is worth noting a mixed geographic context of Hannam, to understand how the specific location helped to mobilise a wide range of art activists, who otherwise would not have participated in a social movement. One geographic part of the Hannam is known as one of the most affluent neighourhoods in Seoul with upmarket detached houses, and Leeum, Samsung Museum of art which boasts the most prominent contemporary and Korean traditional collection of art as a private gallery. Across the street, on the other hand, the other part of Hannam is marked by multiple household-occupied houses, lower floors of which are being increasingly transformed into small experimental and cultural consumption spaces. Standing at the borderline of the wealthiest and the fast-changing neighbourhoods, TOD could draw both classical middle-class cultural consumers and more exploratory, creative minds looking for alternative art and lifestyle.

The particular geographic context contributed to keeping TOD's project by making its space recognised as an alternative art space. The relatively affordable rent was also helpful in continuing the self-generation project. However, the low-rise, relatively old buildings of Hannam became attractive not only to art spaces but also to speculative capital that sought outlets for investment, which in the past, centred on residential (re)development (Shin, 2016). Hannam soon became a symbolic place of commercial gentrification, where many small creative producers that initiated this neighbourhood change were displaced or put under threat of displacement (Kim & Lee, 2018). For the first time in Hannam, TOD spoke up against widespread displacement in the neighbourhood and turned its space into a basecamp for resistance (Figure 1). cause delay[3] in eviction and to protect activists.

An unlikely assemblage

The objective of building a 'boundless' land claimed by TOD conveys the key characteristics of its activism. As an art space and café, TOD aimed to create 'a boundless land where anything we imagine can be built' (Figure 1). TOD accommodated a wide range of activists, artists, researchers, and local media who questioned the current injustice of commercial tenant laws, demolition and eviction and the increasingly exploitive form of gentrification. Instead of producing one unified voice – that often becomes an uppermost, unbreakable goal in conventional USM – the participants gradually developed agendas via meetings and endless performances and exhibitions. Staying boundless becomes particularly challenging

Figure 1 TOD in August 2016

(Courtesy of the author).

at a site of anti-eviction movement, where the private security team or namely, 'eviction team' can take on their job[4] as early as 5 a.m. to deal with the least number of protesters. The rampant eviction practices generate fear among protesters, leading to the hiring of a counter defense measure. After two eviction attempts that caused injury, a performance artist built an iron column at TOD's entrance so that the door[5] cannot fully open, letting in the private securities. A designer group offered furniture that can be erected as a barricade to of the physical barricade and social boundlessness kept the activism intact for over one year.

> "Emerging and established musicians shared a sentiment that gentrification destroyed the independent music scene in Seoul. This sentiment could bridge the musicians to TOD's activism. Inviting the musicians to the Great Asylum, I wanted TOD to become the next Duriban."
>
> (Interview with a musician in July 2016)

Participants included 247 individuals and groups. In terms of the growing participation, we identified and interviewed several core actors. Indie musicians played a notable role in gaining broader support from artists, activists and the general public. Film festivals and public talks helped to keep the site 'boundless' to a large extent, by drawing non-activist, non-artists crowds. When interviewed, most core actors identified themselves as having previous experiences in art activism related to urban issues. Those who identified TOD as their first site of activism, later carried on to other sites, using social relationships made at TOD. A detailed description of the growing role art activism plays at other sites of struggle is beyond the scope of this case study's observation, though symbolic cases are briefly introduced in the next section.

Agendas were built through interactions at breakfast meetings, Disaster Lab, and a multitude of art and culture events held from March 2015 to April 2016. Anti-gentrification was an overarching agenda. What gentrification meant, however, was translated into different life experiences of the participants. For indie musicians, gentrification meant rent increase of affordable stages to nurture emerging musicians.

For business tenants, it meant a direct threat to livelihoods. Young residential tenants who were leading a housing stability movement, identified the 'monstrous' gentrification with their everyday lives, where they were pushed towards basements and rooftop rooms at the outskirts of the city. Culture activists interpreted gentrification as cultural degradation, in favour of corporate chain stores. Some participants had only limited knowledge of what gentrification or displacement meant. However, they joined the movement because they sympathised with close friends or neighbours who unwantedly had to leave for more affordable houses or shops. Despite different vocabularies used, a sense that gentrification was shaking the ground of livelihood and social relations prompted their participation.

4. 'SOCIAL DISASTER', AND THE CHANGING LANDSCAPE OF ANTI-GENTRIFICATION IN SEOUL

Put simply, TOD transformed the tenant-landlord conflict into a social issue. It is a meaningful transformation in Seoul's urban politics, where business tenant displacement and forced eviction in commercial gentrification are too often seen as personal conflicts. TOD situated the seemingly personal conflict within profit-centred urban development and among broadly marginalised inhabitants whose rights were underserved. This section examines the transformation process mainly through focusing on the art activists' efforts to socialise the issue and as a result, the changing political landscape of anti-gentrification movement in the city.

Despite their previous experiences of displacement, the directors of TOD were reluctant to "[let] everyone know that the gallery artists were actually rent-paying tenants". Instead, they chose to "silently leave" every time they were pressured to close down their business and move out. Whenever their experiment of alternative art production settled down, the same situation repeated for the last eight years. This time and for the third time they were asked to leave, TOD directors realised that it was not a mere series of coincidence. Displacement was deriving neither from a particularly unethical landlord nor from a lack of effort. Rather TOD began to weave different forms of displacement of their own and many other vendors, artists and residential tenants into the fabrics of profit-led urban (re)development.

"We decided to speak out at last. Neighbours were silently disappearing, but we did not know. We were blind. Most artists feel ashamed to talk about it. Being evicted as a tenant is nothing to be proud of [. . .] Now we clearly see, this is gentrification, a social disaster. We will record this barbarity as a legacy of the city by all means and by art's means [. . .] Artists say it hurts when it hurts."

(Director of TOD, Hannam Forum in June 2016)

'Social disaster' was used as a metaphor for the rampant violence in commercial gentrification as well as 'legacy of the city', 'monstrous gentrification', and 'urban refugees'. The metaphors were shared and interpreted into different art practices by the participants. The following examples are illustrative of the process where emerging or established artists, journalists, and researchers, including those who had never attended any social movement became active proponents. 'The Great Asylum' music festival held in December 2015 brought particular attention from artists who identified themselves as 'urban refugees' displaced from other neighbourhoods of the city[6] A live octopus was used at a live performance as a metaphor for unleashed speculative capital that flows into the city. In the performance, the octopus destroyed not only miniaturised tenants, but also private security forces and eventually the whole neighbourhood. 'Disaster Lab' was created. Researchers Residency, one of the last residency programmes TOD could host before closing down, went on for two months to archive the activism and neighbourhood changes. 'The Ordinary Scene', a photography exhibition was held at City Hall and National Assembly, displaying photographs made during two years of TOD's struggle. The exhibition resonated with how forced eviction became a 'familiar sight' (Kim, 2010) in the speculative city. All these interpretations were not a neatly organised outcome directed by an elite curator or a heroic political leader. Rather, they can be understood as a constellation of social discontent freely expressed in the most achievable ways.

"Conventional urban social movements emphasised having one united voice to efficiently achieve political goals. Other voices were muted in 'square politics' settings. Unlike them, art activism in the 2000s and 2010s is coming into everyday life. Different people are angry for different reasons, and everyday life becomes sites of struggle. I see TOD as one of the platforms that allow different ways to produce voices in our society."

(Interview with a filmmaker in June 2016)

With the constellation in mind, TOD's activism can set forth a way to better understand the changing political landscape of anti-gentrification movement in Seoul. Art activists' voice for the right to stay put continued to echo after TOD activism. In the ongoing efforts, art activism has drawn political attention beyond the confines of many meaningful but rather unnoticed anti-gentrification movements. Recent actions taken by politicians and following public debates are illustrative of the landscape change. A forceful eviction attempt made by the landlord and hired private security group was stopped though temporarily when a National Assembly member visited the site (the Kyunghang Newspaper 7 July 2016). Likewise, a site visit by Park Won-soon (Dong-A Ilbo, 18 May 2016), the mayor of Seoul Metropolitan Government nullified an uncompromising demolition of a neighbourhood. Both cases involved art activists claiming the right to stay and generated a heated public debate on the legitimacy of current mode in urban redevelopment.

Public discussions were centred on whether it is just to give authority to a private developer to collect residents consent and make a decision. Debates were in part inspired by the fact that earlier decisions made among individuals were repealed by influential political figures' command, taking immediate effects. Taken together, artists-led anti-gentrification activism invoked questions on fundamental democracy of urban redevelopment driven by speculative desires, capitals, and a lack of legitimate process.

At the policy level, growing art activism led to discussions among policymakers and urban practitioners on how to protect business tenants from forced eviction and the Commercial Building Lease Protection Act arguably skewed in favour of landlords. Local governments created ordinances to prevent gentrification (The Kyunghyang Newspaper, 13 July 2017). A bill for amendments to the Commercial Building Lease Protection Act is pending at the National

Assembly (Hankyeoreh 11 July 2018). Timely policy responses were made possible by art activists who prompted instant media reactions and therefore elevated public awareness. It is noteworthy how policy, media, and public attentions fall outside the reach of the conventional urban social movement. Business tenants were particularly distant from tenants right movements. While residential tenants were seen as victims of barbaric urbanisation project and legitimate subjects to claim rights, personal morality or unprofessional business were easily blamed in commercial displacement. The same engine for residential and commercial displacement, albeit in different forms was made visible, through the achievement of TOD's art activism. To describe TOD activism as the one and only driving force for the change might be too linear. However, art activists are shaking the unchallenged engines for speculative urbanisation, creating a meaningful political moment for a coalition.

Notwithstanding the rising hopes and concerns, further practices and conceptualisations remain to be carried out. Clear articulation of what 'collective rights' implies in anti-gentrification movements is one such task left for future art activists. Heterogeneous social groups or individuals with diverse interests are identifying themselves to be 'antigentrification' activists asserting their right to urban spaces. Correspondingly, questions on whose rights are to be advocated in resistance movements are being raised. As the rights claimed by small-business-owning tenants and those of artists can conjoin, intersect, or even collide in messy urban reality, specifying and reconciling different rights subjects will be necessary in future USMs. Conciliating the existing gap between discourses on rights and actual laws/policy would follow. Also, though TOD's exceptionally successful tenant resistance movement empowered other artists and activists, it is worth pointing out that the resolution of the conflict was partially made possible as a result of hierarchical power. Here, by hierarchical power, we mean mass media, legalism, and politically elites whose decisions can be put into force immediately. The resolution for TOD came only after the story was widely broadcasted across the media. In the end, art activists' demands were translated into legal terms by lawyers on behalf of both tenants and landlords. The fact that violent evictions could only be stopped by politicians' visits flags up a problem: that civil society lacks a democratic channel for conflict resolution. Without such a channel, one success story of resistance might not be duplicable elsewhere in a city. The risk of leaving the political responsibility of resolution at the hands of heroic, elite politicians is clear: the voices of political subjects in everyday struggle are left unheard, notwithstanding the meaningful spirit the activism leaves. How to reorient the fundamental process of urban transformation from mundane politics, therefore, remains a future challenge both for site-specific art activism and state institutions.

5. CONCLUSION

The aim of the paper has been to explore how art activism is transforming the urban politics surrounding commercial gentrification in Seoul, through the case of Takeout Drawing. In doing so, we addressed two shifting relationships between art and resistance with regard to gentrification in Seoul: art as a form of resistance to the emerging form of commercial gentrification, and the evolving interplay between the grounded practices of art activism and institutionalised politics. The empirical and theoretical contributions and a point of further investigation are summarised as follows.

First, drawing on our ethnography, we examined how the practices of art activism mobilised various political subjects, unsatisfied by the lack of democracy in urban transformation process, under the over-arching concerns of gentrification. We identify that generating a collective resistance against commercial gentrification is a particularly meaningful outcome of TOD activism, given the current political landscape of gentrification in Seoul. Unlike residential gentrification which is recognised as a threat for life, the political discourse in commercial gentrification is dominated by a widespread narrative on conflicts within middle class – where landlords and business-owning tenants are the main subjects. In this social setting, raising voices as commercial tenants is easily framed as class egoism, while artists are pictured as bystanders or pioneers of gentrification. Against the back-drop of the usual accounts, findings from TOD suggest how art activism can bring together diverse social actors to claim democratic controls over the increasingly exclusive form of commercial gentrification. The coalition evolving around the commercial gentrification opens a space for further theorisation of the shifting spatiality of gentrification in Seoul and accordingly, the reorganisation of political subjects.

Second, the paper contributes to the discussion on the relationship between the site-specific urban social movements and state institutions. Despite the growing intersections between the two forces, there has been an absence of empirical examinations on how grassroots activism and central politics interact in concrete reality. This lack was particularly significant in studies of commercial gentrification, given how the debates have been ignited by a series violent evictions since the late 2000s in Seoul, as outlined in the paper. In this paper, we attempted to respond to this lack by describing how TOD activism encountered and practically used the existing state institutions to bring attention to the struggle. At the same time, we pointed out the potential risk of appealing to the existing institutions or elite politicians with good wills in resolving disputes. Instead, we suggest that a democratic process in which grounded practices form an equally important political channel should be ultimately carved out. This last point marks one of the key challenges art activism faces its struggle against gentrification.

What needs more exploration in future research in art activism and gentrification would be how activism is instrumentalised as a means for making institutional/legal changes. More specifically, the effect of art activism tends to be 'measured' in terms of legal changes, namely, how many years of tenant protection were prolonged in commercial tenant law, or what legal initiatives were introduced at the National Assembly, provoked by the activism. Amendment in laws that prioritise property owners and growth interest over the ordinary people's right to stay put is necessary. However, it should be noted that provoking the sense of collective controls from everyday life politics is another form of social improvement that anti-gentrification movement has brought. For example, a Starbucks coffee shop opened after TOD vacated the space. Does this outcome render TOD's hard-fought struggle for the right to stay put void? Our sense is that the task of reimagination on gentrification-related urban politics can take shape only through the ceaseless grounded efforts. In this vein, TOD's transformation of a tenant-landlord conflict,

often translated as issues of financial compensation or legal disputes, into a fight for the collective production of urban spaces and the right to stay put, are viewed as certain progress. The production and accumulation of empirical observations and theorisations of future tasks hold the promise of a more spatially just city.

NOTES

1. Strong protests in the 1980s and 90s resulted in housing tenants right improvement, though still challenged. Housing tenants receive home loss payments, disturbance payments, temporary accommodation and the right to be rehoused in social housing, whereas business tenants are given disturbance payments. Key money, or premium (Tamura, 2014) paid to a previous tenant by a new tenant, is only partially legalised in Korea, making the resettlement of displaced business tenant difficult.
2. Duriban had invested about £50,000 for a restaurant and was asked to leave with only £1,500 in compensation for a development project. It started squatting and remained there for 531 days, ultimately succeeding in obtaining an alternative restaurant from the developers.
3. Delay is a common strategy to fight an eviction. The task of eviction is 'completed' only the belongings (such as furniture and equipment) are entirely removed out of the property.
4. Eviction is mostly carried out by private security companies (Kim, 2010; Lee, 2012). Private securities, infamously nicknamed 'subcontracted gangsters' or 'thugs', are hired by individual landlords or the state to evict and demolish properties, often in cooperation with or under tacit toleration of public officers. Public concerns on privatised use of violence in urban redevelopment have been raised especially since Yongsan incident in 2009. Physical violence in eviction has become ordinary in East Asian cities (Lee, 2008, p. 17) where enormous financial gains are promised in property (re)development.
5. After conflict resolution in 2016, the iron column was removed in a performance. The entrance door was moved and erected in the yard of Gyeonguiseon Commons, a squat movement to resist eviction-based, private-led development of publicly owned lands.

6. The Great Asylum gave birth to numerous collaborations among musicians who took inspiration from gentrification as their musical motifs. A compilation album entitled *Gentrification* was awarded in the 14th Korean Music Awards in February 2017, raising public awareness of displacement. Most songs in the compilation albums were recorded at struggled sites including TOD.

REFERENCES

Baumgarten, B., Daphi, P., & Ullrich, P. (2014). *Conceptualizing culture in social movement research*. Berlin, Germany: Springer.

Bridge, G., & Dowling, R. (2001). Microgeographies of retailing and gentrification. *Australian Geographer*, 32, 93–108.

Buser, M., Bonura, C., Fannin, M., & Boyer, K. (2013). Cultural activism and the politics of place-making. *City*, 17, 606–627.

Castells, M. (1983). *The city and the grassroots*. California: University of California Press.

Chang, T. (2016). 'New uses need old buildings': Gentrification aesthetics and the arts in Singapore. *Urban Studies*, 53, 524–539.

Dong-A Ilbo (18 May 2016). *Seoul Metropolitan Government will stop this construction by all the means. I may be sued for damages.* (in Korean).

Florida, R. (2003). Cities and the creative class. *City & Community*, 2, 3–19.

Groys, B. (2014). On art activism. *E-flux Journal*, 56, 1–14.

Hankyeoreh (11 July 2018). *The national assembly will pass a bill for amendments to the commercial building lease protection Act?* (in Korean).

Kee, Y., Kim, Y., & Lee, Y. (2014). Sing, dance, and Be merry: The key to successful urban development? *Asian Social Science*, 10, 245–261.

Kim, J. Y., & Lee, S. Y. (2018). Commercial gentrification: Hanmandong from the out-skirts of itaewon to the hot place in gangnam style. In B. D. Choi (Ed.). *Urban regeneration and gentrification*. Seoul: Hanwool (in Korean).

Kim, S. H. (2010). Issues of squatters and eviction in Seoul: From the perspectives of the dual roles of the state. *City, Culture and Society*, 1(3), 135–143.

Kirk, D. (2015). Psy in legal dispute with artists over attempts to evict them from his Seoul coffee house. *Independent*, 22 October.

Krischer, O. (2012). Lateral thinking: Artivist networks in East Asia. *Art Asia Pacific*, 77, 96–105.

The Kyunghyang Shinmun (13 July 2017). *Seongdong Gu Government in Seoul provides social business building.* (in Korean).

Lee, C. K. (2008). Rights activism in China. *Contexts*, 7(3), 14–19.

Lee, K. H. (2012). Violence of private security agents and law; Die neoliberale Staats "macht" und die privatizierte "Gewalt": Eine rechtspolitologische Betrachtung uber Eigentum, Gewalt und Macht. *Democratic Legal Studies*, 48, 13–47 (in Korean).

Lee, S. Y. (2014). Gentrification, displacement, anti-gentrification movements. *Journal of the Korean Geographic Society*, 49(2), 299–309 (in Korean).

Lee, S. Y. (2016). Neil smith, gentrification and Korea. *Space and Society: Journal of Korean Association of Spatial and Environment Research*, 26(2), 209–234 (in Korean).

Lee, S. Y. (2018). Cities for profit: Profit-driven gentrification in South Korea. *Urban Studies*, 55(12), 2603–2617.

Lee, S. Y. (2019). The evolution of housing rights activism in South Korea from 1983 to 2016. In N. M. Yip, M. Martinez, & X. Sun (Eds.). *Contested cities and urban activism – East and west, North and South* (pp. 258–274). London: Palgrave.

Lees, L., Slater, T., & Wyly, E. K. (2008). *Gentrification*. London: Routledge.

Ley, D. (1996). *The new middle class and the remaking of the central city*. Oxford: Oxford University Press.

Lloyd, R. (2002). Neo-bohemia: Art and neighborhood redevelopment in chicago. *Journal of Urban Affairs*, 24, 517–532.

Lloyd, R., & Clark, T. N. (2000). The city as an entertainment machine. *The annual meeting of the American sociological association*. Washington, DC.

Logan, J. R., & Molotch, H. L. (1987). *Urban fortunes: The political economy of place*. Berkeley and Los Angeles. University of California Press.

Luger, J. (2016). Singaporean 'spaces of hope? *City*, 20, 186–203.

Luger, J. (2017). But I'm just an artist!? Intersections, identity, meaning and context. *Antipode*, 49(5), 1329–1348.

Mathews, V. (2010). Aestheticizing space: Art, gentrification and the city. *Geography Compass*, 4, 660–675.

Novy, J., & Colomb, C. (2013). Struggling for the right to the (creative) city in Berlin and Hamburg: New urban social movements, new 'spaces of hope'? *International Journal of Urban and Regional Research*, 37, 1816–1838.

Ok, E., & Kim, Y. (2013). New social movement in the form of cultural practices – a case study of Dooriban movement. *Korean Journal of Communication & Information*, 63, 53–75 (in Korean).

Peck, J. (2005). Struggling with the creative class. *International Journal of Urban and Regional Research*, 29, 740–770.

Pinder, D. (2008). Urban interventions: Art, politics and pedagogy. *International Journal of Urban and Regional Research*, 32, 730–736.

Poposki, Z. (2011). Spaces of democracy: Art, politics, and artivism in the post-socialist city. *Romanian Political Science Review*, 11, 713–723.

Rossi, U. (2019). Fake friends: The illusionist revision of Western urbanology at the time of platform capitalism. *Urban Studies*, 0042098018821581.

Shin, H. B. (2018). Urban movements and the genealogy of urban rights discourses: The case of urban protesters against redevelopment and displacement in Seoul, South Korea. *Annals of the American Association of Geographers*, 108(2), 356–369.

Shin, H. B., & Kim, S.-H. (2016). The developmental state, speculative urbanisation and the politics of displacement in gentrifying Seoul. *Urban Studies*, 53(3), 540–549.

Shin, H. J. (2016). Creative classes and the production of contested places in Hannamdong (Yongsan, Seoul): Another cultural-economic communities of strangers. *Journal of the Economic Geographical Society of Korea*, 19(1), 33–50 (in Korean).

Tamura, F. (2014). The historical background and the legal and social recognition of the premium in Korea and Japan. *Space & Society*, 50, 42–72 (in Korean).

Verson, J. (2007). Why we need cultural activism. In T. Trapese (Ed.), *Do it yourself: A handbook for changing the world*. London: Pluto Press.

Zukin, S. (1989). *Loft living: Culture and capital in urban change*. New Brunswick, NJ: Rutgers University Press.

Zukin, S., Trujillo, V., Frase, P., Jackson, D., Recuber, T., & Walker, A. (2009). New retail capital and neighborhood change: Boutiques and gentrification in New York city. *City & Community*, 8, 47–64.

Index

Note: Page numbers in *italic* indicate a figure and page numbers in **bold** indicate a table or box on the corresponding page.

access to facilities: exclusive 258–259; limited sharing 259–260, *259*
accumulation by dispossession 92–93
activism 356–357, 390–398; and group styles 361–365; and political outcomes 365–370; and tech boom 2.0 357–361; *see also* resistance
affordability: housing 37, 266; rent 308–312
Airbnb 273–274, 275–279, **283–284**, 285–294, 304–305, 307–312, 323–324
alliance building 158–159
ambiguity 346–347
Anglo-American gentrification theory 18–26
Anti-Displacement Coalition (San Francisco) 357, 363, 365–366
anti-gentrification 339–345, **340–342**, 356–357, 390–398; and group styles 361–365; and political outcomes 365–370; and Tech Boom 2.0 357–361; *see also* resistance
art activism 390–398
assemblages 120–123
asset class, real estate as 36–37
Athens 285–294
attachment, racial *see* Racial Attachment Processes
autonomization 156–158
awareness campaigns 344

Bantama, Kumasi, Ghana 248–249, *256–257*, 264–266; characteristics of compound houses 249–252, *250–251*, **252**; and housing transformation 252–255, *253*, 258–262, *259–260*, **261–262**; methods 255–258; and rent gap 262–264; study area 255, *256–257*
Barcelona 277–278, *278*
Buenos Aires 374–375, 385–386; case study neighborhoods 377–380, *378*, **379**; and conceptual understandings of gentrification 375–377; displacement in 380–381; resistance to gentrification in 381–385, *382–384*, **382**

Canlubang 215–217, **215**
capital 177; dismantling the needs of 60–61
capitalism, platform 36–37
capitalism, racial 82–85, 93–94; and imperial terrains 90–93; and neoliberal urbanism 85–87; and the production of raced space 87–90
Cartagena de Indias, Colombia 66–75
China: Xian Village, Guangzhou **xi–xiv**, *xiv*
cities, global 85–87; imperial terrains 90–93; and the production of raced space 87–90
class 36, 106–108, 261–262, **261–262**
classical gentrification 5, 275–276, 287, 300, 302–304; *see also* gentrification
coalition, political 365–370
Cold War 319–321
collective displacement 280
collective identities 344
Colombia 66–75
comparative gentrification studies 19–20, 147–148, 163–164; comparative studies of rural gentrification 152–156, *154–155*; comparative urbanism and urban gentrification 148–152, **149**; comparing rural gentrification in France, UK and US 156–163; skepticism regarding 174–179
comparative urbanism 115–116, 148–152, **149;** gentrification and downward raiding in 133–134; and hybrid gentrification 132–144; and the rural 147–164; skepticism regarding 174–179; thinking through 117–127
comparison, politics of 148, 152
compensation 343
compound houses 248–249, 264–266; characteristics of 249–252, *250–251*, **252**; and housing transformation 252–255, *253*, 258–262, *259–260*, **261–262**; methods 255–258; and rent gap 262–264; study area 255, *256–257*
corporate landlords 36
counter narratives 344
cultural racism 72–73
culture 177

debt 101–109; global mortgage debt 37
defining gentrification xv, 10–14, 134
delaying 343
desakota 205–207, *206*; and booming real estate 212–215, *214*; and the business of building a nation 210–212; and gated suburbia 215–217, **215**, *217*; and the production of space 207–210; and spaces of "destruction" and resistance 217–220, *218*
"destruction" processes 217–220
detachment, racial: organizational racial detachment 67, 71–72; structural racial detachment (SRD) 66–67, 72–75
digital transformations 273–274; and Airbnb 273–274, 275–279, 283–284, 285–294, 304–305,

INDEX

307–312, 323–324; and holiday rentals 275–281; and platform-mediated short-term rentals 300–313; and Tech Boom 2.0 317–326
discipline 226–227, 229, 232–233, **236**, 242–243; economic 240–242; physical 236–238; symbolic 238–239
discrimination, politics of 67, 72–73
dislocations 59, 67, 74–75, 92, **284**; *see also* displacement
displacement 356–357; Buenos Aires 380–381; collective 280; and group styles 361–365; and holiday rentals 275–276, 279–280, *279*; and political outcomes 365–370; and the state 21–23; and Tech Boom 2.0 357–361
dispossession 317–326; accumulation by 92–93; producing 242–243
disputes over urban space 381–385
dot com boom 321–322; *see also* Tech Boom 2.0
downward raiding 133–134; in South Africa 135; in state-subsidised housing 138–142, *141*

economic discipline 240–242
economic processes 73–75
Edinburgh 47–49, *48*
elision of race 85–87
empire, urbanisation of 82–85, 93–94; and imperial terrains 90–93; and neoliberal urbanism 85–87; and the production of raced space 87–90
epistemology of comparative gentrification studies 19–20
ethnography, urban 68
evolution 14–16

favelas 226–227; and discipline 236–242, **236**; and legibility 230–235, 242–243; methodology 229–230; and pacification 233–235, *234–235*; and urban governance restructuring 227–229; and urban upgrading 230–235, **231–232**, *233*
fifth-wave gentrification 32, 35–38, 107
force: removal by government force 74
forgetting 358–360
four waves of gentrification 33–35, *34*, 287
France 156–163

gated suburbia 215–217, **215**
gentrification 3–4, 9–16, 18–26, 91–92, 115–116, 183–184; and Bantama, Kumasi 248–266; and Cartagena de Indias 66–75; classical 5, 275–276, 287, 300, 302–304; conceptual understandings of 375–376; and debt 101–109; defining xv, 10–14, 134; and displacement 21–23; geographies of 7, 117–127, 148, 152, 156, 159, 160, 163–164, **171–173**, **283**, 336, 386; global age of 187–199; histories and trajectories xvi–xvii; Hong Kong 175–176; hybrid 132–144, 253; and Johannesburg 187–199; linguistics of 20–21; and Manila 205–220; as a planetary field ix–xiv, *x*, *xiv*; and Rio de Janeiro 226–243; and the rural 147–164; and time 5–7; transnational 302–306, 312–313; *see also* planetary gentrification
gentrification studies: individualizing and variation-finding strategies in 149–150; theorizing resistance in 337–339; universalizing and encompassing perspectives in 150–152; *see also* comparative gentrification studies
geographies: of gentrification 7, 117–127, 148, 152, 156, 159, 160, 163–164, **171–173**, **283**, 336, 386; of anti-displacement activities 376; of capitalism 59, 213; of inequality 207; of neoliberalism 210; of power 83, 85, 94; of resistance 207, 345–348; of structural violence 49; of the vote 368
Ghana 248–249, *250–251*, **252**, 264–266; characteristics of compound houses 249–252, *250–251*, **252**; and housing transformation 252–255, *253*, 258–262, *259–260*, **261–262**; methods 255–258; and rent gap 262–264; study area 255, *256–257*
global cities 85–87; imperial terrains 90–93; and the production of raced space 87–90
global mortgage debt 37
governance, urban 227–228
government force, removal by 74

Grenfell Tower 82–85, 93–94; and imperial terrains 90–93; and neoliberal urbanism 85–87; and the production of raced space 87–90s
group styles 361–363
Guangzhou, China: Xian Village **xi–xiv**, *xiv*

histories of gentrification xvi–xvii, 6–7
holiday rentals 275–281; *see also* Airbnb
Hong Kong 174–179
houses, traditional (Ghana) 248–249, 264–266; characteristics of 249–252, *250–251*, **252**; and housing transformation 252–255, *253*, 258–262, *259–260*, **261–262**; methods 255–258; and rent gap 262–264; study area 255, *256–257*
housing, state-subsidised 135–136; case study 136–138, *137*; downward raiding in 138–142, *141*
housing affordability 37, 266
housing policy 101; Law 381–382
housing transformation 248–249, *253*, *259–260*, **261–262**, 264–266; changing social class 261–262; characteristics of compound houses 249–252, *250–251*, **252**; conceptualizing 252–255; exclusive access to facilities 258–259; limited sharing of facilities and space 259–261; methods 255–258; and rent gap 262–264; study area 255, *256–257*
hybrid gentrification 133–134, 142–144, 253; case study 136–138, *137*; and downward raiding 133–134, 138–142, *141*; and the South African housing context 135–136

identities, collective 344
ideologies, racial 45, 67–68, 72, 75
immigration, wealthier 306–307
imperial terrains 90–93
inclusion 345–348
income 308–312
individualizing and variation-finding strategies 149–150
informal networks 347–348
informal squatting 344–345
Institute of Urban Dreaming (IUD) xi, **xi–xiv**

INDEX

interpersonal racial attachment (IRA) 66, 70, 72
investment 36
invisibility and invisibilization 239, 243, 347–348; production of 242–243; racial 185, 227; racism invisibilization frames 72, 75; social 233

Johannesburg 187–189, 196–198, *197–198*; conceptual framework 189–191; impact of the regeneration charter 194–196; origins of regeneration policies 191–194

knowledge, local 178
Kumasi, Ghana 248–249, 264–266; characteristics of compound houses 249–252, *250–251*, **252**; and housing transformation 252–255, *253*, 258–262, *259–260*, **261–262**; methods 255–258; and rent gap 262–264; study area 255, *256–257*

landlords, corporate 36
landscapes of power 360–361
Latin American racial ideologies 45, 67–68, 72, 75
Law 341 374–375, 381–387, *384*
legibility, socio-spatial 226–229, 233, *236*, 238, 241, 242–243
linguistics of gentrification 20–21
Lisbon 285–294
local knowledge 178
London 82–85, 93–94; and imperial terrains 90–93; and neoliberal urbanism 85–87; and the production of raced space 87–90

Madrid 300–302, **301**, *306*, 312–313; from classical to transnational gentrification in 302–304, *303*; literature review 304–305; methodology 305–306; and rent affordability 309–312, *310–311*, **312**; and touristic specialisation 307–309, *308*; and wealthier immigration 306–307
Manila 205–207, *206*; and booming real estate 212–215, *214*; and the business of building a nation 210–212; and gated suburbia 215–217, **215**, *217*; and the production of space 207–210; and spaces of "destruction" and resistance 217–220, *218*

marginality 230–233
material shifts 360–361
media 366–368
middle classes 36, 106–108; *see also* class
Milan 285–294
minimization 72
mobilization 159–160
mortgage debt 37

Nanjing 9–10
nation-building 23, 210–212
neoliberalism 85–87, 120–123, 205–210, *206*; and booming real estate 212–215, *214*; and the business of building a nation 210–212; and gated suburbia 215–217, **215**, *217*; and spaces of "destruction" and resistance 217–220, *218*
networks, informal 347–348
nihilisms 324–326
non-newness 6
nuance 177–178

organizational racial attachment and detachment 67, 71–72
organized squatting 344–345
outcomes, political 365–370
Oxford 9–10

pacification s233–236, *234–236*
physical discipline 236–238
planetary gentrification xv–xvi, 45–46, 273–274, 333–334; and Airbnb 273–274, 275–279, 283–284, 285–294, 304–305, 307–312, 323–324; and discursive detachment of race from gentrification 66–75; and Grenfell Tower 82–94; and holiday rentals 275–281; and platform-mediated short-term rentals 300–313; and rent gaps 47–61, 101–109; and resistance 336–348, 356–370, 374–386, 390–398; and Tech Boom 2.0 317–326
platform capitalism 36–37
platform-mediated short-term rentals 300–302, **301**, *306*, 312–313; literature review 304–305; methodology 305–306; and rent affordability 309–312, *310–311*, **312**; and touristic specialisation 307–309, *308*; and transnational gentrification 302–304, *303*; and wealthier immigration 306–307

policing, urban 89–90, 92
policy 123–124, 374–375, 385–386; case study neighborhoods 377–380, *378*, **379**; and conceptual understandings of gentrification 375–377; and displacement 380–381; regeneration policies 187–198; and resistance to gentrification 381–385, *382–384*, **382**
political agendas 366–368
political coalitions 365–370
political outcomes 357, 365–370
political subjects 393–395, 397–398
politics of comparison 148, 152
politics of discrimination 67, 72–73
politics of displacement 356–357; and group styles 361–365; and political outcomes 365–370; and Tech Boom 2.0 357–361
politics of space – time 6–7, 304
postcolonial perspective 124–126
postsocialism 317–326
power 287–288; geographies of 83, 85, 94; landscapes of 360–361
prevention 339–343
public policy 374–375, 385–386; case study neighborhoods 377–380, *378*, **379**; and conceptual understandings of gentrification 375–377; and displacement 380–381; and resistance to gentrification 381–385, *382–384*, **382**
public representations 158–159
public spaces 185, 226–233, 236–239, 242–244, 356–357, 363–368, 381
public sphere 357, 366–368

race 66–75; elision of 85–87; production of raced space 83–84, 87–90, 92; race scholarship 68
Racial Attachment Processes (RAP) 66–67, 75, 80; interpersonal (IRA) 66, 70; organizational 66–67, 71–72
racial capitalism 82–85, 93–94; and imperial terrains 90–93; and neoliberal urbanism 85–87; and the production of raced space 87–90
racial detachment: organizational racial detachment 67, 71–72; structural racial detachment (SRD) 66–67, 72–75
racial ideologies, Latin American 45, 67–68, 72, 75
racialization 66–75, **79–80**, 91–93, 317–326

racial/spatial dispossession 317–326
racism 66–68, 83–88, 320–323; cultural 72–73; invisibilization frames 72
raiding, downward 133–134; in South Africa 135; in state-subsidised housing 138–142, *141*
real estate: as an asset class 36–37; Manila 212–215, *214*
reflections: Cocola-Gant, Agustín **283–284**; Phillips, Martin **171–173**; Rivas-Alonso, Clara **353–355**; Shin, Hyun Bang **29–31**; Vale, Melissa **79–80**; Winkler, Tanja **202–203**
regeneration policies 187–189, 196–198, *197–198*; conceptual framework 189–191; impact of 194–196; origins of 191–194
re-housing 343
reinvention, spatial 358–360
removal by government force 74
rent affordability 308–312
rentals, short-term 275–281, 300–302, **301**, *306*, 312–313; literature review 304–305; methodology 305–306; and rent affordability 309–312, *310–311*, **312**; and touristic specialisation 307–309, *308*; and transnational gentrification 302–304, *303*; and wealthier immigration 306–307; *see also* Airbnb
rent gaps 47–49, *48*, 262–266; and Airbnb 285–294; and capital 60–61; and debt 101–109; and housing transformation 248–255, *253*, 258–262, *259–260*, **261–262**; methods 255–258; and speculation 56–60; study area 255, *256–257*; theory of 49–56, *51*
repertories of contention 334, 363–365
representations, public 158–159
resales 135–136; case study 136–138, *137*
resistance 123–124, 333–334, 336–348; in Buenos Aires 374–386; conceptual understandings of 375–376; in San Francisco 356–370; in Seoul 390–398; spaces of 217–220
restructuring 227–228
Rio de Janeiro 226–227; and discipline 236–242, *236*; and legibility 230–235, 242–243; methodology 229–230; and pacification 233–235, *234–235*; and urban governance restructuring 227–229; and urban upgrading 230–235, **231–232**, *233*
Rose Street, Edinburgh, Scotland 47–49, *48*
rural, the 147–148, 163–164; comparative studies of rural gentrification 152–156, *154–155*; comparing rural gentrification in France, UK and US 156–163

San Francisco Bay Area 356–357; and group styles 361–365; and political outcomes 365–370; and Tech Boom 2.0 357–361
Scotland: Rose Street, Edinburgh 47–49, *48*
segregation 242–243
Seoul 390–398
short-term rentals 300–302, **301**, *306*, 312–313; literature review 304–305; methodology 305–306; and rent affordability 309–312, *310–311*, **312**; and touristic specialisation 307–309, *308*; and transnational gentrification 302–304, *303*; and wealthier immigration 306–307
Silicon Valley 9–10, 319–321
social class 261–262, **261–262**
socio-spatial legibility 226–229, 233, *236*, 238, 241, 242–243
South Africa 187–189, 196–198, *197–198*; conceptual framework 189–191; impact of the regeneration charter 194–196; origins of regeneration policies 191–194
space, production of 177, 207–210
space, raced 83–84, 87–90, 92
space, suburban 205–207, *206*; and booming real estate 212–215, *214*; and the business of building a nation 210–212; gated suburbia 215–217, **215**, *217*; and the production of space 207–210; and spaces of "destruction" and resistance 217–220, *218*
space – time, politics of 6, 304
spatial dispossession 317–326
spatialities 391–393
spatial reinvention 358–360
specialisation, touristic 307–308
squatting 333–334, 338–345, 382–383
state, the 23–24, 37–38, 177; state-designed nexus between gentrification and displacement 21–23
state-subsidised housing 135–136; case study 136–138, *137*; downward raiding in 138–142, *141*
structural racial detachment (SRD) 66–67, 72–75
suburban space 205–207, *206*; and booming real estate 212–215, *214*; and the business of building a nation 210–212; gated suburbia 215–217, **215**, *217*; and the production of space 207–210; and spaces of "destruction" and resistance 217–220, *218*
supply of holiday rentals 277–280, *278*, **279**
symbolic discipline 238–239
symbolic shifts 360–361

Takeout Drawing (TOD) 390–391, 393–398, *394*
taxes 69, 290; dislocations through increases in 74–75
Tech Boom 2.0 317–326, 356–361; and group styles 361–365; and political outcomes 365–370
technologic time, postsocialist 322–324
techno-utopics 317–326
terrains, imperial 90–93
time and temporalities 346; of gentrification 5–7; politics of space – time 6, 304; and resistance 346; technologic 322–324
touristic specialisation 307–308
touristification 36–37, **284**
traditional houses (Ghana) 248–249, 264–266; characteristics of 249–252, *250–251*, **252**; and housing transformation 252–255, *253*, 258–262, *259–260*, **261–262**; methods 255–258; and rent gap 262–264; study area 255, *256–257*
transformation, digital 273–274; and Airbnb 273–274, 275–279, 283–284, 285–294, 304–305, 307–312, 323–324; and holiday rentals 275–281; and platform-mediated short-term rentals 300–313; and Tech Boom 2.0 317–326
transformation, housing 248–249, *253*, *259–260*, **261–262**, 264–266; changing social class 261–262; characteristics of compound houses 249–252, *250–251*, **252**; conceptualizing 252–255; exclusive access to facilities 258–259; limited

sharing of facilities and space 259–261; methods 255–258; and rent gap 262–264; study area 255, *256–257*
transnational gentrification 302–306, 312–313; *see also* gentrification
transnational wealth elites 36

United Kingdom (UK) 19–20, 59, 148, 286; and comparative urbanism 117, 120–122; and discursive detachment of race from gentrification 86–90; and the rent gap 101–105; rural gentrification in 156–163, *162*, **171–173**
United States (US) 3, 7, 13, 15, 19, 45, 82, 92, 183–184; and digital transformations 286–288, 256, 319, 321; and the discursive detachment of race from gentrification 68, 70, **80**; and the rural 148, 152–153, *155*, 156–163, *162*
universalizing and encompassing perspectives 150–152, 156

upgrading 226–227, 230–235, **231–232**, *233*; and discipline 236–242, **236**; and legibility 230–235, 242–243; methodology 229–230; and pacification 233–235, *234–235*; and urban governance restructuring 227–229
urban ethnography 68
urban governance 227–228
urbanisation of empire 82–85, 93–94; and imperial terrains 90–93; and neoliberal urbanism 85–87; and the production of raced space 87–90
urbanism, comparative 115–116, 148–152, **149**; and hybrid gentrification 132–144; and the rural 147–164; skepticism regarding 174–179; thinking through 117–127
urbanism, neoliberal 82–87, 385–386
urban policing 89–90, 92
urban space, disputes over 381–385
urban theory 47, 126, 132, 142–144, 176–177

urban upgrading 226–227, 230–235, **231–232**, *233*; and discipline 236–242, **236**; and legibility 230–235, 242–243; methodology 229–230; and pacification 233–235, *234–235*; and urban governance restructuring 227–229

Vancouver 9–10
vulnerability 380–381

wealth elites, transnational 36
wealthier immigration 306–307
West Africa 248–249, 264–266; characteristics of compound houses 249–252, *250–251*, **252**; and housing transformation 252–255, *253*, 258–262, *259–260*, **261–262**; methods 255–258; and rent gap 262–264; study area 255, *256–257*

Xian Village, Guangzhou, China **xi–xiv**, *xiv*

For Product Safety Concerns and Information please contact our EU
representative GPSR@taylorandfrancis.com
Taylor & Francis Verlag GmbH, Kaufingerstraße 24, 80331 München, Germany

www.ingramcontent.com/pod-product-compliance
Lightning Source LLC
Chambersburg PA
CBHW060453300426
44113CB00016B/2572